CULTURAL GEOGRAPHY

FIFTH EDITION

Greenville, South Carolina

Note: The fact that materials produced by other publishers may be referred to in this volume does not constitute an endorsement of the content or theological position of materials produced by such publishers. Any references and ancillary materials are listed as an aid to the student or the teacher and in an attempt to maintain the accepted academic standards of the publishing industry.

Cultural Geography
Fifth Edition

Coordinating Writer
Dennis Bollinger, PhD

Writer
John Seney, MA

Biblical Worldview
Brian Collins, PhD
William Ostrom, PhD

Academic Oversight
Jeff Heath, EdD
Rachel Santopietro, MEd

Editor
Manda Kalagayan, MEd

Consultant
David Quigley, MEd

Book Concept
Emily Heinz

Cover Concept
Drew Fields

Cover Design
Dan Van Leeuwen

Book Design
Emily Heinz
Dan Van Leeuwen

Project Coordinator
Dan Berger

Page Layout
Sarah Centers

Permissions
Sharon Belknap
Sarah Gundlach
Elizabeth Walker

Illustration
John Cunningham
Emily Heinz
Andy Keylock (Beehive Illustration)
Katy Labadorf
Andrew Pagram (Beehive Illustration)
Kathy Pflug
Briseydi Rouse

Photo credits appear on pages 583–88.
The text for this book is set in Adobe Avenir, Avenir Next by Monotype Typography, Futura by URW, Adobe Helvetica, Adobe Helvetica Neue, Adobe Minion Pro, Adobe Myriad Pro, Adobe Source Han Serif Korean, and Adobe Symbol.

ISBN 978-1-62856-647-5

15 14 13 12 11 10 9 8 7 6 5 4 3 2 1

contents

Ready Reference to Maps iv
Features of the Book v

unit I: The World

chapter 01: Studying the World 2
chapter 02: Physical Geography 18
chapter 03: Earth's Climate 42
chapter 04: The World's People 64

unit 2: The United States and Canada

chapter 05: The United States 92
chapter 06: Canada 118

unit 3: Latin America

chapter 07: Mexico and Central America 142
chapter 08: South America 164

unit 4: Europe and Russia

chapter 09: Northern Europe 190
chapter 10: Continental Western Europe 212
chapter 11: Russia 236
chapter 12: Eastern Europe 258
chapter 13: Southern Europe 284

unit 5: Africa

chapter 14: North Africa 308
chapter 15: Equatorial Africa 330
chapter 16: Eastern and Southern Africa 354

unit 6: The Middle East and Central and South Asia

chapter 17: The Middle East 380
chapter 18: The Caucasus and Central Asia 404
chapter 19: South Asia 426

unit 7: East and Southeast Asia

chapter 20: China, Mongolia, and Taiwan 450
chapter 21: Japan and Korea 470
chapter 22: Southeast Asia 494

unit 8: Oceania and Antarctica

chapter 23: Australia and New Zealand 520
chapter 24: Pacific Islands and Antarctica 542

Glossary 564
Index 570
Photo Credits 583

READY REFERENCE TO MAPS

Physical and Political Maps

Africa 310
Antarctica 546
Australia 522–23
British Isles 192
Canada 120–21
Caucasus 407
Central Africa 333
Central America and the West Indies 145
Central Asia 407
China 452
Continental Europe 215
Eastern Africa 357
Eastern Europe 261
Eastern Mediterranean 382
Korea and Japan 473
Mexico 144
Northern Africa 311
Northern Europe 192–93
Pacific Islands (Oceania) 544–45
Persian Gulf 383
Russia 238–39
Scandinavia 193
South America 167
South Asia 429
Southeast Asia 496–97
Southern Africa 358
Southern Europe 286–87
United States 94–95
Western Africa 332
World Map .... x–xi

Miscellaneous Maps

Climates of the World 63
Language Families of the World 68–69
Vegetation of the World 58–59

FEATURES OF THE BOOK

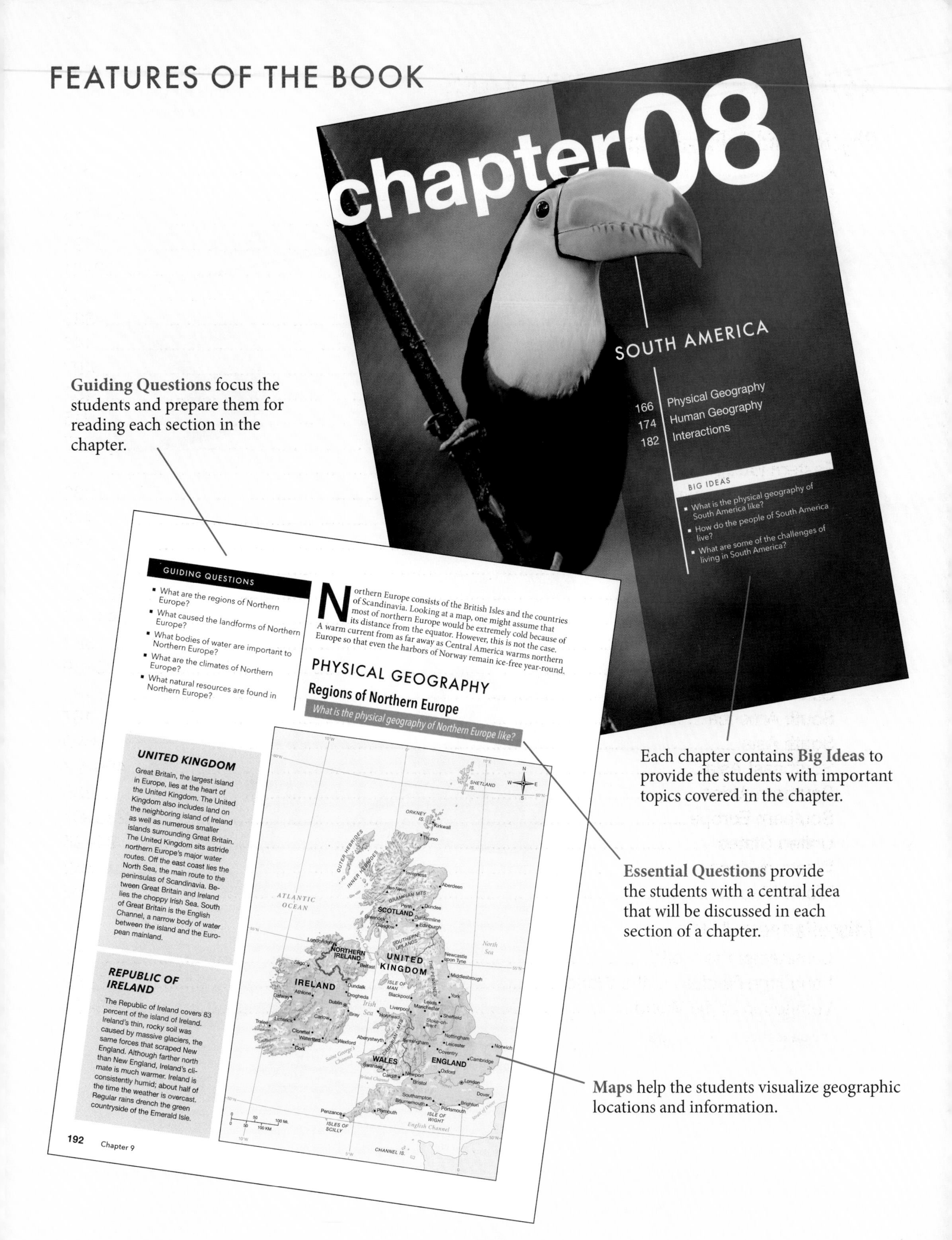

chapter 08

SOUTH AMERICA

166 Physical Geography
174 Human Geography
182 Interactions

BIG IDEAS

- What is the physical geography of South America like?
- How do the people of South America live?
- What are some of the challenges of living in South America?

GUIDING QUESTIONS

- What are the regions of Northern Europe?
- What caused the landforms of Northern Europe?
- What bodies of water are important to Northern Europe?
- What are the climates of Northern Europe?
- What natural resources are found in Northern Europe?

Northern Europe consists of the British Isles and the countries of Scandinavia. Looking at a map, one might assume that most of northern Europe would be extremely cold because of its distance from the equator. However, this is not the case. A warm current from as far away as Central America warms northern Europe so that even the harbors of Norway remain ice-free year-round.

PHYSICAL GEOGRAPHY

Regions of Northern Europe

What is the physical geography of Northern Europe like?

UNITED KINGDOM

Great Britain, the largest island in Europe, lies at the heart of the United Kingdom. The United Kingdom also includes land on the neighboring island of Ireland as well as numerous smaller islands surrounding Great Britain. The United Kingdom sits astride northern Europe's major water routes. Off the east coast lies the North Sea, the main route to the peninsulas of Scandinavia. Between Great Britain and Ireland lies the choppy Irish Sea. South of Great Britain is the English Channel, a narrow body of water between the island and the European mainland.

REPUBLIC OF IRELAND

The Republic of Ireland covers 83 percent of the island of Ireland. Ireland's thin, rocky soil was caused by massive glaciers, the same forces that scraped New England. Although farther north than New England, Ireland's climate is much warmer. Ireland is consistently humid; about half of the time the weather is overcast. Regular rains drench the green countryside of the Emerald Isle.

192 Chapter 9

Guiding Questions focus the students and prepare them for reading each section in the chapter.

Each chapter contains **Big Ideas** to provide the students with important topics covered in the chapter.

Essential Questions provide the students with a central idea that will be discussed in each section of a chapter.

Maps help the students visualize geographic locations and information.

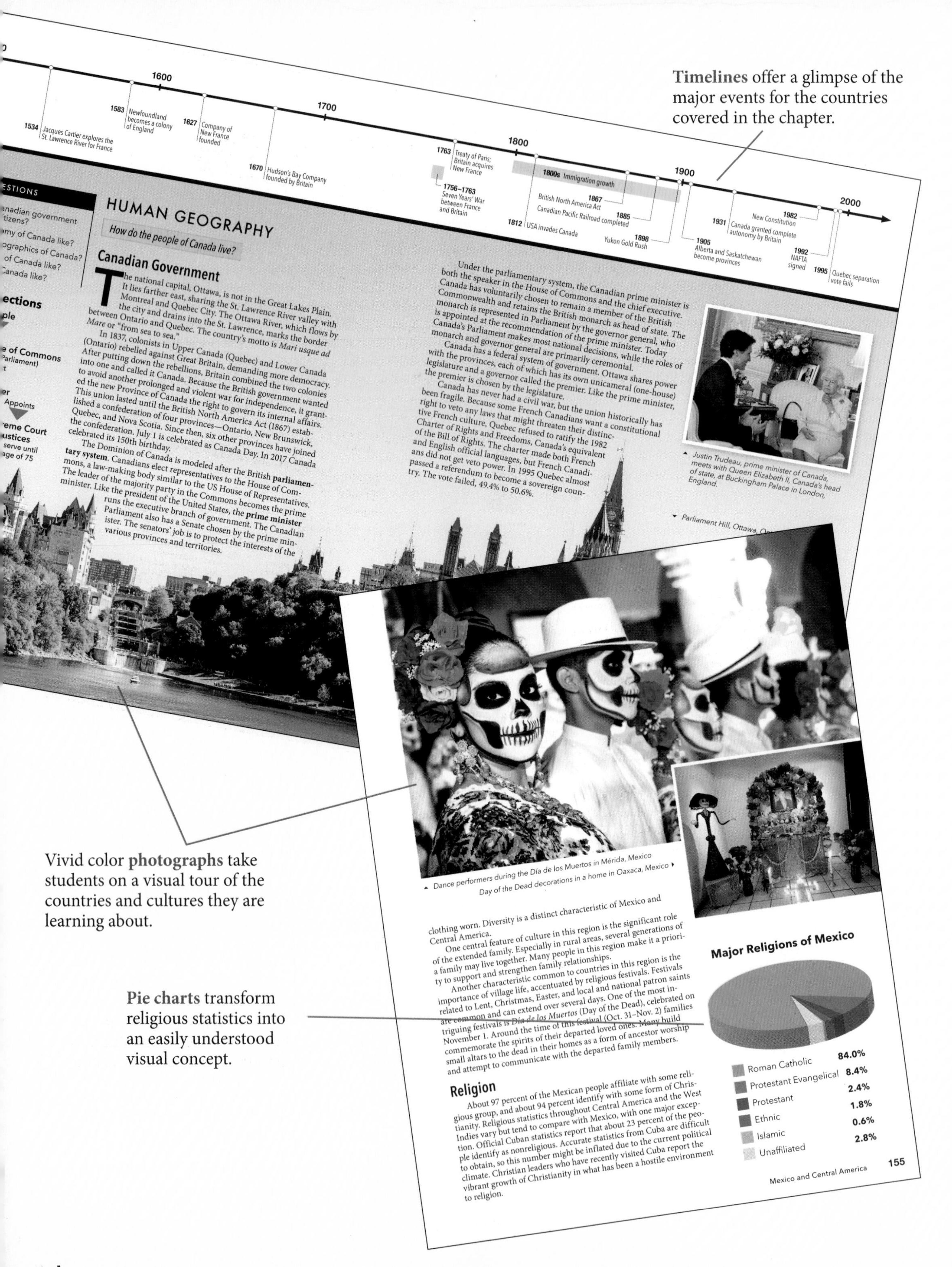

Timelines offer a glimpse of the major events for the countries covered in the chapter.

1534 Jacques Cartier explores the St. Lawrence River for France
1583 Newfoundland becomes a colony of England
1600
1627 Company of New France founded
1670 Hudson's Bay Company founded by Britain
1700
1756–1763 Seven Years' War between France and Britain
1763 Treaty of Paris; Britain acquires New France
1800
1800s Immigration growth
1812 USA invades Canada
1867 British North America Act
1885 Canadian Pacific Railroad completed
1898 Yukon Gold Rush
1900
1905 Alberta and Saskatchewan become provinces
1931 Canada granted complete autonomy by Britain
1982 New Constitution
1992 NAFTA signed
1995 Quebec separation vote fails
2000

HUMAN GEOGRAPHY

How do the people of Canada live?

Canadian Government

The national capital, Ottawa, is not in the Great Lakes Plain. It lies farther east, sharing the St. Lawrence River valley with Montreal and Quebec City. The Ottawa River, which flows by the city and drains into the St. Lawrence, marks the border between Ontario and Quebec. The country's motto is *Mari usque ad Mare* or "from sea to sea."

In 1837, colonists in Upper Canada (Quebec) and Lower Canada (Ontario) rebelled against Great Britain, demanding more democracy. After putting down the rebellions, Britain combined the two colonies into one and called it Canada. Because the British government wanted to avoid another prolonged and violent war for independence, it granted the new Province of Canada the right to govern its internal affairs. This union lasted until the British North America Act (1867) established a confederation of four provinces—Ontario, New Brunswick, Quebec, and Nova Scotia. Since then, six other provinces have joined the confederation. July 1 is celebrated as Canada Day. In 2017 Canada celebrated its 150th birthday.

The Dominion of Canada is modeled after the British **parliamentary system**. Canadians elect representatives to the House of Commons, a law-making body similar to the US House of Representatives. The leader of the majority party in the Commons becomes the prime minister. Like the president of the United States, the **prime minister** runs the executive branch of government. The Canadian Parliament also has a Senate chosen by the prime minister. The senators' job is to protect the interests of the various provinces and territories.

Under the parliamentary system, the Canadian prime minister is both the speaker in the House of Commons and the chief executive. Canada has voluntarily chosen to remain a member of the British Commonwealth and retains the British monarch as head of state. The monarch is represented in Parliament by the governor general, who is appointed at the recommendation of the prime minister. Today Canada's Parliament makes most national decisions, while the roles of monarch and governor general are primarily ceremonial.

Canada has a federal system of government. Ottawa shares power with the provinces, each of which has its own unicameral (one-house) legislature and a governor called the premier. Like the prime minister, the premier is chosen by the legislature.

Canada has never had a civil war, but the union historically has been fragile. Because some French Canadians want a constitutional right to veto any laws that might threaten their distinctive French culture, Quebec refused to ratify the 1982 Charter of Rights and Freedoms, Canada's equivalent of the Bill of Rights. The charter made both French and English official languages, but French Canadians did not get veto power. In 1995 Quebec almost passed a referendum to become a sovereign country. The vote failed, 49.4% to 50.6%.

Justin Trudeau, prime minister of Canada, meets with Queen Elizabeth II, Canada's head of state, at Buckingham Palace in London, England.

Parliament Hill, Ottawa, O...

Vivid color **photographs** take students on a visual tour of the countries and cultures they are learning about.

Dance performers during the Día de los Muertos in Mérida, Mexico

Day of the Dead decorations in a home in Oaxaca, Mexico

clothing worn. Diversity is a distinct characteristic of Mexico and Central America.

One central feature of culture in this region is the significant role of the extended family. Especially in rural areas, several generations of a family may live together. Many people in this region make it a priority to support and strengthen family relationships.

Another characteristic common to countries in this region is the importance of village life, accentuated by religious festivals. Festivals related to Lent, Christmas, Easter, and local and national patron saints are common and can extend over several days. One of the most intriguing festivals is *Día de los Muertos* (Day of the Dead), celebrated on November 1. Around the time of this festival (Oct. 31–Nov. 2) families commemorate the spirits of their departed loved ones. Many build small altars to the dead in their homes as a form of ancestor worship and attempt to communicate with the departed family members.

Religion

About 97 percent of the Mexican people affiliate with some religious group, and about 94 percent identify with some form of Christianity. Religious statistics throughout Central America and the West Indies vary but tend to compare with Mexico, with one major exception. Official Cuban statistics report that about 23 percent of the people identify as nonreligious. Accurate statistics from Cuba are difficult to obtain, so this number might be inflated due to the current political climate. Christian leaders who have recently visited Cuba report the vibrant growth of Christianity in what has been a hostile environment to religion.

Major Religions of Mexico

Religion	Percent
Roman Catholic	84.0%
Protestant Evangelical	8.4%
Protestant	2.4%
Ethnic	1.8%
Islamic	0.6%
Unaffiliated	2.8%

Mexico and Central America 155

Pie charts transform religious statistics into an easily understood visual concept.

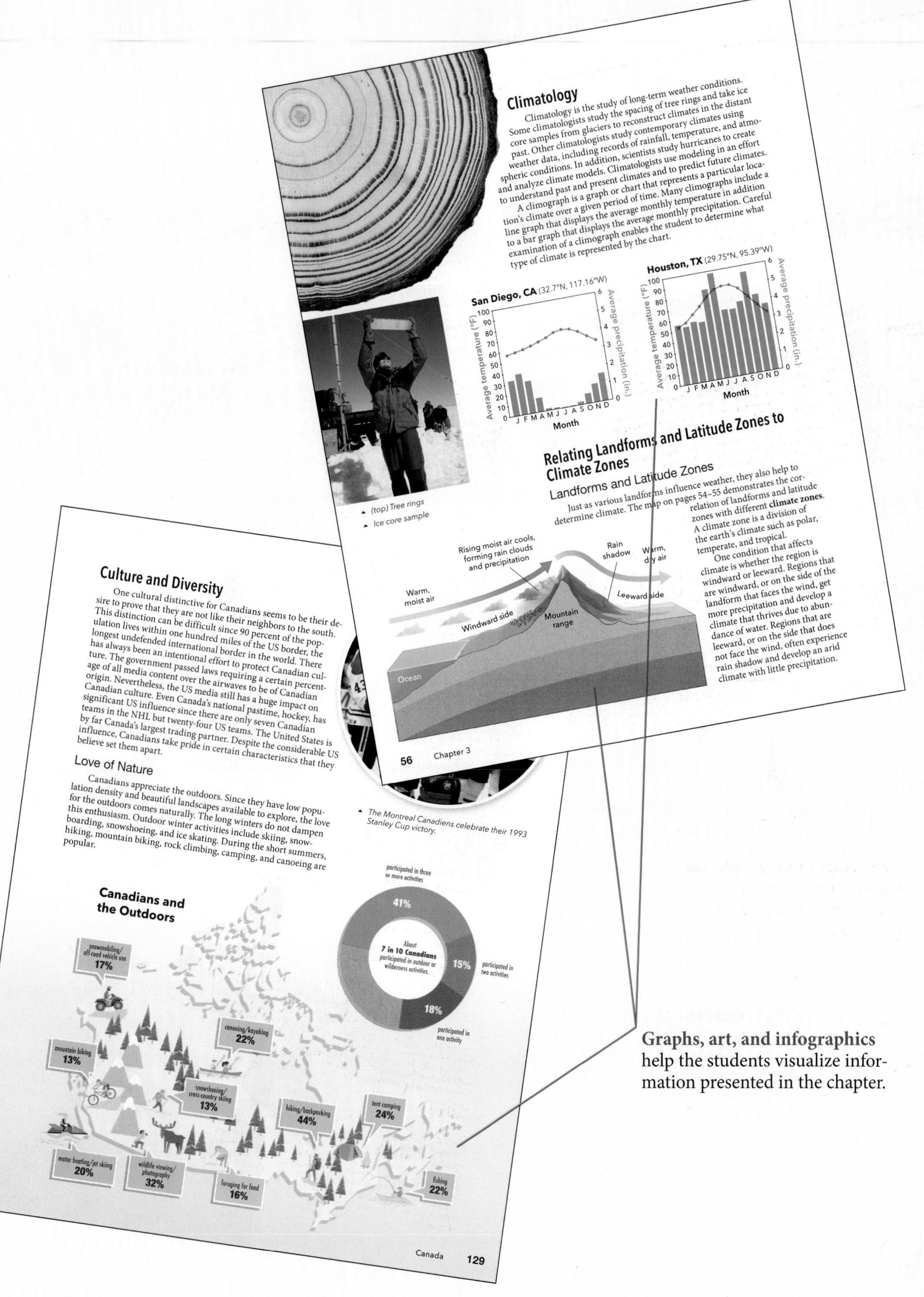

Climatology

Climatology is the study of long-term weather conditions. Some climatologists study the spacing of tree rings and take ice core samples from glaciers to reconstruct climates in the distant past. Other climatologists study contemporary climates using weather data, including records of rainfall, temperature, and atmospheric conditions. In addition, scientists study hurricanes to create and analyze climate models. Climatologists use modeling in an effort to understand past and present climates and to predict future climates.

A climograph is a graph or chart that represents a particular location's climate over a given period of time. Many climographs include a line graph that displays the average monthly temperature in addition to a bar graph that displays the average monthly precipitation. Careful examination of a climograph enables the student to determine what type of climate is represented by the chart.

▲ (top) Tree rings
▲ Ice core sample

Relating Landforms and Latitude Zones to Climate Zones

Landforms and Latitude Zones

Just as various landforms influence weather, they also help to determine climate. The map on pages 54–55 demonstrates the correlation of landforms and latitude zones with different **climate zones**. A climate zone is a division of the earth's climate such as polar, temperate, and tropical.

One condition that affects climate is whether the region is windward or leeward. Regions that are windward, or on the side of the landform that faces the wind, get more precipitation and develop a climate that thrives due to abundance of water. Regions that are leeward, or on the side that does not face the wind, often experience rain shadow and develop an arid climate with little precipitation.

56 Chapter 3

Culture and Diversity

One cultural distinctive for Canadians seems to be their desire to prove that they are not like their neighbors to the south. This distinction can be difficult since 90 percent of the population lives within one hundred miles of the US border, the longest undefended international border in the world. There has always been an intentional effort to protect Canadian culture. The government passed laws requiring a certain percentage of all media content over the airwaves to be of Canadian origin. Nevertheless, the US media still has a huge impact on Canadian culture. Even Canada's national pastime, hockey, has significant US influence since there are only seven Canadian teams in the NHL but twenty-four US teams. The United States is by far Canada's largest trading partner. Despite the considerable US influence, Canadians take pride in certain characteristics that they believe set them apart.

Love of Nature

Canadians appreciate the outdoors. Since they have low population density and beautiful landscapes available to explore, the love for the outdoors comes naturally. The long winters do not dampen this enthusiasm. Outdoor winter activities include skiing, snowboarding, snowshoeing, and ice skating. During the short summers, hiking, mountain biking, rock climbing, camping, and canoeing are popular.

▲ *The Montreal Canadiens celebrate their 1993 Stanley Cup victory.*

Canada 129

Graphs, art, and infographics help the students visualize information presented in the chapter.

▲ The Faroe Islands, Denmark, were formed by volcanic eruptions over many years.

Volcanoes

Iceland is very geologically active, with thirty volcano systems and many moderate earthquakes.

▲ Strokkur Geyser in Iceland; a **geyser** is a hot spring that forcefully ejects hot water and steam from the ground at regular intervals.

CASE STUDY | **Volcanoes in Iceland**

Laying astride the Mid-Atlantic Ridge that separates the North American and Eurasian tectonic plates, Iceland has a long history of volcanic activity. Two recent eruptions are notable. Eyjafjallajökull is a small icecap of Iceland with an elevation of 5,417 feet above sea level. An extended eruption began in the spring of 2010 and was preceded by three thousand small earthquakes. When the volcano erupted in April, melting water from the icecap entered the volcano's vent, and the resulting steam caused an explosion that sent a cloud of volcanic ash high into the atmosphere. This plume of ash contaminated the atmosphere for hundreds of miles and disrupted air travel across Europe for days. By August 2010 the volcano had returned to a dormant state.

A second volcano, Bárðarbunga, is located under Vatnajökull, Iceland's most extensive glacier. It has an elevation of 6,591 feet above sea level. This volcano erupted in August 2014, accompanied by sixteen hundred earthquakes. Bárðarbunga released large volumes of sulfur dioxide, which negatively affected air quality across Iceland. However, because this volcano did not produce a significant amount of volcanic ash, air travel was not seriously affected. By February 2015 this volcano had also returned to a dormant state.

1. Why has Iceland had many volcanic eruptions?
2. What caused Eyjafjallajökull to explode?
3. How did Bárðarbunga's eruption adversely affect air quality?
4. In addition to recently erupting, what did these two volcanoes have in common?

▲ Eyjafjallajökull volcano during eruption

Terms in bold type draw attention to important facts, ideas, or definitions.

Case Studies introduce the students to interesting geographic information and provide questions to ensure understanding.

BELIEFS

Judaism

The religion of Judaism emerged in the wake of the destruction of the Jewish temple in AD 70. Though the roots of Judaism reach back to Moses and Abraham, AD 70 proved to be a decisive turning point. With the temple destroyed, sacrifices ceased and the influential priestly class fell from power. The crushing response of Roman military power also led the rabbis to discourage messianic movements, which stirred up the people against Rome and led to the kind of retribution experienced in Jerusalem in AD 70. In addition, the emerging Judaism faced competition from followers of Jesus, who claimed that Jesus was the Messiah—the one who fulfilled the Old Testament Scriptures and inaugurated the era of the New Covenant.

In this time of upheaval, the Pharisees, a Jewish sect that focused on keeping the Law of Moses, gained ascendency. The rabbis who emerged from this tradition developed rules for interpreting the Jewish Scriptures. These rabbis collected interpretations of laws about agriculture, holy days, rituals, and civic life in a collection known as the *Mishna*. The Mishna was completed in AD 200. Additional traditions about the application of the law can be found in the *Gemara*. Together the Mishna and the Gemara form the *Talmud*. Some Jews believe that the Talmud is inspired just like Scripture. Others deny its inspiration, but they do accept it as an authority for Judaism.

Central to Judaism are monotheism, the Torah, and the election of the nation Israel. **Monotheism** means that adherents to Judaism believe there is only one god. They believe that God created all that there is and that His laws govern the way that all people should live. Evil exists in God's world, but God will one day raise all people from the dead. He will judge the world with justice and mercy. The wicked will be judged for their wickedness. The just will be rewarded. One authority on Judaism notes, "If the balance is equal, then God inclines the scale to forgiveness." Because of the future judgment, humans must choose to do right and repent when they do wrong. Many in Judaism believe that people who work hard enough to overcome sin will be able to do it if they ask God for help. Judaism teaches that God chose Israel to be his special people because of the merits of the patriarchs.

They are unique because God gave them the Torah (Law) and because they worship the one true God instead of idols. Obedience to the Torah is thus a very important part of adhering to Judaism. It identifies a person as being a part of Judaism, which in turn marks him or her as being specially related to God.

▲ A Jewish man reading the Torah in a synagogue

The Middle East 397

Beliefs sections provide a brief examination of various religions and religious concepts.

Global Impacts expose the students to geography-related topics that extend beyond national boundaries and potentially affect many nations.

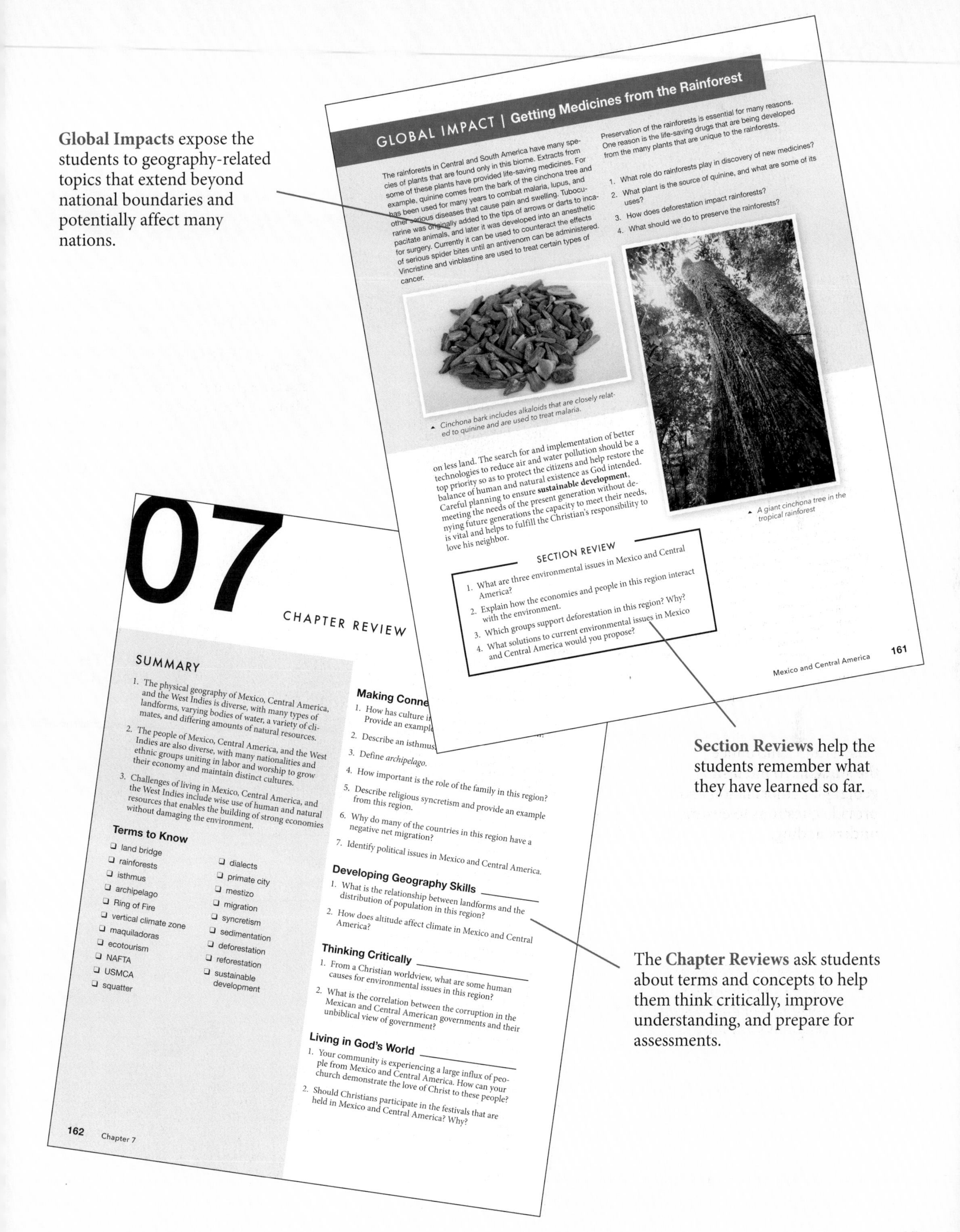

GLOBAL IMPACT | Getting Medicines from the Rainforest

The rainforests in Central and South America have many species of plants that are found only in this biome. Extracts from some of these plants have provided life-saving medicines. For example, quinine comes from the bark of the cinchona tree and has been used for many years to combat malaria, lupus, and other serious diseases that cause pain and swelling. Tubocurarine was originally added to the tips of arrows or darts to incapacitate animals, and later it was developed into an anesthetic for surgery. Currently it can be used to counteract the effects of serious spider bites until an antivenom can be administered. Vincristine and vinblastine are used to treat certain types of cancer.

Preservation of the rainforests is essential for many reasons. One reason is the life-saving drugs that are being developed from the many plants that are unique to the rainforests.

1. What role do rainforests play in discovery of new medicines?
2. What plant is the source of quinine, and what are some of its uses?
3. How does deforestation impact rainforests?
4. What should we do to preserve the rainforests?

▲ Cinchona bark includes alkaloids that are closely related to quinine and are used to treat malaria.

▲ A giant cinchona tree in the tropical rainforest

on less land. The search for and implementation of better technologies to reduce air and water pollution should be a top priority so as to protect the citizens and help restore the balance of human and natural existence as God intended. Careful planning to ensure **sustainable development**, meeting the needs of the present generation without denying future generations the capacity to meet their needs, is vital and helps to fulfill the Christian's responsibility to love his neighbor.

SECTION REVIEW

1. What are three environmental issues in Mexico and Central America?
2. Explain how the economies and people in this region interact with the environment.
3. Which groups support deforestation in this region? Why?
4. What solutions to current environmental issues in Mexico and Central America would you propose?

Mexico and Central America 161

07

CHAPTER REVIEW

SUMMARY

1. The physical geography of Mexico, Central America, and the West Indies is diverse, with many types of landforms, varying bodies of water, a variety of climates, and differing amounts of natural resources.
2. The people of Mexico, Central America, and the West Indies are also diverse, with many nationalities and ethnic groups uniting in labor and worship to grow their economy and maintain distinct cultures.
3. Challenges of living in Mexico, Central America, and the West Indies include wise use of human and natural resources that enables the building of strong economies without damaging the environment.

Terms to Know

- ❑ land bridge
- ❑ rainforests
- ❑ isthmus
- ❑ archipelago
- ❑ Ring of Fire
- ❑ vertical climate zone
- ❑ maquiladoras
- ❑ ecotourism
- ❑ NAFTA
- ❑ USMCA
- ❑ squatter
- ❑ dialects
- ❑ primate city
- ❑ mestizo
- ❑ migration
- ❑ syncretism
- ❑ sedimentation
- ❑ deforestation
- ❑ reforestation
- ❑ sustainable development

Making Conne

1. How has culture i Provide an exampl
2. Describe an isthmus
3. Define *archipelago*.
4. How important is the role of the family in this region?
5. Describe religious syncretism and provide an example from this region.
6. Why do many of the countries in this region have a negative net migration?
7. Identify political issues in Mexico and Central America.

Developing Geography Skills

1. What is the relationship between landforms and the distribution of population in this region?
2. How does altitude affect climate in Mexico and Central America?

Thinking Critically

1. From a Christian worldview, what are some human causes for environmental issues in this region?
2. What is the correlation between the corruption in the Mexican and Central American governments and their unbiblical view of government?

Living in God's World

1. Your community is experiencing a large influx of people from Mexico and Central America. How can your church demonstrate the love of Christ to these people?
2. Should Christians participate in the festivals that are held in Mexico and Central America? Why?

162 Chapter 7

Section Reviews help the students remember what they have learned so far.

The **Chapter Reviews** ask students about terms and concepts to help them think critically, improve understanding, and prepare for assessments.

WORLD MAP

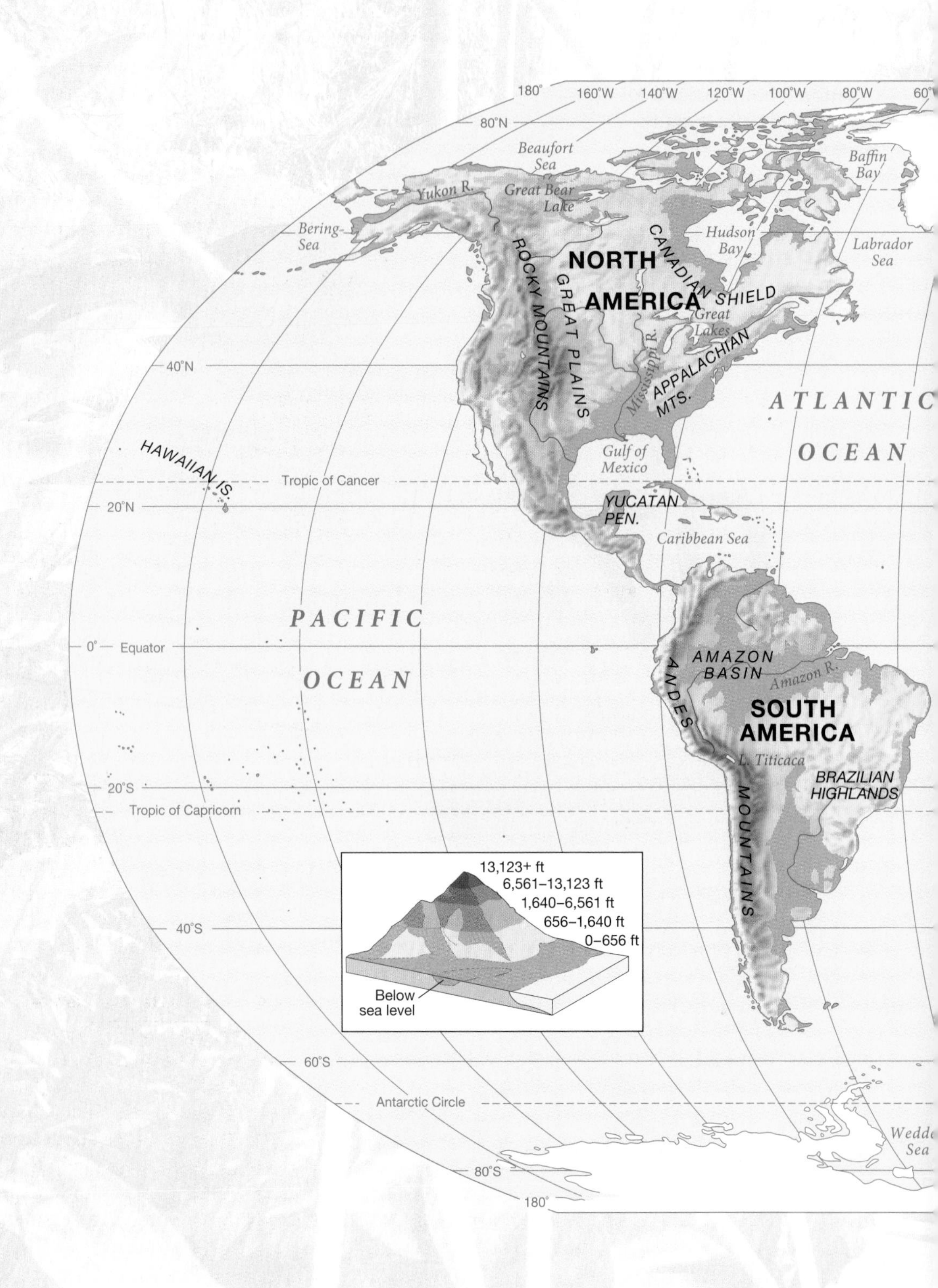

180°
160°W
140°W
120°W
100°W
80°W
80°N
Beaufort Sea
Baffin Bay
Yukon R.
Great Bear Lake
Bering Sea
Hudson Bay
Labrador Sea
NORTH AMERICA
ROCKY MOUNTAINS
GREAT PLAINS
CANADIAN SHIELD
Great Lakes
Mississippi R.
APPALACHIAN MTS.
40°N
ATLANTIC
OCEAN
HAWAIIAN IS.
Gulf of Mexico
Tropic of Cancer
20°N
YUCATAN PEN.
Caribbean Sea
PACIFIC
OCEAN
0° Equator
AMAZON BASIN
Amazon R.
ANDES
SOUTH AMERICA
L. Titicaca
BRAZILIAN HIGHLANDS
20°S
Tropic of Capricorn
MOUNTAINS
13,123+ ft
6,561–13,123 ft
1,640–6,561 ft
656–1,640 ft
0–656 ft
Below sea level
40°S
60°S
Antarctic Circle
80°S
180°
Sea

ARCTIC OCEAN
40°W
0°
40°E
60°E
80°E
100°E
120°E
140°E
160°E
180°
80°N
Barents Sea
Kara Sea
Laptev Sea
Greenland Sea
LAPLAND
Arctic Circle
CENTRAL SIBERIAN PLATEAU
Lena R.
Yenisey R.
Ob R.
URAL MTS.
Baltic Sea
North Sea
NORTHERN EUROPEAN PLAIN
Volga R.
EUROPE
ALPS
Danube R.
Black Sea
ASIA
L. Baikal
Amur R.
KAMCHATKA PEN.
Sea of Okhotsk
60°N
ATLANTIC OCEAN
IBERIAN PEN.
Aral Sea
Caspian Sea
TIEN SHAN
GOBI DESERT
Yellow R.
Sea of Japan
40°N
Mediterranean Sea
ATLAS MTS.
IRANIAN PLATEAU
Indus R.
HIMALAYAS
PLATEAU OF TIBET
Yangtze R.
PACIFIC OCEAN
East China Sea
SAHARA
Persian Gulf
Red Sea
Nile R.
ARABIAN PENINSULA
Ganges R.
Mekong R.
Tropic of Cancer
Arabian Sea
DECCAN PLATEAU
Bay of Bengal
Philippine Sea
20°N
Niger R.
SAHEL
L. Chad
INDOCHINA PEN.
South China Sea
PHILIPPINE IS.
AFRICA
ETHIOPIAN HIGHLANDS
Congo R.
Gulf of Guinea
Equator
CONGO BASIN
L. Victoria
0°
INDIAN OCEAN
ATLANTIC OCEAN
L. Tanganyika
KATANGA PLATEAU
L. Nyasa
Zambezi R.
Coral Sea
GREAT SANDY DESERT
20°S
Tropic of Capricorn
KALAHARI DESERT
AUSTRALIA
GREAT DIVIDING RANGE
N
W
E
S
Tasman Sea
40°S
0
1,000
2,000 Mi.
0
1,000
2,000 Km
60°S
Antarctic Circle
ANTARCTICA
Ross Sea
80°S
180°

unit 1

THE WORLD

chapter 01

STUDYING THE WORLD

4 | Geography: Its Features and Tools
9 | Being a Geographer
12 | Looking at Culture

BIG IDEAS

- What are the tools of geography?
- How can I do the work of geography?
- Why do we have cultures?

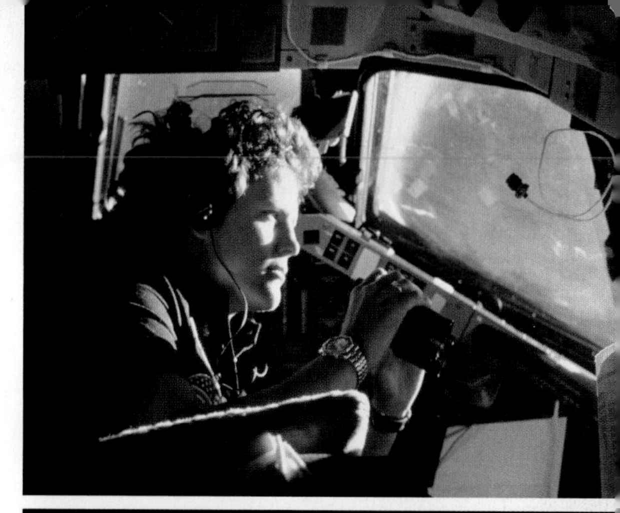

Astronaut Kathryn Sullivan using binoculars for a magnified view of the earth from the space shuttle Challenger

SEEING THE EARTH FROM SPACE

"Kathy Sullivan, who in 1984 became the first American woman to perform a space walk, returned with an abiding awe for the intricate systems that come together to make Earth an improbable oasis. 'The thing that grew in me over these flights was a real motivation and desire . . . to not just enjoy these sights and take these pictures,' she says, 'but to make it matter.'

After retiring from NASA, Sullivan led the National Oceanic and Atmospheric Administration for three years, using the robotic eyes of orbiting satellites to pursue her passion. She says Earth from above is so captivatingly beautiful, she never grew bored looking at it. 'I'm not sure I'd want to be in the same room with someone who could get tired of that.'"

"They Saw Earth from Space. Here's How It Changed Them."
National Geographic, March 2018

The Bible begins with God's creation of the physical realm and the first humans. He creates a man and woman in His own image on the earth He has created. Geography then, is, the stage on which the human drama is acted out.

The earth, however, is more than a backdrop to the human story. God's very first words to Adam include a commission about mankind's role on the earth: "Be fruitful, and multiply, and replenish the earth, and subdue it: and have dominion . . . over every living thing that moveth upon the earth" (Gen. 1:28). These words are often called the **Creation Mandate**.

The Creation Mandate reveals that geography is not incidental to God's plan for Creation. God places Adam and Eve in a garden—a specific geographical place—from the beginning. The mandate also reveals that humans are to fill and subdue the entire earth. Knowledge of geography is required to carry out the Creation Mandate.

Nor does geography become irrelevant as the storyline of Scripture progresses. God chooses a nation to further His plan of redemption and promises it a land in a strategic geographic location. Even at the end of this age, the earth is not abandoned. Instead, the creation is renewed. Though some geographic features are different (Rev. 21:1), nations in specific geographic locations still exist on the new earth (Rev. 21:24). Geography is an important part of God's plan from Genesis to Revelation.

Planet Earth, satellite view

A cliff's-edge view of a Scottish cityscape, with Edinburgh Castle in the distance

A differential GPS being used in a real-time kinematic survey to determine the extent of the Durham canyon flooding in the United Kingdom

GUIDING QUESTIONS

- What are the five themes of geography?
- What are the two types of geography?
- What tools are used in geography?
- What are the features on a globe and a map?

GEOGRAPHY: ITS FEATURES AND TOOLS

What are the tools of geography?

In order to effectively study geography, you must understand its definition, develop a working knowledge of the five themes of geography, and practice using basic tools to develop the craft of being a student geographer.

Definition and Themes of Geography

The word **geography** comes from two roots meaning "earth" and "written description." It can be defined as the detailed study of the earth and the ways people relate to the earth and one another. An important aspect of geography is understanding how people fulfill their God-given role as stewards of God's creation.

Themes of Geography

The study of geography has five fundamental themes: location, place, movement, region, and human-environment interaction.

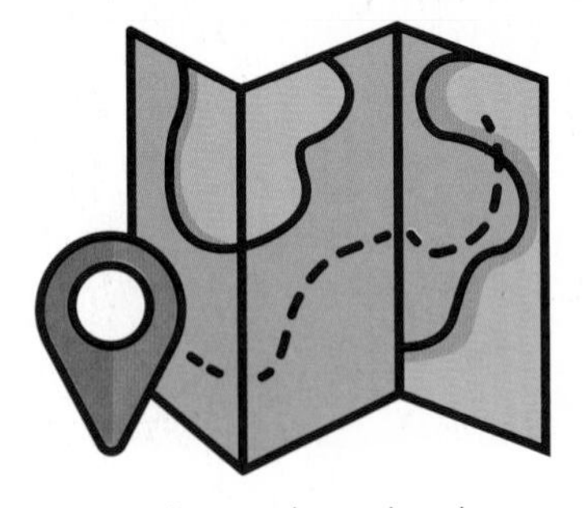

Location: either absolute or relative to one's environment

Place: physical characteristics such as mountains, rivers, soils, and plant and animal life, and human characteristics such as roads, buildings, agriculture, industry, and culture

Human-environment interaction: how people adapt to and modify their environment

Movement: of people, goods, ideas, diseases, etc.

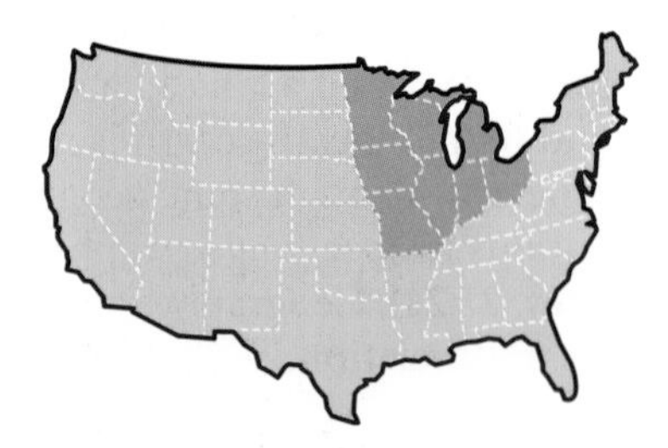

Region: defined by formal boundaries or functions

Planting flowers during Pennsylvania's early spring

As you study geography, remind yourself of these five themes. They will recur many times throughout this book and are essential to a proper understanding of geography. In the simplest terms, geography can be divided into *physical geography* and *human geography*. In this book you will also examine human interaction with the environment.

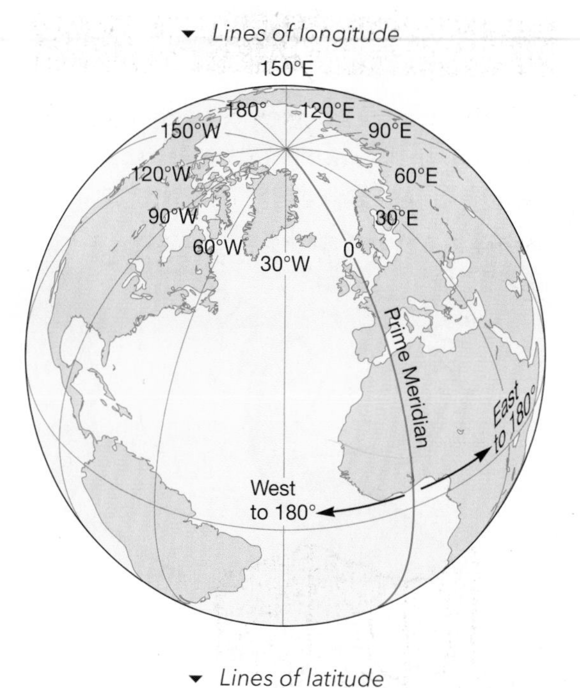

▾ *Lines of longitude*

The Tools of Geography

Much of the visual information about geography appears in one of two forms: a globe or a map. Both of these tools seek to provide models of the earth's surface.

Globe

Globes show information about the earth's surface with almost perfect accuracy. Both a globe and the earth are spheres, and both can be divided easily with lines of latitude and longitude.

The **prime meridian** passes through Greenwich, England, and is designated 0°. Because scientists at the Royal Observatory in Greenwich made the original calculations for modern meridians, their meridian became the basis for all the others. It is also the reference point for the various time zones of the world. The 180° meridian lies directly opposite the prime meridian and is actually a continuation of the same line. Together, these lines form a **great circle** and cut the earth into two equal hemispheres. Every meridian except 0° and 180° is labeled as east (E) or west (W), depending on the hemisphere in which it lies.

Longitude is the distance east or west of the prime meridian measured in degrees. The **equator** is the imaginary line that divides the earth into the Northern and Southern Hemispheres. **Latitude** is the distance north or south of the equator measured in degrees. Imaginary lines run east and west around the earth. They form circles that are parallel to the equator and are therefore called parallels of latitude.

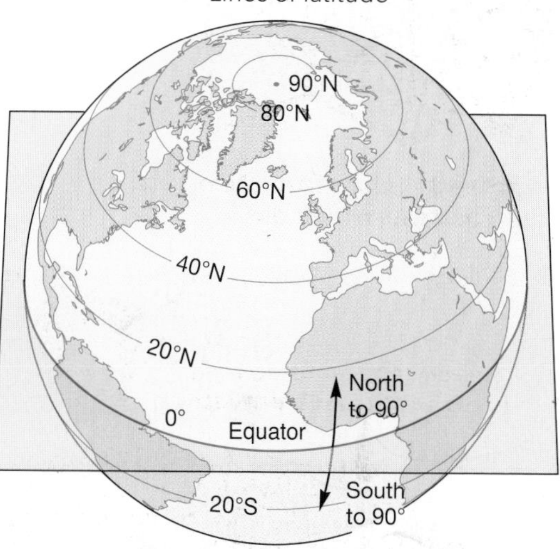

▾ *Lines of latitude*

Maps

Maps are generally flat, show much greater detail, and are more useful than globes. Any method used to show the earth's round surface on a flat map is called a map projection.

When a globe is transferred onto a map, a serious problem known as distortion occurs. The earth's surface is not a flat rectangle like a sheet of paper; it does not flatten without distorting the image. When cartographers (mapmakers) make a map, they try to avoid or reduce the distortion of four features of a globe: area, shape, distance, and direction.

Mental Maps

When someone asks you for directions, you consult a **mental map** to communicate the directions to the person. As you give the directions, the person to whom you are speaking forms a mental map of his own based on what he hears. It might or might not be accurate. A mental map is a person's perception of the world or a part of it based on available knowledge. In addition to boundaries and major physical features, mental maps involve one's cultural perceptions, including biases or prejudices toward the geographic region in question. A person usually views his home area positively but might view "foreign" areas—rightly or wrongly—with a degree of negativity. These perceptions are influenced by a person's home life, the news and entertainment media, and educational experiences. One purpose of studying geography is to expand and improve the accuracy of one's mental map of the world.

Physical Maps

A typical globe is covered by twelve paper strips called gores. If you were to take the gores and lay them flat, you would have a gore map.

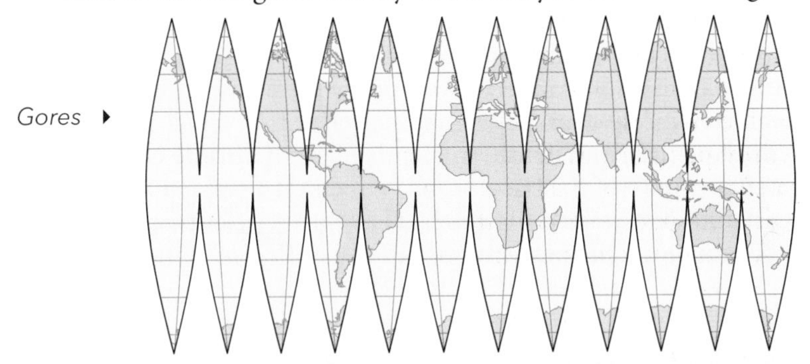

Gores

How accurate is such a map? Areas of land and water are accurate, and compass directions are fairly accurate. Distances also seem to be accurate—an inch equals the same number of miles on every gore. But measuring distances between gores is awkward. The shapes have the most obvious distortions because of all the gaps. Although the gore map is fairly accurate in three respects, it is obviously not very useful as a flat map.

Colorful wooden houses line the shore of Qeqertarsuaq, Greenland, with icebergs visible in the distance.

Most world maps use a variation of the **cylindrical projection**. First, the mapmaker rolls a sheet of paper into the shape of a cylinder around a wire globe with a light inside. Next, he traces the shadows cast by the light and then unrolls the paper to reveal a flat map.

The first important cylindrical projection was published by Mercator in 1569. Not until the second half of the twentieth century was it replaced.

On a Mercator projection, all lines of latitude and longitude look straight. This feature means that compass directions are always constant. Shapes are also accurate. Areas and distances, however, are increasingly distorted the farther one moves north or south from the equator. Greenland, for example, looks larger than the entire continent of South America, although it is really only one-eighth its size.

Known as Goode's Interrupted Projection, this cylindrical projection has several popular variations, including a map that cuts and flattens the earth like an orange peel. It is called an **interrupted projection** because the image is "interrupted" with gaps or cuts. A gore map is another example. Goode's projection is useful because the areas remain fairly accurate and the shapes of continents are less distorted than shapes on the gore map. Unfortunately, Goode's projection distorts distances and all north-south directions.

Cylindrical projection

Mercator projection

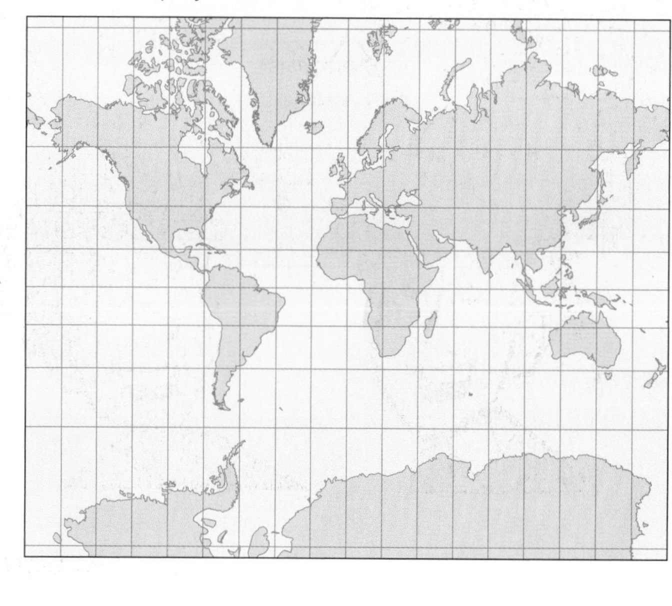

Goode's projection

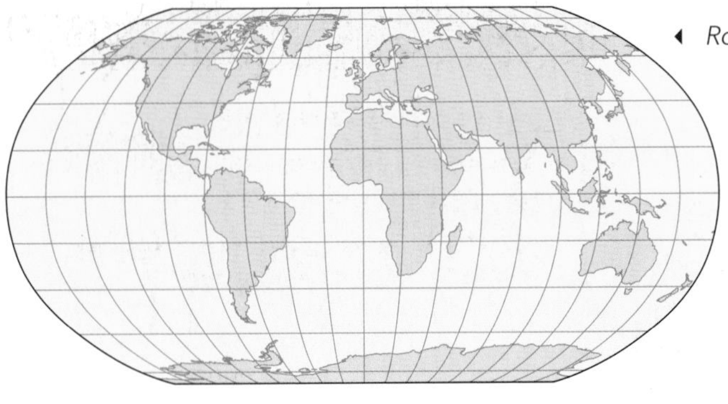

Robinson's projection

Azimuthal projection

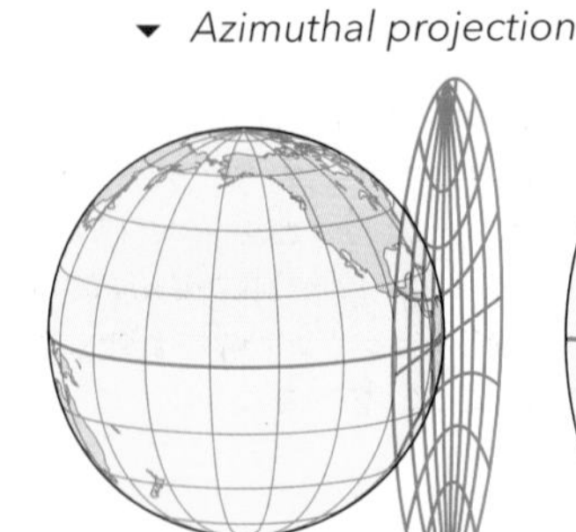

Conic projection

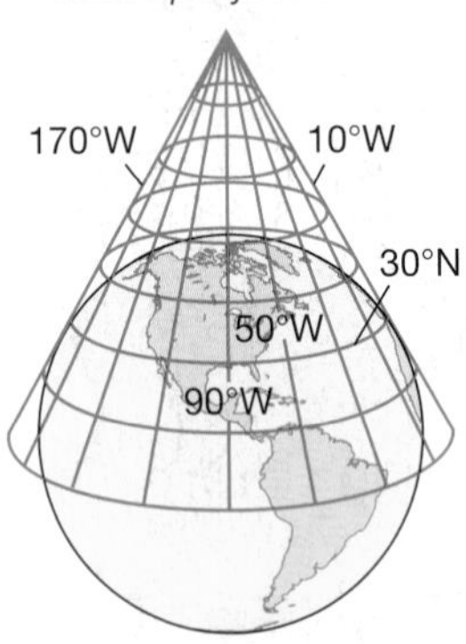

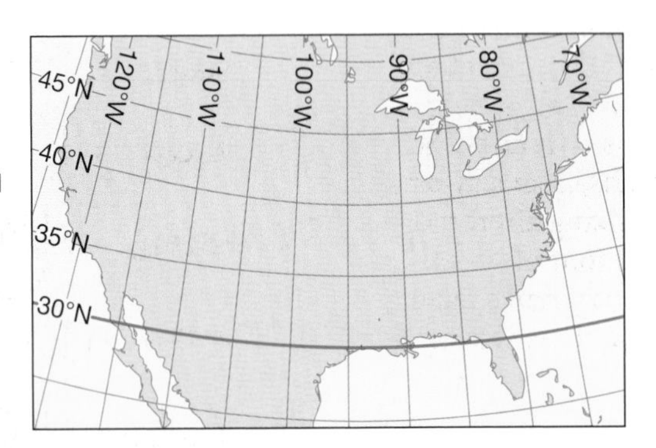

Robinson's projection is popular for textbooks because it combines the best elements from the other projections. Its greatest advantage is that it minimizes all four types of distortions. Everything is distorted, but only a little. Almost every world map in this textbook uses Robinson's projection.

The planar projection, also called an azimuthal projection, uses a flat plane instead of a cylinder. To make the projection, one places a flat sheet of paper on an imaginary wire globe, touching only one point. The shadows traced on this paper form an azimuthal map. The map is most accurate in the center but becomes increasingly distorted near the edges. Therefore, it is useful for compact areas, such as South America and Antarctica, where land is surrounded by water.

To make a conic projection, the mapmaker places a cone-shaped piece of paper on an imaginary wire globe and traces the shadow onto the cone. Then he opens and flattens the cone to make a conic projection. Unlike the planar projection, which touches a single point, the cone touches an entire line of latitude. The conic map is most accurate where the cone touches the line. Away from that line the features become gradually distorted. Thus, it is most useful for showing wide regions, such as the United States.

Students working in groups with tablets

SECTION REVIEW

1. Summarize the Creation Mandate and relate it to the study of geography.
2. Define *geography* and identify its two main branches.
3. What are the themes of geography?
4. How are the features on a globe similar to those on a map? How are they different?
5. What is a mental map? For what geographic activities might this type of map be well suited?
6. Why is an azimuthal projection better for compact areas?

BEING A GEOGRAPHER

How can I do the work of geography?

GUIDING QUESTIONS

- How do I analyze a map?
- What technology can be used to gather geographic information?
- What is the best geographic tool to answer geographic questions?

One of the goals of this textbook is to take you beyond the mere study and understanding of geography to the actual practice of geography. The many benefits of developing geography skills include using maps to plan a trip, utilizing geography-based technology effectively, and knowing how to select the best tools to accomplish a geography-related task.

Map Analysis

Modern maps are the result of **GIS**, or geographic information system technology. These maps are produced using computerized map data, which ensures that the maps remain relatively current and easily accessible. GIS data is collected by engineers who physically survey the land using equipment such as GPS and laser transits. Additional information is gathered through photographs, laser sensors, and height-measuring radar by **remote sensing**, utilizing aircraft or satellites. Some GIS software even provides a virtual tour of streets in many cities. This is made possible by high-speed photographs taken by cameras mounted on vehicles that physically traverse these streets.

Many specialized maps are available, including geological, vegetation, soil, and meteorological maps. Regardless of the type, most maps include symbols that represent features in an abbreviated form. There are three basic types of symbols. Point symbols are used to indicate such things as cities or even buildings, wells, or monuments. Line symbols represent such things as roads, railroads, rivers, and water or power lines. Area symbols indicate bodies of water, swamps, marshes, glaciers, or other physical features.

The meaning of the symbols are shown in a **legend**, which is usually located in a corner of the map. Often located near the legend are two other helpful features, a **compass rose** and a **scale**. The compass rose shows the orientation of the map, that is, whether the top of the map is north, south, east, or west. The scale is a calibrated (marked) line that indicates distance. For maps of large areas, the scale might read, "1 in. = 200 mi." On smaller-scale maps, it might read, "1 in. = 100 ft."

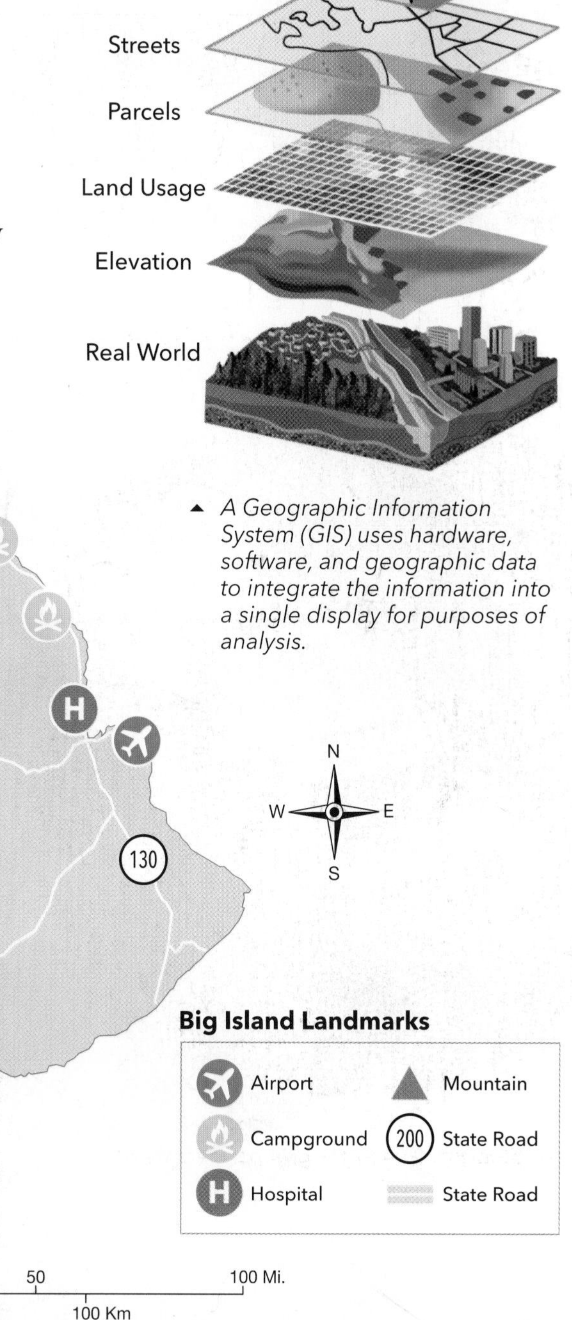

▲ *A Geographic Information System (GIS) uses hardware, software, and geographic data to integrate the information into a single display for purposes of analysis.*

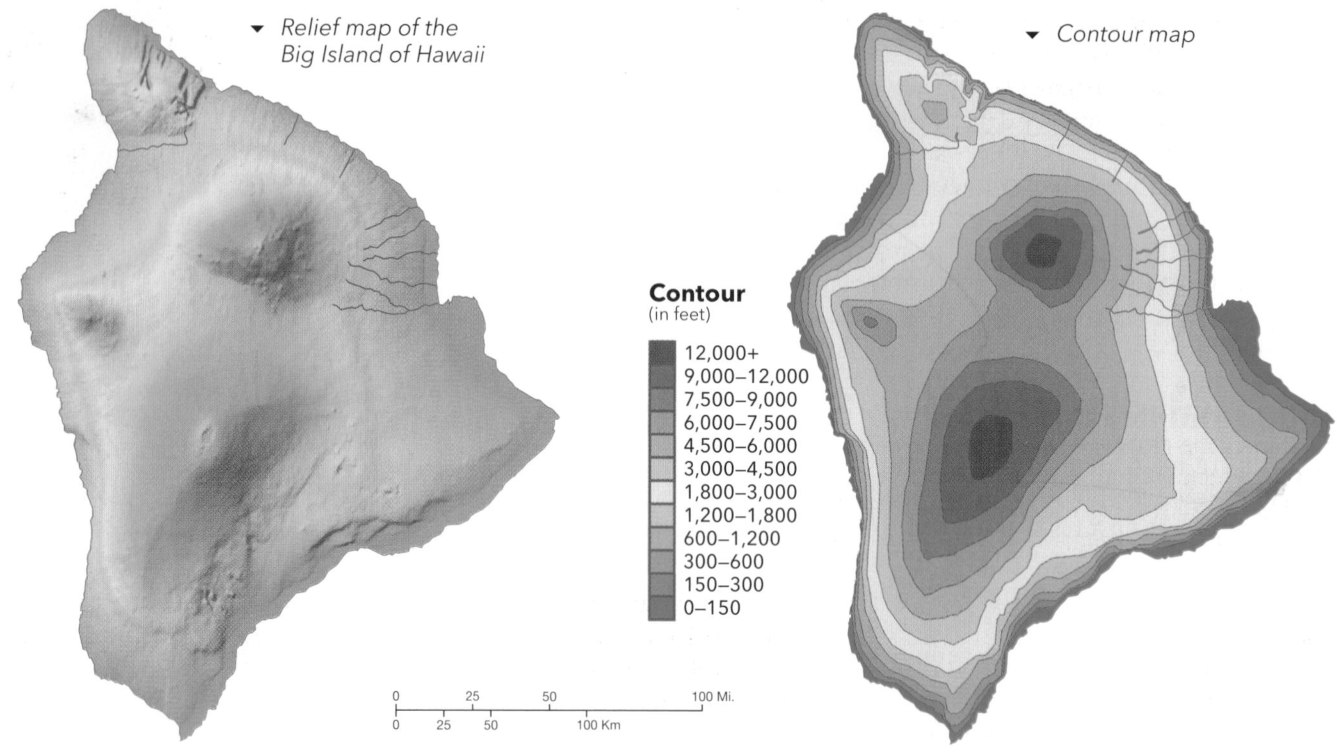

Relief map of the Big Island of Hawaii

Contour map

Satellite image of the Big Island

Any type of map that shows surface features is a physical map because it shows physical things. Physical maps that show specific changes in elevation are called **relief maps**. *Relief* refers to the height and depth of land features in relation to surrounding land. Many relief maps include not only water features such as rivers, but also manmade features, such as dams. Cartographers use **contour lines** of separate colors on a relief map to indicate all points on a map that have the same altitude.

Many of the maps in this book are terrain maps. They use colors to indicate different elevations. On many color relief maps, green represents land near sea level. Yellow or light brown represents a slight rise in land. Dark brown, gray, or white indicates mountains.

Coastline of the Big Island of Hawaii

Another type of map is a **thematic map**. Thematic maps record gathered information about a region or nation's climate, population, or resources. Cartographers produce these maps to communicate information on particular topics and to display their abstract findings.

Technologies Used in Geography

In addition to traditional methods and GIS, another essential tool for geographers is the global positioning system (**GPS**), which is financed and operated by the United States Department of Defense. Although GPS was designed specifically for military use, the government also allows many civilian uses. While the number of satellites varies, about thirty GPS satellites transmit coded signals for a receiver and calculate position, velocity, and time. GPS remains the most precise indicator of location available today. Although civilian use is accurate within five meters, military applications are accurate to within a few centimeters.

China's Resources

FUELS
- Refinery
- Shale oil refinery
- Oil field
- Gas field
- Oil basin
- Major coal mine

NONFERROUS
- Sb Antimony
- Cu Copper
- Pb Lead & zinc
- M Magnesite
- Hg Mercury
- Sn Tin

FERROUS & FERROALLOYS
- Fe Iron ore
- Mn Manganese
- Mo Molybdenum
- W Tungsten

Choosing the Right Geography Tool

Determining the best geography tool to use depends on the need. Planning a trip to a nearby state park might call for the use of a local or state map. Demonstrating the distance from the Hawaiian Islands to a city on the West Coast of the United States might entail the use of a globe. Trying to decide where a city should expand might best be determined by using a GIS map of the city in question. Believe it or not, tracking a teenage driver or a senior family member who has a tendency to get lost might be possible through the GPS on the driver's phone or another device attached to the car. Geographic tools perform many tasks and enable us to answer a myriad of questions.

SECTION REVIEW

1. What items are often found on a map legend?
2. On what kind of map would the scale be 1 in. = 100 mi.?
3. Explain GIS and its potential for providing current information for geographers. Why is current information important?
4. Why is a thematic map helpful in analyzing a country's resources?
5. How does technology help in ways that a paper map or globe cannot?

LOOKING AT CULTURE

GUIDING QUESTIONS

- How can we relate culture to the Creation Mandate and religion?
- How do we define culture and religion?
- How can elements of culture be good or bad?
- How can we analyze culture from a biblical basis?

Why do we have cultures?

The earth is more than a backdrop to the human story. When people obey or live out the Creation Mandate, they start changing the very stage they were placed on. They do this literally: They form the earth into clay bricks that bake in the sun. They use these bricks to build houses and cities. They take raw materials and form them so that beautiful music can be performed. Or they dig metals such as copper, tin, and iron from the earth. And they do this largely in order to turn around and mold and shape the earth even more easily by making plows and backhoes and cranes and all sorts of other tools.

But people do not do this work in isolation. To accomplish the tasks of mining, crafting, farming, and city building—to obey the Creation Mandate—humans work together. And whenever humans get together to create and build, they create something else almost by accident: culture.

From the beginning geography and culture have played key roles in God's purposes for mankind. The earth and its inhabitants are always interacting.

The Spread of the Gospel

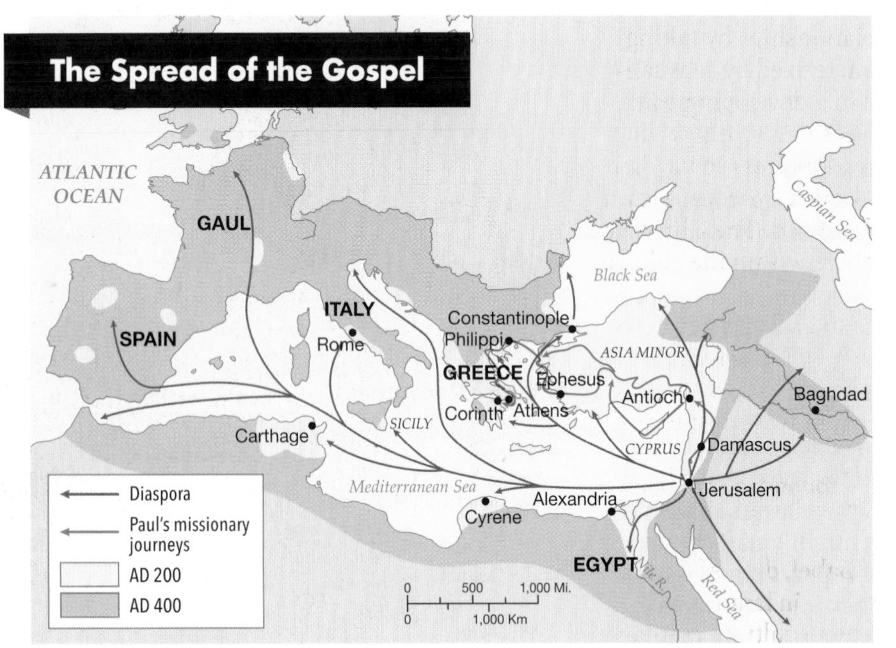

Culture Defined and Related to the Creation Mandate

A **culture** is the system of customs and traditions and habits that a group of people use to make something of their world. Or, put another way, culture is man's response to creation. It includes the technological knowledge necessary for survival. Culture also includes social structures that enable people to live and work together in harmony. Finally, because humans were created as thinking beings designed to worship God, culture includes religion and philosophy.

Making something out of creation is at the essence of the Creation Mandate, which is why some have identified the Creation Mandate as a cultural mandate. Culture is developed by groups of people, not isolated individuals. Thus, the Creation Mandate tells humans to be "fruitful and multiply." When groups of people work together to subdue the earth, as the Creation Mandate requires, culture inevitably emerges.

Positive and Negative Aspects of Culture

For the Christian, aspects of culture that align with God's principles for His creation are positive. Those facets of culture that violate or distort God's principles are negative. Two categories for evaluating culture are structure and direction. Structure is the way that God has intended aspects of culture (including true religion, institutions, and social groups) to be. Direction is the movement away from or back toward God's original intent. When

Brick-field workers carrying bricks on top of their heads in Narayanganj, Bangladesh

Mongol Chinese boy with his lambs

sinners twist culture away from the way God has structured it, they are moving it in a sinful direction. When Christians strive to direct culture back toward God's design, they are restoring positive characteristics of culture.

Christians are to be both at home in and at odds with their surrounding cultures. Christians can be at home in their cultures because they do conform to those cultures in many ways. A Christian banker in New York City wears a suit and tie just like his non-Christian counterparts. And a Christian coffee grower in Colombia uses the same cultivation methods as non-Christian coffee growers. There is no special form of Christian architecture for suburban houses, nor do Christians drive oddly shaped vehicles. And yet a Christian in this fallen world will often be at odds with his culture. A Christian banker will not build professional relationships by taking clients to popular entertainments that are characterized by sensuality, violence, or oppression. A Christian farmer in a developing country will not participate in a culture of corruption to move his product to market. In some cultures, Christians may need to dress somewhat differently from what is considered normal in their culture. In certain cultures some vocations may not be open to Christians. The Christian way of life will sometimes seem laughable to others within the culture (1 Pet. 4:4).

The idea of sojourning, being both at home in and distinct from the surrounding world, remains a significant part of a Christian's mission. By sojourning within the cultures of the world, Christians are to live attractively different lifestyles that will draw people to Christ (1 Pet. 2:12).

Young Indian woman with her baby

Cultural Diversity

With the dividing of people at the tower of Babel, diverse cultures developed. As a result, different people groups vary in languages, customs, and all the other ingredients that make up culture. If Adam and Eve had chosen to exercise the Creation Mandate in submission to God by not eating from the tree of knowledge, it is possible that cultural diversity would have resulted without religious diversity. Tragically, however, religious diversity accompanied the cultural diversity that developed as fallen mankind spread across the earth.

The modern concept of **multiculturalism** teaches that all cultures are equally valid and no culture is better than another. However, the Christian has an ultimate standard by which to evaluate every culture—including his own. With multiculturalism there is the strong assumption that truth is relative to groups of people, but the Bible teaches that truth transcends cultural diversity. With multiculturalism, there is a supposition that people's identities are primarily tied to ethnicity, gender, and class rather than their status as image bearers of God.

Analyzing Culture from a Biblical Basis

Just as the physical world is important to God, so are human cultures. The many global varieties of architecture, dress, speech, music, and even table manners all point to one source: people are image bearers of God. As Christians study the cultures of other people, they should learn to see the good in what other cultures have made of our world. Throughout this textbook we will examine five themes of culture: religion, institutions, social groups, aesthetics, and physical environment.

Afghan boy

World Religions

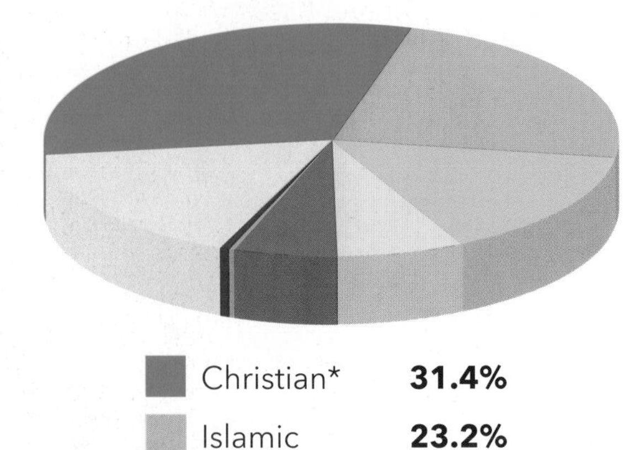

Religion	Percent
Christian*	**31.4%**
Islamic	**23.2%**
Hindu	**15.0%**
Buddhist	**7.1%**
Ethnic	**5.9%**
Jewish	**0.2%**
Other	**0.8%**
Unaffiliated	**16.4%**

* Includes Roman Catholics, Mormons, Jehovah's Witnesses, and Quakers

▾ *A southern Indian family with zebu*

Religion

Religion may be defined as the human response to God and His revelation. True religion is a worship-filled response to the true God in submission to His revelation. False religions are idolatrous replacements of God through the worship of one or more aspects of His creation. Religion is tied to culture because it is closely related to the Creation Mandate. When man fell and became sinful, he did not cease to be a cultural being. The Creation Mandate is repeated in Genesis 9 in the context of a fallen world. However, the cultures of fallen mankind tend to orient away from God and develop in opposition to God's Word. Thus, false religion results. Idolatry is not merely individual. It is cultural, as the raging of nations in Psalm 2 reveals.

Institutions

Institutions are elements of culture that develop around rules, design, and structure. If that seems a bit obscure, just think of a man and woman entering into marriage. It was the first institution and was created by God when He decreed that a man should leave his father and mother and cleave to his wife for life. The next institution was the family, which began with the first children entering the world. The man expanded his role from husband and also became a father. The woman added to her role as wife the role of mother. And the role of child within the family was created.

As mankind multiplied, additional institutions were built around work relationships, city life, and development of civilization. For instance, when Abel became a keeper of sheep, he began to develop patterns of behavior for shepherds. If he hired others to work for him in keeping the sheep, then the roles of employer and employee were created.

Peter identifies government as an institution created by God (1 Pet. 2:13). Policy-making involves both policy and carrying it out. Economics is also closely linked to institutions. There were no employers and employees, conductors and musicians, or government officials when only Adam and Eve existed. But by the end of Genesis 4 these institutions were developing.

Institutions are important for the Christian because they are an integral part of fulfilling the Creation Mandate's commission to develop culture. Institutions provide an effective means of spreading culture across multiple generations and embedding aspects of culture as normal and instinctive.

Social Groups

A social group is any grouping of people who share common characteristics. As in institutions, the family is the foundational social group in any society. At the heart of the Creation Mandate is the command to be fruitful and multiply, and this multiplying is to take place within the context of the family. Thus, from the beginning humans were not meant to function merely as autonomous individuals, but within social groups.

Many social groups are tied to institutions. For example, family relationships, church relationships, neighbor relationships, business relationships, and political relationships are institutions. Even participation in various crafts, hobbies, and interests seems to be tied to related institutions. This would indicate that many social groups are tied to the created order. They can serve to further the Creation Mandate.

Other social groups are not tightly connected to institutions. For example, demographers may study people according to their age, their identity as native or non-native to a particular region, their ethnic background, or their education level. Though not directly related to institutions, these social groups are linked, in one way or another, to the created order.

Aesthetics

A simple definition of beauty is surprisingly difficult to find. However, definitions of this elusive quality often include terms like *property* or *characteristic* and then go on to apply those properties to a person, place, thing or even an idea. What seems to make something beautiful is the pleasing of one or more of our senses, such as sight or sound. God did not create a world to be subdued in a merely functional manner. He created a beautiful world, and He intended humanity to expand, or perhaps multiply, its beauty. While Genesis 4 records the carrying out of the Creation Mandate in the context of the Fall, none of the developments mentioned are themselves evil. Tools, musical instruments, poetry, farms, and cities provide opportunities for humans to make beauty from God's original creation.

Christians need to develop taste in order to see the beauty in things that they at first may not appreciate. This is especially true when studying other cultures. What at first appears repulsive may truly be repulsive because it runs contrary to God's original intent. But it may simply be that one's taste has not been properly calibrated to see something that is truly beautiful as beautiful.

Physical Environment

All people, Christians included, are responsible to exercise good and wise dominion over the earth. This includes being wise stewards of the physical world. Wise stewardship is implied in the fact that God placed Adam and Eve in a garden, which they were instructed to tend. In fact, the command to fill the earth may imply that Adam and Eve were to extend the Garden of Eden to eventually cover the entire earth. Thus, closely related to the Creation Mandate is the responsibility that humans have to care for God's created world.

SECTION REVIEW

1. Define *culture.*
2. What determines whether an aspect of culture is good or bad?
3. What is the origin of cultural diversity? Is it good or bad? Why?
4. Define *religion* and distinguish true and false religion.
5. What are the five themes of culture?
6. Which of the five themes of culture would apply to the following: a family, an island of plastic waste floating in the ocean, Buddhism?

▲ (top) Houses in Amsterdam

▲ Mode Gakuen Cocoon Tower is a 204-meter, 50-story educational facility located in Tokyo, Japan.

CHAPTER REVIEW

SUMMARY

1. The most basic tools of geography are globes and maps. They help us to model the earth's surface.
2. Geographers do their work by using map analysis and geography technology. Use of the proper geography tool depends on the task to be performed.
3. Culture is the system of customs and traditions and habits a group of people use to make something of their world. Positive and negative aspects of culture are evaluated based on their movement away from or toward God's original intent.
4. The Creation Mandate plays an essential role in understanding geography and provides the means by which God intended to populate the earth. Cultural diversity abounds and must be analyzed from a biblical perspective.

Terms to Know

- ☑ Creation Mandate
- ☑ geography
- ☑ prime meridian
- ☐ great circle
- ☑ longitude
- ☑ equator
- ☑ latitude
- ☐ mental map
- ☑ cylindrical projection
- ☑ interrupted projection
- ☑ GIS
- ☑ remote sensing
- ☑ legend
- ☑ compass rose
- ☑ scale
- ☑ relief maps
- ☑ contour lines
- ☑ thematic map
- ☑ GPS
- ☑ culture
- ☑ multiculturalism

Making Connections

1. Briefly describe the five themes of geography.
2. Is 34°52' N a measurement of latitude or longitude? Explain your answer.
3. What are four ways a map can be distorted?
4. How does technology help us learn about the world?
5. Relate culture to the Creation Mandate.
6. Relate religion to culture.
7. Why should Christians care about the environment?

Developing Geography Skills

1. Draw a map of your city and include the location of your church, a post office, a hospital, an airport, and other local points of interest. Include a legend and compass rose. For an additional challenge, draw the map from memory to increase your mental mapping skills.
2. With your parents' permission, download Google Earth and enter your home address in the search bar. Zoom in and out to find churches, hospitals, and businesses on the map. Practice finding the exact location. Record the latitude, longitude, and feet above sea level of the chosen location.

Thinking Critically

1. Why should Christians spend time studying geography in light of the Bible's story?
2. Why are Christians to be both conformed to and distinct from the various cultures of the world?

Living in God's World

1. Chart your mental map of the world by recording your thoughts and impressions about the various regions of the world. Record positive, negative, or mixed views about different regions. Document these

views and the reasons you hold them. As you progress through the course, evaluate your mental map to see how well it conforms to a Christian understanding of these various regions.

2. Maps can play an important role in local church ministry. What are ways that maps could enhance your church's ministry? Formulate a plan. Consider taking it to one of your church leaders to see whether it would be profitable to implement.

CASE STUDY | Mapping Forest Fires with GIS

"A forest fire can be a real ecological disaster, regardless of whether it is caused by natural forces or human activity. It is impossible to control nature, but it is possible to map forest fire risk zones and thereby minimise the frequency of fire, avert damage, etc. Forest fire risk zones are locations where a fire is likely to start, and from where it can easily spread to other areas. Anticipation of factors influencing the occurrence of fire and understanding the dynamic behaviour of fire are critical aspects of fire management. A precise evaluation of forest fire problems and decisions on solution methods can only be satisfactorily made when a fire risk zone map is available. Satellite data plays a vital role in identifying and mapping forest fires and in recording the frequency at which different vegetation types/zones are affected. A geographic information system (GIS) can be used effectively to combine different forest-fire-causing factors for demarcating the forest fire risk zone map. Gorna Subwatershed, located in Madhya Pradesh, India, was selected for this study because it continually faces a forest fire problem. A colour composite image from the Indian Remote Sensing Satellite (IRS) 1D LISS III was used for vegetation mapping. Slope and other coverages (roads and settlements) were derived from topographic maps and field information. The thematic and topographic information was digitised and ARC/INFO GIS software was used for analysis. Forest fire risk zones were delineated by assigning subjective weights to the classes of all the layers according to their sensitivity to fire or their fire-inducing capability. Four categories of forest fire risk ranging from very high to low were derived automatically. Almost 30% of the study area was predicted to be under very high and high-risk zones. The evolved GIS-based forest fire risk model of the study area was found to be in strong agreement with actual fire-affected sites."

A controlled burn in Pench National Park, Madhya Pradesh, India

Reprinted from *International Journal of Applied Earth Observation and Geoinformation*, V.4, by Rajeev Kumar Jaiswal, Saumitra Mukherjee, Kumaran D. Raju, Rajesh Saxena, "Forest Fire Risk Zone Mapping from Satellite Imagery and GIS", Pages No. 1-10, Copyright 2002, with permission from Elsevier.

1. What are two causes of forest fires?
2. What is a forest fire risk zone, and what is the purpose of mapping these zones?
3. What role does GIS play in mapping the risk zones?
4. How does the mapping of potential forest fires help fulfill the Creation Mandate?

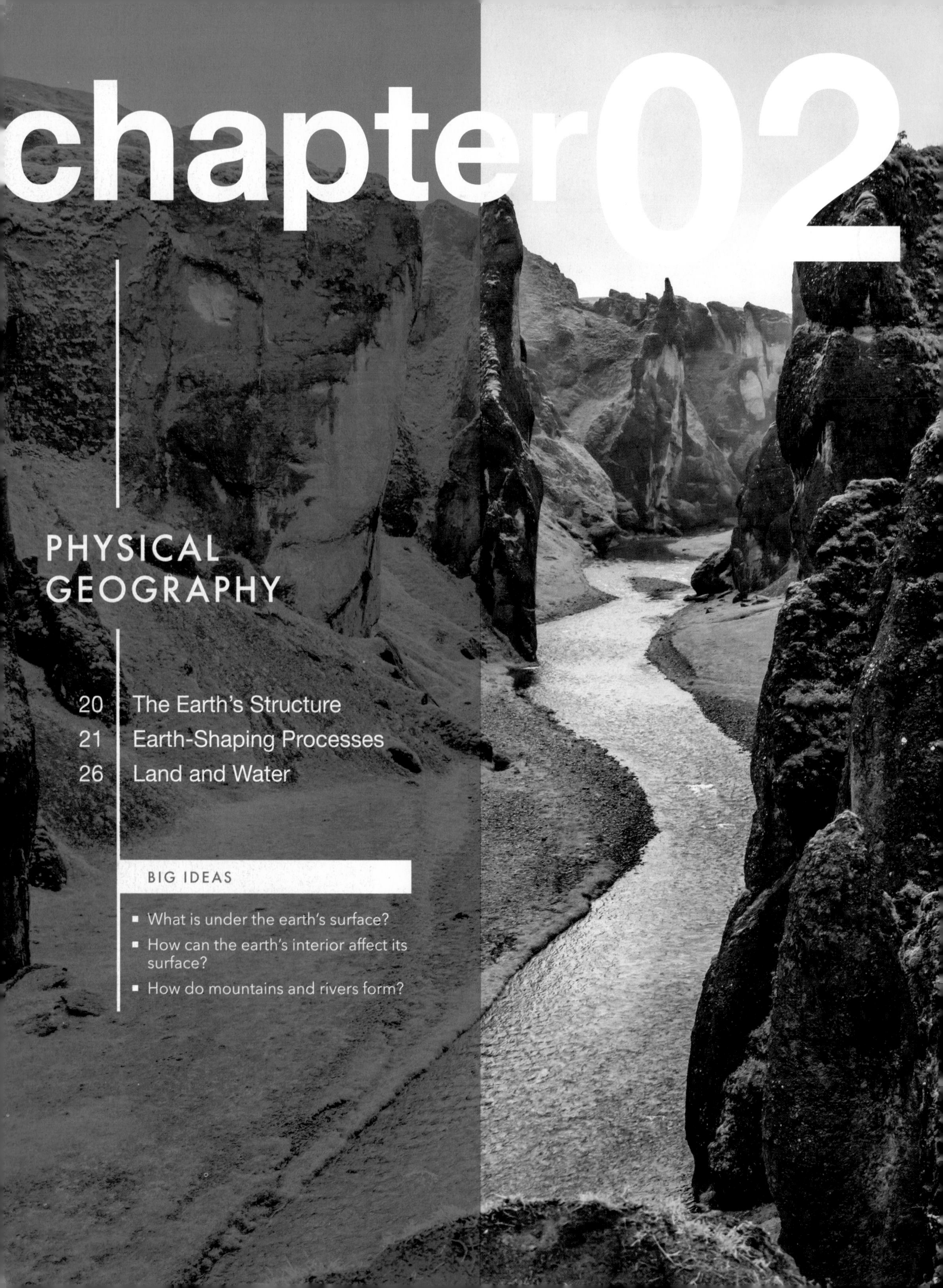

chapter 02

PHYSICAL GEOGRAPHY

20 The Earth's Structure
21 Earth-Shaping Processes
26 Land and Water

BIG IDEAS

- What is under the earth's surface?
- How can the earth's interior affect its surface?
- How do mountains and rivers form?

▲ *Fertile farmland along the Nile, Egypt*

RIVERS: GOD'S PROVISION FOR MANKIND

According to Herodotus, "Egypt was the gift of the Nile." In other words, the Nile made the Egyptian civilization possible. The Nile provided Egyptians an abundant supply of fish and fertile land to grow crops. The Egyptians learned to use irrigation ditches to increase production and substantially increase food supplies. This practice became essential to the survival of people in this part of the world, as illustrated by the biblical account of Joseph in the book of Genesis. Today the Nile is still a major provider of fish and crops and remains a vital water route for transportation.

The psalmist reminds us that God created the earth and all that it contains. He stretched out the heavens "like a curtain," and He "laid the foundations of the earth" so that it will remain forever (Ps. 104:1–5). The earth is not unimportant to God. The earth is God's great masterpiece. Whether we look at marvels such as the Grand Canyon, the savanna of Africa, or a powerful volcano, we see God's handiwork. In a fallen world, that handiwork is marred. The creation groans, awaiting its redemption (Rom. 8:21–22). But even this marred creation testifies to the Creator (Rom. 1:20).

A study of the physical earth is obviously relevant to geography. As we study people and cultures of the earth, we must also understand the structure of the physical space those people inhabit. How did the earth's surface features develop? How do they change? How do people interact with the land and water to use and change them?

▲ *(top) Mount Saint Helens, Washington, USA*

▲ *(middle) Great Barrier Reef, Cairns, Australia*

▲ *(bottom) Antarctica*

◀ *Fjadrargljufur Canyon, Iceland*

GUIDING QUESTIONS

- What are the physical systems of the earth?
- What are the elements of the earth's interior?
- What processes are occurring within the earth's interior?

THE EARTH'S STRUCTURE

What is under the earth's surface?

The Earth's Physical Systems

Scientists have developed models that divide the planet into four parts. The covering of air that surrounds our planet is the **atmosphere**. The earth's crust and the section of the upper mantle that moves with the tectonic plates are the **lithosphere**. All the water on the earth's surface, under the ground and in the air is the hydrosphere. The **biosphere** consists of all the different areas on the earth where life can exist and the living organisms that live there.

The earth is nearly eight thousand miles in diameter. We think of the earth's surface as very rough. But when astronauts view it from space, it seems to them as smooth as the surface of an apple.

The Earth's Interior

The earth seems to be divided into several layers. The thin outer "skin" is called the **crust** and consists mainly of two layers. The bottom layer of basaltic rock spreads over the entire earth. Above that are the oceans and slabs of granitic rock that are many miles thick. Where these slabs rise above the level of the ocean, they form **continents**.

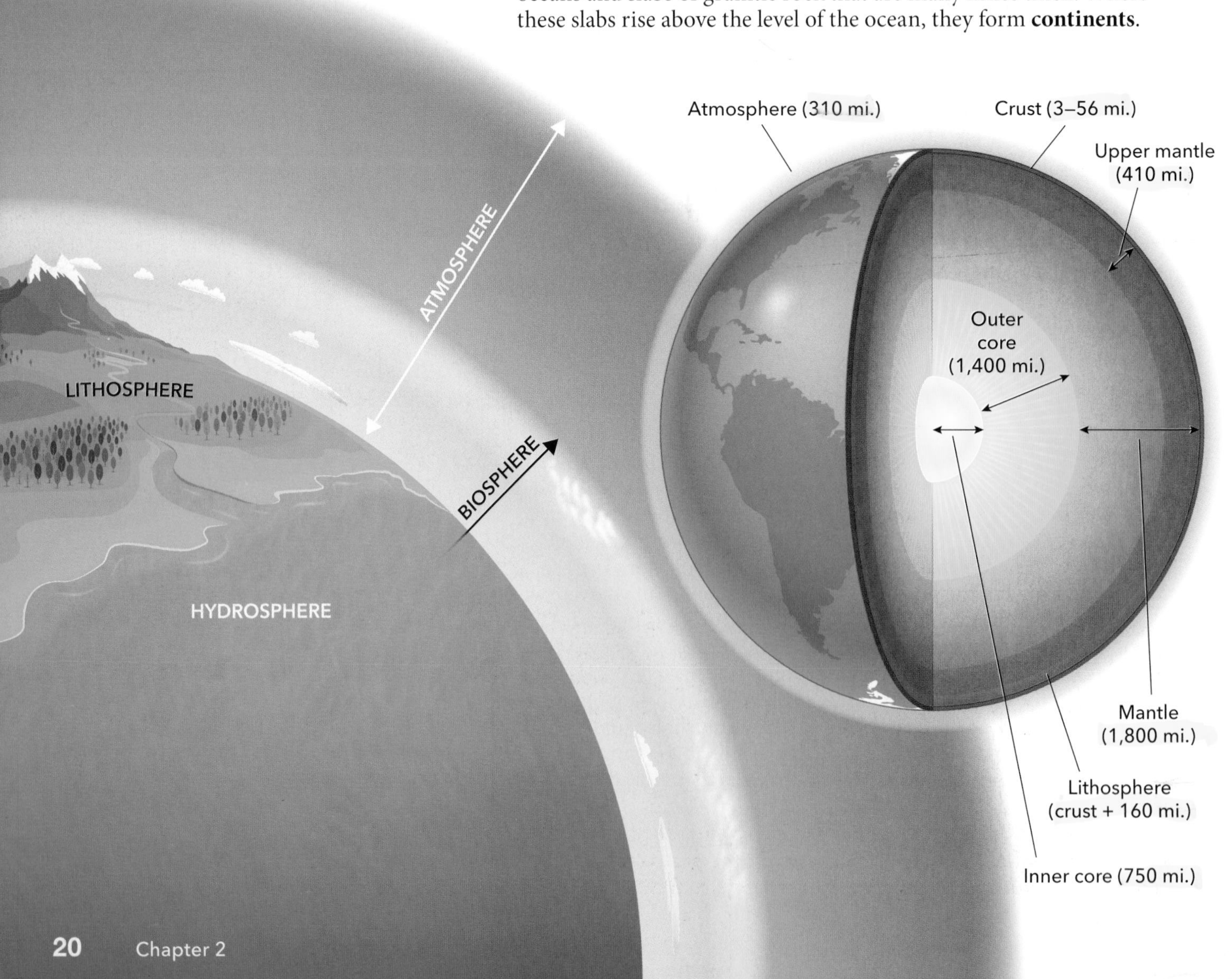

Earthquakes provide tantalizing hints about the secrets that lie below the earth's crust. In 1909 scientists noticed that earthquake waves decelerated abruptly and then accelerated again below the crust. They proposed that the waves were entering a layer of hot, plastic (capable of being shaped) material called the **mantle**. The molten rock in the earth's mantle is called **magma**. It is actually solid rock but flows because it is subjected to intense pressure and temperature (2,372°F). Earthquake waves move faster through the hot, dense mantle than through the crust. Waves from earthquakes also indicate that beneath the mantle is a core, which is divided into a liquid outer **core** and a solid inner core. After studying the magnetism of the earth and its powerful gravity as it interacts with the moon, many scientists concluded that the core might be made of two heavy metals, iron and nickel.

Scientists have theorized that a process of convection occurs in the mantle. **Convection** is the heat transfer that occurs when particles carry thermal energy as they move from one place to another. So as heavy rock material sinks it gets closer to the core where it heats up, gaining kinetic energy, and the magma rises, dragging other material with it. As it rises and gets further from the core, it cools, gets heavier, and sinks back down, thus continuing the process.

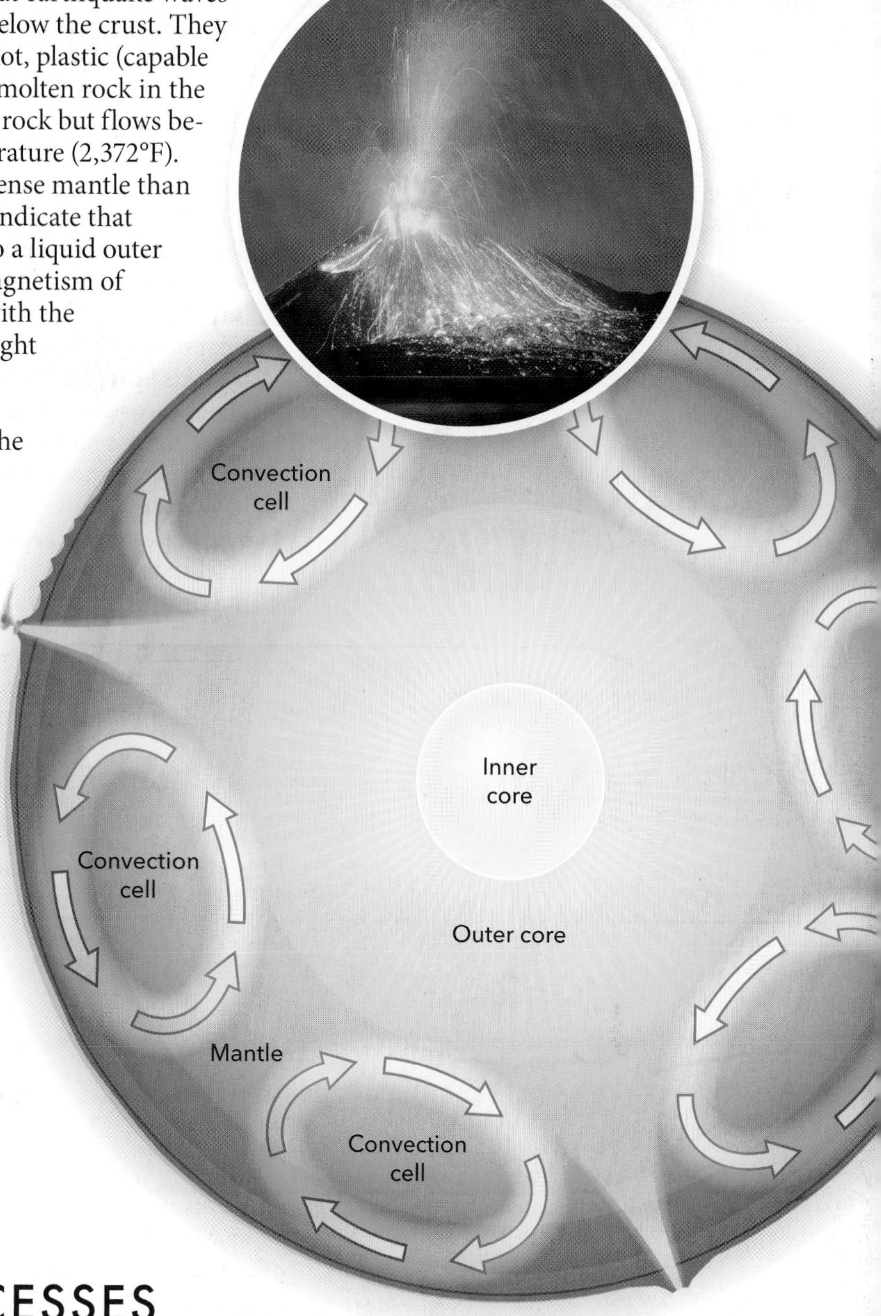

A volcano on the island of Anak Krakatau in Indonesia

Heat transport mechanism within the interior of the earth

SECTION REVIEW

1. List the four physical systems of the earth.
2. What are the three layers of the earth's interior?
3. Describe how the process of convection could be happening in the earth's interior.

EARTH-SHAPING PROCESSES

How can the earth's interior affect its surface?

GUIDING QUESTIONS

- What are the processes that shape the surface of the earth?
- What does the Bible say about these earth-shaping processes?
- How and where do geologists observe physical processes in the interior of the earth?
- How and where do geologists observe the effects of weathering and erosion?

The earth's surface is constantly changing. Since the Flood, two basic processes continue to shape the earth. Internal forces push rocks up, and external forces break rocks down. Both forces help to shape the mountains and other landforms we see today.

Internal Forces

Scientists have proposed that the crust is broken into pieces called plates. According to the **plate tectonics theory**, the plates crash into and pull apart from one another, releasing energy from the earth's

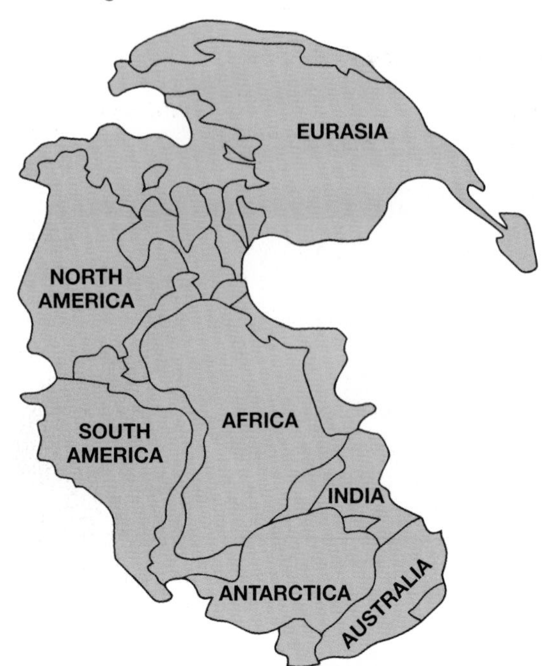

Pangaea

interior and causing earthquakes and volcanoes. This may, in part, explain how God brought about the Flood. The plates continue to move today, resulting in tremors and earthquakes. The engine that moves these giant plates is most likely the process of convection.

If you put the pieces of the earth's crust together like a jigsaw puzzle, especially when the continental shelf is included, you can see how all the continents could have originally been created as one huge landmass. The name Pangaea ("entire earth") is often used to describe this landmass. Some old-earth scientists speculate that the continents must have drifted over millions of years to their present positions. However, the Bible's account of Earth's history does not allow for millions of years. The Bible does teach that the world was once submerged in a worldwide Flood. The evidence seen today can be accounted for by the Flood. The violent upheaval resulting in the shift of tectonic plates during the Flood would have been powerful enough to break apart the supercontinent and set the continents in motion toward their present positions, a process called **continental drift**. This would have occurred over weeks and months rather than millions of years. The plates move today at a speed of two to five centimeters per year. Scientists propose that during the Flood the plates could have had a maximum speed of one meter per second.

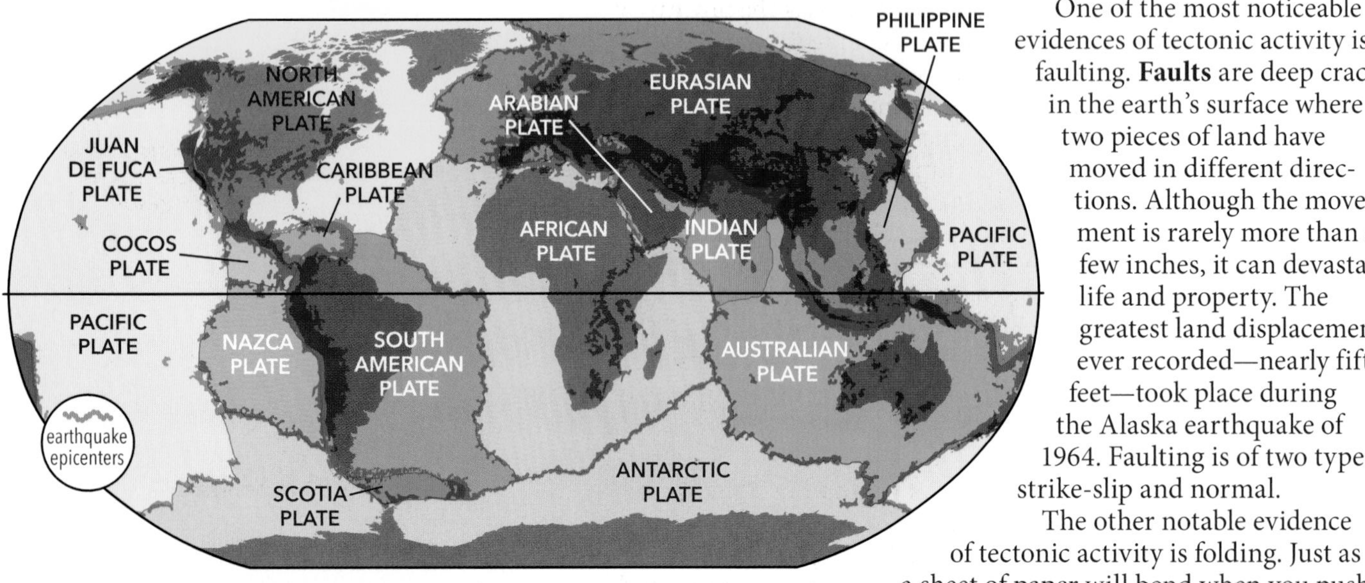

One of the most noticeable evidences of tectonic activity is faulting. **Faults** are deep cracks in the earth's surface where two pieces of land have moved in different directions. Although the movement is rarely more than a few inches, it can devastate life and property. The greatest land displacement ever recorded—nearly fifty feet—took place during the Alaska earthquake of 1964. Faulting is of two types: strike-slip and normal.

The other notable evidence of tectonic activity is folding. Just as a sheet of paper will bend when you push the edges toward the center, so loose sediment can bend upward into a fold when it is pushed from both sides.

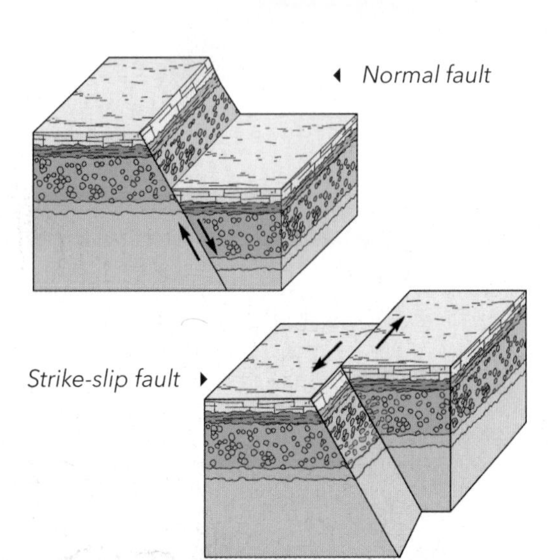
Normal fault

Strike-slip fault

Earthquakes and volcanoes are evidences of powerful forces at work deep within the earth. Although we don't fully understand these internal forces, scientists have some clues. They know that volcanoes and earthquakes are clustered along distinct lines on the earth's surface. Using sonar, scientists discovered that these lines continue under the oceans. The ocean floor is scarred by lines of deep trenches and high ridges.

The Hawaiian Islands are an example of the combined effects of plate tectonics and mantle activity. These islands stretch over 3,600 miles. Moving from east to west they become smaller and smaller. The smallest islands do not even rise above the ocean surface. As the diagram on page 23 shows, there is a hot spot or mantle plume that allows lava from the earth's interior to rise. As the plate moves over the hot spot, an island is created. Since the islands are smaller in the west, the plates must have been moving faster over the hot spot at an earlier time because the islands were not given as much time to form. The volcanoes on the Big Island of Hawaii have been active throughout recorded history, allowing that island to become the largest. This falls right in line with our understanding that during and following the Flood the earth-shaping forces happened at a much faster rate than they are happening today. If the plates had been moving at a constant rate, all the islands would probably be the same size and possibly all connected.

Hawaiian Archipelago formation

NW
Islands are progressively older
SE
Ni'ihau
Kaua'i
Moloka'i
O'ahu
Maui
(Big Island)
Mauna Loa
Mauna Kea
Kīlauea
Lō'ihi
Lithosphere
Pacific plate
Hotspot
Mantle
Motion of the Pacific plate drags the plume head
Mantle plume

External Forces

Landforms do not remain the same. External forces called weathering and erosion wear away the landforms that internal forces have pushed up.

Weathering

Although rocks might seem solid and unmoving, they are constantly weakened by the action of **weathering**. This is the process by which factors or conditions in the environment break rocks into smaller pieces. Weathering can be biological (plants), chemical (water), or physical (formation of ice crystals and temperature changes).

Some kinds of rocks break down more easily than others. Rocks with layers are easily separated. Others shatter under extreme temperature changes. When water collects in pores and freezes, it expands and causes the rock to break. When plants take root and grow, the roots exert tremendous pressure, causing more disintegration. Natural acids from rain, plants, and decaying matter can dissolve some rocks.

Weathering is crucial to life on the earth because it enriches the soil, the thin layer of the earth's surface where plants grow. Weathering produces particles of sand, silt, and clay that mix with humus to form soil. Farmers carefully study their soils to find out which fertilizers will be most beneficial.

A remarkable example of the effects of weathering is the Wave Rock in Western Australia, north of Perth. The rock is made up of granite and has gone through chemical weathering as a result of the groundwater flowing over it. The weathering processes of water and wind have resulted in the rock's unique wave shape.

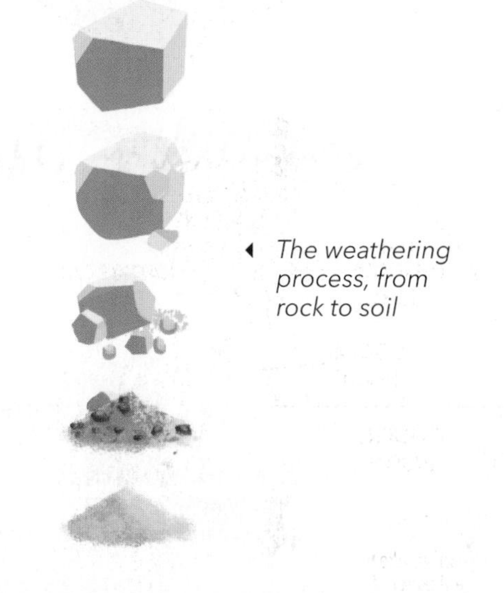

The weathering process, from rock to soil

Wave Rock in Western Australia

▾ A dust storm in Morocco is a kind of wind erosion.

▴ The Geiranger Fjord in Norway is the result of glacial erosion.

Erosion

After weathering breaks down rock into small pieces, those materials are removed by different types of erosion. **Erosion** is the process of wearing away rock and transporting sediments. So while weathering involves the breaking down of material, erosion is movement of those materials.

Wind erosion is the most intense in dry areas, particularly deserts. The abrasive action of tiny particles of sand blown by the wind can, over time, do great damage to landforms. The loss of soil through winds can also be destructive. For example, windstorms devastated American farmers on the Great Plains during the Dust Bowl of the 1930s. "Black blizzards" of choking dust darkened the skies as far away as New York.

Wave erosion alters the shore, creating sea caves, sea stacks, and sea arches. Waves also deposit sand offshore, making sandbars or even entire islands. This process formed many of the popular barrier islands along the North American coast.

Glacial erosion occurs when glaciers, large masses of moving ice and snow, flow downhill under the pull of gravity. Like gigantic bulldozers, glaciers push and scrape the earth in their paths. When glaciers receded to their current locations, they left behind hills of debris known as terminal moraines. Two famous moraines extend across the entire length of Long Island, New York.

Running water, however, is the most powerful force of erosion. It quickly flows through soil and soft rocks, carrying away materials as it goes. During floods, water can carve deep gullies quickly. But water's slow action over years can be just as devastating. Farmers are constantly battling to keep water from eroding their topsoil through normal runoff.

Extraordinary examples of erosion are the U-shaped valleys called fjords, created when glaciers receded and swept away material in a process called **glaciation**. The fjords are deepest near the inland, where the glaciation process was strongest.

Understanding Earth-Shaping Processes

Other than Creation, the Flood was the most significant physical event in history. Genesis 7–8 provides a glimpse of the process leading to the enormous changes the Flood brought to the earth's surface. The Flood also provided a clear distinction between God's original creation and life after the Flood.

Evidence for a **cataclysm** (a violent upheaval or change in the earth's crust) caused by a flood can be found around the world. How that evidence is interpreted depends on one's worldview. Those with a secular worldview have traditionally believed in **uniformitarianism**, the idea that geologic processes have been relatively uniform in activity and rate. Given the geologic evidence for past catastrophic events and processes that have shaped the earth's surface, most professional geologists today call themselves **neocatastrophists**. They continue to reject the biblical account but admit that the current condition of the earth's surface cannot be explained by gradual, uniform processes alone.

▾ *The Colorado River and the Grand Canyon, Arizona, USA*

The same evidence studied through the lens of a Christian worldview provides strong support for the biblical account of a universal flood. From widespread fossil remains, including those deposited on high mountaintops, to miles-thick sedimentary rock units, to deep, sculpted canyons, only a universal flood provides an adequate explanation for the geologic features we see today.

The Flood fractured the earth's surface, and the swirling waters churned soil, vegetation, and animal carcasses together in layer upon layer of sediment. Under the weight of tons of water, thick sediments quickly solidified. Tectonic forces folded and buckled sedimentary strata into unique formations even as they were hardening into rock.

Following the Flood, the global climate likely cooled for centuries due to the large amount of water vapor and volcanic dust in the atmosphere. The accumulation of snow and ice produced a single ice age that may have lasted for several centuries. Evidence for such a glacial period includes not only the remaining icecaps in the polar regions and glaciers in high mountains but also widespread glacial erosional and depositional features in northern Europe, Siberia, and North America. Similar evidence exists in the Southern Hemisphere.

SECTION REVIEW

1. What evidence supports the plate tectonics theory?
2. What are the internal processes that shape the earth's surface?
3. How does Hawaii show evidence of tectonic activity?
4. What is the difference between weathering and erosion?
5. How does the Bible's story help us understand the Earth's surface?

GUIDING QUESTIONS

- How are geology and hydrology relevant to geography?
- What are the different landforms and bodies of water?
- How were particular landforms and bodies of water formed?
- How do people interact with the land and water?
- What does the Bible say about using the earth's resources?

LAND AND WATER

How do mountains and rivers form?

Geography is concerned with the earth's physical features and human activity on the earth. Geology describes what those physical features are and how they change. Hydrology, or a study of the earth's water supply, reveals how human activity has been influenced by bodies of water throughout history and continues to be even today. So both geology and hydrology are important components in a study of cultural geography.

The Major Landforms

God's world is filled with a beautiful variety of land formations. Every variation in the landscape is called a landform. Geographers have classified three major **landforms**—mountains, plains, and plateaus—each of which has played a unique role in human civilization.

Mountains

Mountains stand high above the surrounding landscape. Geographers distinguish them from hills in that hills are generally smaller than mountains, although no set elevation distinguishes the two. Rather, local usage of the terms is the deciding factor.

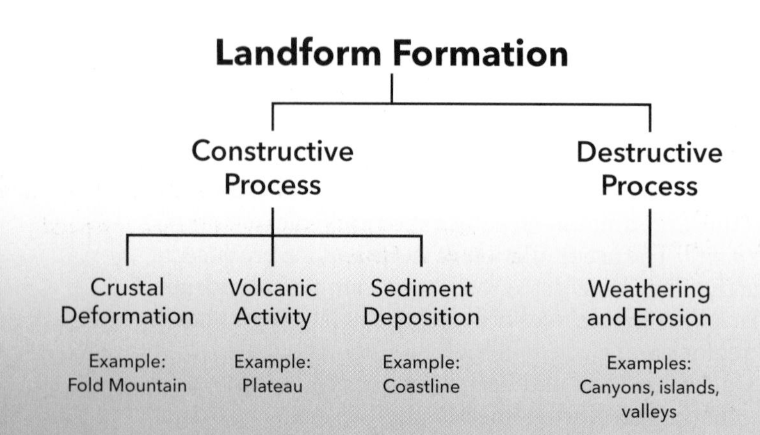

Many mountains stand alone above the surrounding landscape. When several mountains appear together, as in the Rocky Mountains, the formation is called a mountain range. The Rocky Mountain range is so large that it actually contains ranges within ranges, which are then called mountain systems.

The highest mountain range in the world is the Himalayas. The highest peak is Mount Everest, or Chomolungma in Tibetan. Farmers many miles away depend on the rivers that flow from the melting snows of Mount Everest and other Himalayan peaks.

The Himalayas were formed when the Indian and Asian plates collided during the Flood. If you have ever witnessed the results of a collision involving

Mount Everest, Sagarmatha National Park, Khumbu Valley, Nepal

two large vehicles, you can imagine how much greater would be the result of two large landmasses crashing into each other. The tectonic process by which the relatively thin and dense oceanic crust slowly slides down and under the more massive but less dense continental crust is called **subduction**. Mountains that form in this way are called fold mountains. Other examples include the Rockies, the Alps, and the Appalachians. Fault-block mountains are another type. Fault-block mountains occur when pieces of the earth's crust pull apart, causing some blocks of rock to rise and others to fall. The Sierra Nevada range in the western United States offers a classic example of fault-block mountains. Both fault-block mountains and fold mountains are called deformational mountains because tectonic forces seem to have deformed the rocks that were already on the surface.

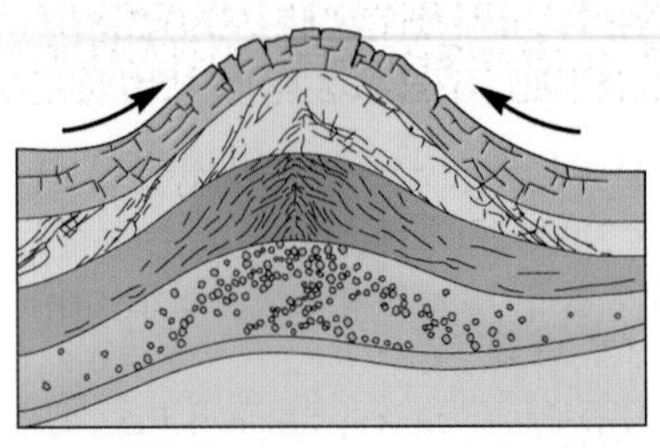

▲ *Fold fault*

In addition to influencing weather, climate, and vegetation, mountains have influenced the pattern of human settlement. Many cities arose near mines, which burrow deep into the belly of mountains. Other cities lie in the fertile valleys of mountain ranges, where they are protected from extreme weather. But in most cases, mountains are too cold, rugged, or infertile for extensive human settlement.

Mountain ranges also hinder travel and contact between people. Populations living in the mountains can easily hide from attack, and social changes are slow to reach them. As you study geography, you will notice that cultures, languages, dialects, and national borders are often defined by mountain ranges.

Plains

In contrast to mountains, **plains** are wide areas of flat land. Some plains that lie in coastal areas, such as the land along the Gulf of Mexico, are called coastal plains. But low elevation does not define plains; plains can also be found at high elevation. For example, nestled among the Andes Mountains of South America is the Altiplano, which averages twelve thousand feet above sea level. Nor are plains always completely flat. For instance, the Great Plains region of North America has many rolling hills.

▲ *The Uyuni Salt Flat in southwest Bolivia is part of the Altiplano Plain.*

Plains are the most valuable landform for farmers. Rivers bring water and sediments from the mountains, and deposits called alluvium settle in the flat plains. Alluvium is often rich in nutrients that enable farms to produce large quantities of food. Therefore, such alluvial plains are the "breadbaskets" of many nations. They are often named after the river that flows through them. For example, the Congo Basin is an alluvial plain named for the mighty Congo River.

Landforms

1. Archipelago: A group of islands
2. Atoll: A ring of low coral islands and reefs surrounding a central lagoon
3. Basin: Area of land drained by a river and its tributaries
4. Canyon: A deep valley with steep sides usually carved by a river
5. Cave: A naturally occurring underground hollow in earth, rock, or ice
6. Cliff: Steep face of rock and soil
7. Delta: The area at the mouth of a river where sediment is deposited
8. Divide: Land that separates river systems
9. Dune: A depositional landform resulting from wind-deposited sand and soil
10. Hill: A natural elevation of the earth's surface rising to a summit; lower than a mountain
11. Isthmus: A strip of land with water on two sides connecting two larger areas to each other
12. Mesa: A flat-topped hill with steep sides
13. Mountain peak: The pointed top of a mountain
14. Mountain range: A series of mountains in the same geographic area
15. Oasis: An area of land in a desert where water and plants are found
16. Peninsula: A piece of land jutting out into water
17. Seacoast: The part of the land adjoining the sea
18. Valley: An area of land between hills or mountains
19. Volcano: A crack in the earth's crust through which molten rock comes to the surface

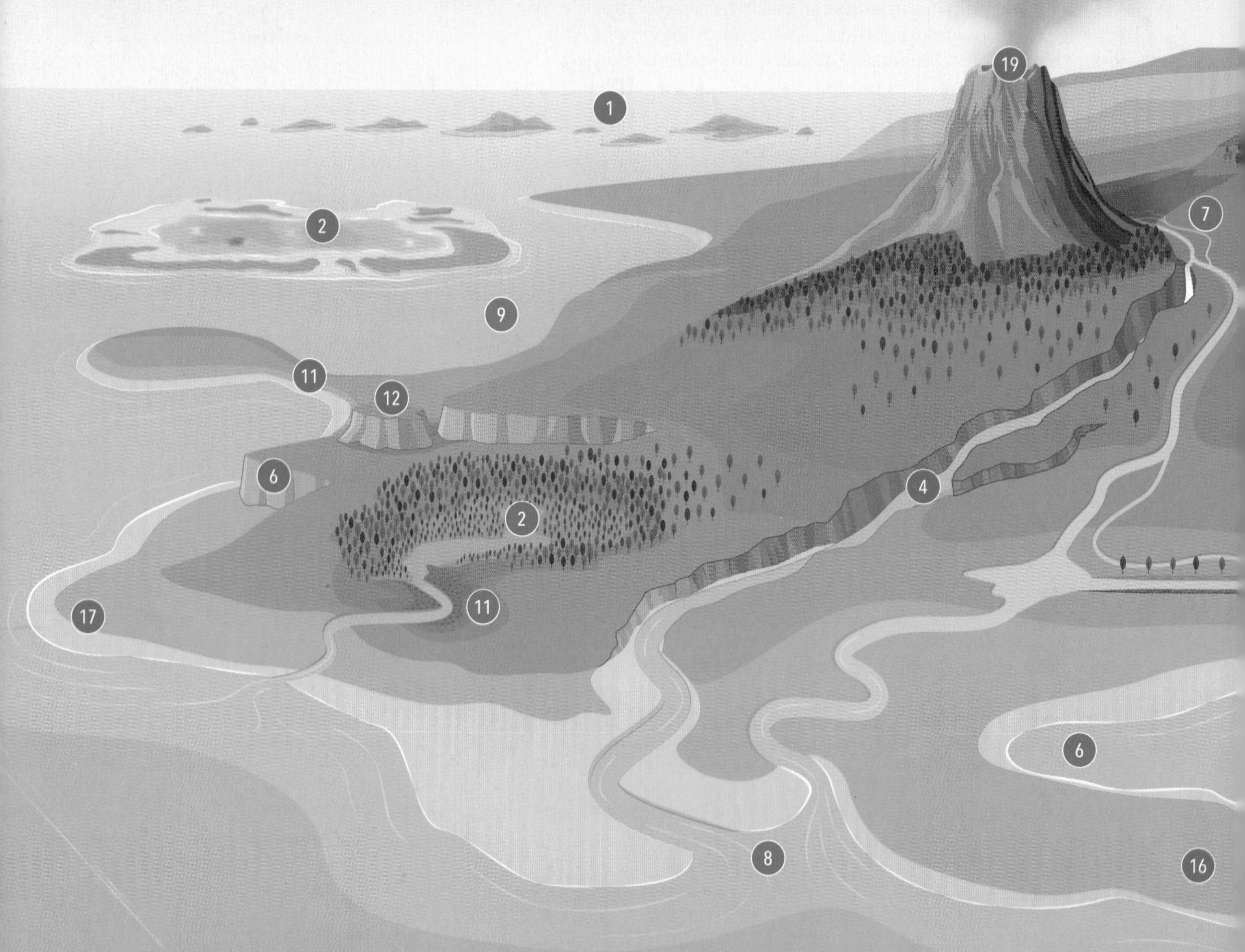

Bodies of Water

1. Bay: An area of water bordered by land on three sides; smaller than a gulf
2. Bayou: A slow-moving stream or a marshy lake
3. River: A large stream
4. Canal: An artificial waterway, usually connected to existing bodies of water
5. Channel: The physical confinement of a river, slough, or ocean strait
6. Cove: A circular or round inlet with a narrow entrance
7. Creek: A small stream
8. Estuary: A semi-enclosed coastal body of water with one or more rivers or streams flowing into it and with a free connection to the open sea
9. Gulf: A part of a lake or ocean that extends so that it is surrounded by land on three sides; larger than a bay
10. Mouth: The point at which a stream empties into another body of water
11. Wetland: Land that is almost always wet; usually classified as a marsh, swamp, or bog

▲ *The Tibetan Plateau is one of the largest in the world.*

Plateaus

Plateaus, a third landform, are wide areas of relatively flat land, like plains, but they rise abruptly above surrounding lands. They resulted from the erosion of soft sedimentary material by the massive movement of the Flood waters. Steep cliffs or slopes mark at least one edge of a plateau. Plateaus are often called tablelands because their surface is sometimes elevated like a tabletop.

The surfaces of plateaus are much more varied than plains, often including hills, mountains, and deep canyons. For example, the Grand Canyon cuts through one of North America's largest plateaus. The most rugged plateaus of the world are often called highlands. Plateaus can occur at almost any elevation. The highest is the Tibetan Plateau, which lies on the northern border of the Himalayan range in Asia.

Plateaus generally have poor soils and few resources other than grass for grazing animals. Many of the world's deserts are located on plateaus.

The Major Bodies of Water

Like landforms, bodies of water play a major role in human life. The three main bodies of water—oceans or seas, lakes, and rivers—are at the heart of a great deal of human activity.

Without a ready supply of fresh water, we would quickly die; therefore, human settlements develop near sources of fresh water. Less than 3 percent of the earth's water is fresh, and more than two-thirds of that water is in polar icecaps and glaciers or is underground. The remaining water, in lakes and rivers, is a precious resource, essential to our growth and survival.

Large bodies of water often provide means for travel and trade. When settlers first arrived in America, they clustered along the coast and rivers rather than moving into the mountains. It was much less expensive to ship food by water than to transport it overland. Ships could carry ten wagonloads of goods for the same price as one cart pulled over the mountains. Food on ships arrived at the marketplace much sooner; the food cost less and was fresher. Even today, water transportation is by far the least expensive way for most nations to ship products to each other, especially if they do not share a land border.

Earth's Fresh and Salt Water

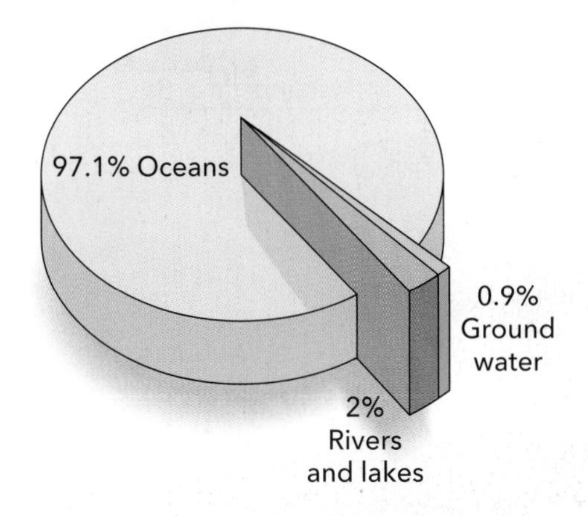

Oceans

The earth is unique in the solar system. To date, scientists have not found liquid water on any other planet or moon, yet water covers 71 percent of the earth's surface, amounting to more than three hundred million cubic miles. Although 97 percent of the water is in the oceans, traces of water can be found on almost every square inch of land.

There are four principal ocean basins in the world: the Pacific, the Atlantic, the Indian, and the Arctic. In the year 2000 the International Hydrographic Organization decided to recognize a fifth ocean. The Southern Ocean, while not a true ocean basin, surrounds Antarctica and extends to 60 degrees latitude. All of the world's seas, gulfs, and bays belong to one of these oceans. Continents generally mark the borders of each ocean. If you look at the world map, however, you will see that the divisions are not always clear. The oceans flow into each other. For this reason, the whole system is sometimes called the **world ocean**.

The oceans provide humans with many blessings—distributing thermal energy from the sun, providing water for rain clouds, and guarding nations from foreign invasion. Ocean waters teem with fish and pearl-producing clams. One often overlooked gift of the sea, however, is its salt. Salt is essential for human health. It has hundreds of uses, from preserving food to being an essential ingredient in many manufactured goods and chemicals.

If we could drink ocean water and pump it into our parched fields, it would solve many of our worst problems. But the high concentration of salt—about 3.5 percent of the total mass of seawater—is harmful to crops and land animals.

With waves averaging thirty to forty feet, the Southern Ocean is no place for the amateur sailor.

Rivers

Water is in constant motion. Unless something gets in its way, water will eventually flow to the ocean. Small streams flow into rivers, which in turn flow into even larger rivers. Rivers that feed other rivers are called **tributaries**. The main river and all its tributaries are called a **river system**. Many of the world's great river systems flow more than two thousand miles from their headwaters (source) to their mouth. Geographers rank river systems by comparing various features, such as length, discharge, drainage area, and navigability.

The most obvious comparison is length. The Nile is considered the longest river, an impressive 4,160 miles. But depending on which tributary one designates as the headwaters, the Amazon might be longer. The longest rivers in the United States—the Missouri River (2,540 miles) and the Mississippi (2,340 miles), which it flows into—are not among the top ten longest rivers. But considered as a river system, the Mississippi-Missouri River (including tributaries of the Missouri) measures 3,735 miles long, giving it a rank of fourth place in the world.

▾ Mississippi River Basin

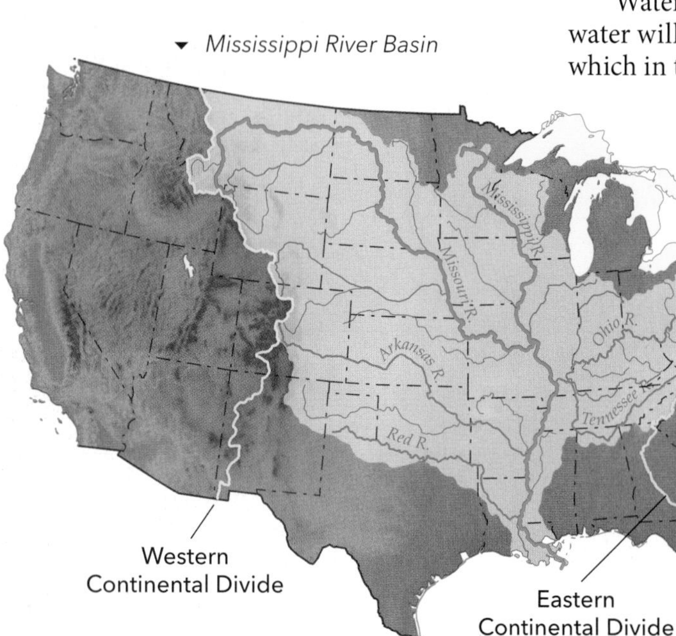

Another feature of comparison is discharge, the amount of water flowing into the ocean. It would take about sixty-three rivers the size of the Nile to match the volume of water that flows from the Amazon. The volume is so large that the water from the Amazon remains fresh and drinkable two hundred miles out into the Atlantic Ocean.

A third feature for comparison is the size of the **drainage basin**, the total land area drained by the main river and its tributaries. The Nile's drainage basin is small and mostly dry and has few tributaries. In contrast, the Amazon River drains a rainforest that covers 40 percent of the continent of South America. The Missouri River has the fifth largest drainage basin (1,244,000 sq. mi.).

A fourth feature of comparison is navigability, or how far up a river oceangoing vessels can travel. Steamboats used to ply the Missouri River more than one thousand miles from the ocean. Barges rely on deep, navigable rivers for carrying goods from their distant sources to coastal cities. The Mississippi River and its tributaries include more than fifteen thousand miles of navigable water, making it the second largest inland water route in the world. The Amazon is the only river system that has more navigable miles than the Mississippi.

Rivers have played a central role in the history of almost every nation. Historically, explorers have used these waters as roads to the interior. Many pioneers who followed the explorers settled near these rivers, and most cities were founded beside rivers. For example, St. Louis sprang up at the point where boats floating down the Missouri entered the Mississippi River. Even where rivers are too shallow for travel, they provide drinking water, irrigation, fish, game, power generation, and recreation. The birthplace of almost every great civilization was somewhere along a river.

▾ The Amazon River

Lakes

Bodies of water fully enclosed by land are called lakes and are remnants of the Flood and the Ice Age. Many cities are located on the shores of lakes because lakes provide fish, drinking water, transportation, and recreation. Lakes make it possible for some cities to be built deep in the interior of continents. Lakes can form in many different ways. Some formed where glaciers cut out valleys and built up dams that kept the meltwater from flowing into the sea. Other lakes formed in basins that were created by tectonic activity. After the basin was formed, it filled with water. Some lakes form in volcanoes. When a volcano becomes inactive, water can collect in the crater, as in the case of Crater Lake in Oregon. When a river changes directions, it can leave a lake behind. Landslides can also cause the formation of a lake when the land dams up a river. Some very large lakes or reservoirs are created when people dam a river. Lake Volta in Ghana is the world's largest reservoir, containing 144 billion cubic meters of water.

The Great Lakes of North America are the largest system of freshwater lakes in the world. This system includes the world's largest freshwater lake (by area)—Lake Superior. The Great Lakes support many large cities, including Chicago and Detroit.

Other continents also have important freshwater lakes. Lake Titicaca, high in the Andes Mountains, is the largest lake in South America (by volume) and the highest navigable lake in the world. Africa's Lake Chad has been the heart of great empires in central Africa. In east Africa is Lake Victoria, the largest lake on the continent (by area) and the second largest freshwater lake in the world.

Lake Baikal, located in Asia, is both the deepest lake and the largest freshwater lake (by volume). More than a mile deep, it holds almost as much fresh water as all of the Great Lakes combined, although its surface area is relatively small.

The Caspian Sea, also in Asia, is the world's largest lake (by both area and volume). Unlike Lake Superior, however, its water is salty. While the water in freshwater lakes is kept clean by rivers or other outlets that carry dissolved minerals downstream, a few drainage basins of the world have no outlet to the ocean. Water collects at the lowest spot, called a depression. The Caspian Sea is actually below sea level. As the water evaporates, minerals are left behind. Though rare, such salt lakes are often large and famous. For example, the Dead Sea, which is nearly 37 percent salt, is the saltiest lake in the world. (Utah's Great Salt Lake is 10–25 percent salt, and ocean water is typically 3 percent salt.)

▲ *North Shore of Lake Superior, Minnesota, USA*

The frozen surface of Lake Baikal, Russia ▶

Seas

Seas are arms of the ocean partially enclosed by land. Seas can vary greatly in size, and some even have seas within seas. For example, a map of the Mediterranean Sea reveals seven arms in the north that ancient peoples called the "seven seas." The Greek and Roman civilizations arose along their shores. Sailors prefer carrying people and goods on the smaller seas because they normally have smaller waves. The shores blunt the blows of the violent storms that batter ships on the open seas, such as the Mediterranean.

Ships need safe places to anchor while they load and unload their cargo. A sheltered body of deep water next to the shore is called a harbor. Good harbors are rare. The water must be deep enough that the ships do not run aground. The shore must encircle enough of the sea to shelter ships from winds and waves that might otherwise drive them into the rocks or sand. A key to the success of America's original colonies was their harbors. Boston, New York, Philadelphia, and Charleston quickly became major port cities because of their great harbors.

▾ *The fishing village of Naousa on the island of Paros, Greece, in the Mediterranean Sea*

SECTION REVIEW

1. What are the three basic landforms on the earth?
2. What type of landform are the Appalachian Mountains?
3. How is crustal deformation a constructive process?
4. Compare and contrast plains and plateaus.
5. What are the advantages to living on a plain? What might be some disadvantages?
6. How are oceans and seas similar?
7. How were most lakes formed?
8. What are the two main reasons that water is important to human activity?

Interacting with Land and Water

As never before, people living today see the world transformed around them. This progress is what we should expect in a world in which God has given humans the abilities to subdue and make use of the creation.

The word *industry* is often used to describe people's hard work to make a living. Although there are many types of jobs, or industries, the basic categories have been around since God made man to exercise dominion over His earth. All industries are primary, secondary, or tertiary. Primary industries are the most basic, which means they relate directly to interacting with land and water. In primary industries people take from the earth materials that are needed for food, clothes, and shelter. There are four types of primary industries: agriculture, fishing, forestry, and mining.

Part of God's Creation Mandate to Adam was dominion over the created world. God intended for Adam to be His steward, or caretaker, of the environment that He had created. The Lord Himself planted the first garden, filling it with plants and foods for Adam and Eve's use. In addition to using the earth to meet basic needs, we should endeavor to make the earth both more productive and more beautiful. This requires us to be careful about how we treat the earth.

Christians should take care of God's creation. It is important to note what God did not say in Genesis 2:15. He did not say, "You are just a part of My creation and are to leave everything the way it is." Today, many believe that people should be viewed as a type of virus on the earth. This contradicts Genesis 1:28–29, where we learn that God has given humanity a special role. The three verbs that exemplify man's job and relation to creation are *tend*, *care*, and *rule*. Sinful humans who damage the creation through pollution and resource depletion are failing to manage the creation wisely. Often these actions stem from prioritizing short-term benefits over long-term flourishing.

The three industry sectors

The Grand Coulee Dam on the Columbia River, Washington, USA

Farming

Contrary to an evolutionary view of human history, mankind did not take millions of years to figure out how to plant seeds and domesticate animals. God taught Adam to be a gardener, and his two sons specialized in the two major branches of agriculture: farming and animal husbandry.

Throughout the ages, farming has supplied most of the earth's food. Planting seeds provides a much more reliable food supply than hunting wild animals and gathering wild fruits. Most farmers produce only enough food to meet the needs of their own households. Such farmers are subsistence farmers. Billions of people in the world still live by subsistence farming.

At the end of the eighteenth century, an agricultural revolution took place in Great Britain and then spread to the United States. Farmers began applying science and machinery to increase their yields, enabling commercial farmers to raise large cash crops for profit and thereby freeing other people to pursue other types of work. Modern cities depend on the steady supply of food from commercial farms.

All farms, whether subsistence or commercial, face the same challenges; they differ only in scale. Drought, disease, and insect plagues can wipe out crops. Windstorms, hail, and floods can devastate fields. In many places, irrigation has reduced the threat of drought, insecticides have limited the threat of insects, and breeding has improved crop yields and resistance to disease. But one major problem remains: loss of soil. Wind and water can wash away soil and nutrients, and certain crops can deplete the soil's nutrients.

Animal Husbandry

The second main form of agriculture is animal husbandry, which also can be subdivided into subsistence and commercial types. Subsistence husbandry, known as nomadic herding, is common in rugged mountains and dry areas where regular farming is difficult. Jabal, a descendant of Cain, became "the father of such as dwell in tents, and of such as have cattle" (Gen. 4:20). Because large herds of animals quickly consume the vegetation in an area, nomads must move frequently in search of fresh pastures.

During the eighteenth century, Europeans developed a second method of animal husbandry called ranching. Wealthy landowners let their herds and flocks graze on enclosed tracts of land. Sheep owners rounded up their sheep to shear them of their wool.

▲ *(top) Farmers grow rice on manmade plateaus in Vietnam.*

◀ *(middle) A Zimbabwean farmer tends to her corn.*

◀ *(bottom) Hawaii once had the largest cattle ranch in the world.*

Freshly caught tuna at a tuna auction in Wakayama, Japan

Fishing

Fishing is an important source of food in many countries. Seafood is the world's second largest export commodity, trailing only oil. Demand has outpaced supply, so the industry is expanding worldwide.

The seafood industry includes essentially two varieties—fish and seaweed—and uses two methods to obtain the products: capture (products gathered in the wild, natural state) and aquaculture (cultivation or farming in a controlled, artificial environment).

Seafood-producing countries are coming under increasing pressure both from conservationists and from within the industry to emphasize sustainability and care of the environment to ensure continuation of the industry. This pressure is leading to a united effort by scientists, conservationists, and the fishing industry. Such efforts to meet human needs while protecting the environment and endangered species are an important part of fulfilling God's expectation of responsible stewardship.

Forestry

Wood is another important resource, and the size of the forestry products industry proves it. When you think about forestry products, you probably think of lumber and paper, but trees have thousands of other unique uses. Fruit, medicine, glues, make-up, fragrances, furniture, and soaps are just some of the other things made from parts of a tree. The most important thing to remember about trees is that they are renewable. While it is true that foresters cut down trees, they also work to protect and sustain valuable forest resources. The most obvious way they do this is by planting new trees. They also thin out some forested areas and remove dead wood in order to reduce the threat of wildfires.

Because logging technology has advanced, it can be done in a more sustainable manner.

Mining

As important as agriculture, fishing, and forestry are, mining has far surpassed them in economic importance. Modern countries spend great sums of money mining three types of resources: metals, nonmetal minerals, and fossil fuels.

Metals

The earth's crust is composed mainly of rock that contains a variety of minerals (solid crystals that occur naturally and have a definite chemical composition). Scientists have identified about three thousand different minerals, but only about one hundred are common.

Metals are the most important type of mineral because of four useful properties: they are shiny, malleable (able to be hammered into sheets), ductile (able to be drawn into wire), and conductive (able to conduct electricity). The first metalworker was Tubal-cain, a descendant of Cain, who became "an instructer of every artificer in brass and iron" (Gen. 4:22).

A one-troy-ounce gold nugget

Metals are of three types: precious metals, common metals, and alloys. The modern production of gold, silver, and platinum is small if measured in tons, but those precious metals are far more valuable than other metal products. They are considered precious for their beauty, durability, scarcity, and trade value.

Common metals get their name because they are mined in great quantities from the earth's surface and are therefore common. Three such metals have been used extensively since ancient times: copper, lead, and iron. Sixty percent of the copper mined today is used in the electrical industry because it is the least expensive conductor of electricity. Lead had been used in paints, but it was discovered that this could be a health hazard. Lead is still used in some products, such as car batteries. More iron is mined each year than all other metals combined. This strong, versatile metal became useful for making cannons, bridges, trains, and other modern machines. The second most common metal on earth is aluminum. It is so difficult to extract from its ore, bauxite, that a process of separating them was not discovered until 1886. The bond holding the elements together in bauxite (hydrogen, oxygen, and aluminum) is very powerful. Aluminum is separated using electrical currents. Because it is lightweight and resistant to corrosion, aluminum is ideal for cars, aircraft, and other machines.

Iron ore

The four metals just mentioned—copper, lead, iron, and aluminum—are useful not only by themselves but also in combination with other metals. Early in history, people learned that they could combine such metals to form alloys. The other six common metals—chromium, manganese, zinc, nickel, tin, and tungsten—are not usually used by themselves but are combined with one or more of the first four metals.

Steel is the world's most important alloy. It is formed by combining iron with the carbon in coal. Nearly all of the world's iron ore is now turned into steel. In a sense, the Iron Age has become "the Steel Age."

The Berkeley Pit copper mine in Butte, Montana, USA, was one of the largest in the world.

Nonmetal Minerals

Many other kinds of minerals play an important role in industry. Limestone is formed mainly from calcite (calcium, carbon, and oxygen). When crushed and mixed with clay, it makes a powder called cement. Adding sand to cement produces mortar. Adding crushed rock to cement makes concrete, the most widely used building material in the world.

Sulfur is another versatile mineral known since ancient times. It has many modern uses. Combined with charcoal and potassium nitrate, sulfur makes gunpowder. It is also used to process petroleum and steel, to produce fertilizer, to improve the strength and texture of rubber, and even to make matches.

Other minerals that have been used since early history include clay (for bricks, plates, pitchers, cups, and bowls); sand (for making glass for windows and bottles); and granite, marble, slate, and sandstone (for monuments and decorative buildings). From phosphates, nitrates, and potassium, we get fertilizers for enriching the soil.

A few minerals contain uranium, a mineral that was used in the first atomic bombs in 1945 and was later used in nuclear reactors. Its high radioactivity makes it very harmful to the human body.

▲ An offshore oil production platform for the exploration of oil and gas

Fossil and Hydrocarbon Fuels

For centuries, people used wind, water, and wood to power their equipment for transportation and manufacture. Gradually, mankind realized the potential of other energy resources—fossil fuels and hydrocarbon fuels. Coal is technically not a mineral but the remains of living things. The Flood waters trapped plants and animals beneath layers of sedimentary rock. The pressure changed this organic matter into its present form. Fuels such as petroleum and natural gas have dramatically changed our way of life.

Coal is a solid rock that occurs in various grades, or levels of quality, depending on the amount of heat produced per pound. The Chinese burned coal for heat more than a thousand years before Christ. In the late eighteenth century, Europeans began using coal to power steam engines. Coal is now used to generate most of the world's electricity.

Petroleum is a liquid hydrocarbon fuel. The ancient Chinese used petroleum that had seeped into pools on the earth's surface; the first commercial oil well was not drilled until 1859. At first, Americans extracted kerosene for lamps and discarded the rest of the oil. But scientists soon realized that petroleum produces much more energy than coal. The invention of gasoline engines turned petroleum into the most important mining product in the world.

Located in many underground oil pools is a hydrocarbon fuel in gaseous form called natural gas. Many scientists believe it is a byproduct of the process that formed petroleum. Natural gas was initially burned off as waste at the first oil wells. However, natural gas is now used as an efficient fuel for generating electricity. Its many residential uses include furnaces, water heaters, dryers, and ovens.

SECTION REVIEW

1. Distinguish the Christian concern for the creation from modern environmentalism.
2. Define *subsistence farming.*
3. Which metal is mined more than any other?
4. What is an alloy, and which alloy is most important?

02 CHAPTER REVIEW

SUMMARY

1. The earth is divided into four physical systems: atmosphere, lithosphere, hydrosphere, and biosphere, and its interior has three layers: crust, core, and mantle.
2. Forces under the surface of the earth started occurring during the Flood to produce the landforms we see today. The forces are still in effect but are not moving at the same speed as during the Flood.
3. Weathering and erosion are external forces working on the landforms of the earth to change them.
4. People interact with the land and water to obtain resources through four primary industries: agriculture, fishing, forestry, and mining.
5. Agriculture has two branches: farming and animal husbandry.
6. Mining has surpassed the other primary industries in economic importance. Metals, nonmetal minerals, and fossil fuels are mined for their usefulness and value.

Terms to Know

- ☐ atmosphere
- ☐ lithosphere
- ☐ hydrosphere
- ☐ biosphere
- ☐ crust
- ☐ continents
- ☐ earthquakes
- ☐ mantle
- ☐ magma
- ☐ core
- ☐ convection
- ☐ plate tectonics theory
- ☐ continental drift
- ☐ faults
- ☐ weathering
- ☐ erosion
- ☐ glaciation
- ☐ cataclysm
- ☐ uniformitarianism
- ☐ neocatastrophists
- ☐ landform
- ☐ mountains
- ☐ subduction
- ☐ plains
- ☐ plateaus
- ☐ world ocean
- ☐ tributaries
- ☐ river system
- ☐ drainage basin

Making Connections

1. What is tectonic activity, and what are its two most notable types?
2. What two formative events in the earth's history occurred only once and will never occur again? How do those events contradict uniformitarianism?
3. How do weathering and erosion work together to shape the earth's surface?
4. What type of landforms are created in a destructive process?
5. How do the different bodies of water benefit humans?

Developing Geography Skills

1. What evidence contradicts the theory of neocatastrophism?
2. What major landforms are in your area?
3. What is the most common primary industry in your area?

Thinking Critically

1. What was the impact of the Flood on the surface of the earth? Support your answer.
2. Read Psalm 24:1 and Genesis 2:15. What principles can be drawn from these verses about the stewardship of natural resources?

Living in God's World

1. What would you say to a friend who says that Christians should not be concerned about the environment because only spiritual things really matter, and God is going to burn up the earth one day anyway? Support your answer with Scripture.
2. How would you respond to a friend who claims that working to save the environment is just as much a part of the Christian mission as seeking to save souls because God intends to save both in the end? Support your answer with Scripture.

CASE STUDY | Oso Landslide

Imagine that you are eating your breakfast on a quiet morning when you hear the sound of a freight train going by (there are no train tracks nearby). You look out your window and see that your neighbor's house is gone. On Saturday, March 22, 2014, at 10:37 a.m., this really happened. A piece of a mountain measuring six hundred feet high by fifteen hundred feet wide had given way in what is called a rotational landslide. The ground, which was a mix of sand, clay, and stones, had become saturated, causing it to detach, slide down, and roll over part of the small town of Oso, Washington.

It took just 138 seconds for the geography of the area to change. The Steelhead Haven community near the base of the mountain was buried by almost two thousand square acres of debris, and forty-three people were killed, making it the single deadliest landslide in US history. Property damages totaled $150 million.

Because the debris was made up of the same ingredients as cement, when it dried it made rescue and recovery efforts almost impossible. The landslide created a dam on the river, which resulted in a lake that county officials had to immediately try to empty because it was hampering search efforts. Almost a mile of the main road was blocked for months.

As people sought answers after this tragedy, several facts came to light. The Stillaguamish River, which ran along the base of the mountain, had been eroding its base for years. The top of the mountain was made up of an unstable mix of dirt, stones, and sand left after a glacier receded.

That March had been the wettest in the history of the area, with 200 percent of normal rainfall. Seven inches of rain had saturated the ground in the two days prior to the slide.

Large-scale logging operations were common in the area. Grandy Lake Forest Associates logged 7.5 acres and did not replant the trees. One acre of the area where they logged was in a restricted water recharge zone.

The extent to which removing trees could cause the landslide is still unclear since there were signs that landslides had occurred in the area long before any logging ever took place. In fact, landslides were known to be common there, most happening in unpopulated areas.

Despite the lack of definitive evidence against the timber company, since the evidence had disappeared with the slide, a judge ruled in 2015 that a case could go forward. In his eventual ruling on the case, "Judge Roger Rogoff wrote that

▾ *Rescue workers attempt to recover victims of the landslide. The scarred mountainside can be seen in the distance.*

'significant evidence' exists from which a jury could determine that a Grandy Lake Forest Associates representative knew 'that logging in the areas . . . would increase the risk of landslide.'" In 2016 the state and the timber company agreed to a $60 million settlement with the survivors.

1. Because of this event how might the people in that community have responded? How might you have responded?
2. What actions might the residents have taken prior to the landslide?
3. After this tragedy one person questioned why people are even logging in the twenty-first century. How would you reply? How might the logging company have acted more responsibly?
4. How does this incident illustrate the relevance of hydrology and geology to geography?
5. How might you respond to a person who blames God for a disaster like this? (Consider Luke 13:4–5 and Romans 8:19–21.)

chapter 03

EARTH'S CLIMATE

45 The Earth and the Solar System
48 The Earth and Its Weather
54 The Earth and Its Climates

BIG IDEAS

- How does the sun influence the earth's climate?
- Why is weather different around the world?
- Why is climate different around the world?

▲ Rice planting

◀ Drying rice after harvest

▼ Birch forest

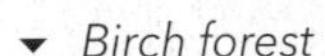

FARMING AND CLIMATE

Farming in tropical climates with an extended rainy season requires human ingenuity and an intimate understanding of weather and climate. For example, in order to grow rice, farmers need to plant the seed in a flooded or irrigated nursery paddy field for one month. Then the young plants are carefully removed from the wet field and replanted in another location where they will be watered for about three months until the plants mature and the grain is ready to be harvested. Then workers separate the rice from the stalks and spread it out to dry in the sun. Farmers perform the final step by separating the rice from the outer husk. All of these steps must be carefully planned and carried out when conditions are right for growing during the rainy season and for processing during the dry season.

The earth is a marvelous creation of God suspended in space and orbiting around our sun. It has just the right amount of gases that form our atmosphere and a balance of conditions that make life possible.

An aloe vera field that is a good example of dry farming. ▶

◀ Storm cloud on the edge of a thunderstorm

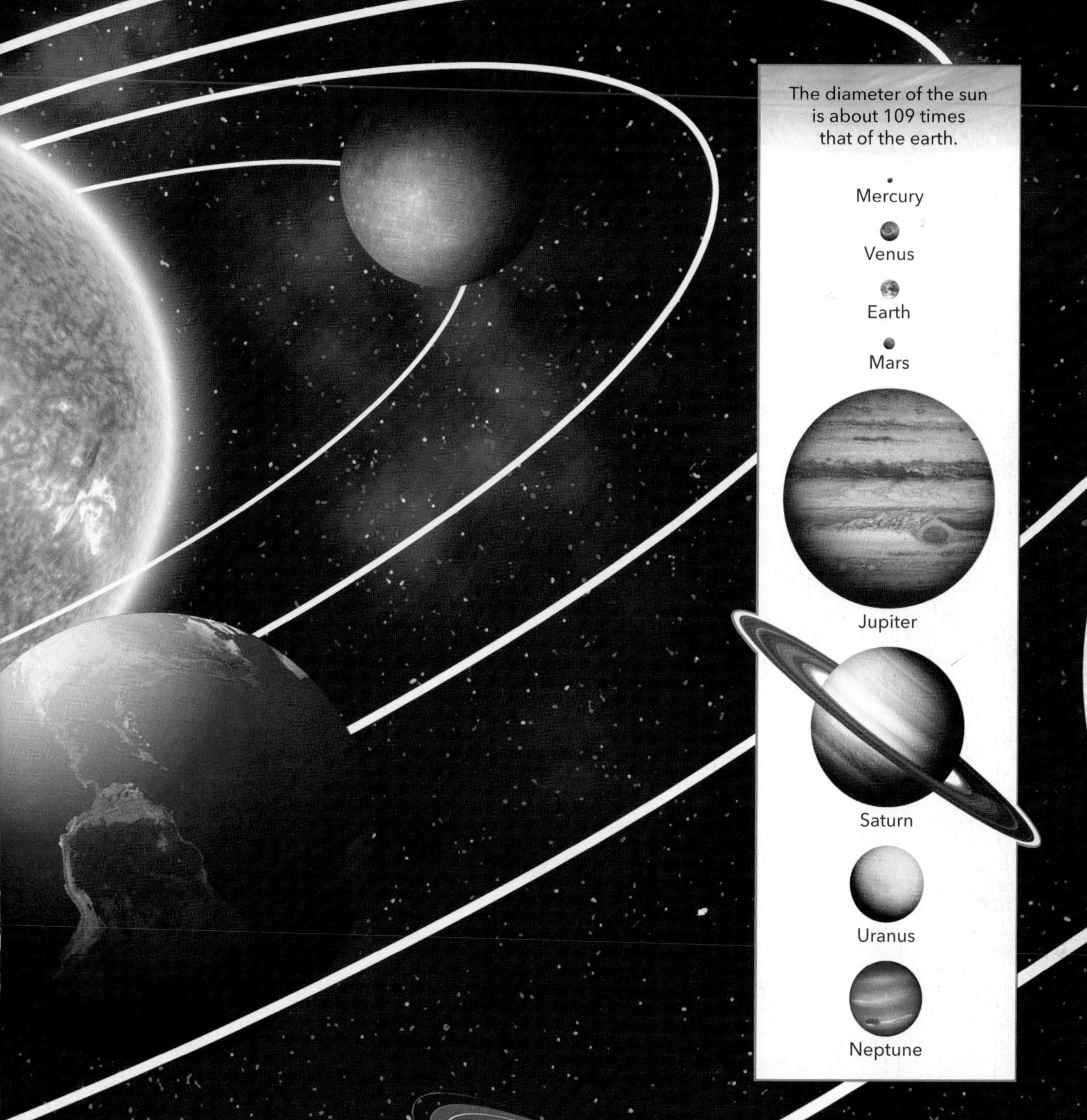

THE EARTH AND THE SOLAR SYSTEM

How does the sun influence Earth's climate?

The Earth's Location in the Solar System

The **solar system** is composed of the sun, planets, small solar system bodies, and other objects held in orbit around the sun by the sun's gravity. The earth is the third planet from the sun and is located about 93 million miles from the sun. It has an **atmosphere**, or envelope of gases, that surrounds the earth and is held in place by the planet's gravity.

GUIDING QUESTIONS

- Where is the earth in the solar system?
- What is the difference between the earth's rotation and its revolution?
- What are the major lines of latitude on the earth?
- How are the earth's place in the solar system and its movements related to latitude zones?

The Earth's Motion

The most obvious motion of the earth is called **rotation**. The earth rotates on its **axis** at a 23½° angle and turns 360° every twenty-four hours. The sun, moon, planets, and stars appear to rise in the east and set in the west.

Less noticeable to people on the earth is the trip around the sun once a year. This motion is the earth's **revolution**. The earth revolves around the sun in an elliptical pattern, and this, combined with the tilted axis, determines how much sunlight reaches different regions of the earth at a given time of the year. As we will see, this pattern affects weather and climate.

Twice each year the length of day and night are approximately equal all over the planet for an instant. This **equinox** occurs at the beginning of spring on March 20 and the beginning of autumn on September 22 or 23 in the Northern Hemisphere. Seasons are reversed for the Southern Hemisphere.

Twice each year the sun reaches its greatest angular distance from the equator, an event known as the **solstice**. The summer solstice occurs on June 21 in the Northern Hemisphere, and the winter solstice falls on December 21 or 22.

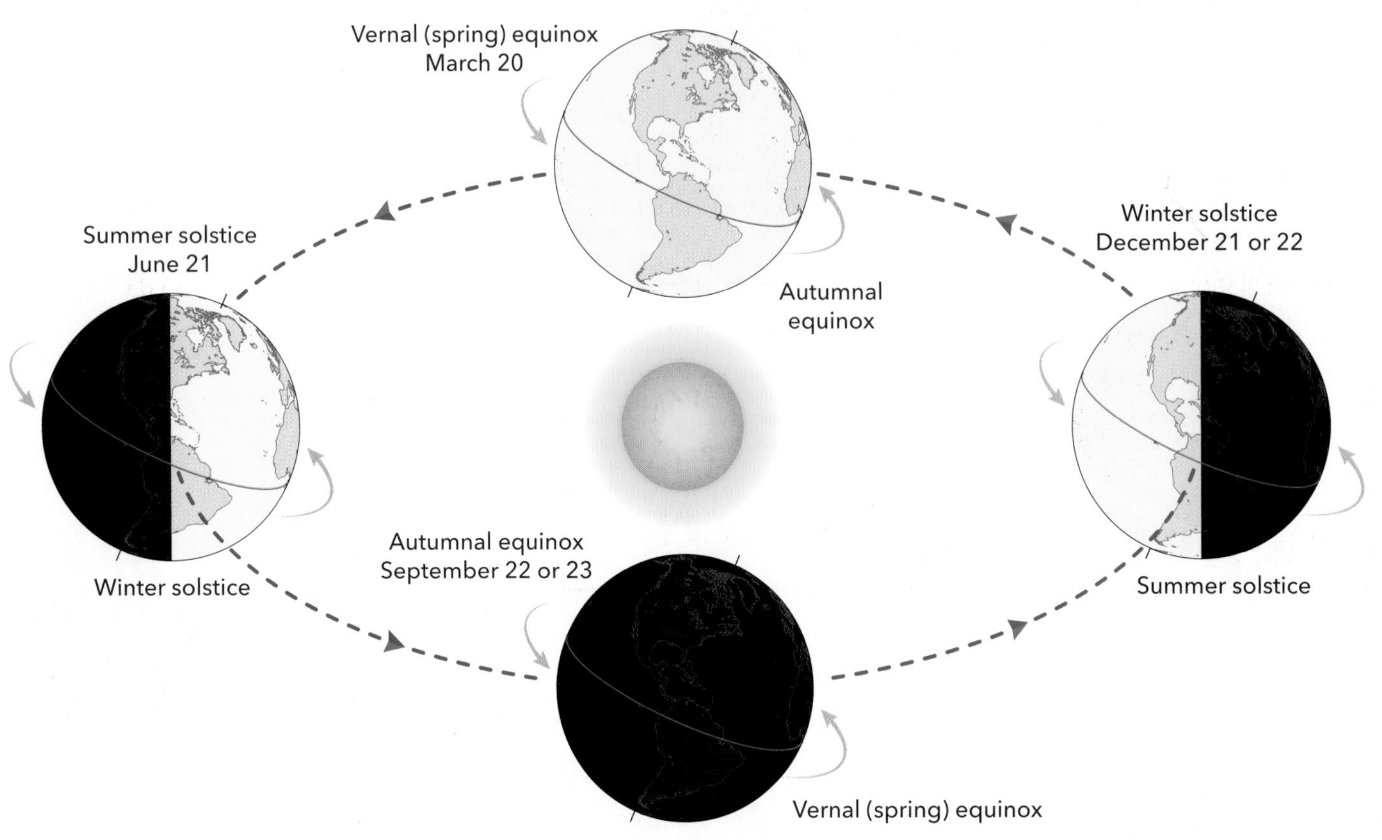

The Earth's Latitude Zones

The sun is the source of most of the thermal energy that warms the earth. The most obvious evidence of the sun's influence is in the seasons. The United States has four seasons, but some places have other kinds of seasons. Near the equator, where the air is always warm, for example, two seasons are evident: rainy and dry. Near the poles, where the air is always cold, the major seasonal change is six months of constant darkness followed by six months of a "midnight sun." All of these changes can be considered seasons. Seasons are caused by the slant of sunlight and the tilt of the earth's axis. These factors explain why different latitudes have different seasons. There are three distinct **latitude zones**. In the zone closest to the equator, the sunlight is always direct, or nearly so. This zone consistently has very warm temperatures and is usually called the **tropics**.

In the middle latitudes the sunlight is nearly direct half of each year, creating seasonal changes from warm summers to cool winters. Because these regions have neither the constant warmth of the tropics nor the extreme cold of the poles, they are called the **Temperate Zone**.

During the long winter nights in the high latitudes, sunlight is always either very slanted or nonexistent. These **polar regions** receive only a small amount of sunlight in winter.

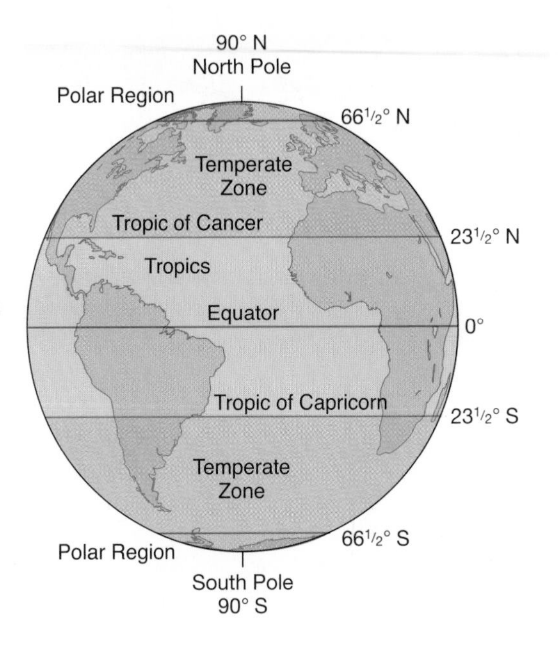

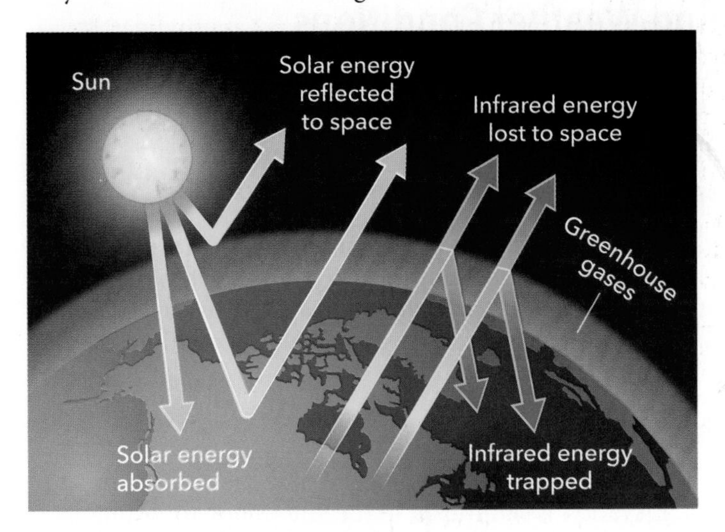

SECTION REVIEW

1. Describe the earth's location in the solar system.
2. What are the two ways the earth moves? Contrast them.
3. Identify the latitude zones on the globe, including the major lines of latitude.
4. How do latitude zones influence seasons?
5. In which latitude zone do you live?

Midnight sun in Iceland at low tide

THE EARTH AND ITS WEATHER

GUIDING QUESTIONS

- How would you define *weather*?
- What conditions are used to describe weather?
- How are landforms and latitude zones associated with specific weather conditions?

Why is weather different around the world?

Weather may be defined as the condition of the atmosphere at a given time and place. Its duration is limited to hours or days. Weather may be described as rainy, cloudy, windy, or sunny with blue skies. Within hours the weather in a given place can change significantly, making it a challenge to forecast precisely. Scientists who study the weather are called meteorologists.

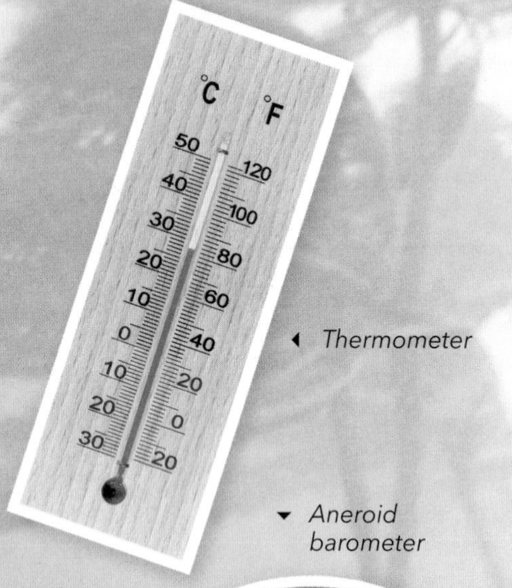

Thermometer

Aneroid barometer

Describing Weather Conditions

The five basic elements of weather include temperature, atmospheric pressure, wind, precipitation, and humidity. Some sources also include cloudiness as an element of weather.

Temperature

Temperature is an indication of the amount of thermal energy in the air. Most people consider temperature to be one of the most important indicators for weather. Meteorologists measure temperature using a thermometer. Measurements are calculated according to either the Fahrenheit or Celsius scale.

Atmospheric Pressure

Atmospheric pressure is the weight of gases in the atmosphere on a surface area. Elevation is significant to the amount of atmospheric gases on a surface area. Atmospheric pressure at ten thousand feet above sea level is lower than the pressure at sea level. At ten thousand feet there is less atmosphere weighing down on a surface area, so the pressure is less. If you have ever flown on a commercial jet, you have probably noticed the change in atmospheric pressure and have felt your ears "pop" as your body adjusted to the change in pressure. Other factors that affect atmospheric pressure are air temperature and moisture. Atmospheric pressure is measured by a barometer.

Wind

The sun's energy is always in motion, even after it reaches the earth's atmosphere. The air carries thermal energy between and within latitude zones. Wind is basically the movement of air caused by the heating and cooling of air masses.

Warm and Cold Air Masses

A large area of moving air with a similar temperature is called an air mass. Warm air masses are warmer than the surface of the earth over which they move; cold air masses are cooler than the surface.

Anemometer

(background) Hurricane winds in Antigua, West Indies

Warm and cold air masses move over the earth in regular patterns. A permanent warm air mass sits over the tropics, where the rays of the sun are direct. At the same time, a cold air mass sits over the polar regions. Warm air is constantly rising at the equator and moving toward the cold polar regions. As the air cools over the poles, it falls and moves back toward the equator. If the sun were the only factor affecting the circulation of air, surface winds in the United States would always blow to the south, and winds in South America would blow to the north.

In reality, however, a large portion of the tropical air mass loses its thermal energy and falls before it reaches the poles. The air drops in the middle latitudes near 30°. Some of the air moves back toward the poles. As the air travels along the surface, it hits frigid air from the poles at about 60° latitude and rises again. Some of this air continues its journey until it finally reaches the frigid poles, where the air drops a second time. The polar air begins moving back toward the equator. As a result of this cycle, the earth has three moving cells of air from the equator to the poles.

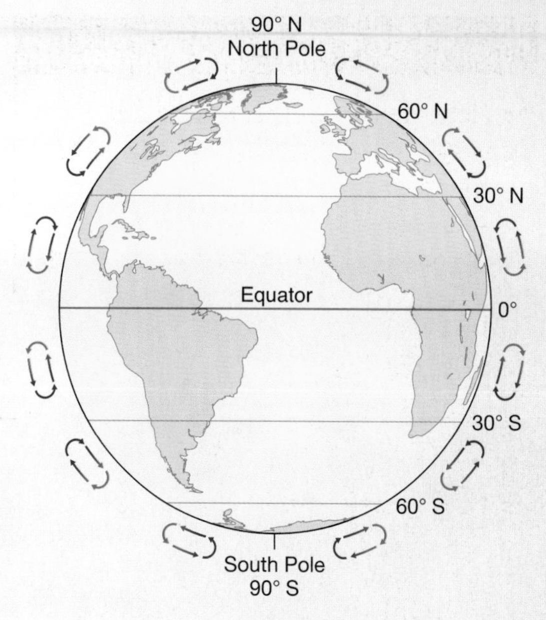

▲ *Air masses*

Coriolis Effect

Few winds blow strictly north or south. The rotation of the earth greatly influences wind direction in something known as the **Coriolis effect**. This phenomenon is somewhat difficult to visualize. You do not feel the earth rotating, but it is moving quite rapidly, at about one thousand miles per hour along the equator and five hundred miles per hour at 30° latitude. The rotation pulls the land out from under the wind. The wind continues to flow straight, but the land beneath it veers away.

Wind Belts

The movement of warm and cold air masses, combined with the Coriolis effect, explains the basic movement of thermal energy around the earth. Winds flow in three belts that circle the globe. These belts influence the world's climate and have also influenced the exploration and conquest of the world.

The hot tropics have the most powerful prevailing winds. Tropical islands are famous for the constant warm winds, called trade winds, that blow over the beaches. Columbus used these steady winds to carry his ships west to the New World. European sailors called them the "northeast trades" because explorers named winds after the direction from which they came, not the direction they were going.

The prevailing winds that blow over the middle latitudes are called the westerlies. They are important because they bring warm air from the tropics to lands far to the north, such as Europe. Less powerful than the trade winds, westerlies still helped Columbus and other explorers sail back east to Europe from the New World.

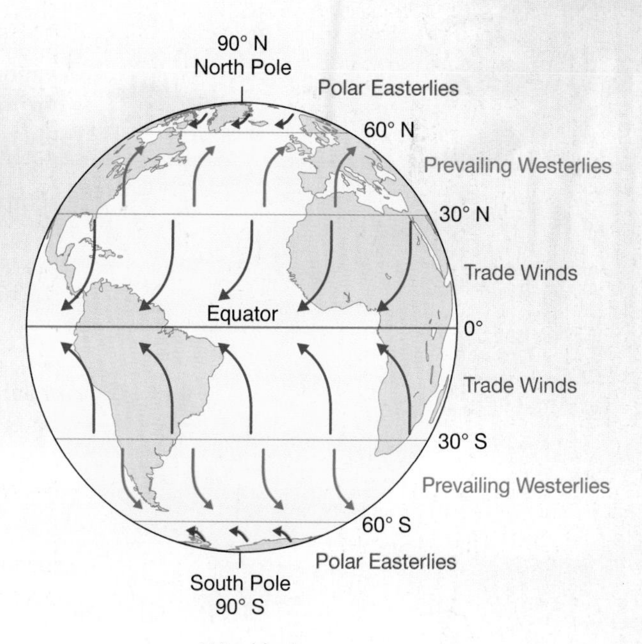

▲ *Wind belts*

▲ *(left) Mount Waialeale in Hawaii*

▲ *(right) The Empty Quarter in Saudi Arabia*

Precipitation

Mount Waialeale in Hawaii has averaged thirty-one feet of rain annually since 1912. In contrast, no record of rain exists for the Empty Quarter (Rub Al Khali) of the Arabian Peninsula. Few places ever see anything near these extremes because the same systems that distribute thermal energy over the land also help to distribute life-giving water.

Water appears in three forms: solid (ice), liquid, and gas (water vapor). Ocean water must change form before it reaches plants and animals on land. This change begins as ocean water absorbs thermal energy. When the liquid water absorbs enough thermal energy, it changes into water vapor in a process called evaporation. When the temperature drops, the water vapor loses thermal energy and changes

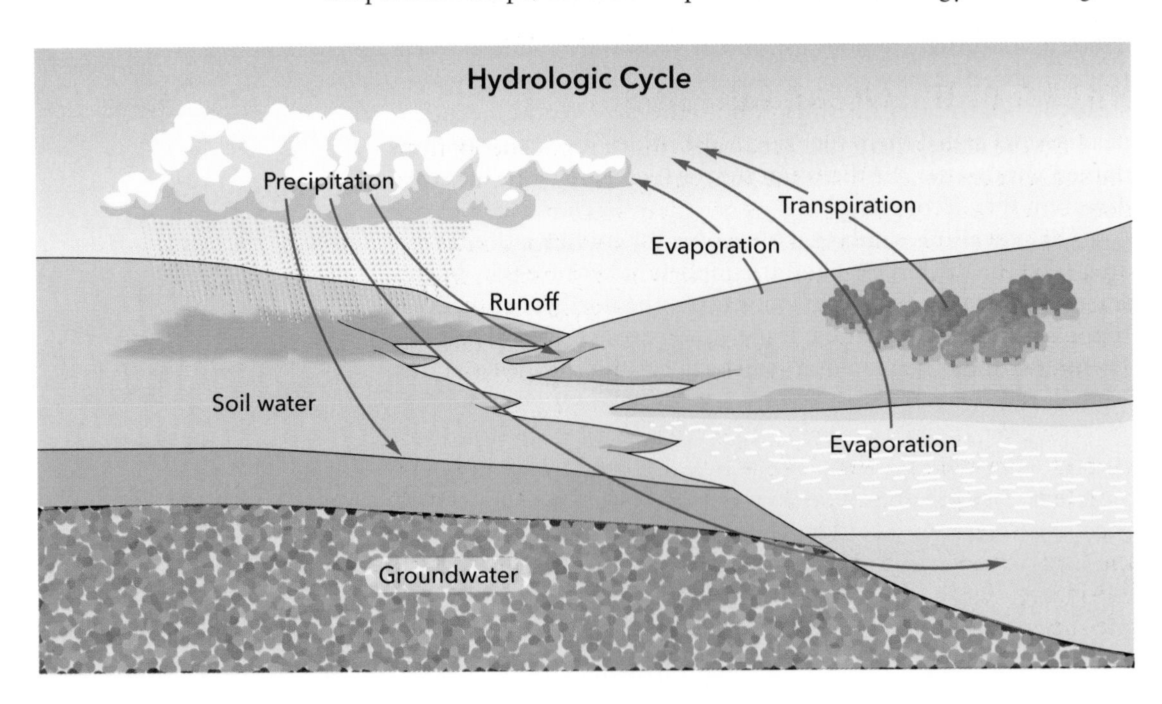

back to a liquid, suspended in clouds as water droplets. This process is called condensation.

When the concentrated water droplets become too heavy to be supported by updrafts of wind, they fall to the earth in a process called **precipitation**. Most precipitation is in the form of rain, but water also can fall in solid form. A sudden drop in temperature causes water vapor to freeze, lose energy, and fall to the earth as snow, sleet, or hail. The process of evaporation, condensation, and precipitation is called the **hydrologic cycle**. The Creator God designed it to replenish the soil, lakes, and rivers with water.

About 80 percent of precipitation occurs over the oceans, but the rest falls on land. The water stays on the earth's surface for only a brief time. Some runs off into rivers or lakes. Some seeps through the soil to become groundwater. Eventually, however, all water returns to the oceans or evaporates, completing the cycle.

▲ *Solar-powered rain gauge*

Humidity

Humidity is the measure of the amount of moisture in a given volume of air at a given temperature. Absolute humidity is the total mass of water vapor present in a given volume or mass of air. Relative humidity is the total amount of water vapor in the air compared to the maximum that could vaporize at the current temperature. In the simplest terms, warm air can retain more moisture and cold air can retain less moisture.

◂ *Hygrometer*

Warm winds carry water vapor into the interior of the continents. Warm air can hold a lot of water vapor, or humidity, because the molecules are very active. Humidity becomes useful when the air cools and returns moisture to the earth's surface. The point at which water vapor begins condensation is called the **dew point**.

Impact of the Ocean Currents

Like the atmosphere, the ocean absorbs thermal energy from the sun. Because water holds thermal energy much longer than air does, oceans are even more consistent than wind in distributing thermal energy. Temperature differences create warm and cold ocean currents that circle the globe, following a pattern similar to the prevailing winds. Water is heated near the equator and moves toward the poles. Cold water from the poles returns to the equator. The presence of continents causes the most obvious variations in these ocean currents.

The prevailing winds help propel surface currents. But ocean currents move more slowly than winds. The normal speed is less than ten miles per hour. The slowest currents are called drifts. In some cases, however, currents may move very fast. For example, the Gulf Stream, which begins in the Gulf of Mexico, flows beyond Florida, up the US Atlantic coast, and to the northeast of the British Isles near the polar region, where it finally weakens and becomes the North Atlantic Drift.

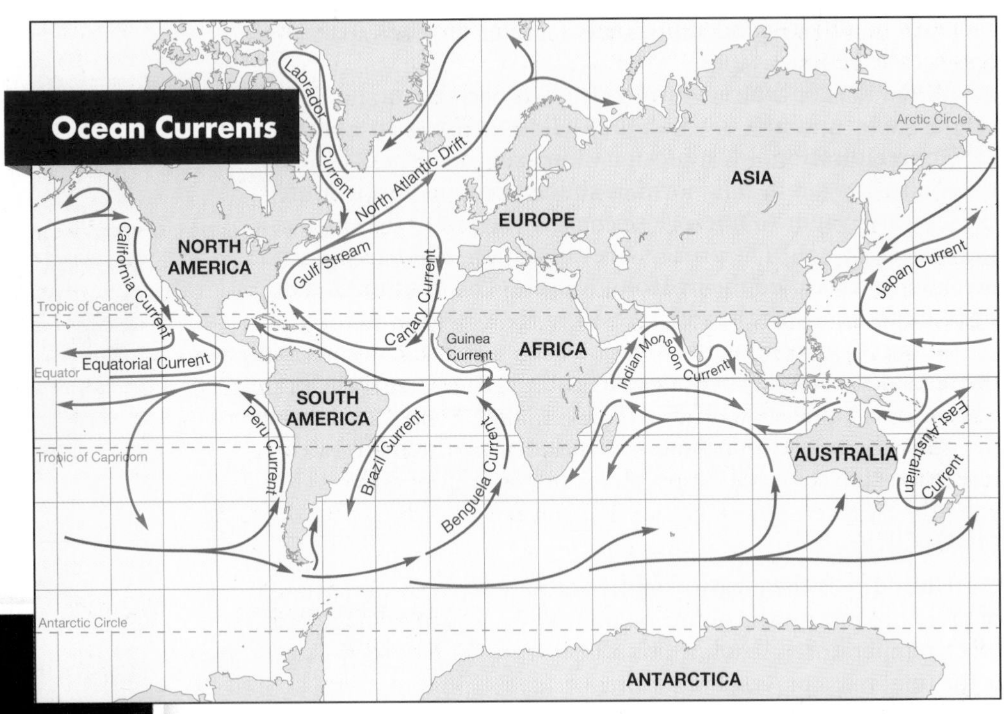

▾ *South America*

BRAZIL

CHILE

The currents flow in circular patterns. That constant circulation of thermal energy in the oceans keeps tropical water from becoming too warm for sea life, and it keeps polar water from freezing solid. Ocean currents also influence the amount of rain that enters the air and falls on the continents. Cold air contains less moisture than warm air does. Therefore, the coast of Chile is a barren desert because the cold Peru Current flows nearby, but Brazil's coast is a tropical rainforest, supplied by the warm Brazil Current.

Relating Landforms and Latitude Zones to Weather Conditions

Landforms

Three situations cause a humid air mass to cool and produce precipitation. One of them is the presence of mountains. When a warm mass of humid air passes over a mountainous area, the air moves upward and cools rapidly. Water vapor condenses into droplets, clouds form, and precipitation quickly follows. Because mountains are often bitterly cold, snow and sleet are common. This precipitation is said to be **orographic**.

Orographic precipitation is common in mountain ranges close to the ocean or big lakes. Large amounts of water enter the air, and prevailing winds drive the water vapor over the mountains. The land beyond the mountains, an area called the **rain shadow**, is usually very dry because little water vapor survives passage over the mountains.

Another important cause of precipitation is the meeting of cold and warm air masses. The warmer air is lighter, so it rises above the cooler, denser air as if it were moving over a mountain range. Rain or snow falls along the line where the two air masses meet. The line is called a **front**. For precipitation to occur, the warm air mass must have water vapor that it gathered over an ocean or large lake. Frontal precipitation is common in the eastern United States, where warm air masses move in over the Gulf of Mexico and the Great Lakes.

A third cause of precipitation is convection, the rise of warm air over a hot surface. In the heart of continents, a large air mass forms when the land cools at night and then heats up rapidly under the summer sun. The hot air is sometimes trapped beneath a cool air mass. When the warm, light air breaks through the cool air above, it rushes upward and cools quickly. Precipitation falls immediately and often violently. Lightning and hail may accompany such storms.

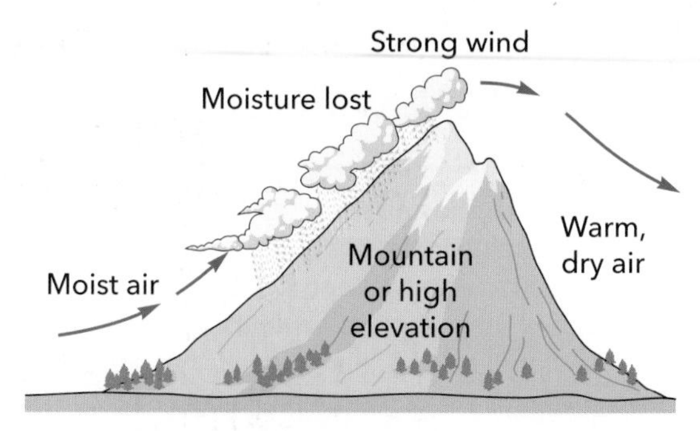

▲ *Orographic precipitation*

▲ *Frontal precipitation*

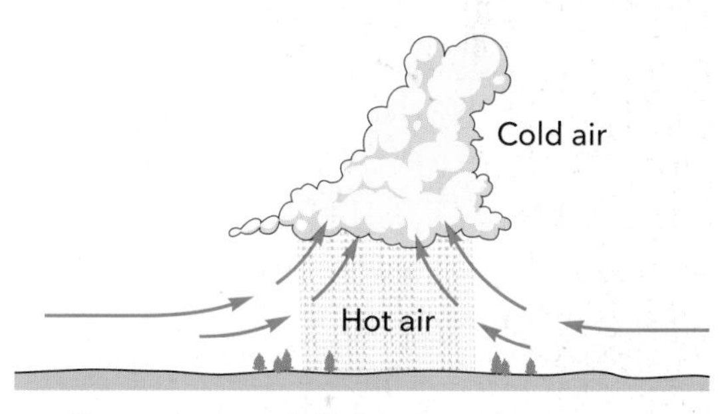

▲ *Convection precipitation*

Latitude Zones

As one might expect, the polar regions in the high latitudes consistently produce cold, dry air. The tropics in the low latitudes develop warm, moist air. However, weather in the temperate zone in the middle latitudes is far more complex. Significantly influenced by continental air masses, weather in the temperate zone varies depending on the humidity and temperature of the region where an air mass originates. In addition, the effect of a given continental air mass can be moderated by proximity to coastal waters or large lakes. The effect can also be intensified by conditions on the ground, such as a valley or other low region that is surrounded by hills or mountains.

SECTION REVIEW

1. What five conditions do meteorologists use to describe weather?
2. Why is atmospheric pressure at five thousand feet above sea level different from atmospheric pressure at one thousand feet above sea level? How is it different?
3. What landforms are associated with specific weather conditions?
4. How do ocean currents influence weather?
5. What are three examples of weather differing in other parts of the world?

▼ *Example of rain shadow on the Tibetan Plateau*

TROPICAL RAINY

The climates in these regions are warm, wet, and found near the equator. Many of these zones receive rain most or all of the year. Others have annual cycles of wet and dry weather. As a result, many of these regions have lush vegetation, large insect populations, and animals that are found only in these climates. About half the world's species of plants and animals are found in tropical rainy climates.

DRY

In deserts, annual precipitation is ten inches or less. Lack of water, not high temperatures, creates deserts. Deserts are often described as arid, which means "lacking moisture." Deserts can occur at any latitude, cold or hot. The ice-covered interior of Greenland is technically a desert!

Semiarid regions receive a few more inches of rainfall than deserts and therefore can support grasses. Pioneers once called the Great Plains of the United States the "Great American Desert," but large parts of it are actually semiarid grassland, where wheat and other grains now grow.

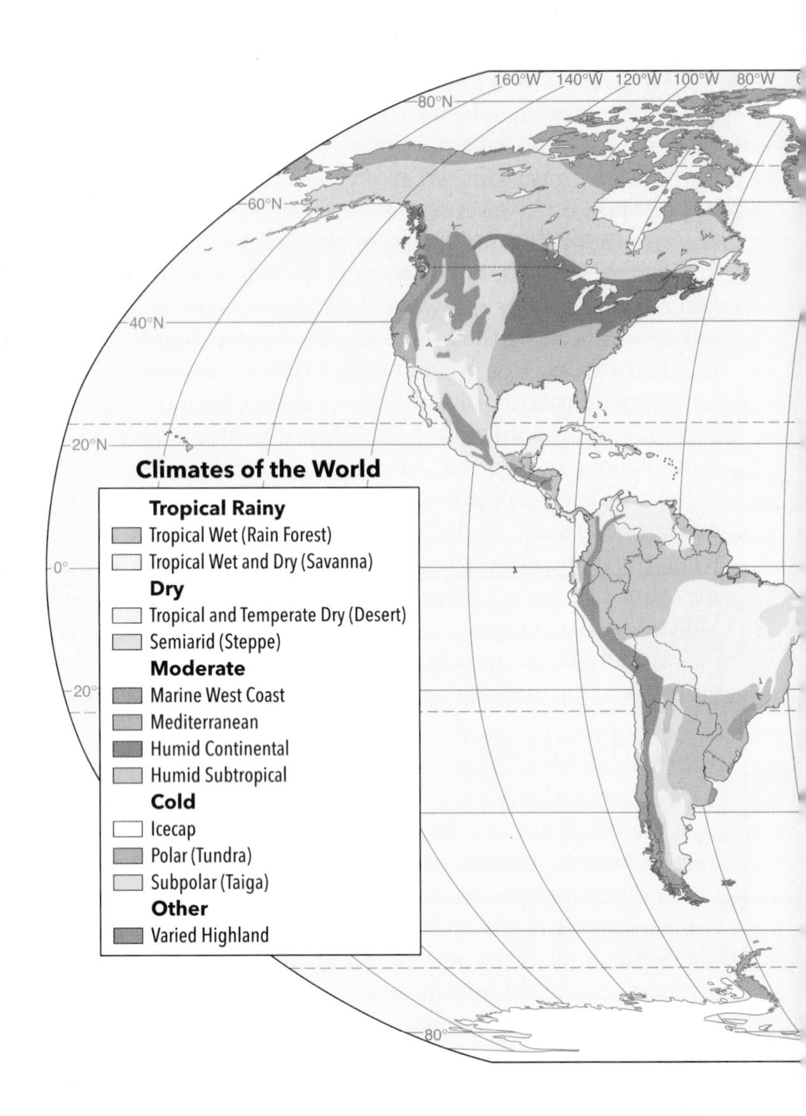

GUIDING QUESTIONS

- What is the difference between weather and climate?
- How do climatologists study climate?
- How are landforms and latitude zones associated with specific climate zones?
- How are biotic zones related to climate zones around the world?
- Why are meteorology and climatology important for geography and creation care?

THE EARTH AND ITS CLIMATES

Why is the climate different around the world?

Depending on a variety of factors, your climate might differ significantly from the climate in another part of the world. Proximity to bodies of water, latitude, and different landmasses significantly influence climate and help explain the different climates that exist around the world.

Comparing Weather and Climate

Weather is the condition of the atmosphere at a given time and place. Weather changes frequently. **Climate**, however, is the average weather in an area over an extended length of time. Factors that influence climate include temperature and precipitation.

Daily changes in weather seldom determine what lives in a region or whether it is a good place for humans. Even a year of record lows or highs in temperature or rainfall does not make much of a difference. There are five broad categories of world climate. This classification system will be used throughout the rest of your textbook.

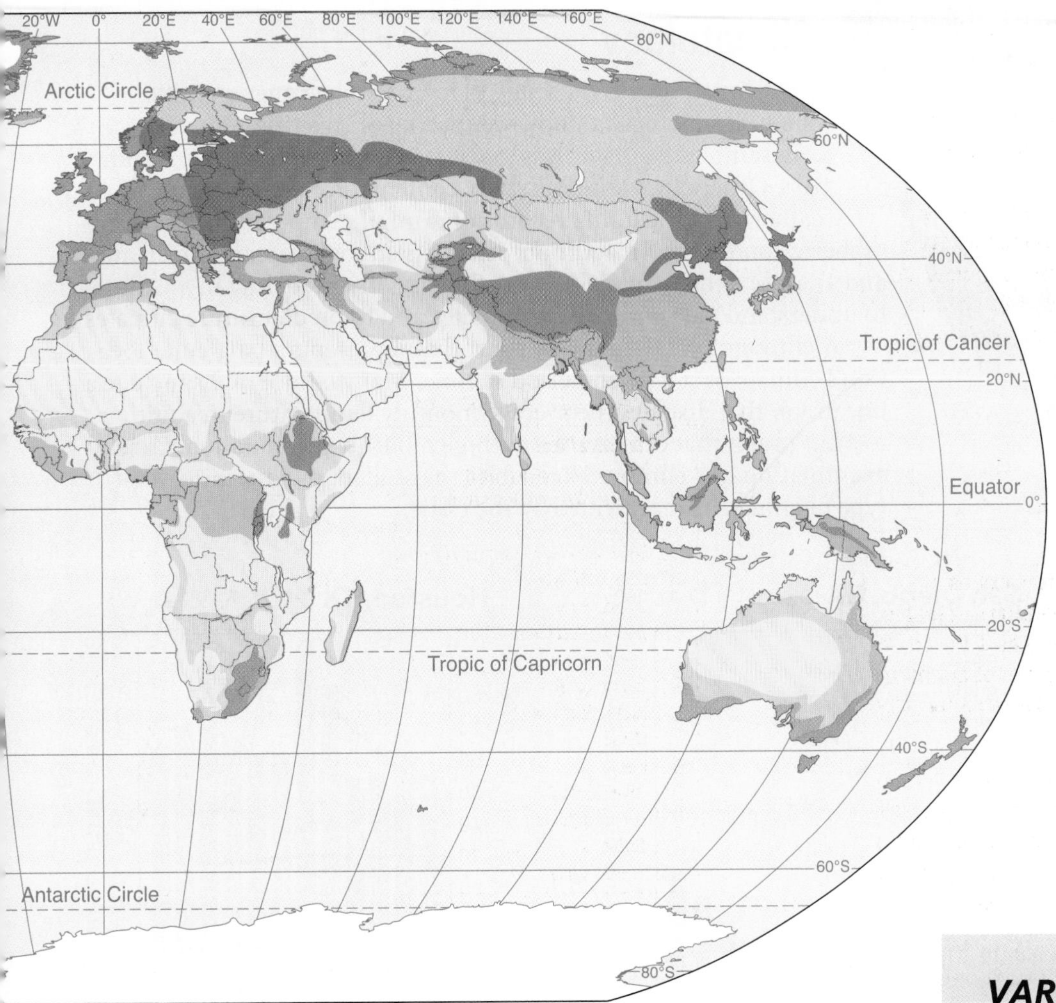

COLD

Some regions receive sufficient rainfall but are too cold to support many kinds of plants. For example, nothing grows on the world's two icecaps in Antarctica and Greenland, which have a thick layer of ice that never melts. Although polar regions are cold year-round, plants grow for a brief period in the middle of the summer, when some of the snow cover melts. Subpolar regions are not as severe in the summer, permitting hardy evergreen trees to grow. Winters are bitterly cold in all three regions, averaging less than 0°F (–18°C).

VARIED HIGHLAND

Another principle is at work in mountains. There are many gas molecules in the air near sea level, where the pull of gravity is greatest. These molecules hold a great deal of thermal energy. As the altitude increases, however, the air becomes thinner and holds less thermal energy. For every one-thousand-foot increase in altitude, the temperature drops about 3½°F. This drop is called the lapse rate. If the temperature at sea level is 65°F, one can expect it to be 30°F at the peak of a ten-thousand-foot mountain.

TEMPERATE

Most of the world's good farmland and major civilizations are located in the four climate regions with moderate rainfall and temperatures. All four climates occur in the middle latitudes, or Temperate Zone. Humid subtropical refers to lands just above the tropics that receive about fifty inches of rain a year, mostly in the summer. The richest farmland in the world is located there.

The other three moderate climates are named after the regions where they occur in Europe: the continent, the Mediterranean Sea, and the west coast. The humid continental region extends far into the interior of the Eurasian continent. Rainfall is adequate but irregular because of the distance it must travel from the ocean to reach the interior. Winters are colder there than in any other temperate region. In the mediterranean climate, little rain falls during the summer, so the land supports few crops without irrigation.

In the marine west coast, which covers most of Western Europe, warm ocean currents bring warm, moist air that blows over the coast and provides regular rainfall. The rain is heavier in the winter than in the summer—about six inches per month in contrast to three inches.

Climatology

Climatology is the study of long-term weather conditions. Some climatologists study the spacing of tree rings and take ice core samples from glaciers to reconstruct climates in the distant past. Other climatologists study contemporary climates using weather data, including records of rainfall, temperature, and atmospheric conditions. In addition, scientists study hurricanes to create and analyze climate models. Climatologists use modeling in an effort to understand past and present climates and to predict future climates.

A climograph is a graph or chart that represents a particular location's climate over a given period of time. Many climographs include a line graph that displays the average monthly temperature in addition to a bar graph that displays the average monthly precipitation. Careful examination of a climograph enables the student to determine what type of climate is represented by the chart.

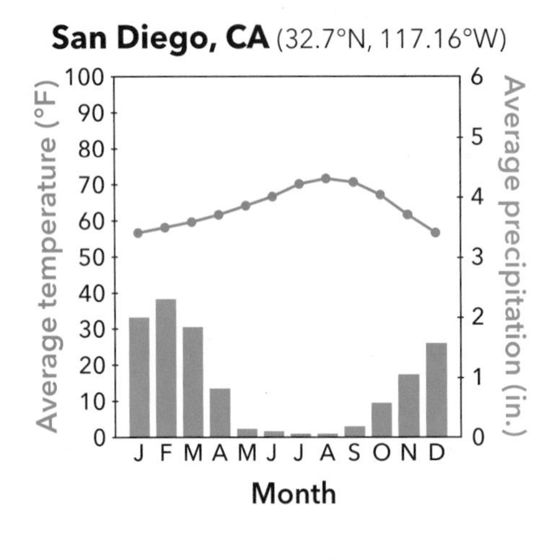

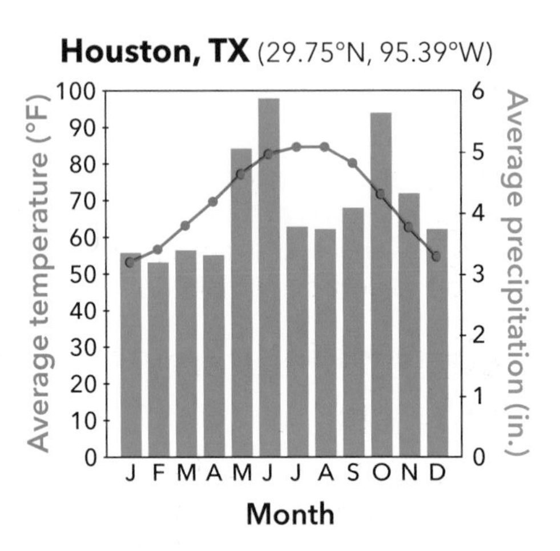

▲ (top) Tree rings

▲ Ice core sample

Relating Landforms and Latitude Zones to Climate Zones

Landforms and Latitude Zones

Just as various landforms influence weather, they also help to determine climate. The map on pages 54–55 demonstrates the correlation of landforms and latitude zones with different **climate zones**. A climate zone is a division of the earth's climate such as polar, temperate, and tropical.

One condition that affects climate is whether the region is windward or leeward. Regions that are windward, or on the side of the landform that faces the wind, get more precipitation and develop a climate that thrives due to abundance of water. Regions that are leeward, or on the side that does not face the wind, often experience rain shadow and develop an arid climate with little precipitation.

Warm, moist air
Rising moist air cools, forming rain clouds and precipitation
Rain shadow
Warm, dry air
Windward side
Mountain range
Leeward side
Ocean

Latitude also plays a role in establishing climate. The angle of the sun's rays in relation to the latitude determines the amount of thermal energy that is retained or reflected. This influences the amount of precipitation, the temperature range, and conditions that make plant, animal, and human life sustainable.

Another factor that influences climate is seasons. The amount of sunlight varies with the seasons. Longer days result in increased warming. Conversely, longer nights result in increased cooling. During the summer solstice more of the sun's rays are concentrated on heating the surface of the earth and fewer are reflected. This process is reversed during the winter solstice.

Anyone who has traveled to a mountain range knows that elevation is related to air temperature. The temperature at sea level is considerably higher than the temperature at ten thousand feet above sea level. As a result, the climate at sea level differs from the climate at a greater elevation.

The presence of large bodies of water like oceans and lakes also has a significant influence on climate. Major ocean currents warm land many miles from the tropics and cool landforms far from polar regions.

Climate Zones

Proximity to the equator determines the climate of landmasses in that region, with only slight variations. Likewise, proximity to the polar regions ensures that the climate there is always cold, varying only in degree. The landforms within the Temperate Zone experience the greatest variety of climates.

Relating Biotic Zones to Climate Zones Around the World

A **biome** is any large region where distinct populations of plants and animals are found living together. Biomes influence how people make a living, what they eat, and even what their homes look like. The unique characteristics of each biome help to explain why human cultures are so different. Biomes can be grouped in three broad categories: forests, grasslands, and wastelands. There are variations within each category.

A map of biotic zones indicates the types of plants that grow in each zone. If you compare the biotic and climate maps, you will see that the regions are similar. Differences between the two maps are caused by local variations in soil and mountains and the presence or absence of rivers.

A biotic map provides information that helps explain why certain animals live in the various zones based on plants available for food. For example, one would expect to find koalas only in areas where there are eucalyptus trees—the koalas' only food.

▲ *(top) Scientists setting up monitoring equipment on a glacier*

▲ *Meteorologists documenting a severe storm with a doppler weather radar truck in the background*

▼ *Grassland in the Masai Mara National Reserve, Kenya*

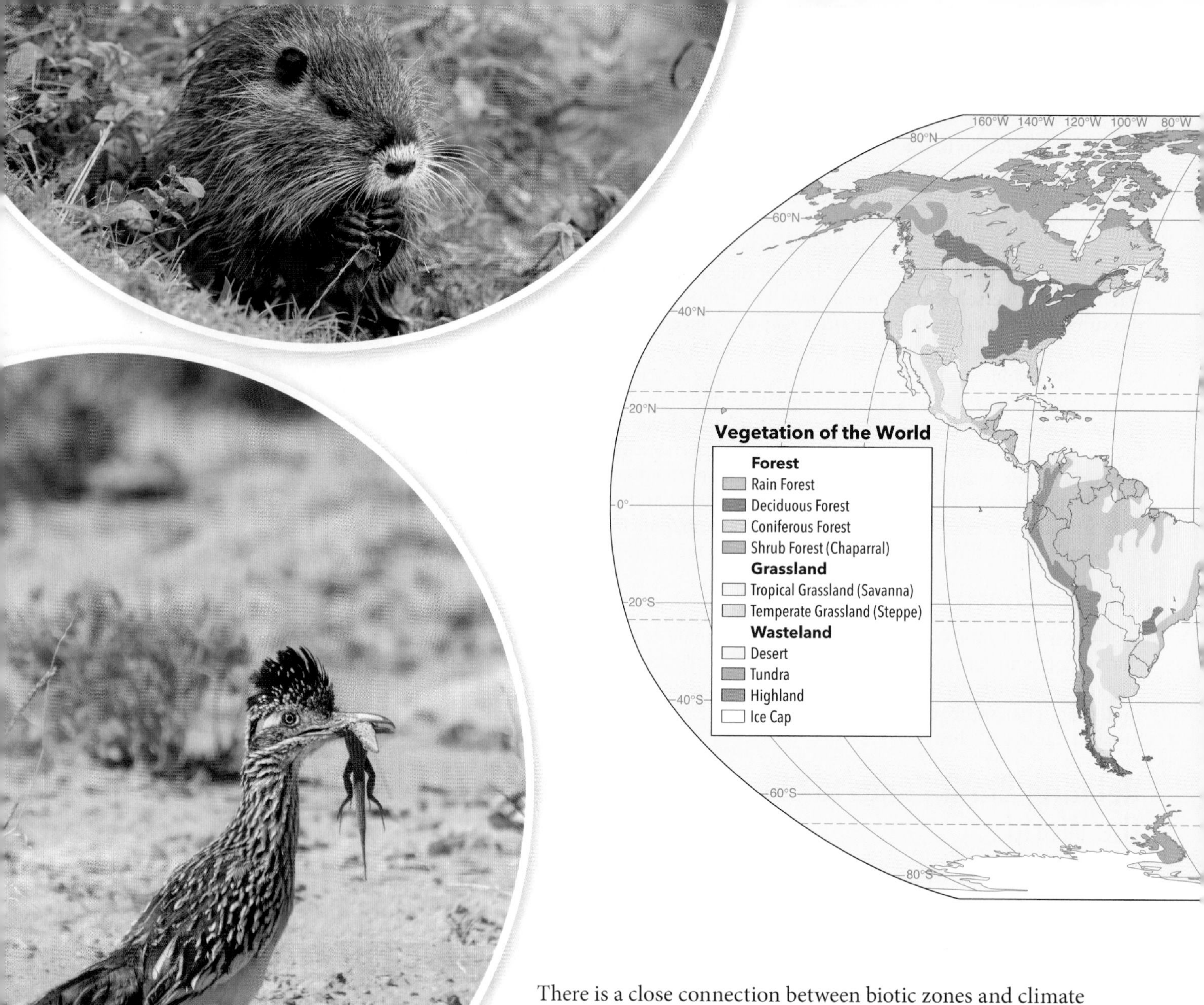

▲ *Young coypu, also known as a swamp beaver or beaver rat, sitting in grass on a river bank*

▲ *Roadrunner with lizard in the Mojave Desert*

There is a close connection between biotic zones and climate zones. Climate plays a pivotal role in determining what forms of life can thrive in a given region.

Importance of Meteorology and Climatology

Meteorology is the scientific study of the atmosphere, including its composition, structure, weather, and alteration. Meteorologists use thermometers, satellite images, and radar to collect data. This enables them to describe the weather. A typical weather report provides information about temperature, atmospheric pressure, wind speed and direction, precipitation, and humidity. Meteorologists provide short-term information about weather and model predicted atmospheric conditions for the near future.

Climatologists collect data in an effort to form theories about past climates, to understand present climate conditions, and to predict possible changes to the earth's climates in the future. They examine changes in weather patterns that might indicate increases in severe weather such as tornadoes and hurricanes. Predicting severe weather is vital and can mean the difference between life and death. Warning of floods and other dangerous conditions from an imminent storm can help people evacuate regions ahead of violent storms and save

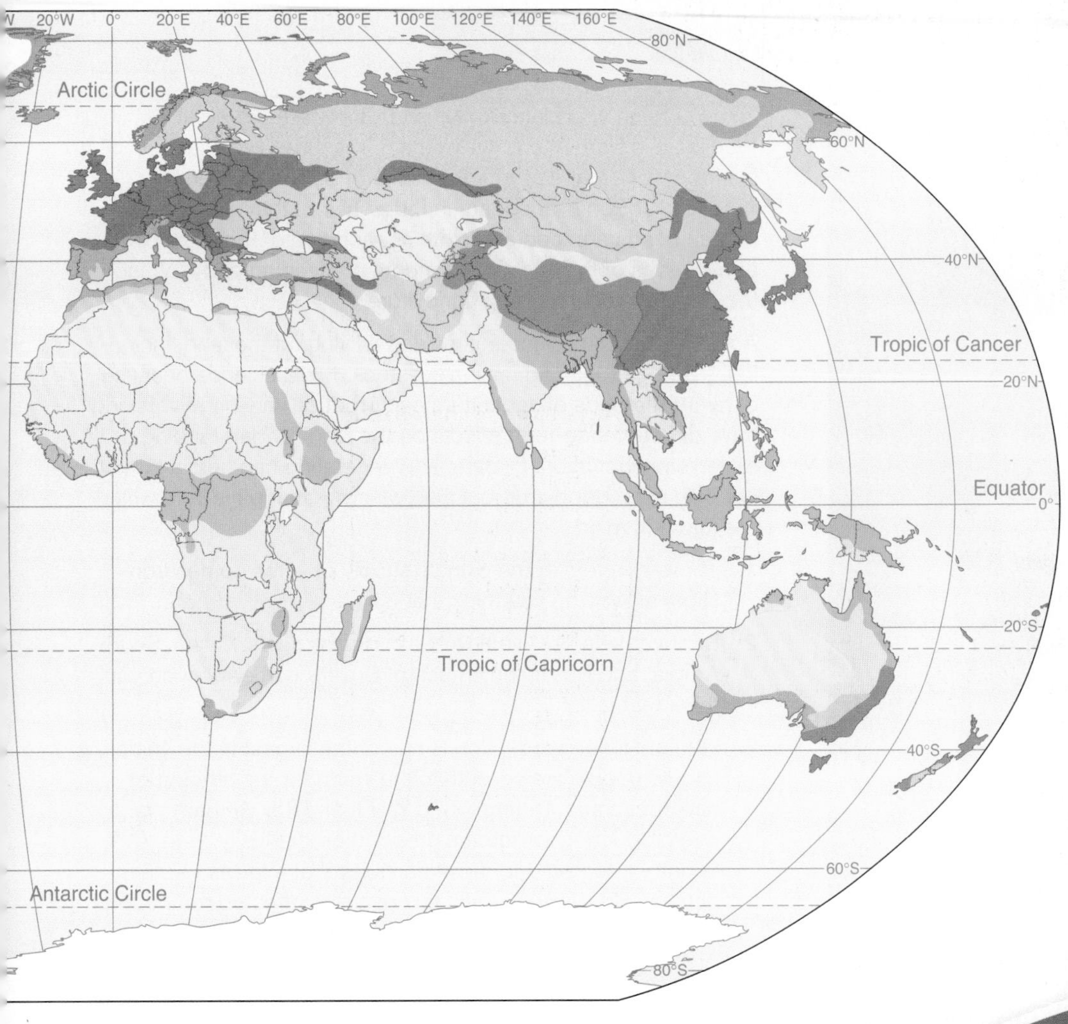

lives. In addition, people are often able to board up windows and construct other barriers to limit the damage caused by flooding and flying debris from high winds. This reduces property damage and mitigates some effects of severe storms.

Given the controversy about global warming, also known as **climate change**, it is imperative for Christians to carefully examine the evidence. Enormous changes resulted from the Flood and its aftermath that extended for centuries. Since the end of the post-Flood ice age, there have been alternating periods of warming and cooling over the last four millennia. Civilizations have expanded and declined due in part to gradually changing climate conditions. Denying that climates change is not an option.

However, the cause of climate change, the extent of climate change, and man's possible role are viable questions. Christians are commanded to think about God's world in light of His Word. It is important to make decisions that demonstrate wise stewardship of the earth's resources. One way

GLOBAL IMPACT | Agriculture around the World

Yams grow in abundance in Nigeria. Beef cattle thrive in Brazil. Rice is an important crop in Vietnam. Mangoes grow in the Caribbean. Farmers produce millions of bushels of corn in America. Cotton is abundant in India. Two of the most basic human needs are food and clothing, and two of the most basic applications of the Creation Mandate are feeding and clothing the earth's people through agriculture.

Agriculture is the science of making a living off the land, including growing crops and raising livestock. It is a science because different methods of agriculture can produce varying results and have different long-term effects on the land. Understanding a region's precipitation, climate, and vegetation can help a farmer not only get a good crop but also wisely manage his land with the future in mind.

1. Three-quarters of the world's supply of yams comes from Nigeria. Why do you think that is?
2. Beef cattle in Brazil are raised in grassy fields. China, Saudi Arabia, and Russia buy much of Brazil's cattle. Why do you think that is?
3. Vietnam's rice production is one of the largest in the world, and its people are seventh in the world for the amount of rice consumed. During World War II and the Vietnam War, rice production in Vietnam dropped dramatically, yet the country attempted to maintain its level of exports to other nations. How do you think this decision affected the people of Vietnam?
4. How are meteorology, climatology, and geography related to agriculture?
5. How is agriculture related to creation care?

◂ *(left) Cotton boll and (right) mango fruit*

▾ *Vietnamese women selling and buying fruits at a floating market, Mekong River Delta, Vietnam*

to show love for others is to avoid actions or processes that waste resources or pollute the planet that God has entrusted to us. Christians should be among the most dedicated conservationists because of the importance that God has placed on the earth in His Word.

Key questions regarding climate change include the following:

- Is the earth warming?
- If so, are people causing it to warm?
- If it is warming because of human activity, is that bad?
- Will solutions that political leaders and scientists suggest fix the problem?

The work of meteorology and climatology, properly performed, can help us understand the current and long-term influence of weather and climate on the earth's surface. This information can enhance the Christian's ability to exercise wise stewardship of the earth.

SECTION REVIEW

1. How are climate and weather different? How are they similar?
2. How do climatologists analyze the world's climate?
3. What do climographs display? What period of time does a climograph usually cover?
4. What is the relationship of landforms and latitude zones to specific climate zones?
5. How are biotic zones related to climate zones around the world?
6. How is the work of meteorology and climatology important to geography?

▾ *Dense tropical rain forest near the Malaysia-Kalimantan border*

03 CHAPTER REVIEW

SUMMARY

1. The earth is the third planet from the sun in our solar system. It rotates on its axis once every twenty-four hours and revolves around the sun once each year. Imaginary lines delineate latitude zones from the equator to the poles.
2. The earth's weather varies from day to day and from region to region. Weather is described in terms of temperature, atmospheric pressure, wind, precipitation, and humidity. Weather is also related to landforms and latitude zones.
3. The earth's climates tend to extend over longer periods than weather does. Climatologists examine evidence from the past, document interaction with landforms in the different latitude zones, and build models to predict changes to the earth's climates.

Terms to Know

- solar system
- atmosphere
- rotation
- axis
- revolution
- equinox
- solstice
- latitude zones
- tropics
- Temperate Zone
- polar regions
- weather
- Coriolis effect
- precipitation
- hydrologic cycle
- dew point
- orographic
- rain shadow
- front
- climate
- climate zones
- biome
- climate change

Making Connections

1. What is the basic cause of all precipitation? Under what three conditions does precipitation usually occur?
2. How does the earth's revolution around the sun determine seasons and weather?
3. What season begins in the Southern Hemisphere on September 23?
4. Define *weather* in your own words.
5. Distinguish absolute and relative humidity.
6. Compare the climate zones.
7. How do climatologists analyze the world's climates?
8. Define *biome*. How does climate influence a biome?

Developing Geography Skills

1. What major landforms are in your area?
2. From what direction do storms approach the area where you live? How does this relate to global wind patterns?

Thinking Critically

1. What is the significance of the greenhouse effect for life on the earth?
2. Analyze the climographs on page 56 and determine the climate represented by each one.

Living in God's World

1. With recent success in unmanned missions to Mars, there is growing interest in sending humans to this planet and establishing a colony. What would be needed to succeed in this endeavor? Would you support or oppose such human exploration? Why?
2. Develop a position on climate change and support your position. (Activity 3 in the *Student Activities* may assist you in this task.)

MAP STUDY | Climates of the World

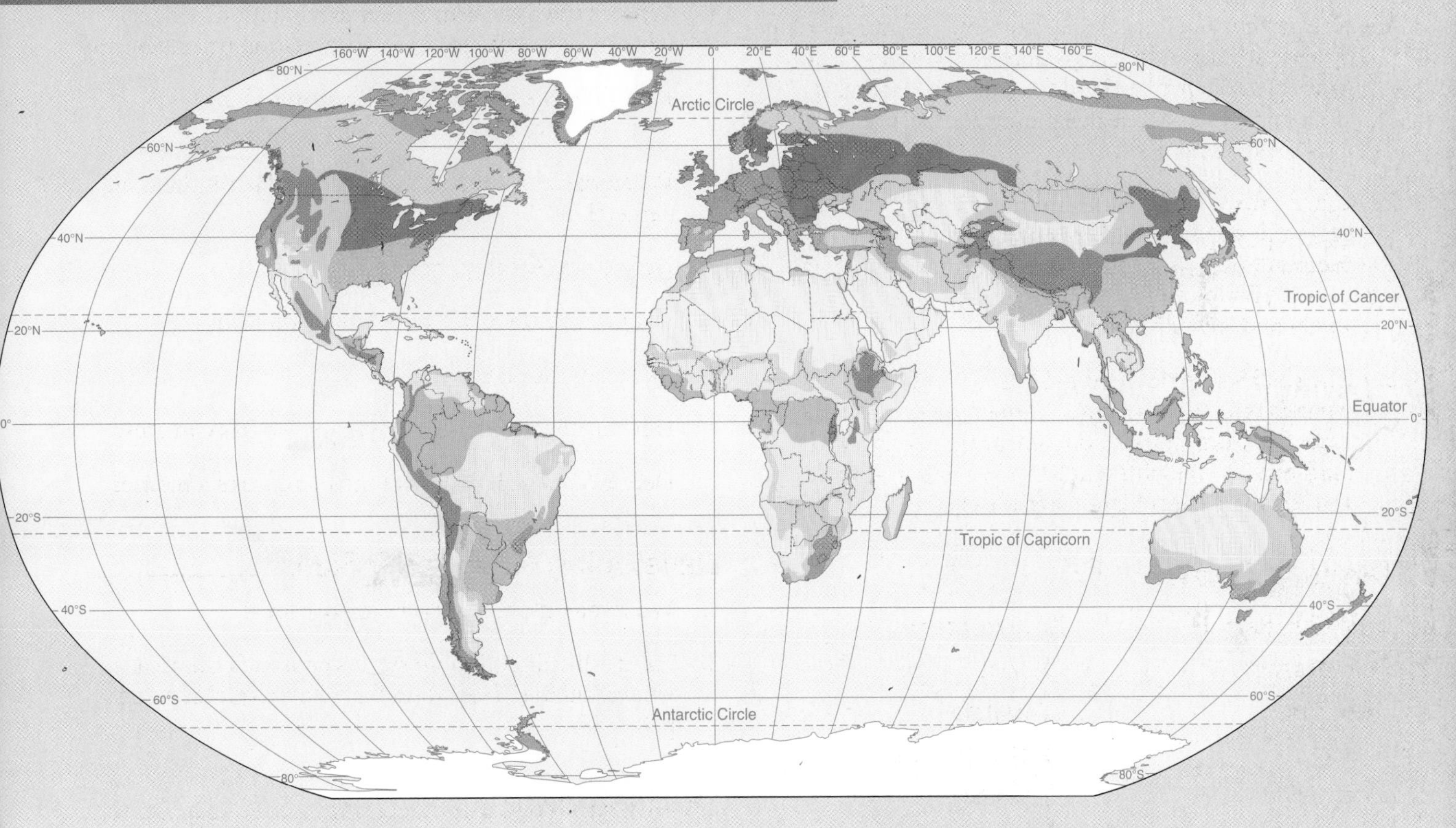

Climates of the World

Tropical Rainy
- Tropical Wet (Rain Forest)
- Tropical Wet and Dry (Savanna)

Dry
- Tropical and Temperate Dry (Desert)
- Semiarid (Steppe)

Moderate
- Marine West Coast
- Mediterranean
- Humid Continental
- Humid Subtropical

Cold
- Icecap
- Polar (Tundra)
- Subpolar (Taiga)

Other
- Varied Highland

1. For each of the five types of climate, identify the continent where it appears most.
2. What is the most common climate at the equator?
3. Where is a humid subtropical climate most common: on the east coast or on the west coast of continents?
4. Compare the rainforests on the biotic map with the tropical wet climate on the climate map. Explain the differences.
5. Why do deserts almost never occur at the equator?

chapter 04

THE WORLD'S PEOPLE

66 Cultures around the World
73 Political Geography
77 Economic Geography
83 World Population and Cities

BIG IDEAS

- How do cultures around the world vary?
- How do governments around the world vary?
- How do people buy and sell things differently around the world?
- How do people and places in the world interact?

The Statue of Liberty in New York City, USA, welcomes immigrants coming by boat.

PRISON NIGHTMARE TO AMERICAN DREAM

For most of the twentieth century, Russia was a Communist nation where it was illegal to read the Bible and worship God. When the Communist regime fell in 1991, the new government began allowing people to leave. Vitaly was one of the first to obtain permission to immigrate to America. He had been imprisoned for his faith, but now he and his family were free to do as they chose. He came to America with his wife and two daughters. He became a truck driver and a part-time pastor. Today he lives with his wife in Oregon and spends most of his time working in his elaborate garden. Though his grandchildren do not speak Russian well, that is something he can accept. In America, they can serve the Lord and pursue their dreams.

Have you ever eaten dinner at a friend's house and encountered foods and ways of interacting that were new to you? Have you ever visited a church and been unfamiliar with the order of service? Have you moved to a different part of the country and found that your classmates and their interests were different from those in your previous school?

In all these instances you were experiencing different cultures. On a larger scale, each region of the world has unique cultural traditions and norms that distinguish it from other regions. Cultural diversity is part of God's plan for the human race as people fill the earth to carry out the Creation Mandate. Studying the rich variety of cultures in the world can be a rewarding experience and can provide Christians with opportunities to connect with and minister to others.

This chapter takes a closer look at the importance of culture in the study of geography. We will examine the elements of culture, types of governments, economic systems, and the use of demographics in describing culture.

A native male dancer in traditional regalia at a powwow in Ohsweken, Canada

(top) Muslim pilgrims pray around the Kaaba in Mecca, Saudi Arabia.

(middle) Tourists in a village in Portugal

(bottom) A Burger King in Dubai, United Arab Emirates, is an example of cultural diffusion.

GUIDING QUESTIONS

- How does culture affect the way people interact with each other?
- How does culture affect the way people interact with their environment?
- How might learning about another culture change how you view the world?

CULTURES AROUND THE WORLD

How do cultures around the world vary?

Culture is the system of customs and traditions and habits that a group of people use to make something of their world. Put another way, culture is the set of unconscious rules by which an individual, family, or society lives. The key word is *unconscious*; most people never question or realize how their culture impacts them. You have been learning those rules since you were born. You do not even realize the depth to which those rules affect your actions. Culture can be likened to tinted eyeglasses. It colors everything you see.

When we try to separate culture from a society or a person and identify why people are the way they are, it is like peeling an onion. You can peel and peel and never seem to get to the center of the vegetable. Culture is so ingrained and multilayered that it affects the very way you walk and carry yourself.

When a person is exposed to a different culture, perhaps by moving overseas, he is suddenly confronted with different customs, assumptions, and "rules." He is then forced to evaluate, adjust, and adapt in order to navigate his new circumstances.

Elements of Culture

Since humans develop culture as image bearers of God in obedience to the Creation Mandate, they ought to develop culture in obedience to God's Word and in a way that reflects His character. However, because of the Fall, humans develop cultures in opposition to God and His ways. As a result every culture manifests good elements as well as bad. Some cultures are more conformed to God and His ways, and others are in greater rebellion against Him.

Chapter 1 addressed some of the elements of culture, including religion, government, and aesthetics. Culture's relation to these elements is somewhat amorphous. Religion and government, for example, react to culture and it reacts back to them, each changing the other. Within a particular culture one of these elements may carry more importance than others and may even absorb the role of the other elements, as illustrated in the two diagrams.

God's Prescribed Domain for Culture
All elements used to glorify God.

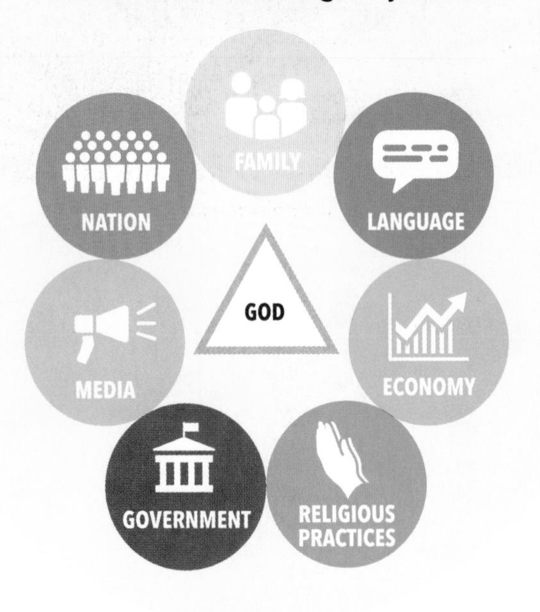

Democratic State
e.g., USA
Elements have greater and lesser importance and are not fulfilling their God-given purpose.

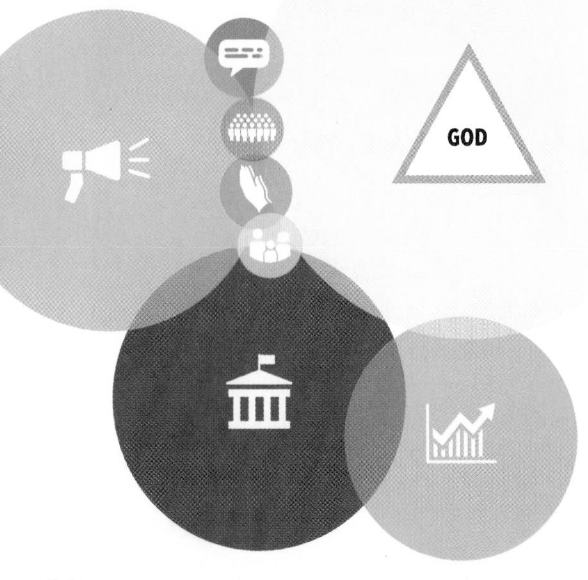

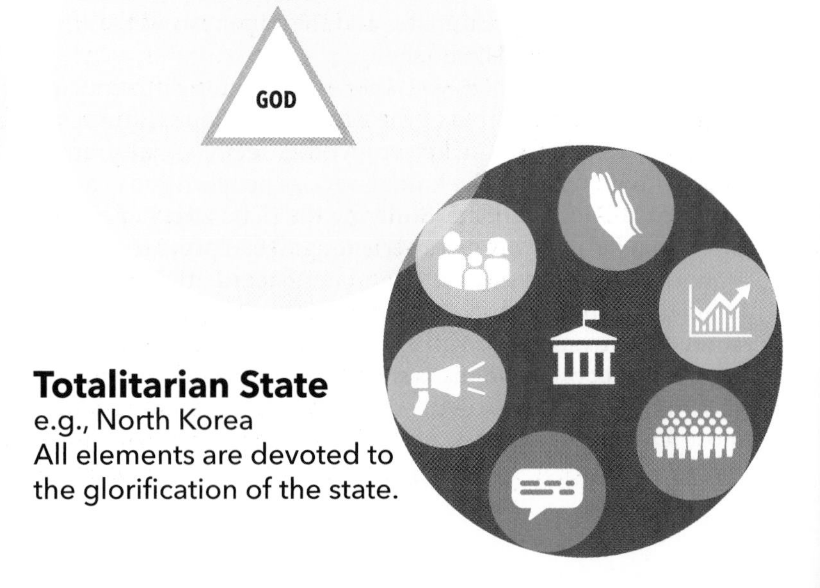

Totalitarian State
e.g., North Korea
All elements are devoted to the glorification of the state.

The Family

▲ *An extended family in Haridwar, India*

The foundation of society is the family. Family life teaches traits that both parents and children need—how to obey, how to serve, how to lead, and how to love. Parents also pass on wisdom to their children. The apostle Paul instructed fathers to bring up their children "in the nurture and admonition of the Lord" (Eph. 6:4).

Every society honors the central role of the family. Certain societies often focus on the nuclear family—a man, his wife, and their children. Other societies typically focus on the extended family—the nuclear family plus grandparents, uncles, aunts, and cousins. Every balanced society honors elders, nurtures children, and emphasizes the central role of the parents.

Fallen societies, however, have taken family responsibilities to extremes. Eastern cultures often worship ancestors or permit polygamy. In contrast, Western cultures tend to overemphasize the rights of individuals, leading to broken families—as reflected in rising divorce rates, dwindling restrictions on abortion, and increasing acceptance of euthanasia. Sometimes the role of the family is filled by other social groups, such as business groups, clubs, or neighborhood community groups.

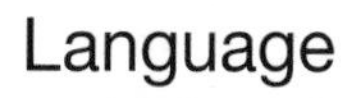

Language

The ability to speak and reason distinguishes humans from the animal world. Man's speech imitates his Maker, who communicates through both His written Word, the Bible, and His living Word, Jesus Christ (Heb. 1:1–2).

After the Flood, the descendants of Noah had one language and one culture. Because the people rebelled and sought to build one great man-centered city, God disrupted human language so that the people could not understand each other's speech. This forced the people to separate into language groups. The locations where different cultures appeared around the world are known as **culture hearths**. The confusing of language at Babel was a judgment, but it was also a blessing. By limiting the power of a united humanity and scattering the human race across the globe, God was placing the peoples of the earth into situations that should have prompted them seek Him (Acts 17:26–27).

What God did at Babel was not the end of the confusing of human language. Since Babel, wherever mountains, oceans, and deserts have prevented people from talking to one another, new languages and cultures have developed.

As of 2019, Wycliffe Bible Translators had identified 7,097 languages spoken in the world. Many linguists recognize at least ten major **language families**, groups of languages that share common characteristics. Because language is the primary means of transmitting culture, the location in which a particular language family is spoken can also be considered a **culture region**. Ninety-nine percent of people speak a language that belongs to one of the ten major families. The most prominent language family is the Indo-European family. Indo-Europeans account for nearly half the world's total population.

▲ *The Museum of the Bible in Washington, DC, USA, includes a room displaying Bibles that have been translated into hundreds of languages.*

Many primitive societies rely on word of mouth to transmit culture. But advanced societies use written languages to keep more accurate and complete records. Writing allows the rapid spread of culture. Before 1900 less than 10 percent of the world's population was literate. Now approximately 86 percent of the world's people can read. Literacy among youth worldwide is 91 percent.

Non-Christian anthropologists blame missionaries for the destruction of languages and culture. Yet, the spreading of the gospel by missionaries has been the main instrument for preserving culture. Missionaries often create written languages for those who formerly had none and thus rescue languages that were destined to die. In spite of a concerted effort over the past seventy years to translate the Bible into every language, only about seven hundred languages have a complete Bible. At least two thousand languages still do not have even a single verse written in the language.

Religious Groups

Religion is key to continuing a culture since it is what gives people a sense of purpose in life. Religion provides a culture with both a set of beliefs and a formal code of conduct that regulates how people should live and worship. Religion—or the rejection of religion—guides all other expressions of culture, including holidays, dress, and even food preparation. Sadly, many of the world's cultures have departed from the worship of the one true God into different forms of idolatry.

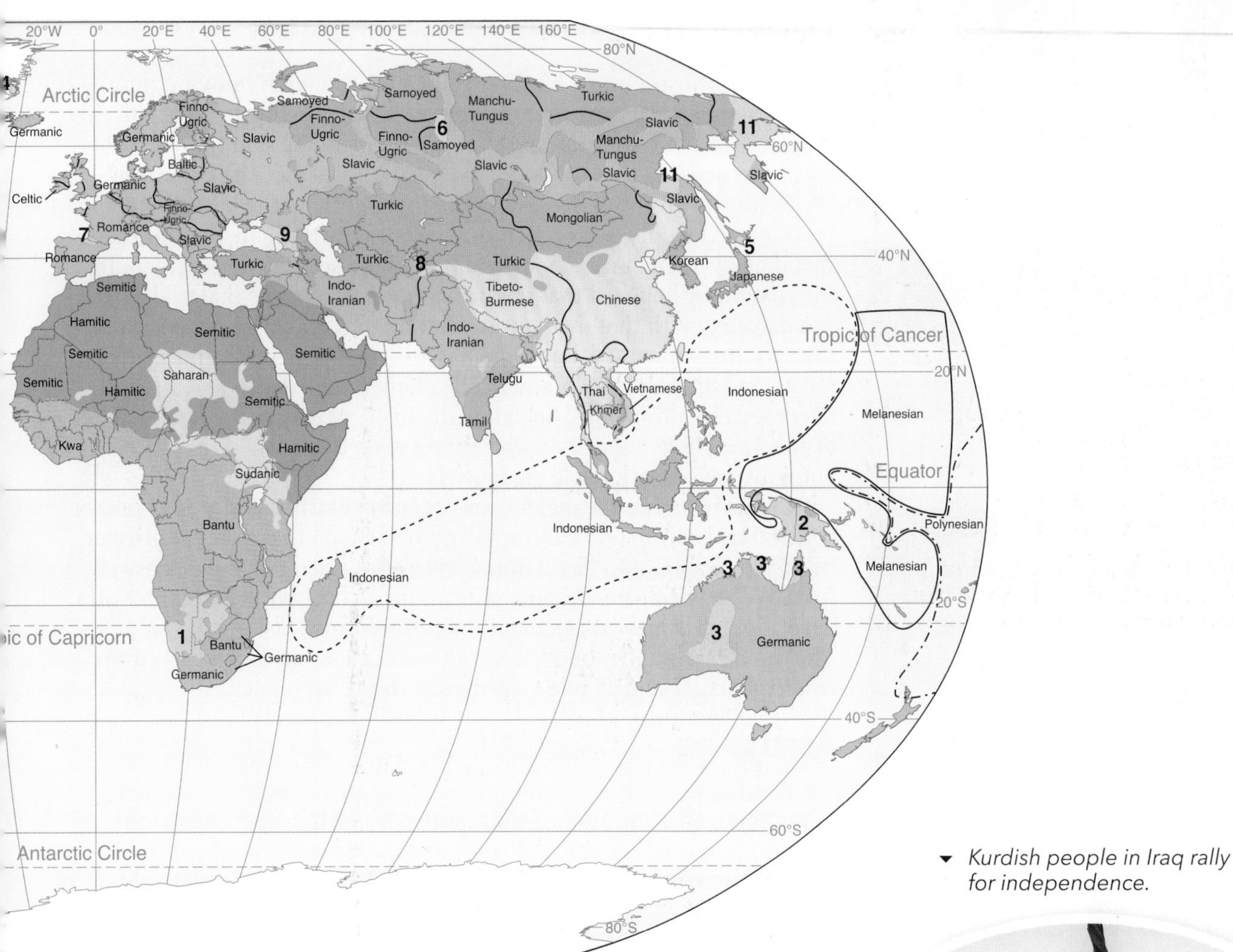

The Nation

After the Tower of Babel, nations arose to transmit culture. A **nation** is a large group of people with a common history and language who have developed a strong sense of identity. Even after a nation loses control of its homeland, it often retains its identity. For example, Israel remained a nation even after foreign nations drove the Hebrews out of the Promised Land. Today, we often call the Kurdish people of the Middle East a "nation," although they are divided among five separate countries.

According to Acts 17:26, God has directed the settling of all the **ethnic groups**, or nations, of the world. The Greek word translated "nation" is *ethnos*, from which we get the word *ethnic*. The English word *nation* comes from a Latin root meaning "born." Both of these words share the idea of a "common birth."

Nation is often confused with related words. *Nation* refers primarily to people, but *country* refers to the land of the people, and *state* refers to the institution that governs the people. A *tribe* is a large group of people who share a common ancestor and is usually governed by elders. A *nation-state* is a nation of people that has established its own government, or state. When one nation conquers other nations beyond its borders, it creates an *empire*. Governments that rule over many nations are called *multinational states*.

▾ *Kurdish people in Iraq rally for independence.*

▲ The invention of the smartphone has had a dramatic effect on culture.

Media

If you hear the word *media*, things such as videos, movies, internet, and music may come to mind. But media actually goes back to the first time ink or paint was put to paper. So it can be said that media has influenced culture for good and bad almost since the beginning.

With the invention of new technologies during the past thirty years, the effect of media on culture has dramatically increased. Teens spend an average of nine hours a day viewing some type of screen. In the past many believed that media was neutral and the material a person digested with that media was what mattered. Now we can see that the very instrument of the media has an effect. The platforms of social media and texting have dramatically changed the depth and strength of personal relationships. Social media influencers are the new shapers of culture. These are people who have a wide following on the internet but may have questionable credentials.

Media has been the major cause of **cultural diffusion**, the spread of cultural traits from one culture to another. Given the apparent prosperity of Western nations, less affluent countries often borrow extensively from Western culture. Because of mass media, people around the world have adopted American elements of culture, from fashion to fast food. The rapid rise of cities and mass communication has aided this cultural convergence, resulting in a growing similarity among cultures.

▲ A fun run is an example of cultural aesthetics.

Aesthetics

Aesthetics is what we often think of when the topic of culture is brought up. Music, dances, foods, festivals, clothes, and architecture are common types of cultural aesthetics. Some less obvious examples of cultural aesthetics could be a "fun run," a Friday night high school football game, or a community garden. The cultural values of a nation can dictate its aesthetics and the way the land is developed and used. For example, in South Korea the only things built on mountaintops are Buddhist temples or an occasional tower. This results in a growing megalopolis with islands of treed hills. Roads are also built in conformity to this value system: a tunnel will be built through a mountain, leaving the top unspoiled. Contrast that example with other countries where the road would be built right over a small mountain because it is more cost-effective. The physical environment may also be shaped by a culture's recreation and entertainment preferences. For example, many Western nations are dotted with golf courses and large plots of land devoted to amusement parks. In the United Arab Emirates, resorts are built on intricately designed man-made islands.

▼ Mountains are not developed in Seoul, South Korea, despite the need for space.

Rise of the Third-Culture Mentality

Some people grow up in two different cultures—the one they are born into and the one that they move into with their family because of job or ministry. Missionary children, children of diplomats, children in military families, and those whose parents work in international business fall into this category. Although these individuals are better able to recognize strengths and weaknesses in the cultures they inhabit, they do not strongly identify with either one. They are called third-culture kids because they identify most strongly with others who have grown up in similar situations. Their primary cultural ties are to like-minded people rather than to a particular place. The number of people in this category is growing, due in part to increasing markets in the global economy.

A group of third-culture kids from an international school

Third-culture kids have the advantage of understanding different cultures and can more easily see the world from other people's perspective. They usually have a high degree of adaptability from having to adjust to living in different countries. They are often able to speak multiple languages. These traits make them attractive to employers. However, third-culture kids also face unique challenges. They sometimes lack a sense of belonging since they cannot call any place home.

Because all cultures are affected by sin, Christians of every culture are required in their daily lives to evaluate cultural norms and practices to see what pleases God and what is sinful. Like third-culture kids, Christians are called to live for Christ in many different cultures, which means they must appreciate them to a degree. But, also like third-culture kids, they cannot be entirely at home in any culture of this age.

Describing and Comparing Cultures

To compare cultures, cultural anthropologists have created a variety of categories to describe the cultural values that people hold. Even though there are exceptions within each category, the effort to describe and categorize still has value. Another challenge with categorizing cultures is that they are not static. They are changing from generation to generation, and in the internet age they are changing even more rapidly. This explains why you see the world differently than your parents do; you are living in slightly different cultures.

Each cultural value can be placed on a continuum between two extremes. The extremes are labeled as high-context and low-context. Neither of these extremes is completely right or wrong. There are biblical virtues and sinful traits found with both extremes. Christians must seek to find the God-honoring balance between the two by evaluating both sides in the light of Scripture.

In high-context cultures, communication relies on implied and nonverbal cues through body language, a person's status, and tone of

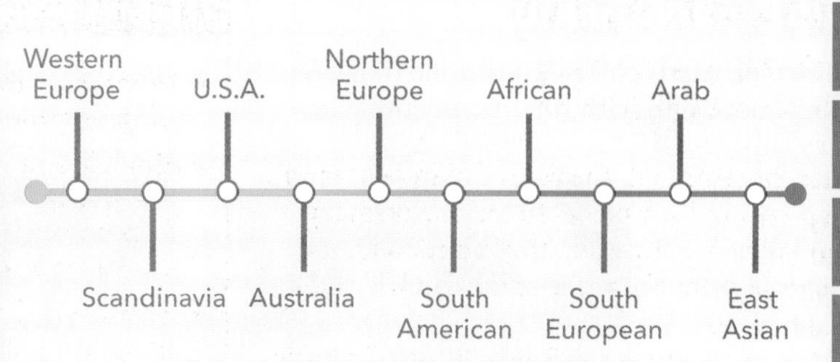

voice. In such cultures, an event will be considered more important than its appointed starting time. So you could expect to find people arriving at church an hour after the service is scheduled to begin. Likewise, the service might continue for the rest of the day. These cultures value relationships over any tasks that need to be completed. Personal space is not a significant issue since the relationship is most important. People will avoid confrontation in this type of culture since harmony is most valued. Usually they will not reveal a lack of knowledge. For example, if you ask for directions from someone in this type of culture, he will confidently give you directions. But later you may discover that he had no idea where the destination was. The important thing for him was to avoid revealing any vulnerability. To people from a low-context culture this is viewed as dishonest. People from high-context cultures tend not to be crisis oriented, meaning they will not look ahead to a potential problem but instead will deal with the problem as it comes.

In a low-context culture, communication is done primarily through verbal language. The very words being said are most important. In this type of culture, events are scheduled to begin and end. It is inappropriate to be late or to go beyond the time allotted for the event. Completing the task is more valuable than a relationship. So it can be expected for a boss to correct an employee and not be too concerned about hurt feelings. The individual takes priority over the group, so personal space is respected and valued. It is permissible to confront someone about something he or she needs to correct, and it is all right for someone to reveal a personal fault or a lack of knowledge.

A particular culture may have elements from both high- and low-context, as in the case of Latin culture. Such cultures are called multi-active.

SECTION REVIEW

1. Why might being in a different culture cause discomfort and confusion?
2. Why is language so important to culture?
3. Why did God divide mankind by multiplying languages?
4. How do cultural values affect what happens to the environment?
5. What are some of the differences between high-context and low-context cultures?
6. How does culture affect the way people interact with each other?

POLITICAL GEOGRAPHY

How do governments around the world vary?

God instituted human government, the rule of man over man. He gave rulers the power of life and death for one primary purpose: restraining violence. By executing murderers, the government shows respect for the value of human life and helps deter other murders (Gen. 9:6).

The Bible defines the duties of government (Rom. 13:1–6). Its basic responsibilities are to ensure justice (Ps. 72:4), to provide for defense and public safety, to promote morality (1 Pet. 2:14), to provide a framework for addressing poverty (Deut. 15:12-15), and to provide order.

Ensuring justice entails a system of laws and courts to settle disputes between citizens. Defense entails a police force to protect law-abiding citizens from domestic criminals and military forces to protect citizens from foreign attack. When no form of governing authority exists and people are doing whatever they want, a state of anarchy results.

For a government to be fair and stable, it must be good. Repeatedly in the book of Proverbs, God states that rulers who obey His law will enjoy stability and peace (Prov. 16:12; 20:28; 25:5; 29:4). So why do wicked people and countries sometimes seem to prosper? The Lord temporarily exalts whom He will. Babylon was "a golden cup in the LORD's hand" (Jer. 51:7), destroying Jerusalem in 586 BC and carrying the Jews away as captives. God eventually judged that empire for its sin. No nation that rejects God's Word will ultimately escape divine judgment.

Types of Governments

Governments can be classified in many ways. The most basic way, however, is according to the ruler's source of power. Romans 13:1 teaches that all governments, whether secular or religious, receive their ultimate authority from God.

Authoritarian governments hold power by claiming an authority higher than that of the people they govern. A government where one individual rules is an **autocracy**. Autocracies are usually unitary systems of government in which all the power lies in the central government. An autocracy is like a **dictatorship**, but a dictatorship can have more than one person ruling, usually by the authority of the military. Most dictatorships are viewed negatively.

Monarchies are the oldest form of single-rule government. Monarchs, usually kings or queens, receive their authority by birth. An absolute monarch rules as he pleases. Although monarchies were far more common in the past than they are now, a few absolute monarchies still exist (e.g., Saudi Arabia, United Arab Emirates, and Jordan). Another type is a limited or constitutional monarchy, in which the people have limited the power of the monarch by law. The monarch functions more as a figurehead; the real power belongs to an elected legislature. The most powerful leader of the elected assembly supervises the writing of laws and heads the bureaucracy that executes the laws. Great Britain is an example of such a government.

A **theocracy** is an authoritarian system of government in which the clergy rule and claim that their authority comes from God, Allah, or some other deity. Almost all theocracies today are in the Islamic world, as in Iran, Yemen, and Afghanistan.

GUIDING QUESTIONS

- What does the Bible say about the role of government in society?
- How does a nation's government affect the way people interact with each other to promote justice and to preserve and conserve resources?
- How do governments of different nations affect each other?

The Supreme leader of Iran, Ayatollah Ali Khamenei, and other government leaders pray after a meeting in Tehran, Iran.

▲ *The Greek parliament in Athens, Greece, is an example of a representative democracy.*

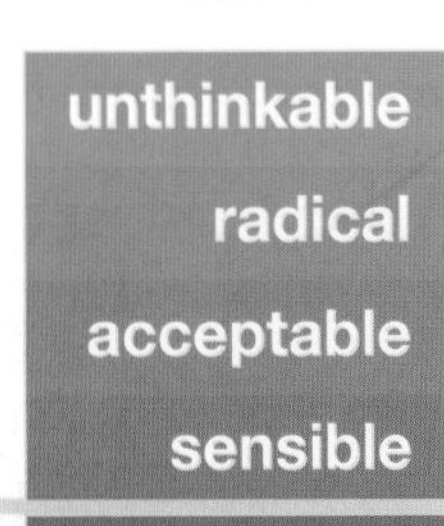

An **oligarchy** is a small group of people holding ultimate authority. Authoritarian governments usually establish their own political party and allow no opposition to their actions. These are common in undeveloped and developing countries.

The different authoritarian governments can be placed on a continuum of varying levels of freedom. The extreme form of authoritarian government is a totalitarian government, which allows the least amount of freedom. These governments tend to make decisions about almost every detail of the people's lives. Citizens must get permission before they can perform activities that others would take for granted. North Korea is the most repressive totalitarian government today.

Elected governments rely on the consent of the people to remain in power. The word **democracy** is often used to describe elected governments. Democracy originally described a government in which a broad segment of the population ruled. The first direct or pure democracies arose in Athens and some other ancient Greek city-states. Adult male citizens could vote on laws and other issues that came before the government. However, given the size of many modern nations, most democracies today are indirect or representative democracies, called **republics**, where the people elect representatives who vote on laws. The people have an opportunity to voice their opinions and even to run for office if they wish. In a republic the citizens elect their national leader, generally known as the president, who supervises the bureaucracy while the legislature writes laws. Republics usually have a federal system in which power is distributed among the local, state, and national governments.

A nation's type of government is influenced by culture. It would be difficult to quickly change a republic to a totalitarian state without an armed takeover since a nation accustomed to having freedom would not easily give it up. It may seem strange, but it is also difficult for a nation to move from an autocratic government to an elected form since the people are not accustomed to having freedom. Russia and Iraq are examples of this.

The culture must be changed gradually over time for citizens to accept a different type of government. A theory called the Overton Window has been proposed to explain how governments or other groups try to move the culture toward a policy they desire. For instance, gay marriage was not a culturally acceptable public policy twenty years ago, but policymakers worked over time to move the issue into the culturally acceptable window.

Government and the Environment

▲ *Bogd Khan Uul National Park, Mongolia*

Governments have an important role in preventing pollution or rectifying pollution for the good of their citizens. They greatly influence the environment within their borders for the positive or the negative. One obvious way is keeping land from being developed. Examples of this are national parks, wilderness areas, and wildlife refuges. Almost every country in the world has some amount of protected land. Venezuela has the largest percentage of protected land at 53%. Excluding small island nations, Turkey has the least with .02%. The first protected land, Mount Bogd Khan Uul, was established in Mongolia in 1783. That was followed by the Yellowstone National Park in 1872.

Usually the needs of the citizens take precedence over any desire to protect the environment since, to some extent, even authoritarian governments must please the people. In China new coal plants are opened regularly despite the impact on air pollution since there is a constantly growing need for electricity production. Wealthy nations tend to have the luxury of putting more restrictions on industries that affect the environment.

Often, the principle of local governmental control provides the best results for achieving a balance between preserving the environment and using a locality's resources. Local citizens care most about the land where they live and also depend on it for their livelihood. Christians should press for the restoration of the created world in the present in anticipation of what God will finally and fully do in the future. A polluted and depleted world is also a harmful world for humans. Caring for creation is a way of loving one's neighbor.

International Relations: Friend and Foe

Every nation is concerned about its relations with other countries. The set of principles that guides a government's international relations is called its **foreign policy**. Just as individuals have different levels of relationships with each other, countries have different levels of relationships. Factors such as ethnic ties, geographic closeness, ideological agreement, common language, religion, and common enemies can cause countries to be friends. Opposing views on these issues can cause them to be foes.

▼ *British and American soldiers patrol together in Afghanistan.*

The relationship of the United States and the United Kingdom is an example of a strong national friendship that has existed for almost two hundred years. It is the result of economic, ethnic, religious, and ideological ties. The ultimate example of unity is forming an alliance to wage war against a common enemy, which the United States and the United Kingdom have done many times, starting with World War I.

Throughout history we can see that powerful nations tend to vie for cultural and political leadership over their weaker neighbors. The powerful nations consider the weaker neighbors they try to influence to be their sphere of influence. Nations can influence their neighbors through foreign trade and foreign aid. But the most obvious, although not necessarily the best, way to influence neighbors is the threat of military attack.

Political boundaries affect a nation's stability, its government, and its relationship to its neighbors. **Natural borders**, such as oceans, mountains, rivers, and deserts, make for the most stable borders. For example, oceans and seas have helped protect countries like the United States, the United Kingdom, and Japan from invasion. River boundaries can be less stable since rivers have a tendency to change their path. An example is the border between Nicaragua and Costa Rica at the San Juan River. Disputes over this river border date back to the 1800s. In 2015 the International Court of Justice ruled against Nicaragua for violating Costa Rica's sovereignty and establishing a military presence in the area.

Geometric borders are the most unstable. These borders are straight artificial lines usually following longitude or latitude lines. These are found all over the world, but they mostly occur in Africa and the Middle East. Because those who drew the lines rarely took into account the different ethnic groups living in the area, conflicts are common. One of the most dangerous borders separates India and Pakistan. The border was drawn by the British before they gave up control of India. They intended to segregate the Hindu and Muslim populations and thereby turn a **cultural boundary** into a political one. When India was split between Muslim Pakistan and Hindu India, 14 million people had to quickly migrate to the land of their respective religion. One million people died in the ensuing warfare. There is no geographic logic to this border, and it has led to the worst possible outcome—a standoff between two nations possessing nuclear weapons.

If two countries have disagreements, their diplomats must get together to try to prevent a war. **Diplomacy** is the art of negotiating agreements between nations. Formal agreements between nations are called treaties. Nations can negotiate two kinds of treaties. They can either talk to their enemies and sign a peace treaty or make strong military alliances with their friends, agreeing to help each other in case of attack.

SECTION REVIEW

1. Identify some statements about the purpose of governments from the following Scriptures: Psalm 72:4; Romans 13:1–7; 1 Peter 2:13–16; Deuteronomy 15:12–15.
2. Where does an absolute monarch obtain his authority? a dictator? a president?
3. What is the main difference between a pure democracy and a republic?
4. In what ways can the government affect the environment?
5. Why do some political boundaries lead to conflict?

The separation barrier on the West Bank in Israel is an example of a geometric border.

ECONOMIC GEOGRAPHY

How do people buy and sell things differently around the world?

The earth's resources are neither unlimited nor evenly divided among the nations. Each country must make difficult choices about the best way to develop and distribute its resources, goods, and services. The study of the process by which people and countries make such choices is called **economics**.

The Creator owns all of the earth's resources (Ps. 24:1; 50:10). Humans are merely stewards, placed in charge of the creation to use and develop its resources for His glory (see Gen. 1:28). Every system for making economic choices should be evaluated in light of that fact. The governments of the world generally have economic systems that can be classified as capitalist, socialist, or mixed economies.

National progress and wealth are also dependent on a stable government. People are more willing to work hard, take risks, and invest in business if they are free and if their government encourages such efforts and works to protect them from exploitation or external attacks.

GUIDING QUESTIONS

- How does a nation's economy affect how people interact with each other?
- How does a nation's economy affect the way people interact with their physical environment?
- How is a nation's economy affected by the economies of other nations?

Economic Systems

Capitalism

Elected governments and republics tend to have a capitalist, or free-market, economy. It is called free-market because businesses can freely compete in the marketplace for buyers with little interference from the government. People who take risks to start businesses are called entrepreneurs.

Capitalism is an economic system in which private individuals own most of the factors of production and make most economic decisions. Capital is money and equipment (buildings, tools, computers, and vehicles).

Capitalism, by valuing private property and giving rewards for labor done, adheres to the norms that God built into creation better than many of the alternative systems. For this reason it has done more than any other economic system to lift people out of poverty. However, every system created by fallen humans has problems. Critics have long expressed concerns that capitalism disrupts traditional societal structures such as family and local community and that it leads people to view everything through the lens of a market. Christians have noted that people with large amounts of capital have power, and there needs to be some check on this power so that it is not used to oppress people (Isa. 5:8; Amos 8:4–6). Nevertheless, in a sinful world capitalism does tend to channel the profit motive in mutually beneficial ways, and it allows the power of wealth creation to be dispersed.

▲ *A street market in Cusco, Peru, is an example of capitalism.*

Socialism

During the nineteenth century, opponents of capitalism developed an alternative system called socialism. Under **socialism**, the government owns the major industries and promises to make production decisions for the welfare of society. Socialist governments are normally oligarchies. In a socialist or **command economy**, the government determines which industries are developed, where they are built, and what they produce. Few business people are willing to take risks with capital because much of the profit goes to the government in the form of high taxes.

▲ *People wait in line outside a supermarket in Caracas, Venezuela, where socialist policies caused a lack of goods.*

The most extreme form of socialism is called **communism**, which is a totalitarian form of government under which the government owns everything.

More than just an economic system, socialism is a worldview with particular ideas about what is wrong with the world and how to correct it. Inequality is the chief problem that socialism seeks to solve. Common ownership of all property is the proposed solution. Socialists have tended to think that people will do right when everyone is equal and no one is competing for possessions.

Christians recognize that when people amass wealth and power they often oppress other people (cf. Amos 4:1; Isa. 5:8). But the Bible never holds out absolute equality as the ideal. It seems that even in eternity some people will have more responsibility than others, and some individuals more rewards than others (Luke 19:16–19; 1 Cor. 3:12–15). Private property also seems to persist through the millennial period (Mic. 4:3–4; Zech. 3:10). Because socialism runs contrary to the way God designed his world to work, it has led to economic hardship and tyranny in the nations that have attempted most strenuously to put it into practice.

Mixed Economies

Many countries whose socialist economies collapsed adopted a **mixed economy** that attempted to combine elements of capitalism and socialism. In a mixed economy, private citizens can own property and businesses, but the government closely regulates their choices. In spite of socialism's poor record, even some leaders in capitalist countries have sought to move toward mixed economies. China provides an example of a mixed economy in which citizens can now own property. Ironically, the United States has been moving closer to a mixed economy for a number of years. In 1995 the United States ranked fourth in economic freedom; by 2018 it ranked twelfth.

Economic Measurement

Most people think of wealth as the ownership of things, such as cattle, land, or money. But real wealth is the ability to produce new things. Consider the biblical example of Jacob. His wealth was not in the size of his flocks and herds but in the plentiful offspring his animals produced each year to feed and clothe his growing family. The more a country produces each year, the more its people can eat and enjoy that year, and the better prepared they will be for the next year.

The most common measurement of a country's wealth is the gross domestic product (**GDP**). The GDP is the monetary value of all the goods and services produced for sale within a country's borders over the course of a year. This measurement includes primary, secondary (manufactured goods), and tertiary (service sector) industries. GDP means little, however, until it is divided by the population of the country. A more meaningful measurement is per capita GDP, the value of products divided by the number of persons living in a country.

A high per capita GDP does not always mean that a country has a lot of **industry** or that the average worker makes a lot of money. Several rich countries, such as the United Arab Emirates and Qatar, have a high per capita GDP because primary industries ship valuable exports like oil, but a few rich sheiks and bureaucrats receive the money. The majority population of these countries are migrant workers who do not see this wealth. In Qatar's case 90 percent of the population consists of foreign-born workers.

Economic Prosperity

What makes some countries rich and others poor? This is not an easy question to answer. Possessing natural resources is not essential for having wealth. Japan's industries have thrived even though its islands lack natural resources. On the other hand, the Democratic Republic of Congo's mines are rich in resources, but its per capita GDP is among the lowest in the world. Nations can be placed into different highly subjective categories based on their economic strength and development. **Highly developed countries** have advanced infrastructure and industrialization. They tend to have a high per capita income and standard of living. **Newly industrialized countries** have transitioned from primarily agricultural industries to goods-producing industries. **Developing countries** have a lower per capita GDP, and their economies are primarily based on agriculture. Factors impacting a nation's development include governmental institutions, geographic location, and religious beliefs about material goods.

A situation called the poverty trap occurs when poor countries have weak or corrupt institutions that result in deeper poverty for the nation. Consider an agriculture minister who finds himself in charge of a budget of $200,000 to be used for the nation's farm development, and his salary is $10,000 a year. He can choose to pocket most of the budget, guaranteeing a better life for his family, or be honest and use the money the way it was meant to be used. He can easily rationalize keeping the money. In fact, in many developing countries keeping it is expected. In turn, the people avoid paying taxes by every possible way, which weakens the institutions and destroys the rule of law in every step of the cycle. Geographic location also plays a major role in whether a nation is rich or poor. As the map shows, the closer a nation is to the equator, the lower the per capita GDP.

Corruption is a major problem for developing countries.

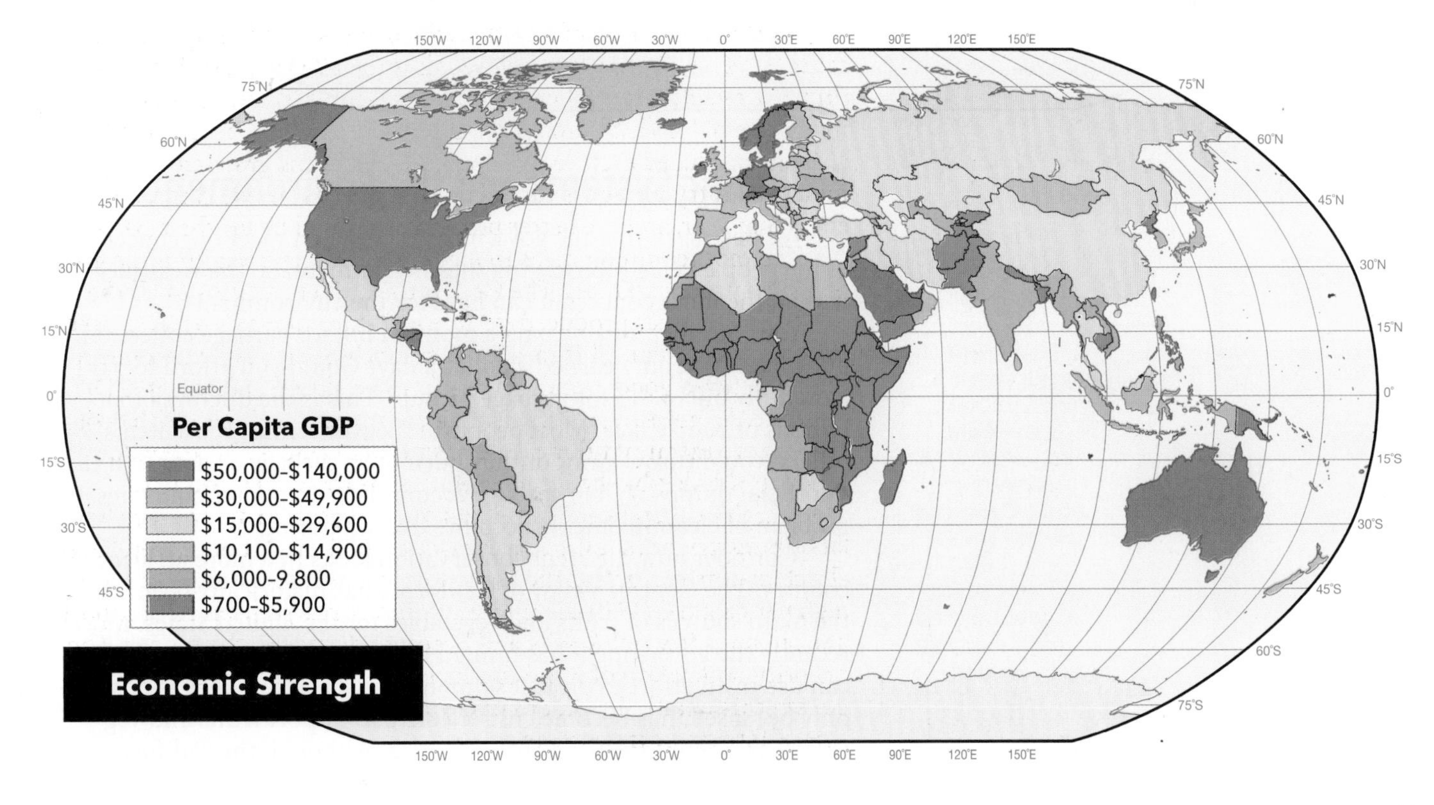

Economic Strength

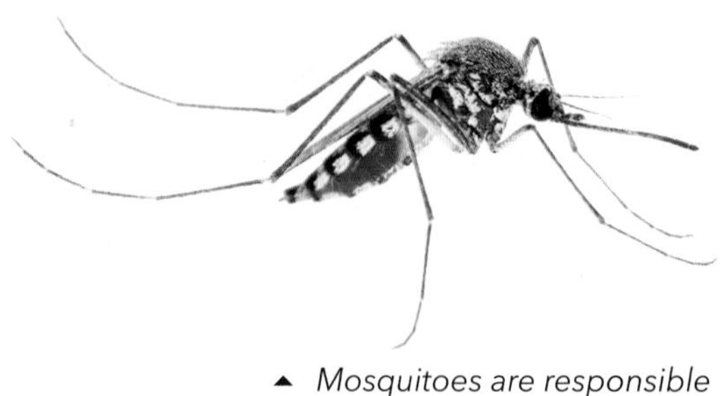

▲ *Mosquitoes are responsible for transmitting diseases like malaria and yellow fever.*

Many reasons have been suggested for this phenomenon. Diseases, particularly malaria, are more prevalent along the equator. This can cause a vicious cycle of workers being disabled and the nation having to allocate more resources for health care, which results in less national wealth spent on development. The weather in the tropics also allows for diseases and insects that kill plants and animals. Nations in other regions take for granted the natural purging that winter frost provides by killing bugs and weeds.

Religious belief also affects prosperity. For example, according to Hinduism, karma determines a person's fate. So poverty is a person's punishment and there is nothing he can do about it. Contrast that philosophy with the teaching that God wants all Christians to be wealthy. Both views are incorrect, but the former can be especially paralyzing to a nation in poverty.

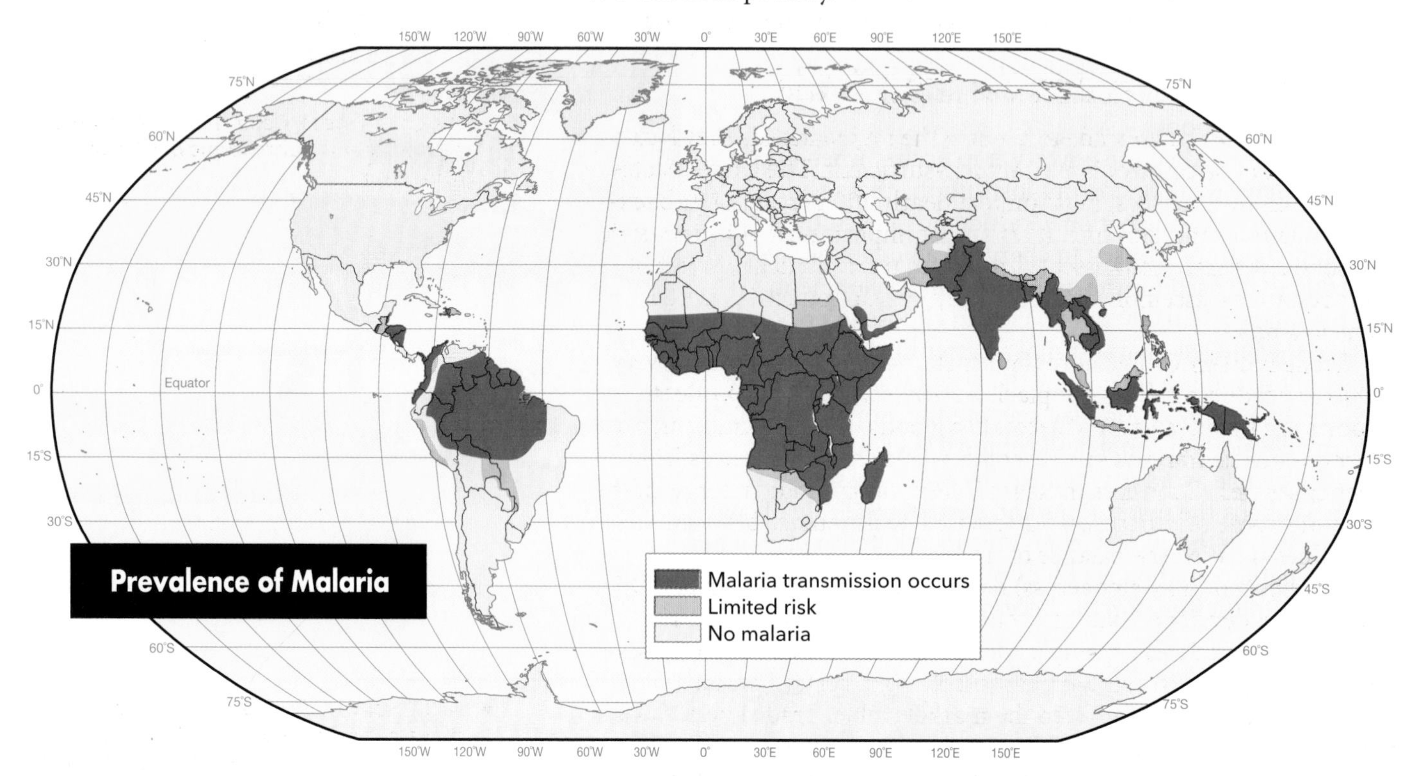

Economic Systems and the Environment

We have seen that the government must first meet the concerns of the people before conserving the environment. So the wealthier the nation, the more concern it can have for the environment.

Your family probably pays a monthly bill for garbage collection, but what if you only earned a dollar a day? Could you afford to pay a monthly bill of $15 for garbage pickup? This is the dilemma that billions of people face. Most people in the world must reuse items others would throw away, or they burn their garbage or deposit it in unofficial dumps. When garbage accumulates in poorer countries, the problem of cleanup quickly becomes overwhelming.

Consider how different conservation looks in a more affluent country. The Central Valley of California has historically been one of the main sources of fruits and vegetables for the United States. More recently the government has limited the amount of water the farmers can use in an effort to protect salmon habitats. This policy is possible only because it has become cost-effective to import fruits and vegetables from Central and South America. Although the California farmers suffer, there is not a national outcry since prices remain stable. Contrast this with France, where in late 2018 the government tried to impose high gas taxes to combat climate change. The people rioted in the streets against the policy because they could not afford the tax. The government quickly reversed its decision.

Today the countries of the former USSR are still reeling from the environmental polices of the past. This was exemplified during the 2014 Winter Olympics when even after Russia spent $50 billion on the location, hotel guests still saw a sign on the faucets that said, "Do not use water on your face because it contains something very dangerous." The irony is that earlier Soviet thinkers thought their plan, as opposed to capitalism, would benefit the environment. They thought their policies would start "a new relationship between society and nature." Today huge areas of Kazakhstan and the Ukraine are uninhabitable because of the Soviet Union's environmental legacy.

▲ *A sign in Wasco, California, USA, protests the fact that water to farms has been turned off.*

Economic Interaction through Trade

Nations depend on trade to acquire the raw materials they lack. No individual or country is entirely self-sufficient. The United States, though rich in resources, must import nearly 100 percent of its bauxite, manganese, and graphite. It also must import most of its industrial diamonds, platinum, tungsten, chromium, tin, and nickel. Without these resources, assembly lines for many critical industries would come to a halt.

Trade is essential for more than exchanging raw materials. Every industry needs a market—people or businesses to buy its products. Exports are the primary and secondary goods that a country ships to other countries. Imports are the goods that a country receives from other countries. Countries measure international trade in terms of the monetary value of exports and imports. The difference between these two values is called the balance of trade.

Landlocked (no water access) nations have lower per capita GDPs. Even within developed nations, coastal areas have higher GDPs. International trade has multiple advantages. It allows a nation to have a variety of goods. If a nation has a surplus of a certain product, it can trade the product and keep the market stable. Trade lowers costs because companies are competing to make things better and more cheaply. It spurs production efficiency because companies must limit waste in order to make a profit. It provides for resource specialization, which means companies focus on what they are good at and outsource the rest. International trade is also a bulwark for peace between the nations. When nations are dependent on trading with each other, they

▼ *Advances in shipping and logistics via container ships and ports like this one in Bangkok, Thailand, are major reasons for increased trade around the world.*

GLOBAL IMPACT | Globalization

Globalization tends to break down cultural and economic borders. It results in cultural diffusion. The primary vehicle of globalization is the spread of technology, particularly the internet. People who otherwise would be cut off from one another can now communicate instantly.

There are both positive and negative effects of the internet and globalization. All segments of life in the developing world have been improved through the spread of technology. Doctors now have access to knowledge and expertise from all over the world. Environmental engineers can share creative ways to provide clean water. Businesses have access to markets and lending sources. Missionaries are able to communicate much more easily.

Negative effects include a rise in unsafe working conditions and exploitive labor practices, even to the point of human trafficking. Additionally, because of cultural diffusion, nations are losing their unique cultures and traditions. There is also upheaval among the people of industrialized and newly industrialized nations as manufacturing jobs move to other parts of the world.

1. Identify positive aspects of globalization.
2. Why would some say that globalization is another term for the "Americanization" of the world? Do you think that description is accurate?
3. How does globalization affect jobs in developed and newly industrialized nations?
4. Why might a totalitarian state object to its people having access to the internet?

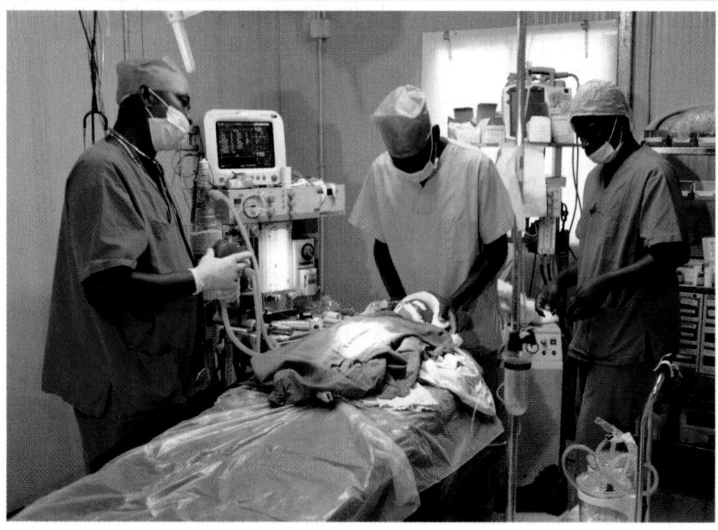

Technology has allowed doctors like these in Mogadishu, Somalia, the ability to perform more advanced medical procedures.

tend to avoid aggressive actions that their trading partners might see as hostile.

Occasionally, countries have disputes over trade. Though those conflicts can lead to war, countries have other weapons at their disposal. Tariffs are taxes on imports and exports. In theory, if the United States places a high tariff on Japanese automobiles, sales of Japanese cars will drop and domestic sales will increase. (In reality, because consumers are sometimes willing to pay the higher prices for the foreign-made products, domestic sales may continue to languish.) Another weapon is an embargo, a ban on importing or exporting certain products or trading with a particular country.

SECTION REVIEW

1. What is the main difference between capitalism and socialism?
2. Which economic model do you think is most effective?
3. What is GDP, and how does it differ from per capita GDP?
4. How does the health of institutions affect the wealth of a nation?
5. How does the economy affect what happens to the environment?
6. What are import and export taxes called?

WORLD POPULATION AND CITIES

How do people and places in the world interact?

The study of human populations and their characteristics is called **demography**. Demographers use statistics to show what has happened with a population and to predict what the population will be like in the future.

GUIDING QUESTIONS

- How do a nation's demographics affect how people interact with each other?
- How do a nation's demographics affect the way people interact with their physical environment?
- What is a population pyramid?
- How do demographics, economy, government, and culture relate to patterns of human settlement?

Population Growth and Decline

Demographers use vital statistics such as the number of births, marriages, divorces, and deaths to describe a particular population. These statistics are helpful in shaping our understanding of people and cultures. They are "life signs" that indicate a culture's health and vitality.

Population Growth

Countries measure population increase by comparing the number of births and deaths each year as well as the number of immigrants coming in and the number of those leaving. The number of children born per one thousand people is called the crude **birthrate**. In 2018 the United States had a crude birthrate of 12.4 (12.4 live births for every one thousand people). Demographers must also calculate the number of people who die each year per one thousand people, called the crude **death rate**. In 2018 the United States' crude death rate was 8.36. Subtracting the number of deaths from the number of births (12.4 – 8.36) provides the rate of natural increase. It is 4.04 per one thousand, or 0.4 percent. Immigration accounted for 1.05 million new people coming into the country, resulting in a final growth rate of .71% for 2018. The number of those leaving the United States is not tracked and is probably not significant.

▲ *Crowds of people in Istanbul, Turkey*

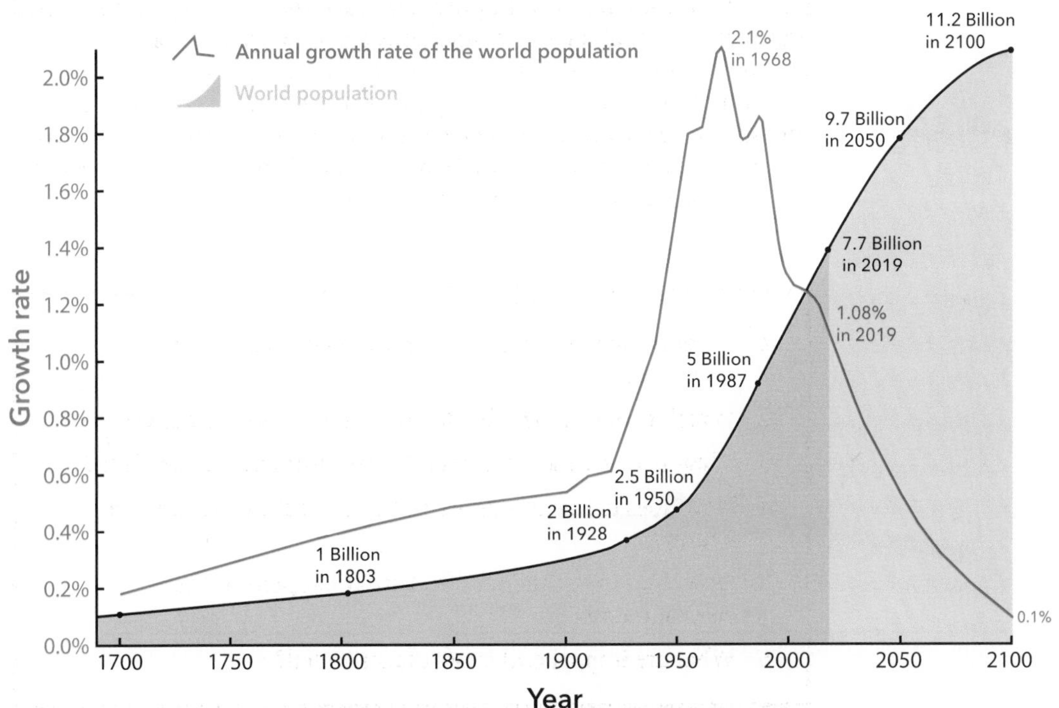

Though Christians and non-Christians alike are discouraged by high death rates, activists oppose high growth rates. Activists seek to decrease the world's growth rate, which is now about 1.1 percent but is already in a downward trend. Growth peaked in 1968 and has decreased ever since. The Bible provides a different perspective on birth and death. Suffering and death are the inevitable consequences of sin in this fallen world (Rom. 8:22), and having children is a sign of God's blessing as families obey God's Creation Mandate. In the midst of sorrow and death, children offer hope of new life (Ps. 127:3–5).

▲ *With declining birthrates and death rates, there is a shortage of people to take care of the elderly. Nursing homes like this one in France are looking to robots as an answer.*

Life Expectancy

Before the Flood, people lived long lives; Methuselah lived a record 969 years. Life expectancy fell dramatically after the Flood. Abraham still lived to 175 years, but David lived to be only 70. Since Bible times, life expectancy has fluctuated depending on several factors, including war, disease, and food supply.

Advances in technology and medicine have done much to increase life expectancy. Better crops and new vaccinations have practically eliminated the effects of malnutrition and some common diseases that once took countless lives. Life expectancy in the United States in 1901 was 47 years for men and 50 for women; by the turn of the next century it was 77 years for men and 80 years for women. As of 2018 it was approximately 76 years for men and 81 years for women. Life expectancy has begun to drop, however, partly as the result of the drug epidemic and the rising number of suicides.

Fertility Rate

Another statistic that illustrates the health of a culture is the fertility rate, the average number of children being born per couple. Statistics show that an average of 2.1 children per couple is the number required for a country's population to replace itself. If a country has a number lower than that, its population is said to be in decline. At present, fertility rates worldwide are going down. Many countries have a rate that is below the 2.1 replacement level. The 2018 US rate was 1.76. Japan reached a low of 1.26 in 2005. With people living longer, countries are facing a new economic crisis. The elderly depend on the young to

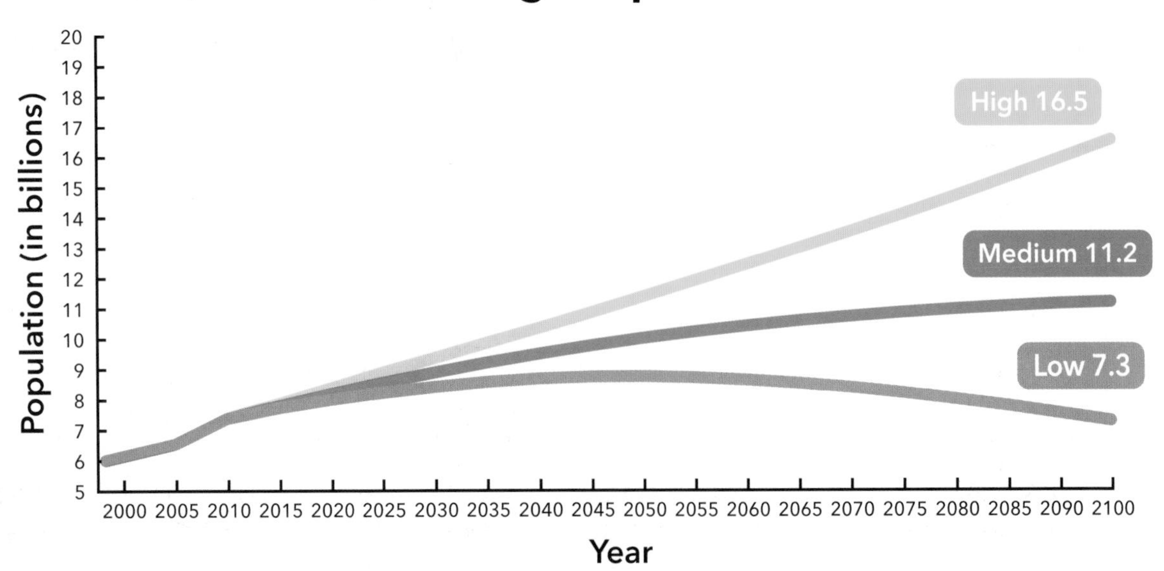

support them in their retirement years. Because there are fewer young people now working, governments are running out of money to support their elderly populations. Consequently, some governments have resorted to offering couples cash incentives to have children.

Some demographers made dire predictions in the past. They said the earth would soon be unable to support its population and that hundreds of millions of people would die of starvation. Obviously, this did not happen. Yet still there are doomsayers who see the world's population as the problem and population control as the solution. How does a Christian navigate this debate? The answer is not to ignore the statistics altogether. Rather, we must seek models that provide a more accurate picture of how vital statistics are affecting the earth and its people.

DEMOGRAPHIC TRANSITION MODEL

Demographers use the **demographic transition model** to describe what has happened with populations and what will happen. Population pyramids are like a snapshot that shows the current population of a country according to age.

Stage 1: Most of the world before the Industrial Revolution: high birthrate/high death rate.

Stage 2: Medical advances and improved sanitation causes death rates to decline. Least developed countries are in this stage today: high birthrates/lower death rates.

Stage 3: Improved economic conditions; children don't impact economic health as much. Birthrates begin to decline; death rates continue to decline.

Stage 4: Stabilization stage: both the birthrate and the death rate are low. Developed world just completing this stage.

Stage 5: Will fertility rates continue to decline, causing an overpopulation of older people compared to the young?

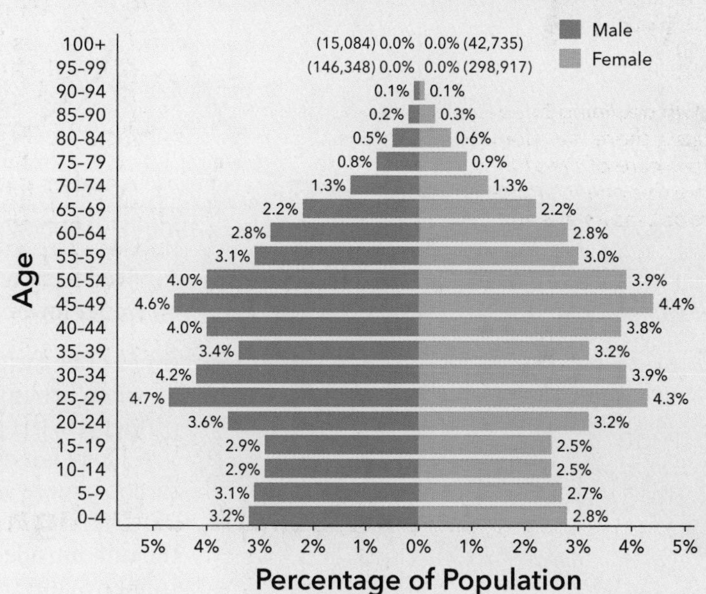

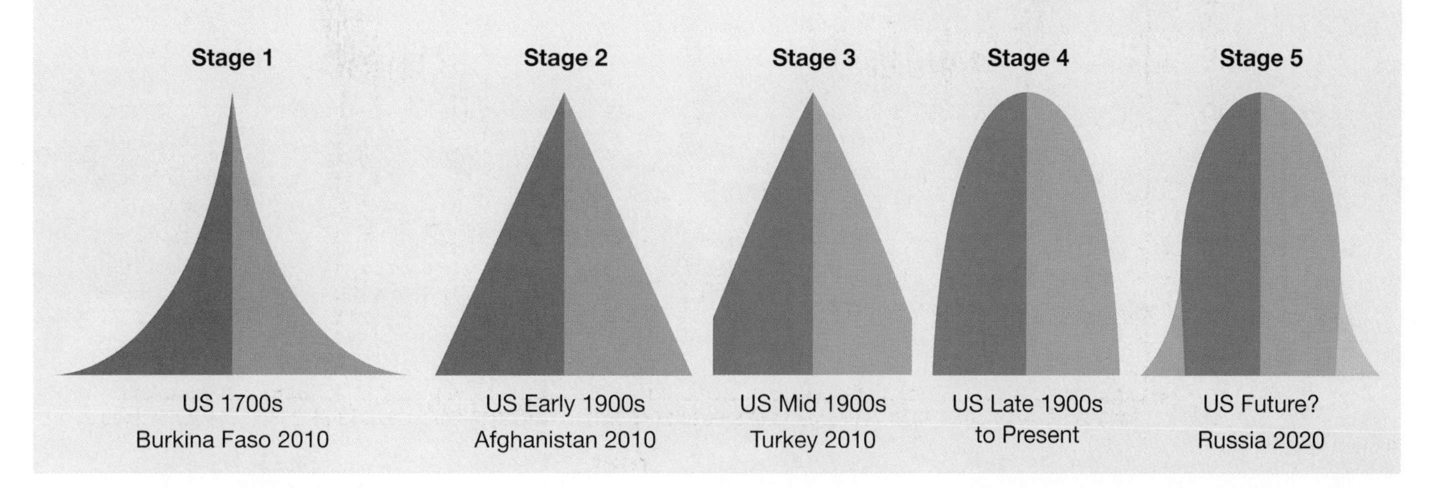

Population Distribution

Demographics deal not only with population growth or decline. They can also be used to identify different trends in the movements of people. **Population distribution** is the term used to describe where people choose to live.

A key date for a nation is when it switches from majority rural to majority urban. For the US we can see it was 1917; for China that happened in 2010. India is one of the few nations that still have a rural majority, but it is projected to reach urban majority in 2046. Fifty-five percent of the world's people live in an urban area.

Urbanization

No hard and fast rule distinguishes the different types of communities. Usage of terms such as *city*, *town*, or *village* varies. For simplicity, demographers have divided populated areas into two broad categories: urban and rural. Urban areas have a large number of buildings and people in a small area, and rural areas have few buildings and people in a large area. According to the definitions of the US Census Bureau, rural communities have populations of less than 2,500 and urban areas have populations greater than 2,500.

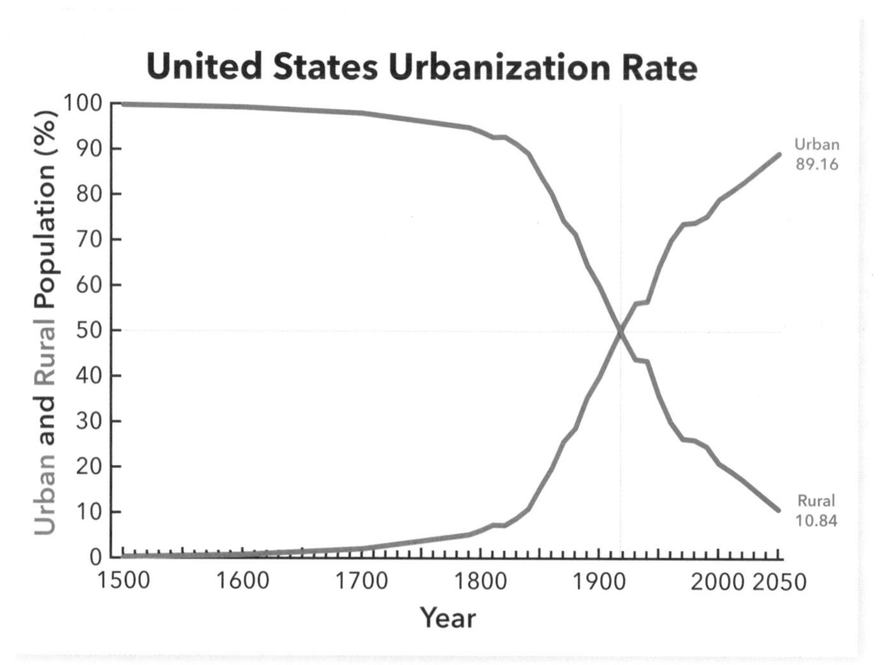

The size and number of communities have increased throughout most of history. Since the Industrial Revolution, however, the move to urban areas has accelerated as people have left their farms and small villages to seek opportunities in big cities. Two hundred years ago, 95 percent of Americans lived on farms, but now fewer than 5 percent do. The growth of urban areas at the expense of rural areas is called **urbanization**.

Urbanization has been linked to lower fertility rates. In rural areas children are an asset, but in urban areas they can be considered a liability. Family and religion sometimes offer the greatest external pressure on a couple to have children. So when urbanization results in a separation from family and religious influences, the pressure to have children is reduced.

There is a cycle fueling urbanization. As more people move to cities for jobs, more services are needed, so more jobs are created. And the pattern of more people/more jobs keeps repeating. Urban sprawl, or the uncontrolled expansion of urban areas, happens as the city grows. In many countries, the city center becomes the prime real estate and

Urbanization is happening rapidly in Rio de Janeiro, Brazil, as slums are built next to the more developed city.

the optimal place to live. As poor people from rural areas move to the city, they move into slums on the fringe. As more people become wealthy and move into the inner city, it grows outward and overtakes the slums. Thus the poorer areas move further out.

The situation is the opposite in the United States. A very small part of the downtown is considered prime real estate, but most of the desirable property is in the suburbs, an area between urban and rural areas that offers proximity to urban benefits but without the attending problems. As the suburbs become more urban, people move out farther. The areas between the downtown and the suburbs often get neglected and become unlivable.

▲ *People live in the narrow band along the Nile River, Egypt.*

Population Density

Population density is the average number of people who live on each square mile (or kilometer) of land. The most densely populated countries are city-states like Macao and Monaco. Some larger densely packed countries are Bangladesh, with 2,753 people per square mile, and South Korea, with 1,329 per square mile. The United States has a population density of 86 people per square mile.

Population density is a fairly good indication of crowding, but people are not spread evenly across the landscape. They generally cluster around good farmland. Nearly all the Egyptian people, for example, live in a narrow band of land along the banks of the Nile River and in the Nile Delta. Thousands of square miles of that desert country are virtually uninhabited.

Demographers have developed an even more accurate way to measure population density. They take into account the amount of arable land (land that can be used to plant crops). For example, only 2.9 percent of Egypt's 386,660 square miles of land is arable. By comparing the total population to the arable land, demographers find the physiological density. Egypt's physiological density is more than six thousand people per square mile. The lower the physiological density, the easier it is for a nation to feed itself.

We can see how the demography of a nation or region can affect the way the peoples of that area interact with one another. In a less dense rural area, people interact with each other differently than in a dense urban area. An illustration of this is the green light waiting time test. When the traffic signal turns green and the car in front does not move, what is the response of the car behind? In urban areas, drivers are typically much quicker in sounding the horn.

Many groups are concerned about the increasing size of cities, the loss of wilderness, and the decline in rural societies. But the Bible has a different perspective on urbanization and population density. God meant for the earth to be subdued. He provided Israel with walled cities in the Promised Land, and He made provisions to ensure that the land would not return to its wild state (Deut. 7:22). The ultimate destination of His people is not a wilderness but the New Jerusalem, a massive city that will cover nearly two million square miles and be filled with people.

The following chapters examine urban areas—why they arose and what they show about human geography—as well as rural areas. You will discover some of the natural limitations God has placed on human settlement and identify some of the awesome natural wonders found around the world.

SECTION REVIEW

1. What four statistics are used to compute the rate of increase of a population?
2. What are the main reasons for recent increases in life expectancy?
3. What does a population pyramid illustrate?
4. Why have rural populations decreased in most developed nations?
5. How do a country's demographics affect the way the people interact with each other—the difference between rural and urban?
6. Should Christians oppose urbanization and the utilization of wilderness areas? Support your answer.

04 CHAPTER REVIEW

SUMMARY

1. Language is the main transmitter of culture. Other factors include religion, media, family, government, nationhood, media, and aesthetics. World cultures can be described as high-context, low-context, or multi-active.
2. Governments can be classified by the source of their authority. Authoritarian governments are more restrictive than elected governments.
3. World economies are generally described as capitalist, socialist, or mixed. Per capita GDP is the measurement of the value of the goods produced by each person in the country. Countries are either highly developed, newly industrialized, or developing. The more wealthy the country, the better the environment. Trade is key for the prosperity of a nation.
4. Demographics, or a population's birth, death, fertility, and immigration statistics, enable demographers to try to predict what will happen with a population. The study of demography also includes population distribution and population density.

Terms To Know

- ❑ culture hearths
- ❑ language families
- ❑ culture region
- ❑ nation
- ❑ ethnic groups
- ❑ cultural diffusion
- ❑ autocracy
- ❑ dictatorship
- ❑ theocracy
- ❑ oligarchy
- ❑ democracy
- ❑ republics
- ❑ foreign policy
- ❑ natural borders
- ❑ geometric borders
- ❑ cultural boundary
- ❑ diplomacy
- ❑ economics
- ❑ capitalism
- ❑ socialism
- ❑ command economy
- ❑ communism
- ❑ mixed economy
- ❑ GDP
- ❑ industry
- ❑ highly developed countries
- ❑ newly industrialized countries
- ❑ developing countries
- ❑ demography
- ❑ birthrate
- ❑ death rate
- ❑ demographic transition model
- ❑ population distribution
- ❑ urbanization
- ❑ population density

Making Connections

1. Which cultural institution guides all the other manifestations of culture?
2. What is the most widespread language family in the world?
3. What are the characteristics of a totalitarian government?
4. Why do coastal regions have a higher GDP?
5. What is the demographic transition model?

Developing Geography Skills

1. Why are some countries poor even though they have valuable raw materials?
2. Consider the population pyramid. What stage is the population in? What predictions can you make about the population?

United States of America (2018)

Population: 328,835,763

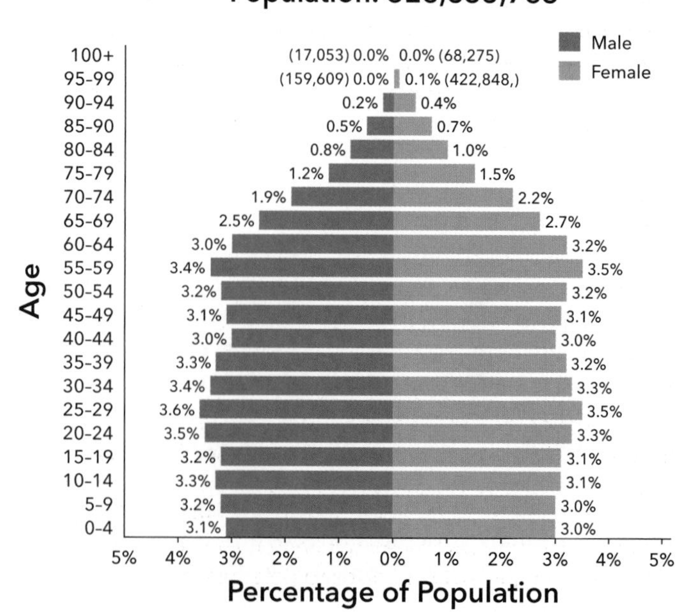

Thinking Critically

1. Why does China have a high GDP but a low per capita GDP?
2. What can Christians learn from third-culture kids about how to relate to various world cultures?

Living in God's World

1. Different demographic issues affect how missionaries will go about reaching the people of a certain country. Use the CIA Factbook or Operation World websites to find demographic data on a country. How might a more rural or wealthy demographic change a mission strategy? Write a brief paragraph explaining how the information may be helpful to a missionary.
2. Formulate a biblical position on the role of government with regard to either the environment or the economy.

CASE STUDY | Urban Sprawl: Phoenix, Arizona

Phoenix, Arizona, is built in a hostile desert environment with no river, coast, or port, yet it is one of the fastest growing regions in the country. Phoenix is the fifth-largest city in the United States and is part of an expanding metropolis with twenty-five separate cities. It can take two hours to drive from one end to the other. Since the 1970s it has grown 55 percent.

Many factors made Phoenix a desirable place to live: the invention of air conditioning, construction of dams providing cheap water, cheap open land, ideal weather, and a business-friendly government. Water there has ironically been some of the cheapest in the country because of government subsidies.

Sprawl has happened in Phoenix for many reasons. There seemed to be a limitless amount of flat desert land to build on. The ability to build convenient freeways made it practical to commute many miles. As more cars used the roads, the roads expanded to more lanes, bringing even more cars to fill them, and the cycle continued. It was much more cost-effective to build on the fringe than to revitalize the inner city.

There are two other factors to consider. As of 2019 the Colorado River basin system has been losing water volume from overuse. If Lake Mead, which supplies the Southwest with water, reaches a certain water level, it will no longer be able to come out past the dam since the lake is "v" shaped. Everything downstream from Lake Mead will dry up. The other factor is that of zoning, the ability of cities to determine what can be built on a piece of land. Residential, commercial, and industrial zones have been historically widely separated in Phoenix, which made having a car essential. A proposed solution for this is to create multi-use zones.

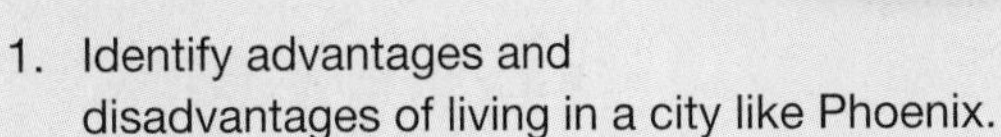

1. Identify advantages and disadvantages of living in a city like Phoenix.
2. How might each of these affect sprawl: demographics, economics, government, cultural values?
3. In what type of place would you like to live: a high-density city, lower-density suburb, or rural area? What cultural categories do those preferences demonstrate about you?
4. How might aging demographics (people working later in life) and the fact that children are living with their parents longer affect sprawl?
5. What could the government do to lessen sprawl without being heavy-handed?

unit 2

GEODATA | Activity

Cultural Geography *Student Activities*

You will have the opportunity in Chapter 6 to complete a geodata activity for the United States and Canada in the Student Activities.

Background image:
Niagara Falls viewed from the United States

NORTH AMERICA

chapter 05

THE UNITED STATES

94 Physical Geography
102 Human Geography
112 Interactions

BIG IDEAS

- What is the physical geography of the United States like?
- How do the people of the United States live?
- What are some of the challenges of living in the United States?

▲ Glacier National Park, Montana

NATIONAL PARKS, AMERICA'S GREAT CONSERVATION

As a result of the vision and inspiration of men like Teddy Roosevelt, the United States set aside millions of acres of American land and established national parks. This decision preserved vast regions that abound in magnificent scenery and wildlife habitats for future generations to enjoy and for people from around the world to visit and admire. America's first national park was established on March 1, 1872, during the administration of Ulysses S. Grant. It extends across parts of Wyoming, Montana, and Idaho. The most recent national park to date is Indiana Dunes National Park, which was designated a national park in February 2019.

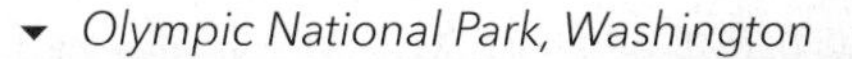

▼ Olympic National Park, Washington

▲ (top) Joshua Tree Landscape in the Yucca Brevifolia Mojave Desert, Joshua Tree National Park

▲ President Theodore Roosevelt with pioneer conservationist John Muir on Glacier Point in Yellowstone National Park in 1906

◀ Delicate Arch, Arches National Park, Utah

GUIDING QUESTIONS

- What are the regions of the United States?
- What caused the landforms in the United States?
- What bodies of water are found in the United States?
- What are the natural resources of the United States?

THE PACIFIC MOUNTAIN RANGES

Along the Pacific coast of the United States is a series of mountain ranges interspersed with low valleys. The mountains are part of a system called the Pacific Mountain Ranges.

THE GREAT BASIN

Between the Rocky Mountains and the mountains along the Pacific coast is a lowland area called the Great Basin, which includes most of Nevada and a large part of Utah. On the north is the Columbia Plateau. To the south is the Colorado Plateau.

THE ROCKY MOUNTAINS

The mountains that mark the western boundary of the Great Plains are the Rocky Mountains. The Rockies form the Western Continental Divide. Waters that flow down the eastern side of the mountains run into the Mississippi River and to the Gulf of Mexico, whereas waters that flow down the western side run into the Pacific Ocean.

In many ways, the United States of America is unique among the countries of the world. It is blessed with enormous amounts and varieties of natural resources and fertile croplands. Its population is a mixture of practically every people and culture on earth, each of which has made valuable contributions to the cultural landscape, yet the nation has developed its own distinct culture.

PHYSICAL GEOGRAPHY

Regions of the United States

What is the physical geography in the United States like?

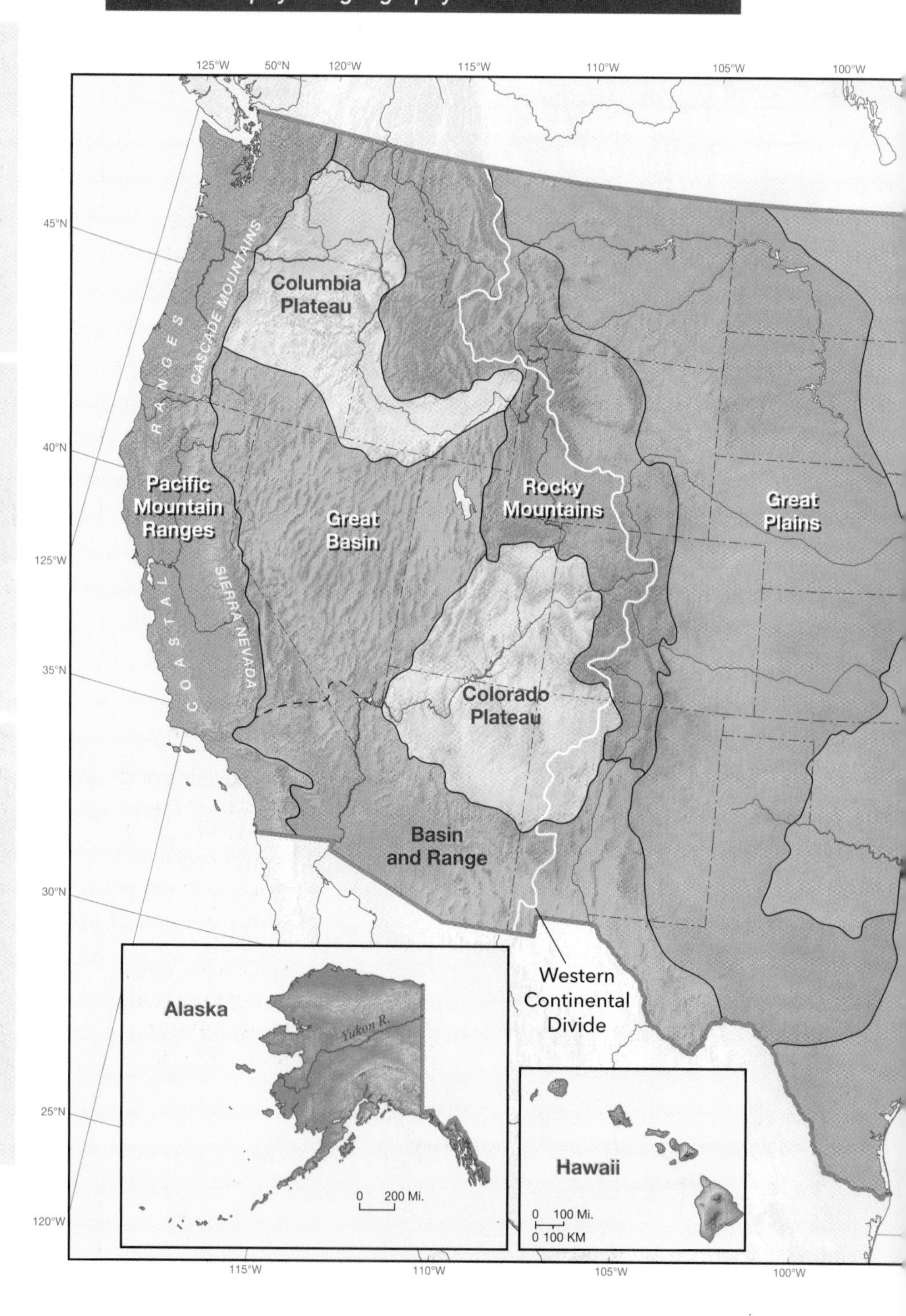

THE GREAT PLAINS

West of the Central Plains lies another plains region called the Great Plains, which begins about the ninety-eighth meridian and stretches to the base of the Rocky Mountains. The altitude rises gradually from about one thousand feet above sea level in the east to about five thousand feet against the mountains in the west.

THE CENTRAL PLAINS

West of the Appalachians, settlers discovered the fertile rolling hills, forests, and prairies of the Central Plains, which stretch about a thousand miles across the heart of the country. The Mississippi River, its tributaries, and the Great Lakes provide numerous water transportation routes.

THE APPALACHIAN MOUNTAINS AND PLATEAUS

Located west of the Piedmont, the Appalachian Mountains extend from eastern Canada southward into northern Alabama. These mountains form the Eastern **Continental Divide**. Waters flowing from the eastern side of the mountains empty into the Atlantic Ocean. Waters flowing from the western side empty into the Great Lakes or the Gulf of Mexico by way of the Mississippi River.

THE PIEDMONT

The Piedmont lies west of the Coastal Plains and forms the foothills of the Appalachian Mountains. This region extends from New York to Alabama.

THE COASTAL PLAINS

The sandy plains along the coast of the Atlantic Ocean and the Gulf of Mexico are called the Coastal Plains. In the south the Gulf Coastal Plain extends up through the Mississippi River Valley into the Midwest.

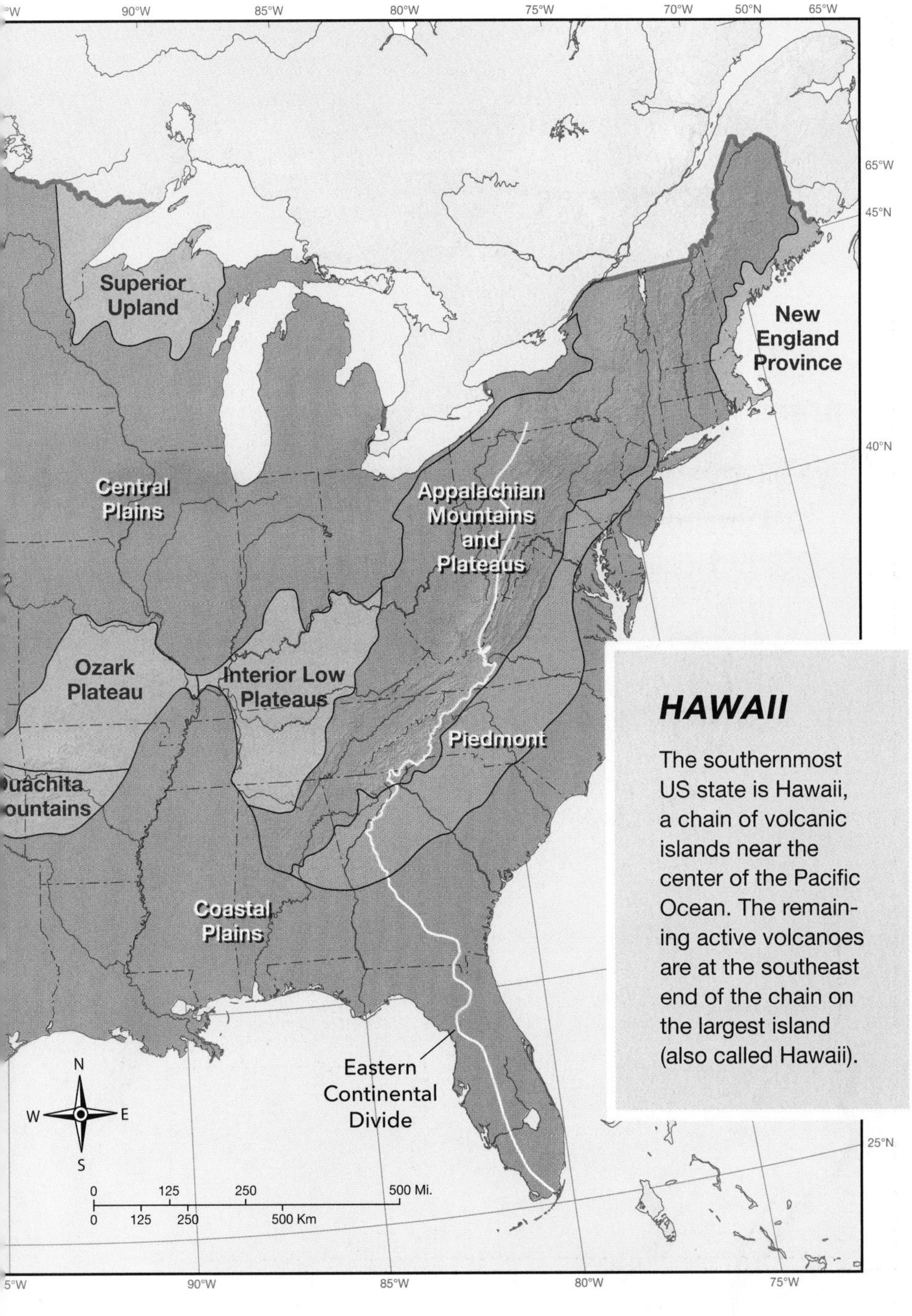

HAWAII

The southernmost US state is Hawaii, a chain of volcanic islands near the center of the Pacific Ocean. The remaining active volcanoes are at the southeast end of the chain on the largest island (also called Hawaii).

ALASKA

Alaska is separated from the "lower forty-eight" by Canada. Although Alaska is far to the north of the northwestern states, its geographic regions are a continuation of those we have mentioned in the lower forty-eight states. Coastal mountains rim the Gulf of Alaska, reaching their highest elevations in the Alaska Range. In northern Alaska, the Brooks Range is the northern end of the Rocky Mountain chain.

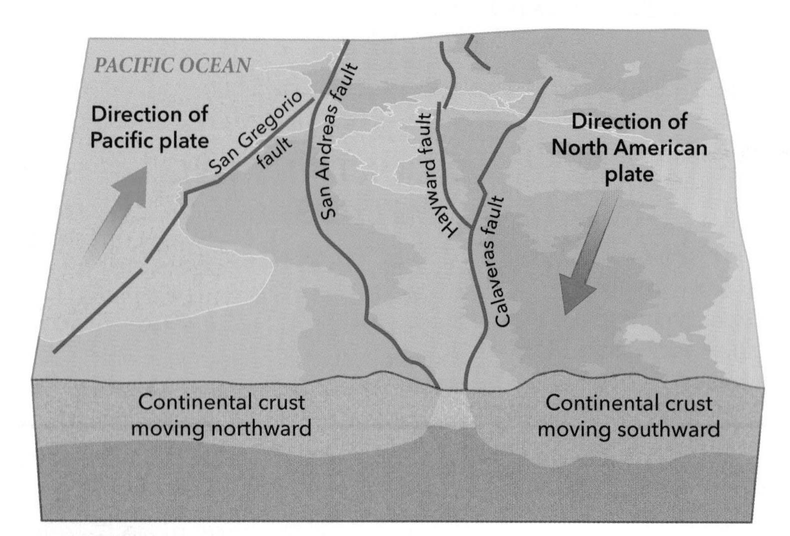

▲ *Plate tectonics in the United States*

Physical Landforms

The landforms of the United States are the result of several factors including plate tectonics, faults, folding, volcanic activity, weathering, and erosion.

Plate tectonics and faults formed the Pacific, Rocky, and Appalachian mountain ranges. Volcanic activity formed the plateaus and dry basins between the Pacific and Rocky Mountains. Biological, chemical, and mechanical weathering have occurred in many parts of the United States. Erosion from wind, water, and glaciation has also produced many of the current landforms.

▼ *Olympic Mountain Range in Washington State*

▼ *Rocky Mountains in Colorado*

◂ *(circle) Folded layers of sedimentary rock in Brookings, Oregon*

▼ *(bottom) Folded rocks of Sevehah Cliff in the John Muir Wilderness, in Sierra Nevada, California*

The joints in the rocks in the background are an example of either frost wedging or thermal expansion/contraction. The round stone in the front was most likely weathered by water forces, another example of mechanical weathering.

Artist's Palette on Artist's Drive in Death Valley, California

Mount Saint Helens

Worthington Glacier

Monzogranite rock formation displaying wind erosion in California

Eroded lone rock formation at the Children's Pool in La Jolla, California

Inner Grand Canyon catching day's first rays

Columbia R.
Great Salt Lake
SIERRA NEVADA
ROCKY MOUNTAINS
Platte R.
Colorado R.
GRAND CANYON
Arkansas R.
Red R.
PACIFIC OCEAN
Western Continental Divide
Yukon R.
Rio Grande
0 200 Mi.
0 200 Km
0 100 Mi.
0 100 Km

Bodies of Water

The United States is blessed with many lakes, rivers, tributaries, and **aquifers** that provide an abundance of water for many parts of the country. An aquifer is an underground layer of water-bearing rock or sediment from which groundwater can be extracted. Many of the lakes were formed as a result of glacial activity. The direction a river flows is determined by the continental divides. The longest river in the United States is the Missouri, flowing 2,340 miles from its **headwaters**, or source, in Montana to the Gulf of Mexico.

Climates of the United States

Prevailing wind patterns in North America are generally from west to east across the central section of the continent. The warm Japanese Current flows across the northwest coast, bringing plentiful rains to that region. A cool ocean current blows by the coast of California, giving that area a mild mediterranean climate with dry, sunny summers and mild, wet winters.

These westerly winds have an important influence on the climate patterns of the United States. As they flow over the Pacific coastal mountains, they lose much of their moisture. Therefore, on the eastern side of the mountains, the winds are cooler, milder, and drier, producing arid conditions for this rain shadow area, which includes the Great Basin and the desert Southwest. Although such areas are very hot during the daytime, they lose their heat quickly at night.

After the winds pass the Great Basin, they must climb over the Rocky Mountains, losing on the western slopes of the Rockies any moisture they might have picked up. On the eastern side, the rain shadow effect once again prevails. The area of the Great Plains immediately east of the Rockies typically receives only ten to twenty inches of precipitation a year.

The temperatures of the Great Plains are affected greatly by the warming and cooling of the great landmass of the heart of the North American continent. In temperate regions, this continental effect results in wide temperature extremes, hot in summer and cold in winter. For example, temperatures might average in the 80s and 90s in summer but dip to below 0° in winter. A place at the same latitude on the west coast might have temperatures that rarely exceed 80° or go below 30°.

In the eastern United States, two basic climates predominate. The northern half is influenced by not only the westerly flow of air across the plains but also the cold winds that sometimes dip down from Canada. The East has a generally cool, humid climate. The winters are cold, and the summers are hot. Precipitation totals range from twenty to more than forty inches a year. States around the Great Lakes also get "lake-effect snows" since the air picks up moisture as it crosses the Great Lakes. States of the Northeast are sometimes subjected to dramatic storms known as "nor'easters," which, as their name indicates, move in from the northeast over the North Atlantic.

The South is influenced by not only the westerly flow of air across the continent and occasionally the cold Canadian air but also the warm, moist breezes from the Gulf of Mexico. Average temperatures are much milder in the South than in the North. Temperatures along the Gulf coast rarely dip below freezing. When the warm, moist air

Between June and November, the southern Atlantic and Gulf coasts are susceptible to hurricanes and tropical storms that develop in the Atlantic Ocean off Africa and move across the Atlantic and through the Caribbean.

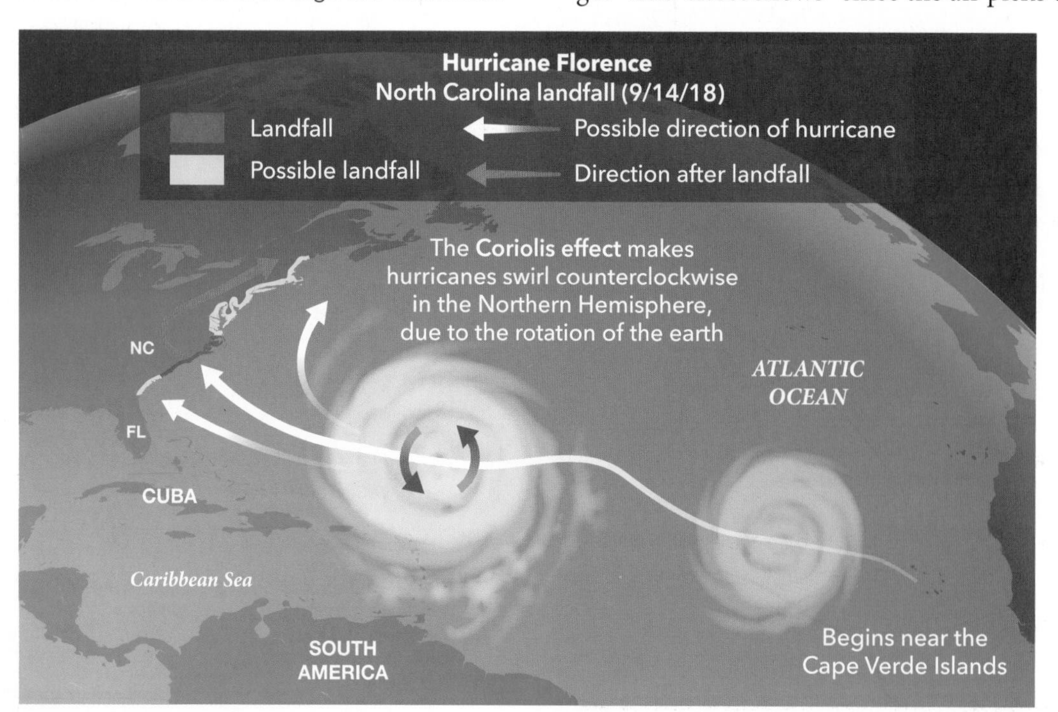

from the Gulf moves northeast and meets the cooler air moving southwest, violent thunderstorms and tornadoes occur in the summer and snowstorms in the winter, especially in the border states that divide the North from the South.

Resources of the United States

God has graciously blessed the United States with an abundance of natural resources. Whatever resources it lacks, it is able to obtain through trade with other countries. Of the resources that it does possess, the United States has more than enough for its own needs and trades the excess to other nations that need them.

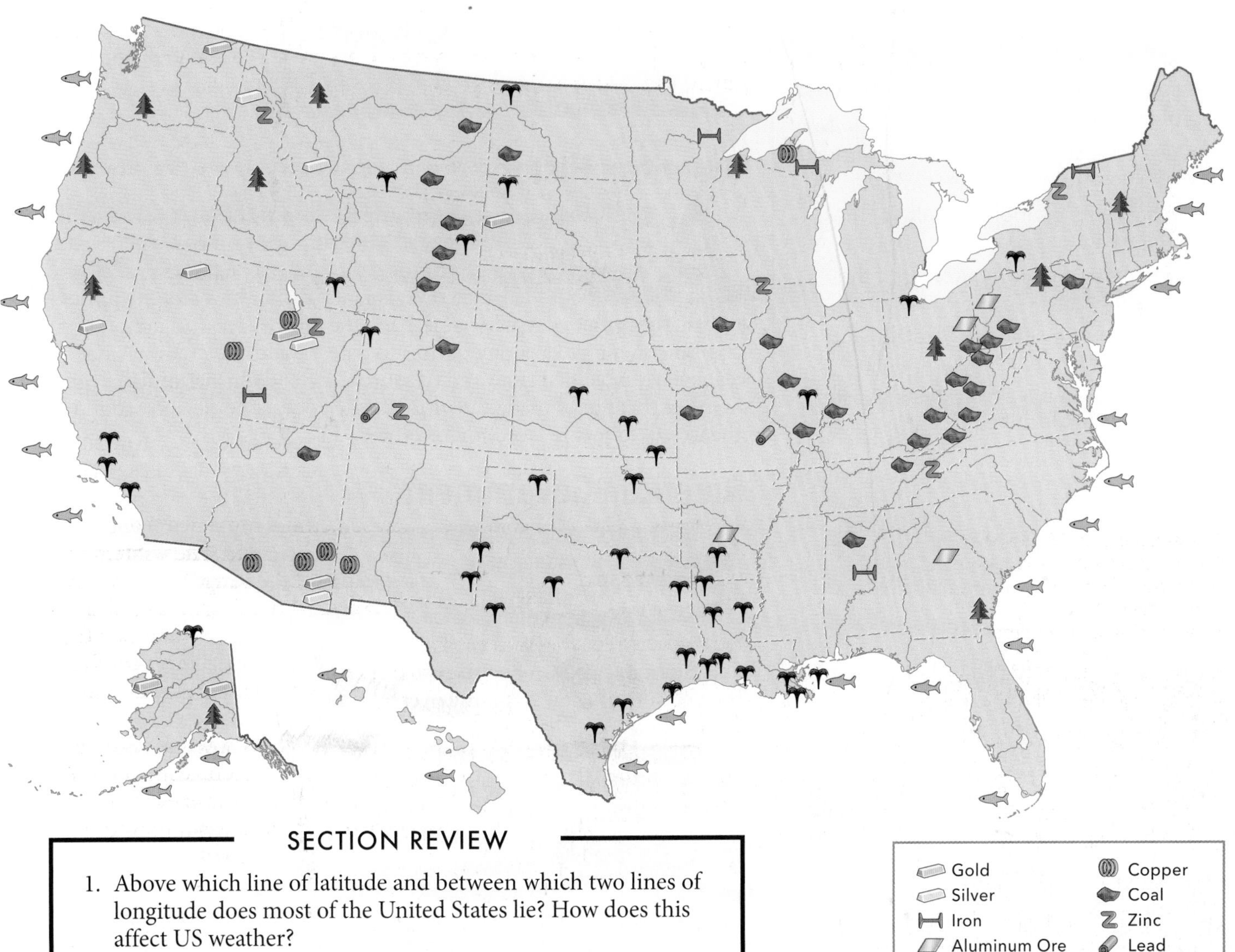

SECTION REVIEW

1. Above which line of latitude and between which two lines of longitude does most of the United States lie? How does this affect US weather?
2. Define *continental divide*. What earth-shaping processes caused the continental divides in the United States?
3. What causes weathering? What examples of weathering are prominent where you live?
4. Define *aquifer*. Which type of water source supplies water to your home?
5. What influences the basic climate where you live?
6. What natural resources are found where you live?

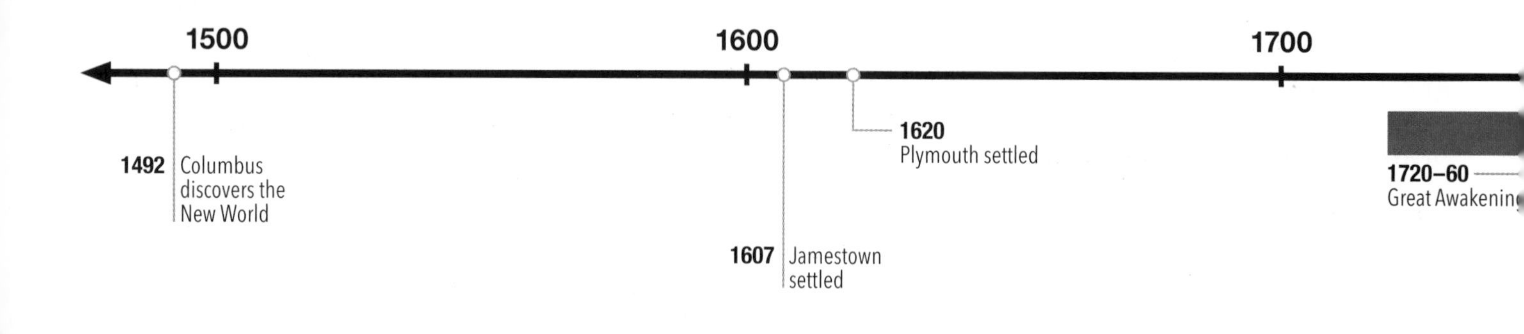

GUIDING QUESTIONS

- How has the United States changed over time?
- How does the US government interact with its citizens?
- What is the economic health of the United States?
- What are the demographics of the United States?
- What are the cultural characteristics and diversity in the United States?
- Is religion in the United States based on biblical teaching?

HUMAN GEOGRAPHY

How do the people of the United States live?

American History

America's history is one of migration, expansion, consolidation of people and territory, and diversification. The United States has often been referred to as the melting pot of several cultures. While history reveals many difficulties and inequities during this process, America has been the most successful nation to combine so many varying cultures to date. In addition, many Americans have expended time and treasure to defend our nation's liberty. Some of them have made the ultimate sacrifice, at home and around the world, to secure freedom for others.

American Government

The United States government functions as a federal republic, meaning that supreme power rests in the people and their elected representatives, and that power is shared between the national government and the governments of the fifty states. There are also various local governments within each state—counties, townships, boroughs, and cities. Each state government functions under a constitution, with the US Constitution being the overriding governing document, or "law of the land."

The Tenth Amendment of the Constitution delegates certain powers to the national government and reserves all other powers to the individual states. The Constitution also includes the principle of separation of powers, which divides the national government into three distinct branches: legislative (Congress), executive (the president), and judicial (Supreme Court and other lower courts). Each branch has its own powers, responsibilities, and limitations. State governments are organized similarly. The separation of powers principle is designed to prevent any elected official or branch of government from becoming too powerful.

The foundation of American freedom, as set forth in the Declaration of Independence, proclaimed and included the "unalienable rights" of "life, liberty, and the pursuit of happiness." These rights were further specified in the Constitution and subsequent amendments. One important right of Americans is that of participating in their government at all levels by voting, speaking or publishing their opinions, or even running for public office.

1800 — 1900 — 2000

- **1775–83** American Revolution
- **1861–65** Civil War
- **1869** First transcontinental railroad completed
- **1903** Wright brothers' first successful flight
- **1914–18** WW I
- **1929** Stock Market Crash
- **1939–45** WW II
- **1964** Civil Rights Act
- **1969** First man on the moon
- **2001** Major terror attacks on US

CASE STUDY | Mount Rushmore

This rock face was originally known to the Lakota Sioux as *Tunkasila Sakpe* (The Six Grandfathers). A wealthy American investor, Charles E. Rushmore, spent time in the Black Hills of South Dakota in the late 1800s and jokingly suggested that this mountain be named after him. This mountain became famous for the four sixty-foot-high heads that gaze from its side. They are the work of American-born sculptor Gutzon Borglum, who began the carving when he was sixty years old and spent the rest of his life creating his masterpiece. The mountain, which has been called a "shrine to democracy," features the likenesses of George Washington, Thomas Jefferson, Theodore Roosevelt, and Abraham Lincoln. The sculpted heads of the presidents on Mount Rushmore took nearly fifteen years to complete. The site was dedicated by President Calvin Coolidge in 1927, and the work continued into the administration of Franklin D. Roosevelt, being completed in 1941. The four presidents were chosen to represent the birth, growth, development, and preservation of the nation.

1. What does the original name of this mountain tell you about the history and culture of the United States?
2. What does this monument tell you about how Americans viewed their presidents?
3. Why do you think the sculptor, Gutzon Borglum, chose these four presidents?
4. Locate background information about Gutzon Borglum.

American Economy

The US economy is a system of free enterprise capitalism in which private individuals own most of the factors of production and make most of the economic decisions. Those individuals—or groups of individuals formed into corporations—can compete with other individuals or companies to earn money. Tension has always existed, however, between those who want unrestricted economic freedom and those who advocate government control or regulation of various aspects of economic activity. Christians might advocate a third approach that opposes unrestricted economic freedom, which might lead to abuse, and also opposes government control because God created a world with multiple institutions, including government and businesses. Most Christians would recognize the importance of some government regulation to ensure justice, but many would oppose government seizing control over businesses.

The United States moved dramatically toward government control during the Great Depression of the 1930s and during World War II, and, with few exceptions, that trend has continued. Nonetheless, the United States still has one of the freest economies of any nation in the world. Its phenomenal material success is a direct result of the degree of its freedom.

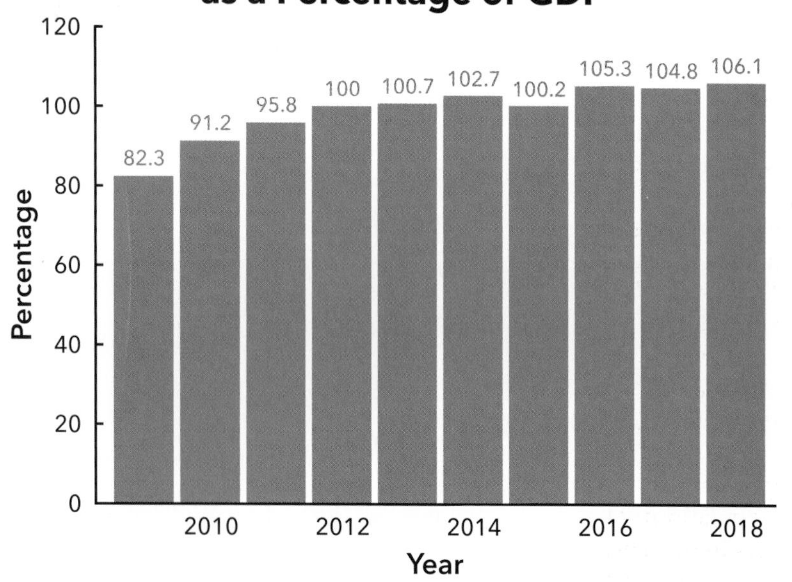

Lowest: 31.8% 1981

Highest: 118.9% 1946

In 2017 the GDP of the United States was estimated to be $19.5 trillion. Of that figure, 0.9 percent came from agriculture. That percentage is deceptive, however, because America's farmers literally feed the world. America's farmers are the most productive in the world. On average, an American farmer produces food and other related products for about 155 people.

Nineteen percent of the GDP is industry, and an amazing 80 percent is services. The per capita GDP in 2017 was $59,800. One cause of concern is the national debt, which is 78.8 percent of the GDP and growing. Six percent of government expenditures are payments of interest (not principal) on the national debt, while spending on national defense is around 15 percent. The combined expenses incurred by the ongoing war on terrorism and relief for victims of an unprecedented number of natural disasters in the last decade only worsen the problem, making it harder to pay down the national debt.

American Demographics

A major part of studying geography is understanding demographics. The goal of such study is to understand better who the people are and why they live as they do. It includes the population count, of course, but it also includes much more.

Migration patterns have changed over the course of our nation's history. One of the early developments that brought the vast regions between the Atlantic and Pacific Oceans together was the construction of the transcontinental railroad, which was completed in 1869. This encouraged westward expansion. The Industrial Revolution that spread from England to America resulted in a growing population in the Northwest and the Great Lakes regions, an area that became known as the **Manufacturing Belt**. Beginning in the 1960s manufacturing declined in this region as companies moved to the **Sunbelt** in the South and Southwest.

In 2018 the United States had an estimated population of 329.3 million. Of those, 82.3 percent lived in urban areas, places with a population of 50,000 or more. This number also includes those who lived in suburbs, areas between cities and rural settings.

▲ *Pedestrians in New York City*

The 2010 census showed that forty-nine states increased in population, although the greatest growth has been in the Sunbelt. The increased growth there might be the result of increased numbers of retirees who move from the cooler North to the warmer climates of southern states.

The census also noted that total US growth was 9.7 percent. The growth of individual states ranged from a low of -0.6 percent (Michigan) to an impressive 35.1 percent (Nevada). Five states had a growth rate above 20 percent; six states had a population increase ranging from 1.3 to 4.3 million. The most heavily populated areas continue to be the Northeast and the West Coast, although other metropolitan areas are also growing.

The growth of minority groups continued, especially among the Hispanic population. Many minority populations tend to cluster in certain regions—Hispanics and Native Americans in the West and Southwest, black Americans along the southeastern seaboard and in the Deep South, and Asian Americans in the West.

The non-Anglo population is growing in all fifty states. For example, the non-white population of Texas was 57 percent of all Texans, the largest group of which was Hispanics. The statistics are similar for California and New Mexico. A similar circumstance exists in Hawaii, where the largest minority group is Asian. Five states (Maryland, Mississippi, Georgia, New York, and Arizona) have about 40 percent minority populations. It is estimated that more than half of the nation's population will be minorities by 2050.

In 2018 the birthrate of the United States was approximately 12.4 (12.4 live births per 1,000 people in the general population). The average lifespan of an American is 80.1 years. Advances in preventive health care, better medicines, and improved technology are leading to the "graying" of the US population. More people are living longer, and the average age of Americans is increasing. The number of Americans who are 65 years of age and older is expected to double by 2050.

SECTION REVIEW

1. Describe the US form of government.
2. How would you describe America's economic health?
3. What percentage of Americans live outside urban areas?
4. How do demographers predict the population of the United States will change by 2050?
5. How has America changed over time?

American Culture and Diversity

American culture has been enriched over the years by people groups migrating to our country. Many immigrants from Asia, Eastern Europe, Africa, and Latin America initially lived in enclaves where others spoke their language and shared their customs. However, succeeding generations have moved into mainstream American culture. Some of these enclaves still exist, including Little Italy, Chinatown, Little Tokyo, and Little Havana, but they are now showplaces of the varied cultures represented. Many words that have become a part of our vocabulary came from other countries and cultures. For example, *zucchini*, *espresso*, *cappuccino*, *linguini*, and *pasta* are terms brought from Italy. *Bodegas* (corner stores in New York), *guacamole*, *jalapeño*, and *tortilla* came from the Spanish language.

▲ *Bodega in Brooklyn, New York*

Diversity

Just as diversity characterizes the geography of the United States, it also describes the American people. Very few Americans can trace their ancestry to Native American ethnicity; most are descended from immigrants who brought to their new home diverse languages, customs, and traditions. Through hard work and determination, the early settlers eventually built a strong, prosperous, and united country. They shared a respect for Christian values and a willingness to endure personal sacrifice. They were also unified by certain core values.

Core Values

Core values forge a common culture and bind a people together. For Americans from the colonial period to the present, those ideals have been freedom, equality, individualism, and growth. American Christians must evaluate these values from a biblical worldview. These values can be lived out in ways that reflect God's purposes for His people. But they can also be understood and lived out in ways that are contrary to God's Word and will.

Freedom

Abraham Lincoln declared in the Gettysburg Address that the United States was "conceived in Liberty." This statement echoes Patrick Henry's cry on the eve of the American Revolution, "Give me liberty or give me death!" Americans have always valued freedom, but they have not always agreed on what it means. For many Americans liberty is primarily about freedom from authorities or laws. Liberty is the freedom to do whatever one wants. This was not the view of the Pilgrim or Puritan forefathers, however. The Pilgrims and Puritans had a great deal to say about liberty, but the liberty they valued was the freedom to submit to Christ their King and His law.

Alongside the liberty to do right came the Enlightenment ideal of political liberty. The English philosopher John Locke, along with others, focused on a person's right to life, liberty, and property, rights that came from the "state of nature." Thomas Jefferson in the Declaration of Independence altered it to read "Life, Liberty, and the pursuit of Happiness." Their ideas, which were radical in an age of kings and nobles, centered on the right of the people to govern themselves. Political liberty has taken firm root in the United States. It is an essential part of the American political system.

Equality

Another core American ideal is that of equality. Equality is a powerful concept, and it can be applied in many different ways. For instance, one can declare all humans equal by virtue of their humanness. Or one can speak of equality of opportunity, equality of income, equality of outcomes, or equality of authority. Americans also expect equal application of justice under the law.

Americans differ about which kinds of equality are good or bad. Political liberals often work toward equality of outcomes. Political conservatives often object that in a free society, some citizens will achieve more than others and inequality will result. Efforts on the part of the government to ensure equality of outcome will result in a curtailment of some liberty.

Christians recognize that liberty is not an absolute good, so they must evaluate what is being gained and lost in particular situations. Nor is every kind of equality an absolute good. The equality of all people as humans is biblical because all humans are created in the image of God. But the Bible does not see inequalities of possessions or power as necessarily evil. Some inequalities will persist through eternity (Matt. 19:28; Luke 19:17–19), and attempts to remove all inequalities will inevitably result in injustice.

JOHN WINTHROP ON LIBERTY

"There is a liberty of corrupt nature, which is affected both by men and beasts, to do what they list [want]; and this liberty is inconsistent with authority, impatient of all restraint; by this liberty, sunuis omnes deteriores [we are all the worse for it]; . . . But there is a civil, a moral, a federal liberty, which is the proper end and object of authority; it is a liberty for that only which is just and good; for this liberty you are to stand with the hazard of your very lives."

From a 1645 speech that was published in Cotton Mather's *The Life of John Winthrop (1702)* Nehemias Americanus.

www.matherproject.org/node/33

▾ *Replica houses at the Plimoth Plantation in Plymouth, Massachusetts*

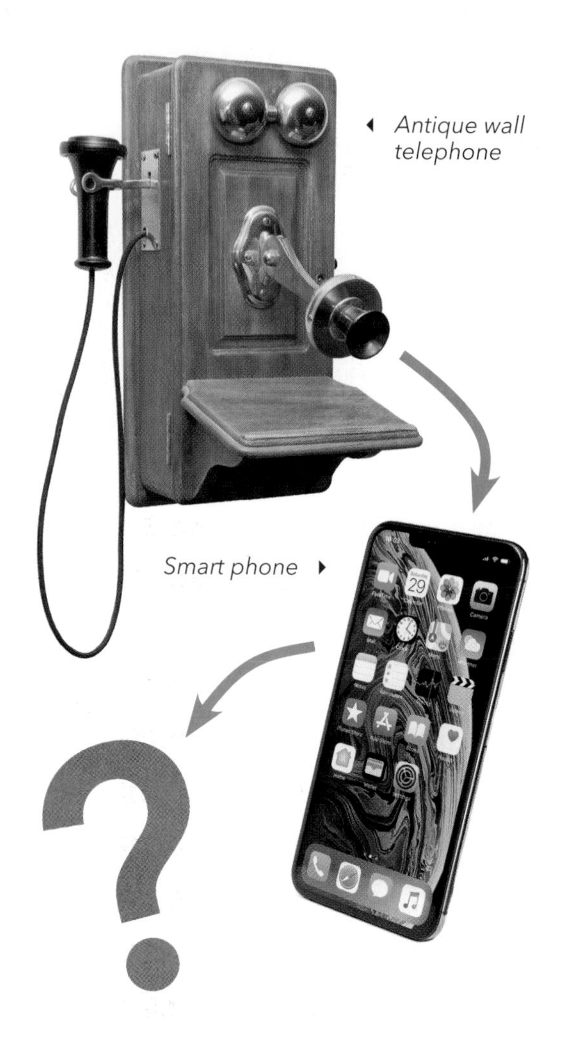

Antique wall telephone

Smart phone

Individualism

Americans celebrate the ideal of the self-reliant individual, often at the expense of the group or society. The independent American spirit contributed to a work ethic that encouraged capitalism and economic success for many. The roots of this spirit run deep in Western civilization, beginning with the ancient Greeks and Romans and reinforced in the Renaissance and the Enlightenment, when philosophers declared that individuals had natural rights.

Once again the Christian recognizes that individualism is not an unqualified good. On the one hand, the Bible stresses the individual and his or her need of salvation. On the other hand, the Bible teaches that all Christians are to gather into a community, the church. Weekly Christian worship is a communal event. The Bible teaches that we are to help those in need, the poor, and especially widows and orphans. Not every person can afford to take care of himself. A French observer of American society in the 1830s, Alexis de Tocqueville, observed in *Democracy in America* that the Christian religion in this country countered some of the selfishness that resulted from individualism.

Growth

Americans also value growth. From the beginning Americans pressed westward, expanding the borders of their territory. As the nation grew, so did the roads, canals, and railroads that connected its growing towns and cities. Factories sprang up beside rivers, and crops filled fertile valleys. American inventors developed new ways to communicate, travel, and work. In time the United States emerged as an industrial leader and then as a world power.

From a Christian perspective, much of this growth is good. But like the other American core values, growth is not an unadulterated good. When Andrew Jackson removed the Cherokee Indians from their lands or Polk seized land belonging to Mexico, growth ceased to be good because it was being valued for itself rather than as a means for glorifying God and loving others.

Old building and walking path along the Erie Canal in Chittenango, New York

Religion in America

Depending on where you live, your community might have many churches or other houses of worship. Religious structures near you might be used by evangelicals, one of the mainline Protestant groups such as Lutheran or Methodist, Roman Catholics, Mormons, Jehovah's Witnesses, Jews, Muslims, Sikhs, and others. Many of the first Europeans who arrived to America from Europe sought religious freedom and fled religion-based persecution. Religion has played an important role in several periods of American history.

A modern religious philosophy that seems to be unofficially embraced by many teenagers and young adults in America is known as moralistic therapeutic deism (**MTD**). Those who embrace MTD accept the existence of God as Creator and believe that He wants people to be good, wants them to be happy, is available if needed but is not involved in our daily life, and takes good people to heaven upon death.

However, America is also home to a growing number of people who reject any religious affiliation and consider themselves non-religious. Some prefer to call themselves secularists and may oppose any contact with religion or religious symbols. The United States remains one of the most diverse nations in the world, allowing virtually any religion and opposition to religion to enjoy equal protection.

While religion has influenced the history and values of the United States, American culture has also influenced the concept of religion. For example, most Americans who affiliate with one religious group tolerate or accept those from a different religious group. It would be considered un-American to verbally or physically oppose others simply because of their religious affiliation.

Major Religions of the USA

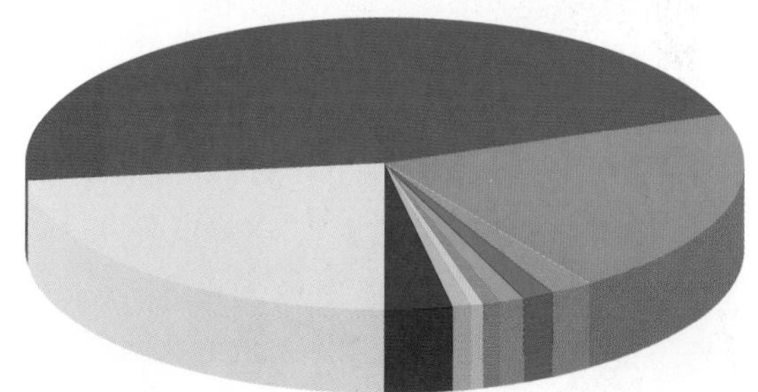

Religion	Percent
Protestant	**46.5%**
Roman Catholic	**20.8%**
Jewish	**1.9%**
Mormon	**1.6%**
Islamic	**0.9%**
Jehovah's Witness	**0.8%**
Buddhist	**0.7%**
Hindu	**0.7%**
Other	**3.3%**
Unaffiliated	**22.8%**

BELIEFS

Evangelicalism

Originally the term ***evangelical*** referred to Protestants as distinguished from Roman Catholics. Evangelicals believed in justification by faith alone, salvation through Christ alone, and the final authority of Scripture. Until the eighteenth century the words *protestant* and *evangelical* were synonymous. By the eighteenth century many Protestant churches had compromised the truth, and followers of rational religion in the United States rejected the Bible as God's Word and the deity of Jesus. At this point *evangelical* became a designation for orthodox Protestants. Due to a series of spiritual awakenings, the nineteenth century was the evangelical century for the United States. Churches grew as people came to Christ.

Evangelicals played key roles in higher education. They also worked together to form societies that promoted reading, Bible distribution, and many other issues. The twentieth century began with a struggle to prevent liberalism from gaining access to and eventually seizing control of many evangelical institutions. The evangelicals lost most of these battles and started new institutions. Evangelicals in the twentieth century sought to maintain their cultural influence. They remained a significant American subculture, but they no longer dominated major American institutions as they had earlier in American history. Because of evangelical political involvement in the late 20th and early 21st century, *evangelical* became a political label. Political pollsters identified certain voting demographics as evangelical even though some of the people so identified rarely attended church. There remains a debate among evangelicals about whether the movement should be defined primarily by adherence to key theological truths or by social characteristics.

Traditional Protestant church in Williamstown, Massachusetts ▸

Mormon Temple in Salt Lake City, Utah

BELIEFS

Mormonism

Mormonism is a made-in-America religion. Joseph Smith founded the Mormons in New York in 1830, a time in which the democratization of the United States led numbers of Americans to abandon orthodox churches and develop new variations. Smith claimed to have been visited by an angel named Moroni, who revealed that all churches of the time were false and showed Smith writings on golden plates, which he was to translate and share with others. The result was the Book of Mormon. The book tells about the lost tribes of Israel, who allegedly migrated to America about 600 BC during the Babylonian Captivity. Smith called the new church that arose from these teachings the Church of Jesus Christ of Latter-Day Saints (LDS). Those who followed Smith were persecuted and driven from New York, first to Ohio, then Missouri, and finally Illinois, where Smith was jailed and later killed by a mob. Brigham Young assumed leadership and led the group to what is now Utah.

Though Joseph Smith taught that all other churches were false, today Mormons seek to be accepted as a legitimate Christian denomination (though the claim that Mormonism restored a gospel lost by all other churches is still Mormon teaching). Many Americans accept this Mormon claim to be a Christian denomination. Mormons say they love Jesus, they raise model families, and they are often good citizens who contribute to their communities. Nevertheless, Mormonism differs from the fundamental doctrines of Christianity.

Mormonism has four sacred books: the King James Version of the Bible, the Book of Mormon, *Doctrine and Covenants*, and *Pearl of Great Price*. Unlike evangelical Christians, however, Mormons do not believe that all of their sacred books are without error. For instance, Mormons claim that the Bible has been corrupted, has errors in it, and is missing some passages. The Book of Mormon, however, is considered to be without error. It primarily tells the story of alleged Israelite groups that made their way to America. *Doctrine and Covenants* is the book that teaches Mormon doctrine. This book has been revised several times. In Mormon thought, the President and Prophet (a man elected by Mormon leaders) can receive new revelation that can alter older revelation. For instance, in 1890 a supposed revelation called for the end of polygamy, and in 1978 a new revelation allowed black men into the Mormon priesthood.

The Mormon understanding of salvation differs from orthodox Christian views. It consists of several levels. Mormons will say that everybody will be saved by grace alone, but this simply means that everyone will rise from the dead and live forever. It does not mean that the person will spend eternity with the Father god or escape eternal suffering. There are various levels of salvation with varying degrees of suffering as well as a couple levels where there is no suffering. To attain the highest level, a person most have been married in a Mormon temple and obeyed the Celestial laws faithfully. These people may become gods with their own spirit children, just as all humans are the spirit children of the Father god. In Mormon teaching Jesus was a spirit child of the Father god who became a god himself.

The Celestial commandments that good Mormons must keep include faith, repentance, baptism by immersion, confirmation by the Holy Ghost (given by the laying on of hands of LDS priests), and various temple ceremonies. Mormons believe that spirits in spirit-prison can receive Mormonism after death, but they cannot leave the spirit-prison until someone has been baptized for them. For this reason Mormons have compiled a huge database of genealogical information about millions of people.

Joseph Smith, founder of the Mormon Church

Another aspect of American culture's influence on religion is the democratic approach that many take. If a group of Baptists or Presbyterians, for example, disagrees about church polity or a particular religious issue, the dissenters can simply open a new house of worship. There tends to be less loyalty to a strict denominational approach and more acceptance of multiple interpretations in America than in many other parts of the world.

America's democratic approach to religion has also been combined with American consumerism in religion. For example, while many American Christians choose their church based on its faithfulness to worship God according to the Scriptures, many others shop for the church as another market commodity. For some it is a social organization that facilitates networking in the community; others look at church as an additional entertainment venue. Some want their church to be a political advocacy group or to provide social services to the community. And still others want to hear weekly motivational talks or for the church to provide emotional therapy. Many American churches have become skilled at marketing themselves to these religious consumers.

SECTION REVIEW

1. What are the four core values that traditionally bind Americans together?
2. How do many Americans define freedom or liberty? How does that view differ from the Puritan concept of liberty?
3. Does equality of opportunity guarantee that all Americans will have an equal amount of the nation's wealth or an equality of outcome? Why?
4. Why do Americans disagree about which kinds of equality are good or bad?

GLOBAL IMPACT | Terrorism

Though terrorism is not new or unique to the United States, Americans have been the target of terrorist attacks since the 1970s. American embassies and military bases abroad have been attacked on several occasions. However, the first World Trade Center bombing in 1993 brought the threat of terror home. Sadly, it took the second attack on multiple American targets on September 11, 2001, to result in a significant increase in military and financial resources designed to destroy terrorist organizations that threatened the United States. Despite many military successes, the threat continues due to the changing forms of terrorism and the decentralization terrorists have employed to survive.

1. In what other countries might you expect to be affected by terrorism?
2. What event in history prompted Americans to declare war on terrorism?
3. Why is terrorism difficult to eradicate?

▲ *Aerial view of the Pentagon following the 9/11 attack in 2001*

GUIDING QUESTIONS

- How do America's economy and its people interact with the environment?
- What are environmental issues in the United States?
- What are causes and effects of environmental issues in the United States?
- What are possible solutions to environmental issues in the United States?

FRACKING

Hydrologic fracturing, or fracking, has recently become a popular way of accessing natural gas that was previously too expensive to extract. The spread of hydrologic fracturing in states like Pennsylvania has created thousands of jobs and has resulted in lower natural gas prices. But people in some communities are concerned that fracking will pollute their water and endanger their communities. What if you served on a state or local committee tasked with deciding whether to allow fracking in your state? You will have an opportunity to examine this issue in Activity 3 in the *Student Activities*.

▲ *Fracking rig*

INTERACTIONS OF PEOPLE AND PLACES

What are some of the challenges of living in the United States?

Interaction with the Environment

About 150 million people in a myriad of jobs constitute the American workforce. In order to produce billions of dollars worth of goods and services each year, resources must be supplied, a vast transportation system must be in place, and markets at home and abroad need to be replenished. Industry fuels America's economy, but in doing so it affects the environment. Activities that affect the environment include mining, drilling, automobile and factory exhaust, and combustion of fuels to produce energy.

The list of environmental issues in the United States continues to grow as people become aware of the human impact on the environment. Many people are genuinely interested in addressing these issues. Others see economic or political advantage in proposing changes to address the human footprint on the environment. Christians should carefully examine the information and make decisions that demonstrate wise stewardship and love for one's neighbor. We will examine three broad environmental categories: water, air, and land.

Water

Every American wants to have clean water and enough of it to sustain life. However, some areas of the United States suffer from **drought** due to insufficient rainfall or populations that have grown larger than the water supply can sustain. More regions are facing potential water shortages than ever before. In addition, many communities depend on water drawn from aquifers because there is no large body of water nearby from which to draw clean water. Drawing too much water in these areas can result in **groundwater depletion**. Many industries also require large amounts of water for production, irrigation, or cooling in their manufacturing process. Human and industrial usage of water results in millions of gallons of water that must be treated before it can be recycled into the water supply.

▼ *Cracked earth resulting from drought*

Air

Just as important as clean water is the air that we breathe. Anyone with a sensitivity to contaminants in the air, ranging from strong perfume to smog, has probably experienced the terrifying sensation of not being able to breathe. Even though God has designed our atmosphere and plants that clean the air, humans need to be careful to minimize air pollution and find ways to sustain their livelihoods without producing contaminants.

Land

In regions where cities are growing, over-population and urban sprawl can occur. Land is stripped of trees and vegetation and covered with concrete and asphalt. In the past, many areas were virtually deforested to accommodate human expansion. This expanding human footprint has had serious environmental consequences.

America's economy requires vast amounts of natural resources, many of which are extracted from the earth by surface or underground mining. These efforts can disrupt local water tables or contaminate water sources through the runoff. Mining is necessary, but if it is left unmonitored or if problems are uncorrected, land can be scarred and left unusable for current and future generations.

One of the reasons for the high productivity of American farms is the use of pesticides to control infestation and limit crop damage from insects. However, these chemicals can also seep into groundwater, rivers, and lakes and contaminate drinking water.

Another use of land in the United States is the storage of waste. Americans are consumers of goods to a degree not seen in many parts of the world. When the many things that land in our trash containers are taken away by garbage trucks, they end up in landfills that can accumulate mountains of trash. In many cases, trash releases methane or other gases that vent into the air.

▲ *Open pit copper mine*

▼ *Trees damaged by acid rain*

Reasons for Environmental Issues

Coal-fired, and to a lesser extent gas-fired, energy plants that produce the ever-growing volume of electricity needed to sustain our economy send toxic gases into the atmosphere and contaminate the air. Two serious results are acid rain and smog. **Acid rain** develops when sulfur dioxide and nitrogen oxide combine with water vapor that then falls to the earth as rain. Acid rain damages buildings and plants, and pollutes water and soil. **Smog**, a haze or cloud, results when smoke and other pollutants in the atmosphere combine. Factory and automobile exhaust significantly contribute to the development of smog and can make breathing difficult. Cities where smog is a major threat often issue smog alerts and encourage people to wear masks or avoid going outside.

Americans also tend to use large amounts of water, compared with many other nations in the world. Estimates of daily use of water per household vary from around 150 to 400 gallons. Many parts of our nation have been blessed with ready access to enough water to care for daily needs and even many luxuries, including irrigated lawns, swimming pools, and regular car washes. In addition, American industry uses nearly 50 percent of the country's water supply. Consequently there is a great demand for clean water, and the demand on municipal systems that recycle our water is enormous.

Our nation has also been blessed with millions of acres of trees, many of which have been harvested to satisfy America's insatiable need for wood products. In the past, **clear-cutting**, or the total removal of all trees in a given area, has scarred the land when poorly executed and has decimated many **old-growth forests**. Old-growth forests are forests that are populated with mature trees which have not experienced significant disturbances. In some cases this has resulted in soil erosion and loss of wildlife habitat.

Another negative effect of human activity has been **eutrophication**. This refers to the increase of nutrients in a lake or stream, often the result of a runoff from farmland. Eutrophication causes an increase of algae and bacteria, reduces oxygen levels, and increases the cloudiness of the water. Without remediation, this process can make a body of water unable to sustain marine life.

Due to a variety of factors, species of plants and animals not native to the United States have been brought here. While some are harmless, others wreak havoc on a region's environment and are classified as **invasive species**.

Kudzu
Imported from Japan; rapid growth and very difficult to control

Tumbleweed
Imported in flaxseed from Russia; no serious threat

Privet
Imported from Europe; difficult to control

Zebra mussels
Imported by ships in ballast water; possible carriers of deadly avian botulism

Burmese pythons
Escaped from breeding facilities during hurricane, devastating wildlife in the Florida Everglades

Africanized bees
Known for violent attacks in large numbers that can be deadly for animals and humans

Proposed Solutions

Ideas about how to deal with pollution vary widely and range from extreme and economy-crushing to practical and affordable. Scientists are finding ways to lower automobile emissions and factory exhausts that pollute the air. Solutions as simple as planting trees and expanding green spaces can also have a positive impact on the air we breathe.

In addition to using cleaner-burning coal and natural gas and capturing CO_2 emissions, there is expanded use of renewable energy in the forms of hydroelectric, solar, and wind. These renewable resources hold the promise of additional sources of energy production.

Automobile companies are producing more fuel-efficient vehicles, vehicles that run on fuel cells using hydrogen and oxygen, and electric vehicles. Research into biofuels that can be produced using renewable resources such as certain grasses, algae, and waste continues to hold great promise.

While scientists are working on major solutions, every American can demonstrate wise stewardship. Reducing waste through recycling and purchasing new products made from recycled materials can significantly lessen the human impact on the environment.

Water might be one of the easiest resources to conserve. There are many devices that reduce water flow, including toilets, shower heads, and flow-restricted faucets. In areas where water is scarce, many people are replacing moisture-consuming lawns with stones or mulch. Given that most people in the world survive using much less water than Americans currently do, further consideration of how we are using this resource can result in better conservation. In addition to conserving water, keeping the water supply clean is an important factor in protecting this vital resource.

Emerald ash borer
Threatens to destroy ash trees, a $25 billion per year industry

SECTION REVIEW

1. What are three environmental issues in the United States?
2. What human activities result in environmental problems in the United States?
3. Explain how America's economy and people interact with the environment.
4. List any invasive species where you live.
5. What solutions to current environmental issues would you propose?

Row of wind turbines

05 CHAPTER REVIEW

SUMMARY

1. The physical geography of the United States is diverse, with many types of landforms, varying bodies of water, a moderate climate, and abundant natural resources.
2. The people of the United States are also diverse, with many nationalities and ethnic groups uniting in labor and worship to produce a distinctly American culture.
3. Challenges of living in the United States include wise use of human and natural resources that maintains a strong economy without damaging the environment.

Terms to Know

- ❑ Continental Divide
- ❑ aquifer
- ❑ headwaters
- ❑ Manufacturing Belt
- ❑ Sunbelt
- ❑ core values
- ❑ MTD
- ❑ evangelical
- ❑ drought
- ❑ groundwater depletion
- ❑ acid rain
- ❑ smog
- ❑ clear-cutting
- ❑ old-growth forest
- ❑ eutrophication
- ❑ invasive species

Making Connections

1. Draw a map and label the regions of the United States.
2. How has American culture influenced religion in the United States?
3. What limits should a Christian place on American core values?
4. Compare modern-day religious ideas in the United States with biblical teaching.
5. How can Christians demonstrate concern for the environment?

Developing Geography Skills

1. What river is found in your area? How has a continental divide affected its direction?
2. In what region of the United States do you live? Is your region's climate more affected by winds from Canada or the Gulf of Mexico?

Thinking Critically

1. What are some causes and effects for environmental issues in the United States?
2. Choose an issue currently being debated in American culture and identify how the core values of freedom, equality, individualism, or growth are being assumed in the arguments.

Living in God's World

1. Imagine you have developed a friendship with a Mormon in your neighborhood. He says that he is confused and even a little disappointed that you do not consider him a Christian since he also loves Jesus. Plan a conversation that you would like to have sometime with him.
2. Identify some of the reasons why biblical Christianity appears to be declining in many parts of the United States. Outline biblical ways that Christians should respond to this decline, drawing on Matthew 5:3–16.

CASE STUDY | Off-Shore Drilling

While numbers vary depending on the source, the supply of off-shore natural gas in the United States is measured in trillions of cubic feet. Off-shore crude oil supplies are measured in billions of barrels. Why would Americans not want to take advantage of these immense resources and approve off-shore drilling? A frequent reason given for opposition is the possibility of oil spills. Another objection is the threat to coastal tourism because the drilling platforms disrupt the scenic view. Supporters of off-shore drilling point out the extraordinary efforts that oil companies expend to extract these resources with minimal impact to the environment. Improving technologies are also making off-shore drilling less visible by replacing huge oil derricks with underwater systems that pump the resources to facilities on land for processing.

▲ *Oil and gas drilling rig*

1. Does the United States have abundant oil and gas resources along its coastal waters? In what numbers are these resources measured?
2. Why do many people object to off-shore drilling?
3. Why do other people support off-shore drilling?
4. If you lived in a coastal community that was debating this issue, which side would you support? Why?

chapter 06

CANADA

121 Physical Geography
126 Human Geography
134 Interactions

BIG IDEAS

- What is the physical geography of Canada like?
- How do the people of Canada live?
- What are some challenges of living in Canada?

Old Town, Quebec City, Quebec, at twilight in autumn ▸

▴ *Children playing ice hockey in picturesque Banff National Park, Alberta*

Immigrants celebrating Canada Day in Saint John, New Brunswick ▸

CANADA'S NATIONAL PASTIME

What can unify a vast country with huge open spaces, two official languages, and a plethora of ethnicities? The answer for Canada is hockey. To survive the long winters, Canadians invented the sport of hockey when they strapped on skates and went to play on the frozen ponds until the sun went down. Children in Canada learn to skate shortly after they learn to walk. With the changes in society and the introduction of less expensive sports, you might think hockey would begin to lose its luster, but that is not the case. Free hockey lessons and leagues are offered to new immigrants as a way to acculturate them into Canada. Hockey is even commemorated on the "loonie," the Canadian dollar coin.

◂ *A member of the Royal Canadian Mounted Police, "Mounties," at the Calgary Stampede rodeo*

GUIDING QUESTIONS

- What are the regions, landforms, and bodies of water of Canada?
- What is the climate of Canada?
- What are the natural resources of Canada?

Canada has the second-largest land area in the world, 3.86 million square miles. It boasts the longest coastline, 151 thousand miles, which includes the coastlines of its more than fifty-two thousand islands. Yet it has a relatively small population, 35.9 million as of 2018. This unusual combination offers Canada great benefits. Canadians are able to make a comfortable living, enjoy the blessings of both rural and urban environments, and export large quantities of raw materials. Canada continually ranks high on any list of favorable countries, whether that be most admired, safest, freest, or most respected countries in the world. Canadians say the best traits of their country are its nature and landscapes, its cultural diversity, and its values.

THE CANADIAN SHIELD

The largest region of Canada is a solid mass of hard rock that makes up nearly half of Canada's land surface. It includes the mainland, or Labrador, part of Newfoundland and Labrador. It also includes most of Quebec, Ontario, Nunavut, the northern parts of Manitoba and Saskatchewan, and the eastern part of the Northwest Territory.

THE WESTERN CORDILLERA

The chain of mountains that stretches from Alaska to the southern tip of South America is called the Western Cordillera. **Cordillera** means "a chain of mountains." The cordillera covers most of British Columbia, Yukon, and a sliver of Alberta.

THE ARCTIC AND INNUITIAN MOUNTAINS

This region consists almost entirely of Nunavut but also includes a small piece of the Northwest Territory. The Arctic is one of the earth's great archipelagos, or island groups. The islands in the south are mostly flat with some rolling hills; they are made up of sedimentary rock. Nine of these islands exceed ten thousand square miles in area. The Innuitian Mountains dominate the northern islands. These mountains are made up of igneous and metamorphic rock.

PHYSICAL GEOGRAPHY

Regions of Canada

What is the physical geography of Canada like?

Canada makes up 40 percent of the North American continent. The country is shaped like a giant basin, with the Hudson Bay as its lowest point and mountains on the eastern and western coasts. Canada has seven physical regions, ten political divisions called **provinces** (which are similar to US states), and three territories.

THE GREAT LAKES-SAINT LAWRENCE LOWLANDS

This region covers the finger of southern Ontario and a small part of Quebec. It extends from Quebec City to Detroit and contains Canada's major eastern cities. This small region extends farther south than the states of Maine, Vermont, and New York, and it is home to over 50 percent of Canadians.

THE INTERIOR PLAINS

Lying between the Canadian Shield and the Canadian Rockies, the Interior Plains are the breadbasket of Canada and include western Manitoba, southern Saskatchewan, most of Alberta, and half of the Northwest Territory. A few low hills bring variety to this flat plain.

The northern border of this region is the Arctic Ocean; the eastern border is the giant Lake Winnipeg. In the north, there are two other large lakes, Athabasca and the Great Slave Lake.

THE HUDSON BAY LOWLANDS

The main part of this region is the land south of the Hudson Bay, which is northern Ontario and the northeastern corner of Manitoba. The region also includes a couple of islands in the northern part of the bay which are part of Nunavut. The swampy lowlands and coastal plains along the Hudson Bay have little soil and are made up of sedimentary rock.

THE APPALACHIAN MOUNTAINS

This region includes the provinces of Nova Scotia, New Brunswick, and Prince Edward Island; Newfoundland Island; and eastern Quebec's Gaspe Peninsula. It is composed of low rocky mountains, hills, valleys, and coastal fjords. The mountains are an extension of the Appalachian range in the United States.

Physical Landforms

The Canadian Shield is the dominant feature of Canada. It is a broad region of surface igneous rocks that may be the result of large lava flooding due to massive tectonic activity. Glaciers that formed during the Ice Age also might have carved out the thousands of lakes and marshes in the shield. This mass of glaciers, called the Laurentide Ice Sheet, gave the area its rounded hills.

The northern plains differ from plains in the United States in that after the Flood there was probably a large inland sea left behind. The small shellfish fossilized in the sea and are now a resource in the form of oil sands.

(top) The Jakeman Glacier on Ellesmere Island in Nunavut, far above the Arctic Circle

(bottom) The Canadian Shield, Georgian Bay, Ontario

The Western Cordillera was shaped by the Cordilleran Ice Sheet, which merged with the Laurentide Ice Sheet at the continental divide. The coastal mountains were formed from uplift.

Bodies of Water

Canada is surrounded by three oceans: the Atlantic Ocean to the east, the Arctic to the north, and the Pacific to the west. Canada holds 20 percent of the world's fresh water. Much of it is locked away in the Arctic ice, but it is also held in the more than 250,000 lakes, including the Great Lakes.

On the Atlantic coast between Nova Scotia and New Brunswick is the Bay of Fundy, one of the seven wonders of Canada. It is noted for having the highest tides in the world. One hundred and ten billion tons of water flow in and out of the bay every six hours.

The thousands of lakes in the Canadian Shield support vast, extensive forests. In the cool forests live large numbers of animals, including moose, beaver, and black bear. Swarms of insects appear during the warm months. The Hudson Bay moderates the temperature of the region during the summer, but during the winter the bay freezes. Cold arctic air persists for most of the year. The many ponds and streams around the bay make the area a favorite home of many birds. It is also famous for being a home to polar bears. Churchill, Manitoba, claims the title of "Polar Bear Capital of the World."

In the west large rivers dominate. The Mackenzie River, the largest river in Canada, is also one the longest river systems in North America. It winds northward from the Great Slave Lake to the Arctic Ocean. The Fraser and Columbia Rivers are the major bodies of water in the Cordillera.

▲ *High tide (above) and low tide (below) in the Bay of Fundy are dramatically different.*

▼ *Polar bear mom and cubs in Churchill, Manitoba*

Climates of Canada

Canada is known for being cold, though the climate varies regionally. In the east the climate is cool year-round, but the Gulf Stream keeps the climate from becoming too harsh. Summer temperatures average 61°F, while the winter averages 32°F. The frigid Labrador Current carries Arctic water and icebergs past the coast.

A subpolar climate dominates the Canadian Shield. The summers are mild and short. The winters are long and harsh. Needleleaf evergreen trees, such as spruce, fir, and pine, are nearly the only trees that grow, and they become increasingly stunted as one travels north. These coniferous forests, called *taiga*, cover most of the Central Provinces. In the northernmost extremes is the **timberline**, the point beyond which trees cannot grow at all. The terrain gives way to tundra, which is land that is frozen year-round.

The timberline is the height beyond which trees do not grow, as this photo of Jasper Park, Alberta, depicts. The timberline is also the latitudinal limit for trees to grow, as in the Arctic regions.

▲ *The CN Tower and Toronto skyline at sunset*

The area around the Great Lakes, where more than 25 percent of Canadians live, has a humid continental climate that escapes the frigid extremes found farther north. Summer temperatures rise into the eighties, and farmland remains frost-free for about six months. Because Toronto is on the leeward side of the lakes, it is spared the lake-effect snow that Buffalo, New York, just 62 miles away, endures during the winter.

Above 66° latitude is a polar or tundra climate. Winter temperatures often fall to –30°F or lower. Summer temperatures rarely climb above 50°F, and they stay above freezing for only about two months. Permafrost keeps large plants from growing, but small lichens and other tiny plants and bushes grow in colorful profusion during summer's brief thaw. From November to February it is dark all day. From May to August there is around-the-clock sunlight.

In the interior plains the climate is affected by latitude and the continental effect, which occurs because land heats up and cools down more dramatically than water, causing harsh weather. Summer temperatures can climb to 100°F, whereas winter nights often drop below 0°F. As one travels farther north, it becomes considerably more chilly. Southern Alberta has a unique weather phenomenon called **Chinook winds**. These winter winds cause dramatic warming for a period of one to three days. They occur about thirty times a year and are the result of warmer dry air that is created as it comes over the western mountains. In Pincher Creek, Alberta, the temperature rose from -2°F to 72°F in one hour in 1962. Because the plains lie in the rain shadow of the Rocky Mountains, rainfall is scarce. Most areas receive only about fifteen inches of precipitation per year, mainly in the summer.

The warm Japan Current gives the coast of British Columbia a marine-west-coast climate. The coast enjoys the most pleasant climate in Canada. Although winters are wet, temperatures generally stay above freezing. In the summer they rarely climb above 80°F.

▲ *Crab fishermen unloading their catch at Pleasant Bay, Nova Scotia*

Resources of Canada

Fishing was historically the leading industry in the east. Not long after explorers discovered Canada, fishing boats from many parts of Western Europe were braving the icebergs, fogs, and storms to harvest fish. Cod became the most important commercial fish, but haddock, flounder, and herring were also abundant. The continental shelf off the southeast coast of Newfoundland extends far out into the Atlantic Ocean, providing a perfect fish "nursery." The comparatively shallow waters (averaging six hundred feet) receive plenty of sunlight, and the warm Gulf Stream mixes with the icy, oxygen-rich Labrador Current, encouraging explosive growth of plankton and other fish food. Unfortunately, this thriving industry has been greatly depleted because of **overfishing**. The fishing industry is still important, but the catch has changed from cod to lobster and crab.

Under Labrador's rugged mountains lie zinc and one of the largest iron ore deposits in Canada. In New Brunswick lead, copper, and zinc are mined. The forests also provide lumber. Farmers in the south grow potatoes. Prince Edward Island, a tiny island in the Gulf of St. Lawrence, is arable lowland that is sometimes called Canada's Million-Acre Farm. The fertile soil has a distinct red color from rusted oxides.

In the Great Lakes region, the rich soil and more moderate weather make for excellent farming. Dairy farms, orchards, vegetable gardens, and grain fields dot the countryside. This is also sugar maple country. The national symbol of Canada, the maple leaf, comes ablaze with color in the fall. The maple tree's sap is used to make maple syrup, a major export of Canada.

The valuable furs of beaver, mink, otter, and muskrat lured many hardy Frenchmen during the early seventeenth century. Fur is still a billion-dollar industry for Canada. Forestry products are also an important industry in the Canadian Shield. Under the shield lie important mineral resources miners can extract, including rich deposits of iron, copper, nickel, gold, lead, zinc, cobalt, diamonds, and uranium. Canada is one of the world's leading producers of uranium. Hydroelectricity is a valuable resource of the shield region. The largest dams are in Churchill Falls, Newfoundland and Labrador and James Bay, Quebec. The energy produced here benefits not only Canada but also areas of the United States. The Arctic is rich in oil, gas, lead, zinc, and silver. The difficulty is in extracting the minerals since the weather is so harsh.

With improved seed and irrigation equipment, the interior plains became a key supplier of wheat. Canada is one of the world's largest exporters of wheat. Tall grain elevators that rise from the flat landscape are a frequent sight. These "skyscrapers of the prairie" hold mounds of wheat and barley. Canada's barley and flax harvests are among the largest in the world. The grasslands also support a beef cattle industry, mainly in Alberta. East-central Alberta contains 1.7 billion barrels of oil. Canada is among the world leaders in the number of proven oil reserves. The oil here does not naturally come in liquid form but has to be processed from the bitumen soil to get the liquid.

Fish, trees, and minerals are the natural resources in the west. The fertile soil of the Fraser River valley supports many orchards, and salmon fill the rivers. Salmon and king crab are also fished heavily along the Pacific Coast. The tall, dense forests of Douglas fir, red cedar, and hemlock that cover the mountains make British Columbia a leading producer of lumber and other forest products. Zinc, copper, and gold are mined in the Western Cordillera.

▲ *The first step in making maple syrup is tapping the trees of their sap.*

◀ *Canadian maple syrup*

▼ *A king crab*

▼ *Wheat harvest, Three Hills, Alberta*

SECTION REVIEW

1. What earth-shaping processes formed the Canadian Shield?
2. What are some of the most significant bodies of water in Canada?
3. How does its latitude affect Canada's temperature? What helps to moderate the temperature in some regions?
4. Why did fish thrive off the Newfoundland coast? What happened to them?
5. What are Canada's important renewable and nonrenewable resources?

1500 | 1600 | 1700

1534 Jacques Cartier explores the St. Lawrence River for France

1583 Newfoundland becomes a colony of England

1627 Company of New France founded

1670 Hudson's Bay Company founded by Britain

GUIDING QUESTIONS

- How does the Canadian government interact with its citizens?
- What is the economy of Canada like?
- What are the demographics of Canada?
- What is the culture of Canada like?
- What is religion in Canada like?

HUMAN GEOGRAPHY

How do the people of Canada live?

Canadian Government

The national capital, Ottawa, is not in the Great Lakes Plain. It lies farther east, sharing the St. Lawrence River valley with Montreal and Quebec City. The Ottawa River, which flows by the city and drains into the St. Lawrence, marks the border between Ontario and Quebec. The country's motto is *Mari usque ad Mare* or "from sea to sea."

In 1837, colonists in Upper Canada (Quebec) and Lower Canada (Ontario) rebelled against Great Britain, demanding more democracy. After putting down the rebellions, Britain combined the two colonies into one and called it Canada. Because the British government wanted to avoid another prolonged and violent war for independence, it granted the new Province of Canada the right to govern its internal affairs. This union lasted until the British North America Act (1867) established a confederation of four provinces—Ontario, New Brunswick, Quebec, and Nova Scotia. Since then, six other provinces have joined the confederation. July 1 is celebrated as Canada Day. In 2017 Canada celebrated its 150th birthday.

The Dominion of Canada is modeled after the British **parliamentary system**. Canadians elect representatives to the House of Commons, a law-making body similar to the US House of Representatives. The leader of the majority party in the Commons becomes the prime minister. Like the president of the United States, the **prime minister** runs the executive branch of government. The Canadian Parliament also has a Senate chosen by the prime minister. The senators' job is to protect the interests of the various provinces and territories.

Federal Elections

The People

Elect

Members of the House of Commons
(Lower house of the Parliament)

Defacto elect

Prime Minister

Selects → All 105 Members of the Senate (Upper house of the Parliament)

Appoints → Supreme Court Justices who serve until the age of 75

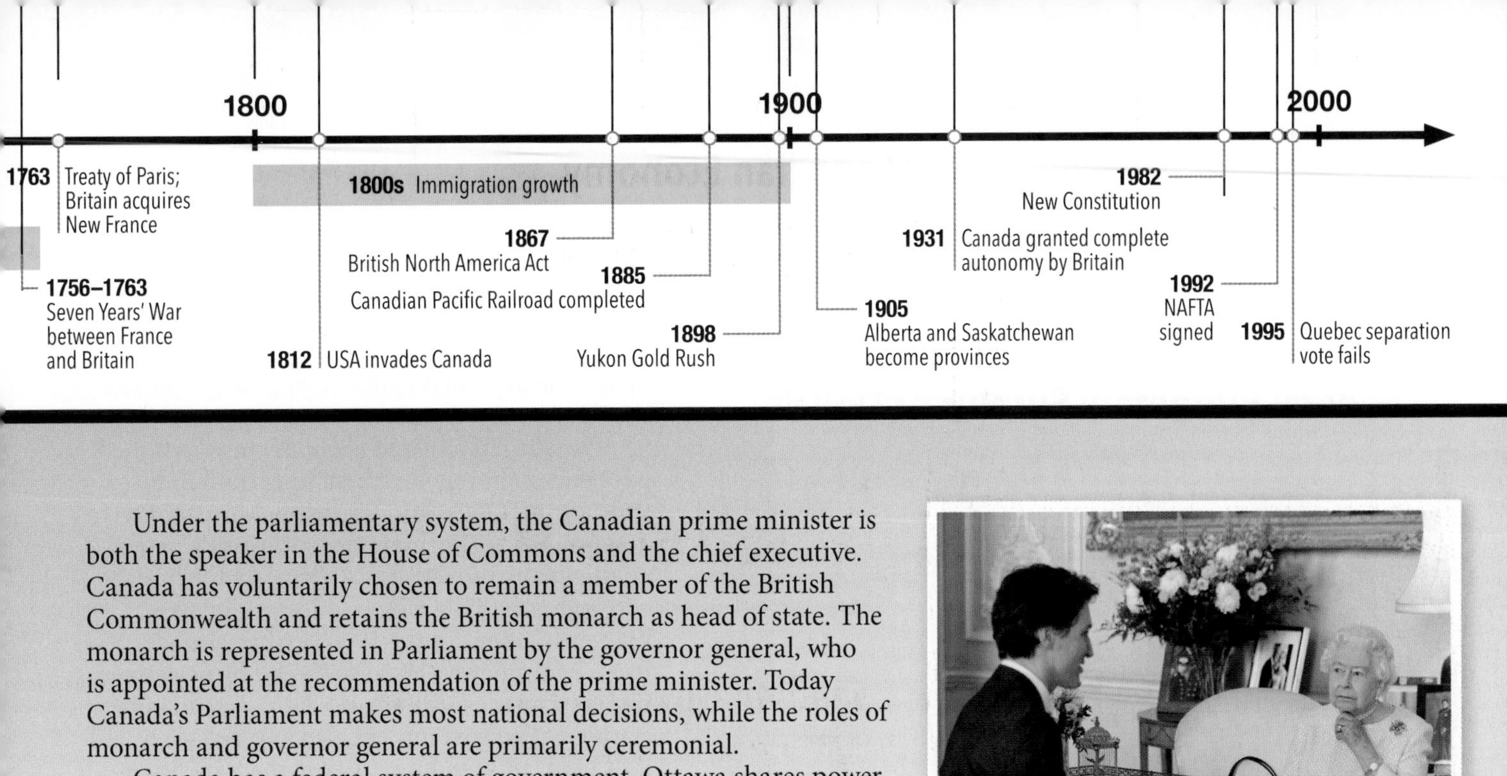

Under the parliamentary system, the Canadian prime minister is both the speaker in the House of Commons and the chief executive. Canada has voluntarily chosen to remain a member of the British Commonwealth and retains the British monarch as head of state. The monarch is represented in Parliament by the governor general, who is appointed at the recommendation of the prime minister. Today Canada's Parliament makes most national decisions, while the roles of monarch and governor general are primarily ceremonial.

Canada has a federal system of government. Ottawa shares power with the provinces, each of which has its own unicameral (one-house) legislature and a governor called the premier. Like the prime minister, the premier is chosen by the legislature.

Canada has never had a civil war, but the union historically has been fragile. Because some French Canadians want a constitutional right to veto any laws that might threaten their distinctive French culture, Quebec refused to ratify the 1982 Charter of Rights and Freedoms, Canada's equivalent of the Bill of Rights. The charter made both French and English official languages, but French Canadians did not get veto power. In 1995 Quebec almost passed a referendum to become a sovereign country. The vote failed, 49.4% to 50.6%.

▲ *Justin Trudeau, prime minister of Canada, meets with Queen Elizabeth II, Canada's head of state, at Buckingham Palace in London, England.*

▼ *Parliament Hill, Ottawa, Ontario*

Canadian Economy

Canada has one of the largest economies in the world. The country has transitioned from being totally dependent on agriculture and mineral exports to being more service-based. Sixty percent of the people work in the service sector (healthcare, education, tourism, etc.). Even so, exports have a great impact on the economy. When the price of oil goes down, the people feel the effect.

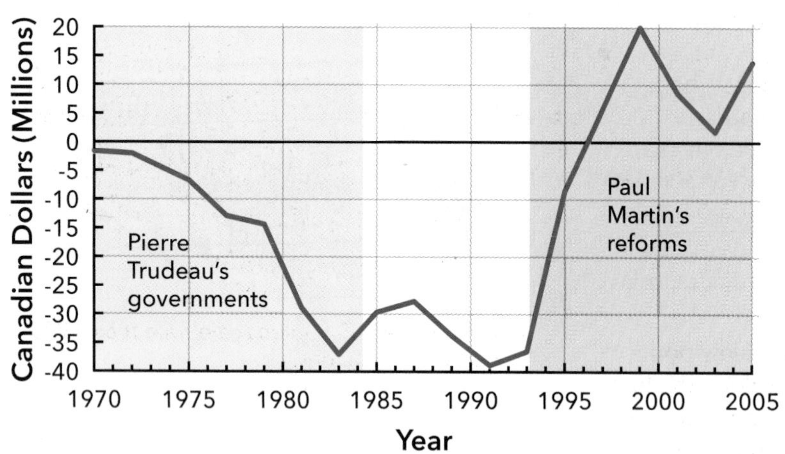

Canada has a mixed economy in which the government has involvement in certain industries. In the 1960s and 70s, Prime Minister Pierre Trudeau made Canada more socialist by nationalizing many industries, particularly the health-care industry. This move led to vast debt and higher inflation. In the 1980s Prime Minister Brian Mulroney reversed the trend by privatizing Air Canada (airline) and Petro-Canada (gas stations). The government also lowered taxes, but it did not cut spending. In 1995 the Wall Street Journal labeled Canada "an honorary member of the Third World" because of its high debt and devalued dollar. Canada then cut spending by 15 percent and privatized the railroads and the air traffic control agency. These measures put Canada in good fiscal health, with balanced budgets and low debt. As a result, Canada now has a higher economic freedom rating than the United States.

Consumers are taxed twice on purchases. There is a GST (goods and services tax), or national sales tax, and a PST (provincial sales tax). Because of these taxes, the high cost of shipping, and the fact that Canada cannot buy in volume, prices for goods are significantly higher in Canada.

Canada has a national health-care system. Doctors are not directly employed by the government but are reimbursed for their services. Health care is administered by the individual provinces and funded by people's taxes. Some provinces, like British Columbia, do charge a premium based on income. Because someone can show up at a clinic and not be charged for services, medical care has the illusion of being free. Canadians spend almost $5,000 a year per capita in taxes for health care. While the system works well for preventative care, long wait times are the defining characteristic of the service. Most Canadians give high marks to their doctors and accept the wait times. Dental care and prescription medicine continue to be private, so individuals must pay for those.

Canadian Demographics

Canada has been below the 2.1 fertility rate needed to maintain the population since 1971. And the birthrate has declined by more than a point over the last two decades. Even so, the population grew from almost 31 million in 2000 to over 35 million in 2018. How is the country growing? Immigration is the answer. Canada ranked eighteenth in the world in 2017, with a net migration rate of 5.7 migrants per 1,000 people. Since the mid-1940s Canada has been mostly urban. So even though Canada has vast open land and very low population density overall, most Canadians live in highly dense urban areas such as Toronto, Montreal, and Vancouver.

Culture and Diversity

One cultural distinctive for Canadians seems to be their desire to prove that they are not like their neighbors to the south. This distinction can be difficult since 90 percent of the population lives within one hundred miles of the US border, the longest undefended international border in the world. There has always been an intentional effort to protect Canadian culture. The government passed laws requiring a certain percentage of all media content over the airwaves to be of Canadian origin. Nevertheless, the US media still has a huge impact on Canadian culture. Even Canada's national pastime, hockey, has significant US influence since there are only seven Canadian teams in the NHL but twenty-four US teams. The United States is by far Canada's largest trading partner. Despite the considerable US influence, Canadians take pride in certain characteristics that they believe set them apart.

▲ *The Montreal Canadiens celebrate their 1993 Stanley Cup victory.*

Love of Nature

Canadians appreciate the outdoors. Since they have low population density and beautiful landscapes available to explore, the love for the outdoors comes naturally. The long winters do not dampen this enthusiasm. Outdoor winter activities include skiing, snowboarding, snowshoeing, and ice skating. During the short summers, hiking, mountain biking, rock climbing, camping, and canoeing are popular.

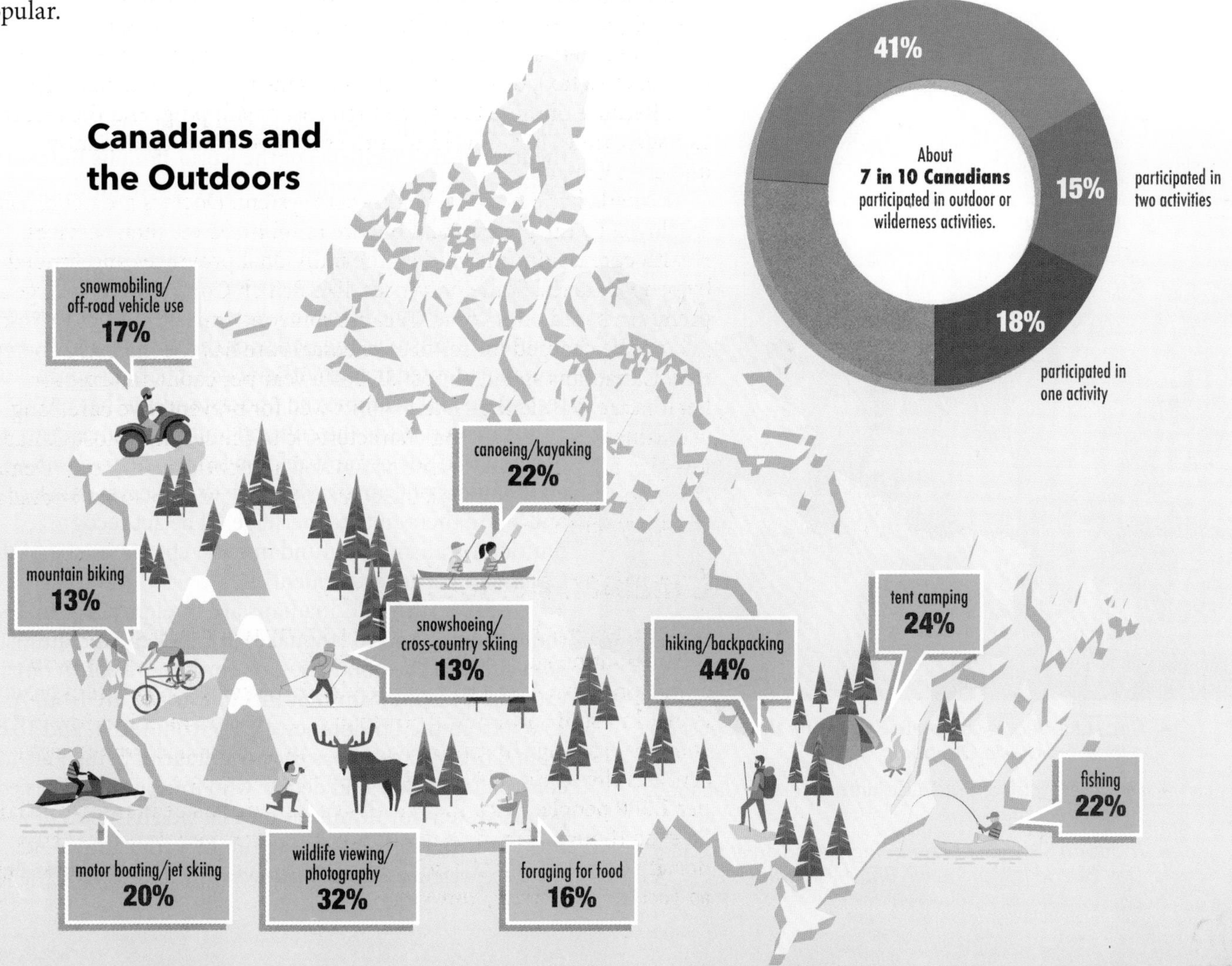

- (top) Québécois celebrate Saint John the Baptist Day, a local holiday in Quebec.
- (middle) Victoria, British Columbia, retains Canada's British heritage.
- (bottom) Sikhs celebrate being Canadian at a Canada Day Parade in Vancouver, British Columbia.

Multiculturalism

Canadians value the idea that they are **multicultural**. They use the term cultural "mosaic," which means the varied peoples who settled Canada have retained the distinct and colorful attributes of their diverse cultures. This is admirable when those attributes align with the Bible. This policy was imperative early on in holding a nation of two European peoples together.

French

When the English defeated the French on the Plains of Abraham in Quebec, they began to enforce British law and customs. But the need to keep the peace quickly overtook the principle of applying British law to the whole nation. In 1774 Britain passed the Quebec Act, which allowed that province to retain French civil law and its French identity. Eighty percent of the population of Quebec is French-speaking; they call themselves **Québécois**.

English

On the opposite side of the country, British Columbia's capital, Victoria, sits on the southern edge of Vancouver Island. Victoria is one of the few Canadian cities where British Canadians have been careful to keep British traditions intact. The streets and houses look much like those of British cities, and many of the people speak with a distinctly British accent. Evidence of British influence is widespread, from the double-decker buses to the formal arrangements of the world-famous Butchart Gardens. Flowered walks and ivy-covered buildings add to Victoria's charm.

Other Nations

In 1971 Prime Minister Pierre Trudeau put forward multiculturalism as the policy of the nation, and in 1988 Canada adopted it as an official act. The act sought "to recognize and promote the understanding that multiculturalism reflects the cultural and racial diversity of Canadian society and acknowledges the freedom of all members of Canadian society to preserve, enhance and share their cultural heritage." The act recognized multiculturalism as "a fundamental characteristic of the Canadian heritage and identity."

Today a fifth of Canadians are foreign-born. In Toronto more than 140 languages are spoken, and almost 50 percent of the population of Toronto was born outside Canada. Most new immigrants to Canada are from Asia: 15.6% from the Philippines, 12.1% from India, and 10.6% from China. Canada has the advantage of being able to control its borders and decide who immigrates. It has a points system for immigration that weighs a potential immigrant's English language ability, education, and work experience. Canada allows immigration for the purpose of family reunion. They also allow a large number of refugees to settle in the country every year.

First Nations

One significant group, however, was not allowed to retain its culture, the native or "**First Nations**" peoples. They make up 4.9% of the Canadian population and have a higher birthrate than other groups. Comparatively, the US has a 2% native population. Like the United States, Canada has a troubled historical relationship with its native peoples. Beginning in the 1880s, residential schools were formed to make the native people assimilate. Their purpose was to "kill the Indian in the child." Many native children were forcibly taken from their parents; this continued into the 1970s. The last school closed in 1996. These schools were mainly located in the western provinces and have an evil legacy of abuse and even death. Sadly, much of the abuse was done in the name of Jesus since the schools were run by so-called Christians. The teachers in these schools may have had good intentions, yet the core mission was unbiblical. Because of incomplete record keeping, it is hard to know many children died.

▲ *Cree students and their teacher at All Saints Indian Residential School, Lac La Ronge, Saskatchewan, March 1945*

GLOBAL IMPACT | The Olympics

The mission of the Olympics is to build a better world through sport. Cities have looked at hosting the Olympics as a way to present themselves to the world. Canada has hosted the Olympics three times. The 1976 Montreal Summer Olympics was an opportunity for the French and British Canadians to come together, which was symbolized by a French Canadian athlete and an English Canadian athlete lighting the torch at the same time. But the games were a massive financial failure for the city. Not until 2006 did Montreal finally pay off the bill; the legacy of those games was one of waste and corruption.

The 1988 Calgary Winter Games is considered by many to be the greatest Winter Olympics ever. It was filled with many impressive athletic performances and did not send the city deep into debt, yet when Calgary had an opportunity to pursue hosting the 2026 winter games, the people of the city soundly rejected the idea.

▼ *Millennium, the Athletes Village that was built for the Olympics, has been repurposed.*

Vancouver learned from the mistakes of other Olympic cities and repurposed its 2010 Winter Olympic facilities for continued use by its residents. They planned a permanent use of the buildings and parks before they were built. The city has brought in many more sporting events and conventions after the Olympics. Approximately 2,500 people have permanent jobs that would not have been available otherwise. Vancouver is the model for how the Olympics can benefit a city in the long term.

1. In what ways might an event like the Olympics provide a source of national pride?
2. Do you think the Olympics should change locations every year, considering the cost? Explain.
3. How did Vancouver show that it had learned lessons from previous Olympic cities?

▲ *Justin Trudeau's cabinet exhibits the Canadian value of diversity.*

The official number ranges from 6,000 to as high as 50,000. In June of 2008 Prime Minister Stephen Harper, a professing Christian, made a formal apology to the First Nations on behalf of the government and people of Canada for creating and running the residential schools.

Today missionaries minister to the First Nations with the truth that they do not have to become white to be saved. One of the former residential school properties is now a Bible camp so that something that was meant for evil has become something good.

Tolerance

Canadians are proud to say that they are the most tolerant people in the world. The generalizations that Canadians are open-minded, politically correct, polite, devoted to the common good, and apologetic flow from this value. Many point to John Humphrey as the modern originator of Canada's tolerance movement. He was a Canadian diplomat who submitted the Universal Declaration of Human Rights to the United Nations in 1948.

Canadians seek to exemplify this trait by having diversity in government. Prime Minister Justin Trudeau ensured that his cabinet included an equal number of women and men. There were also two First Nation members and three from the Sikh community. Canadians' love of tolerance makes for a pleasant society when it causes people to respect others and treat them kindly and politely. This is also what Christians should be known for, the Golden Rule (Matt. 7:12).

Canadian tolerance, however, has gone beyond acceptance of other ethnicities to the tolerance of behaviors, and the culture determines what behaviors are to be tolerated. Generally, behaviors are considered acceptable as long as they do not seem to harm others. Canada was among the first countries to legalize gay marriage. Other behaviors that were extreme in the past but are tolerated now include allowing children to change their gender even if the parents object, legalizing of marijuana, and some legalizing of prostitution.

The pressure to conform to this kind of thinking is only increasing, which, ironically, is not very tolerant. Christians may find themselves accused of committing hate crimes when they present a biblical perspective on behaviors such as homosexuality.

Major Religions of Canada

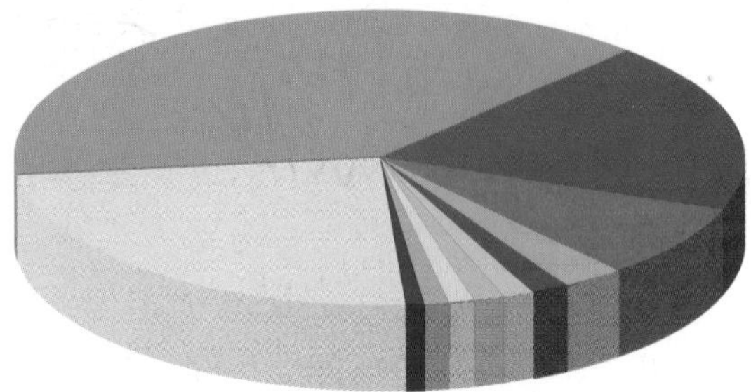

Religion	Percent
Roman Catholic	**39.0%**
Protestant	**18.6%**
Protestant Evangelical	**8.0%**
Islamic	**2.9%**
Orthodox	**1.6%**
Hindu	**1.5%**
Sikh	**1.4%**
Buddhist	**1.0%**
Jewish	**1.0%**
Other	**1.1%**
Unaffiliated	**23.9%**

Religion in Canada

In 1971, 90 percent of Canadians identified as Christian. In 2019, only 67 percent called themselves Christian, even when the term Christian was interpreted broadly. Christianity is not being pushed out by one particular religion but rather by the lack of religion. Although the numbers of minority religions such as Islam, Buddhism, and Hinduism have grown with the influx of immigrants, the largest numerical growth has been among the "nons," people who do not belong to any particular religion. Even in Canada's largest denomination, the United Church, some of the clergy are departing from a belief in God. The issue drew international attention when, after much debate within the denomination, an atheist minister was allowed to keep her position. Although that was an extreme case, a recent survey showed that

BELIEFS

Native Religions

There are 634 First Nation tribes in Canada with fifty distinct languages. Though each tribe's religion has unique characteristics, we can make some broad statements about these religions.

These native religions are **animist**, which means they believe that every natural thing has a soul. Animals, birds, mountains, and rivers are all spiritual beings. When a living thing dies, it continues on in the spirit world. A shaman has the ability to contact and control these spirits.

These religions are centered on the quest for power. The people seek the power to avoid negative things and the power to have good things. If someone is experiencing something bad, he must appease the offended spirit. If someone wants something favorable to happen, he must please the spirit that is believed to control that issue.

Another commonality of these religions is the belief in guardians who protect them. For one tribe it is the bear. Males, at the time of puberty, will go on a vision quest, a solitary journey into a remote area for fasting and praying. Their goal is to have an encounter with one of these spirits.

Some of the signature symbols of the native religions in North America are totem poles and sweat lodges. Like most human religions, these are works based and focused on the present material world.

A number of First Nations peoples have identified as Christian. In spite of the abuse they endured from so-called Christians, they still found Christ. There are challenges, however, as the youth seek to revive the old ways. In the James Bay Cree Nation, the tribal council had a sweat lodge demolished in 2010. "The Council hereby unanimously declares that the sweat lodge is to be dismantled and removed, and that all sweat lodge practices in the community immediately cease. Oujé-Bougoumou will continue to uphold its faith in and guidance by God."

◂ Totem poles are part of the native religion of Canada.

▾ A traditional Iroquois sweat lodge at the Grand River Reservation, Ohsweken, Ontario

only 34 percent of the clergy believe in the God of the Bible. Fifty-one percent of the United Church clergy were pantheists, meaning they believe that God inhabits everything. Others were atheist, agnostic, or believe God is a metaphor. Canadians tend to feel that religious conviction is a purely personal choice, which goes along with their value of tolerance. So whatever an individual believes is fine as long as he does not say that what he believes is the truth.

SECTION REVIEW

1. What two European countries competed for control of Canada?
2. In what ways is the Canadian government similar to the US government? In what way is it dissimilar?
3. How did Canada improve its economy?
4. How is the population growing in Canada?
5. What is multiculturalism, and how does it affect the way Canadians interact with one another?
6. Why can the god of pantheism not be the God of the Bible?

GUIDING QUESTIONS

- How do Canada's economy and demographics affect how its citizens interact with the environment?
- What are environmental issues in Canada, and what are their causes?
- What are possible solutions to Canada's environmental issues?

INTERACTIONS OF PEOPLE AND PLACES

What are some of the challenges of living in Canada?

Canada spent $12.6 billion on the environment in 2016. This represents a sizable commitment by the Canadian government and the people themselves. In general, Canadians see themselves as environmentalists.

One symbol of shared commitment to conservation in Canada and the United States is the Waterton-Glacier International Peace Park. This is the only cross-national park in the world. Three-quarters of it is Glacier Park in Montana, and the other part is the Waterton Lakes Park in Alberta. It is a World Heritage Site and is known as "the crown of the continent." There are also a large number of Canadian entrepreneurs seeking solutions to environmental problems for their country and the rest of the world.

▲ The Prince of Wales Hotel in Waterton Lakes National Park, Alberta

While its citizens tend to be better at protecting the natural environment, Canada, like the United States, is doing poorly at keeping its urban environment clean. The problem stems from a greater tolerance for the drug and alcohol culture that causes people to live on the streets. In cities like Vancouver and Toronto, it is becoming more common to see tent camps with their associated trash and human waste. In Vancouver thousands of discarded needles are collected in city parks every week.

Canada has many environmental issues, but there are five main ones dealing with the waters, mining, and hunting. The Arctic Ocean has been changing over the past years. NASA imagery has shown a decline in the older, thick ice sheet, which has led to the belief that the Arctic Ocean will soon be ice-free during the summer.

Interaction with the Environment

Water

In the Great Lakes, which are actually one connected water system, water moves from Lake Superior through all the lakes and into the Atlantic Ocean. Since Lake Erie and Lake Ontario are at the bottom of this system and many cities are built along their shores, they have become more polluted than the other lakes. In the 1960s Hamilton harbor in Toronto was covered with a thick layer of oil. The water actually caught fire at the point where the Cuyahoga River flows into Lake Erie. This was a wake-up call as to the extent of the pollution problem. Fish and bird populations declined, and many of them were born with deformities.

▲ Oil sands mining near Fort McMurray, Alberta

Land

In the west a big issue has been the oil sands. For many people, any exploitation of the bitumen soils in Alberta to obtain oil is unjustified. But even Prime Minister Justin Trudeau, one of the most outspoken world leaders on the subject of climate change, said, "No country would find 173 billion barrels of oil in the ground and just leave it there."

The mining of minerals is another large source of income for Canada, both domestically and internationally. The country is the leader in managing mining operations around the world. As far as managing the environmental effects of mining, Canada does not have a great track record. With the invention of large earthmoving machines, open-pit mining became more common.

Seal hunting in Canada has been a controversial issue primarily because the thought of a cute seal being killed is unthinkable to many. Other countries have banned the importation of seal products. Some activists have tried to differentiate between the commercial seal hunt and the seal hunts of the indigenous Inuits, but that is not easily done.

Reasons for Environmental Issues in Canada

Water

Whether the melting of the ice sheet is due to human impact (anthropogenic) or just a continuation of the natural warming since the last Ice Age is unclear. As of 2019 various studies have shown that the Antarctic ice sheet has actually been growing in the winter months. So the fear of rising sea levels has not been realized.

The effect of the melting in the Arctic has led to the opening of the Northwest Passage during the summer. The hope of finding such a passage originally brought explorers to Canada. Thus the trend of the waters having less ice during summer would actually benefit shippers and Canada in particular by shortening shipping times and the distance between Asia and Europe.

Who owns the Arctic Ocean? Canada claims it is part of their national waters, so if someone wants to traverse the ocean they must inform and pay Canada. The United States challenged this claim, saying the waters were international. In 1985 a US Coast Guard cutter went through without Canada's permission. After that incident the two countries came to an agreement that the United States would inform Canada before sailing through the Arctic. The Arctic could be a source of international conflict as Russia, China, the United States, and Canada all vie for control of the area.

The pollution problem in the Great Lakes originally stemmed from raw sewage, polychlorinated biphenyls (PCBs), and dioxins being dumped into the lakes. More recently the problem has been invasive algae blooms that feed on the nitrates coming from the runoff of fertilizer used on the fields of nearby farms.

The Canadian Coast Guard icebreaker Louis S. St-Laurent *makes its way through the ice in Baffin Bay, Canada.*

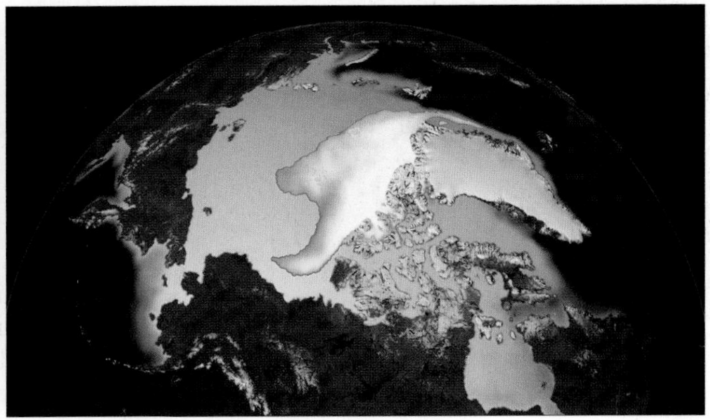

The satellite images show sea ice coverage in 1980 (left) and 2012 (right). Multi-year ice is shown in bright white, while average sea ice cover is shown in light blue to milky white.

Land

There are three issues with the processing of bitumen soil to obtain the oil. Tailing ponds are created to hold the byproduct waste. A large amount of water is used and is contaminated by the cleaning agents used to process the soil. There are scars on the land left after the dirt is dug up.

When miners remove minerals, the runoff of mine waste tailings affects drinking water and destroys fish populations. The pits leave permanent scars on the earth. Gold and uranium mining companies were less responsible in the past. They mined all the minerals, closed the mines, and then left, leaving the cleanup for someone else. A gold mine in the Northwest Territories left tons of arsenic waste, which is a dangerous poison. When the company went bankrupt, the government had to find a way to deal with the waste. The solution was to freeze the rock that the waste was contained in.

One issue with seal hunting is that although commercial hunters are merely interested in obtaining the pelts, the Inuit hunters use every part of the seal. The Inuits have depended on the sale of pelts for their livelihood. When the sale is banned, it affects them more dramatically than non-native groups. Over the years the hunters have gone to great lengths to kill the seals humanely, but now they are required to attend classes on how to do this before hunting. Another issue is that some seals killed in the open sea are wasted because they are unretrievable.

▲ *Inuit hunters pulling a dead seal behind their snowmobile*

Proposed Solutions

Fortunately, when sea ice melts it is less dense and does not raise the sea level. But from a political standpoint, Canada will need to plan how to protect its territory. Canada and the United States must work together to limit Russia's and China's actions in the ocean for two reasons, one environmental and the other strategic. Russia and China are not as concerned about harming the environment and sea life as Canada and the United States are. And Russia and China have shown a propensity to militarize disputed areas. To hold their claim to the area as internal waters, Canada must build more infrastructure in case of emergencies in order to rescue ships that need help. This is a common practice of nations making territorial claims.

In 1972 the United States and Canada signed the Great Lakes Water Quality Agreement, which started a unified effort between the two nations to clean the Great Lakes. Initially the effort was focused on stopping the continued pollution. That goal has been accomplished to a large extent. No longer are raw sewage, PCBs, and dioxins flowing into the lakes. It is now possible to swim in Hamilton Harbor—something that was previously inconceivable. The national agencies are now focused on cleaning the Great Lakes. They realized that the PCBs and dioxins take many years to leave naturally. They identified 48 areas of concern and began to physically clean up those areas. The cost has been estimated at $3.5 billion. Entrepreneurs have also invented new ways of fertilizing fields so that the fertilizer does not run into the lakes and cause algae to grow.

Canadians have discovered many ways to make mining the oil sands more environmentally friendly. In 2014 a scientist from the University of Saskatchewan wondered why some plants were able to grow in the tailing ponds created by mining companies. She discovered a fungus which allowed plants to grow in the ponds, and not only do the plants survive, but with the fungus they have the potential of cleaning the ponds. The oil companies say they will fill the mine pits with clay and sand left over after the extraction process. A new process called In-Situ does not require pits or tailing ponds to be created at all. In this process steam is pumped into the ground to extract the oil from the bitumen.

Because mining companies were not taking responsibility for the cleanup, there has been a change in policy. Now before the mine is dug, a plan is made for what happens after it is closed. For example, after diamonds are mined the pits are filled with water. Once the water quality is found to be good, dikes are broken so that the pits are included in the surrounding wetland system, becoming a habitat for fish.

Canadian officials say the number of seals has rebounded so that today they are almost at the same number as when the European explorers first arrived. With international opposition it is likely that the seal hunt will soon end due to a lack of markets for the products. As the indigenous groups lose their traditional way of making a living, however, instances of suicides and substance abuse tend to increase.

SECTION REVIEW

1. How does Canada show its commitment to taking care of the environment?
2. How has tolerance given rise to urban pollution? What solution would you suggest?
3. List three environmental issues in Canada.
4. What is the cause of environmental problems in the Great Lakes? What are some of the means of environmental success in the lakes?
5. How does the change in mining practice demonstrate the biblical value of stewardship?
6. Why might the seal hunt demonstrate a conflict in the modern value system?

▾ *The Ekati Diamond Mine, Northwest Territories*

06

CHAPTER REVIEW

SUMMARY

1. Canada has seven regions that were shaped through plate tectonics and two huge glacial sheets. Canada has 20 percent of the world's fresh water and is bordered by three oceans. Canada has a cold climate, but the east and west coasts are moderated by maritime air currents. Canada has rich natural resources in its oil reserves and agricultural abundance.
2. Canadians are noted for a love of the outdoors, multiculturalism, and tolerance. Population growth has been through immigration. The growth of the nonreligious is the largest religious shift. The government is a parliamentary democracy. Canada's mixed economy has recently returned to fiscal health.
3. Canadians are environmentally conscious. They look to take advantage of new summer shipping lanes through the Arctic. There has been success in cleaning up the Great Lakes. They have sought to find a balance in obtaining natural resources like bitumen oil and minerals while still protecting the environment.

Terms to Know

- ❑ cordillera
- ❑ province
- ❑ timberline
- ❑ Chinook winds
- ❑ overfishing
- ❑ parliamentary system
- ❑ prime minister
- ❑ multicultural
- ❑ Québécois
- ❑ First Nations
- ❑ animist

Making Connections

1. What geographic features are shared by Canada and the United States?
2. How does Canada's latitude affect its climate and where people live?
3. What are the four people groups of Canada?
4. What is unique about the clergy in Canada's largest protestant denomination?
5. Who is the head of state in Canada?
6. What kind of government does Canada have?
7. What are two inventions that help to limit the environmental impact of mining oil sands?

Developing Geography Skills

1. Why is southern Ontario such an important region of Canada?
2. Why are Canada's northern territories valuable despite their cold climates?

Thinking Critically

1. Why would Canadians seem to look past the troubled people with addictions living on the city streets but be very concerned over the death of seals?
2. What has been the result of a demilitarized border between Canada and the United States?

Living in God's World

1. Write a letter to a missionary in Canada. Ask why he became a missionary to Canada, what parts of the culture he learned to adopt, and what aspects of Canadian culture needed to be challenged by the gospel.
2. Canada has a Christian heritage but an increasingly secular population. Write a paragraph that explores ways to overcome the evangelistic challenges.

CASE STUDY | Canada's Enforcement of Tolerance

Like other Western countries that have become more secular, Canada has decided that tolerance is necessary for people with different ethnicities, beliefs, and behaviors to live together in peace. In one sense this is a biblical value because God calls His people to live peaceably with all people (Rom. 12:18). On the other hand, tolerance has become a slippery word. Used in the context of secularism, the word *tolerance* actually means accepting beliefs and behaviors that violate biblical standards. Living peaceably with people of diverse backgrounds and beliefs is a good thing. But when governments, in the name of tolerance, force their citizens to accept ideas and behaviors that violate deeply held religious beliefs, then tolerance ceases to be tolerance.

The clearest example in Canada's recent history is the government's position on human sexuality. According to Canada's secularists, gender identity, gender expression, and sexual preference are pliable. People are free from creational principles to redefine these things as they see fit. Canada passed a law in 2016 (Bill C-16) requiring citizens to address people by their self-designated gender rather than their birth gender. Bill C-16 is unique in that it compels, under threat of penalty, government sanctioned speech. The law effectively criminalizes those who sincerely believe that God determines a person's biological gender at birth, whether male or female.

Jordon Peterson, a Canadian psychologist and university professor, has gained international attention for his public stance against coerced speech. Although he is not a Christian, he freely borrows from various religious traditions in an effort to push back against the moral confusion in the West, a confusion that he believes is the result of prioritizing individual "rights" over personal responsibility. His main argument is that Western societies must recover their lost emphasis on personal responsibility.

▲ *Prime Minister Justin Trudeau marches in the Vancouver Pride Parade on July 31, 2016, along with his family.*

1. What does Genesis 1:27 say about gender identity?
2. What type of government might put rules on what words you may say?
3. From verses like 1 Timothy 2:4 and 2 Peter 3:9, what can be said about how God feels about people with gender issues?
4. How does Jordan Peterson inadvertently make the point that "all truth is God's truth"?

unit 3

GEODATA | Activity

Cultural Geography *Student Activities*

You will have the opportunity to complete a geodata activity for Latin America in the Student Activities.

Background image:
Arco de Santa Catalina in Antigua, Guatemala, with restored colonial architecture

LATIN AMERICA

chapter 07

MEXICO AND CENTRAL AMERICA

144 | Physical Geography
150 | Human Geography
158 | Interactions

BIG IDEAS

- What is the physical geography of Mexico and Central America like?
- How do the people of Mexico and Central America live?
- What are some of the challenges of living in Mexico and Central America?

- ▲ *View of St. Lucia's Twin Pitons in the West Indies*
- ◀ *Mayan woman making corn tortillas by hand*
- ▼ *The Palacio de Bellas Artes (Palace of Fine Arts) in Mexico City*

- ▲ *(top) Suspension bridge in the jungle in Central America*
- ▲ *(bottom) Colorful houses in Guanajuato, Mexico*

MEXICO CITY, MAGNIFICENT AND CHALLENGING

Although Mexico City has beautiful lakes and parks, it has been called the worst-located city in the world. As one of the world's most populated cities, its teeming mass of humanity is packed, at 7,200 feet above sea level, into the broad Valley of Mexico, where the Sierra Madre Oriental and the Sierra Madre Occidental meet. The surrounding mountains trap air pollution in the valley and create a daily health hazard.

GUIDING QUESTIONS

- What are the regions of Mexico and Central America?
- What caused the landforms of Mexico and Central America?
- What bodies of water are important to Mexico and Central America?
- What are the climates of Mexico and Central America?
- What natural resources are found in Mexico and Central America?

Latin America lies south of North America. The people of this region speak one of the languages descended from ancient Latin—Spanish, Portuguese, Italian, or French, also known as the Romance languages.

Latin America has two main subregions: Central America and South America. Mexico and Central America consist of the nations and islands that lie between the United States and South America. The region forms a **land bridge** between North and South America. Several empires vied for control of this area, which has become a vibrant blend of native Indians, Europeans, Africans, and Asians. Local superstition has blended with Roman Catholicism, and local words have blended with Latin languages. Even different ethnicities have mixed, creating a diverse culture.

MEXICO

The two Sierra Madres join to form one range near the twentieth parallel and continue into neighboring Guatemala. These mountains were formed by upward pressures along the edges of tectonic plates.

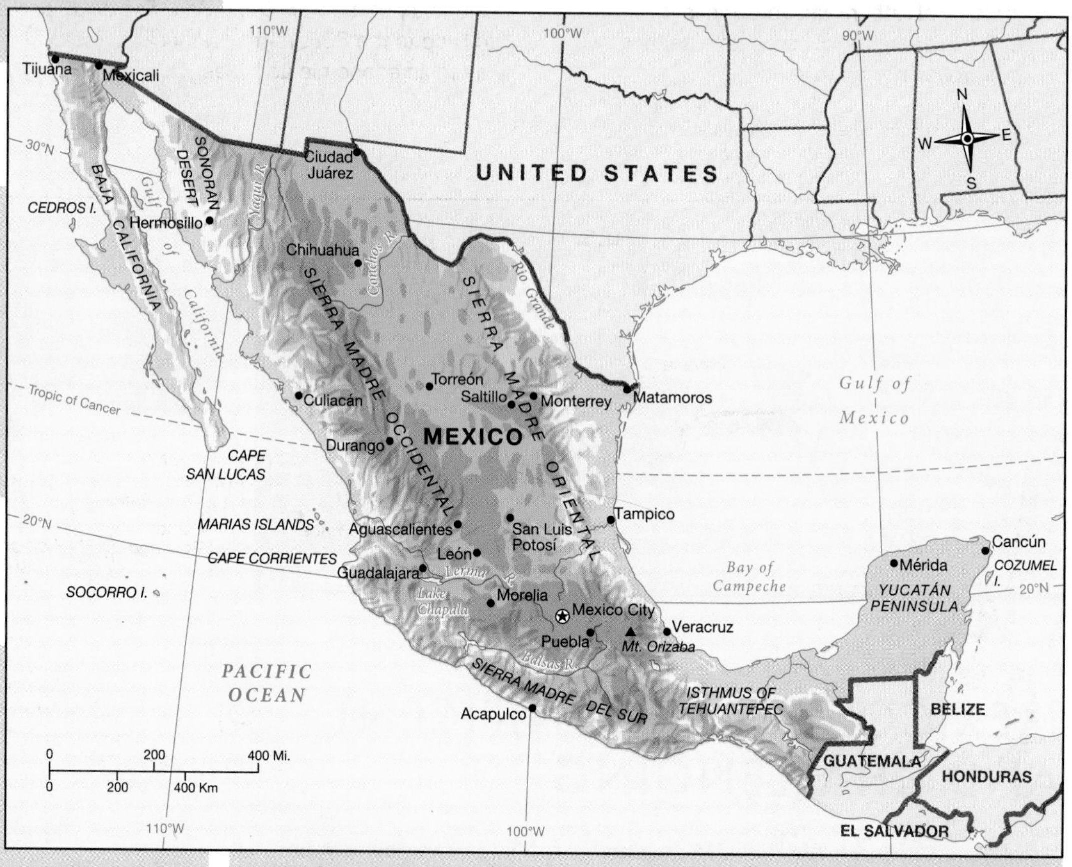

PHYSICAL GEOGRAPHY

Regions of Mexico and Central America

What is the physical geography of Mexico and Central America like?

Northern Mexico

Northern Mexico's geography is much like that of the American Southwest—hot, dry, and generally flat desert.

Mesa Central

The vast Mexican Plateau, bordered by the two Sierra Madres, dominates the landscape of Mexico. Most of Mexico is too dry for farming. But during the rainy season in the late spring and summer, easterly trade winds from the Caribbean Sea blow over the southern end of the Mexican Plateau, bringing adequate water for crops.

The Southern Tropics

Savannah covers the coastal areas, although it gives way to mangrove swamps in some parts. In the interior, colorful parrots, chattering monkeys, tapirs, and other exotic animals roam the lush **rainforests.** Rainforests are dense jungles filled with biodiversity. They are usually located in tropical regions that consistently have heavy rainfall.

CENTRAL AMERICA

An **isthmus**, or narrow land bridge, connects Mexico with South America. Seven small countries lie in this region, known as Central America. Although they stretch southward over one thousand miles, all seven countries would fit into the state of Texas, with enough space left for Georgia.

Central America is similar to southern Mexico. The mountains of the Western Cordillera continue south along the Pacific shore.

THE WEST INDIES

The Bahamas

The Bahamas, a cluster of coral islands north of the Greater Antilles, differ from the other mountainous islands of the West Indies. Because they are formed from coral rather than volcanic lava, all of the islands are low and have neither mountains nor good soils.

The Greater Antilles

The Antilles islands are the crests of an underwater mountain chain, or **archipelago**. The western range consists of the four largest islands—Cuba, Hispaniola, Puerto Rico, and Jamaica.

The Lesser Antilles

The Lesser Antilles are a chain of smaller islands that form the eastern boundary of the Caribbean Sea. The chain curves southward from Puerto Rico to the South American coast. Tourism, fishing, and farming are the main economic activities.

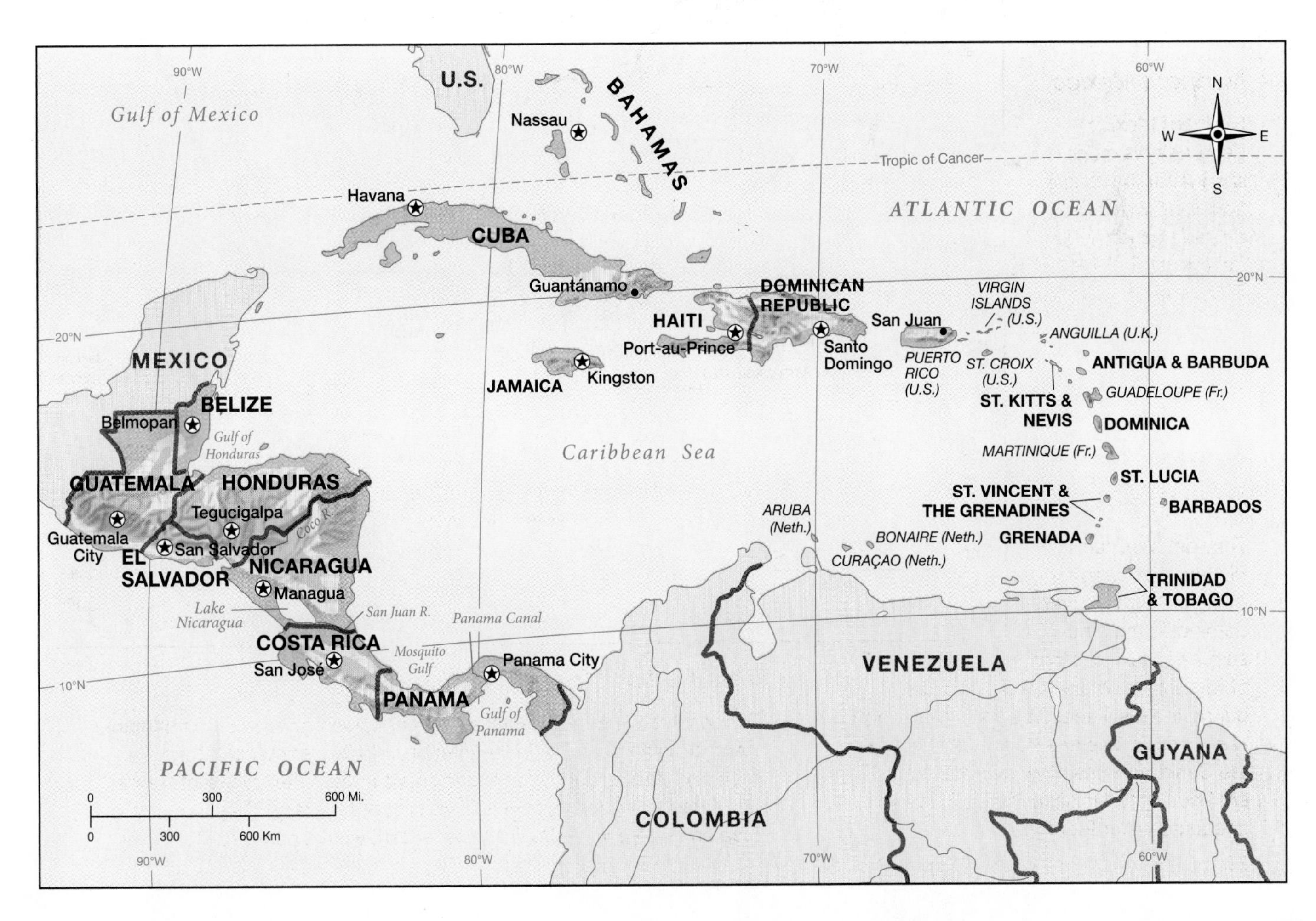

Physical Landforms

The Ring of Fire is a path of volcanic activity in the Pacific Ocean. This ring extends about 25,000 miles and includes the boundaries of seven significant tectonic plates. About 75 percent of the world's volcanoes are located along this path.

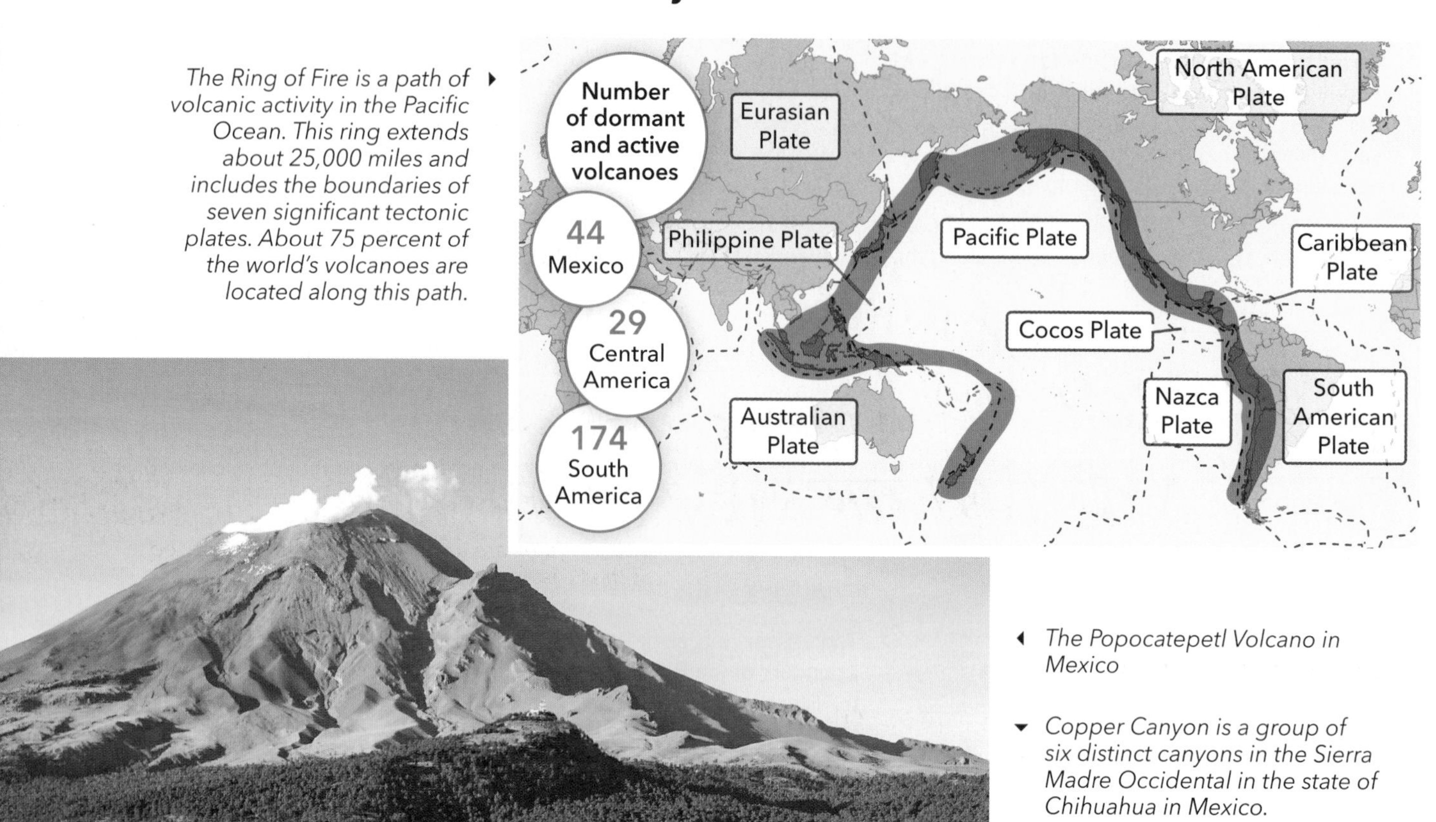

The Popocatepetl Volcano in Mexico

Copper Canyon is a group of six distinct canyons in the Sierra Madre Occidental in the state of Chihuahua in Mexico.

▲ Waterfall in the Costa Rican rainforest

▲ The mogotes are unusual limestone hills located in the West Indies.

Bodies of Water

Given the low level of precipitation in parts of this region, rivers and lakes provide a significant source of water in Mexico and Central America.

GLOBAL IMPACT | The Panama Canal

Construction of a canal through Central America saved ships several thousand miles when transporting goods between the Atlantic and Pacific Oceans. French engineers had attempted to build a canal across Panama in 1882 but gave up after seven years and twenty thousand deaths from diseases, such as yellow fever, bubonic plague, and malaria. Before Americans began construction, they drained the mosquito-infested swamps. Construction began in earnest in 1907, with the building of the Gatún Dam that created a 163-square-mile lake. Next came six pairs of locks. Finally, though plagued by landslides, American workers dug the Gaillard Cut, a channel across the Continental Divide. The S.S. *Ancon* made the first trial crossing in August 1914, and President Woodrow Wilson officially opened the $340 million canal on July 12, 1920.

The Panama Canal Authority has recently undertaken significant construction to widen and modernize the canal. In addition, two new flights of locks were built to allow larger ships to use the canal and handle the expected growth in ship traffic. The construction cost $5.25 billion. The new locks became operational in 2016.

1. Why is the Panama Canal so important to transportation?
2. Why was it important to drain the swamps prior to construction?

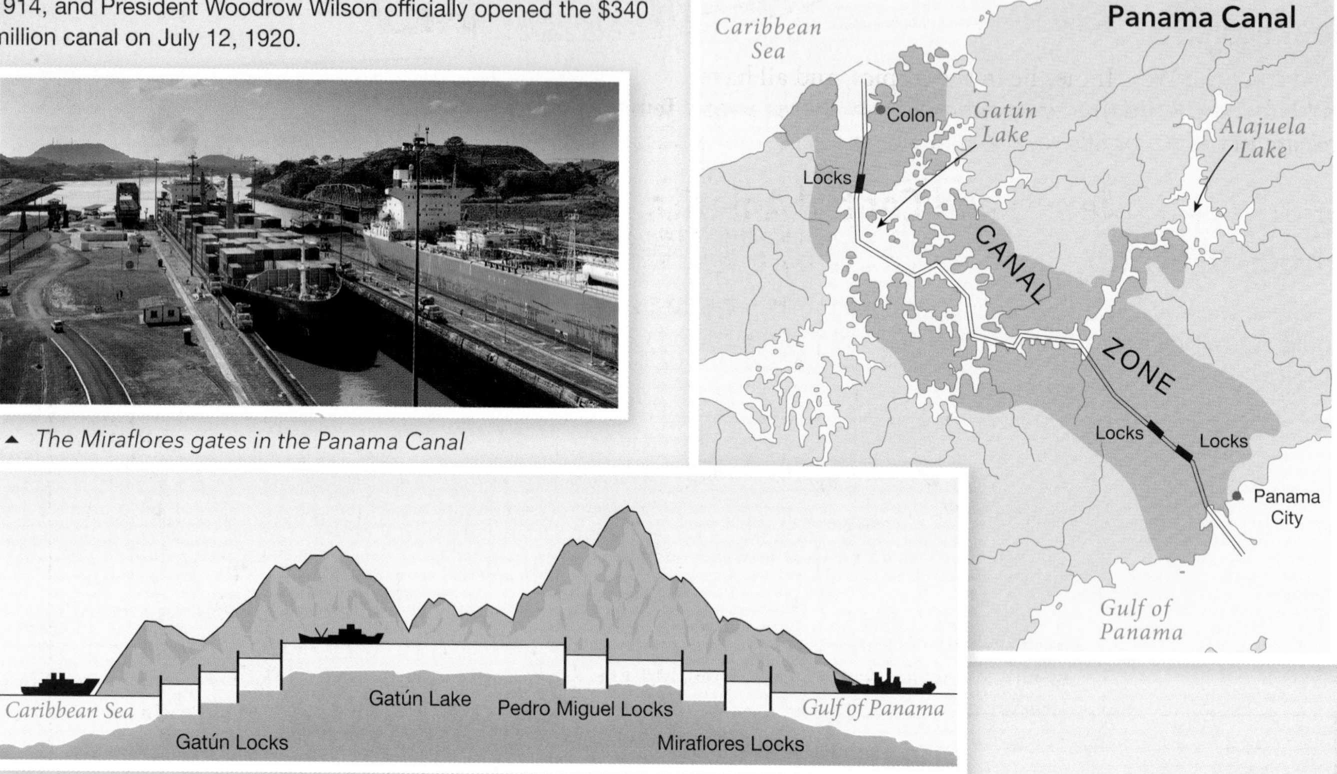

▲ *The Miraflores gates in the Panama Canal*

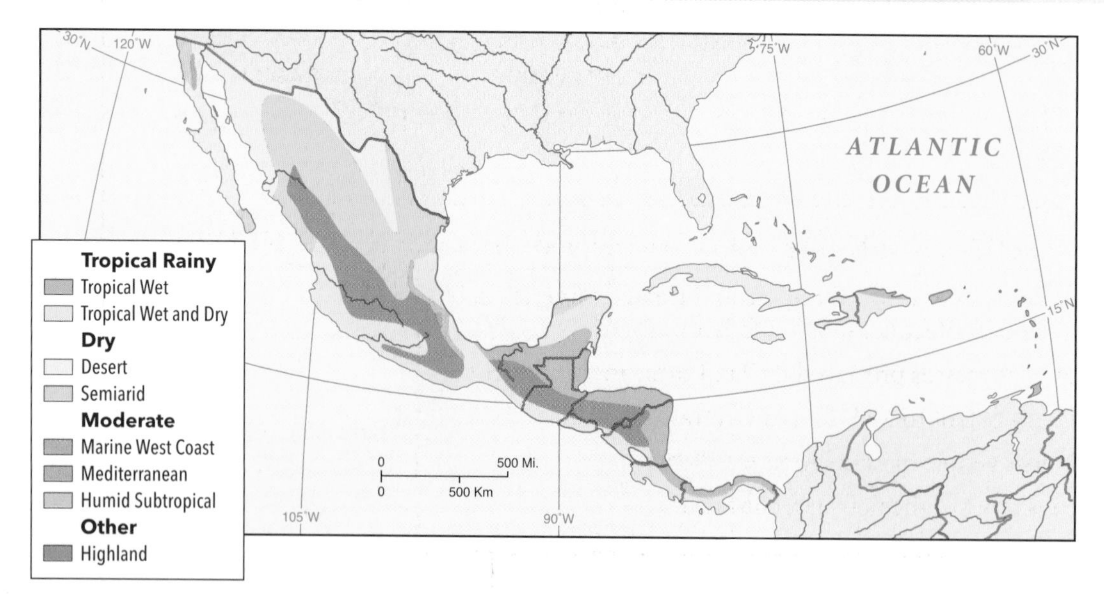

Climates of Mexico and Central America

Climates in this region include tropical wet, tropical wet and dry, desert, semiarid, mediterranean, humid subtropical, marine west coast, and highland. Local climates are affected by their proximity to the sea, elevation, latitude, and local topography.

Mexico

The climates of Mexico range from desert in the north to subtropical in the south. Altitude plays an important role in a region's climate.

Central America

The eastern coast receives more than one hundred inches of rain from trade winds blowing over the Caribbean Sea. But the Pacific Coast, which lies in the rain shadow, receives only forty inches of rain. Most people live in the comfortable *tierra templada* of the highlands.

West Indies

Most of the West Indies lie in the tropics, and all have a mild climate. Rainfall averages about thirty inches a year. Temperatures are in the 70s or 80s year-round, and the vegetation is lush.

Mexico's Vertical Climate Zones

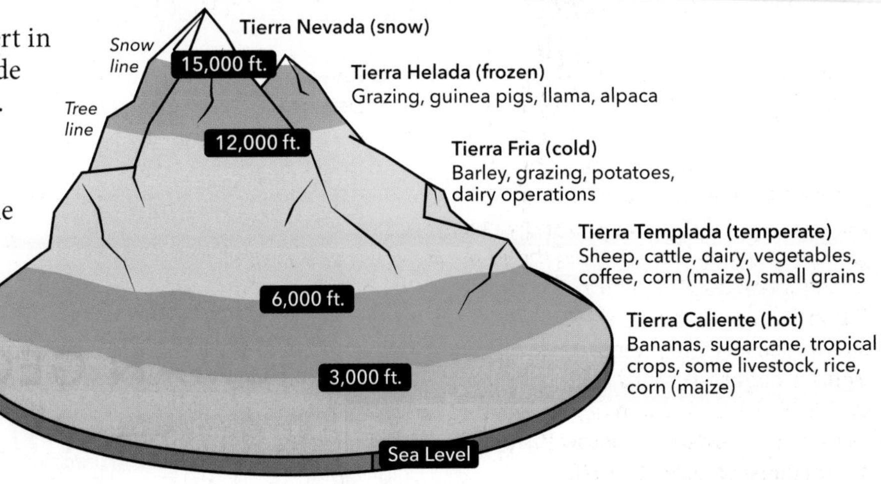

Resources of Mexico and Central America

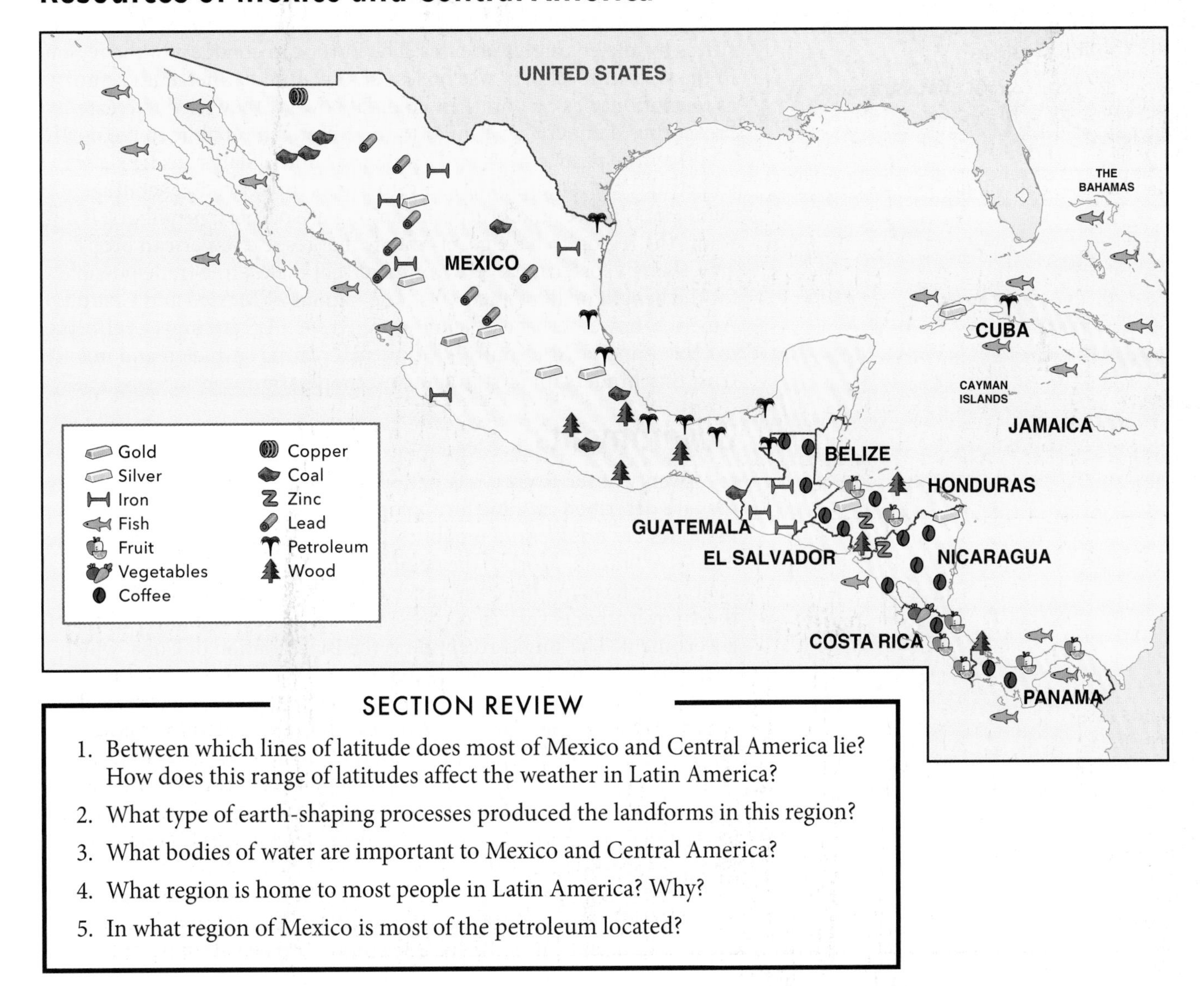

SECTION REVIEW

1. Between which lines of latitude does most of Mexico and Central America lie? How does this range of latitudes affect the weather in Latin America?
2. What type of earth-shaping processes produced the landforms in this region?
3. What bodies of water are important to Mexico and Central America?
4. What region is home to most people in Latin America? Why?
5. In what region of Mexico is most of the petroleum located?

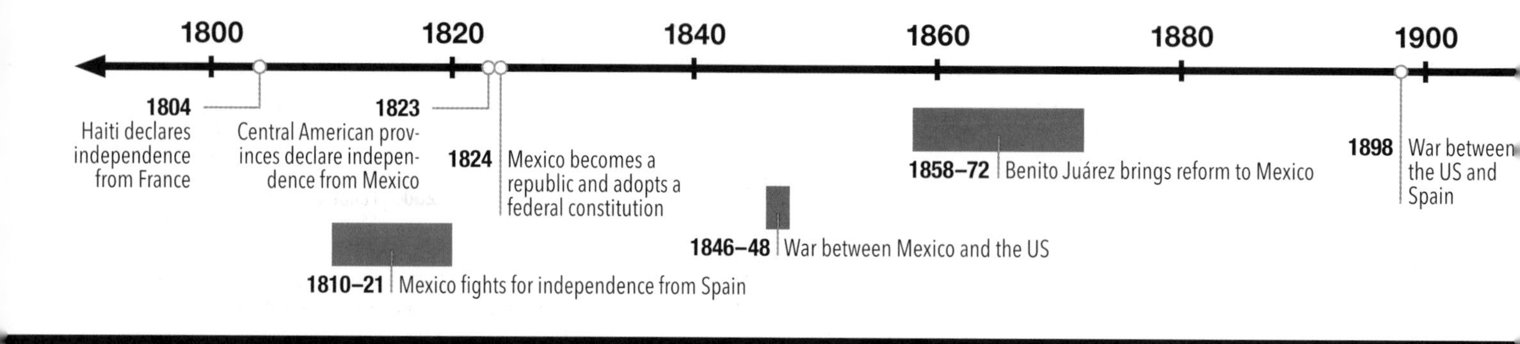

GUIDING QUESTIONS

- How have Mexico and Central America changed over time?
- How do the Mexican and Central American governments interact with their citizens?
- What is the economic health of Mexico and Central America?
- What are the demographics of Mexico and Central America?
- What are the cultural characteristics and diversity in Mexico and Central America?
- What forms of religion are practiced in Mexico and Central America?

HUMAN GEOGRAPHY

How do the people of Mexico and Central America live?

History

The history of this region has been influenced by the blending of several cultures and ethnicities. Such mixing of people groups was not without conflict. Mexico and Central America have a violent past, stretching back to the bloody wars and human sacrifices by ancient native empires. The European conquest of the region in the sixteenth century was no less bloody. In the nineteenth century, as revolutionaries cast off their colonial powers, they tried to create prosperous democracies similar to the American republic to the north.

Over the past century and a half, the United States has tried, sometimes not too diplomatically, to use its influence to encourage democracy, peace, and prosperity among its southern neighbors. It wants the region to have governments that respect American property, thereby fostering an environment that makes free trade possible for the benefit of all participants. The nations of Mexico and Central America, however, have often interpreted such US attempts as efforts to exert imperialistic control over them, creating suspicion and mistrust that hinders understanding and cooperation.

Governments

Twenty of the twenty-one nations in this region have governments that are described as some form of republic or democracy. Most of the republics are *presidential* republics, emphasizing the dominance of the executive branch. Most of the democracies are *parliamentary* democracies, emphasizing the dominance of the legislative branch. While these governments vary in degrees, they are all representative forms of government. The single exception is the island nation of Cuba, which currently remains a Communist regime.

The interaction of government with its citizens varies with each country and culture found in this region. However, the republics and democracies imply the central role of their citizens to elect officials who will represent them and be responsive to their needs. Again, Cuba remains a significant exception since government officials answer to unelected Communist leaders and allow the people little or no voice in their government.

Technically, the Mexican government subsidizes medical and hospital care and makes it available to all Mexican citizens. However, publicly subsidized medicine is inferior to private care, and the

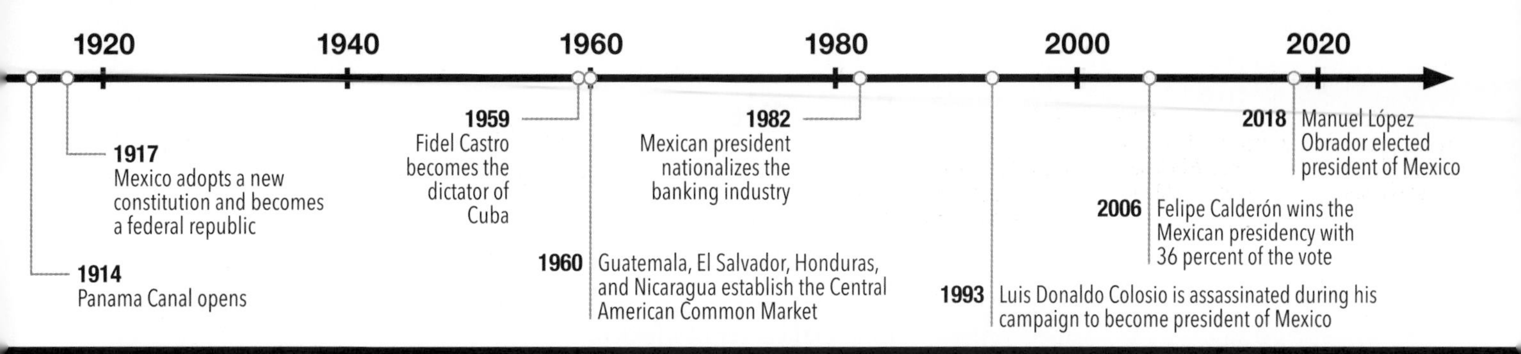

A rally in support of Mexico's president Andres Manuel López Obrador

quality of care varies from urban areas to rural areas. Mexicans who can afford quality care go to private physicians and private hospitals. In rural areas and among the poorest Mexicans, modern medicine is not affordable, not available, or not trusted. Many continue to go to traditional healers for folk remedies.

Sadly, the Mexican government's treatment of its people is inconsistent, and many crimes go unreported because of a lack of confidence in the police and judicial system. Bribes are common, and police corruption is rampant. Impoverished Mexicans tend to be subject to arbitrary arrests and long periods of imprisonment before going to trial. Violent drug cartels often threaten the safety of many Mexicans, and this violence even marred the 2018 election with the murder of more than 130 people preceding that election. Often political candidates or other public officials are targeted by the drug cartels due to the officials' opposition to corruption. A majority of Mexican people embrace the hope that corruption can be ended, and López Obrador was elected president of Mexico, in part, by pledging to end corruption.

Mexico's newly elected President Obrador delivers a speech during the inauguration in Mexico City in December 2018.

Economies

Mexico

Mexico has a mixed economy. The importance of Mexico City and the greater metropolitan area cannot be overstated. This area generates about one-quarter of the country's GDP. Mexico City is also the financial center of Mexico.

Mexico has a dynamic industrial base, and its workers produce goods related to electronics, oil production, energy, and various types of manufacturing that supports many sectors, including the US auto industry. Companies from the United States and Japan have also built manufacturing plants in northern Mexico, known as **maquiladoras**, where goods are manufactured and sent for final assembly to the companies that own the plants.

Tourism also brings significant income to Mexico. It is the fourth largest source of foreign exchange for the country. In particular, **ecotourism**, tourism that emphasizes exotic, natural environments with the goal of supporting conservation efforts, helps make Mexico one of the ten most visited countries in the world.

Mexico is also a major trading partner with Canada and the United States. **NAFTA**, the North American Free Trade Agreement, has resulted in significant economic growth for Mexico. However, this agreement led to large trade deficits with the US and resulted in President Trump proposing a replacement of NAFTA with **USMCA**, the US-Mexico-Canada Agreement. This agreement was signed by President Trump on January 29, 2020.

▲ *Poás Volcano*

▼ *Chichen Itza pyramid on the Yucatán Peninsula*

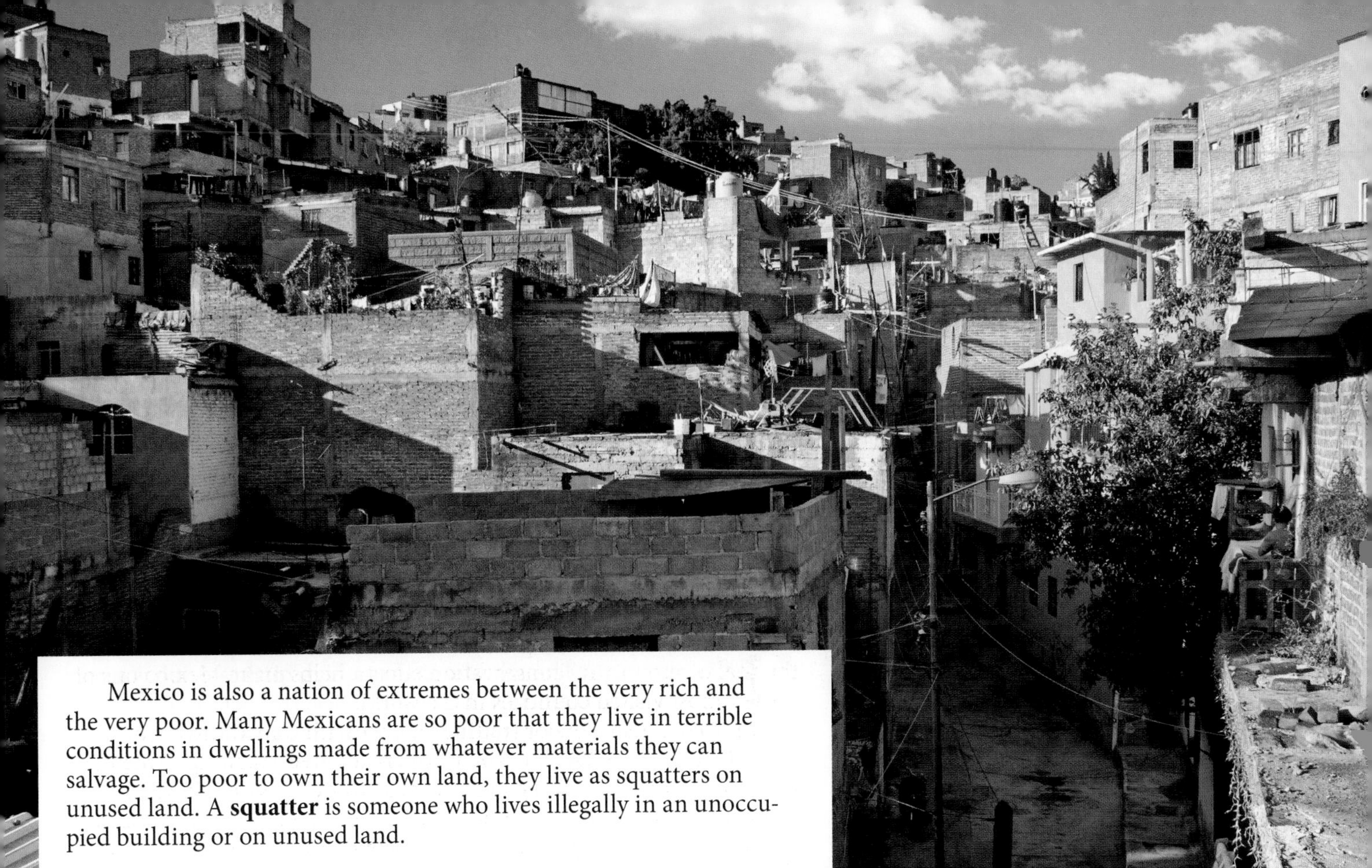

Mexico is also a nation of extremes between the very rich and the very poor. Many Mexicans are so poor that they live in terrible conditions in dwellings made from whatever materials they can salvage. Too poor to own their own land, they live as squatters on unused land. A **squatter** is someone who lives illegally in an unoccupied building or on unused land.

Central America

Most Central American nations produce sugar, bananas, coffee, and beef. In addition, Belize has income from tourism and crude oil. Nicaragua has gold resources in addition to its crops. Panama's economy is positively impacted by the Panama Canal.

▲ *(top) Shanties; housing for the poor on a hillside in Guanajuato, Mexico*

The West Indies

Common crops in the Greater Antilles include coffee, rice, sugar, mangoes, and corn. Tourism, fishing, and farming are the main economic activities in the Lesser Antilles. Tropical fruits and vegetables are common crops, and some farmers also raise sugar cane, cotton, or coffee.

Immigration

The complicated issue of immigration can be viewed in a variety of ways, depending on a particular country's perspective. For the United States, legal immigration has been an accepted part of the nation's history, because America is a land of immigrants. Mexico and some of the Central American countries have strictly limited the number of migrants from other countries due to the stress that migrants place on their economies and native labor forces. Illegal immigration has been widely opposed in North and Central America because of the threats accompanying many illegals, including violence, drug smuggling, human trafficking, and gang activity. Recent organized caravans from Central America attempting to enter the United States after passing through Mexico have highlighted the economic and political problems in some Central American countries and the need to provide better ways to determine the legitimacy of claims for asylum.

▲ *Coffee beans*

Demographics

While Spanish is the most frequently spoken language in this region, several other European languages are also spoken. There are also many local languages, known as **dialects,** spoken in Mexico, Central America, and the West Indies.

Mexico

In 2019 Mexico had an estimated population of 133.3 million. Of that number, most live in the middle of the country. Nearly one-fourth of the people live in or around the nation's capital, Mexico City. This concentration of the nation's population in a single city makes Mexico City a primate city. A **primate city** is the largest city in a country and is significantly larger than other cities in that country.

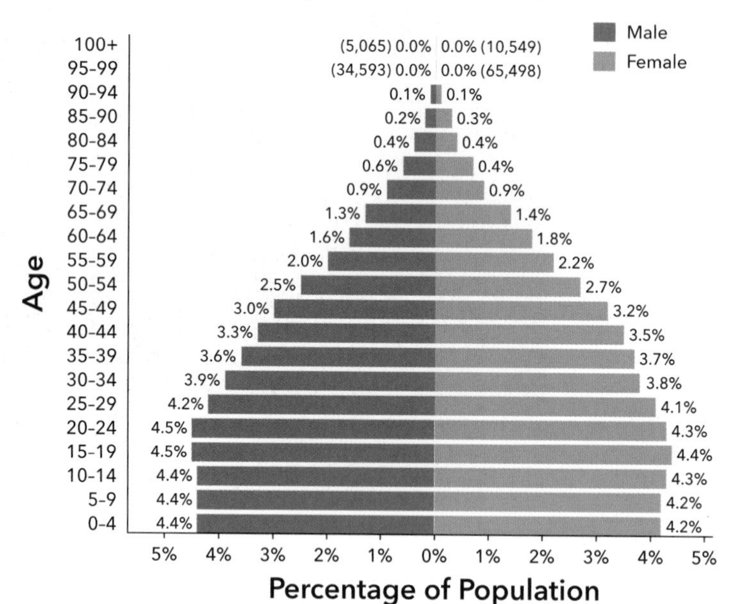

The people of Mexico are a reflection of their history, with **mestizos** (Amerindian-Spanish) forming the majority and Amerindians and others (mostly European) rounding out the population.

Though Mexico has a high birthrate, it has a very meager growth rate and a negative net migration rate. The steady **migration** (movement of people to a new area) of Mexican people north to find work in the United States explains these troubling numbers.

Central America

Populations in the Central American countries vary from a high of 15.46 million in Guatemala to a low of 360,000 in Belize. Statistics of ethnicities vary by country and include mestizo, indigenous, and other (ranging from Mayan to African).

Birthrates in the Central American countries are also high. However, due to circumstances similar to those in Mexico, the growth rates are minimal at best. Economic challenges also contributed to negative net migration rates in most of the Central American countries. Central Americans compose a rapidly increasing number of immigrants trying to enter the United States across the southern border.

The West Indies

Populations in the West Indies vary from a high of 11.4 million in Cuba to a low of 50,000 in St. Kitts and Nevis. Statistics of ethnicities vary by country, but the populations are a blend of those descended from African, European, Hispanic, and East Indian ethnic groups.

Birthrates in the West Indies countries are high as well. However, the growth rates remain low. Economic challenges also contribute to negative net migration rates in most countries in the West Indies.

Culture and Diversity

Mexican and Central American cultures are the product of the compilation of many ethnic groups and nationalities. This blending of cultures has resulted in great diversity. Even the national languages have traces of terms brought to this region from Europe and ancient languages that developed among the Amerindian civilizations prior to European contact. Foods and forms of music vary, as do types of

▲ *Dance performers during the Día de los Muertos in Mérida, Mexico*

Day of the Dead decorations in a home in Oaxaca, Mexico ▶

clothing worn. Diversity is a distinct characteristic of Mexico and Central America.

One central feature of culture in this region is the significant role of the extended family. Especially in rural areas, several generations of a family may live together. Many people in this region make it a priority to support and strengthen family relationships.

Another characteristic common to countries in this region is the importance of village life, accentuated by religious festivals. Festivals related to Lent, Christmas, Easter, and local and national patron saints are common and can extend over several days. One of the most intriguing festivals is *Día de los Muertos* (Day of the Dead), celebrated on November 1. Around the time of this festival (Oct. 31–Nov. 2) families commemorate the spirits of their departed loved ones. Many build small altars to the dead in their homes as a form of ancestor worship and attempt to communicate with the departed family members.

Religion

About 97 percent of the Mexican people affiliate with some religious group, and about 94 percent identify with some form of Christianity. Religious statistics throughout Central America and the West Indies vary but tend to compare with Mexico, with one major exception. Official Cuban statistics report that about 23 percent of the people identify as nonreligious. Accurate statistics from Cuba are difficult to obtain, so this number might be inflated due to the current political climate. Christian leaders who have recently visited Cuba report the vibrant growth of Christianity in what has been a hostile environment to religion.

Major Religions of Mexico

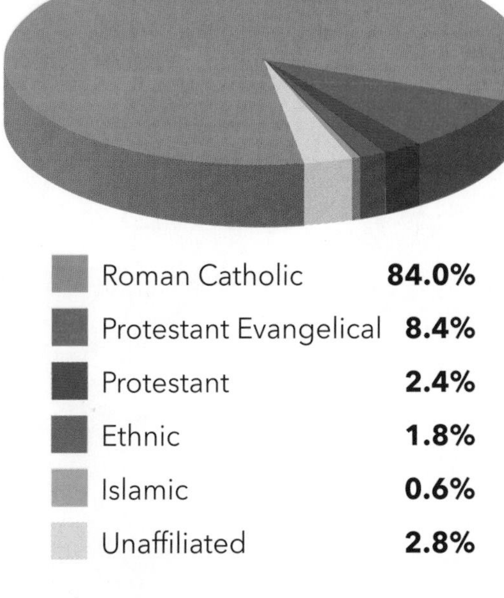

Roman Catholicism

Roman Catholicism is one of the largest religions in the world with almost a billion members. It is led by the bishop of Rome, who is called the pope. The headquarters of this religion is the country of Vatican City. Catholicism developed in Western Europe during the medieval period, and it now has a worldwide presence.

While Catholicism teaches the necessity of God's grace for justification and Christ's death for forgiveness of sin, Catholicism teaches that neither God's grace nor Christ's death is sufficient alone to accomplish salvation. Hence the Roman church stresses the need for sacraments. Catholicism insists that only as individuals cooperate with God's grace in the following seven sacraments is grace made effective for them.

According to Roman Catholicism, baptism removes original sin from a person. Children of Roman Catholic parents are baptized as infants. At baptism a person is regenerated by the Holy Spirit and is made righteous before God. Baptism, or the desire to be baptized, is necessary for salvation.

Confirmation is a means of receiving strengthening grace from the Holy Spirit. It is usually received when a Catholic child reaches an age of understanding. Even though baptized Catholics are purified and made right with God at baptism, they can still lose this purity by sinning. Mortal sins especially put them in danger of eternal judgment.

Penance is the sacrament that restores a person to a state of grace with God. To receive penance, the person must be truly sorry in his heart for his sin, confess his sin, and make satisfaction for his sin. For a small sin, the satisfaction may be reciting the "Our Father" (the Lord's Prayer) or the "Hail Mary" a set number of times.

The eucharist is the central sacrament in Roman Catholic worship. In the eucharist the bread and wine of the Lord's Supper are believed to become in their essence the actual body and blood of Jesus (though in appearance and taste they remain bread and wine). The eucharist is said to be a sacrifice which makes present Christ's sacrifice on the cross.

Marriage, or matrimony, is also considered a sacrament. Actual grace from God is given to the couple in the wedding to enable their union.

Holy orders is the sacrament given to those who are ordained as deacons, priests, or bishops. At ordination a priest receives the power to absolve sins through the sacrament of penance and to consecrate the bread and wine so that it becomes the body and blood of Christ in the eucharist.

Extreme unction, more commonly called last rites or the anointing of the sick, is the sacrament given to a person who is dying. It provides grace so that the dying person does not go to hell because a mortal sin obviated the grace of justification.

Historically, Roman Catholicism has had a strong presence in Latin America. Protestant missionaries were not permitted in Latin American countries until the nineteenth century. However, after liberal governments gained control, many Latin American countries passed laws to limit the influence of the Roman church. It was seen as a supporter of the wealthy oppressors, with some notable exceptions such as Bartolomé de las Casas.

Beginning in the twentieth century, Pentecostalism has proved a significant rival to Catholicism. Nevertheless, Catholicism retains a strong influence on the culture of this region as demonstrated in the various festivals and holidays that are still celebrated. The significance of Latin America to Catholicism may be indicated by the choice of an Argentinian as pope in 2013.

▲ *The Church of Vinales, Cuba*

◀ *Religious parade in Antigua, Guatemala, featuring a float with Christ and the cross*

Given the blending of cultures in Mexico and Central America, it comes as no surprise that different forms of religion have also combined to form a religious **syncretism**, the blending of aspects of various religions to form a new religion. Voodoo and Santeria, for example, have combined Catholicism and traditional African religions. Indigenous people have also blended elements of folk religion, including superstition, magic, and ancestor worship, with Catholicism.

Evangelical Christians have been increasing in number in this region as well. Eight percent of people in Mexico identify as evangelicals. Other nations in this region that have a significant percentage of evangelicals in their populations include Nicaragua at 29.93 percent, the Bahamas at 35 percent, and St. Vincent and the Grenadines at 36.8 percent.

A MISSIONARY'S ENCOUNTER WITH DEATH

Mike and Faith Goldfuss, Mexico City

Death often strikes without warning in Mexico, and embalming is rare. Instead, the family holds a wake or all-night vigil that very night, followed the next day with the burial or cremation. During the vigil, they bring the body in a casket into the house and set up some candles with lots of flowers. Neighbors and family members come and stay for the whole night. When a family member of someone in my church dies, I am often asked to preach. I make it a point to remind those attending, "This morning, none of us thought we would be here tonight." Given the strong Roman Catholic influence, family members and friends often do rosaries and prayers for the dead person, but I always mention Hebrews 9:27 and the fact that this day is coming for everyone who is in attendance. Then I preach to the people who are there and urge them to think of eternity, and the fact that Jesus died to forgive sinners and He obeyed in order to give them perfect righteousness.

During one wake, the widow asked me to preach three times. These were three tremendous opportunities to give the gospel, and between preaching sessions, my wife and I had very good conversations with some of the people at the vigil. Realizing the importance of always being ready to give an answer for the hope that is in us, we have made ministry opportunities, including speaking at wakes, a central part of our work in Mexico.

▾ *Burning candles is an integral part of worship for many.*

1. Contrast the way many Mexicans prepare and honor their dead with how the dead are prepared and honored in your culture.
2. What is the significance of Hebrews 9:27 regarding preparation for death?
3. What would you say if you were asked to speak at the funeral of a friend or relative?

SECTION REVIEW

1. How have Mexico and Central America changed over time?
2. Use a graphic organizer to contrast Mexico's economy with the economies of Central America and the West Indies.
3. Describe the demographics of Mexico and Central America.
4. Define *primate city*.
5. What are some cultural characteristics and examples of diversity in Mexico and Central America?
6. How have Mexican and Central American cultures influenced religion?

INTERACTIONS OF PEOPLE AND PLACES

GUIDING QUESTIONS

- How do Mexico and Central America's economies and their people interact with the environment?
- What are environmental issues in Mexico and Central America?
- What are causes and effects of environmental issues in Mexico and Central America?
- What are possible solutions to environmental issues in Mexico and Central America?

What are some of the challenges of living in Mexico and Central America?

Interaction with the Environment

About 54.5 million people in a myriad of jobs constitute the Mexican workforce, and millions more work in the Central American countries. In order to produce billions of dollars' worth of goods and services each year, resources must be supplied, a vast transportation system needs to be in place, and markets at home and abroad need to be replenished. Industry and the service industry fuel the Mexican and Central American economies, but in doing so these activities affect the environment. Actions that affect the environment include mining, drilling, automobile and factoy exhaust, logging, and combustion of fuels to produce energy.

Another factor of human interaction with the environment in this region is the extreme poverty of many of the people. When the question is one of survival from day to day, stewardship of resources and sustainability of the environment are not realistic concerns.

Water

Many industries in this region use water in production and then contaminate water supplies by discharging industrial waste into rivers. Since the governments in this region have limited resources to monitor and prevent these forms of pollution, many rivers and lakes in this region have high levels of pollution.

Another form of water-related pollution occurs when sedimentation occurs. **Sedimentation** is the washing of sediment from construction and farming sites by rain that transfers soil to the ocean, where it settles in the reef systems. This process can destroy coral beds and threaten marine life, especially if fertilizers are present in the sediment.

A tourist boat traverses a river filled with trash in Mexico.

Air

The growing use of automobiles and trains for transportation has led to severe air pollution in Mexico and Central America. Some of the poorest air quality in the world has been recorded in Mexico City and other Central American cities. Industrial pollution also plays a key role in air pollution, as does naturally occurring volcanic activity, which intensifies the sulfur dioxide in the air.

Land

In addition to the environmental impact of construction, mining, and storing trash, deforestation and soil erosion in Mexico and Central America have an enormous impact on the environment in this region. Centuries of tree removal for logging, farming, and grazing have drastically depleted the millions of acres of coniferous and deciduous trees that once covered most of central Mexico and Central America. Despite this environmental tragedy, deforestation continues due to ongoing construction, the increased planting of avocado groves to meet the growing demand, and clearcutting to grow coca plants to meet the increasing market for cocaine, especially in North America.

▲ *View of Mexico City with visible air pollution*

▼ ***Deforestation****, the process of removing trees for logging, farming, or grazing, is shown here in Guatemala.*

One consequence of deforestation has been severe erosion. Without trees to provide stability for the soil, precious topsoil has been washed away. Areas that could once sustain agriculture have become scarred and barren.

Reasons for Environmental Issues

Air contaminated with various chemicals produces acid rain. Smog produced by combined smoke and airborne pollutants (natural and manmade) makes the air dangerous to breathe and contributes to many health issues.

The industrial and household pollution that ends up in the water supplies of these countries contributes to the difficulty of maintaining access to clean water. Between the chemical contaminants and bacterial parasites, safe drinking water is becoming scarce. Inadequate water treatment, or in many cases no water treatment, makes this essential resource a potential carrier of diseases.

Soil erosion in Costa Rica

Decimation of old-growth forests and clearcutting have grown out of the conflicting interests of farmers, ranchers, and landowners with conservationists. Farmers, ranchers, and landowners want cleared land for farming, grazing, or construction. Conservationists want to limit the clearing of land in order to prevent erosion and promote a sustainable environment for future generations.

Proposed Solutions

Since poorer countries lack resources to protect the environment, economic improvements are essential to enable these governments to fund environmental solutions. It is vital that each citizen exercise wise stewardship of resources. This includes **reforestation**, or the replanting of trees, and utilization of modern technology to grow more food

GLOBAL IMPACT | Getting Medicines from the Rainforest

The rainforests in Central and South America have many species of plants that are found only in this biome. Extracts from some of these plants have provided life-saving medicines. For example, quinine comes from the bark of the cinchona tree and has been used for many years to combat malaria, lupus, and other serious diseases that cause pain and swelling. Tubocurarine was originally added to the tips of arrows or darts to incapacitate animals, and later it was developed into an anesthetic for surgery. Currently it can be used to counteract the effects of serious spider bites until an antivenom can be administered. Vincristine and vinblastine are used to treat certain types of cancer.

▲ *Cinchona bark includes alkaloids that are closely related to quinine and are used to treat malaria.*

Preservation of the rainforests is essential for many reasons. One reason is the life-saving drugs that are being developed from the many plants that are unique to the rainforests.

1. What role do rainforests play in discovery of new medicines?
2. What plant is the source of quinine, and what are some of its uses?
3. How does deforestation impact rainforests?
4. What should we do to preserve the rainforests?

▲ *A giant cinchona tree in the tropical rainforest*

on less land. The search for and implementation of better technologies to reduce air and water pollution should be a top priority so as to protect the citizens and help restore the balance of human and natural existence as God intended. Careful planning to ensure **sustainable development**, meeting the needs of the present generation without denying future generations the capacity to meet their needs, is vital and helps to fulfill the Christian's responsibility to love his neighbor.

SECTION REVIEW

1. What are three environmental issues in Mexico and Central America?
2. Explain how the economies and people in this region interact with the environment.
3. Which groups support deforestation in this region? Why?
4. What solutions to current environmental issues in Mexico and Central America would you propose?

CHAPTER REVIEW

SUMMARY

1. The physical geography of Mexico, Central America, and the West Indies is diverse, with many types of landforms, varying bodies of water, a variety of climates, and differing amounts of natural resources.
2. The people of Mexico, Central America, and the West Indies are also diverse, with many nationalities and ethnic groups uniting in labor and worship to grow their economy and maintain distinct cultures.
3. Challenges of living in Mexico, Central America, and the West Indies include wise use of human and natural resources that enables the building of strong economies without damaging the environment.

Terms to Know

- ❑ land bridge
- ❑ rainforests
- ❑ isthmus
- ❑ archipelago
- ❑ Ring of Fire
- ❑ vertical climate zone
- ❑ maquiladoras
- ❑ ecotourism
- ❑ NAFTA
- ❑ USMCA
- ❑ squatter
- ❑ dialects
- ❑ primate city
- ❑ mestizo
- ❑ migration
- ❑ syncretism
- ❑ sedimentation
- ❑ deforestation
- ❑ reforestation
- ❑ sustainable development

Making Connections

1. How has culture in this region influenced religion? Provide an example.
2. Describe an isthmus.
3. Define *archipelago*.
4. How important is the role of the family in this region?
5. Describe religious syncretism and provide an example from this region.
6. Why do many of the countries in this region have a negative net migration?
7. Identify political issues in Mexico and Central America.

Developing Geography Skills

1. What is the relationship between landforms and the distribution of population in this region?
2. How does altitude affect climate in Mexico and Central America?

Thinking Critically

1. From a Christian worldview, what are some human causes for environmental issues in this region?
2. What is the correlation between the corruption in the Mexican and Central American governments and their unbiblical view of government?

Living in God's World

1. Your community is experiencing a large influx of people from Mexico and Central America. How can your church demonstrate the love of Christ to these people?
2. Should Christians participate in the festivals that are held in Mexico and Central America? Why?

CASE STUDY | An Immigrant's Story

This account was written by a girl named America, who immigrated to the United States when she was a young child.

▲ *Village of Tampico, Mexico*

"I was born in Tampico, Mexico. I lived with my mom and my dad. . . .

"I was two years old when I came to the United States. . . . I remember we lived in a small apartment, but then we moved into a bigger apartment. In that apartment I lived with fifteen people. They were not all family members, but some of them were friends of my family. It was just that they were all barely arriving to the United States, and we decided to all live together to pay the rent together. . . . It was very hard to live with a lot of people because it was very crowded and noisy all the time, but I liked having all my uncles around. . . .

"When I started school no one around me knew how to speak English, and so it was very hard. But my mom found a way to teach me English even though she did not know the language herself. . . . In Pre-K, my teachers knew Spanish and would speak to me in Spanish. My mom would get really mad because I wasn't learning any English. So she had to try harder to teach me English.

"Now I live in an apartment with only my mom, my brother, and my dad. My dad has come a long way. When he got here, he started cleaning restaurants at night with a company, and now he has his own company cleaning restaurants. He's an employer, and I am very proud of him because of that."

Green Card Youth Voices: Immigration Stories from an Atlanta High School. 2018. 79–80.

1. Why did so many migrants initially share the same apartment?
2. What was a major challenge when America attended school in the United States?
3. How did America learn English?
4. Why do you think the teachers spoke to her in Spanish?
5. Why was America's mother upset with the teachers?
6. Do you think America's father was a hard worker? Why?
7. Describe a biblical position on immigration.

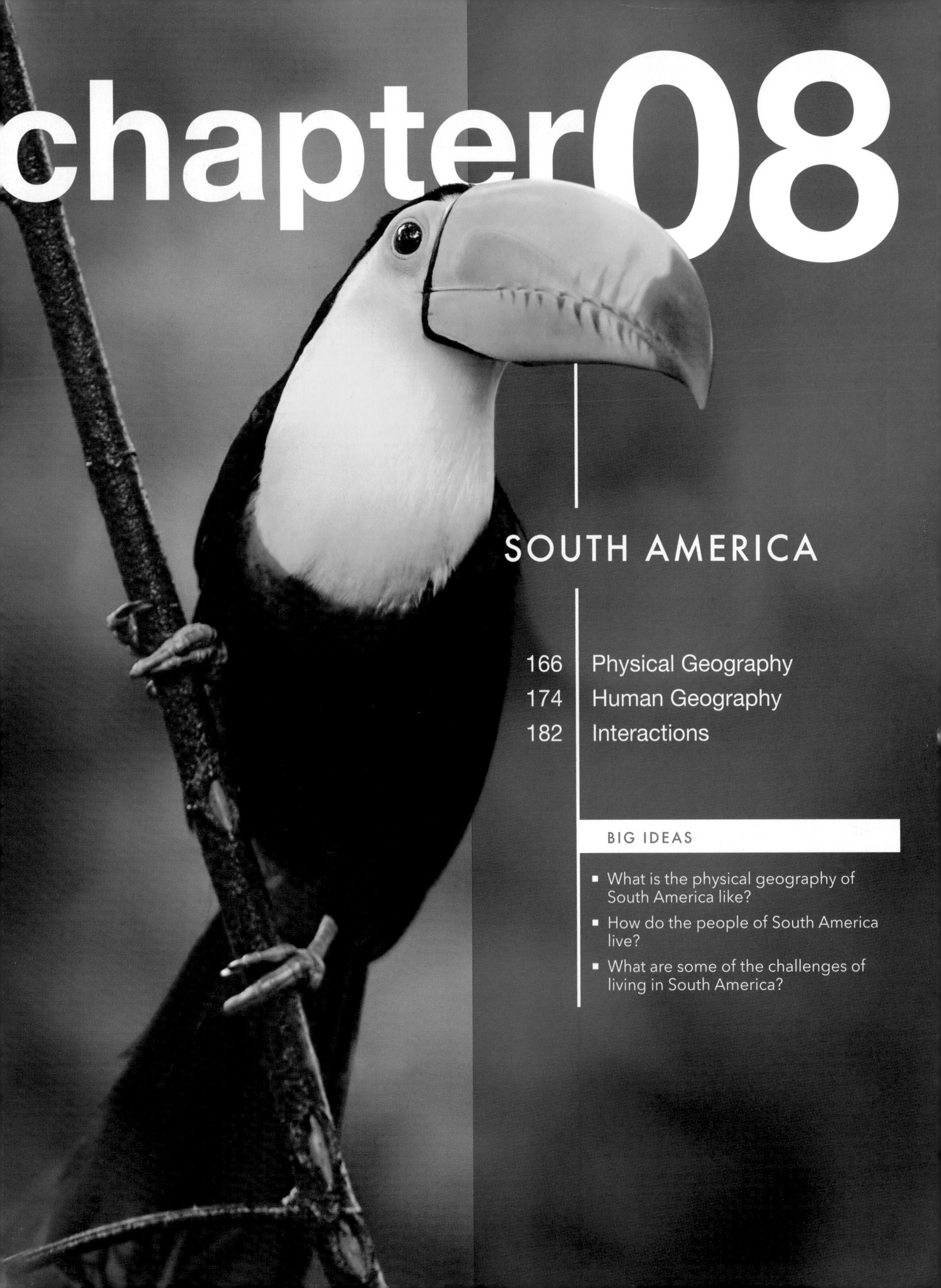

chapter 08

SOUTH AMERICA

166 | Physical Geography
174 | Human Geography
182 | Interactions

BIG IDEAS

- What is the physical geography of South America like?
- How do the people of South America live?
- What are some of the challenges of living in South America?

▲ *Machu Picchu, Peru*

MACHU PICCHU

Why would someone build an amazing city high in the mountains? Machu Picchu was built about AD 1450 as a retreat for Incan rulers. It was abandoned after the Spanish conquered the Incan empire. The city rises precariously between two craggy peaks high in the Peruvian Andes about sixty-five miles west of the Amazon Basin. Machu Picchu has been named one of the New Seven Wonders of the World. Somehow Inca craftsmen carried supplies up to the five-acre plateau, 7,875 feet in the clouds. Pure white granite temples, palaces, and dwellings served about fifteen hundred people. Without mortar or iron tools, the engineers cut stones that fit together perfectly. Even the earthquakes of recent centuries have not toppled them. The Incas also hauled dirt from the valley to provide soil for vegetable gardens on the slopes. In 1911 Hiram Bingham III was, with the help of a native boy, the first Western archaeologist to find Machu Picchu. Because the Spanish conquistadors never discovered the city, Bingham found a treasure trove of artifacts.

▲ *(middle) Peruvian women practicing traditional weaving*

▲ *(bottom) The Plaza Grande, Quito, Ecuador*

◂ *A keel-billed toucan*

South America is a continent of diverse topographies, climates, plants, animals, natural resources, peoples, and cultures. South Americans have adapted to living in the vastly different regions of the continent, from the high altitudes of the Andes Mountains to the dense jungles of the Amazon basin to the barren and cold Patagonia region. While the geographic features of South America are majestic, they have tended to isolate people groups. The nations f the continent have sporadically attempted to achieve their potential through increased international trade, better resource management, and more regional interaction.

GUIDING QUESTIONS

- What are the regions of South America?
- What caused the landforms of South America?
- What bodies of water are important to South America?
- What is the climate of South America, and how is it related to its location on the globe?
- What are the natural resources of South America?

PHYSICAL GEOGRAPHY

What is the physical geography of South America like?

Regions of South America

The South American continent resembles the shape of an ice cream cone. It contains six main geographic regions that fall into two categories, highland or lowland.

THE HIGHLAND REGIONS

The Guiana Highlands

This plateau region covers the southern part of Venezuela and most of Guyana, Suriname, and French Guiana. It is a rugged plateau that runs parallel to the north coast, separating Venezuela's Caribbean coast from the Amazon Basin. Whereas Spain and Portugal controlled most of South America, three other European powers founded small colonies on the coast below the Guiana Highlands. These colonies became known as the Guianas. This region contains Angel Falls and Cuquenán Falls, two of the highest falls in the world.

The Brazilian Highlands

These highlands cover half of Brazil and run parallel to the east coast. Like the Andes, the Brazilian Highlands greatly influence river drainage on the continent. Most waters flow down the highlands into two great water systems—the Amazon in the north and the Río de la Plata in the south. Paulo Afonso Falls, one of the world's most powerful falls, is in this region.

Andes Mountains

The Andes Mountain Range, the longest in the world, begins in Venezuela near Lake Maracaibo and runs down the west side of the continent. The Andes are part of the Western Cordillera, which includes the Cordilleras in Canada, the Rockies in the United States, and the Sierra Madres in Mexico. In Colombia, the Andes divide into two, the Cordillera Occidental and the Cordillera Central. They continue through parts of Ecuador, Peru, and Bolivia. The Andes mountain system reaches its highest peaks in Argentina, where nine of the Western Hemisphere's ten highest peaks exist. The tallest of them all is Aconcagua, at 22,834 feet. The mountains make up all of Chile.

There are three notable subregions in the Andes. The *Altiplano* is a high plateau that has an average elevation of 12,000 feet. It is on the east side of the mountains and covers most of Bolivia and part of Peru and Argentina. The *Atacama Desert* covers the northern twelve hundred miles of Chile and extends into parts of Peru, Bolivia, and Argentina. *Patagonia* is the subregion that includes Chile's archipelago and all of southern Argentina. It consists of mountains, deserts, and high plains and is bordered by the Atlantic, Southern, and Pacific Oceans. Three hundred miles to the east of Patagonia lie the Falkland Islands, which are a little smaller than Connecticut. Argentina and Great Britain fought over these islands in 1982. Today they still belong to Great Britain.

THE LOWLAND REGIONS

Orinoco River Basin

This region includes parts of Venezuela and Colombia. The Orinoco River is the third-longest river on the continent. A subregion called the ***Llanos*** consists of broad grassy plains that cover the northeastern corner of Colombia and central Venezuela. The northernmost rivers of the Llanos flow into the Caribbean Sea, but the southern rivers flow into the Amazon River.

Amazon River Basin

This is the largest river basin in the world, covering 40 percent of South America. It includes all the land drained by the Amazon and its tributaries. It is like a giant bowl collecting water from the Andes, Guyana, and Brazilian Highlands. It includes parts of the countries of Colombia, Ecuador, Peru, Brazil, Guyana, Suriname, Venezuela, and Bolivia.

Río de la Plata Basin

This drainage basin, the second-largest in South America, includes parts of Bolivia, Brazil, Argentina, and Uruguay and all of Paraguay. The region includes three subregions. The *Gran Chaco* is a lowland plain that is mostly in Argentina but also covers parts of Bolivia and Paraguay. It is flat and dry but is covered by shrubs and forest. *Pantanal* is the world's largest wetland. About 80 percent of the land is flooded during the rainy season. It includes an area of eastern Brazil and part of Bolivia and Paraguay. Argentina's low plains around the Río de la Plata are called the ***Pampas***. Most of the nation's people, industry, and agriculture are there. The Pampas cover all of Uruguay and part of Brazil.

Physical Landforms

The Andes Mountains dwarf the mountains of North America. They are part of the ring of fire and were formed after the plates collided, causing uplift. The red sands, barren rock, and salt flats bear mute testimony to the Atacama Desert's reputation as the driest desert on earth. It gets less than 1 mm of rain a year because of the rain shadow effect of the Andes and the unique ocean current.

▲ *Cotopaxi is one of the highest active volcanoes in the world at 19,347 feet.*

▼ *Mount Chimborazo ranks 38th tallest in the Andes at 20,702 feet, but its summit is actually the farthest point from the center of the earth because of the earth's bulge at the equator.*

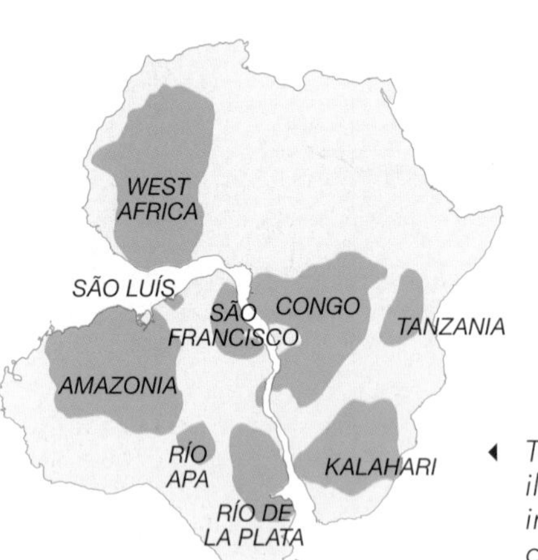

◀ *The Brazilian Highlands have geologic similarities to their corresponding seashore in Ghana, possibly showing evidence for continental drift, that Africa and South America were once joined.*

▼ *The Gran Chaco is stone free because it is filled with the alluvial debris (loose soil that came down the rivers) from the Andes to the west and the Brazilian Highlands to the east.*

Chile's archipelago is similar to Alaska's Inside Passage. Glaciers have carved deep gorges that the ocean flooded to form fjords.

▾ *The huge, block-shaped mountains, called tepuis, in the Guiana Highlands were formed by erosion. The tepuis are examples of* ***escarpments****. On the top are savannas. The highest tepui, Mount Roraima, is 9,219 feet.*

▴ *Atacama Desert*

▲ People live on floating islands made out of reeds on Lake Titicaca in Peru.

▼ Catatumbo lightning, Lake Maracaibo, Venezuela

▼ An aerial view of the Amazon River near Manaus, Brazil

Bodies of Water

South America is surrounded by three of the world's oceans, the Atlantic, Pacific, and Southern. The Caribbean Sea is the large body of water in the north.

Titicaca is a lake located on the border of Bolivia and Peru. It is one of the highest navigable lakes in the world. Many native settlements dot the shore. By volume, it is the largest lake in South America. Some Uru Indians actually live on the water itself, building islands from the totora reeds that grow along the water's edge. The Uru also use the versatile totora for fuel, animal food, baskets, mats, houses, and boats. The shores of Lake Titicaca became the center of the Tiahuanaco Empire, which preceded the Incas. The Incas believed that the first man and woman were created on an island in the lake.

Lake Maracaibo, the largest lake in South America, sits south of the Caribbean Sea, so close that the lake water has a greater salinity than other lakes. It is the site of the majority of Venezuela's oil reserves. There is a unique weather phenomenon here called Catatumbo lightning. Almost 300 days a year, lightning occurs where the Catatumbo River enters Lake Maracaibo, so NASA has declared the location the lightning capital of the world.

Rivers are a vital part of South American life. They are a means of transportation, a habitat for thousands of species, a source of power, and the lifeblood of the rainforests. The Amazon River holds multiple records for world rivers. It drains the largest area and carries the largest volume. It pours 20 percent of the world's fresh water into the Atlantic. The river runs 4,075 miles, which is second in length to the Nile only by a little bit. At its mouth, the Amazon is 37 miles wide.

Angel Falls is the world's highest uninterrupted waterfall. It is in the Guiana Highlands of Venezuela and is part of the Orinoco River system. The water drops 3,212 feet from the top of a tabletop mountain.

The Río de la Plata was the center of Spanish settlement in the east. It is the widest **estuary**, or ocean inlet, on the Atlantic coast. The mighty Paraná and Uruguay Rivers flow into the Río de la Plata. These navigable rivers are essential for three nations: Argentina, Paraguay, and Uruguay.

The Strait of Magellan is a passageway in the south between the Atlantic and Pacific Oceans. It lies almost totally in Chile's territorial waters. It is 350 miles long and ranges from two to twenty miles wide. It is named for Ferdinand Magellan, whose fleet sailed through the strait in 1520 and whose crew ultimately became the first to circumnavigate (journey around) the earth. Until the construction of the Panama Canal, the strait was the main shipping route between the Atlantic and Pacific Oceans.

▲ *Angel Falls, Venezuela*

Climates of South America

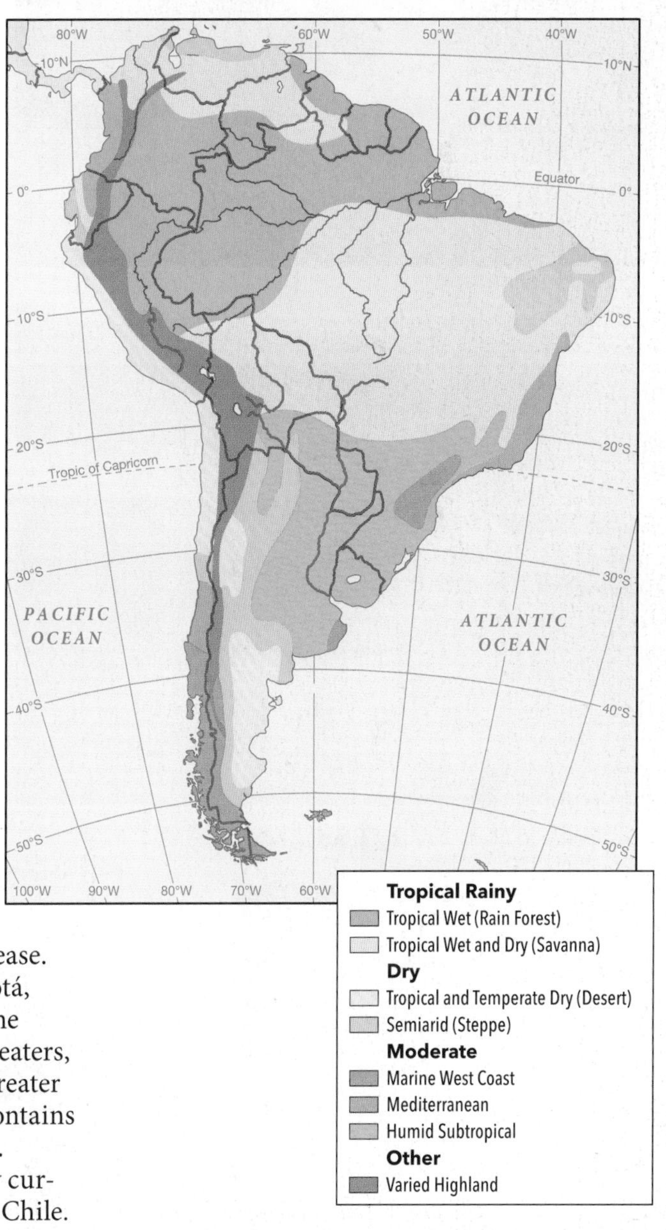

The wider portion of South America is located in the tropics between 23.5° N and 23.5° S, so there is not much seasonal temperature variation for most of the continent. There are two main factors that affect the climate. One is the **Intertropical Convergence Zone,** which is the area encircling the earth at the equator in which the northeast and southeast trade winds converge. Called the doldrums by sailors, this zone causes the wet and dry seasons for areas it covers. The other factor is the altitude of a certain region. The higher the elevation the more temperate the climate.

The Amazon rainforest has a very steamy, uncomfortable climate. Temperatures hover between 75°F and 95°F throughout the year. Many areas receive more than one hundred inches of rain annually. Although there is technically a wet season, from December to May, and a dry season, the differences are not so much in the amount of rainfall since rainfall occurs on average 200 days a year. The main cause of the wet season is the runoff from the Andes, which causes flooding.

Unlike the Amazon Basin, the Brazilian Highlands have a more distinct rainy season half of the year. The reason for the difference is that the Amazon always receives direct sunlight, which heats the surface and causes regular afternoon showers (by convection precipitation, which you studied in Chapter 3). But in the highlands, the direct rays of the sun shift every six months. The rainfall begins in November when the sun shifts over the highlands. When the sun shifts back north in May, the land cools, cold air rises, and the rains cease.

In the cities that sit on the plains of the Andes, such as Bogotá, Quito, and La Paz, the weather is spring-like year-round since the cities are so high. People leave home in the morning wearing sweaters, but by the afternoon they are wearing short sleeves. There is a greater chance of getting sunburned at these altitudes because the air contains less water vapor to protect against the ultraviolet rays of the sun.

The Peru, or Humboldt, ocean current is a cold, low salinity current that dominates the waters off Ecuador, Peru, and Northern Chile.

It is responsible for causing the Atacama Desert. The climate is so dry that some places in the desert have no recorded rainfall. The Peru Current might hurt the climate, but it supports one of the world's best sardine fishing grounds.

The climate in the southern half of South America is quite different from the tropical north. The Pampas region in Argentina has a semiarid climate that supports vast grasslands. Half of the people of the Pampas live in Buenos Aires, Argentina's capital. Buenos Aires is ideally located near the mouth of the Paraná River on the Río de la Plata. The humid subtropical climate provides much more rain than the semiarid areas in the western and southern Pampas. Winter temperatures rarely drop below freezing, even in July, the coldest month in the Southern Hemisphere. The climate is colder in the mountains and more temperate in the lowlands. The temperatures in Patagonia are similar to those of Canada's cold Maritime Provinces since they share the same distance from the equator.

▾ *A Peruvian man picking coffee cherries*

▴ *Cattle in Mato Grosso, Brazil*

Resources of South America

South America is extremely rich in natural resources, and these countries depend heavily on the income from their exportation. The resources are so numerous and diverse that it is almost easier to list the resources that are *not* prevalent in South America!

Roughly 60 percent of the world's coffee comes from South America. Brazil, Colombia, and Peru are the main sources. Each country produces its own unique type of beans. While Brazil produces the most, Colombia is renowned for the quality of its coffee.

South America exports many fruits and vegetables. Ecuador is a major exporter of bananas and cacao (a plant that is used to make chocolate, cocoa, and cocoa butter). Since Chile and Argentina have the reverse seasons of the Northern Hemisphere, they are able to sell various common fruits and vegetables to the Northern Hemisphere when it is the off-season there, including cherries, blueberries, apples, avocados, and more. This arrangement is possible because of free trade agreements and advanced shipping methods. Some plants, like quinoa and brazil nuts, can only be found in South America. Quinoa is a grain grown in Peru that is noted for its high vitamin content. Brazil is currently the top producer of sugar, providing 51 percent of the world's supply.

Raw quinoa grains ▸

Raw uncut emerald gemstones

In recent years the countries of Ecuador and Colombia have become major cut flower producers because of their steady climates. Ecuador is currently first in the world for rose production and third for flower production overall. Since Colombia ranks second, it is likely that a rose you purchase in the United States came from South America.

South America supplies around 23 percent of the world's beef. Brazil ranks second to the United States in beef production. The Pampas, with its wide grassland, is perfect for raising livestock. Argentina, Uruguay, and Paraguay also produce a lot of cattle, most of it being exported to Europe and Asia. Fish are an important resource, especially on the Pacific Coast. Ecuador is a leader in shrimp production.

The forests of the Amazon are a valuable resource. The mahogany and rosewood trees there are some of the most profitable hardwoods in the world.

South America is rich in minerals, including gold, silver, copper, iron ore, and tin. Chile and Peru are responsible for almost 40 percent of the world's supply of copper. Near the southwestern border of Bolivia, Chuquicamata has one of the world's largest open-pit copper mines. Colombia is rich in emeralds, providing almost 90 percent of the world's supply. Chile has one of the world's few natural deposits of sodium nitrate, which is used to make explosives and fertilizer.

South America accounts for 8.5 percent of the world's yearly oil production, as of 2019. Venezuela has the greatest amount of proven oil reserves. The reserves are in the form of oil sands, as in Canada. But because of mismanagement Venezuela actually produces less oil than its neighbor Brazil. Other countries with significant oil production are Colombia, Ecuador, and Argentina.

Natural Resources of South America

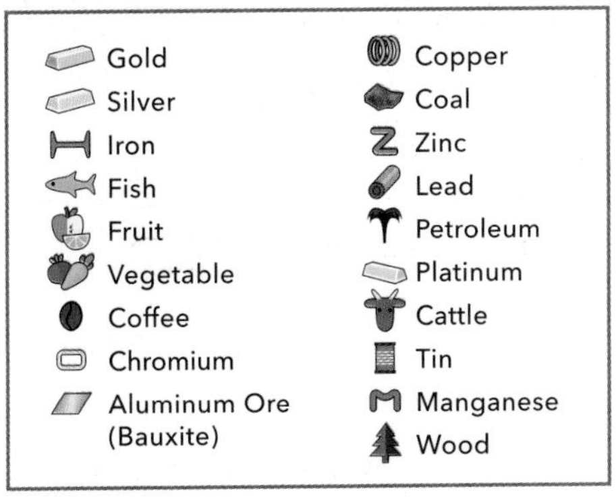

SECTION REVIEW

1. How are the regions of South America categorized?
2. What earth-shaping activity caused the Andes Mountains? Why would they have so many volcanoes?
3. Which records does the Amazon River hold?
4. Why would the cities in the Andes have cooler temperatures despite being located on the equator?
5. List five natural resources of South America.
6. Why would Ecuador and Colombia be the largest producers of flowers?

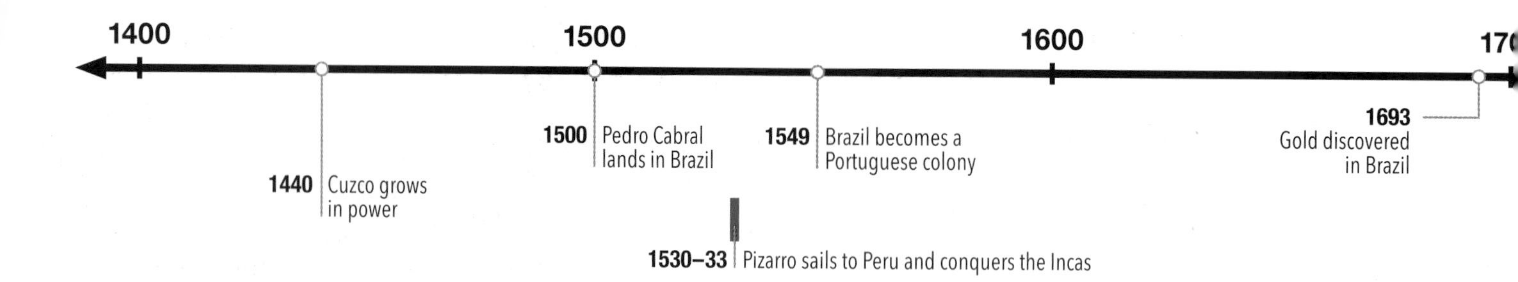

GUIDING QUESTIONS

- How has South America changed over time?
- How do the governments of South America interact with their citizens?
- What are the economies of South America like?
- What are the demographics of South America?
- What are the cultural characteristics of South America?
- What are the religions of South America, and how do they interact with the culture?

HUMAN GEOGRAPHY

How do the people of South America live?

Governments

In general, South American countries have fragile governments with many challenges. The South American nations were free from colonial rule by the 1820s with the exception of the Guiana nations. Suriname and Guyana obtained their independence in the 1960s and 1970s from the Netherlands and Great Britain respectively. French Guiana is still a district of France. Since the 1820s most of the countries have oscillated between military dictatorships and socialist governments. The end result seems to be the same: lack of freedom with one group repressing the other.

This map ranks the countries as of 2019 based on their political and economic freedom. These rankings change from year to year. For example, both Venezuela and Colombia were ranked as moderately free in the late 1990s.

There seems to be a cycle in which a militarist dictator or a group of generals called a **junta** comes to power, promising to bring law and order. The dictator is usually backed by wealthy landowners. He tends to overstep his bounds and rule harshly, imprisoning or killing his opposition. The poor people are overlooked by the government, so they rise in opposition and cause a change in government through election or **coup d'etat** (a sudden illegal seizure of the power of government). They bring in a socialist leader who promises to help the poor. The leader has little experience in government and cannot fulfill his or her promises. Eventually, the economy and society start to collapse. The leaders impose greater controls, along with imprisoning or killing their opposition. Then a powerful general steps in to bring order, and the cycle repeats. Both the right and left governments are characterized by corruption, in which public money goes to make the leaders wealthy. Overall, in recent years, this cycle has been moderating for the continent, the swings between the right and left becoming less radical. But that is no consolation for the people of Venezuela, who are currently experiencing great suffering as a result of poor governance.

Chile is an example of success, and since 1990 that country has not experienced these oscillations between the left and right. It is currently the most stable nation in South America. The Chilean poorer classes voted Salvador Allende, a Marxist, as president in 1970. But his efforts to redistribute land ruined the economy and sparked a coup in 1973. General Augusto Pinochet took power and ruled with an iron fist for nearly two decades. Although Pinochet relied on secret police to keep

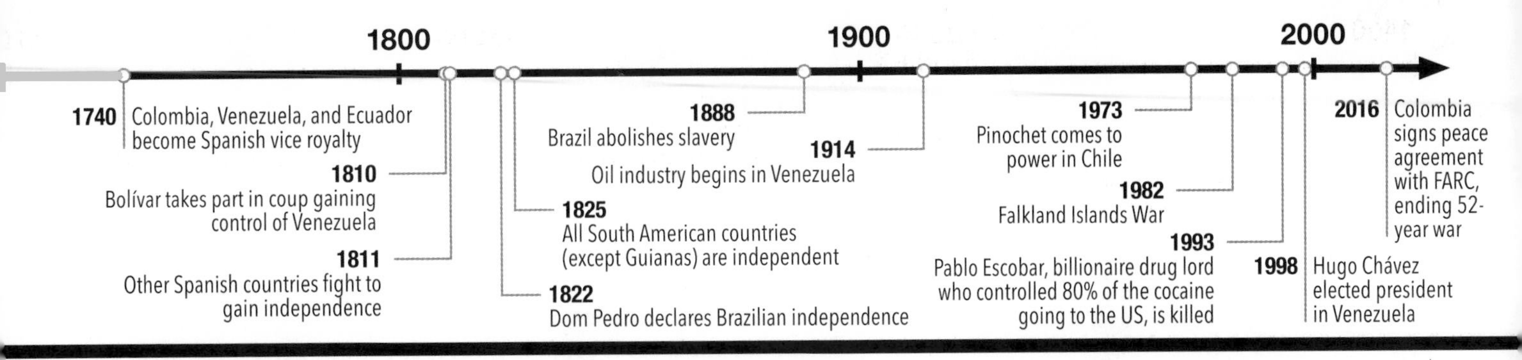

political power, he also introduced the first free-market reforms in South America. This happened because he put a group of economists known as "the Chicago boys" in charge of the economy. They were Chileans who had studied at the University of Chicago under Milton Friedman, the conservative economist behind the transformation of the US economy in the 1980s. So while Pinochet's brutal policies repressed political freedom, the "Chicago boys" brought economic freedom and turned Chile into an economic dynamo. In 1989 Pinochet allowed the people to vote on whether or not to continue his military dictatorship. They chose democracy instead. So today Chile enjoys both political and economic freedom.

Colombia and Peru have sought to follow Chile's policies. In 2016 Colombia made a peace agreement with the communist FARC rebels, whose brutal attempts to institute a Communist government in the country had resulted in over 200,000 deaths. While the people will need generations to heal from the impact of the war, Colombia's economy has grown after the peace agreement because of increased tourism and the fact that they do not have to spend money fighting the rebels.

Venezuela, on the other hand, has followed the Cuban model of government. In 1998 Hugo Chávez was elected president. He nationalized companies and consolidated his power. In 2013 he died and was succeeded by Nicholas Maduro, a former bus driver, who continued Chávez's policies. The result has been mass emigration out of the country, no electrical power in the capital, women having to sell their hair to buy food, and people having to get water from storm drains. The situation there continues to worsen.

Ecuador and Bolivia have followed the socialist model of Venezuela to some extent. Ecuador's new constitution has the unique provision of acknowledging the rights of nature, the only constitution in the world to do so.

▲ *Handbags and paper cranes made of Venezuelan bolivars are sold on the sidewalk as a way to get some value out of the virtually worthless Venezuelan money.*

Economies

We have seen that the strength of a nation's economy is directly related to its governmental policies. There is no better illustration of this truth than in South America. Geography is partially an obstacle to economic success. The mountains and jungles prevent easy movement of goods. This disadvantage is balanced by the abundant natural resources that the countries possess.

Brazil has the largest economy but is fourth in per capita GDP. Chile is in first place with almost double the per capita GDP of Brazil. The clearest evidence for the value of free institutions is the fact that Venezuela ranks first in proven oil reserves, more than Saudi Arabia and Canada, but ranks last in per capita GDP for South America and next to last in all of the Americas, beating only Haiti.

▲ *The Pacific Alliance logo*

There is not much trade or cooperation between the South American countries, and that is one of the main problems. Numerous organizations desire to address this issue. In general, they have been ineffective. The two main organizations are the Mercosur Alliance created in 1991 and the Pacific Alliance created in 2011. These two organizations represent distinctly different philosophies of governance in relation to the economy.

The Mercosur Alliance includes the nations of Brazil, Paraguay, Argentina, and Uruguay. Its members tend to desire more control over their economies. Venezuela was a member, but its membership was revoked in 2016. This alliance has seen flattened economic growth. Consequently, Uruguay would like to leave the alliance, since it shares more in common with Chile.

The Pacific Alliance includes the countries of Chile, Colombia, Mexico, and Peru, which all border the Pacific Ocean. The alliance emphasizes free trade between its members and the rest of the world. The governments tend to be more relaxed in their control of the

▼ *A Daimler-Chrysler automobile factory in Brazil*

economy. The organization has been much more successful in its short existence than any other Latin American organization of its kind.

Peru is notable for its success and is becoming the economic model for South America. It has the fastest growing economy because it has little debt and has not followed the policies of Venezuela. Peru is seeking to be the business startup and tech capital of Latin America, making it a more service-based economy and not solely dependent on the sale of natural resources. Brazil is notable because it has the largest manufacturing base in South America. Brazil manufactures cars, airplanes, electrical machinery, paints, and many other products.

Demographics

If it were a single country, South America would be the third most populous country in the world with almost 419 million people, but since it is a continent, it exceeds only Australia in the number of people. Brazil makes up over half the population of South America. The average fertility rate of South America is 2.0. In general, the poorer nations have a higher rate. Brazil has drawn the attention of demographers as it has the lowest fertility rate at 1.75, which has been declining steadily. The factors of urbanization and wealth have had the same effect on Brazil as they have worldwide, but the researchers discovered an added issue in Brazil—telenovelas (soap operas). The women portrayed on TV "have it all," a career and family. They usually have only one or two children, so it seems the women of Brazil have followed suit.

South America is a hollow continent, as most of the people live near the coasts. Ethnically, the continent loosely divides into five regions. The northern nations of Ecuador, Colombia, and Venezuela have a mestizo majority. The Guianas that were colonized by the French, Dutch, and English are made up of the descendants of slaves brought in by the Europeans. The majority are ethnically East Indian, and the largest minority is of African heritage. The southern nations of Uruguay, Argentina, and Chile are characterized by majorities of a more distinctly European ethnic heritage. Bolivia and Paraguay are the two landlocked nations. Bolivia is the only country with a majority of indigenous or Amerindian population. The tribes share a common language, Quechua. Paraguay has a mestizo majority.

Brazil contains half of the continent's land, so its people resemble the rest of the continent, with a mestizo majority in the north, a European majority in the south, and indigenous tribes in the vast Amazon jungle. Ninety-seven percent of the uncontacted peoples of the world live in the Amazon. South America is the most urbanized region of the world, with around 80 percent of people living in cities.

▾ East Indian

▴ Mestizo

▴ Bolivian

▴ European

Culture and Diversity

South American culture is similar to that of Mexico and Central America. As you learned in Chapter 4, Latin culture is **multiactive**, meaning it has characteristics of both high-context and low-context cultures. Views on time, personal space, and relationships are like that of high-context cultures. Social events do not begin until well after the scheduled time. People do not require much personal space and generally greet each other with much affection. Latin Americans tend to find their identity in their family, so they desire not to displease their family or relocate. It is common for children to live with their parents until they get married. Latin culture also resembles low-context cultures in some ways. People are not ruled by their effort to avoid shame or shaming others, and they do not conceal their emotions. The literal meaning of words is what is meant when speaking.

Because Brazil was colonized by Portugal, Brazilians speak Portuguese, while the remainder of the continent, with some exceptions, speaks Spanish. In Guyana, which was a British colony, the official language is English. In Suriname, they speak a form of Dutch, and in French Guiana, French is the official language. Ecuador and Bolivia have a large number of Quechua speakers.

One negative aspect of Latin America's culture is its history of violence. It is ranked as the most violent region in the world. Thirty-nine percent (excluding regions in open war) of the world's murders occur in this region, yet it only accounts for 9 percent of the world's population. It is difficult to understand how such a beautiful place and such vibrant people could be so violent. Policymakers point to the drug trade, poverty, and the lack of law enforcement as causes of the violence. Another issue that may play a part is the legacy of the conquistadors and the violent practices of the ancient peoples. However, the South American people are not doomed to this legacy.

Over 1.4 million Venezuelans have fled to Colombia in recent years. They have been welcomed. Here they are served a meal at the Divina Providencia migrant shelter in Cúcuta, Colombia.

People straining to watch a soccer game in Cartagena, Colombia

In South America key cultural aesthetics relate to sports, foods, and festivals. Soccer, or fútbol, is the cultural glue that unites the people of the Latin American nations. It is called "el jogo bonito," or the beautiful game. When their national fútbol team is playing, people clear the streets and gather around screens in cafés, homes, and stores.

South American foods reveal the mix of European and indigenous cultures. It is arguably some of the best food in the world since the people generally still take the time to cook with traditional ingredients and methods. Countries like Colombia take pride in the variety of their unique fruits. A person could try a different kind of fruit juice every day for a long time without repeating.

As in Mexico, South Americans enjoy festivals, most notably **Carnival**, which literally means "farewell to meat" since the festival occurs before Lent, when Catholics are to give up meat for forty days. Rio de Janeiro, Brazil, has the most famous Carnival celebration. In 2019 the president of Brazil criticized the raucous party atmosphere and debauchery that occur during this festival. Uruguay has the longest Carnival, lasting forty days. In Ecuador, the festivities include a five-day water balloon fight.

Some of the exotic fruits grown in South America

Peruvians celebrating Carnival in Lima

▲ *Pope Francis from Argentina, the first Latin American pope*

Major Religions of South America

Religion	Percentage
Roman Catholic	**70.4%**
Protestant Evangelical	**18.7%**
Ethnic	**3.7%**
Protestant	**1.3%**
Islamic	**0.6%**
Buddhist	**0.2%**
Hindu	**0.1%**
Other	**0.8%**
Unaffiliated	**4.2%**

Religion

The people of South America are very religious. Even those who do not practice a religion or personally believe in God tend to be cultural Catholics. In 2013 Cardinal Bergoglio, from Argentina, became the first pope from Latin America, taking the name Pope Francis.

From the time it entered Latin America, Catholicism was linked to the state. The constitutions of South America have reflected this church-state relationship. In recent years, however, a divergence from the church is evident in the new constitutions. For example, in 1991 Colombia replaced a reference to the "Sacred Heart of Jesus" with a more universal "God." While such changes may seem small, they represent a significant distancing of the state from the Roman Catholic Church.

With the rapid growth of the prosperity version of Pentecostalism, however, many people have merely replaced one tainted gospel for another. The major hindrance to evangelism is that the majority have accepted an incorrect gospel and believe they are already Christians. A Latin American pastor has said, "Latin America needs to be re-evangelized because it has been inoculated with the wrong message. Therefore, people have developed 'antibodies' to the real gospel."

In spite of this, there are many positive things happening. Latin American Christians are going as missionaries to the Middle East, where they are more accepted than North American missionaries. All but one of the reasons Catholics give for switching to Pentecostalism are positive. The top three were seeking a personal connection with God, seeking a different worship style, and wanting a greater emphasis on morality. In light of this trend, an important subset ministry is ethnomusicology, in which musicians create theologically sound, culturally appropriate hymns and songs for the church to use.

BELIEFS

Pentecostalism

Pentecostalism arose in America from a Methodist-Holiness tradition. Christians in this tradition sought a second blessing, or a second gift of the Holy Spirit following conversion. This blessing was believed to be an aid to holy living. In the Pentecostalism that emerged in the United States early in the twentieth century, speaking in tongues came to be seen as the sign of this blessing. During this same period, a number of Pentecostal groups began. At first they were looked upon with skepticism, even by others in the Holiness tradition. However, as Pentecostals moved into the mainstream by the middle of the twentieth century, they gained greater respect.

Pentecostal and Charismatic churches are diverse. They hold in common the belief in miraculous gifts such as tongues and healing. But many differences also exist. Initially, the gift of tongues was defined as the ability to speak in unknown foreign languages. However, tongues are now described as ecstatic speech rather than human languages. While most Pentecostals and Charismatics hold to the biblical doctrine of the Trinity, Oneness Pentecostals teach that God exists as a singular spirit who reveals Himself in many ways, including Father, Son, and Holy Spirit. Traditional Pentecostals continue to believe that the baptism of the Holy Spirit is a second blessing following conversion. Charismatics who are not from a Holiness background may hold that the baptism of the Holy Spirit occurs at conversion or at water baptism. Given this diversity, it is difficult to give a doctrinal description of Pentecostalism beyond noting the emphasis on the Holy Spirit and miraculous gifts.

Pentecostal church services appeal to people whose culture is emotional and colorful. With the additional aspects of being healed and finding wealth, the appeal to Latins is complete. Speaking directly to God and being able to talk to Him about their personal issues are two other reasons Latins have given for turning to Pentecostalism.

SECTION REVIEW

1. What two countries are responsible for colonizing the majority of South America?
2. What characterizes the governments of South America?
3. What are the two main economic alliances in South America? Why does one alliance outperform the other?
4. What countries have a majority of people of East Indian ethnicity? Why is that the case?
5. How do Latin Americans display their multiactive culture?
6. Why is Pentecostalism appealing to Latin Americans?

Aerial view of the city of Rio de Janeiro, Brazil, with the statue of Christ the Redeemer

GUIDING QUESTIONS

- How do South American economies and demographics affect how the citizens interact with the environment?
- What are the environmental issues of South America?
- What are the causes and the effects of environmental issues in South America?
- What are possible solutions to environmental issues in South America?

▾ *Solar plant in Chile*

INTERACTIONS OF PEOPLE AND PLACES

What are some of the challenges of living in South America?

Most of the governments and people of South America understand the need to protect the rainforest and to ensure the survival of the people and animals that call it home. Since the 1980s there has been an increasing amount of outside pressure and money given toward protecting the Amazon rainforest. With the fluctuation in governments, however, especially in Brazil, efforts to protect the rainforest have also fluctuated. Priorities change as economies stagnate and poverty grows.

Venezuela showed its commitment to the environment by having the largest percentage of protected land in the world. Most of the land was set aside between the 1950s and the '90s. Since then illegal mining and logging have persisted because the government lacks the will and resources to enforce the protection of the land.

The more wealthy countries have invested in renewable energy. Chile has massive solar power plants in the Atacama Desert. Colombia and Argentina have built new mass transit systems and improved their old ones. South America is a world leader in clean-energy public transport systems. Colombia is making efforts to protect its forests by increasing the amount of area designated as national parks by 31,000 square miles. The country hopes to bring an end to deforestation by 2030.

GLOBAL IMPACT | The Amazon Rainforest, the "Lungs" of South America

You may think that rain produces rainforests. Actually, it's the other way around. Rainforests produce rain as the leaves on trees "exhale" both water vapor and oxygen. This water vapor produces clouds that make rain. Though some rain comes from other places, the Amazon rainforest generates up to half the rainfall in the area.

But when we cut down too many trees in a rainforest, there's a point at which the rainfall that the remaining trees produce isn't enough to keep them alive. In fact, cutting down too many trees could eventually shrink the mighty Amazon. Cutting down 40 percent of the trees in the Amazonian rainforest could reduce precipitation in the area by 43 percent!

People need rainforests, not just for the health of the environment but also because they are beautiful. God wants us to enjoy and thrive in His resource-filled world. But He also wants us to wisely use those resources to meet the needs of people who bear His image while keeping a mind toward the future. When Brazil began monitoring the Amazon with satellite images in 2007, deforestation dramatically dropped. But in 2013, there was an uptick in deforestation as the Brazilian government loosened restrictions on protected lands around the Amazon.

1. What resources do the trees provide as they "exhale"?
2. How might cutting too many trees in the Amazon shrink the river?
3. How might a Christian worldview shed light on the problem of deforestation in the Amazon?

Interaction with the Environment

There are four main environmental issues in South America: polluted and overused water, deforestation, illegal mineral extraction, and how all of these issues affect the tribes that call the rainforests home.

Water

Many of Brazil's cities face water scarcity issues. The people of the cities like São Paulo, the largest city in South America, are suffering from having their water intermittently shut off. There are not enough reservoirs to keep the water during times of abundance. Rivers have raw sewage and chemicals flowing into them. In northern Colombia, the Wayúu people are suffering because the Ranchería River has been dammed and redirected to support coal extraction. The Riachuelo River on the edge of Buenos Aires is one of South America's most polluted rivers. It has had an average of 90,000 tons of heavy metals dumped into it every year.

▲ *Pollution along the banks of the Riachuelo River, Buenos Aires, Argentina*

Land

An increasing number of Brazilian settlers are moving into the rainforest, both legally and illegally, to exploit its riches—minerals, farmland, and lumber. Farmers have attempted to grow crops in the rainforest. A few cacao and rubber plantations thrive along the banks of the Amazon. You might think that heavy rainfall would make productive soil, but the soil is actually very thin. Insects and rapid decay deprive the soil of humus. In a process called **leaching**, constant rains dissolve nutrients in the soil and carry them away. Loggers are felling the forests to extract valuable hardwoods, such as mahogany and ebony. But because the trees hold the soil in place, deforestation is depleting the soil, rendering the land useless for future generations.

A major element in the early exploration of the continent was the search for gold. The same attitude continues today in many ways. People search for mineral wealth with no concern for the effect they have on the environment. Mining contributes to deforestation, scarred land, and lack of water.

The tribal peoples are part of the Amazon jungle, and they depend on it for their home. Their knowledge of the plants and animals of the rainforest is quite extensive. Their existence has been a major factor in holding back the development of the rainforest. But as the rainforests shrink and the tribes come into contact with illegal miners, cocaine traffickers, and loggers, they face extinction due to loss of their land. Other factors affecting the declining indigenous population are the exposure to different diseases which they have no immunity to and illegal invaders who fight against and even murder the indigenous people when they meet them.

Reasons for Environmental Issues in South America

As farms wear out the soil, the farmers look for more land to develop, and the demand for water increases. The world is looking to South America for its food. Brazil and Argentina are projected to be the top food suppliers by 2050, the main crops being soybeans, sugar, and cattle.

Brazil is rolling back laws protecting the forest. Governments have instituted selective logging rules in areas they want to keep as forest. But they have not been able to enforce them, so clear-cutting goes on. Bolivia has recently changed its policy and removed the special protected status of the large TIPNIS National Park so that a road for development access can be built.

Much of the problem stems from illegal mining and government's short-sightedness, trying to obtain wealth now in the cheapest way. There have been few efforts to develop less intrusive mining practices, and open-pit mining is widespread. Colombia, Ecuador, and Peru have been accused of routinely ignoring the negative environmental and social impacts of developing oil and gas fields.

There are three different views about the tribes living in the jungles. One is that they should not be interfered with but left to live as they have. The second view is that they are obstructing progress, that their land should be developed, and they should modernize or disappear. The third view is that these tribes are people, not zoo animals. They need and desire to hear the gospel. If no one reaches out to them, they will disappear, along with the rainforest. Those who hold this view believe there can be a balance between keeping the people group and their culture intact while introducing change.

Tribes living along the Pisqui River, Peru, are in danger as the forest shrinks.

Proposed Solutions

The solutions to the water issues are also solutions to deforestation since improved water management means less expansion of farmland areas. There have been some limited initiatives to help farmers conserve water. Some farmers are paid to implement "nature-based solutions" that copy natural processes, allowing water to be stored in the ground. Many farmers operate "water neutral," using only the water on their land.

Land conservation is one area where education and technology really could help. Farmers could learn improved farming practices, such as planting trees to hold back erosion and loss of soil. Although not the best solution, many indigenous peoples with more resources have resorted to vigilantism, protecting the rainforest themselves. In Colombia the former FARC rebels are being employed through a grant from Norway to protect the forests.

One solution to illegal mining and logging has been to provide indigenous and other peoples with a means of reporting instances so that they can raise awareness of the issue. South Americans have brought lawsuits against the international mining companies in the courts of their home countries, with limited success.

It seems inevitable that indigenous tribes will be affected by outside contact since the governments have already shown an inability to protect them. Even if they were left alone, continued malnutrition, infant mortality, and internal wars would likely mean their eventual extinction. Likewise, if their land was open for unfettered development, the tribes would become extinct. When tribes are presented with the gospel, they often accept it wholeheartedly because they have been living in fear of the spirits for centuries. As Christians come in, they also bring medical expertise, and as the people grow in their faith, negative aspects of their culture, such as child sacrifice and child marriage, cease, while the positive elements remain. With the provision of resources, indigenous Christians are able to reach out to uncontacted tribes. The tribes find economically viable means of survival and become strong advocates for the sustainability of the rainforest.

▲ *Arara indigenous chief Tatji patrols the Arara land in Para state, Brazil, to protect the forest.*

▲ *Locals selling souvenirs and handicrafts in Barcelos, Brazil*

SECTION REVIEW

1. How does the health of the economy affect what a South American country can do for the environment?
2. Why is the soil poor in the Amazon?
3. What responsibilities do governments have for the water supply?
4. Thinking back on earlier chapters, what are some other solutions to the problem of poor mine management in South America?
5. Why would tribal peoples be the best advocates for the rainforest?

08 CHAPTER REVIEW

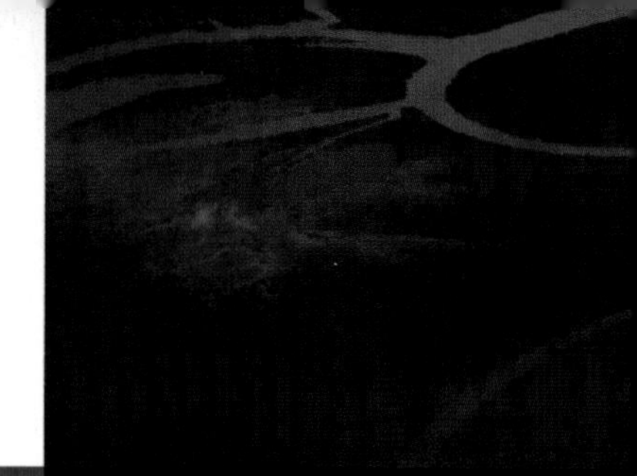

SUMMARY

1. South America has three highland regions and three lowland regions. The Andes are part of the "ring of fire" and were formed when the plates collided. The rivers are important to the survival of the forest and the continent. The climate is mostly tropical but is temperate in the higher altitudes. The continent is very rich in agriculture and mineral wealth.
2. South America's governments are generally fragile, historically oscillating between military and socialist dictatorships. The continent is split between two trade organizations, one that pursues more governmental control over the economy and one that is more free-market. The culture is multiactive, made up of diverse people. Violence is a negative heritage of the region. Although very strong, the Catholic church has been losing people to the Pentecostal church.
3. South America's environmental issues are numerous. The most important issue is preserving the Amazon rainforest. Illegal mining with no concern for the environment is a big problem. New methods in farming help to conserve water. The tribal peoples, who are the key protectors of the rainforest, are facing extinction. They need to hear the gospel.

Terms to Know

- ❑ Llanos
- ❑ Pampas
- ❑ escarpments
- ❑ estuary
- ❑ Intertropical Convergence Zone
- ❑ junta
- ❑ coup d'etat
- ❑ multiactive
- ❑ Carnival
- ❑ leaching

Making Connections

1. What are the two main factors impacting the climate of South America?
2. What are some of the most important exports of South America?
3. What are five different general ethnic regions in South America?
4. Considering the causes, what are some policies to stem the violence in South America?
5. Why is the Amazon rainforest so valuable?
6. What are good reasons for the leadership of South American countries to invest in water infrastructure?

Developing Geography Skills

1. Choose a city in South America to live in. Describe how your life would change if you moved there.
2. What lessons could Brazil learn from the United States in regard to settling its frontier?

Thinking Critically

1. Why do those concerned about the environment want Brazil to stop developing the Amazon? Should other nations have a say in Brazil's decisions?
2. How does a biblical worldview help make sense of Chile's economic success compared to Venezuela's economic failure?

Living in God's World

1. Imagine that you are a Christian missionary working among indigenous people in South America. Write a letter to an anthropologist who opposes your work on the grounds that you are corrupting the people's culture.
2. Compose a brief paragraph that explains why Christians should support the use of the earth's resources while also being concerned about the damaging effect of activities such as deforestation.

CASE STUDY | Two Cities Experiment with Gondola Lift Systems

Medellin, Colombia, was known as the drug and murder capital of the world. It had the highest murder rate in the 1990s. Both the rich and the poor feared for their lives. The rich hid their wealth so as not to get kidnapped for ransom, while the poor in the slums had to pay tribute to gangs for "protection."

Starting in 2000 the citizens elected city leaders who were determined to bring reform. The city incorporated the haphazard slums into the city proper, hoping to lower violence and poverty. The slums were built on the steep mountainside. The roads were narrow and built in a random fashion, which made it difficult for the residents to commute to work. The difficult location also gave the middle class no desire to journey there.

The centerpiece of this effort to include the slums was a gondola lift system that connected them with the central city metro system. The city also built an extensive series of escalators to bring people to the gondola station. Now a commute that had taken an hour could be done in less than 15 minutes. Along with the gondolas, the city built libraries, parks, and schools to attract the middle class to areas that were historically segregated between the rich and poor. As things changed, the people's attitudes also changed. They felt empowered to improve their community, not to just accept the poverty and violence.

Medellin became the shining example in Latin America for successfully bringing the people of notorious slums out of poverty. Many other South American nations sought to copy this model.

Rio de Janeiro, Brazil, has many of the same problems as Medellin. It has informal developments, segregated from the main city, where the poor people live. In 2011 the city built a gondola with the goal of including the *favela*, or slum, in the city and generally improving Rio before the Olympics. But the leaders did not make a comprehensive plan or include the residents in their planning as Medellin had. They hoped that the gondola would be the single solution. But the people lacked basic necessities, such as a sewer system. The city's geography also played a part in the gondola's failure since its beginning and ending points were not convenient for the residents. Today the gondola is not running and serves as a reminder that there are no easy solutions to the problems of the urban poor. Solutions require long-term commitment from both the city leaders and the residents.

1. How did violent crime affect everyone in Medellin?
2. In what two ways did the leadership of the city seek to help the people of the mountainside?
3. How would the ability to commute from the slums to the city for work bring money into the community?
4. What did the leaders of Rio neglect in their effort to change the slums?
5. What kind of city would a gondola benefit? Identify a specific one.

unit 4

GEODATA | Activity

Cultural Geography *Student Activities*

You will have the opportunity to complete a geodata activity for Europe and Russia in the Student Activities.

Background image:
River Moika in Saint Petersburg, with Saint Isaac's Cathedral in the background

EUROPE AND RUSSIA

chapter 09

NORTHERN EUROPE

192 Physical Geography
200 Human Geography
206 Interactions

BIG IDEAS

- What is the physical geography of Northern Europe like?
- How do the people of Northern Europe live?
- What are some of the challenges of living in Northern Europe?

Northern lights in Ilomantsi Sonkaja, Finland; Orthodox chapel

Saint Finbarr's Oratory on Barra Lake in West Cork, Ireland

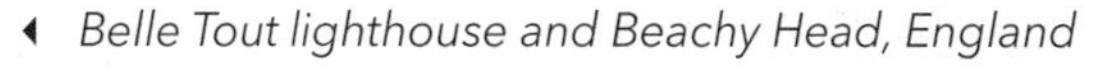

Belle Tout lighthouse and Beachy Head, England

Viking ship off the coast of Greenland

LAND OF THE VIKINGS

Imagine living along the coasts of Europe between the eighth and eleventh centuries AD and being in dread of the sudden appearance of Viking ships. With a fierce-looking dragon head at the bow, these ships carried brutal warriors who raided and terrorized towns near rivers or coasts all over Europe and beyond. During these three centuries, Vikings also seized territory, built settlements, and spread Nordic culture throughout Europe. Vikings contributed to the development of the English language, and the Nordic words *window*, *gang*, *angry*, *flaw*, and *threat* are part of our vocabulary. Vikings helped to spread commerce throughout Europe and reintroduced coinage for trade. Viking settlers also founded the Irish capital city of Dublin.

Ruins of Dunluce Castle in Northern Ireland

GUIDING QUESTIONS

- What are the regions of Northern Europe?
- What caused the landforms of Northern Europe?
- What bodies of water are important to Northern Europe?
- What are the climates of Northern Europe?
- What natural resources are found in Northern Europe?

Northern Europe consists of the British Isles and the countries of Scandinavia. Looking at a map, one might assume that most of northern Europe would be extremely cold because of its distance from the equator. However, this is not the case. A warm current from as far away as Central America warms northern Europe so that even the harbors of Norway remain ice-free year-round.

PHYSICAL GEOGRAPHY

Regions of Northern Europe

What is the physical geography of Northern Europe like?

UNITED KINGDOM

Great Britain, the largest island in Europe, lies at the heart of the United Kingdom. The United Kingdom also includes land on the neighboring island of Ireland as well as numerous smaller islands surrounding Great Britain. The United Kingdom sits astride northern Europe's major water routes. Off the east coast lies the North Sea, the main route to the peninsulas of Scandinavia. Between Great Britain and Ireland lies the choppy Irish Sea. South of Great Britain is the English Channel, a narrow body of water between the island and the European mainland.

REPUBLIC OF IRELAND

The Republic of Ireland covers 83 percent of the island of Ireland. Ireland's thin, rocky soil was caused by massive glaciers, the same forces that scraped New England. Although farther north than New England, Ireland's climate is much warmer. Ireland is consistently humid; about half of the time the weather is overcast. Regular rains drench the green countryside of the Emerald Isle.

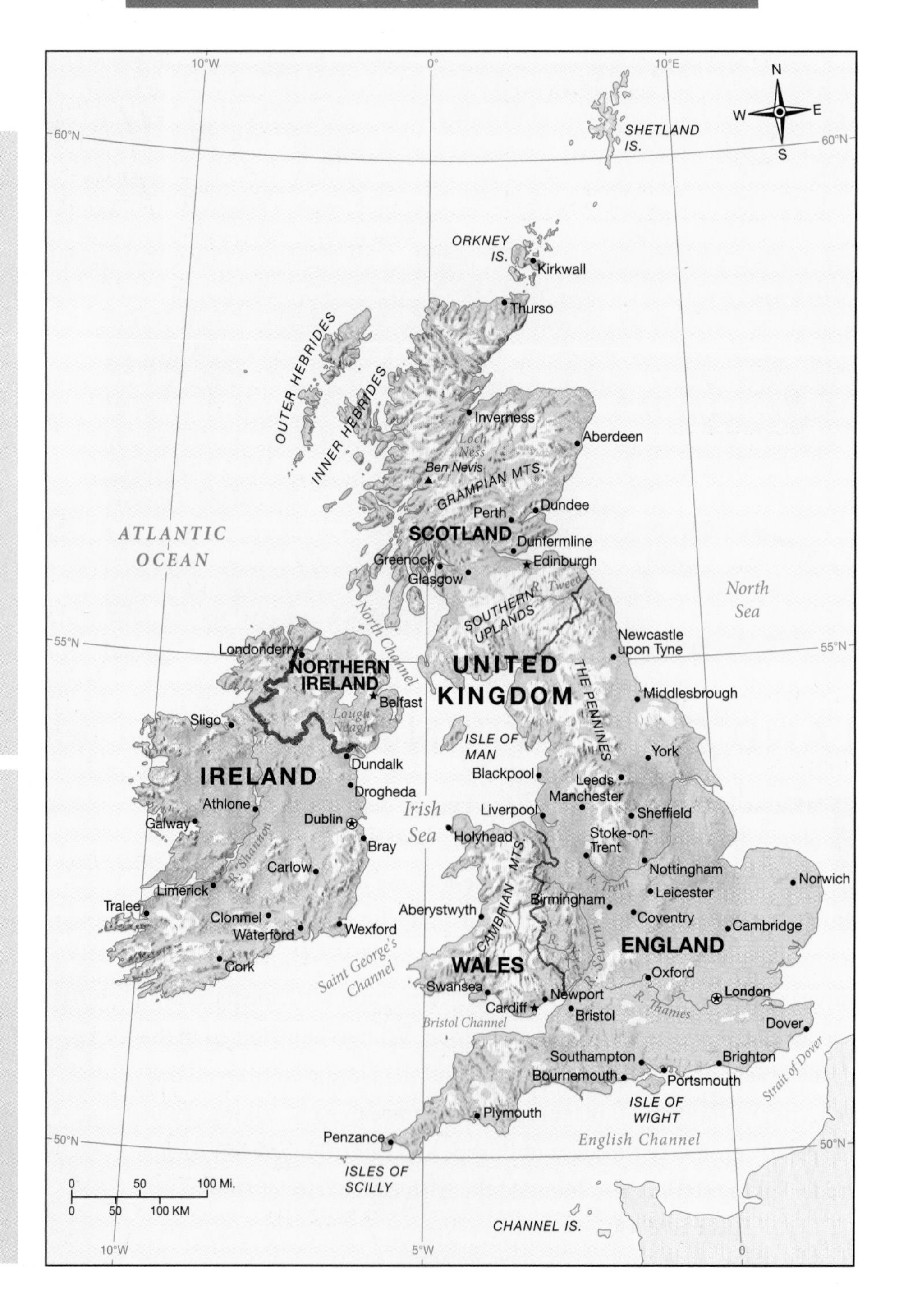

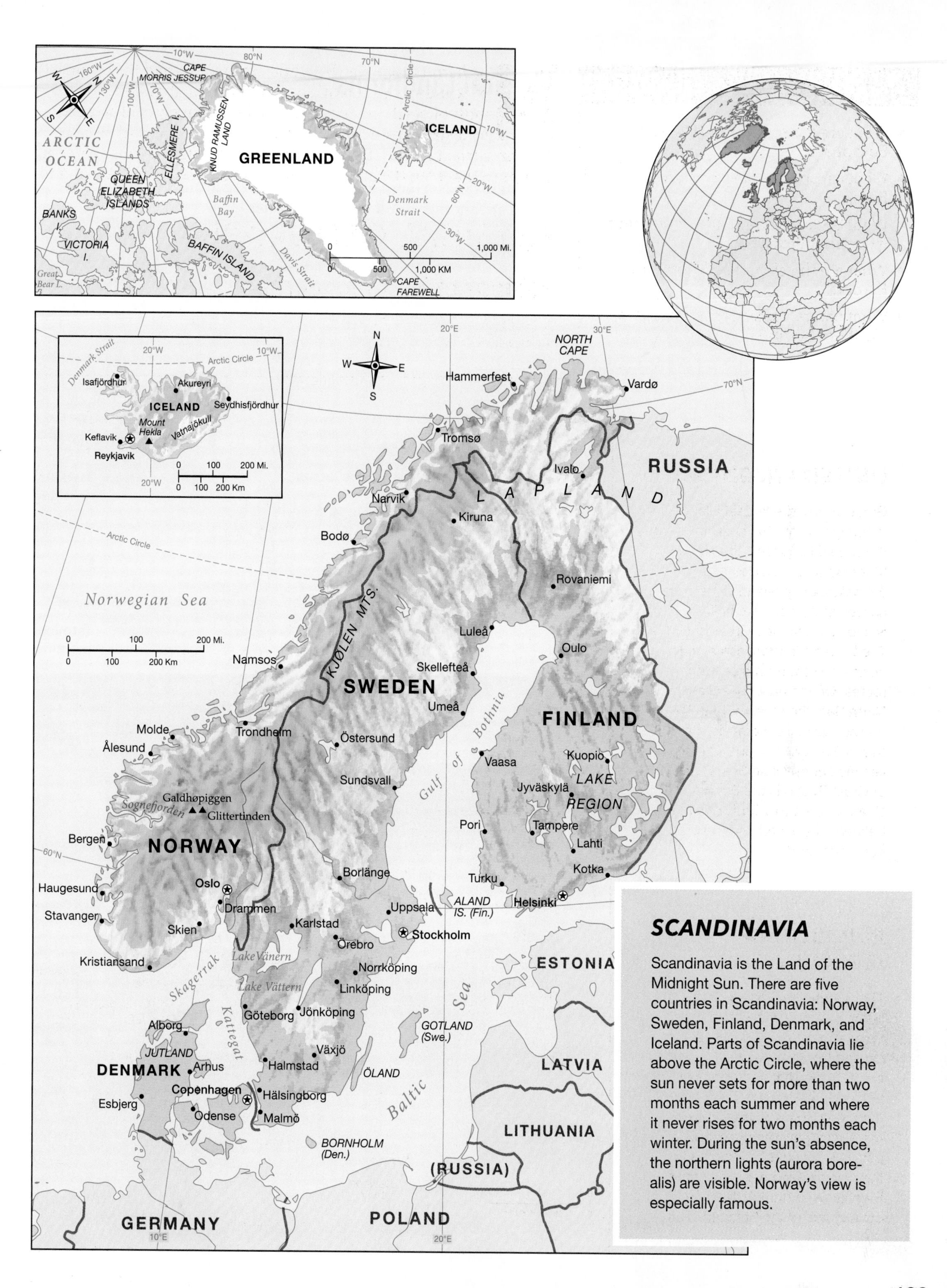

SCANDINAVIA

Scandinavia is the Land of the Midnight Sun. There are five countries in Scandinavia: Norway, Sweden, Finland, Denmark, and Iceland. Parts of Scandinavia lie above the Arctic Circle, where the sun never sets for more than two months each summer and where it never rises for two months each winter. During the sun's absence, the northern lights (aurora borealis) are visible. Norway's view is especially famous.

Physical Landforms

Plate Tectonics

Plate tectonics caused folding or faulting and formed many of the mountains in Northern Europe. Others were formed by volcanoes, which are another result of shifting plates.

Glaciers

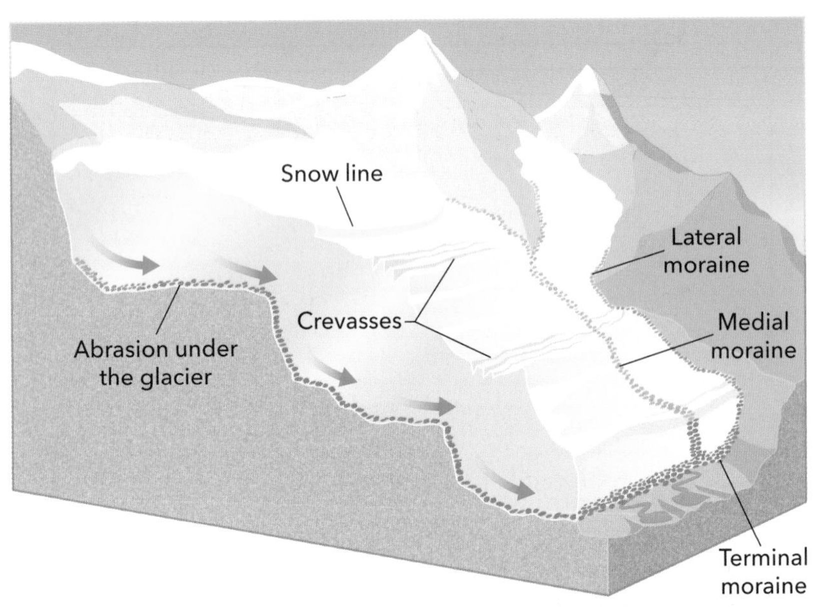

▲ ***Glaciers*** *cover about 11 percent of Iceland; the largest, Vatnajökull, is up to 1,300 feet thick.*

▼ *Glaciation scraped the plains and steepened the mountains.*

A ***fjord*** *is a long, narrow, deep inlet between steep cliffs that glacial motion carved into the land during the glacier's movement to sea level. Following the melting of the glacier, the fjord filled with sea water. Some fjords are over 4,000 feet deep.*

The Faroe Islands, Denmark, were formed by volcanic eruptions over many years.

Volcanoes

Iceland is very geologically active, with thirty volcano systems and many moderate earthquakes.

Strokkur Geyser in Iceland; a **geyser** is a hot spring that forcefully ejects hot water and steam from the ground at regular intervals.

CASE STUDY | Volcanoes in Iceland

Laying astride the Mid-Atlantic Ridge that separates the North American and Eurasian tectonic plates, Iceland has a long history of volcanic activity. Two recent eruptions are notable. Eyjafjallajökull is a small icecap of Iceland with an elevation of 5,417 feet above sea level. An extended eruption began in the spring of 2010 and was preceded by three thousand small earthquakes. When the volcano erupted in April, melting water from the icecap entered the volcano's vent, and the resulting steam caused an explosion that sent a cloud of volcanic ash high into the atmosphere. This plume of ash contaminated the atmosphere for hundreds of miles and disrupted air travel across Europe for days. By August 2010 the volcano had returned to a dormant state.

A second volcano, Bárðarbunga, is located under Vatnajökull, Iceland's most extensive glacier. It has an elevation of 6,591 feet above sea level. This volcano erupted in August 2014, accompanied by sixteen hundred earthquakes. Bárðarbunga released large volumes of sulfur dioxide, which negatively affected air quality across Iceland. However, because this volcano did not produce a significant amount of volcanic ash, air travel was not seriously affected. By February 2015 this volcano had also returned to a dormant state.

1. Why has Iceland had many volcanic eruptions?
2. What caused Eyjafjallajökull to explode?
3. How did Bárðarbunga's eruption adversely affect air quality?
4. In addition to recently erupting, what did these two volcanoes have in common?

Eyjafjallajökull volcano during an eruption

Bárðarbunga volcano

Bodies of Water

The many rivers of Northern Europe have been used for transportation over the centuries. Perhaps most famous in England is the River Thames, which flows across the southern region and through London. Lochs, deep and narrow lakes formed from glaciers, are found in Scotland. Lough Neagh, in Northern Ireland, is the largest freshwater lake in the British Isles.

The rivers of Norway, Sweden, and Iceland are less navigable due to the terrain. Norway and Iceland have magnificent fjords, and Norway has high waterfalls. Norway's bodies of water provide hydropower for production of electricity. Iceland's waters are geothermally heated to provide hot springs and energy for the country.

▲ *Lough Neagh in Northern Ireland*

The famous Loch Ness, home of the fabled Loch Ness monster ▶

In northern Sweden rivers descending from the mountains provide hydroelectric power for the nation. Sweden has lakes in the south that are connected by canals. This combination of lakes and canals enables transportation of goods and people across this region of the country.

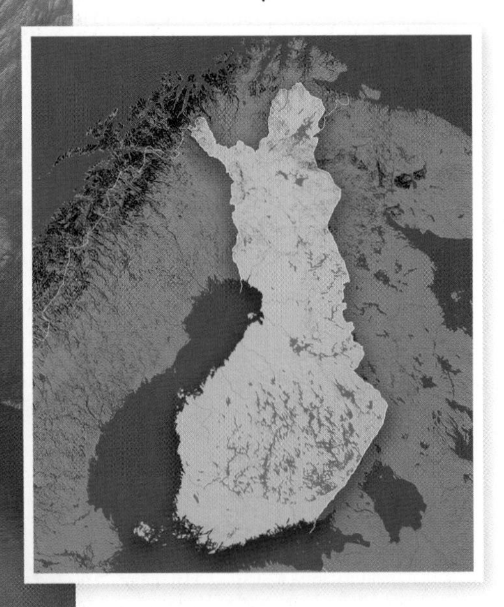

◀ *About 10 percent of Finland is covered with lakes and rivers that were carved by glaciers and filled with water by melting glaciers.*

◀ *Magnificent view of Kjerag rocky plateau, with waterfall and Lysefjord below*

Climates of Northern Europe

Climates in this region include marine west coast, humid continental, subarctic, and tundra. Local climates are affected by their proximity to the sea, elevation, latitude, and local topography. The climates of Northern Europe are moderated by the **North Atlantic Drift**.

The United Kingdom, Denmark, and some of the coastal areas of Norway and Sweden have a marine-west-coast climate. In general, their summers are warm and their winters are cool, but they avoid the extreme cold that many countries at the same latitude experience. Given their proximity to large bodies of water, these regions receive large amounts of precipitation, ranging from 20 to 98 inches per year.

▲ *Denmark has a strait called "The Great Belt" (see arrow on map) that effectively cuts the country into parts. In the 1990s a massive bridge was constructed that united the two regions of Denmark.*

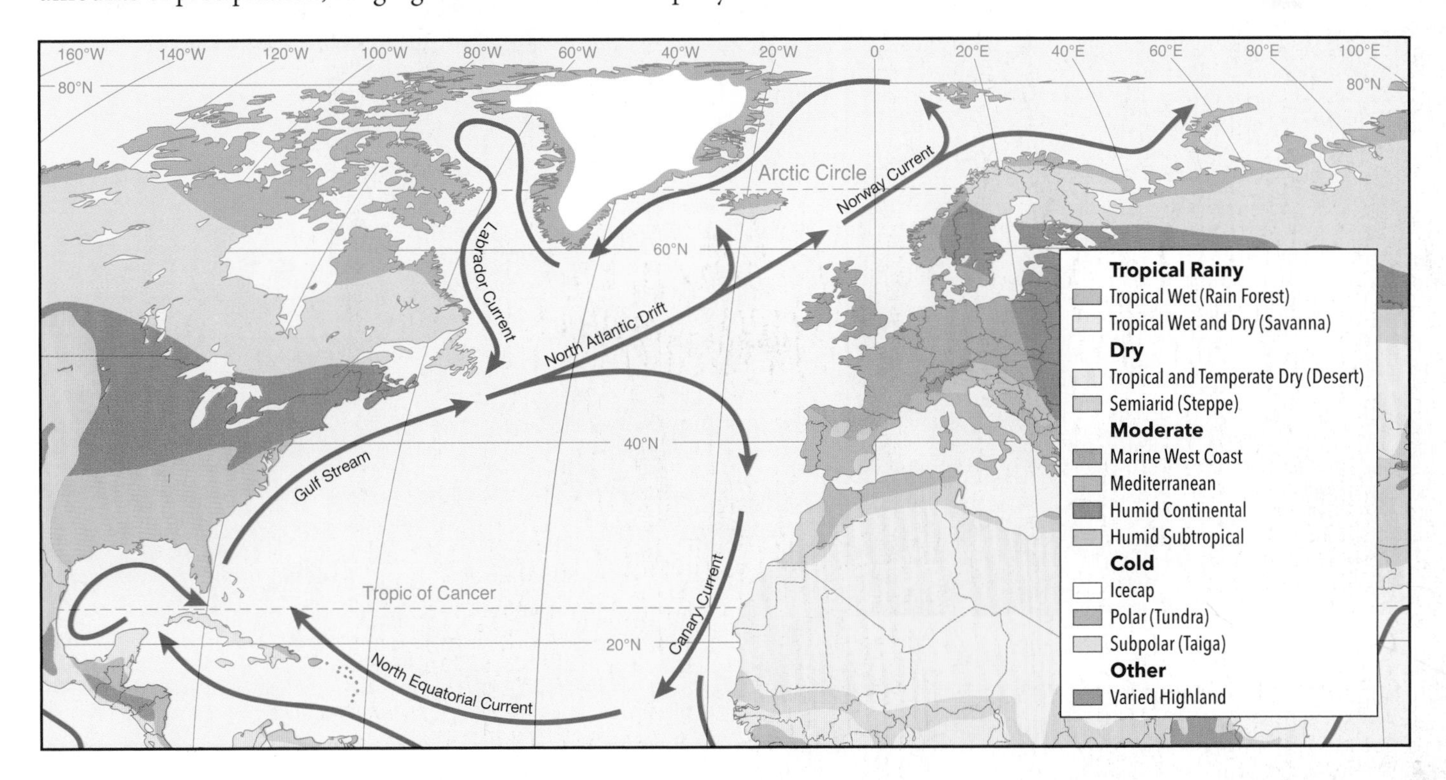

◂ *Lake Thorsø in Denmark has a humid climate.*

The southern parts of Sweden, Finland, and Norway have a humid continental climate. Summer temperatures range from 70° to 80°, while winter temperatures fall below freezing and are brisk and cold. These regions typically receive significant precipitation.

A subarctic or polar climate is found in the northern regions of Norway, Sweden, Finland, and the southern region of Iceland. Winters in this climate are long and extremely cold, while the summer is brief and cool or moderate. This climate receives little precipitation.

Tundra covers much of Iceland and Greenland. Limited vegetation can survive in this harsh climate, and the limited precipitation is mainly in the form of snow. Temperatures remain near or below freezing most of the year, and the short summers remain very cool.

Resources of Northern Europe

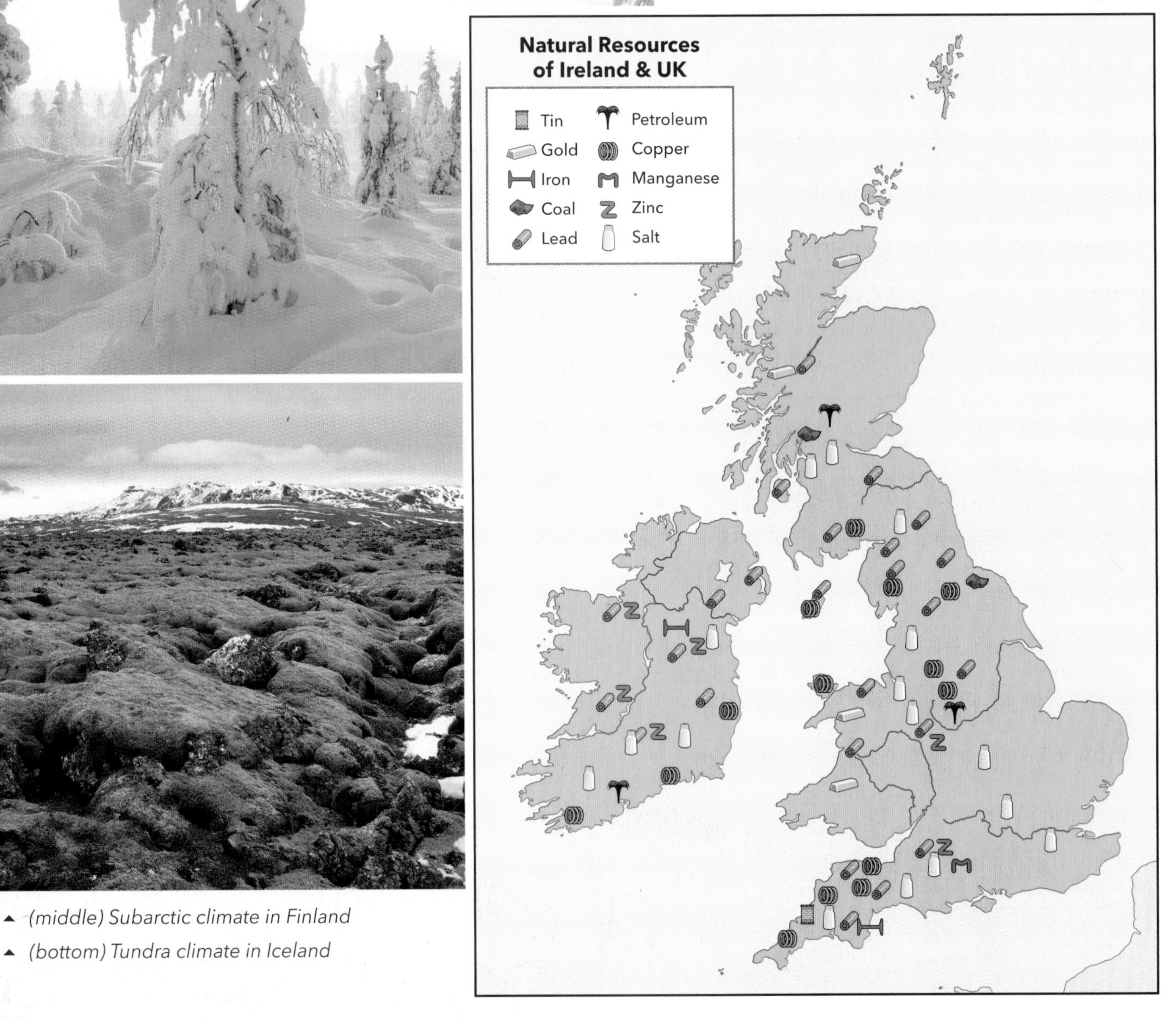

▴ *(middle) Subarctic climate in Finland*

▴ *(bottom) Tundra climate in Iceland*

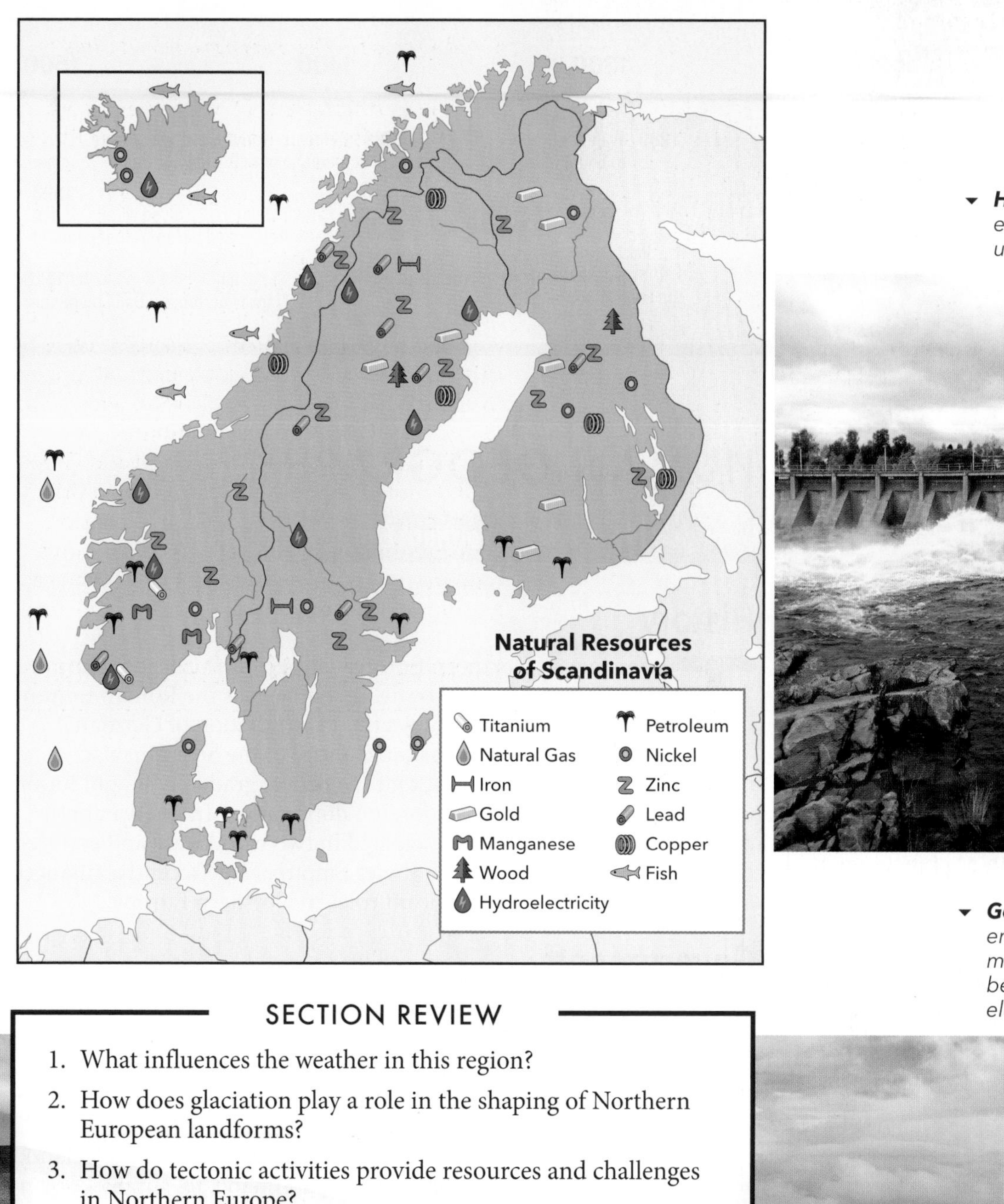

▾ ***Hydroelectric energy*** *is energy generated by the use of running water.*

▾ ***Geothermal energy*** *is the energy in steam heated by magma intrusions that can be harnessed to generate electrical power and heat.*

SECTION REVIEW

1. What influences the weather in this region?
2. How does glaciation play a role in the shaping of Northern European landforms?
3. How do tectonic activities provide resources and challenges in Northern Europe?
4. Why are there many kinds of climates in Northern Europe?
5. What do you think makes a body of water significant in Northern Europe?
6. What resources are common to most of the countries in Northern Europe?

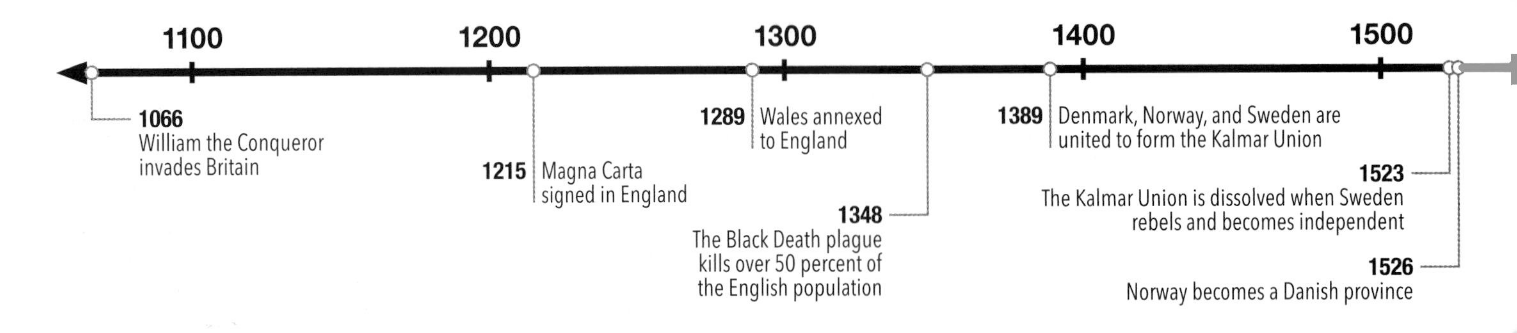

GUIDING QUESTIONS

- How has Northern Europe changed over time?
- How do the Northern European governments interact with their citizens?
- What is the economic health of Northern Europe?
- What are the demographics of Northern Europe?
- What are the cultural characteristics and diversity in Northern Europe?
- What forms of religion are practiced in Northern Europe?

HUMAN GEOGRAPHY

How do the people of Northern Europe live?

History

The history of Northern Europe has been influenced by immigration, invasion, and trade. As far back as the Roman Empire, the British Isles were subject to the migration of Germanic tribes and Roman invasion. Control of the Scandinavian nations also changed over time, and the people gradually fought for or negotiated their freedom from foreign domination. In the twentieth century, Northern Europe participated in two world wars and endured the threat of destruction by the Soviet Empire. More recently, alliances and trade have taken on significant roles in Northern Europe.

Governments

While there are subtle differences in forms of government, the people of Northern Europe all have some level of representation, and any remaining monarchies have become largely ceremonial. Great Britain has a parliamentary constitutional monarchy. Norway, Sweden, and Denmark have constitutional monarchies. Ireland has a parliamentary republic, and Iceland and Finland are simply known as republics.

All the nations in Northern Europe are also **welfare states**, states that assume primary responsibility for the social welfare of their citizens "from the cradle to the grave." While a government guarantee of economic welfare and medical care might sound attractive, it comes at a tremendous cost. These countries impose high taxes on their citizens in order to pay for the health care that government-controlled facilities are able to provide. Often government panels determine what level of care will be available, depending, in part, on age

▾ *Seat of the Danish Parliament in Copenhagen, Denmark*

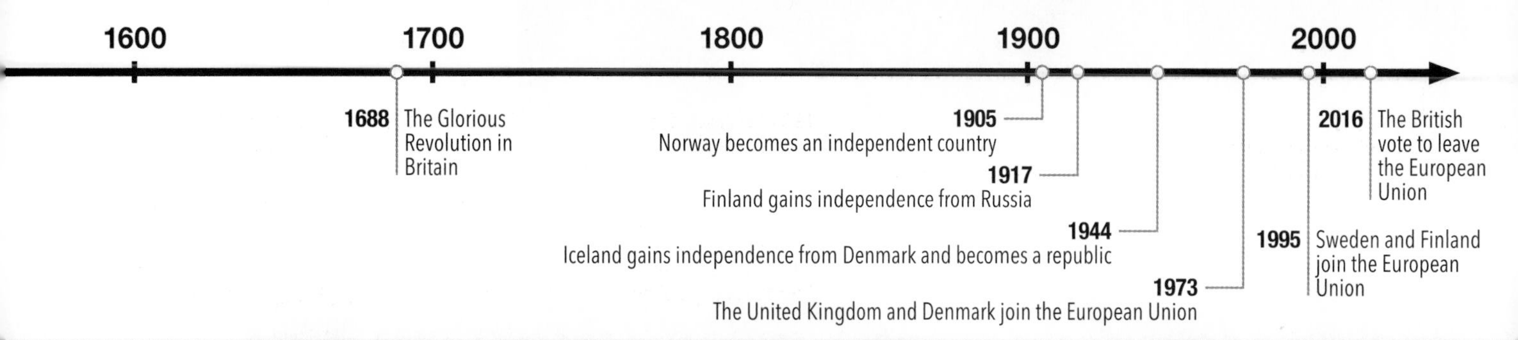

and cost. Private care is available only for those who can afford it. Those who have no choice but to use public health care often experience long waits to see a nurse, tolerate crowded conditions, have limited access to medical resources, and endure long delays in order to receive advanced testing or treatments.

A trend in Scandinavian countries is the conclusion that health care options must include **euthanasia**, or so-called "mercy-killing," in the form of physician-assisted suicide. During this process, patients either are given an injection that ends life quickly or are allowed to die slowly as a result of food and liquids being withheld. Even in Europe, questions about the morality of this procedure provoke continued debate.

Jaguar, British automobile

Economies

The United Kingdom's market economy is the largest economy in Northern Europe, with a GDP of nearly $3 trillion. As in all of the Northern European countries, most workers in the United Kingdom are employed in the services sector. Industries include the manufacture of machine tools, electrical power equipment, automation equipment, and railroad equipment. The United Kingdom also has thriving shipbuilding, aircraft, automobile, electronics and communication equipment industries.

Ireland also has a market economy and produces pharmaceuticals, various chemicals, and medical devices. Irish companies also build computer hardware and develop computer software. Ireland currently has the highest economic growth rate in Northern Europe.

Norway has a mixed economy that has benefited greatly from the discovery and development of petroleum and natural gas reserves. Industries include shipping, fishing, shipbuilding, pulp and paper products, timber, and mining. Norway is also a major smelter of aluminum from imported bauxite. This process requires an enormous amount of electricity, and Norway has a vast supply of electricity provided by the country's hydroelectric power plants.

Rolls Royce jet engine for the Airbus 350 aircraft

◂ *Saab JAS 39 Gripen jet fighter, manufactured in Sweden*

▾ *Ball bearing manufactured in Sweden*

Sweden has a mixed economy with recent fiscal restructuring that has led to a growing national prosperity. Industries include iron and steel, precision equipment, timber, pulp and paper products, and automobiles.

Denmark has a mixed economy that has developed a competitive export market. Industries include the manufacture of wind turbines, pharmaceuticals, medical equipment, pulp and paper products, iron and steel, and machinery and transportation equipment.

Finland also has a mixed economy. Industries include various metal products, electronics, different types of machinery and scientific instruments, and pulp and paper products. Finland is also a major builder of ships and has constructed some of the world's largest cruise ships.

▾ *Cruise ship originally manufactured in Finland*

▾ *Aerial view of Meyer Turku shipyard in Finland with a cruise ship under construction*

Iceland also has a mixed economy. While many Northern European nations have a significant income from tourism, Iceland has recently enjoyed a surge in this industry. Regular volcanic eruptions have attracted many people to this country. Industries includes fish processing, aluminum smelting, medical equipment, and pharmaceuticals.

Demographics

Most countries in Northern Europe have their own national language, although many of the people speak English or German in addition to their native tongue. Some minority groups, such as the Romani and Sami in Finland, have their own languages.

United Kingdom

In 2019 the estimated population in the United Kingdom was 66.9 million. Although the United Kingdom has many large cities, none rise to the level of a primate city. In each of the countries that compose the United Kingdom, the native populations of British, Scottish, Welsh, and Irish make up the combined majority. Minority groups include those from Africa, the Caribbean, Asia, Pakistan, and mixed.

Ireland

The physical island of Ireland is divided between the small region of Northern Ireland and the majority of the island, which is known as the Republic of Ireland or simply Ireland. Northern Ireland was settled by British Protestants in the seventeenth century. It remains a part of the United Kingdom. Most of the people living in Ireland identify with the Roman Catholic Church.

In 2019 the estimated population of Ireland was 4.8 million. The majority of the population is Irish. Minorities include people from other European countries, Asia, and Africa.

Scandinavia

In 2019 the combined estimated population of Scandinavia was 27 million, with Sweden having the largest population at 10 million and Iceland having the smallest population at 0.3 million. However, several cities in Scandinavian countries are primate cities. For example, Reykjavik, Iceland's capital, is home to half of the island's population. An astounding 80 percent of people in Sweden live in and around Stockholm, that nation's capital.

As in the United Kingdom, Scandinavian populations have majorities that are native to their countries. Minorities are composed of other Europeans, Russians, Turks, and refugees from war-torn regions such as Iraq and Syria.

Satellite image of Norway, Sweden, and Finland at night, with a red arrow pointing to Stockholm

The changing of the guard at the castle in Edinburgh, Scotland

Girls' football (soccer) teams compete in a public tournament in Sweden.

Sollus Highland Dancers on Derry Walls in Scotland

Culture and Diversity

Each country in Northern Europe has a distinct national culture. To whatever extent diversity within a country has occurred, it has often resulted from immigrants who have brought aspects of their culture with them. One characteristic of many Europeans is a love of sports, foods, and forms of music that reflect their particular culture. Northern Europeans also pride themselves on being tolerant of other cultures, as demonstrated by acceptance of refugees from other countries.

Scandinavians celebrate several unusual events. Finland and Sweden celebrate St. Knut's Day on January 13 and use this occasion to take down their Christmas trees and race around in sledges and sleighs. Denmark celebrates "30 and Unmarried" by giving titles and gifts to singles in their community. A single woman is called a "Pepper Maid," and a single man is called a "Pepper Man." The unmarried are given a pepper shaker on the eve of their thirtieth birthday. The contest known as the "wife-carrying competition" began in Finland and has become very popular in Scandinavia. As one might expect, male contestants carry their wives on their shoulders and race to be the first to cross the finish line.

Major Religions of the UK

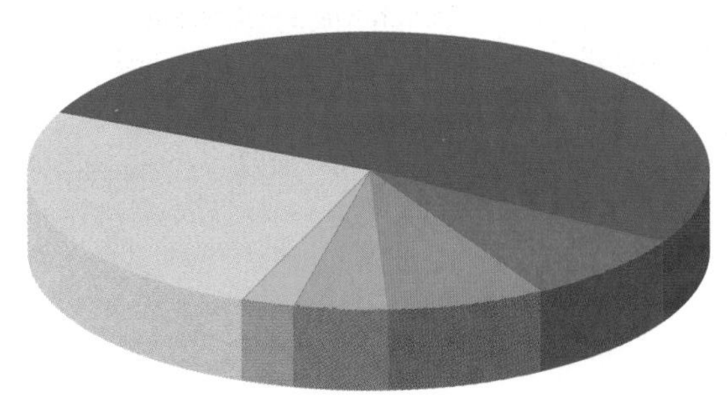

Protestant	**51.9%**
Protestant Evangelical	**7.9%**
Roman Catholic	**7.7%**
Islamic	**4.4%**
Hindu	**2.4%**
Unaffiliated	**25.7%**

Religion

With the exception of Ireland, Northern Europe has historically been primarily Protestant. However, the trend is toward non-Christian forms of religion or practical secularism. Prevalence of some form of Christianity in Northern Europe ranges from 67.5 percent in the United Kingdom to 90 percent in Iceland. Those indicating no religious connections vary from 8.6 percent in Iceland to 30 percent in Sweden. The recent arrival of immigrants from Islamic countries has contributed to a growing Muslim population.

Among young people between the ages of sixteen and twenty-nine in Northern Europe, religion is becoming irrelevant, and they would identify as being nonreligious. One reason for this decline is the failure of parents to pass on a religious identity to their children. One consolation is that those who remain active in church tend to be committed to their faith.

BELIEFS

Secularism

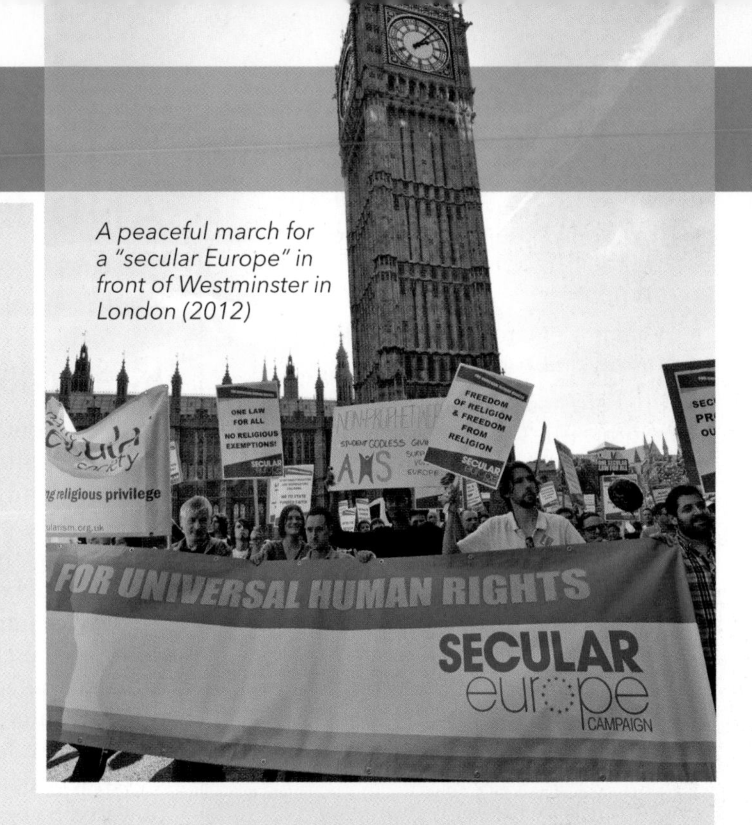

A peaceful march for a "secular Europe" in front of Westminster in London (2012)

Secularism may be defined as a belief system that rejects or excludes religion. Secularism emerged in Europe as a response to the wars of religion. Secularists thought that if religious reasoning could be excluded from politics, law, education, and anything else that a society does together, then religious wars would cease. Religious people could still attend places of worship, and they could talk about their religions among themselves. But religion would be banished to the private sphere. In public, religion would have no place. A neutral secularism would keep the peace between warring religions.

Proponents of secularism also proposed a "secularization thesis," which stated that as the world modernized, religion would wither away. Religion would no longer be needed to explain how the world works or to give moral reasons for how people ought to live. Science could provide these answers. But in the last decades of the twentieth century, several prominent sociologists noticed that the secularization thesis simply was not true. At first the United States was singled out as the exception to the rule. Though their country is modern and technologically advanced, large numbers of Americans are not only religious but also believe that their religion (often evangelical Christianity) speaks to every aspect of their lives. It soon became clear that Western Europe was the real exception in the world. The rest of the world is becoming more religious while Western Europe (and American higher education) clings to secularism.

This raises the question of why secularization has failed. In the first place, secularization is not inevitable, as its proponents claimed. Where secularization has flourished, it has done so because its supporters gained positions of influence and power. This highlights the second failure of secularism. Secularism claims to be a neutral place of common ground in contrast to various religions. But secularism is not neutral. It has its own ideology. It dictates which areas of life religion can speak to and in which areas it must be silent. It bars some voices from speaking in the public square. Secularism is willing to protect religion as long as religion is irrelevant. But when a Christian argument is mounted in public, the secularist shuts down the discussion. But this raises a third problem with secularism. Secularists want to refer to justice, equality, liberty, and other such concepts. But what do these concepts mean? Secularism cannot answer this question. There is no value-neutral formula for determining what is just. Moral and religious meaning must be smuggled in somehow.

Philosopher and Harvard professor Michael Sandel notes, "Asking democratic citizens to leave their moral and religious convictions behind when they enter the public realm may seem a way of ensuring toleration and mutual respect. In practice, however, the opposite can be true. Deciding important public questions while pretending to a neutrality that cannot be achieved is a recipe for backlash and resentment. A politics emptied of substantive moral engagement makes for an impoverished civic life. . . . To achieve a just society we have to reason together about the meaning of the good life, and to create a public culture hospitable to the disagreements that will inevitably arise."

SECTION REVIEW

1. How has Northern Europe changed over time?
2. How do the Northern European governments interact with their citizens?
3. How would you describe the economies of Northern Europe?
4. Describe the demographics of Northern Europe.
5. What are some cultural characteristics and examples of diversity in Northern Europe?
6. How have the patterns of immigration to Northern Europe affected its culture and religion?

INTERACTIONS OF PEOPLE AND PLACES

What are some of the challenges of living in Northern Europe?

GUIDING QUESTIONS

- How do Northern European economies and their people interact with the environment?
- What are environmental issues in Northern Europe?
- What are causes and effects of environmental issues in Northern Europe?
- What are possible solutions to environmental issues in Northern Europe?

Interaction with the Environment

About 33.5 million people in a variety of jobs constitute the workforce of Great Britain, and millions more work in Ireland and Scandinavia. As in other countries studied to date, the people produce large quantities of goods and services each year, gather and process vast amounts of resources, and transport them to markets all over the world. The manufacturing industry and the service industry power the Northern European economies, and in doing so these labors affect the environment. Actions that directly or indirectly affect the environment include the usual suspects: mining, drilling, automobile and factory exhaust, logging, and combustion of various fuels to produce energy.

Much industry and energy production in the United Kingdom is powered by coal-fired plants. This has produced dangerous levels of air pollution. In addition, outside the urban areas many homes are heated by low-grade coal that produces significant pollution. Another source of heat in many homes is **peat**, which is inexpensive but smoky. Burning of peat, or dense layers of partially decayed plant material, is also believed to release significant amounts of carbon dioxide into the air.

Most Scandinavians are very sensitive about their interaction with the environment and work to minimize any negative impact. As a result, Finland is known as one of the cleanest environments in the world.

(top) Men cutting peat from a bog in Ireland

(bottom) A peat-turf fire in Ireland

An automated waste collection system in Helsinki, Finland

Reasons for Environmental Issues

United Kingdom and Ireland

Water

As in other developed nations, water in the United Kingdom and Ireland is polluted by chemicals from industry and agriculture. Given the concentrated populations, filtering water to make it safe for human consumption remains an enormous challenge.

Air

Industrial cities in these countries play a major role in air pollution. In fact, the twelve cities in the United Kingdom with the greatest air pollution are all major industrial cities. Of course, automobiles also produce significant air pollution. It is interesting to note that the term *smog* was first used to describe the air in London.

Land

In addition to the environmental impact of construction, mining, and waste management, erosion remains an ongoing problem. During World Wars I and II, the United Kingdom experienced major deforestation, and the wooded land was reduced to about 5 percent. By way of contrast, during this same period, other Northern European countries retained from 25 to 75 percent wooded land. Currently about 13 percent of the United Kingdom and about 10 percent of Ireland is wooded. (Following World War II, the United Kingdom and Ireland designated areas of **green space**, an area of grass, trees, or other vegetation set aside in an urban area.)

▾ *(top) Green space in London, England*
▾ *(bottom) Smog in London (2014)*

Scandinavia

The Scandinavian countries have experienced significant water pollution in the form of acid rain from other countries. In addition, these countries have to contend with pollution caused by runoff of chemicals from industry.

As with water pollution, most of the air pollution in Scandinavia originates in the United Kingdom and other industrialized European nations. Using hydroelectric and geothermal power, the Scandinavian countries have been able to minimize their own negative impact on the air and water.

Proposed Solutions

The countries of Northern Europe have developed economies and the financial resources to maintain current solutions and develop future solutions to various forms of pollution. All are committed to reducing water and air pollution and are actively working to develop or increase clean sources for energy.

United Kingdom and Ireland

The United Kingdom has determined that diesel-powered vehicles are significant air polluters. The government is working with industries to replace these vehicles with electric and hybrid cars. Of course, cleaner sources of electricity production will be key to the expansion of electric vehicles. Plans in the United Kingdom are underway to shut down or convert coal-fired energy plants by 2025. An additional source of clean energy is the increased use of windmills, in part by developing windmill farms at sea. Ireland is drilling deep wells to access geothermal energy as another source of energy.

Efforts are also underway to increase the rate of reforestation in the United Kingdom, with a goal of achieving 15 percent of land as wooded by 2060. Support is growing in Ireland as well for an increased percentage of wooded land.

Scandinavia

Scandinavia's wealth of energy-producing resources through hydroelectric and geothermal power provides these countries with a major advantage in clean energy production, with the result of minimal water and air pollution. In addition, Denmark and others have developed effective windmill technology to capture the wind's energy and turn it into electricity.

Scandinavian countries have been proactive in the areas of sustainability planning. Legislation to protect forestry has been in place about one hundred years and has resulted in significant improvement in wooded land. Careful management of the forests has enabled Scandinavian countries to maintain thriving timber, wood pulp, and paper industries while maintaining a healthy percentage of wooded land.

▲ *Reforestation on a Norwegian hillside*

SECTION REVIEW

1. What are three environmental issues in Northern Europe?
2. Distinguish how the different countries of Northern Europe have responded to the problem of deforestation.
3. Explain how the economies and people of Northern Europe have interacted with the environment.
4. In addition to what you find in the text, what solutions to current environmental issues in Northern Europe would you propose?

CHAPTER REVIEW

SUMMARY

1. The physical geography of Northern Europe was shaped by tectonic activity, volcanic activity, and glaciation. Various natural features provide great sources of energy as humans harness these resources.
2. The people of Northern Europe are varied by nationality and yet similar in the enjoyment of common activities, including sports, ethnic foods, and regional music. These societies are highly developed, and the people are exceptionally productive.
3. A major challenge of living in Northern Europe is wise use of human and natural resources that enables the building of strong economies without damaging the environment.

Terms to Know

- ❑ glacier
- ❑ fjord
- ❑ geyser
- ❑ North Atlantic Drift
- ❑ hydroelectric energy
- ❑ geothermal energy
- ❑ welfare states
- ❑ euthanasia
- ❑ secularism
- ❑ peat
- ❑ green space

Making Connections

1. How has religion in this region historically influenced culture?
2. Describe what causes a fjord.
3. What resource is required to extract aluminum from bauxite? What two Scandinavian countries have the resources to efficiently perform this process?
4. How has geothermal energy impacted Scandinavia?
5. Why is secularism not a neutral ideology?
6. Why do you think many of the countries in this region have a mixed economy?
7. Identify political issues in Northern Europe.

Developing Geography Skills

1. What is the relationship between landforms and the distribution of population in this region?
2. How has glaciation affected the landforms of Northern Europe?

Thinking Critically

1. Evaluate euthanasia from a Christian worldview.
2. What should a Christian think of secularism based on what the Bible teaches?

Living in God's World

1. Evaluate the secular understanding of liberty from a biblical worldview. What happens to a society when a biblical view of liberty is rejected in favor of a secular view?
2. As a Christian, do you think it would be better to live in a welfare state or one that has limited provisions for those in need? Why?

NORTHERN EUROPE

List your answers on a separate sheet of paper.

1. ____ Norway
2. ____ Sweden
3. ____ Iceland
4. ____ Finland
5. ____ Denmark
6. ____ Ireland
7. ____ Greenland
8. ____ Northern Ireland
9. ____ England
10. ____ Scotland

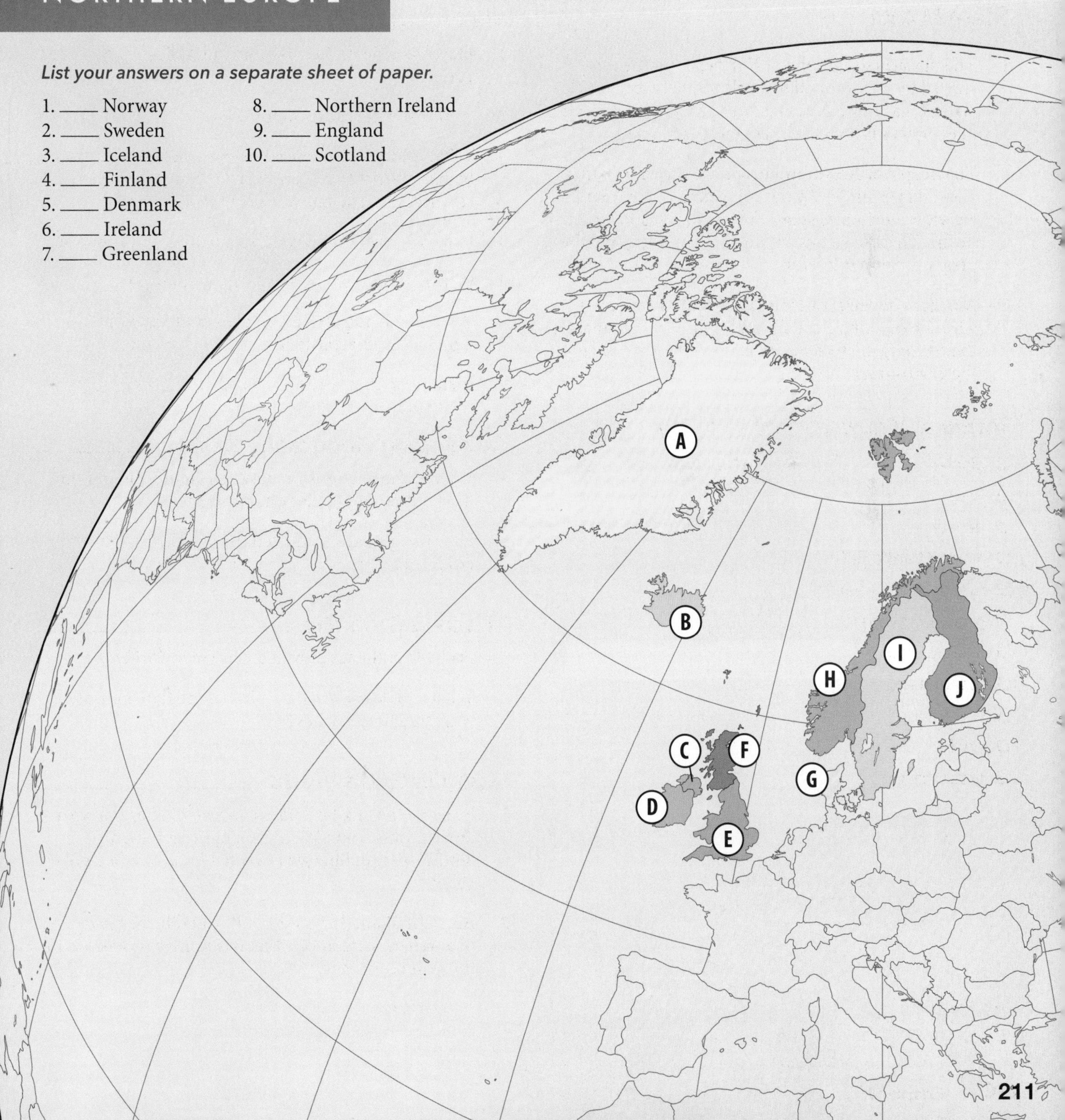

chapter 10

CONTINENTAL WESTERN EUROPE

214 | Physical Geography
222 | Human Geography
230 | Interactions

BIG IDEAS

- What is the physical geography of Continental Western Europe like?
- What are the people of Continental Western Europe like?
- What are some of the challenges of living in Continental Western Europe?

▲ *The Prinsengracht canal, Amsterdam, the Netherlands*

▲ *The Victory Column in Berlin's Tiergarten park, Germany*

▲ *Saint Stephen's Cathedral, Vienna, Austria*

CAFÉ CULTURE

The sidewalk café is an iconic institution in France. Cafés first appeared in Paris in the seventeenth century. French intellectuals gathered at these "coffee shops" to discuss new ideas. The name *café* comes from what was originally the only item served, *café au lait* (coffee made with steamed milk). Since that time cafés have expanded their menus, but the concept of a place with a pleasant atmosphere for patrons to slow down, watch passersby, read a book, or socialize with friends remains the same.

On the evening of November 13, 2015, a series of coordinated terrorist attacks in Paris targeted the people at cafés. Many people were killed and injured. In the days immediately following the attacks, the cafés were empty, but the people regained their courage. "Je suis en terrasse" (I am on the café terrace) became the slogan used to defy terrorists. By returning to their café tradition, the people were sending a message that the terrorists had not won.

▼ *The Le Bon Georges Café, Paris, France*

◀ *The Matterhorn rises above Zermatt City, Switzerland.*

Continental Western Europe's largest nations are France and Germany. The region has a rich heritage. Germany is the home of the Reformation, and France had an instrumental role in early US history. Western Europe has unsurpassed cultural achievements in art, music, and architecture. During the twentieth century, the European continent was turned upside down by militarists, Fascists, and Communists. As Europeans look forward to the middle of the twenty-first century, the region faces many challenges. The only thing certain is that there will be change.

GUIDING QUESTIONS

- What are the regions of Continental Western Europe?
- What caused the landforms of Continental Western Europe?
- What bodies of water are important to Continental Western Europe?
- What is the climate of Continental Western Europe, and how does it relate to its location on the globe?
- What are the natural resources of Continental Western Europe?

PHYSICAL GEOGRAPHY

Europe is called a peninsula of peninsulas because it is a large peninsula jutting off Asia with many other peninsulas extending off the main one. This chapter covers the part of Western Europe that lies in the middle of the main peninsula. There are four physical regions in Europe. As one moves from north to south, the elevation rises.

Regions of Continental Western Europe

What is the physical geography of Continental Western Europe like?

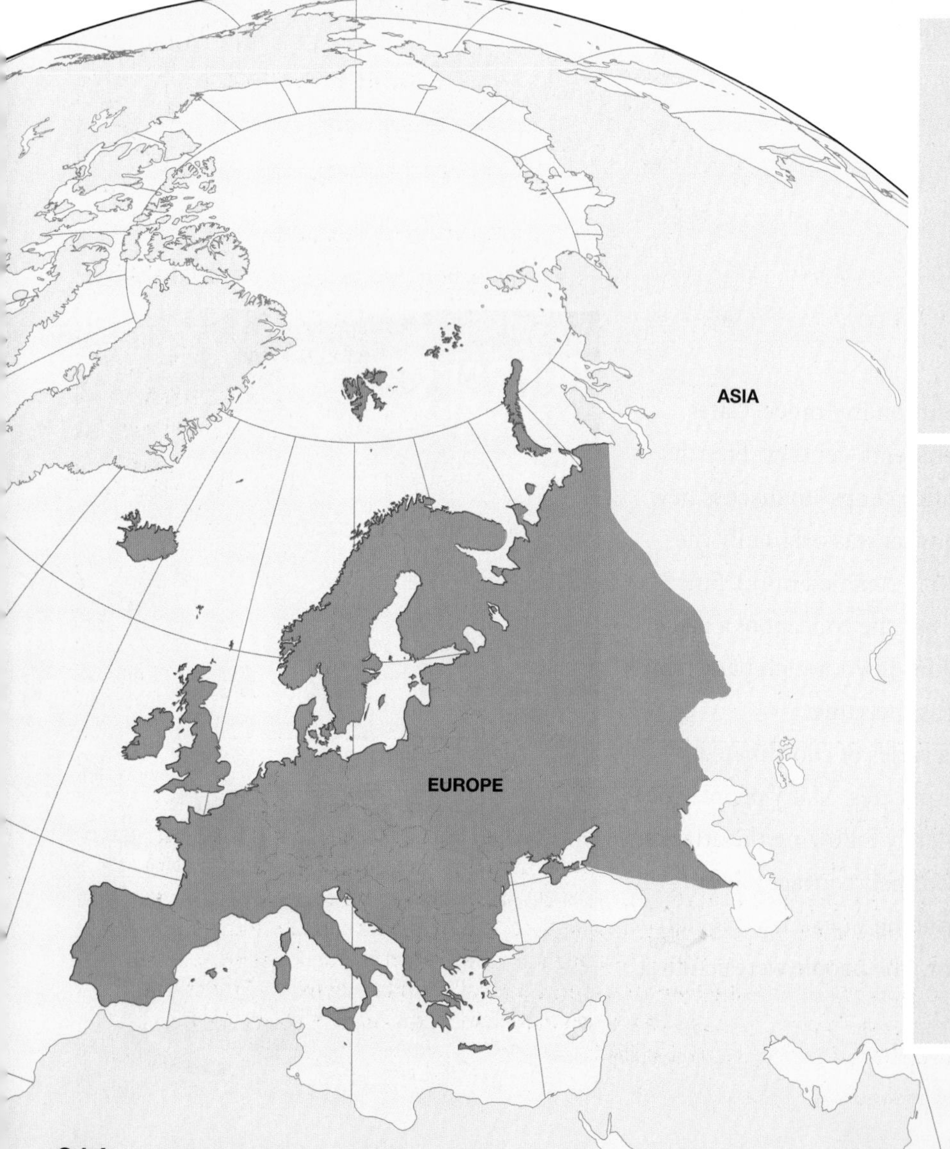

THE WESTERN UPLANDS

The Brittany Peninsula of France is the only area in Continental Western Europe that is part of the western uplands. It is characterized by rocky and rugged cliffs facing the English Channel. Historic Normandy is the eastern border of the upland region. Normandy was the location of the Allied invasion in France during World War II on June 6, 1944.

THE CENTRAL UPLANDS

The central uplands is a series of plateaus, hills, and low mountains. The system begins with the Massif Central of France and stretches through the low Jura Mountains of Switzerland. This region includes the Ardennes, a series of forested rolling hills in Luxembourg and southern Belgium. The uplands advance eastward covering most of Germany, all of Czechia (also known as the Czech Republic), northern Austria, and Poland. The Black Forest in the southwest along the French border was so named because in the Middle Ages the forests of fir and pine were so dense they appeared dark.

THE GREAT EUROPEAN PLAIN

The Great European Plain covers the north of the European continent, extending from France, through Russia, all the way to the Ural Mountains. This is the largest physical region of Europe. It includes the low countries of the Netherlands and Belgium, so called because the land is flat and mostly below sea level. The plain covers the northern half of Germany. It continues around the central uplands of France, creating a corridor called the Aquitaine Basin, which borders the Pyrenees and ends at the Mediterranean Sea. The Great European Plain is the geopolitical superhighway of Europe since over the centuries it has been the route of invaders.

THE ALPINE MOUNTAIN SYSTEM

The Alpine Mountain system forms a great snowy barrier severing the southern peninsulas of Europe from the rest of the continent. It is the third-largest mountain system in the world. The Alps are the principal mountains in this system, extending from France all the way to Albania. They are grouped into three main divisions: the Western Alps, Central Alps, and Eastern Alps. The Western Alps lie in France and Italy, while Switzerland contains the Central Alps. The Eastern Alps spread south from Germany, across Austria, and into Eastern Europe. Between Switzerland and Austria is the tiny principality of Liechtenstein, located on the east side of the Rhine River. The Alps descend into the Mediterranean Sea and form the French island of Corsica, while the Pyrenees form a natural boundary between France and Spain. These two mountain ranges are separated by the Aquitaine Basin.

Physical Landforms

The Massif Central is a series of small mountains and plateaus. It was formed through volcanic activity.

Caves like this one, the Grotto Cave on the French/Swiss border, are common in this area. The nearby Gouffre Mirolda is the deepest cave in Europe.

Polders *are parcels of low-lying land reclaimed from the sea through the use of* ***dikes****.*

Mont Blanc, near the Italy/Switzerland border, is the highest mountain in the Alps at 15,771 feet.

The Verdon Gorge in southern France was formed by the Verdon River. It is one of the largest canyons in the world.

The Alps were formed as the African tectonic plates collided with the European tectonic plates.

(top) The Danube River and modern Vienna, Austria

(middle) The Rhine River in the Ruhr Valley, Germany

Bodies of Water

Continental Europe is surrounded by a number of seas. The Baltic Sea is in the north, and Germany is the only country in this region to have access to this sea. Because the channel between the Atlantic and the Baltic is narrowed by the Danish islands of Sjaelland and Fyn, Germany built a shortcut, the Kiel Canal, through its interior which connects the North Sea to the Baltic Sea. Germany, the Netherlands, and Belgium have coasts on the North Sea. The Netherlands reclaimed much of its land from this sea. A popular saying claims that "God created the earth, but the Dutch created the Netherlands." Belgium has done the same to a lesser extent. France by far has the most access to the open sea. Between Britain and France is the English Channel. In the southwest is the Bay of Biscay, and south of France is the Mediterranean Sea.

The navigable rivers of Europe were elemental to its success since it is a continental region and many of the areas are landlocked. The rivers are important for trade, transportation, and agriculture production.

The Danube is the second-longest river in Europe and is classified as an international waterway. The river begins in the Black Forest in Germany, passes through Austria and Eastern Europe, and drains into the Black Sea. Vienna, the capital of Austria, is built on its banks.

The Elbe is another important river for Germany, flowing the opposite direction of the Danube. It begins in Czechia and flows through the heart of eastern Germany and into the North Sea. It served as part of the border between democratic West Germany and Communist East Germany.

The Rhine River begins in Switzerland, forms part of its border with Germany, and flows through several important regions of Germany.

The village of Silvaplana and Lake Sils, Switzerland

The Seine River flows through the middle of Paris, France.

It also forms part of Germany's border with France before it winds west into the Netherlands. At the lower end of the river, where the Ruhr River flows into the Rhine, is an industrial megalopolis called the Ruhr, the largest industrial region in Europe.

The Loire is the longest river in France. It begins in the Massif Central, flows north, forms an estuary in Nantes, and empties into the Bay of Biscay. The Loire River valley is famous for its vineyards.

The Seine River, France's second longest, begins in the central uplands and flows north into the English Channel. The Seine is known as the river of Paris since it flows through the center of the city.

The water from the snowcapped Alps drains west into the Rhône River, which flows south into the Mediterranean Sea. The Rhône River valley was historically the main overland route between Mediterranean Europe and Continental Western Europe.

Alpine lakes are the most important bodies of water in Switzerland and Austria. Glaciers gouged out several long, narrow lake basins on the Swiss plateau. The two largest are Lakes Constance and Geneva, at each end of the plateau. The Rhine and the Rhône flow from these lakes, respectively. Other large lakes include Lake Neuchâtel, Lake Lucerne, and Lake Zurich.

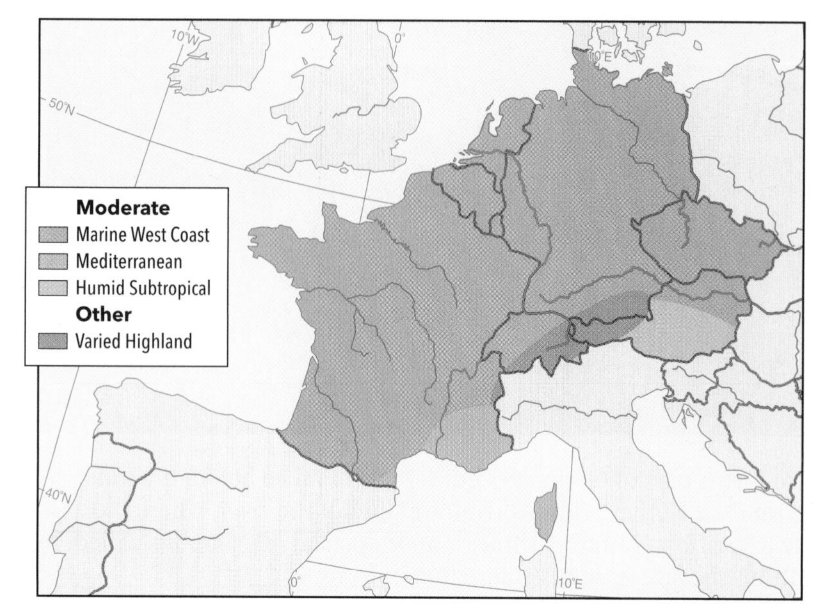

Climates of Continental Western Europe

Continental Western Europe sits high in the northern latitudes between 43°N and 55°N. The northern United States and southern Canada share these latitudes, but Western Europe does not share the same climate as those places since it is exposed to westerly winds that moderate the temperature. It has a marine-west-coast climate. Paris and Amsterdam do not receive much snow in the winter since they lie near the sea. As one moves further inland, the continental climate becomes stronger, making for greater extremes between the winter and the summer.

In the Alps people can experience a warm, dry wind in the winter, called a **foehn**, which blows in from the south. This is similar to the Chinook winds in Canada. Although the winds keep the climate mild, they can cause a sudden **avalanche,** which is a large amount of snow that detaches and moves down the mountain.

▾ *Sugar beets*

Resources of Continental Western Europe

The most important natural resource of Continental Western Europe is its fertile soil, caused by the deposit of **loess**, a fine-grained soil carried by the wind. All the nations have a significant amount of arable land. France and Germany have the most, with 33 percent being devoted to agriculture, while Switzerland has the least, with only 10 percent used for farming. France leads Europe in wheat production and is second in the world for sugar beet production. The fertile river valleys produce grapes and vegetables. Both France and Germany are world leaders in barley production. Germany is a large producer of rye, wheat, potatoes, and sugar beets. The Netherlands is a leader in flower production. They also grow many types of vegetables.

Dairy cattle roam the hills of the Alpine system nations. This area is famous for its dairy products such as cheese, yogurt, and milk chocolate. Germany, Belgium, Austria, and Switzerland are timber-rich nations and are leaders in sustainable forest production.

Coal is a major resource for France, Germany, and Belgium. Currently, Germany supplies about 5 percent of the world's coal. Copper is also found in large amounts in Germany. Hydroelectric power is the most significant resource in the Alpine system countries. These nations harness the power of the rushing water coming off the Alps to produce electricity. The Netherlands and Germany have some reserves of natural gas and oil, especially in the North Sea. All these countries are yearly increasing their use of wind energy. The Netherlands uses on and offshore wind turbines to harness the power.

▾ *The Netherlands is a major producer of tulips.*

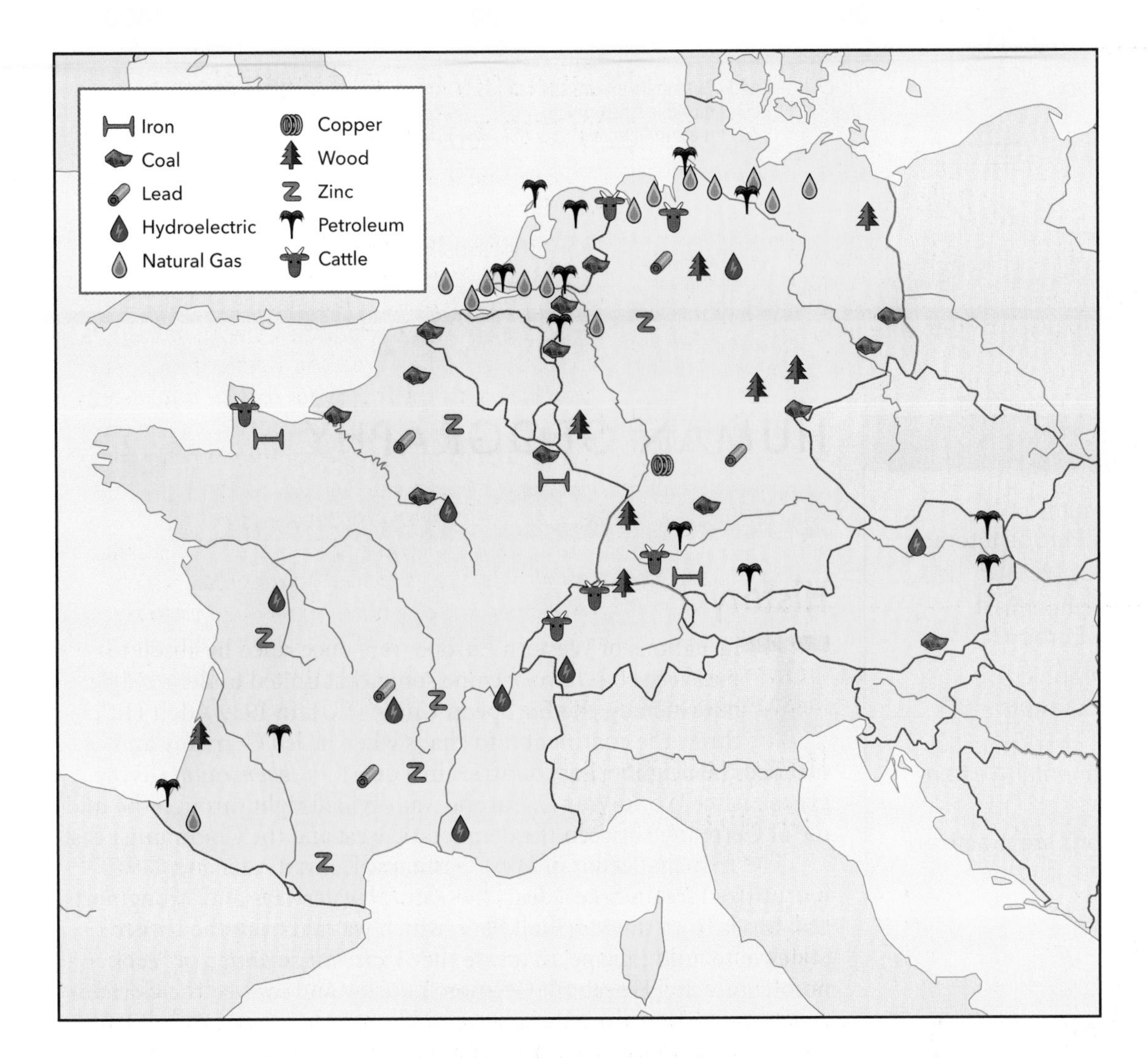

SECTION REVIEW

1. What is the largest region of Europe? Why would this region be so important?
2. What does the Netherlands do to reclaim land?
3. List the landforms in Western Europe related to the following earth-shaping processes: glaciers, tectonics, and the movement of water.
4. Compare the climate of Continental Western Europe with that of the same latitudes in North America. Why might it be so different?
5. What is the most important natural resource in this region? How could this have led to the region's success and significance through the centuries?

1300 | 1400 | 1500 | 1600

1291 Swiss confederation formed

1440 Gutenberg invents the movable type printing press in Germany

1517 Luther posts the Ninety-Five Theses (October 31)

1572 St. Bartholomew's Day massacre of French Protestants

1619 First stock exchange in the world opens in Amsterdam

GUIDING QUESTIONS

- How do the governments of Continental Western Europe interact with their citizens?
- What is the economic health of Continental Western Europe?
- What are the demographics of Continental Western Europe?
- What are the cultural characteristics and diversity in Continental Western Europe?
- What forms of religions are practiced in Continental Western Europe?

HUMAN GEOGRAPHY

How do the people of Continental Western Europe live?

History

The nations of Western Europe were once ruled by absolute monarchs but have become somewhat united under a single bureaucracy, the European Union (EU). In 1939 Adolf Hitler threw the continent into chaos when he led Germany and invaded the neighboring countries in a quest for *lebensraum* (living space). After World War II, Europe was divided right through the middle of Germany between the democratic west and the Communist east.

The first chancellor of West Germany, Konrad Adenauer (1949–63), utilized free-market ideas, the natural waterways and strong ports, and funds from the Marshall Plan, which was aid from the United States to rebuild Europe, to create the *Wirtschaftswunder*, or "economic miracle." He rebuilt German industry and revived the German economy. By 1955 the nation was producing more goods than it had before the war, despite the loss of East Germany.

In contrast, East Germany fell further and further behind. Its Communist government greatly hindered economic development. As its chief sponsor, the Soviet Union, started to show signs of weakness, the East Germans became more courageous and began protests. In October 1989 East Germany's Communist leader resigned. The Berlin Wall had been built to keep the people of the East in and was a symbol of the conflict between the East and the West. Protesters, joined by the wall's guards, tore down the Berlin Wall. The two Germanies formally reunited on October 3, 1990.

Since 1815 France has gone through four kings and five republics. It has been a parliamentary republic since 1870. The present constitution was passed in 1958. Today France retains only a small portion of its once mighty empire that spanned four continents. The country has a socialist government with national health care and free college.

People celebrate the fall of the Berlin Wall in November 1989.

1700 — 1800 — 1900 — 2000

1683 Battle of Vienna; the Turks besiege Vienna for two months before being defeated

1789 French Revolution

1804–14 Napoleon is emperor of the First French Empire

1815 Congress of Vienna; Battle of Waterloo

1830 Belgium becomes independent

1871 Otto Von Bismarck unifies Germany

1914–18 WWI

1933 Hitler comes to power in Germany

1939–45 WWII

1957 Treaty signed establishing the European Economic Community

1961 Berlin Wall is built

1990 East and West Germany reunited

Governments

The **European Union** (EU) is an organization of twenty-eight countries, as of 2019. It evolved from a modest beginning in 1952 when it was the European Coal and Steel Community. The goal was to unite German and French interests and stop the two nations from invading each other. With the signing of the Maastricht Treaty in 1992, the current EU was created. It seeks to be a community of nations that can compete on the world stage economically and politically and also counterbalance the United States. The vision is to turn Europe into something like the US so that the individual nations are like US states governed by a federal government headquartered in Brussels, Belgium.

The EU nations use the euro (€) as a common currency. The EU is an extremely complex bureaucracy, which seems to be purposeful. It includes a parliament consisting of representatives allotted in proportion to the population of each nation. The European Commission, includes a president, vice-president, and a representative from each member nation and fills the role of the executive branch. The European Court of Justice is the judicial branch.

The EU enforces many regulations that seem burdensome to individuals and businesses. Extensive rules regulate everything from the quality of fruits and vegetables to how much electricity a certain appliance can use. Partly because of these rules, the United Kingdom voted in 2016 to leave the EU, a decision known as BREXIT, but separation proved difficult.

The EU does not have a military but relies on each individual nation for defense. The majority of EU members are also members of **NATO**, a defense alliance founded after World War II to counter the Soviet Union. NATO also has its headquarters in Brussels. If a NATO country is attacked, all the other NATO nations will come to its defense. Each country is required to spend a portion of its GDP on defense. The United States, being the biggest defense spender, has accused Europe of taking it for granted. While many of the EU nations do not spend the required GDP percentage, they do spend a lot. The greater problem seems to be a lack of defense coordination between the countries. To fix this issue there have been proposals for forming a united EU army, which would seem logical as the EU morphs into a federation.

Switzerland stands separate from the EU and NATO. In 1515 Switzerland adopted a policy of neutrality regarding Europe's wars and refused to join organizations that could jeopardize that neutrality. The Swiss government is one of the most democratic in the world. The cantons, divisions of the country, are united as a federal republic, but the people can demand a popular vote on any issue by submitting

▲ *The European Union Parliament headquarters, Brussels, Belgium*

▼ *President Francois Mitterrand of France and Chancellor Helmut Kohl of West Germany celebrate a new spirit of unity between their countries on December 22,1984, in Verdun, France.*

a petition with sufficient signatures. While not a member of the EU, Switzerland is part of the Schengen Area, which gives it some of the benefits of membership, such as visa-free travel.

The Swiss take advantage of the mountains for their defense. A defense system called the Swiss National Redoubt includes the strategic placement of artillery and the ability to blow up tunnels so that invading armies cannot enter the country. Mandatory male conscription requires every Swiss male to spend a number of months in the military.

▲ *The defensive bunker and cannon near Gotthard Pass, Switzerland, was once part of the Swiss National Redoubt. Now it is a museum.*

Economies

The nations of Continental Western Europe have per capita GDPs that rank within the top twenty in the world. Germany, with its diversified economy, is by far the economic powerhouse of Europe. It includes leading numbers in the agriculture, manufacturing, and service sectors. Thirty-seven of the Fortune 500 companies are headquartered in Germany. It has a high percentage of government spending for various entitlements (benefits guaranteed to the public) and is second only to France for the amount of government spending.

France has the third-largest economy in the EU as of 2019. Its two largest industries are chemical manufacturing and tourism. France is the most visited country in the world. The French government directly controls 56 percent of the national economy; that's the highest percent age of governmental control for any of the **G20** countries (world's top economies). France has the weakest economy of all the countries in Continental Western Europe, with the highest unemployment and the lowest per capita GDP. President Macron tried to decrease public spend ing and raise fuel taxes, which led to the "yellow vest" protests in 2019.

Switzerland has the strongest economy in this region, centering on the banking and tourist industries. The country ranks high on global innovation and competitiveness indexes. Government spending accounts for only 33 percent of the economy, which puts it third least among the G20. The country has almost double the per capita GDP of France and ranks second in the world for highest per capita GDP. First place is held by a country slightly to the north, Luxembourg, but the population there is very small. Switzerland also has very low unemployment.

▼ *A "yellow vest" protester flies the French flag as part of a national general strike, February 2019.*

The EU economy as a whole is hindered by the weaker performing economies of countries like Greece, Italy, and Portugal. The people are accustomed to receiving benefits from public spending, but the economies have not been able to support those spending levels. Economists have noted that Europe lacks the adaptability and agility of the United States economy. Europe has Airbus to compete with Boeing in the airplane industry, BMW and Volkswagen to compete with Ford and GM in the automotive industry, but no counterpart to Microsoft, Amazon, or Google.

Demographics

With one exception, the nations of Continental Western Europe have seen a significant decline in their birthrates. The fertility rate in Germany collapsed in the late 1960s. As of 2019 it is 1.5, which is well below the 2.1 number needed to replace the population. In 2019 the country crossed a threshold; there are now more people over the age of 30 than under. It is predicted that by the end of the twenty-first century the population will be the same as it was in 1950. All of this could change, but it is the reason the government has given for deciding to bring in over a million immigrants from the Middle East and Africa. They are needed to make up for the babies who are not being born.

France is the lone exception. It did not have the dramatic drop in births in the 60s and has been able maintain a fertility number just under the 2.1 replacement level. As demographers studied this, they found two factors keeping the birthrate up in France. The government has a long history of providing benefits for working mothers, and it

GLOBAL IMPACT | Refugees from North Africa and the Middle East

Syrian migrants and refugees march through Turkey toward the Greek border, hoping to eventually reach Western Europe.

Through the first two decades of the twenty-first century, countries like Iraq, Afghanistan, Syria, and Libya were embroiled in wars and much upheaval. Civilians fled as Islamic extremists took more territory and committed horrible atrocities. Many of those fleeing went to Europe. There were two categories of refugees: asylum seekers, most coming from UN refugee camps, and economic immigrants. Many of those escaping the wars experienced atrocities, especially the women and children. Christians in Syria and Iraq suffered the most but proportionally were not able to get to Europe since they were kept out of the UN refugee camp system. Hundreds of thousands of immigrants came on boats that were not seaworthy. The world was horrified to see a picture of a Syrian boy's body that washed up on a beach in Turkey. He had drowned when his migrant boat capsized.

Germany opened wide its doors to these refugees and has taken the most by far. Angela Merkel, who was then Germany's chancellor, used the slogan "We can manage this." As the number of new arrivals rose from year to year, European feelings changed. In many small German towns, the majority of the population was now new immigrants. In Berlin and Bremen, over 40 percent of the elementary school students spoke little to no German. Public opinion shifted dramatically against the immigrants after New Years Eve 2015, when twelve hundred women were assaulted, mainly in Cologne. There were also three major Islamic terrorist attacks: the 2015 Paris attacks, a 2016 Brussels airport bombing, and a 2016 Berlin Christmas market attack, when a truck drove into the crowd. In 2006 there were 257 arrests related to jihadist activities in the EU. By 2017 that number was 705.

In 2016 Merkel seemed to apologize for the way the government had handled the refugee crisis, saying she still would have opened the doors but that the government could have handled it better. As of 2019 the numbers of those seeking asylum had decreased to pre-2015 levels.

A German police officer entertains a newly arrived migrant boy who is waiting for a bus in Munich, Germany.

1. Why is there a refugee crisis in Europe?
2. How did Europeans react to the refugees initially? What events caused public opinion to change significantly toward the refugees?
3. How could EU governments help refugees to assimilate?
4. How should Christians in the EU respond to the refugee crisis?

has been culturally acceptable in France for mothers to work outside the home. In Germany however, there is still a stigma associated with having the "state" rear children. So the researchers concluded that there is a paradox; when both parents work outside the home they have more children.

France is the most ethnically diverse nation in Continental Western Europe as a result of people immigrating from the former French colonies in North Africa. France does not allow any official collection of statistics on ethnicity and religion. The country aims to have a "French society" rather than a multicultural society. For Germany, Turkish is the largest minority, making up 4 percent of the population.

The nations of this region have an average life expectancy of 81.8 years, which would rank 23rd in the world if it were a single country. Switzerland has the highest life expectancy, and Germany ranks last among these nations. These nations have an average urbanization rate of 82 percent, the Low Countries being the most urbanized and the Alpine system nations being the least.

▲ *This house in Engelberg, Switzerland, exemplifies low-context culture through its orderliness and attention to detail.*

Culture and Diversity

The people of Germany, Austria, and Switzerland are the epitome of a low-context culture. For every occasion, punctuality is important. An important clue to this is the fact that Germany and Switzerland are known for producing precision clocks and watches. These countries are very task oriented, which is seen in the quality of their manufactured goods. A key low-context cultural trait is crisis planning. The Swiss have prepared shelters for 114 percent of their population in case of nuclear war. High-context cultures, on the other hand, tend to roll with the punches, not planning ahead for possible tragedies.

The German language is very precise, which is another characteristic of a low-context culture. Many German words have been adopted by English speakers, such as *angst, gesundheit, kaffeeklatsch, kaput,* and *kindergarten*. These are borrowed because there is no English equivalent to express precisely the intended meaning.

▼ *People sit outside to enjoy the sunny weather at the Viktualienmarkt biergarten in Munich, Germany.*

As France sits geographically between Spain and Germany, it also fits somewhere between the multiactive Latin culture in Spain and the very low-context culture of Germany. As American soldiers during World War II crossed from France into Germany, they took note of the change in aesthetics. The German farms were much more orderly, in spite of the war. The French are very proud of their culture. In fact, the very word *culture* has its origins in the French language. Between the seventeenth and nineteenth centuries, French language and culture reigned supreme in Europe. It was the language spoken by the kings from England to Russia. Today there is the *Académie française,* which was founded in 1635 to protect the French language. It consists of forty people known as the *immortels* (immortals).

Relationships can exist on the surface level for a long time in these nations. In France a common topic of conversation is a person's public transportation route home. Germans are known for being friendly, but it is also difficult to build strong relationships since these nations place a lesser value on having many relationships.

French cuisine is legendary. People come from around the world to learn French cooking, which is considered an art form. The different peoples of this region have a particular expertise in baked goods.

France is known for its baguettes and croissants. Germany has Black Forest cake, pumpernickel bread, and pretzels. Luxembourg is famous for raisin bread. In addition to Belgian waffles that are famous worldwide, the country has Couque de Dinant, a sweet biscuit. The Netherlands has Dutch apple pie, and Switzerland has the Swiss roll cake and Zopf, which is bread that is braided.

Classical music is still popular across the different age groups in these nations. Beethoven, Bach, and Brahms were from Germany. Vienna, Austria, is known as the capital of classical music since it was the home of Mozart, Johann Strauss, and Franz Schubert.

▾ *People of all ages enjoy a Vienna Philharmonic Orchestra concert at the Schoenbrunn Palace, which was the summer residence of the Habsburg imperial family.*

▴ *A German pastry chef displays his authentic Black Forest cherry cake in Triberg, Germany.*

◂ *Belgian waffles*

Religion

Christians owe much to Western Europe since it was the home of reformers like Martin Luther who rediscovered "the just shall live by faith." For years the center of Christian thought was in Germany, Switzerland, the Netherlands, and the United Kingdom. The Reformation gave rise to the cultural achievements of Western Europe. Europe's advances in law, science, and other fields occurred in part because of its Christian worldview.

France and Austria remained Roman Catholic. In France many Protestants died for daring to preach and witness. The situation changed in 1789 with the French Revolution. Since that violent upheaval in France, the country has remained a secular state and was one of the first to do so. As a result, a high percentage are atheists, and a majority are nonreligious in spite of still claiming the label Catholic.

When the Notre Dame Cathedral in Paris burned in 2019, it symbolized the state of Christendom in Europe, not only for Roman Catholics but also for Protestants. The French were saddened not by the loss of a religious symbol but by the loss of a cultural symbol. As plans for rebuilding took shape, there were calls to make it into a secular shrine and put a sustainable greenhouse on top.

While the majority of Western Europeans would still identify as Christian, the fact makes no difference in their lives. They are practical atheists. During the last few decades, the Netherlands, in particular, has embraced almost every form of moral vice and sought freedom from moral restraint, with dire consequences. Freedom to practice deviant lifestyles has limited the liberty of Christians to teach about many topics from the Bible because the state has instituted anti-discrimination legislation.

Major Religions of Western Europe

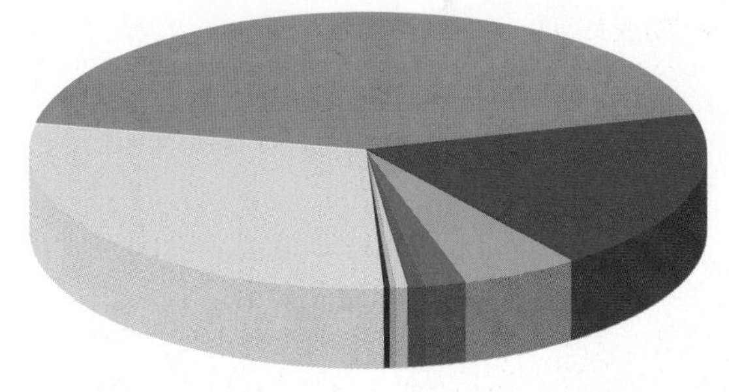

Religion	Percentage
Roman Catholic	**42.9%**
Protestant	**18.8%**
Islamic	**5.7%**
Protestant Evangelical	**1.9%**
Ethnic	**.8%**
Buddhist	**.6%**
Hindu	**.2%**
Other	**.3%**
Unaffiliated	**28.8%**

BELIEFS

Atheism/Agnosticism

Does God exist? More and more people in Western civilization are answering this question in one of two ways. Some people claim God does not exist, and they are rather certain about it. These people are called atheists. Others are less certain. They prefer to claim that human beings are unable to know for sure. These people are called agnostics. The agnostic basically admits ignorance about the question of God's existence. In both cases, there is a degree of disbelief in God.

Before the Enlightenment, the intellectual framework of Europe was biblical Christianity. Enlightenment thinkers opened the door to atheism by cutting off man's intellectual dependence on God's revelation. The authority of the Bible was replaced with the authority of independent human reasoning. Skepticism about the Bible and theological claims, however, did not immediately win over most people. Atheism simply could not offer a compelling explanation for the origin of the world.

The theory of evolution, popularized by Charles Darwin in the nineteenth century, gave atheism the explanation to the origin of the universe it was looking for. The scientific enterprise gradually shifted from an endeavor to understand the world God had made to a field of study that could be used to challenge God's existence. Atheist Richard Dawkins claims that evolution is "the only game in town, the greatest show on earth." Atheists and agnostics routinely claim that the existence of God has been either disproved or rendered suspect by scientific inquiry. The world, they claim, can now be explained solely by natural causes. No supernatural explanations are needed. Thus, miracles are denied, as are the human soul and the afterlife.

In one sense, atheists and agnostics deny the existence of any kind of supernatural deity. But a deeper look reveals that one particular deity is considered the most suspect. It is the personal, triune God of the Bible. Popular atheistic writers and speakers are often candid about this.

Scripture teaches that atheists and agnostics know on some level that God in fact does exist (Rom. 1:19–20). They even know some of God's attributes—He is almighty and all-knowing. In addition, they have a sense of accountability to God for violating His law (2:11–18). Of course, atheists and agnostics dispute this claim. They assert that they are simply allowing science to govern their thinking, not any personal bias against God.

Disbelief in God is nothing new. David wrote in one of his psalms that the person who says in his heart "there is no God" is a fool (Ps. 14:1). The human heart is in opposition to God, according to Scripture (Matt. 6:24; Rom. 8:7). A proper Christian analysis of atheism and agnosticism must take this truth into account. Atheism and agnosticism are not neutral belief systems. They are, according to biblical Christianity, human ideologies constructed in opposition to God.

▲ *(top) Charles Darwin*

◀ *Richard Dawkins*

Before World War II there were 9.5 million Jews living in Europe. The continent was home to 57 percent of the total Jewish people in the world. By the year 1945, the number was down to 3.8 million as the result of the **Holocaust,** Hitler's attempt to systematically murder every Jewish person within his sphere of influence. Today there are about 1.3 million Jews living in Europe, the majority of them in France. This accounts for about 9 percent of the worldwide Jewish population.

▲ (left) The Notre Dame Cathedral, Paris, before the fire of April 15, 2019. (right) The Notre Dame Cathedral, Paris, burns on April 15, 2019.

The growing number of Muslims has caused tension in Western Europe. France has the greatest percentage of Muslims. The government has been trying to come up with policies to change the way the religion looks and is practiced in France. They want to create a "French Islam" rather than an "Islam in France." Their goal has been to reduce radicalization and assimilate the Muslims into French culture. In 2011 France passed laws that banned women from wearing the full-face Islamic veil. Belgium passed laws that banned any clothing that obscured the identity of the wearer in a public place.

EU governments are involved with churches and synagogues through the collection of taxes to support the particular religious body. In Germany, Switzerland, and Austria, church and synagogue members are taxed around 1 percent. Churches in Germany depend on this tax for 70 percent of their income. Currently, mosques do not participate in this tax, but there are proposals to change that. Almost one third of Germany's mosques are owned by the Turkish government, and Germany would like to lessen that influence.

▲ Muslim girls and women demonstrate against the Islamic headscarf school ban during a march in Strasbourg, France.

SECTION REVIEW

1. Considering a map and history, why do you think Alpine countries like Switzerland and Austria would want to be neutral?
2. What are the main goals of the European Union?
3. How might the central control of an economy make it hard for industries to adapt to the rapidly changing demands of the world economies?
4. Why has France not experienced a great decline in birthrates? Can you think of other possible reasons that were not mentioned?
5. How do Germany and Switzerland show that they are low-context cultures?
6. Considering the cultural values of France, why would they want to create a "French Islam"? Do you think this is possible?

GUIDING QUESTIONS

- How do Continental Western Europe economies and demographics affect how citizens interact with the environment?
- What are the environmental issues of Continental Western Europe?
- What are the causes and effects of environmental issues in Continental Western Europe?
- What are possible solutions to environmental issues in Continental Western Europe?

INTERACTIONS OF PEOPLE AND PLACES

What are some of the challenges of living in Continental Western Europe?

Continental Western Europe is probably the most environmentally conscious region of the world. These countries have implemented policies to reduce pollution, and the people have embraced these efforts. The German-speaking nations are leaders in environmentally friendly buildings. Thirty percent of the energy of any new building in Germany has to come from renewable sources. Many homes and buildings are *Passivhäuser*, or passive houses. These buildings use very little energy from power plants and are almost totally self-sufficient. Though upfront construction costs are enormous, it suits the culture since the people there are not as mobile as in other nations.

In Switzerland people must buy special garbage bags. A resident only pays for garbage that is actually collected rather than a monthly rate for a can that may or may not be full. Thus they have an incentive to produce as little garbage as possible. In France, supermarkets have initiated a campaign against food waste by discounting and selling disfigured produce that would otherwise be discarded. It is called the Inglorious Fruits and Vegetables campaign and has been a huge success. The Dutch are known for using bikes for everyday travel. There are more bikes than people in the Netherlands. The Dutch have invested heavily in bike-friendly infrastructure so that 70 percent of travel in the cities of the Hague and Amsterdam is done on bicycles.

▲ (top) An illustration of a Passivhäus

▲ (bottom) Ugly fruits and vegetables are sold as part of campaign against food waste.

▼ Cycling is the main form of transportation in Dutch cities.

GLOBAL IMPACT | High-Tech Dutch Dikes

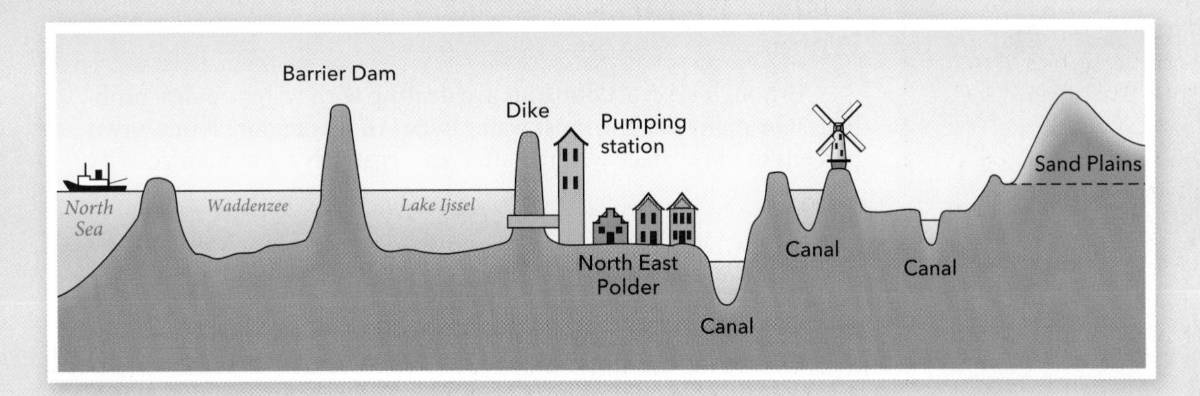

The Dutch and dikes go together. The Dutch have been building them for centuries. However, one daring project in the twentieth century far surpassed any previous attempt to capture land from the sea.

The first challenge was to control the floods along the Zuiderzee, an arm of the North Sea that reaches into the heart of the country. Storm surges in the North Sea would sometimes fill this inlet and flood the coast. In 1931 the Dutch completed a nineteen-mile-long dam called the "Enclosing Dike," which crossed the Southern Sea. Rivers slowly turned the enclosed portion of the sea into a freshwater lake called Lake Ijssel (Inner Lake). The portion beyond the dam became known as the Waddenzee.

The next challenge was to drain parts of the Ijsselmeer to obtain more land for housing and farming. Building the dikes, draining the water, and preparing the land for settlement took many years. Now, four large polders exist that a few years ago were covered by the salt waters of the Zuiderzee. The Flevoland Polder, the largest, covers over one hundred thousand acres.

1. What significant event was occurring in the world during the 1930s? Why might this have been one of the reasons for the project?
2. How might the Dutch knowledge of building dikes be useful to the whole world today?

▼ *The Oosterschelde Barrier is a high-tech dike.*

Interactions with the Environment

Water

Although several countries are dealing with water quality problems, Germany has the most water issues in this region. Ninety-two percent of the surface water is affected negatively by human activity.

Air

The most significant environmental issue for this region is air pollution. Although it has improved over the years, many large cities in this region still exceed the World Health Organization's maximum level during various times of the year. Previous chapters have discussed the problem of air pollution. One unique issue in Europe is that the pollution degrades the monuments and statues.

Land

The forests have been damaged by acid rain. Smaller countries such as Belgium and the Netherlands face the pressure of spreading urbanization. Belgium has a very small amount of protected land compared with other countries of the world.

▲ *A sculpture eroded by pollution*

▼ *Air pollution, Paris, France*

Reasons for Environmental Issues

Fifty percent of the air pollution is caused by vehicle emissions. The French drive a greater percentage of diesel cars and trucks than other nations. Diesel-burning vehicles produce more pollutants than other vehicles. Other causes of air pollution include coal and oil-fired power plants as well as manufacturing industries. At different times of the year, wind from the south brings the sands of the Sahara Desert to Europe. Air pollution is especially bad during the winter when high pressure and cold air keep the particulates from dissipating.

The culprits behind the water problems in Germany are twofold. Fertilizers and pesticides used in agriculture are seeping into the rivers, as in other nations. A unique reason in Germany is related to one of its strengths, engineering. Engineers manipulated the rivers to be straighter so that larger container ships could travel down them. Many fish species have dropped dramatically in numbers because of this. The natural filtering process that happens as a river winds is also limited by the straightening.

Proposed Solutions

The nations of Continental Western Europe are already aggressively pursuing environmentally friendly policies. Paris has instituted bans on private vehicles for certain days. Luxembourg has made all public transportation free, and Paris is considering the same. Germany has Energiewende, which is the planned transition to low carbon energy sources so that 60 percent of the energy will come from renewable resources by 2050.

PARIS BAN ON CARS

5 2018
4 2019
3 2022
2 2024
1 2030
0

Cars banned from Paris by year

The Paris Crit'Air System assigns colored stickers to cars from the oldest, most emitting cars, like low-standard diesel (5) to electric and hydrogen cars (0).

Only 0 is allowed in Paris after 2030

SECTION REVIEW

1. Consider the environmentally friendly practice examples from Germany, Switzerland, France, and the Netherlands. What traits do these initiatives have in common that make them successful?
2. How do the Dutch exhibit the Creation Mandate?
3. Considering the physical geography and demographics of the Netherlands, why might it be ideal for them to use bicycles?
4. Why was it necessary for Germany to engineer its rivers?
5. Considering that France is the second leading producer of nuclear energy, how could this strength provide a solution to the air pollution problem?

A state of the art train system, Luxembourg City, Luxembourg

10 CHAPTER REVIEW

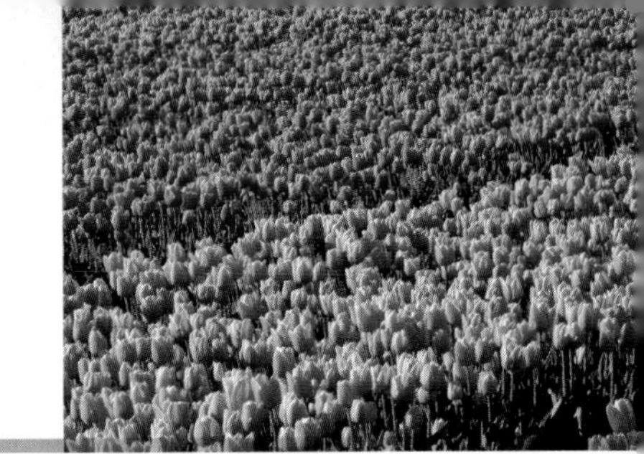

SUMMARY

1. Continental Western Europe has four physical regions. It is flatter in the north and more mountainous in the south. Rivers that provide access to the sea are important since much of the region is inland. It has a marine-west-coast climate. Arable land is the largest resource.

2. After World War II the European Coal and Steel Community was formed to unify the interests of Germany and France. It has become the European Union, which began in 1992. Germany is the largest economy in Europe. Birthrates have been falling significantly in all countries except France. The cultures of Germany, Austria, and Switzerland are the most low-context in the world. The French are proud of their food, art, and architecture. Christianity is in decline, while governments are struggling to integrate Muslims.

3. Western Europeans are very committed to a healthy environment. The worst issue is air pollution from vehicles and burning coal. Many waterways are polluted by agricultural runoff. Europeans are transitioning to renewable energy and free public transportation to address air pollution.

Terms to Know

- ❑ polder
- ❑ dike
- ❑ foehn
- ❑ avalanche
- ❑ loess
- ❑ European Union
- ❑ NATO
- ❑ G20
- ❑ Holocaust

Making Connections

1. How were the Alps formed?
2. What important area is on the Rhine River? How might the river be advantageous for this area?
3. Why is Protestantism significant in Germany's history?
4. Why were the majority of French people saddened when the Notre Dame Cathedral burned?
5. Why would countries like Belgium and the Netherlands not have much protected land?
6. Describe how World War II had a deep effect on Western Europe that persists to the present day.

Developing Geography Skills

1. How do the rivers in Western European countries contribute to their prosperity?

2 What effect do the Alps have on European culture and geography?

Thinking Critically

1. What are two cultural-geographic reasons that Western Europe has been so influential in world history?
2. Western European countries are generally considered secular, though many have tax-funded state churches. In contrast, the United States is not considered a secular nation and does have separation of church and state. What distinguishes separation of church and state from secularism?

Living in God's World

1. Write a paragraph explaining how Christians and the church as a whole can remain relevant, biblically sound, and influential in the culture rather than becoming a cold, ancient institution as in Western Europe.
2. How should a Christian respond according to a biblical worldview to the influx of Muslim refugees?

CASE STUDY | Farming Technology in the Netherlands

Chrysanthemum flowers in a Dutch greenhouse being tended by a semi-automatic robotic spraying device

The Netherlands is about the size of Maryland. It is densely populated, lies far north of the equator, and yet is a leader in feeding the world. How is this possible? The Dutch study how to grow food better and apply what they learn. They have a long history of experimenting with foods. Before the seventeenth century, carrots came in a variety of colors. Dutch farmers created an orange carrot through breeding, in tribute to their prince, William of Orange. It became so popular that carrots of other colors disappeared.

In the 1970s the Netherlands was industrializing and the agricultural sector was shrinking. As this push toward manufacturing and service industries grew stronger, the farming unions representing those who did not want to change their occupation pushed back. But for the agriculture industry to continue in the country, it would have to become more efficient and make a profit.

The University of Wageningen is the agriculture research center of the country. Researchers work to find solutions for the farmers of the Netherlands. The university's stated goal is to improve food quality for the entire world. They receive 25 percent of their income from private companies so that they work hand in hand with companies and farmers to put what is being learned in the labs into practice. This is called agribusiness.

Because of these partnerships and a commitment to productivity, the farmers were able to double their potato yields and grow crops such as tomatoes for a profit. They have done this by automating. They use tractors that drive themselves. They use drones to monitor and tend to individual plants. The drones also take pictures to collect massive amounts of data on the fields so that the farmer can target areas of need and leave plants alone that are doing fine. Because of this targeting, farmers use 90 percent less water. They use little to no pesticides since the drones can zap weeds with a laser or a small spritz of weed killer.

A Dutch farmer said, "Precision farming is basically doing the right thing at the right place at the right time."

1. Why did the Netherlands have to innovate their farming practices?
2. What is the core structural change that led to the success?
3. How do they use technology to improve yields?
4. In what ways might the new techniques help the environment?
5. How might the new techniques in farming be helpful for the whole world?

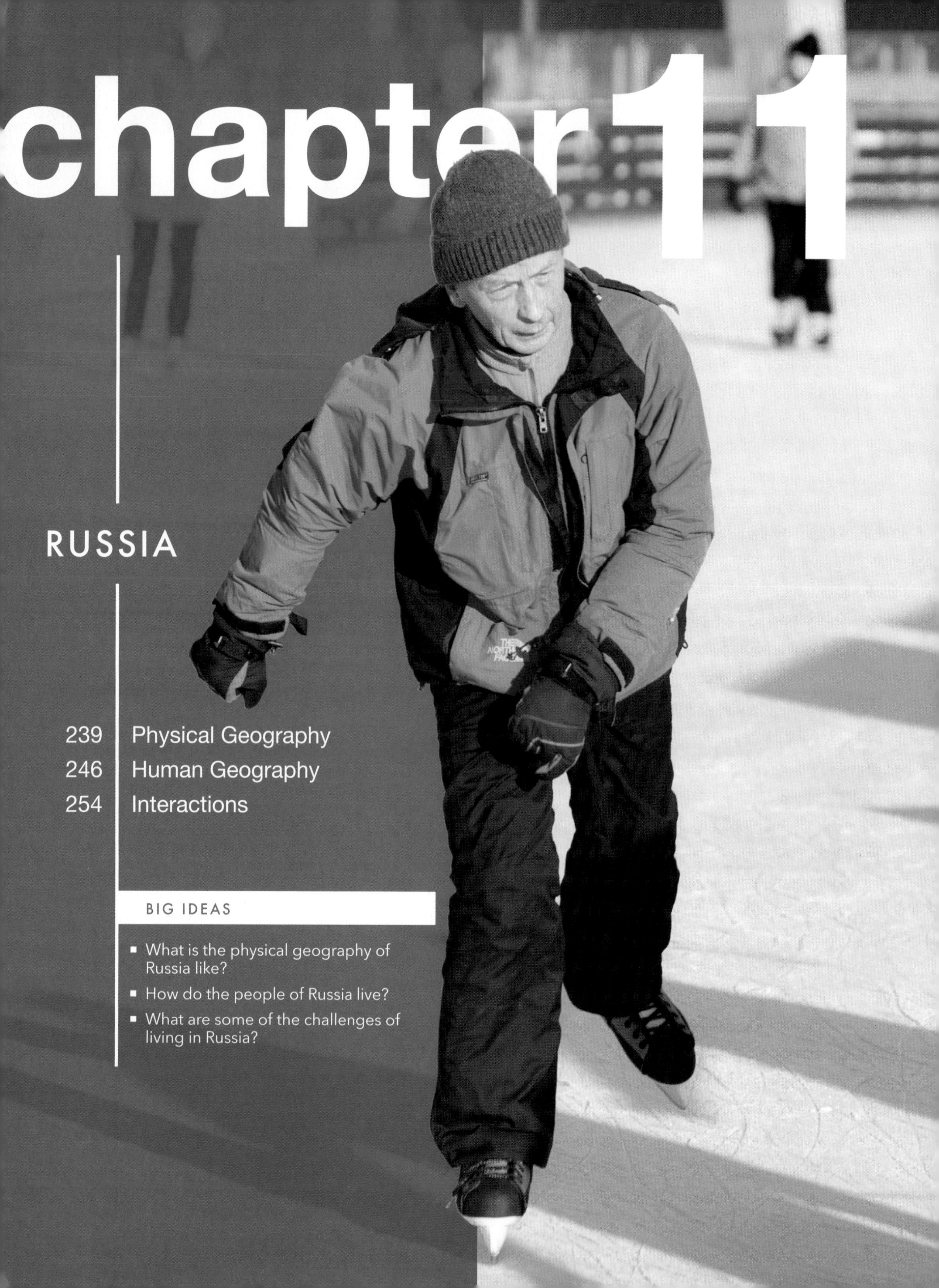

chapter 11

RUSSIA

239 | Physical Geography
246 | Human Geography
254 | Interactions

BIG IDEAS

- What is the physical geography of Russia like?
- How do the people of Russia live?
- What are some of the challenges of living in Russia?

▲ *Tabyn-Bogdo-Ola Plateau, a steppe in Siberia, Russia*

▲ *(top left) Snowcapped top of Mount Dykh-Tau*

◂ *Trans-Siberian Railway at Lake Baikal, Siberia, Russia*

▾ *Long-distance sleeping car on the Trans-Siberian Railway*

TRAVELING ON THE TRANS-SIBERIAN RAILWAY

Imagine taking a trip across Russia on the **Trans-Siberian Railway**. This line extends 5,778 miles from Moscow in the west to Vladivostok on the Pacific Ocean, and the trip can take up to seven days. The trip would take you through eight time zones, and you would pass through mountain ranges and other varied terrain. The various scenes you observed from your window would be breathtaking, including a glimpse of Lake Baikal. You would be following a route used by the Russians during both world wars and by German Jews who used the railway to escape Europe during the Holocaust. This could be the trip of a lifetime!

◂ *Man skating on a sunny winter day in Moscow*

GUIDING QUESTIONS

- What are the regions of Russia?
- What caused the landforms of Russia?
- What bodies of water are important to Russia?
- What are the climates of Russia?
- What natural resources are found in Russia?

With more than one-tenth of the world's land area, Russia is easily the largest country on earth. From east to west, Russia is nearly 5,600 miles across. From north to south, Russia extends about 1,850 miles. Russia borders fourteen countries; the only other country to join Russia in this achievement is China. Russia is "lost" in a vast expanse of lowlands without clear natural borders, except the frigid ocean in the north and the Caucasus Mountains in the southwest.

With great size has come great opportunity. Russia has a vast wealth of natural resources. Russia has several obstacles, however, that affect its ability to use these resources properly.

Perhaps the greatest obstacle is its Soviet past. Russia was the largest part of the Union of Soviet Socialist Republics for most of the twentieth century. The Soviets misused many of Russia's physical

NORTHERN EUROPEAN RUSSIA

The nation's capital, Moscow, and the city of St. Petersburg dominate this region of Russia. Most Russians live in this area, specifically around Moscow. The East European Plain also extends through this region.

SOUTHERN EUROPEAN RUSSIA

While the Volga River originates in Northern European Russia, it has increasing significance as it flows into Southern European Russia. The Don River also serves as an important resource here.

and human resources. As a result, Russia has faced the dual tasks of cleaning up the mismanagement of the Soviet era and learning how to manage the land well.

PHYSICAL GEOGRAPHY

Regions of Russia

What is the physical geography of Russia?

In addition to nine mountain ranges, this country stretches across steppes, an extended taiga, and plains.

ASIAN RUSSIA

Asian Russia comprises all of the country east of the Ural Mountains. This region is a study in contrasts, with vast plains such as the West Siberian Plain, plateaus such as the Central Siberian Plateau, and vast mountains that outline this region.

Physical Landforms

Plate tectonics caused folding or faulting and formed many of the mountain ranges in Russia. Others were formed by volcanoes. Two mountain ranges form the geographic border between Europe and Asia: the Ural Mountains in the north and the Caucasus Mountains in the south.

▲ *The Caucasus Mountains in Elbrus National Park, Russia; an example of mountains formed by folding or faulting*

Mount Elbrus ▶

Glaciation helped to shape the mountain ranges, plains, hills, and plateaus. The Great European Plain extends into Russia. Although the plain covers only 20 percent of Russia, a majority of the population

Big Aktru Glacier in the Altai Republic in Russia ▶

▲ Chernozem in the Saratov region of Russia

lives there. Rich black topsoil, known as **chernozem**, is located on this plain and provides bountiful harvests for the nation when rainfall is adequate.

Eastern Russia lies along the Pacific Rim, and volcanic activity along with glaciation shaped many of the landforms in this part of Russia.

Klyuchevskoy Volcano in the Russian Far East ▶

▼ (background) The Ural Mountains in Russia

Bodies of Water

Given the vast expanse of this nation and the extremes of terrain and weather, Russia's rivers, its manmade canals and waterways, and its key lakes serve as vital transportation routes.

The Volga River provides a vast highway of commerce and serves as a hub of Russia's shipping transportation. The Volga River has also been utilized to provide enormous amounts of hydroelectric energy. The Volga is the longest river in Europe at nearly 2,200 miles long. The Don River, at 1,224 miles long, is another vital waterway to transport goods.

Over several decades Russians have dug canals and developed waterways to enhance their ability to transport raw materials, finished goods, and people across Russia. These manmade routes have strategically connected important rivers and lakes to greatly expand the use of the nation's bodies of water. These include the Volga–Baltic Waterway and the White Sea–Baltic Canal. The White Sea–Baltic Canal connects the two largest lakes in Europe to this extensive water transport system.

▲ *Timber cargo ship in the Svir River, Volga-Baltic Waterway, Russia*

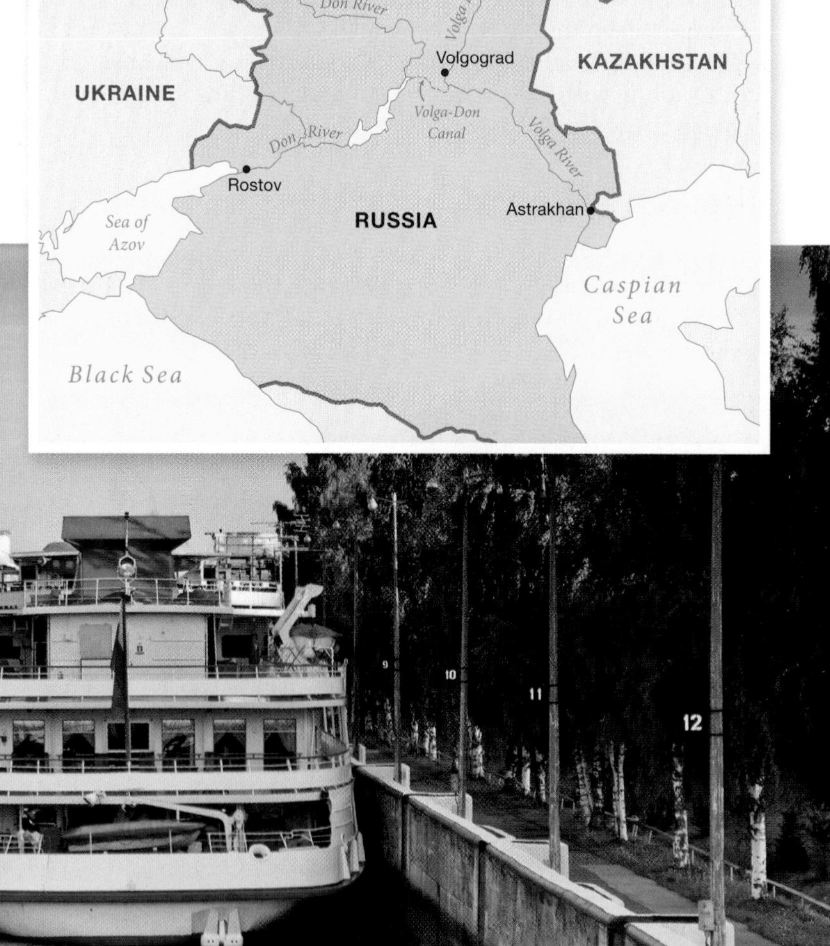

The Volga-Don Canal connects the Don and Volga Rivers. ▶

▼ *A ferry ship full of passengers in a lock on the Volga-Baltic Canal in Vytegra, Vologda Oblast, Russia*

▲ *Satellite image of Lake Baikal*

Lake Baikal was formed by tectonic activity in the Baikal Rift Zone, where tectonic plates are slowly separating. Lake Baikal is the seventh-largest lake in the world. This lake is over one mile deep, 395 miles long, and up to fifty miles wide.

Baikal seals, a freshwater species, sunbathe on the shore. Over nine hundred animal species in the lake are found nowhere else in the world. These include many unusual fish that swim near the lake's surface. The black and frigid depths are virtually lifeless and little explored.

Lake Baikal has beautiful blue waters, like the Great Lakes in the United States, but it lacks many other advantages. It has no navigable outlet to the ocean. While the climate is better there than in much of the area around it, the lake surface remains frozen from January to May.

Winter scene of Lake Baikal ▶

Climates of Russia

Climates in Russia include humid continental, subarctic, semiarid, and polar. In much of Russia, **permafrost**, the layer of soil beneath the surface that remains frozen throughout the year, limits the types of vegetation that can grow and support human life.

▼ *Permafrost in the Yamal Peninsula in Russia*

▲ (left) Northern European Russia and Siberia have a subarctic climate, with winter temperatures that dip below -90°F and summer temperatures that average 50°F.

▲ (right) Russian territory along the shore of the Arctic Ocean has a polar climate.

Southern European Russia has a humid continental climate. Given the vast landmass and great distance from large bodies of water, this region experiences **continentality**, climate conditions that form over the interior of a large landmass and are characterized by temperature extremes such as hot summers and extremely cold winters.

Moscow is colder than most capitals of Europe. Its climate is determined by its location in the interior of the continent, far from the moderating influence of the oceans. During the summers, temperatures average

Taiga in West Siberia ▶

▼ The region along the Lower Volga and Caspian Sea, along with portions of southern Siberia, has a semiarid climate. This region typically has a higher elevation and has mild summers and cold winters.

in the sixties. Winters are harsh and snowy, with an average January temperature of less than 20°F. In most summers adequate rainfall reaches this far inland, but rains are unpredictable and crops often fail. Deciduous forests lie south of Moscow, with aspen, oak, and linden; but much of this growth has been cleared for agriculture, settlement, and industry. Evergreen trees grow in increasing numbers north of Moscow.

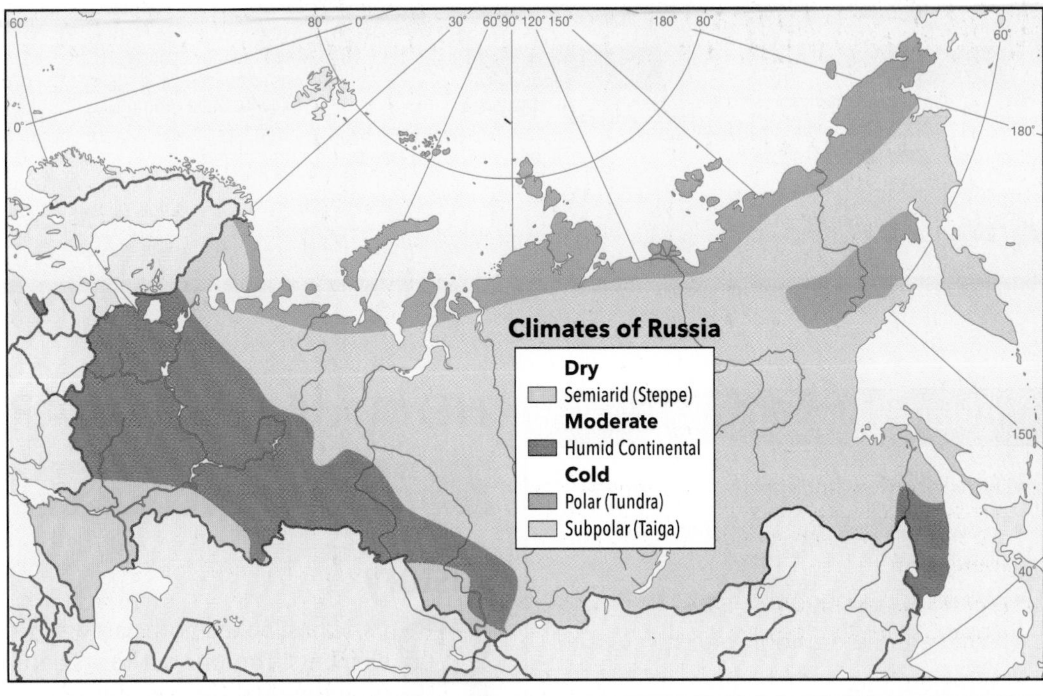

Resources of Russia

Russia is a land rich with resources, and many of these resources are estimated to be in great abundance. Some obstacles to accessing these resources include harsh climates, natural barriers, and remote locations. These obstacles make retrieval and transportation of resources difficult.

▾ *Russia produces substantial energy through harnessing hydroelectric power. There are currently 102 hydropower plants with a potential of 500 if this resource were fully developed.*

SECTION REVIEW

1. Between which lines of latitude does most of Russia lie?
2. How was Lake Baikal formed?
3. What renewable form of energy is abundant in Russia?
4. What bodies of water are important to Russia?
5. Only about one-third of Russia is inhabited. Based on what you have learned in this section, explain why this is true.
6. What resources are abundant in Russia?

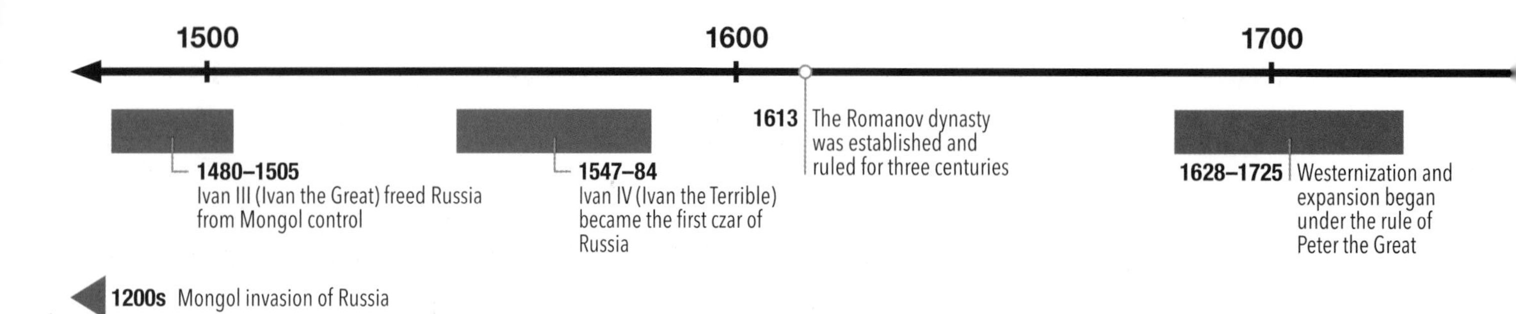

GUIDING QUESTIONS

- How has Russia changed over time?
- How does the Russian government interact with its citizens?
- What is the economic health of Russia?
- What are the demographics of Russia?
- What are the cultural characteristics and diversity in Russia?
- What forms of religion are practiced in Russia?

HUMAN GEOGRAPHY

How do the people of Russia live?

History

Russia has looked both east and west. Its culture has borrowed elements from the authoritarianism of Asia and the emphasis on individual rights in Europe.

Like the countries of Eastern Europe, Russia has suffered under the heel of many Asian tribes, including Scythians, Huns, and Slavs. Modern Russians are descendants of the Slavs and speak a Slavic language. Russia encompasses many different nationalities.

Czarist Russia

A total of twenty-four czars ruled Russia from 1547 to 1917. A **czar** was similar to an emperor or king. The czars and czarinas (female rulers) were autocrats; they had no established limits on their authority and power. While some rulers sought to improve the lives of the Russian people, others instituted policies that enslaved and impoverished the people. During World War I under the last czar, Nicholas II, Russia experienced humiliating defeats. In the resulting confusion, Vladimir Ilich Lenin led the Russian Revolution in 1917 and executed the last czar the following year.

Soviet Rule

In 1922 Lenin created the Union of Soviet Socialist Republics (USSR). This union gave limited power to several "republics." Communists claimed Russia was no longer an empire but a land of equals. Joseph Stalin, Lenin's brutal successor, extended the empire deeper into Europe than any czar could have dreamed possible. After a secret agreement with Adolf Hitler, Stalin seized Moldova, Lithuania, Latvia, and Estonia in 1940, bringing the total number of Soviet republics to fifteen. After the defeat of Hitler during World War II, Stalin extended the "Iron Curtain," the area under Soviet control, to lands as far west as Germany. Russian expansion into Eastern Europe resulted in many countries becoming **satellite states**, or nations that were controlled by Russia. Under the brutal rule of Stalin and others, millions of Russians died through starvation, mass executions, or other ruthless means.

After World War II, the USSR (also known as the Soviet Union) competed with the Western Allies. Soon the competition involved primarily the USSR and the United States. As the USSR expanded Communist influence, the United States sought to limit this expansion.

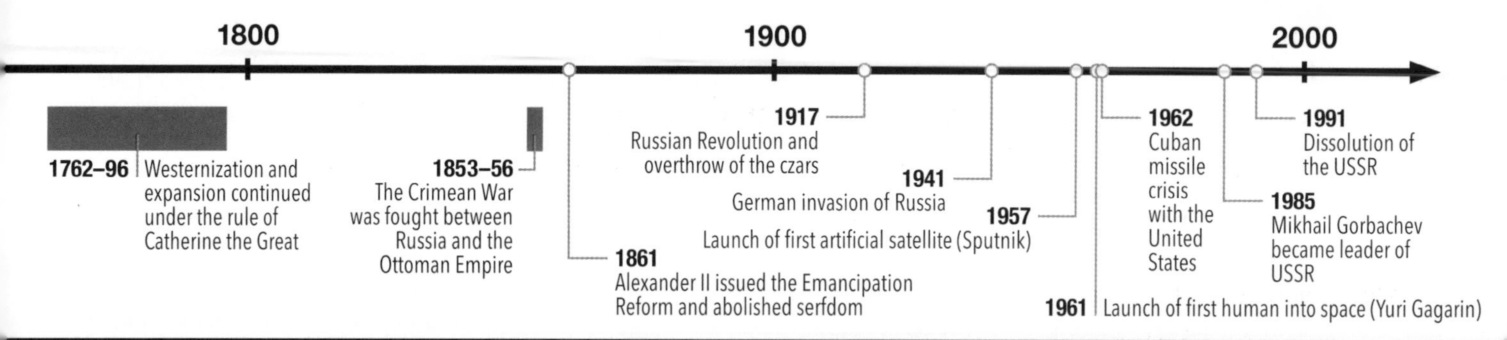

Both powers built up weapon arsenals, including nuclear weapons. Both the United States and the USSR feared that the other power would attack. This period was known as the Cold War.

▾ *Muscovites line up at a grocer's in Moscow in 1990. Shortages of food and other items were common in the Soviet Union.*

Soviet Collapse

By the 1980s the Soviet economy lagged far behind that of the West. Soviet premier Mikhail Gorbachev instituted the reforms known as **perestroika**, or "restructuring," and **glasnost**, or "openness." Perestroika brought more free-market policies and some private ownership of property. Glasnost opened the Soviet Union to the West. However, instead of stabilizing the Soviet Union, these reforms hastened its demise. The people of the Soviet Union had tasted freedom, and they wanted more.

The entire system collapsed in 1991, as the leaders of the various republics declared independence. Boris Yeltsin, the president of the largest republic—Russia—joined the others. By December 25, Gorbachev was a ruler without a country, and he quietly resigned. In the place of the Soviet Union, Yeltsin formed the Commonwealth of Independent States (CIS) to retain economic ties among the former Soviet states.

Yeltsin's tenure was marked by political and economic turmoil, and those conditions (along with declining health) led to his resignation in 1999. His successor, Vladimir Putin, increased the power of the president and moved Russia back toward a more centralized government.

▴ *(left) Soviet president Mikhail Gorbachev at a press conference, 1991*

▴ *(right) Russian president Vladimir Putin hosts a meeting of the Russian Security Council at the Kremlin on May 10, 2017, in Moscow, Russia.*

Government

Russia currently has a federation form of government that is technically a federal semipresidential republic. Shortly after the collapse of Soviet rule, Russia encountered problems of **devolution**, a passing down or "de-evolution" of power. Under the Soviet Union, Moscow had regulated everything. Even the train schedules in Siberia used Moscow time. With the breakup, Moscow initially shifted some responsibilities to local governments. This transition, though necessary, threatened to tear Russia apart because some local areas enjoyed their new powers and wanted more, perhaps even independence.

Political Divisions

Russia has many different names for its political divisions. An *oblast* is a large region or administrative district similar to a state or province, and Russia has fifty oblasts. There are also ten large, sparsely populated areas, mostly in the north, that are called *okrugs*, or areas. Moscow and St. Petersburg stand alone as Russia's two federal cities. Russia also has six *krais*, or territories, governed by Moscow.

Over thirty ethnic minorities have their own districts and have signed treaties with the government that give them a measure of self-rule. But the twenty-one autonomous republics have the most population, power, and status.

The political divisions have been distinguished by the degree of autonomy that they possess. The autonomous republics have the most freedom, followed by the oblasts, krais, okrugs, and federal cities. Because the administration of these different divisions was cumbersome, Russian president Vladimir Putin reorganized the various political divisions into seven federal districts based on geography. These federal districts allow Moscow to govern Russia more effectively.

Branches of Government

In 1993 the Russian people voted for a new constitution that separated powers among three branches of government: executive, legislative, and judicial. While these branches sound similar to those of the United States, they are not, in fact, coequal branches of government.

Most of the power resides in the executive branch, which is led by a president. Instead of a vice president, the next official in line is the prime minister. The president chooses a prime minister with the consent of the State Duma. In 2005 Putin gained the authority to appoint the governors for each of the oblasts in lieu of elections. This move by Russia's executive branch greatly increased its power and weakened the independence of the oblasts.

Russia's legislature, known as the Federal Assembly, is divided into two houses, the Federation Council and the State Duma. The Federation Council consists of two representatives from each political division in the Russian Federation. The State Duma is composed of elected representatives from throughout Russia.

Russia's judicial branch of government has a Supreme Court that functions much like the Supreme Court of the United States, although it has little independent authority. It also has a Constitutional Court that examines the constitutionality of Russia's laws.

Government Interaction with Its Citizens

The Russian government provides universal health care for its citizens, but health-care services are limited. As in other parts of the world, medical care tends to be more readily available in the big cities than in rural areas. Following an economic downturn in 2014, medical facilities in Russia have experienced reduced government funding and are chronically understaffed. Those who cannot afford private care typically endure long waits for medical care.

Russians also receive a free eleven-year education. College admission is competitive, and Russian colleges are transitioning to a student-paid system in addition to government scholarships. As a result, just over half of Russians have a college or graduate degree. Russian higher education places an emphasis on science and technology, medicine, mathematics, and aerospace research.

Historically, Russian rulers, from czars to Communists and currently president and prime minister, have treated the people poorly. Centuries of abusive rule under the czars contributed to the Russian Revolution in 1917. Poor living conditions, massive military spending, and disregard for the people contributed to the collapse of the Soviet Union in 1991. While economic and living conditions for most Russians have gradually improved in the last three decades, it is still dangerous for Russian citizens to disagree with the government. Protesters have been beaten and arrested, and wealthy citizens who have run afoul of political leaders have been tried and imprisoned on questionable charges.

▾ *Moscow is a primate city with 12.4 million people as of 2017 and is one of the financial centers in Europe.*

The Russian government also controls the media. Television stations that broadcast across Russia are carefully monitored and consistently report from a pro-government position. Stories about President Putin and other leaders are highly favorable of everything they do or support. Reporters serve as little more than government proponents.

A person who opposes official government policy in an authoritarian state is known as a **dissident**. Russian dissidents at home and abroad have mysteriously disappeared, have been executed by gunmen, or have been poisoned with rare toxins that imply official government involvement. Disagreement with the ruling powers is not tolerated and can be fatal.

Economy

Russia has a mixed economy. Much that was formerly owned by the government has now undergone **privatization**, the transition from government to private ownership of industries. Given the changes following the collapse of the Soviet Union, Russia's economy can also be referred to as a transition economy and an emerging upper-middle income economy. However, this upper-middle income economy is unevenly divided geographically, with a large percentage of the GDP being created in the region around Moscow. A significant percentage of Russia's revenue comes from exporting petroleum and natural gas. Another important source of income is derived from exporting precious metals such as platinum and zinc. In 2017 Russia's GDP was an estimated $4 trillion.

During the Cold War the Soviet Union developed a large and sophisticated arms industry, with military exports including combat aircraft, air defense systems, ships, and submarines. This industry has continued in Russia and brings the country substantial revenue from the foreign purchase of these weapons.

As in many other developed countries, most workers are employed in the services sector, and about one-fourth are employed in industries. Nearly 10 percent of Russians work in agriculture.

Another legacy of the Soviet Union is the black market. The **black market** is an illegal underground or shadow economy. During the Soviet era it supplied wealthy Russians with high-priced goods that were generally not available in stores or markets in the Communist nation. Even today the black market thrives in Russia and continues to represent about 20 percent of Russia's GDP as of 2019.

Demographics

In 2019 the estimated population in Russia was 143.9 million. Eighty percent of the Russian population consists of native Russians, and Russian is the official language. Significant minorities include Tatar, Ukrainian, Bashkir, Chuvash, and Chechen, and there are nearly 200 different ethnic groups and indigenous groups living in Russia (based on a 2010 census).

Eighty percent of the Russian population lives west of the Ural Mountains. Reasons for this concentration of people include rich soil for farming, ready access to waterways, greater employment opportunities, and a milder climate.

▲ *(top) Russian S-300 mobile air defense missile system*

◂ *Russian military helicopter*

GLOBAL IMPACT | Population Decline in Russia

Russia's population decreased by at least a half million people nearly every year from 1991 to the mid 2000s. Multiple issues have caused this destructive trend. Russia has had a low birthrate, one of the lowest in the world. The fertility rate has also been among the lowest in the world. In addition, Russia has a high rate of abortions. As of 2010 the abortion rate was 37.4 per 1,000 women aged 15–44, the highest rate reported in UN data. Due to the low quality of health care, many of the women in Russia who undergo an abortion risk serious injury or death from complications during the abortion procedure.

Other issues leading to premature deaths in Russia include alcoholism, drug addiction, and HIV/AIDS. Russians buy over two billion liters of vodka, wine, and beer each year and suffer from the dire consequences of alcohol consumption, including disease, homicide, and suicide. As many as 2.5 million people in Russia are addicted to drugs, and another five million are believed to abuse drugs. Russia also has one of the highest and fastest growing rates of HIV/AIDS. This epidemic primarily affects Russia's young people.

1. What role has abortion played in the declining population of Russia?
2. What impact does alcohol play in the premature death of Russians?
3. How has drug use impacted the Russian people?
4. What health epidemic has spread primarily among younger Russians?

▲ *A mother and her son at a playground in Russia*

Music in Russia ranges from folk to classical.

A Russian folk music group in traditional clothing in a remote village along the Volga River

Culture and Diversity

As the largest country in the world and one that combines dozens of ethnic groups, Russia has a rich and varied culture.

Music and Dance

Russians love to celebrate, whether it is a birthday, wedding, or other event. Celebration calls for food and singing. If the conversation around the table begins to wane, someone from the family will often break out in song, and the others quickly join. Subjects range from traditional Russian songs to Soviet ballads. Many favorite Russian songs are about love, especially unrequited love.

Dance in Russia ranges from folk to ballet.

Russian ballet dancers performing Swan Lake

One form of Russian song is called a *chastushka*. It is usually a humorous improvisation based on recent local news, sung by two competing performers. The singers are accompanied by a stringed instrument similar to a guitar or by a Russian accordion.

Russian composers have also contributed to the world of classical music. Composers include Anton and Nikolay Rubinstein, Pyotr Ilyich Tchaikovsky, Sergei Rachmaninoff, and Igor Stravinsky.

Schi, a traditional Russian cabbage soup

Food

A typical Russian meal starts with a first course of soup. The most famous kind is called *schi*. Schi is cabbage soup made with carrots, onions, potatoes, and beef. Russians eat a lot of potatoes—boiled, mashed, or fried. Potatoes are often served with homemade pickles. Wild mushrooms are a specialty in Russia. There are many delicious ways to serve mushrooms, such as fresh mushroom soup or mushrooms fried in sour cream. For a truly special occasion, Russians love caviar served on white bread with butter. Caviar also tastes good with *blini*, a traditional dish similar to crepes. Appetizers such as beet salad or Olivier salad are fairly common. Olivier salad,

▲ *Examples of Russian cuisine, including borscht, pelmeni, herring, marinated mushrooms, salted cucumbers, vinaigrette, sauerkraut, rye bread, pancakes, and cheese pastry*

▲ *Russian Olivier salad*

also known as "Russian salad," is made with diced potatoes, beef, pickles, carrots, peas, and mayonnaise. Russians also love *pelmeni* and *pirozhki*. Pelmeni are small dumplings filled with meat. Pirozhki are bread rolls filled with cabbage, mushrooms, fish, meat, or apples and then baked. Every meal ends with hot tea plus chocolate candies, pastry, or homemade cakes. As in many other cultures, meals in Russia provide an excellent opportunity for fellowship.

Sports

Russians love sports. Russian soccer teams are very popular along with most winter sports, including hockey. Russia has also produced many Olympic medal winners, and its athletes are among the world's finest.

Russian gold medal champions in ice hockey at the 2018 Winter Olympics ▸

Major Religions of Russia

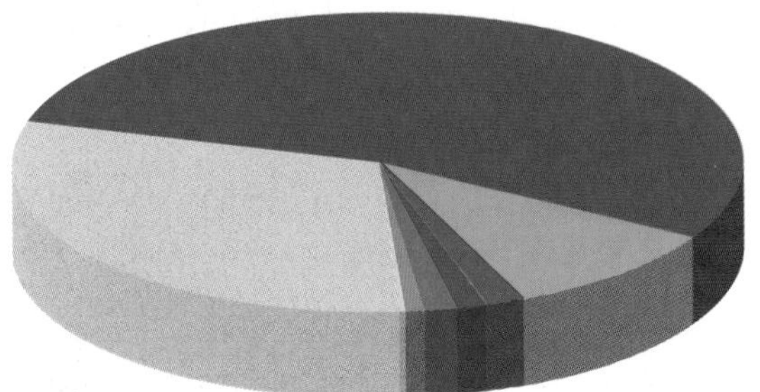

Religion	Percentage
Orthodox	**54.0%**
Islamic	**10.0%**
Ethnic	**1.7%**
Protestant	**1.5%**
Protestant Evangelical	**1.2%**
Roman Catholic	**1.0%**
Buddhist	**0.3%**
Unaffiliated	**30.3%**

Religion

Historically Russians have been religious. Under the influence of the czars, they developed their own form of Orthodox church that closely resembled the Eastern Orthodoxy that originated in Constantinople and the Byzantine Empire. Some czars used the church to monitor and control the people. After the Muslim Turk conquest of Constantinople in 1453, the Russian Orthodox Church became the "mother" of other Orthodox churches in eastern Europe. Despite seven decades of Communist rule and official hostility to religion, about 54 percent of Russian people retain a connection to the Russian Orthodox Church. The Russian constitution guarantees freedom of worship. Traditional religions such as Siberian Shamanism are also on the rise, as are Hinduism and Islam. As in many countries, less than 10 percent attend services regularly.

BELIEFS

Eastern Orthodoxy

The Eastern churches, led by Constantinople (modern-day Istanbul, Turkey), followed an increasingly different path from the Western churches, led by Rome. The Eastern churches finally broke from Rome in 1054, when the pope demanded that they acknowledge his supreme authority. The Eastern churches became known as the Eastern Orthodox churches. The two churches refused to cooperate until 1965, when they agreed to restore friendly relations.

Eastern Orthodoxy agrees with Roman Catholicism and traditional Protestants on several points. All three groups hold to the Trinity, the two natures of Christ, and the inspiration of Scripture.

Eastern Orthodoxy also shares some beliefs with Roman Catholicism that are distinct from those of many Protestant groups. For instance, both groups have a hierarchy that includes deacons, priests, and bishops. In both groups the Eucharist (Lord's Supper) is a central part of worship. Both groups also differ from Protestants in giving church tradition an authoritative role alongside Scripture and denying that salvation is by grace alone through faith alone in Christ alone. Instead, they teach that God and humans cooperate to bring about salvation.

Serious differences also exist between the Roman and Eastern churches. While Roman Catholics allow paintings and statues of saints as part of their worship, Eastern churches confine icons to flat painted images. In Eastern Orthodoxy a church is a body of Christians overseen by a bishop. The bishops are all equals, although some are more highly regarded than others. In the West the Bishop of Rome, or the pope, claims authority over all other bishops. This was one of many factors that led to a split between the two groups.

The Eastern Orthodox also reject the doctrine of original sin, as held by both Protestants and Catholics. The apostle Paul taught that all humans are born guilty because of Adam's sin (Rom. 5:12); the Eastern Orthodox deny this. The Orthodox Church also denies Paul's teaching that the human will was corrupted by the Fall (Rom. 3:11) so that people will not come to God apart from grace (Eph. 2:8–9). Instead, they teach that humans are affected by sin but remain basically good.

Along with Protestants and Catholics, the Orthodox Church teaches that Christ was offered as a sacrifice in His death. But unlike Western churches, the Orthodox deny that Christ's sacrificial death was offered to the Father to satisfy divine wrath over sin.

The Orthodox Church suffered a serious setback when Islam pushed its way up from the Middle East and into Eastern Europe. This shift, however, has caused some peoples in Eastern Europe to hold tightly to the Orthodox Church. For instance, over 90 percent of Greeks belong to the Greek Orthodox Church.

▲ (top) Saint Basil's Cathedral was built in the sixteenth century at the order of Ivan the Terrible. It was confiscated by the Communists and turned into a museum. Orthodox worship resumed in 1997.

▲ (bottom) Russian Orthodox priest blessing Easter eggs and kulitches

SECTION REVIEW

1. How has Russia changed over time?
2. How well does the Russian government protect the rights of its citizens and ensure that justice is carried out?
3. How would you describe the economy of Russia?
4. Describe the demographics of Russia.
5. What are some cultural characteristics and examples of diversity in Russia?

GUIDING QUESTIONS

- How do the Russian economy and Russia's people interact with the environment?
- What are environmental issues in Russia?
- What are causes and effects of environmental issues in Russia?
- What are possible solutions to environmental issues in Russia?

▲ *Peat is another source of energy in Russia for some power plants.*

▼ *Pulp mill in Russia's Bratsk forestry complex*

INTERACTIONS OF PEOPLE AND PLACES

What are some of the challenges of living in Russia?

Interaction with the Environment

Following the rule of the czars, Communist leaders seized control of industries and exerted great pressure on workers to catch up with Western nations. As a result, the environment suffered from poor stewardship and massive disregard for the long-term consequences of damaging the soil, water, and air in order to increase production. Further damage occurred with the German invasion during World War II and the wholesale destruction of many areas in Russia. Following World War II, Communist officials renewed the push to modernize industry and increase production at any cost. Russians are dealing with nearly one hundred years of harming the environment. With a workforce of about 76 million people as of 2017, manufacturing and services provide the most jobs and consume the most resources. Most power is produced by coal-fired plants, and significant air pollution has resulted.

Another impact on the environment has been the large-scale production of radioactive materials. This has resulted in the contamination of large areas where these devices were produced and are being stored.

Reasons for Environmental Issues

Water

For many years water in Russia has been polluted by chemicals from industry and agriculture, including pesticides. Many Russian rivers and lakes contain oil, lead, iron, arsenic, harmful bacteria, radioactive materials, and nitrates that contaminate the water. As a result, millions of Russians lack access to safe drinking water.

Air

Air quality in the industrialized regions of Russia is some of the worst in the world. The growing number of automobiles adds to the already severe air pollution, as do wildfires that can burn for weeks or months. While statistics vary, thousands of Russians die each year from complications caused by polluted air.

Land

Regions of Russia have contaminated soil due to chemical and oil spills and **nuclear waste** (radioactive byproducts of the manufacture of nuclear energy and nuclear weapons). Due to logging, fires, and destruction of trees by pollution, Russia is also being deforested at the alarming rate of 40 million acres per year. To make matters worse, up to 40 percent of the harvested trees go to waste due to clearcutting and inefficient logging. As in other countries, this massive removal of trees has resulted in extensive erosion and loss of valuable topsoil.

Proposed Solutions

While Russia has a growing economy and vast natural resources, continued economic improvements will be essential to provide the enormous financial resources needed to clean up decades of dumping and improper storage of many hazardous materials. The culture of corruption that has hampered the needed reforms must be rejected. In addition, laws designed to reduce or eliminate the various forms of pollution must be vigorously enforced in order to discourage the continued illegal activities. Legitimate advocacy groups that bring the corruption and illegal polluting activities to light should be supported by the Russian government, and the temptation to punish these groups must be resisted.

On a positive note, some Russian companies are working on ways to provide safe drinking water and are developing technologies to solve other environmental issues such as air pollution. These efforts should have popular and government support for the good of the Russian people.

▲ *(top) Air pollution in St. Petersburg, Russia*

▲ *(bottom) Deforestation in Russia*

▼ *Storage units for radioactive waste in Murmansk, Russia*

SECTION REVIEW

1. What are three environmental issues in Russia?
2. How has Russia responded to the problems of water and air pollution?
3. What has caused pollution to land, air, and water in Russia?
4. What solutions to current environmental issues in Russia would you propose?

11 CHAPTER REVIEW

SUMMARY

1. The physical geography of Russia was shaped by tectonic activity, volcanic eruptions, and glaciation. Russia has an abundance of natural resources that provide a vast economic potential as these elements are accessed and developed.
2. The people of Russia are ethnically varied and yet similar in the enjoyment of common activities, including ethnic foods, regional music, and sports. This society is transitioning into a highly developed status but is also threatened by many destructive elements, including alcohol and drug abuse, low birthrates, and the erosion of liberties recently won.
3. A major challenge of living in Russia is the destructive consequences of many decisions made by the Soviet Union. Russians are struggling to make wise use of human and natural resources in ways that build a strong economy without further damaging the environment.

Terms to Know

- ❑ Trans-Siberian Railway
- ❑ chernozem
- ❑ permafrost
- ❑ continentality
- ❑ czar
- ❑ satellite states
- ❑ perestroika
- ❑ glasnost
- ❑ devolution
- ❑ dissident
- ❑ privatization
- ❑ black market
- ❑ nuclear waste

Making Connections

1. How has government influenced religion in Russia?
2. Describe continentality.
3. List a landform in Russia related to glaciation and one for tectonics.
4. What natural resource is abundant in Russia from which to extract aluminum? What abundant energy source is used to process aluminum?
5. How has nuclear energy affected Russia?
6. What is *chernozem*?
7. Why do you think Russia's economy is in transition?
8. Identify political issues in Russia.

Developing Geography Skills

1. What is the relationship between landforms and the distribution of population in this region?
2. How has glaciation affected the landforms of Russia?

Thinking Critically

1. How does Russian construction of canals and waterways demonstrate, in part, the Creation Mandate?
2. Evaluate the Soviet rule of Russia.

Living in God's World

1. Write a brief essay that defends viewing the human population as a nation's most valuable asset. How should this position affect Russian government policy?
2. Relate religion in Russia to the presence of government corruption and a culture of drug and alcohol addiction.

CASE STUDY | Tower in the Taiga

Ecologist Ernst-Detlef Schulze clips into a safety harness as he rests on a platform almost one thousand feet above the treetops of the Siberian taiga. He takes a dizzying look down. Schulze spearheaded a group of German researchers that have erected and manned a "sniffing" tower, almost as tall as the Eiffel tower, called the ZOTTO in the Siberian taiga.

The taiga is the largest land biome in the world, home to many of the longest rivers in the world. The Siberian taiga is the lungs of Europe, similar to Amazonia in South America. The goal of these researchers from the Max Planck Institute is to "smell" gases generated and used by the Russian taiga, the largest continuous forest on Earth. And they set their sights high.

These scientists are trying to see if the forests of northern Russia are speeding up or slowing down climate change. Trees consume carbon dioxide, but climatologists are concerned that thawing bogs in Siberia could release large amounts of methane, another greenhouse gas like carbon dioxide. They are also concerned about massive logging in Siberia. But it is difficult for scientists to fully understand what is happening on such a large scale. This is one of the challenges of science.

1. What are scientists monitoring on the taiga?
2. What positive role does the taiga play in the environment?
3. What is the effect of thawing in the taiga?
4. What role do you think massive logging plays in relation to the health of the taiga?

▲ *This tower in the Amazon is similar to those found in the taiga.*

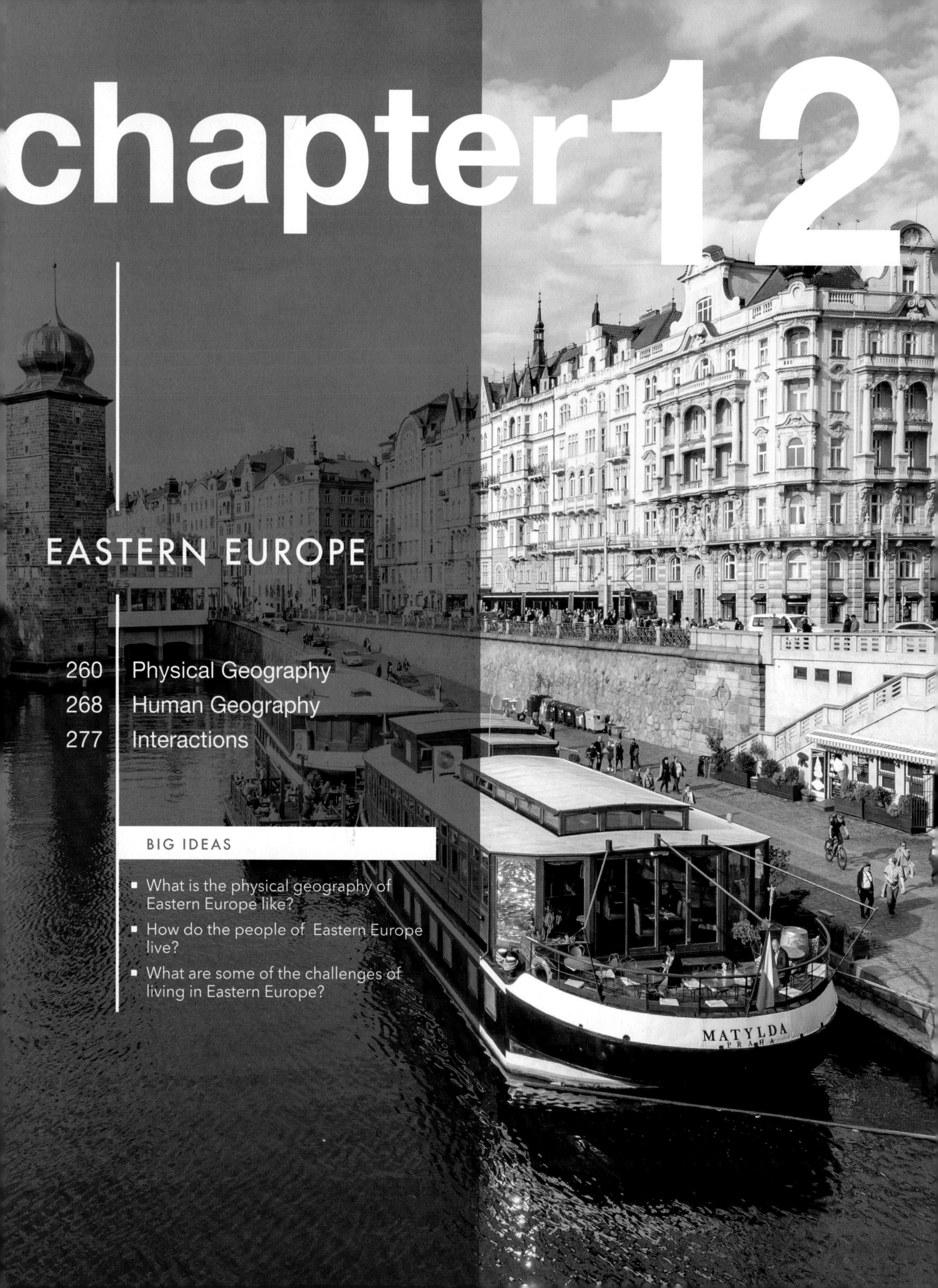

chapter 12

EASTERN EUROPE

260 Physical Geography
268 Human Geography
277 Interactions

BIG IDEAS

- What is the physical geography of Eastern Europe like?
- How do the people of Eastern Europe live?
- What are some of the challenges of living in Eastern Europe?

▲ (top left) Cloasterf Saxon Village, Transylvania, Romania

▲ (top right) Old Market Square, Tallinn, Estonia

◀ Prague, Czechia, and the Vltava River

THE TOMBS OF WAWEL CATHEDRAL

In 1973 archaeologists were permitted to open a royal tomb in the Wawel Cathedral of Kraków, Poland, to study the remains. The cathedral is the burial place for most Polish kings. The tomb they opened was that of King Casimir IV. A few days after the tomb was opened, four of the scientists died. A total of fifteen of those involved in the excavation died early deaths. Some attributed the deaths to a curse, but the actual cause was a toxic fungus that escaped after the tomb was opened.

The Polish-Lithuanian Commonwealth was one of the largest countries in the world during the fifteenth and sixteenth centuries, encompassing most of north-central Europe, but in 1795 it was wiped from the map. The Wawel Cathedral and the adjoining Wawel Castle serve as a magnificent monument to this empire and the kings that led it. Kraków amazingly survived World War II when the other large Polish cities were demolished, first by German bombs then by Russian bombs. Karol Józef Wojtyła served at this cathedral, later to become Pope John Paul II, arguably the most influential modern pope.

(middle) The Wawel Cathedral, Kraków, Poland ▲

(bottom) Inside the Wawel Cathedral, Kraków, Poland ▶

GUIDING QUESTIONS

- What are the regions of Eastern Europe?
- What caused the landforms of Eastern Europe?
- What bodies of water are important to Eastern Europe?
- What is the climate of Eastern Europe, and how does it relate to its location on the globe?
- What are the natural resources of Eastern Europe?

Because Eastern Europe as a region includes twenty separate countries, it has many different cultures, peoples, and lands. Its one commonality is that for most of the twentieth century it was under the control of the Soviet Union. As a result, Eastern Europe generally lacks the material prosperity that is characteristic of Western Europe.

Eastern Europe has appropriately been called a **shatter belt,** a region that is under continual political pressures and is often fragmented by warring internal factions and heavily influenced by surrounding rival countries. Consequently, the size, shape, and number of countries have frequently changed. The borders of some countries shifted back and forth, depending on the military success of their powerful neighbors. Each time a nation revolted against its conquerors and set up a new country, it was conquered again and divided among the victors, as was the case with Poland.

PHYSICAL GEOGRAPHY

Regions of Eastern Europe

What is the physical geography of Eastern Europe like?

This region is a buffer between Russia to the east and Germany to the west and between "Christian" Europe and Muslim West Asia, to the southeast. Physically, Eastern Europe is divided between the Great European Plain in the north and the Alpine mountains in the south.

ALPINE MOUNTAIN SYSTEM

The Alpine system in Eastern Europe is dominated by the Carpathian Mountains, which form the eastern boundary of the system. The mountains give way to the Great European Plain at the Dniester River in Ukraine. There are many subranges within the Carpathian Mountains. The highest subrange, the Tatra Mountains, rises in the far north along the border of Poland and Slovakia. The Tatra range is the continental divide, separating the rivers that flow north into the Baltic Sea and the rivers that flow south and east into the Black Sea. Four nations share parts of the Carpathians—Poland, Slovakia, Ukraine, and Romania.

The Balkan Peninsula is a mountainous land that juts down from Europe into the Mediterranean Sea. The peninsula has five different ranges, four of them in Eastern Europe. The Dinaric Alps begin in Italy and run parallel to the Adriatic Sea, covering Slovenia, Croatia, Bosnia-Herzegovina, and Montenegro before ending in northern Albania. To the east are three ranges that run east to west. The Transylvanian Alps cover central Romania. The Balkan Mountains border the Great European Plain in central Bulgaria, and the Rhodope Mountains cover southern Bulgaria, extending into Greece.

CENTRAL UPLANDS

The Central Uplands is the smallest physical region of Eastern Europe. These uplands cover all of Czechia and a small part of Poland and Slovakia. The Sudeten Mountains and the Bohemian Massif are the main geographic features of this region. The Sudetens are low mountains which form the northern border of Czechia and Poland. The Bohemian Massif takes up the middle of Czechia. It is a plateau area of rolling hills and plains. The famed Bohemian Forest is on the western border of Czechia and Germany. The Erzgebirge range, meaning "Ore Mountains," is in the northwest.

THE GREAT EUROPEAN PLAIN

Over half of Eastern Europe is covered by this plain. Because it is so large, it gives Europe the lowest average elevation of any continent. Estonia, Latvia, Lithuania, Belarus, and Moldova are entirely within the Great European Plain. Ninety percent of Poland is on this plain. These nations have lacked security because of the flat, open topography. Most of Ukraine sits on this plain, making it a breadbasket. The plain hooks around the Alpine system to include eastern Romania and northern Bulgaria. It ends on the north shore of the Black Sea.

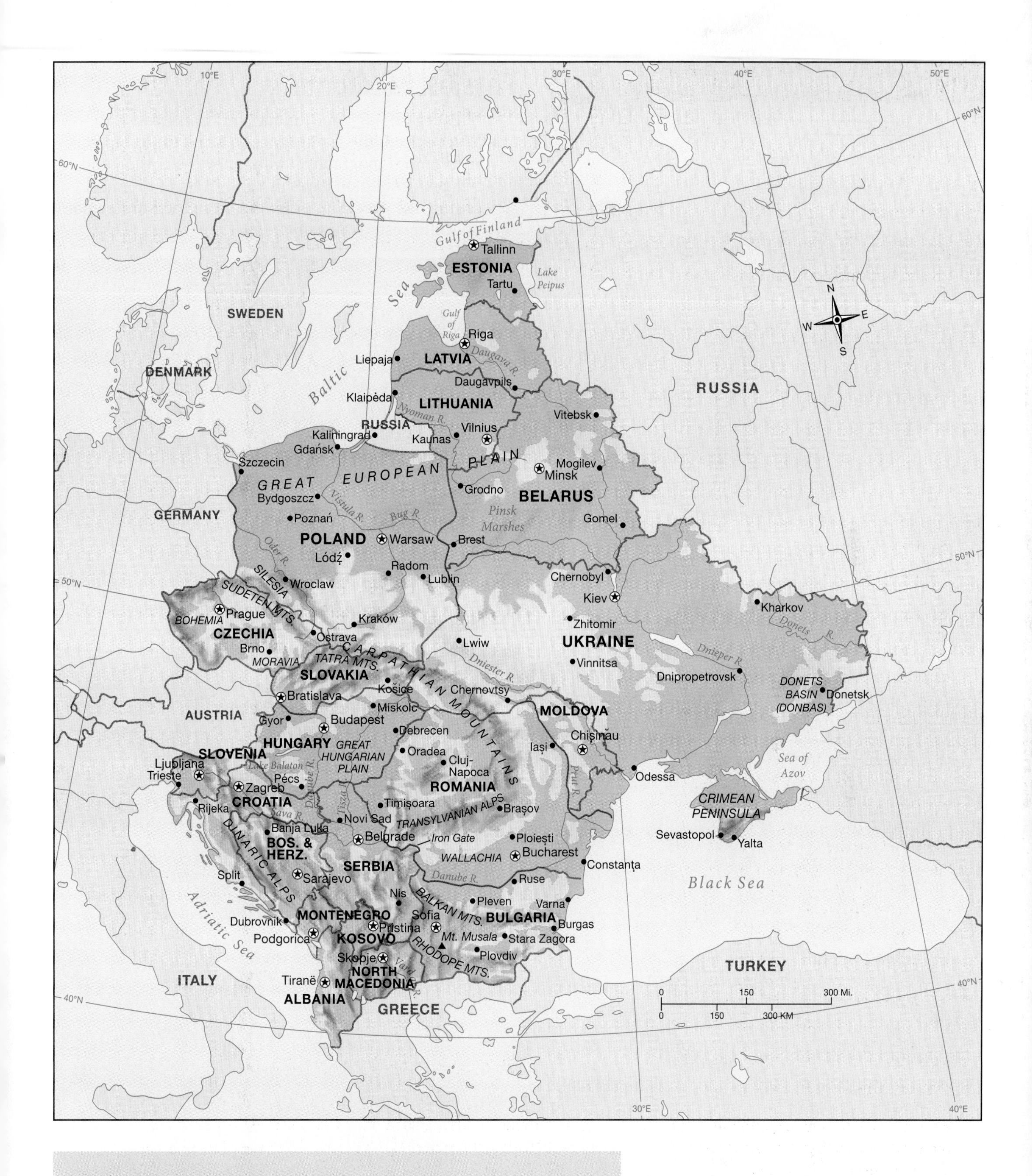

THE GREAT HUNGARIAN PLAIN

The Great Hungarian Plain, or Great Alföld, is a basin in the center of the Alpine system. It comprises eastern Croatia, northern Serbia, and most of Hungary. The Danube River flows through the center of the plain.

Physical Landforms

This region has some unique landforms related to soluble rocks in the Alpine system. **Karst topography** is the term for topography produced by the erosion and collapse of solution caves in thick strata of chemical sedimentary rocks. It originates from the Karst region in southwestern Slovenia.

▲ *Gerlachov Peak in Slovakia is the tallest (8,711 feet) peak of the Carpathians. It is composed of flysch, which is a series of sedimentary deposits.*

▲ *Karst topography is famous for its sinkholes, natural bridges, and limestone caves.*

◀ *The Pinsk (or Pripet) Marshes are the largest marshlands in Europe, extending about three hundred miles on the drainage basin of the Pripyat (or Pripet) River, a tributary of the Dnieper River. The marshes, which lie in Belarus and Ukraine, yield potash for fertilizers.*

▼ *The Great Alföld, a plain of flat land and rolling hills, covers most of Hungary. It formed when block-fault mountains submerged into an inland lake. Then the area was filled with fertile soil by the Danube.*

Bodies of Water

Eastern Europe has three prominent seas. The Baltic Sea is in the north and borders the nations of Poland, Lithuania, Latvia, and Estonia. The capitals of Estonia and Latvia, Tallinn and Riga, are ports on the Baltic. The Adriatic Sea is in the southwest with coasts on Slovenia, Croatia, Montenegro, a twelve-mile piece of Bosnia-Herzegovina, and Albania. The Black Sea is a large inland sea in the southeast. Its water is anoxic, meaning it lacks oxygen because there is rare movement between its upper and lower layers. The Sea of Azov is a smaller sea to the north of the Black Sea. The control of this sea has been disputed between Russia and Ukraine.

The Danube River is the most important river of this region. It is Europe's second-longest. Three Eastern European capitals sit on its banks: Bratislava, Slovakia; Budapest, Hungary; and Belgrade, Serbia. The Danube flows east from the Great Alföld through a break in the Carpathian Mountains called the Iron Gate. Steep rock walls, 530 feet apart, guard both sides of this gorge. The Danube then flows east through a broad fertile plain shared by Romania and Bulgaria. Romania's capital, Bucharest, is located on a tributary of the Danube. The Danube widens and flows through swampland before it reaches the Black Sea.

▲ *(top left) The Swallow's Nest Castle on the Crimean Black Sea coast*

◀ *The Danube River splits the city of Budapest, Hungary.*

▼ *A sculpture of Decebalus guards the Iron Gate on the Danube River. Decebalus was a first-century Romanian king who fought against the Romans. The sculpture was completed in 2004.*

The Dnieper River, the third-longest in Europe, is a Ukrainian national symbol. It begins in Russia, flows through eastern Belarus, and continues south through the heart of Ukraine. Kiev, the capital of Ukraine and the most populous city in all of Eastern Europe, lies at the junction of the Dnieper and Desna Rivers.

▲ *The Dnieper River winds through Kiev, Ukraine.*

Another significant river in this region is the Dniester River, which flows through western Ukraine and all of Moldova. The Vistula and the Oder are important rivers in Poland. Warsaw lies on the Vistula River, which flows into the Baltic Sea and is a major shipping artery through the central plains. The Oder begins in Czechia and flows through the resource-rich and formerly disputed region of Silesia in Poland. It forms the German-Polish border before it empties into the Baltic Sea.

Plitvice Lakes National Park in Croatia includes sixteen clear blue, green, or turquoise lakes that vary in color throughout the year. Along with the lakes are hundreds of waterfalls. They are the result of sedimentation. As the water flowed over the limestone and chalk, it moved material and created natural dams, causing lakes to form.

▼ *Plitvice Lakes National Park, Croatia*

Dry
Semiarid (Steppe)
Moderate
Marine West Coast
Mediterranean
Humid Continental
Humid Subtropical

Climates of Eastern Europe

The warm marine-west-coast climate of Western Europe gradually gives way to a colder climate in the heart of the Eurasian continent. The term for this type of cold, wet climate is a humid continental climate. Precipitation averages between twenty and thirty inches a year. Summer temperatures often reach the eighties, and freezing temperatures persist through much of the winter. The steppes in eastern Ukraine are too dry to support forests but not to the extent of being a desert. The mediterranean climate in the Balkans is very comfortable. The climate is created by the Mediterranean Sea, resulting in dry summers and mild winters.

▲ *A vineyard in Moldova*

Resources of Eastern Europe

As in Western Europe, Eastern Europe's most valuable resource is arable land, since most of the region is on the Great European Plain. These countries grow crops that do well in the colder climate, such as hardier grains and root vegetables. The Great Alföld has the most fertile soil in Eastern Europe. The top grain crop is rye, which is related to wheat. It is easier to grow but not as popular as wheat. Poland and Belarus rank at the top in the world for rye production. Eastern Europe produces a large percentage of the world's barley, a cereal grain which is also used for animal feed. Ukraine is a world leader in barley and flaxseed production. Flaxseed is turned into cooking oil or used as a nutritional supplement because of its fiber content. It can also be used in the production of linen. This region produces a percentage of the world's wheat, with Ukraine being the main source. Many of the world's potatoes and sugar beets come from Eastern Europe.

Moldova, Ukraine, and Hungary are leaders in growing grapes. Moldova is especially dependent on grape production. At the end of the Soviet era, the government made an effort to fight alcoholism. As one of the initiatives, they destroyed many Moldovan vineyards. Small-scale sheep farming is common in Romania, Bulgaria, and Hungary.

Belarus, Latvia, Estonia, and Poland are leaders in the production of peat. The nations that border the Baltic Sea produce almost all of the world's amber, a gemstone made of fossilized tree sap. Much of the world's coal comes from Eastern Europe. The main location of the coal is on the Czech-Polish border. Ukraine produces iron ore. The foothills of the Alps are rich in timber. The mountain nations also produce a great amount of hydroelectricity. Estonia's marshes are rich in oil shale.

▲ *Amber gemstones*

▲ *A shepherd watches over his flock in the Carpathian Mountains in Transylvania, Romania.*

▼ *(background) A field of flax*

▼ *Flax flowers*

SECTION REVIEW

1. Why is Eastern Europe considered a shatter belt?
2. What is the largest marshland in Europe, and in what countries is it located?
3. What characterizes the water of the Black Sea? What might one deduce about the sea life in it because of that characteristic?
4. What kind of earth-shaping process could form marshlands?
5. Which geographical region has both marine-west-coast and humid continental climates in Eastern Europe?
6. How might the climate play a part in what crops are grown? What ways might farmers work around this to produce different crops?

1300 | 1400 | 1500 | 1600

1237–40 Mongols rule much of Eastern Europe

1348–50 The Black Death kills a huge percentage of the people in Europe.

1025 Poland declares independence, emerges as major European power

1349–1430 Polish-Lithuanian Commonwealth dominates Eastern Europe

GUIDING QUESTIONS

- How has Eastern Europe changed over time?
- How do the governments of Eastern Europe interact with their citizens?
- What is the economic health of Eastern Europe?
- What are the demographics of Eastern Europe?
- What are the cultural characteristics and diversity in Eastern Europe?
- What forms of religions are practiced in Eastern Europe?

HUMAN GEOGRAPHY

How do the people of Eastern Europe live?

History

The fact that both World Wars began in this region testifies to the amount of upheaval the people have experienced. In World War II alone the nations in this region lost close to 20 million people. It could be said that the Eastern European people are suffering from generational post-traumatic stress, with increasing intensity as one travels east.

Former Soviet Bloc Nations-North and Central

When Germany invaded Poland it set off World War II. By 1941 Germany had conquered all the countries of this region. By April of 1945 the Soviet Union had conquered all of the countries. The Soviet Union forced the Eastern European countries to join the **Soviet bloc**, a string of semi-independent countries behind the Iron Curtain ruled by puppet governments taking their orders from Moscow.

In the 1980s Lech Walesa, the head of the Solidarity trade union in Poland, demanded changes. In response Poland went under martial law, Solidarity was outlawed, and Lech Walesa was put in prison. As the Soviet Union weakened, however, it could not stop Walesa and Solidarity. Solidarity was one of the groups that led the way in bringing an end to communism in Eastern Europe. The "year of surprises"—1989—showed the world just how unpopular the Soviet system was among the people. In a few remarkable months, all the countries within the Soviet bloc cast off communism and threw open their borders to the West. Walesa later became the first president of free Poland, introducing many economic reforms.

▲ *The Prague Spring in 1968 was one of two major uprisings in Central Europe. The other was in Hungary in 1956. The Soviet Union stopped the uprisings by driving tanks into the cities.*

Lech Walesa and Pope John Paul II ▸

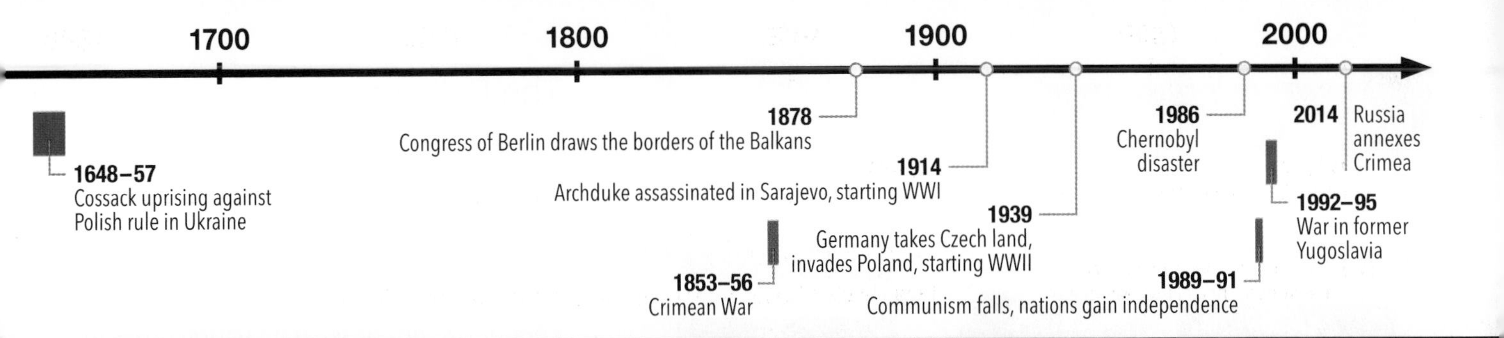

Former Soviet Republics

The word *Ukraine* actually means borderland. Along with Belarus and Moldova, Ukraine was a part of the Soviet Union and did not get to retain even the illusion of independence. Prior to 1991 Ukraine was independent for only a few years. In 1922 it became part of the Soviet Union. The Holodomor, or terror-famine, occurred from 1932 to 1933 when 7–10 million people died of starvation, mainly in Ukraine but also in Belarus, Moldova, and Russia. The famine was orchestrated by Joseph Stalin to put down Ukrainian resistance to **collectivization**, when the state takes ownership of the farms and puts people there to work the land. As a result of the famine, when the Germans invaded many Ukrainians sided with them.

After its independence in 1991, the transition to a democratic form of government proceeded slowly. In 2004 there was a contentious campaign between pro-Western Viktor Yushchenko and pro-Russian Viktor Yanukovych. Yushchenko was poisoned but survived, though he was severely scarred. He lost the election, despite widespread support. Because many suspected fraud, large groups of Ukrainians protested the results. Due to the persistence of the people, another election was held, and this time Yushchenko won. This became known as the "Orange Revolution" since the pro-Western Ukrainians wore orange as a sign of their support. But the tensions with Russia would not end there. In 2010 Yanukovych did become president only to be removed from office in 2014. Russia considered this removal to be a move against their interests. They surreptitiously invaded and annexed the Crimean Peninsula.

▲ *President Viktor Yushchenko of Ukraine, with scars from the poisoning, speaks to the US Congress in 2006.*

◄ *The Orange Revolution, Kiev, Ukraine*

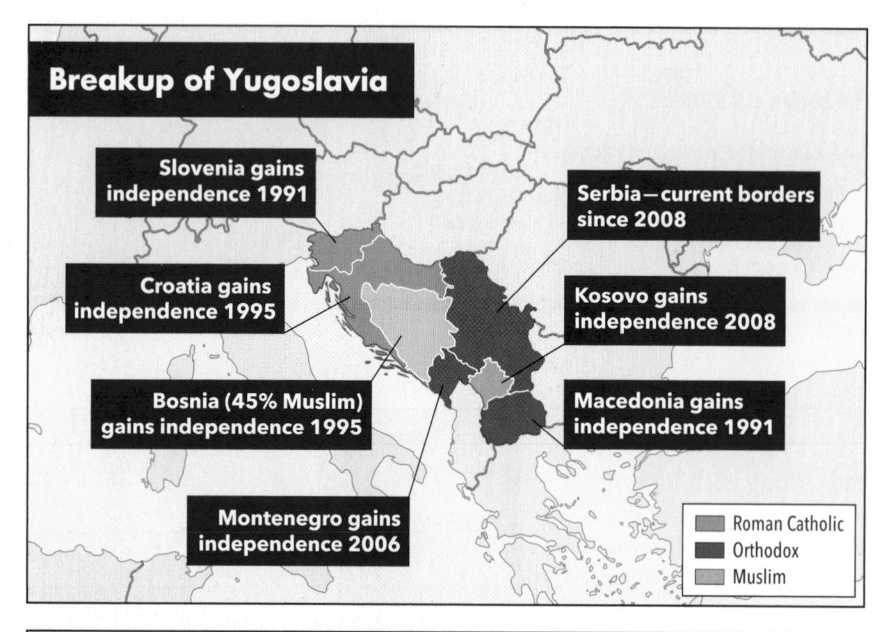

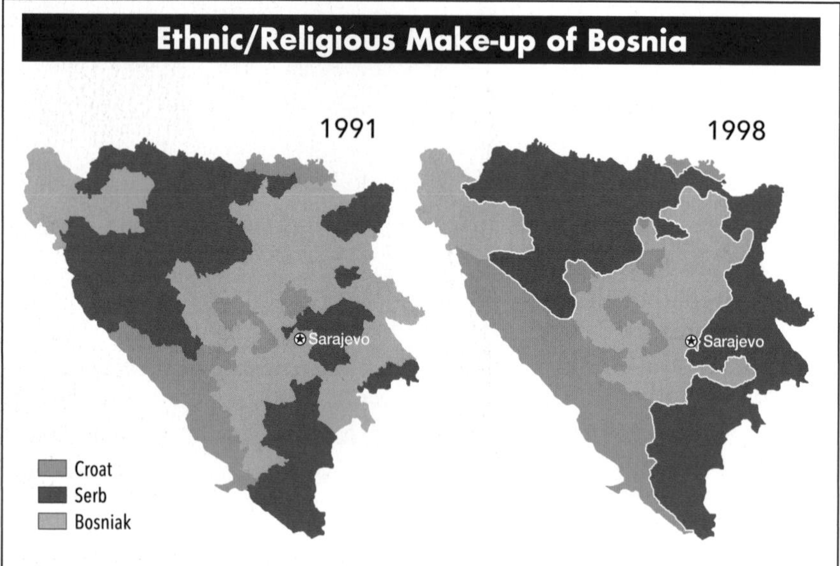

The Balkans

The Balkans' rugged ranges once isolated numerous tribes that migrated into the region, causing them to develop separate cultural identities. The terrain encouraged disunity and conflict between these peoples. The Balkans are a complex knot of two dozen separate nationalities in ten countries. The tendency of ethnically and religiously diverse territories to break up into small, hostile nations is called **Balkanization**.

Yugoslavia was the largest country in the Balkans during the twentieth century. It was held together by the power of a Communist dictator. When communism fell in 1991, a bitter civil war erupted. Conflicts arose because the borders of the Yugoslav ethnic states did not match with where the corresponding ethnicities lived.

Bosnia and Herzegovina's quest for independence proved to be the bloodiest. It was in the center of Yugoslavia and had a slim majority of Muslim Bosniaks. Serbs and Croats composed the minority. Neither the Serbs nor the Croats wanted an independent Muslim Bosnia. For almost four years Sarajevo, the capital, was under siege by Bosnian Serbs aided by the Yugoslav army, which was largely composed of Serbs.

▾ *The mountainous terrain of the Balkans is a cause of disunity.*

The Bosnian Serbs committed **ethnic cleansing**, the mass killing or expulsion of an ethnic or religious group, against the Bosniaks. The world could not believe something like this could happen in "modern" Europe. NATO forces entered the conflict in order to stem the violence and restore stability. In 1995 President Bill Clinton brokered a peace agreement called the Dayton Peace Accords. The agreement, however, did not completely resolve the discord. NATO soldiers remained until 2004 to enforce the fragile peace.

Kosovo, an area of southern Serbia with a predominantly Muslim-Albanian population, enjoyed some autonomy during the Communist era. Tension with Serbia resulted in the Kosovo War from 1998 to 1999. The United Nations brokered a peace agreement and sent in a force to govern Kosovo. As of 2019 the United Nations does not recognize Kosovo as a separate nation, and there is still a force of 3,500 NATO soldiers, called KFOR (Kosovo Force), to keep the peace.

▲ (top) Bosnian soldiers fire back at Serbian snipers shooting at civilians in Sarajevo, Bosnia and Herzegovina, in 1992.

▲ (bottom) Refugees from Srebrencia, Bosnia and Herzegovina, who fled after more than eight thousand Bosniaks were murdered in 1995

Governments

The people of this region consider the term "Eastern Europe" derisive. It includes the connotations of poverty, weakness, and Soviet domination. The Baltic nations have more in common with Scandinavia, particularly Finland. Czechia, Slovakia, Croatia, Poland, Hungary, and Slovenia call themselves Central Europe since these lands were all part of the Holy Roman Empire. The Balkan nations have more in common with the southern nations of Italy, Greece, and Turkey. In the future "Eastern Europe" will probably refer to a much smaller region. But as of now these countries share the goal of trying to emerge from the dark shadow of Soviet communism and find their place in the world. Some have had more success than others.

By 1991 communism was a despised philosophy by most of the people of Europe, yet many of the new leaders had been proponents of it just a year or two prior. These leaders were now in charge of the privatization and democratization of their countries. Countries that had spent a shorter time under communism and had more competent leadership found transition to a democratic form of government less difficult. Countries where communism was more firmly entrenched had a much more difficult time.

Since almost all of these nations are members of the EU, or are in the process of joining, they share the same governmental structure as the Western EU nations. In general they oppose the idea of the EU progressing to a United States of Europe. They desire to retain their sovereignty and have moved to protect some of their industries, rather than letting the forces of free trade have full control. On the

issue of immigration, there has been heated disagreement with the West. Poland and Hungary took the lead, but all the Eastern countries seemed to be in agreement that they were not going to open their doors to immigrants and refugees from Muslim nations.

The nations of the Eastern EU and the Western EU share the same tensions as countries that have a distinct urban/rural divide. The East feels disenfranchised and condescended to since it lacks the wealth of the more populous and prosperous urbanized Western EU, while the West feels like it is supporting the East. Corruption is a major problem for many of these countries, especially in Romania, Bulgaria, and Moldova.

In 2001 the United States started looking to the Eastern European countries for new allies. The region was called the "new Europe" since the countries seemed more agreeable to partnering with the United States. The Eastern NATO countries spend a greater percentage of their wealth on defense than many in the West and have been open to placing American missile defense systems as well as American military aircraft on their soil. They do this because of their continued fear of Russia, especially in Estonia, which feared it would be next for invasion after Russia annexed Crimea.

Ukraine has been trying to join the EU for a number of years, but those efforts have been undermined by Russia. Both Ukraine and Moldova are having trouble just keeping control of their territory. Both have breakaway states loyal to Russia. In 2019 it seemed the people of Ukraine decided to go a different direction by electing Volodymyr Zelensky, a comedian who had played the role of president for four years on a TV show. Belarus stands apart from the rest of Eastern Europe as it has close ties with Russia. It has been under a dictatorship since the end of the USSR, never really turning away from communism.

Economies

In 1991 the major issue was how to return ownership of everything back to the people. Never before had a Communist country (in which the state owns the means of production) transitioned to a market-driven economy. How does a country sell the companies and industries the government owns? Czechia introduced reforms that strengthened the economy rapidly. To return the property to the people, leaders distributed vouchers to private citizens in an experiment called mass privatization. Each adult became a shareholder in the nation's various industries. After a brief period of economic hardships, the country swiftly regained its vigor. Estonia introduced a flat income tax and quickly reaped the rewards of a robust economy. Other countries did privatization in a much more haphazard manner. Some countries still have state ownership of many industries.

Eastern Europe's top economic hindrance for the foreseeable future is the lack of a skilled workforce. The nations are racing to create new industries and modernize old ones so that they can provide high quality jobs and thereby entice the youth to stay and work. Many young workers have moved to Western Europe where there are more desirable jobs. In an effort to keep the young people from moving away, Poland passed a law in 2019 which waived income taxes for everyone under the age of twenty-six who makes below $22,500 per year.

Demographics

Eastern Europe has significantly low birthrates. There has been a decline in population here because the people are not having babies; they are emigrating. The countries also are not allowing immigrants from Muslim nations to come in. In 1992 there were approximately 310 million people in Eastern Europe; as of 2019, there are about 291 million. Eastern Europe ranks in the middle as far as the level of urbanization. The average percentage of urban population is in the low 60s, which is less than the upper 80s of Western Europe and the Americas but more than the 40s and 50s of Asia and Africa.

The majority of Eastern Europeans are Slavic. They migrated into Europe from further east between AD 500 and 1000. There are three main Slavic groups divided by religion and culture. The Western Slavs (Poles, Czechs, Slovaks, and others) have more ties with Western Europe. They use the Roman alphabet and are predominately Catholic. The Eastern Slavs (Russians, Ukrainians, and Belorussians) and Southern Slavs (Serbs, Croats, Bosnians, Slovenes, Macedonians, and Montenegrins) belonged to the Byzantine Empire, sharing its Eastern culture and Cyrillic alphabet. Because the Southern Slavs have Muslim minorities, they are slightly differentiated from the Eastern Slavs.

The non-Slavic peoples live in the Baltics, Romania, Moldova, Hungary, and Albania. Since the people of the Baltic countries speak various Finnic (related to Finland) languages, their cultural ties are in Scandinavia. The Romanians and Moldavians are the same ethnically, having descended from a mixture of Roman soldiers and native peoples. Their language is the only one in Eastern Europe that developed from Latin. Hungarians are descendants of Magyar tribes from the East who invaded Central Europe in AD 896, enslaving the Slavic and Germanic peoples. They speak a Uralic language associated with the Ural Mountains. Albanians speak a unique Indo-European language. Their roots are somewhat a mystery, but they seem to be distantly related to Greeks.

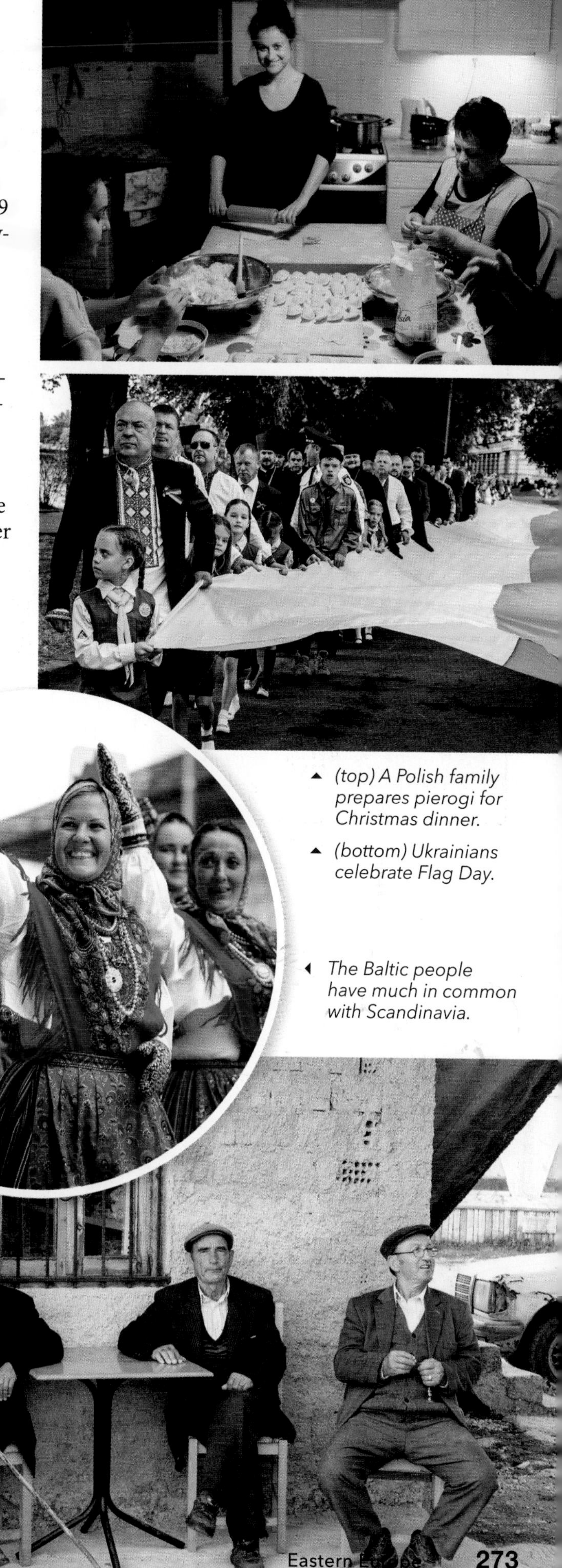

(top) A Polish family prepares pierogi for Christmas dinner.

(bottom) Ukrainians celebrate Flag Day.

The Baltic people have much in common with Scandinavia.

Albanians are a distinct people group distantly related to Greeks.

▲ *Romani teens*

A large ethnic minority in Europe is the Romani. They have been derogatorily referred to as Gypsies. Although the precise origin of the Romani remains uncertain, they have been genetically linked to people from northwest India. These dark-complexioned people migrated to Europe by the fourteenth century. They were mistakenly thought to be Egyptians, thus the term *gypsy*.

The Romani limited their contact with the outside world and consequently preserved their own tribal language, laws, and customs. Their work reflected the life of wanderers. Some took seasonal jobs as circus performers, musicians, and acrobats. Others worked as peddlers, smiths, tinkers, woodcarvers, hangmen, undertakers, dogcatchers, or horse traders. They developed an unfortunate reputation because of the few who were tricksters or thieves. Hitler targeted the Romani as "undesirables" and ordered the execution of about 400,000 of them during the Holocaust.

Today, many Romani have settled and joined the modern world. Others have replaced their wagons with campers. Governments throughout Europe are seeking to incorporate the Romani population into the general populace. While the Romani have spread all over the world, their greatest numbers are in Bulgaria, Romania, and Hungary.

Culture and Diversity

Generally, the people of northern areas of Eastern Europe, such as the Baltics, tend to be reserved while those in the southern areas, such as the Balkans, are more warm and friendly. The northerners say that they are reserved and unsmiling because they value authenticity.

Communism affected every aspect of the culture. During those years the state created a tangible atmosphere called "the fear." The state accomplished this through its secret police and the control of every institution. The perception was that the state knew everyone's thoughts so that the internal fear was as powerful as the police in controlling the individual. Since neighbors would report on each other's "illegal" behavior, the people closed themselves off from one another and to this day have found it very difficult to trust. The tendency to distrust people and institutions is changing as new generations who have not experienced "the fear" come along, but it persists in those who are middle-aged and older.

▼ *People dance in traditional costumes in Budapest, Hungary.*

Many countries are reviving their pre-Communist cultural heritage. They are teaching their children the cultural and religious traditions (not necessarily the religious beliefs). They are bringing back the dances and clothing of the past.

The people of Eastern Europe seem to have two cultural commonalities: drinking and gardening. Twelve of these countries are in the top twenty for per capita alcohol consumption. The first three are Belarus, Moldova, and Lithuania. Czechs are known for being world leaders in beer consumption, with a per capita rate of over 37 gallons a year.

The people of Eastern Europe are expert gardeners because it was essential for survival. As they continue to transition to a market economy, the younger generations do not need this skill, but as of now it has continued. Because the gardens are not as necessary for survival, the people of this region are able to devote more space to growing flowers than before.

The most visible reminder of the Soviet era is the architecture built in the Brutalist style, rows and rows of rectangular, drab buildings. Aesthetically it is extremely depressing. The more wealthy countries, like Poland, have been able to demolish some of it. They have even gone to the effort of finding pre-World War II photos to rebuild the area with buildings that resemble ones from the 1700s and 1800s. The poorer countries have tried things like adding bright colors to the buildings or cladding, which are façades, to lessen the monotony.

▲ *A Ukrainian vegetable garden*

▼ *Old Town Market Place, Warsaw, Poland, in 1945 (left) and in 2009 (right)*

▼ *A mass of Brutalist-style apartment buildings from Soviet times, Kharkiv, Ukraine*

▲ *Christians "March for Jesus" in Gdansk, Poland. The banners and t-shirts say "Jesus loves you" and "March for Jesus."*

Religion

The main philosophy of life seems to remain atheistic, even though Central Europeans identify as Catholic, Easterners as Orthodox, and a large number of people in the southern Balkans as Muslim.

It has been said, "The blood of the martyrs is the seed of the church." In many ways persecution demonstrates the true character of Christians to the rest of the world and leads to a stronger faith among believers. But persecution has also been effective in limiting the spread of the gospel. Eastern Europe is a great example of the effectiveness of persecution. The Communist governments were successful at instilling an atheistic/materialistic philosophy in the people. Throughout the twentieth century, stories of Christian heroism in the face of intense persecution filtered out to the West. There was some limited undercover missionary work, and Bibles were smuggled in. The Bible had been outlawed, and even the Orthodox church looked down upon people owning a Bible, so it was a precious possession of believers.

In the years that followed the fall of the iron curtain, missionaries poured in, but the majority served on a short-term basis. As missionaries came in, hundreds of thousands of Christians (from Ukraine, especially) left for the United States and Canada.

Unlike Western Europeans, Eastern Europeans value the idea of religion, and they seem to be more open to the gospel. The small Protestant churches in Central Europe resemble modern American Protestant churches while the Protestant churches in Ukraine and Romania have retained their historic cultural styles of worship. Romania, Ukraine, and Moldova have the greatest number of evangelical believers and have embraced the call to missions by sending out missionaries. For a number of years, Ukrainian public schools have been teaching a Christian ethics course based on biblical teaching.

Religions of Eastern Europe

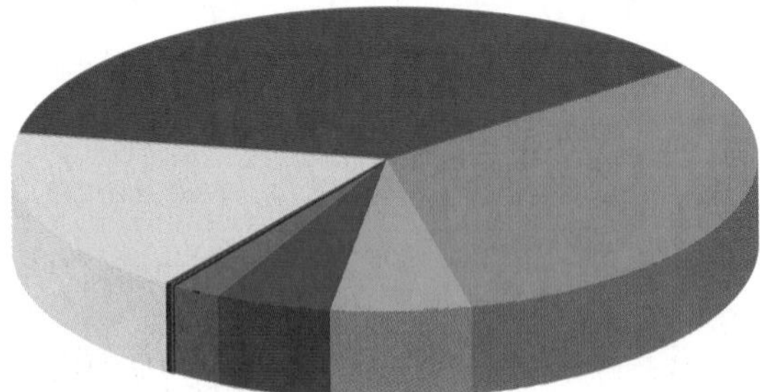

Religion	Percent
Orthodox	36.9%
Roman Catholic	31.7%
Islamic	5.9%
Protestant	5.0%
Protestant Evangelical	2.3%
Ethnic	0.1%
Other	0.3%
Unaffiliated	17.8%

Majority Catholic: Poland, Lithuania, Slovakia, Hungary, and Croatia
Majority Orthodox: Macedonia, Montenegro, Bulgaria, Romania, Belarus, Ukraine, Moldova, and Serbia
Majority Muslim: Kosovo
Majority Unaffiliated: Estonia and Czechia

SECTION REVIEW

1. In what ways have the peoples of Eastern Europe suffered?
2. Why would the Eastern European countries not want to be part of a "United States of Europe"?
3. Why might these countries be having such a hard time keeping their youth, and why are the youth able to leave?
4. How are Romanians and Moldovans unique compared to their neighbors?
5. How did the former governments change the culture of Eastern Europe?
6. Why might the Ukrainian Protestant church be one of the strongest in Eastern Europe?

INTERACTIONS OF PEOPLE AND PLACES

What are some of the challenges of living in Eastern Europe?

GUIDING QUESTIONS

- How do the economies and demographics of Eastern Europe affect how the citizens interact with the environment?
- What are the environmental issues of Eastern Europe?
- What are the causes and effects of environmental issues in Eastern Europe?
- What are possible solutions to environmental issues in Eastern Europe?

As previously mentioned, a country's economic health is related to its ability to pursue environmental health. The map on page 272 provides a general idea of how well the countries of Eastern Europe are addressing pollution, deforestation, and the cleanup of waste. The Baltics and Poland, in particular, have made great progress in cleaning up their Soviet-era waste and lessening their amount of continued pollution. One unique positive aspect of Eastern Europe is its amount of underdeveloped farmland. While the Dutch are trying to make farming profitable by going high-tech, some Romanians are trying to make a profit by retaining their no-tech farming. Many Romanian farmers still use horses and hand tools to grow and harvest crops. This less intrusive farming has been lauded by outsiders as an example of the perfect harmony of people and nature. Because the farms have not been industrialized, they continue to grow genetically diverse crops—unlike the rest of the world, which grows a very limited variety of popular crops. Genetically diverse plants have a greater natural ability to combat diseases and pests. These farmers are selling products like jams, honey, breads, and relishes made in the traditional manner. They sell the products over the internet. Because these products are of such high quality, they are able to sell them at a higher price. They are also opening the farms to tourists. Whether this can be expanded and be profitable enough to keep the children on the farm is yet to be seen. Just as the innovation of Dutch tech farming will benefit the whole world, so Romania's knowledge of less invasive farming methods and their biodiverse crops will benefit the whole world.

Romanians use traditional methods to farm.

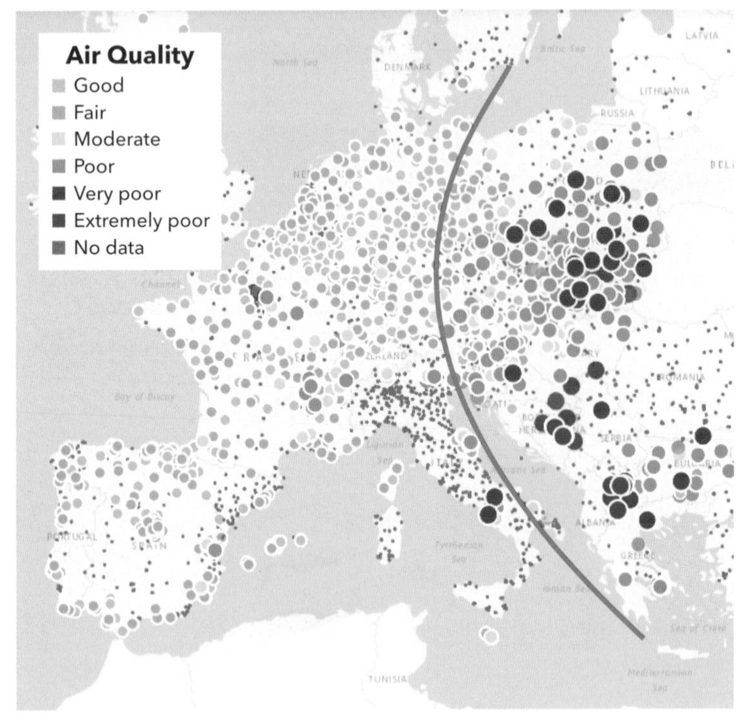

▲ *The iron curtain of air pollution*

Interaction with the Environment

Water

Water pollution is also a big problem in this region. In many of the poorer countries, raw or poorly treated sewage flows into the rivers and seas. The Danube River is still heavily polluted. Czechia, Poland, and the Baltics have at least been able to assess the problem, finding 95 percent of the water unsafe for drinking.

Air

There is an "iron curtain" of air pollution in Europe. Western Europe struggles with air pollution in the cities, especially in the winters, but Eastern Europe has much higher levels of pollution year-round and not just in the cities.

Land

While places like Romania are commended for their lack of industrialized farming, Moldova and Ukraine suffer from the contamination of their soil through the overuse of pesticides and fertilizers. The farms are experiencing a lack of fertility. The land also has high levels of contamination from heavy metals. Belarus and Ukraine have to deal with radiation-contaminated land not only from Chernobyl but other leftover nuclear waste. Bosnia still has land mines throughout the country placed there during the war in the 1990s.

▼ *Workers clear landmines in Bosnia, long after the conflict has ended.*

GLOBAL IMPACT | Chernobyl

▾ *Chernobyl's reactor number 4, a few weeks after it exploded*

On April 26, 1986, the worst single environmental disaster in history occurred at the Chernobyl nuclear reactor number 4 in Pripyat, Ukraine. At the time Ukraine was still a part of the Soviet Union. During a test to see whether backup power would work, the reactor blew up, melted down, and spewed huge amounts of radioactive material into the air. The radiation was four hundred times the amount of radiation of the bomb dropped on Hiroshima. The outside world did not learn about the accident until two days later when the radiation cloud reached Sweden, setting off detectors.

The reactor had serious design flaws, most notably the lack of a concrete-steel containment building which every other nuclear reactor worldwide had. This structure would have contained the radioactive material after the explosion. Helicopters had to dump sand and boron on top to put out the fires, but the radioactive material was also burning through the ground toward water tanks below. Firefighters sacrificed their lives to put out the fire. The room where their clothes were piled is still one of the most radioactive places on earth. Three men volunteered to walk into the reactor building to empty the water tanks manually, thus preventing a second greater explosion. Amazingly, they survived the task.

Like most manmade disasters, this event was the result of a series of errors. It seems the ultimate cause was the Soviet Communist political system, a system that valued the "greater good" over individual initiative and party loyalty over competence. It was a system that punished people for taking responsibility and rewarded dishonesty. The last General Secretary of the Soviet Union, Mikhail Gorbachev, believed that this accident played a part in the collapse of the Soviet Union.

▴ *Almost four thousand human "biorobots" had to clean the highly radioactive debris off the roof of reactor number 3. At first robots were tried, but they quickly broke down because of the radiation. Each man could work no longer than forty seconds before the radiation dose received was the maximum dose a person should receive in his entire life. The stripes on the image are caused by radiation damage.*

Today there is a one-thousand-square-mile exclusion area around Chernobyl. The area will be unsafe for permanent habitation for twenty thousand years. In the end, the death toll from this disaster was less than predicted. A total of 31 died immediately after the explosion and during the weeks that followed. There is a disagreement over the true number of cancer deaths related to the accident. The reasonable range seems to be between 5,000 and 57,000.

◂ *The abandoned city of Pripyat, Ukraine, today, with the nuclear plant in the background*

1. Why would the world have to learn indirectly about this accident?
2. How might the fear of taking responsibility for mistakes cause worse accidents to happen?
3. Considering nuclear power can generate abundant electricity with only steam emissions, should it be abandoned as a result of Chernobyl? Why or why not?

Reasons for Environmental Issues

Sewage flows freely today because many cities do not have wastewater treatment facilities or the facilities are inadequate. Flood management is also poor so that flooding is common and the water can quickly get polluted. There are many toxic waste dumps leaking hazardous chemicals into the rivers, seas, and ground water.

The air pollution stems from the use of old, inefficient coal power plants. People also still burn wood or poor-quality coal to heat their homes in the winter. They tend to drive cars that were not built with modern emission standards.

There was little regard during the Soviet years to conserve the environment since there was an abundance of land and people. During that time production quotas in farming and manufacturing took precedence over the environment. Collectivization meant that all farms followed the same practices since government controlled all the land.

Proposed Solutions

The best solution to all the environmental problems is continued economic expansion. As these countries are able to move to service sector industries, there will be less pollution and more money for the continued cleanup from the years of environmental neglect. Poland has committed to have 15 percent of its power coming from renewable sources in 2020. They are building two nuclear plants after avoiding that power source for obvious reasons.

The EU has taken the lead in formulating plans to clean up the Danube. But the Eastern European countries pushed back, saying the plans hinder their economic development. In 2011 a commission presented the "European strategy for the Danube region," a plan to balance ecological and economic interests. It takes a generational effort to clean up the water, but the first step is forming a plan.

Employees of the Romanian Waters Authority collect water samples in the Danube River.

Ukraine has had to spend a large percentage of its national wealth to clean up Chernobyl. Following the disaster, the Soviets built a sarcophagus over the top of the reactor that was designed to last thirty years, but by 1996 it had already deteriorated so much that it was allowing large amounts of radiation to escape. While Ukraine made some repairs, the need for a permanent structure was obvious. In 2018 a French company led an alliance of European companies to secure the reactor for one hundred years. From contract signing to completion, the project took eleven years. They began construction

Chernobyl New Safe Confinement

Capacity

Durability
100 years

Wind speed
158-206 M/h (level three tornado)

Resources

Workers on-site
1,200

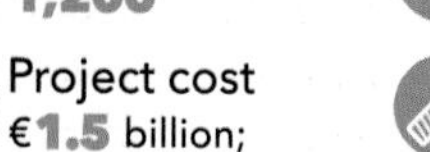
Project cost
€**1.5** billion;
US **$2.3** billion

Nations
27

Screws used
500,000

Timing

Construction began
2010

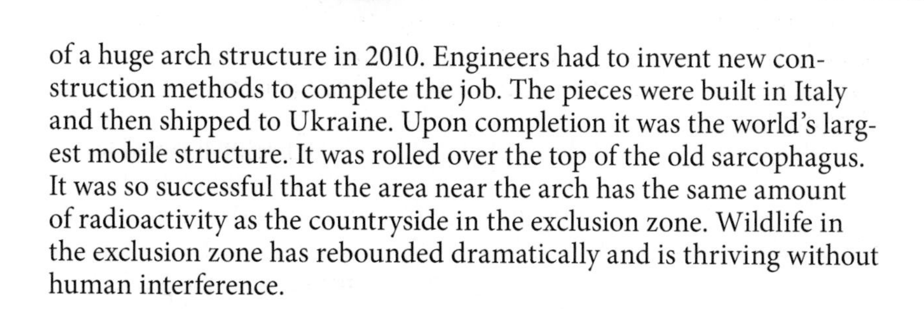

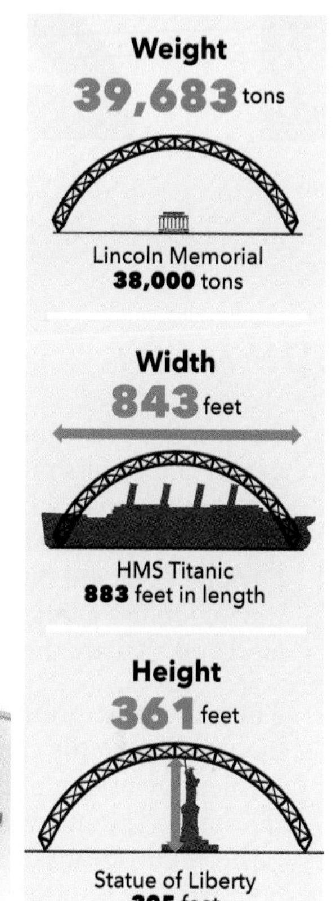

of a huge arch structure in 2010. Engineers had to invent new construction methods to complete the job. The pieces were built in Italy and then shipped to Ukraine. Upon completion it was the world's largest mobile structure. It was rolled over the top of the old sarcophagus. It was so successful that the area near the arch has the same amount of radioactivity as the countryside in the exclusion zone. Wildlife in the exclusion zone has rebounded dramatically and is thriving without human interference.

SECTION REVIEW

1. What are the benefits of Romanians making their farming styles profitable? What are their major obstacles?
2. Why is the air pollution in Eastern Europe so much worse than in Western Europe?
3. Why might collectivized farms have been more susceptible to poor environmental practices?
4. What positives can you infer from the past environmental disasters of Eastern Europe?
5. Compare the cleanup story of Chernobyl to stories of environmental cleanups in previous chapters. What are some common themes?

12 CHAPTER REVIEW

SUMMARY

1. Eastern Europe is mostly flat because the Great European Plain covers most of the region. Karst topography (caves and sinkholes) is caused by the erosion of chemical sedimentary rocks. The Black Sea and the Danube River are the largest bodies of water. Most of the region has a humid continental climate. Arable land and coal are the two most important resources.

2. There are three groups of countries: former Soviet bloc nations in the central and northern regions, former Soviet republics in the east, and the Balkans in the south. The majority are members of the EU. Most Eastern Europeans are Slavic while as many as seven countries are of other ethnicities. Communism had a big impact on the culture. Catholicism is predominant in the west, while Orthodox religions dominate the east and Islam the south.

3. The greatest environmental advantage of this region is the amount of untouched or lightly impacted land, especially in Romania. The former Soviet Republics have by far the most environmental issues. The Chernobyl explosion was the greatest single environmental disaster in history. Eastern Europe is beginning to implement cleanup plans as countries grow their economies.

Terms to Know

- ❑ shatter belt
- ❑ karst topography
- ❑ Soviet bloc
- ❑ collectivization
- ❑ Balkanization
- ❑ ethnic cleansing

Making Connections

1. What are the positive and negative aspects of Eastern Europe being dominated by the Great European Plain?
2. Contrast the Baltic States and the Balkans.
3. Why might the Romani be looked down upon in Europe?
4. How might the years Eastern Europe was under communism be considered lost years?
5. What two forms of Christianity are most common in Eastern Europe? Which of the two is associated with Western Europe?

Developing Geography Skills

1. Based on the map on page 261, why would Russia have an interest in the countries of the Eastern Plains?
2. Look at the map on page 272. What conclusions can be made about the relationships of religion, geographical location, levels of freedom, and economic health?

Thinking Critically

1. How have the Balkans exhibited Balkanization? How have the many mountains of the Balkans contributed to Balkanization?
2. What are the potential benefits and problems of keeping out new immigrants and refugees?

Living in God's World

1. God created His world with built-in laws. Explain what laws of creation communism may have broken. Think about both scriptural teaching regarding money and the effects of communism on economies and families.
2. How does the idea of ethnic cleansing run counter to the fact that everyone is created in the image of God? Consider Joshua 2:9 and 11:19. How was God's command to the Israelites different from the ethnic cleansing of the Bosniaks?

CASE STUDY | Separatist Movements

▲ *A woman shows her house hit by shelling in the conflict between Russian backed separatists and the Ukrainian army.*

This region is a shatter belt, and even today Ukraine and Moldova are struggling with open rebellion among some of their citizens. Estonia and Latvia fear that their ethnic Russian populations have more loyalties to Russia than to their home country. These difficulties are the legacy of Joseph Stalin, who relocated ethnic Russians into these countries 70 to 85 years ago.

As of 2019 Ukraine is in the midst of a significant war that began in 2014 and has not received much attention from the Western media. It involves an area a little smaller than West Virginia called the Donbass region which is made up of the Luhansk and Donetsk oblasts. The war began when the Ukrainian government made a move away from the EU toward Russia, which the people soundly rejected. The majority of Ukrainians want to be part of the EU. Russian special forces quickly took the Crimean Peninsula, with its 77 percent Russian majority population. But the Ukrainians were not so quick to give up the Donbass region, and Russia does not want to risk the international condemnation of openly invading. So a low-intensity conflict continues, with casualties reaching 13,000 as of 2018.

Because Ukraine is not a member of NATO, it is vulnerable to Russia. The United States and the European Union have enacted sanctions against Russia because of the Crimean annexation and their continued support for the rebels in Donbass. After peace talks, a security zone was created between the Ukrainian forces and the rebels, but artillery fire is still traded across the security zone regularly.

Moldova has similar issues with its eastern state of Transnistria. In 1992, after Moldova became a country, the state of Transnistria, which is one-third Moldovan, one-third Ukrainian, one-third Russian, wanted to remain part of Russia. The Transnistrians looked fondly at Soviet times. Since Moldova had no means of holding onto the territory, it had to let it go, but the Moldovan government will not acknowledge Transnistrian independence officially, and neither will any other country in the world.

1. Why would Russia not want Ukraine to become a member of the EU?
2. Why might Ukraine want to hold onto its territory even though a majority of the population within the Donbass region does not want to be part of Ukraine?
3. How might events during the Soviet era play a part in this conflict?
4. Why might some people desire a return to the days of the Soviet Union?

chapter 13

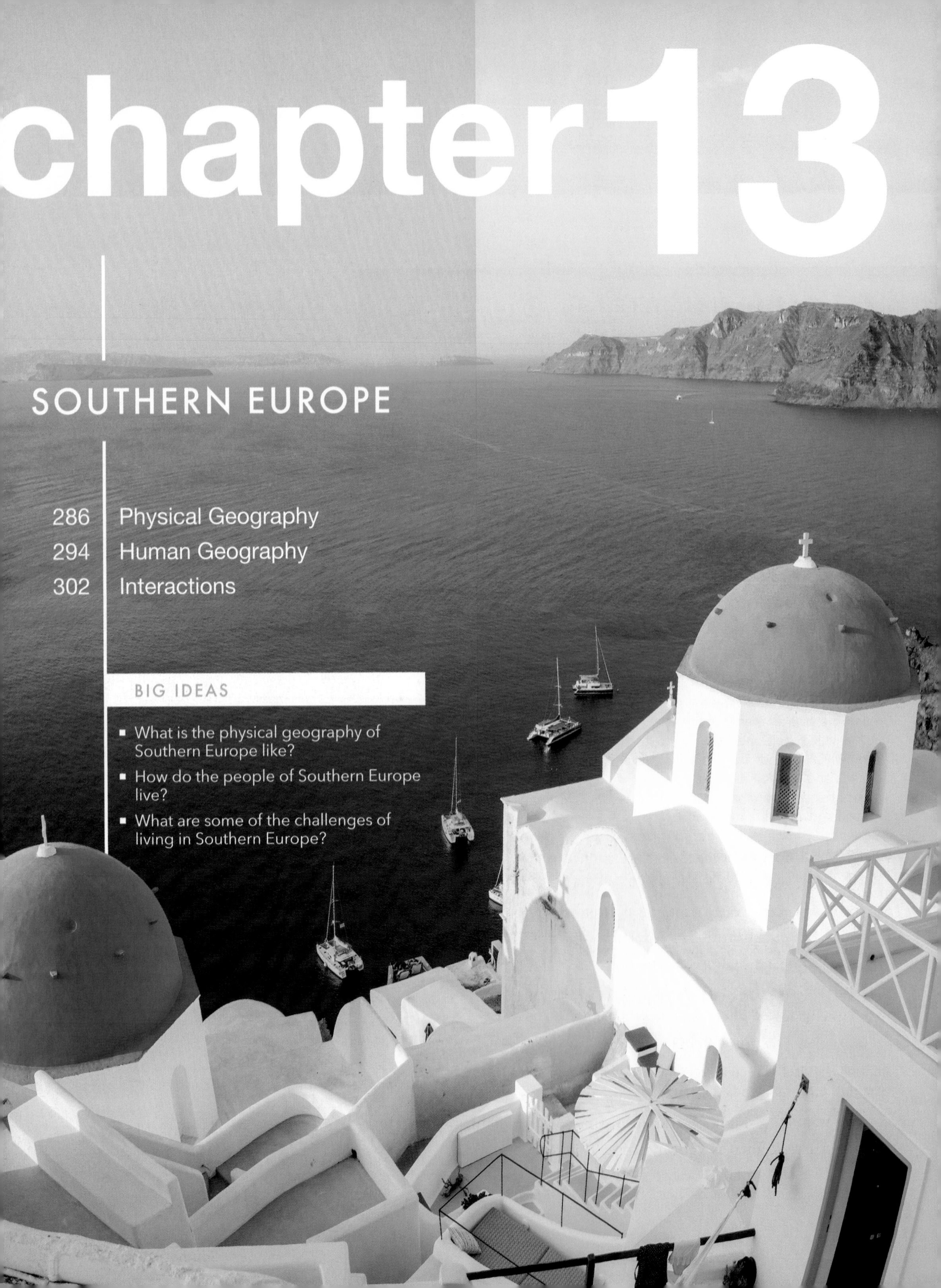

SOUTHERN EUROPE

286 Physical Geography
294 Human Geography
302 Interactions

BIG IDEAS

- What is the physical geography of Southern Europe like?
- How do the people of Southern Europe live?
- What are some of the challenges of living in Southern Europe?

▲ *Ruins of the Forum in Rome*

Medieval bridge of the Besalu in Catalonia, Spain ▶

◀ *Greek village*

ROME THE CITY, THE EMPIRE

The story of Rome the city began nearly 2,800 years ago as various fortified villages eventually merged to become one city that was founded, according to legend, by brothers Romulus and Remus. Rome became the capital of the Roman Republic, which transitioned into the Roman Empire. With the collapse of the empire, Germanic tribes ravaged Rome, and the city fell into disrepair for centuries. The rise of Italian city-states brought the Italian peninsula and the city of Rome back into prominence, especially during the Renaissance. Modern metropolitan Rome has a population of 4 million and the distinction of containing a tiny state, known as Vatican City, within its boundaries.

The Pena National Palace in Sintra, Portugal ▶

GUIDING QUESTIONS

- What are the regions of Southern Europe?
- What caused the landforms of Southern Europe?
- What bodies of water are important to Southern Europe?
- What are the climates of Southern Europe?
- What natural resources are found in Southern Europe?

Southern European nations are located on three peninsulas that jut out into the Mediterranean Sea, so these nations are also referred to as Mediterranean Europe. The people of this region have made many contributions to the Western world, including philosophy, language, navigation, and mathematics.

Ready access to large bodies of water affords these nations many benefits. The sea offers food, provides harbors, and moderates the climate.

Proximity to water by four of these nations has also resulted in shipbuilding and travel by sea. Transportation to and from these nations has continued from ancient times to the present. Trade has also been a vital part of the economies of these nations.

IBERIAN PENINSULA

The Iberian Peninsula received its name from ancient Greek explorers and is mentioned in Greek writings as early as 500 BC. The Romans added an "h" to the beginning of the name (Iberian), but otherwise, the name has remained unchanged for over 2,500 years. This peninsula touches the Atlantic Ocean on the west and the Mediterranean Sea on the east. Three countries are located on this peninsula: Portugal, Spain, and Andorra.

Portugal lies on the west coast of the Iberian Peninsula. Given its ready access to the sea, Portugal became a seagoing nation and was among the first during the Age of Exploration to establish colonies and trading posts as far away as China.

Over 80 percent of the Iberian Peninsula lies in Spain. Spain's capital, Madrid, is perched on a plateau over two thousand feet high, and is the highest capital in Europe. A high plateau called the *Meseta*, or "tableland," extends from Madrid across most of interior Spain.

Nestled high in the Pyrenees Mountains, Andorra lies between Spain and France. Its name may have come from an old Moorish word meaning "thickly wooded place," but it is indeed a mixture of Spain and France. The official language is Catalán. Isolated by steep mountains in their fertile valleys, the Andorrans lived as farmers and shepherds when Charlemagne, according to tradition, granted them independence in exchange for help in fighting the Moors.

PHYSICAL GEOGRAPHY

Regions of Southern Europe

What is the physical geography of Southern Europe?

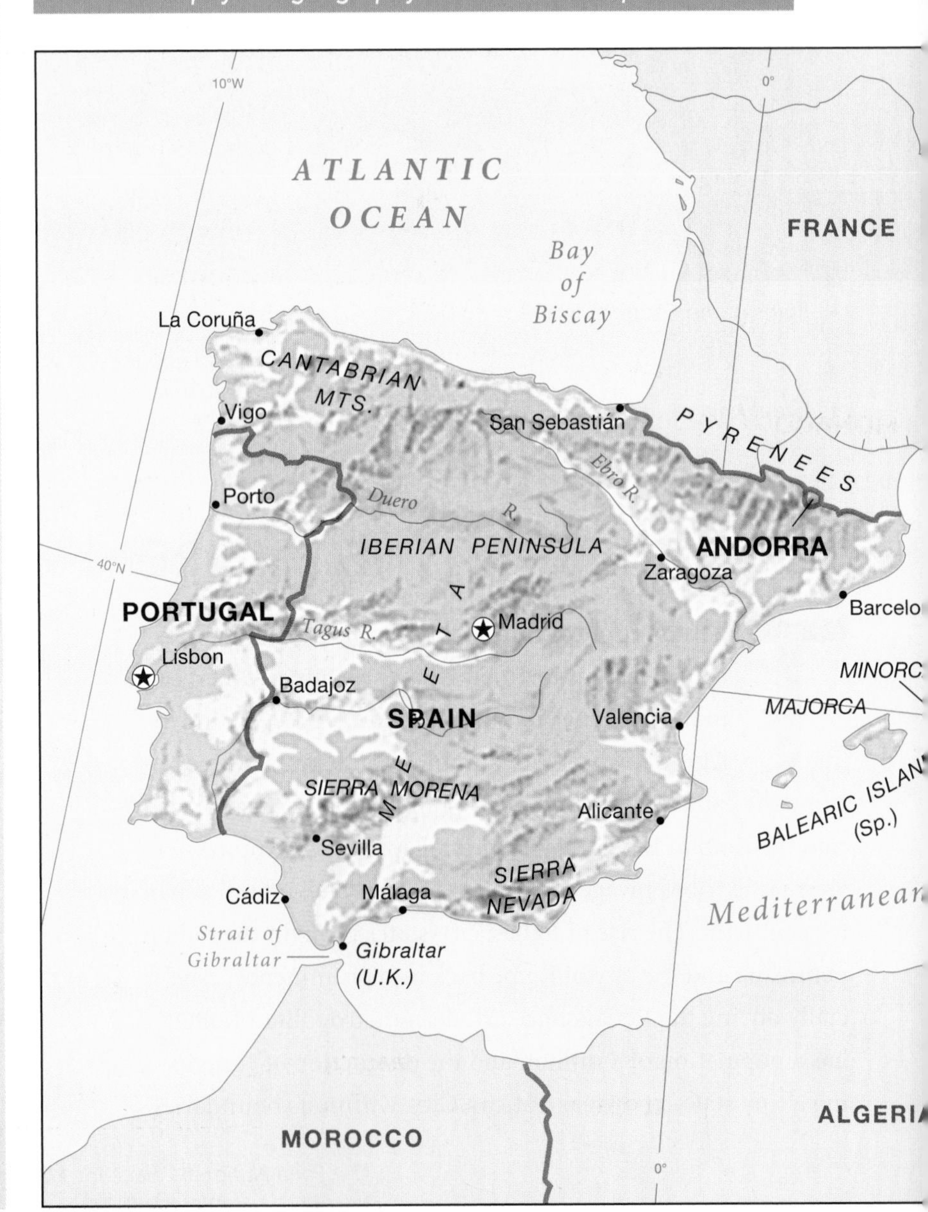

ITALIAN PENINSULA

Italy occupies a long and narrow boot-shaped peninsula. The Alps form the top of the boot, while the toe reaches almost to Africa. Italy's coastline stretches for 4,722 miles and is known more for its beautiful beaches and resorts than its natural harbors. Nearly three-fourths of the country's land is either hilly or mountainous. The Apennine Mountains run the length of the Italian peninsula.

The island country of Malta is located about sixty miles south of Sicily in the Mediterranean Sea. The country consists of the two islands of Gozo and Malta as well as a few smaller islands. On Malta, a series of low hills dominates the terrain. Gozo is primarily a flat island with rocky soil and few rivers.

SOUTHERN BALKAN PENINSULA

Greece occupies the southern tip of the Balkan Peninsula, which juts out of Europe at the eastern end of the Mediterranean. Greece's terrain is mostly rough and mountainous, but about 30 percent of the country has arable soil. Greece also controls many islands located near the peninsula.

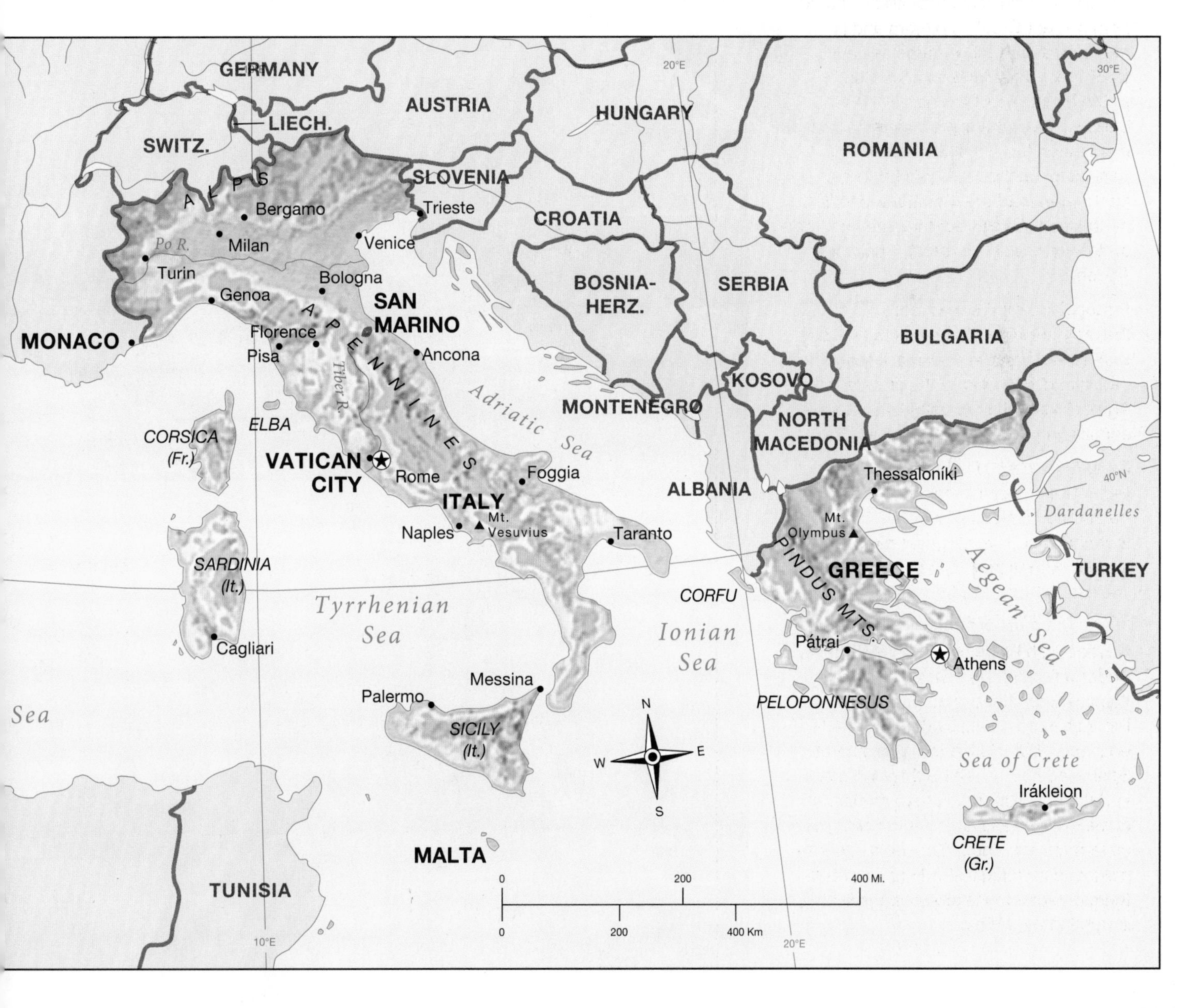

Physical Landforms

Plate tectonics caused folding or faulting and formed many of the mountain ranges in Southern Europe. Other mountains were formed by volcanoes. Glaciation shaped the mountains and formed the valleys. Two mountain ranges form the geographic boundary between Continental Europe and Southern Europe: the Pyrenees north of Andorra and the Alps north of Italy. The Pyrenees Mountains are flat-topped massifs. A **massif** is a mountain formed by fault-line movement.

Pyrenees Mountains

Mountaineers on a glacier plateau in Italy

The ruins of Pompeii with Mount Vesuvius in the background

The snow-covered Alps in northern Italy ▸

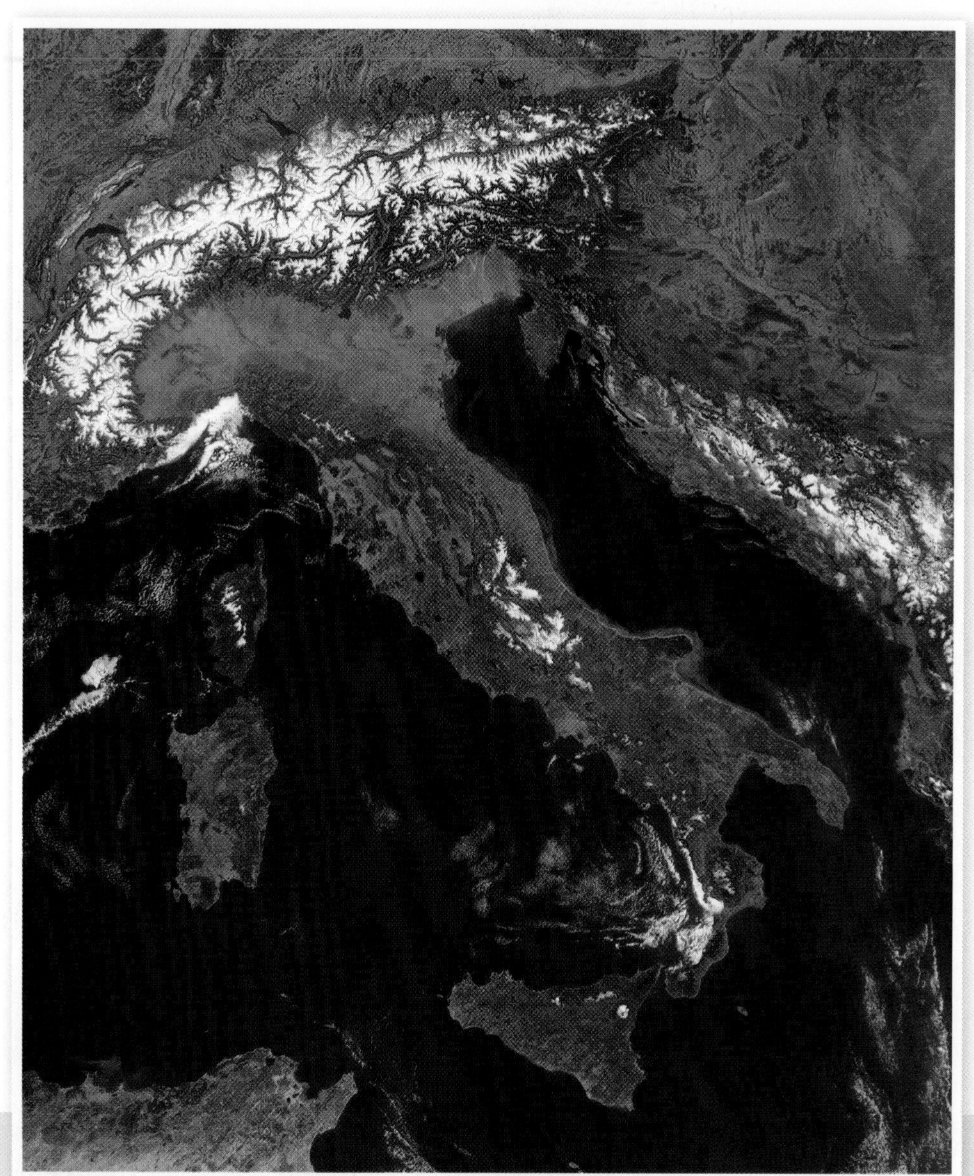

Bodies of Water

Oceans and Seas

Southern Europe touches five large bodies of water. Portugal and Spain have coasts along the Atlantic Ocean. Spain and Italy have coasts along the Mediterranean Sea. The Adriatic Sea extends along the eastern side of the Italian Peninsula, and the Ionian Sea lies south of the Italian Peninsula and west of Greece. The Aegean Sea lies east of Greece.

▾ *A view of the Aegean Sea*

▲ *Douro River in Portugal*

Rivers

Three significant rivers flow through Portugal and Spain: the Tagus, Douro, and Guadiana Rivers. Andorra has a single drainage basin that forms the Gran Valira. While Italy has several rivers, one of the most important is the Po River in northern Italy. This river deposits rich soil that enables extensive farming of vegetables, grapes, wheat, corn, and barley. In addition, the Po River is navigable by large ship as far as Turin, near the French border. Other rivers in Italy include the Adige, Tiber, and Piave. Important rivers in Greece include the Maritsa, Struma, Vardar, and Haliacmon. In addition to transportation, many of these rivers provide hydropower for production of electricity.

GLOBAL IMPACT | Venice: Queen of the Adriatic

▼ *Flooding in Venice's St. Mark Square during the Acqua Alta, an annual high tide of the Adriatic Sea*

The magnificent city of Venice, called by some the "Floating City," was constructed in the Venetian lagoon between the mouths of the Po and Piave Rivers in northern Italy at the north end of the Adriatic Sea. The city spreads across 118 islands, and construction was supported by driving posts of alderwood into the silt and soft clay. Workers laid Istrian limestone over these wooden piles to support the buildings that were built over them. The city is divided by canals, and areas of the city are connected by four hundred bridges. Built originally to escape the marauding Germanic tribes, this city grew to become a sovereign city-state and was known as the Republic of Venice from 697 to 1797. Venice became a rich and powerful city by maintaining a monopoly on trade in silk, grain, and spices for centuries. Venice also became the staging ground for the Crusades in the thirteenth century and a center of Renaissance activity in the fourteenth century. However, the city has also struggled for centuries to control the flooding from the Adriatic that naturally occurs every year between autumn and early spring. Modern issues include too many tourists for the city's resources to accommodate, gradual sinking of the city between one and two millimeters each year, and increased frequency of low-level flooding that often makes the first floor of buildings unusable.

1. Where is Venice located?
2. How would a person move from one area of the city to another?
3. What annual event causes problems in the city?
4. What would you consider to be the greatest modern challenge for this city? Why?

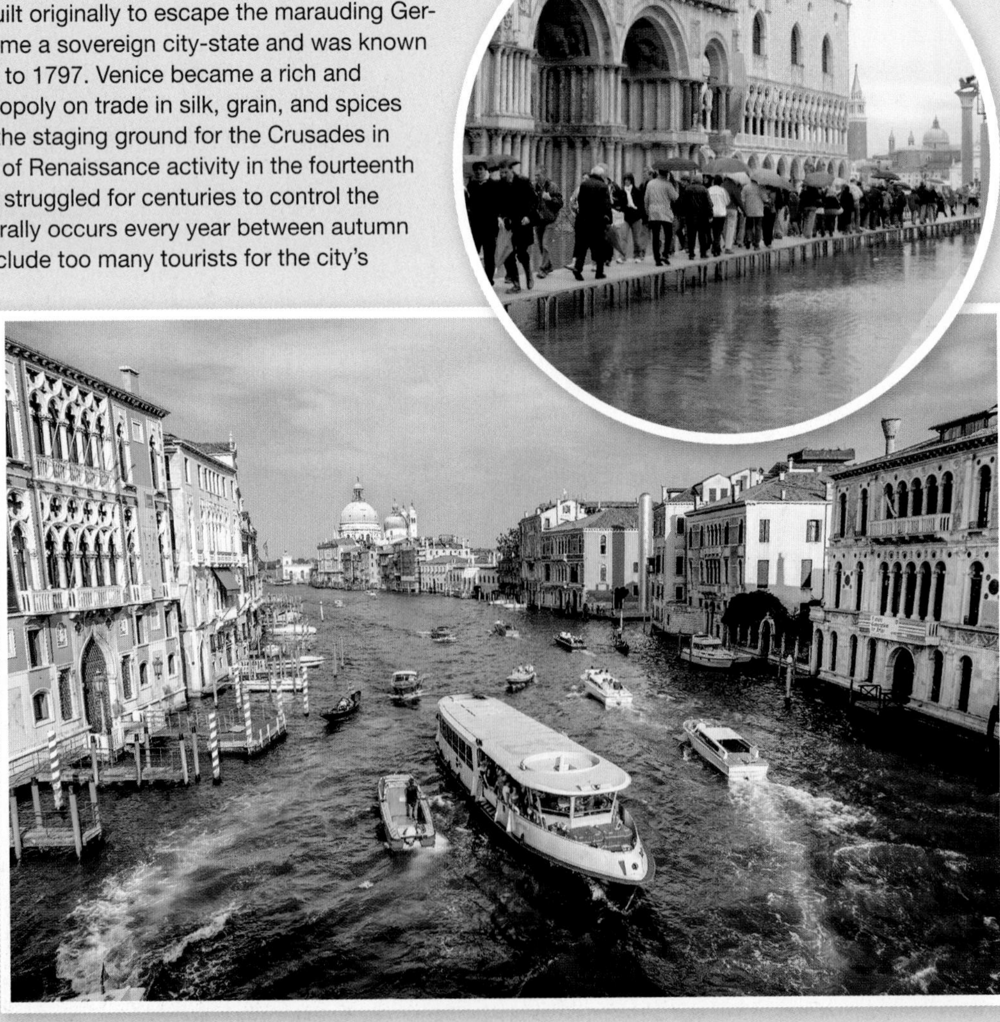

Venice, Italy ▶

Climates of Southern Europe

The climates of Southern Europe vary based on proximity to large bodies of water and elevation. Climates include various forms of mediterranean, semiarid, continental, and tundra.

Portugal's climate is primarily warm mediterranean. Spain's climates vary by location and include a hot summer mediterranean climate, a warm summer mediterranean climate, a semiarid climate, and a warm summer continental climate.

Andorra has two regions that result in two major climates. Valleys have a temperate climate, while higher elevations have a tundra climate.

Italy has similar variations in climate. The inland northern area of Italy enjoys a cool, humid subtropical climate. Along the coasts residents enjoy a mediterranean climate. Temperatures in Italy tend to be low in the winter and moderate in the summer.

Greece's climate is predominately mediterranean and varies in the level of moisture. The mountains in Greece have a tundra climate at higher elevations.

Example of the warm climate in Spain along the Mediterranean coast

Vineyards thrive in the humid climate of the Piedmont in Northern Italy.

Example of the temperate climate near the Pyrenees Mountains in Andorra

Greece enjoys a mediterranean climate.

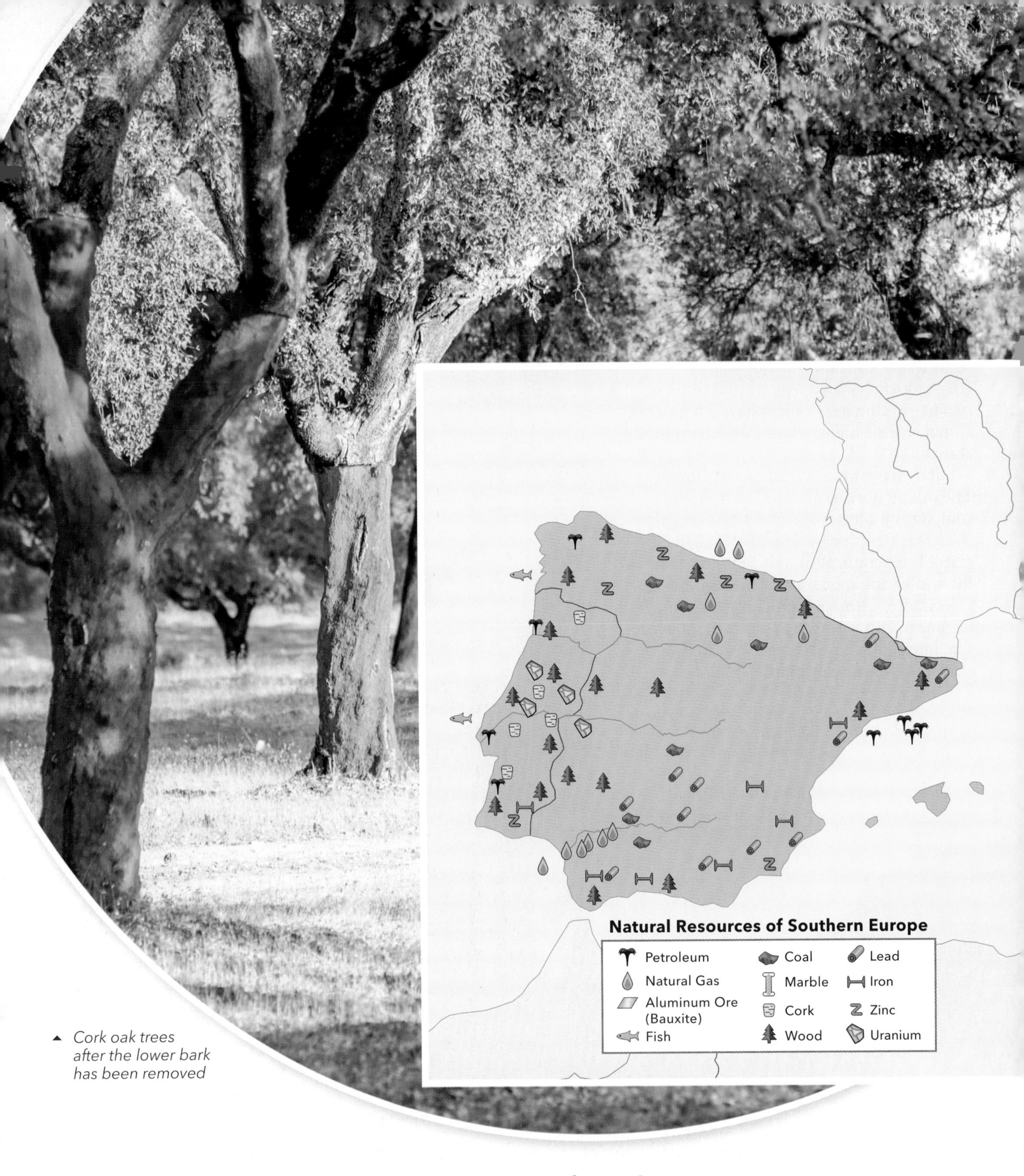

▲ *Cork oak trees after the lower bark has been removed*

Resources of Southern Europe

Southern Europe has a variety of resources, including common items such as iron ore, zinc, lead, copper, and coal. Rarer materials include small deposits of diamonds, gold, and uranium.

SECTION REVIEW

1. Between which lines of latitude does most of Southern Europe lie?
2. How do the latitude of Southern Europe and its proximity to bodies of water affect its climate?
3. What bodies of water are important to Southern Europe?
4. What renewable resource is abundant in Portugal?
5. What resources are abundant in Southern Europe?

500 | 400 | 300 | 200 | 100 | 0 | 1300

509–27 BC Roman Republic

479–323 BC Hellenic Period in Greece

1300–1400 Renaissance begins in Italy

GUIDING QUESTIONS

- How has Southern Europe changed over time?
- How do the Southern European governments interact with their citizens?
- What is the economic health of Southern Europe?
- What are the demographics of Southern Europe?
- What are the cultural characteristics and diversity in Southern Europe?
- What forms of religion are practiced in Southern Europe?

HUMAN GEOGRAPHY

How do the people of Southern Europe live?

History

Iberian Peninsula

Various groups settled in this peninsula over time. Successive waves of invaders seized control of this peninsula and made use of its strategic location.

Portugal

Roman forces invaded in the third century BC. Visigoths and other Germanic tribes seized lands in the fifth century AD. Muslim forces invaded the peninsula in 711. Not until the eleventh century did Portugal become an independent state. In the fifteenth century Portugal briefly expanded to become a world power before going into decline in the sixteenth century. The military deposed the monarchy in 1910, and Portugal was ruled brutally by a dictatorship until 1974. The dictatorship was overthrown, and the new government granted many rights and freedoms to the Portuguese people.

Spain

Spain's main provinces were united in 1469 when Isabella I, queen of Castile, married Ferdinand II of Aragon. Most Spaniards are Roman Catholic, and Castilian Spanish is the primary language of business and government.

In 1936 the country was engulfed in a bloody civil war when Spain's military revolted against the country's newly formed Republican government. The fascist victor, Francisco Franco, ruled as a dictator from 1939 to 1973. After Franco's death, Juan Carlos became king of Spain. He pushed democratic reforms, and in 1978 Spain adopted a constitution. The government began to increase local control by allowing the election of regional parliaments. In an attempt to bolster the country's economy, Spain joined the European Economic Community (now the EU) in 1986.

Andorra

During the eighth century AD, this region served as a buffer zone between the Frankish kingdom under Charlemagne and Islamic invaders advancing from Spain. For centuries Spain or France dominated Andorra. During the Napoleonic wars Andorra remained

▾ *Andorra's national flag*

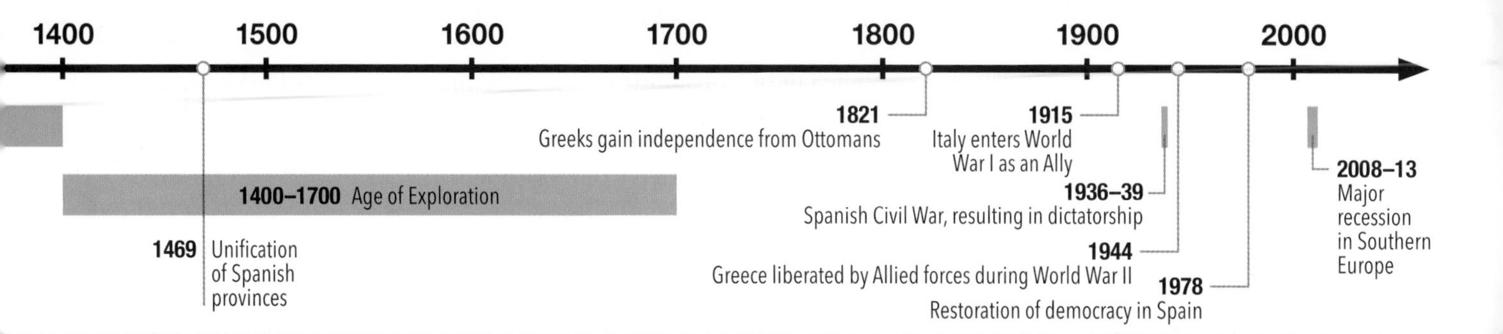

neutral and avoided conflict. Again, during World War II, Andorra maintained its neutrality.

Italian Peninsula

Italy's history can be divided into three main periods with several subdivisions. Ancient Rome began as a kingdom in 753 BC and lasted until the establishment of the Republic in 509 BC. Rome transitioned into an empire in 27 BC and lasted until AD 476.

Italy's second period of history parallels the time called the medieval period. Germanic tribes overran the Italian peninsula, and chaos ensued until the renewal of cities on the peninsula due to increased trade and the resulting wealth.

The development of the **Renaissance**, or rebirth of the arts, beginning in the fourteenth century inaugurated Italy's third period of history: modern Italy. While art, literature, and architecture excelled during this period, political division continued. The political movement to unite the Italian peninsula, called the *Risorgimento*, succeeded in unifying the country with the capture of Rome in 1870. The fascist period of Italy's history began under Benito Mussolini and lasted until 1946. Itay's current form of government as a republic began in 1946.

Malta has been inhabited for thousands of years and has been important for shipping and navies due to its harbors and location in the Mediterranean Sea. About AD 60 the apostle Paul was shipwrecked on Malta (Acts 27:27–28:11).

Balkan Peninsula

Greek history can be divided into five periods. Ancient Greece is dated from 1100 BC to 146 BC. During this period city-states developed. A **city-state** is an independent state consisting of a city and its surrounding territory. Two famous city-states on the Greek peninsula were Athens and Sparta. Following war between the leading city-states and the resulting decline, the ruler of Macedonia, a land north of Greece, united the two regions. His son, Alexander the Great, conquered the Persian Empire and spread Greek culture to the borders of India. Fracturing under Alexander's successors led to decline, and Greece entered its second period, Roman control from 146 BC to AD 324. With the moving of Rome's capital to Constantinople in the fourth century, Greece entered the Byzantine period from 324 to 1453.

▾ *Artist's reconstruction of the Acropolis in Athens*

The fall of Constantinople to Ottoman invaders in 1453 brought the Greek peninsula under Ottoman control, its fourth period lasting from 1453 to 1821. The struggle for independence from the declining Ottoman Empire led to Greek independence in 1821 and the commencement of modern Greece.

Government

Southern European governments are similar in function and in their giving a voice to the people through regular elections. They provide similar forms of representation, collect taxes to provide education and health care, and provide for the defense of their citizens. Some of these basic functions of government have existed in these countries for only a few decades, while others have been in place longer. All of the Southern European countries are also members of the European Union.

▼ *Spanish Parliament in Madrid, Spain*

▲ *Session of the Andorran Parliament in Andorra-la-Vella, with French president Emmanuel Macron participating*

Type of Government

Portugal has been a republic since 1834. Spain endured a dictatorship until 1978, when it became a parliamentary constitutional monarchy. Greece won its independence in 1821 and had various forms of government until democracy was restored in 1974. Italy became a parliamentary republic in 1978, and the Andorran people approved a constitutional referendum in 1994 that made their country a parliamentary democracy. Malta gained its independence from Britain in 1964 and is now a republic. Note the emphasis on a written form of law in the terms *constitutional* and *republic* and the emphasis on representation in the term *parliamentary.*

Education

All Southern European countries provide taxpayer-funded education for their children. The governments of Spain, Andorra, and Italy provide free and compulsory education between the ages of six and sixteen. Portugal's government provides free and compulsory education until the age of eighteen. Greece has a more structured educational system that provides free compulsory education beginning with primary school from the ages of six to twelve. Then the Greek students are routed either to a form of high school or to a vocational school, depending on various factors. Greek universities provide the third level of education.

Andorra's educational system is unique due to its proximity to both Spain and France and the large populations of Spanish and French students in Andorra. As a result, the schools located near France are French and receive financial support from France. The schools that are located near Spain are Spanish and receive financial support from Spain.

Health Care

Portugal has a taxpayer-funded National Health Service as well as a voluntary private health insurance. The National Health Service charges user fees to discourage abuse of the system. Portugal has public hospitals run by the state, social hospitals funded by private donations, and private hospitals for those who can afford them. Significant differences between these hospitals include wait times for service and the number of services available, with the private hospitals having the shortest wait times and the greatest number of services.

Spain and Italy have offered limited universal health care since 1978. Officials have recently endeavored to decentralize Spain's health care in order to better care for patients. The health care in Spain and Italy is supported by high taxes and suffers from long waits for service, limited care, and lengthy delays in seeing specialists, problems that plague most universal health-care systems.

Andorra and Greece also offer limited universal health care and allow those who can afford it to use private health care. Many of the features of universal health care are found in these countries as well, but Andorrans also have the option of purchasing private health insurance in addition to the state health insurance that is funded by taxation.

▲ *Andorran ski resort*

Economy

The service sector drives all of the Southern European economies, with 74–95 percent of the people working in services. Manufacturing and farming vary from 5 to 24 percent of these economies.

The estimated GDP in 2017 for these countries varied from $3 billion (Andorra) to $2.3 trillion (Italy). The workforces varied from just under forty thousand (Andorra) to nearly twenty-six million (Italy).

Portugal, Spain, and Italy have mixed economies. Greece and Andorra have free-market economies. Southern Europe suffered from an economic slump during the first decade of the twenty-first century, and all of the countries have had to make economic adjustments to recover. Greece was especially hard-hit due to a large national debt and the large number of citizens receiving government assistance or retirement payments. Attempts to restructure Greek debt, overcome widespread corruption, prevent tax evasion, and reduce the high unemployment have met with mixed results.

All the Southern European nations depend on tourism to strengthen their economy. However, Andorra and Greece have excelled in attracting tourists and their dollars. Greece relies on historic sites, long coastlines, islands, and beaches to draw foreigners, and more than thirty million tourists visited Greece in 2018. Andorra has transformed from an agricultural economy to a tourism-driven economy by building ski resorts in its many mountains and selling duty-free products. Andorra has also developed extensive hiking trails to attract tourists. Religious shrines and Romanesque churches attract many observers. Andorran banking has also attracted large financial deposits from abroad due to its tax haven status.

Demographics

In 2018 the combined estimated population of Southern Europe was 78.7 million, with Spain having the largest population at 47.7 million and Andorra having by far the smallest at 76,000. In most of these countries, the native population maintains a clear majority with some minority population. Andorra is distinct in that less than 50 percent of its population is native Andorran. Spanish, French, and Portuguese make up nearly half of Andorra's population.

In addition to a majority of Portuguese nationals in Portugal, Moldovians, Romanians, Russians, Bulgarians, and Venezuelans make up the minority population. Native Spanish make up the majority of their country's population, and Morrocans and Romanians contribute to Spain's total population. While Italians constitute a majority of Italy's population, Germans, French, Greeks, and Albanians also live there. Just over 90 percent of Greece's population is composed of native Greeks, and a minority of Italians and Albanians also reside there.

Culture and Diversity

Cultures of Southern Europe are a blend of earlier cultures, some of which are ancient. For example, Portuguese culture combines Celtic, Phoenician, Iberian, Germanic, and Roman elements. For many in Southern Europe, the rhythm of labor, leisure, and meals is different from that experienced by many Americans. Shops often close in the afternoon due to the heat, and many people take afternoon naps. Meals tend to be more deliberate and last longer as families fellowship around the dinner table.

Portuguese musicians playing a duet with a Portuguese guitar and an acoustic guitar

Music and Dance

In each of these cultures, music and dance are central elements. Each Southern European country has distinct cultural attire, dances, and music that are a blend of the various groups that contributed to its culture and history. All the Southern European countries also have modern forms of music. In addition, Portuguese music is a blend of traditional/folk and classical. Spanish music is predominately traditional and varies by region. Andorran music is primarily folk. Italian music ranges from folk to classical. Greek music blends traditional with Byzantine.

Spanish folk dancing in traditional costumes

▲ *Greek traditional dancing at the fort of Heraklion, Crete*

Italian folk dancing ▶

Food

Portuguese cuisine includes extensive use of seafood, rice, and chicken. Spanish cuisine varies across Spain's seventeen regions. However, a common course in Spanish homes is *paella*, a rice dish that may be topped with a variety of meats, including seafood.

Andorran cuisine includes the national dish *escudella* (hearty stew flavored with chicken legs or chicken neck and pig snout), *trinxat* (a fried mixture of mashed potatoes, cabbage, and leeks), *cargols* (snails), and *embotis* (cured meats including sausages, hams, and black puddings).

Italian cuisine varies by region but includes many foods that are familiar, including a variety of pastas, pizza, and espresso coffee. Tomatoes and olive oil are two key ingredients in many Italian dishes.

Greek cuisine features locally grown grains, grapes, and olives. Greek meals often include *moussaka* (an eggplant- or potato-based dish with ground meat), followed by *baklava* (dessert made of layers of phyllo dough and nuts, sweetened with syrup or honey), and thick coffee.

▲ *Paella, a typical Spanish food*

▼ *Baklava*

Escudella, a Catalan soup often served at Christmas ▶

A game of futsal in Lisbon, Portugal

Sports

While soccer tops the list of favorite sports in many Southern European countries, you might be surprised at the long list of sports that are very familiar. Cycling, basketball, volleyball, tennis, golf, and various forms of hockey are also very popular throughout this region. Portugal and Greece have even developed an indoor version of soccer, called ***futsal***, where two teams of five compete for goals. In addition, the countries with ready access to water enjoy many water sports. Andorra's landforms provide ideal conditions for hiking and skiing.

Religion

Roman Catholicism is the predominant form of Christianity found in most of Southern Europe. While other forms of Christianity and different religions have the right to assemble, they represent a tiny minority, with the notable exception of Greece. About 80 percent of the people of Portugal identify as Roman Catholics. Small groups of Protestant groups are found in this country, and less than 20 percent identify as "none" or "unspecified."

Until 1992 religious groups not recognized by the state were subject to persecution. Modern Spain is rapidly becoming a multireligious society in a secular state. Spaniards who associate with some form of Christianity represent about three-quarters of the population, while those who consider themselves nonreligious represent nearly one-fifth. Muslims constitute a small but growing presence, and Evangelical Christians make up a tiny fraction of the Spanish population. Many of the Evangelicals in Spain are immigrants, and they have increased the Evangelical population in the last five decades. They meet in small congregations throughout Spain.

Major Religions of Southern Europe

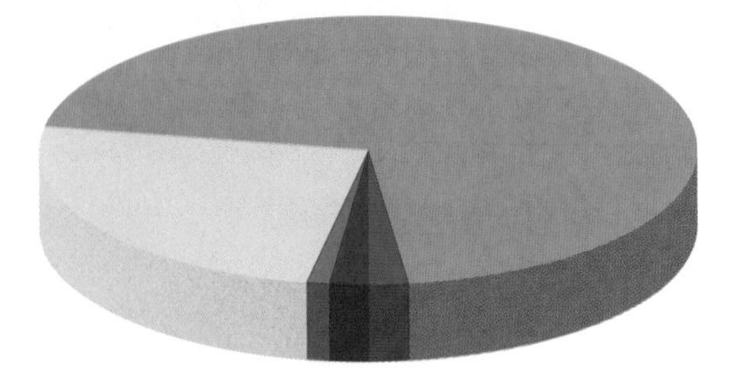

Roman Catholic	**70%**
Protestant	**2%**
Other	**2%**
Protestant Evangelical	**1%**
Unaffiliated	**25%**

The pope leads the Roman Catholic Church from Vatican City, sometimes referred to as the Holy See. The tiny country, completely surrounded by the city of Rome, obtained independence by the Lateran Treaty in 1929. With less than one thousand residents and an area of only one-sixth of a square mile, it is the smallest country in the world.

While the Roman Catholic Church remains the established church in Andorra, freedom of religion has been guaranteed since 1993. The vast majority of the people affiliate with some form of Christianity. Just under 10 percent are nonreligious, and Muslims represent a small but growing presence. Evangelical Christians may number a few hundred.

Malta is over 90 percent Roman Catholic but does allow freedom of worship. The minority is composed of various religious groups and a small percentage of agnostics or atheists.

At nearly 92 percent, Greek Orthodoxy remains the dominant form of Christianity in Greece. In addition, there is a tiny representation of Evangelicals, Muslims, and nonreligious in Greece.

MISSIONS IN EUROPE

Missionaries to Europe face a unique challenge. The people of Europe have had the gospel preached among them longer than any other part of the world except for the Middle East and North Africa. Of these three regions only Europe successfully resisted Muslim invasions. As a result, Europe has a long Christian heritage. The Reformation took place in Europe. Christians from Europe stood at the forefront of Christian missions in the eighteenth and nineteenth centuries. But at that time many Europeans began to doubt the Bible's truthfulness. In the last half-century, church attendance has dropped in many European countries. In some Roman Catholic countries church attendance may be higher, but the need for the gospel is just as great. Missionaries and pastors in Europe face the challenge of bringing the gospel to people who are familiar with a nominal form of Christianity (Christianity in name only) and therefore are not interested in the biblical message of the gospel.

The value that Europeans place on community and compassion provides an open door for Christian ministry. Europeans believe that churches should be involved in compassionate outreach to those who are most vulnerable. Christians who show the love of Christ in meeting people's temporal needs are therefore more likely to find opportunities to minister to people's eternal needs. While the former ministry should never replace evangelism, it is a valid means of displaying the love of Christ in a way that opens doors for evangelistic ministry.

▲ *Reformation Wall in Geneva, Switzerland*

1. Why is mission outreach to Europe challenging?
2. Why is Europe no longer active in sending out missionaries?
3. Why is it difficult to effectively communicate the gospel to many Europeans?
4. How might missionaries in Europe demonstrate Christ's love?

SECTION REVIEW

1. How has Southern Europe changed over time?
2. How well do the Southern European governments provide for the education, health, and safety of their citizens?
3. How would you describe the economies of Southern Europe?
4. Describe the demographics of Southern Europe.
5. What are some cultural characteristics and examples of diversity in Southern Europe?

GUIDING QUESTIONS

- How do the Southern European economies and people interact with the environment?
- What are environmental issues in Southern Europe?
- What are causes and effects of environmental issues in Southern Europe?
- What are possible solutions to environmental issues in Southern Europe?

▲ *Waste, garbage, and dirt floating in the Mediterranean Sea near Cyprus*

INTERACTIONS OF PEOPLE AND PLACES

What are some of the challenges of living in Southern Europe?

Interaction with the Environment

Southern European nations have striven to bring their economies and workforces into the twenty-first century. Industries and tourist regions have been promoted in order to bring much-needed money to these countries. Unemployment and underemployment have created unstable societies in Southern Europe. As a result the governments have endeavored to attract companies and make use of resources that produce enough jobs to meet human needs. Success in creating jobs also provides taxable incomes that pay for the many services these countries have promised to their citizens. Many resources, including timber, have been consumed for centuries, and too often little thought was given to replacing or wisely stewarding these resources.

Reasons for Environmental Issues

Given the variety of governments in some of these countries over several decades, little attention has been paid to adequate processing of pollutants and wastes. Economic and political struggles have also hindered a robust response to environmental issues.

Water

The transition from an agricultural to an industrial or tourist economy led to a neglect of the problems of runoff of chemicals, processing of waste, and proper care of water sources. Access to clean water is an ongoing issue, and the effort to maintain effective water treatment facilities remains a priority in these nations.

Air

The growth of industrial centers in many of these countries has resulted in significant air pollution. Increased use of automobiles has also contributed to contamination of the air. The priority has often been financial gain, and the environment has suffered as a result. Financial struggles have often left these governments ill-equipped to rally the resources needed to protect the air.

Land

Effective removal and processing of trash remains a major problem. These countries often lack sufficient land for proper storage of their nation's trash and struggle to bring this problem under control.

Removal of replaceable resources such as timber has led to erosion and loss of valuable topsoil. In addition, forms of plant life that have thrived in wooded areas have been depleted. Loss of soil has resulted in a reduction of farming land in a region that has little to spare due to the many mountains where agricultural use of land is difficult if not impossible.

◂ *Chemical runoff from a deserted open-pit mine in Portugal*

▲ *This dam on the Douro River on the Spain/Portugal border produces hydroelectric power.*

Proposed Solutions

The nations of Southern Europe currently have growing economies. Continued economic prosperity will be essential in order to pay the enormous cost of reducing the human impact on the environment and replacing certain resources. For example, Greece has significant potential for increasing use of hydropower to produce electricity and thereby reducing its use of polluting fuels. Spain has a goal of producing 70 percent of its electricity production by hydropower in 2030 and achieving zero percent emissions in electricity production by 2050. Continued development of nuclear and wind energy will also help reduce air pollution.

Portugal needs to aggressively address its deforestation issues by planting new trees. Spain, Italy, and Greece have taken up the challenge of rebuilding their forests, with differing levels of commitment. Andorra seems to be maintaining its forests and managing this important resource for future generations.

Southern Europe is especially vulnerable to the economic well-being of other nations in Europe and beyond. When those economies prosper, they buy more goods produced in this region, and more tourists come to enjoy the many natural and historical attractions that abound in Southern Europe. Conversely, when other national economies contract, trade decreases, and the number of tourists declines or they tend to spend less money when they do visit. These fluctuations can have a devastating influence on Southern European economies and their ability to pay for needed tools to reduce pollution or develop cleaner methods for producing energy.

SECTION REVIEW

1. Explain how the Southern European economies and people have interacted with the environment.
2. What are three environmental issues in Southern Europe?
3. How has Southern Europe adjusted from agricultural to diversified economies?
4. What solutions to current environmental issues in Southern Europe would you propose?

13 CHAPTER REVIEW

SUMMARY

1. The physical geography of Southern Europe was shaped by tectonic activity, volcanic eruptions, and glaciation. Southern Europe has varying supplies of natural resources that provide an economic potential as these elements are accessed and developed. Features of this region and its historical cultures have attracted millions of tourists every year.
2. The people of Southern Europe are ethnically varied and yet similar in the enjoyment of common activities, including ethnic foods, regional music, and sports. These societies are transitioning into a highly developed status but are also threatened by their dependency on strong economies in other parts of the world to support trade and tourism.
3. A major challenge of living in Southern Europe is the need to make wise use of human and natural resources in ways that build strong economies without further endangering the environment. A goal for the nations of Southern Europe would be to become less dependent on foreign economies to ensure the prosperity of their own.

Terms to Know

- ❑ massif
- ❑ Renaissance
- ❑ city-state
- ❑ *futsal*

Making Connections

1. Describe a *massif* and provide an example found in this chapter.
2. What earth-shaping processes are at work in the region of Southern Europe near the Alps and Pyrenees?
3. How do landforms affect the climates in Southern Europe?
4. In what country in Southern Europe would you like to live? Why?
5. Why do you think Southern European economies are in transition?
6. Identify political issues in Southern Europe.
7. How has a long history of access to forms of Christianity influenced religion in Southern Europe?
8. How has deforestation affected Southern Europe?

Developing Geography Skills

1. How do landforms influence the distribution of population in this region?
2. How has glaciation affected the landforms of Southern Europe?

Thinking Critically

1. Select one of the countries in this chapter and analyze its influence in world history.
2. How has religion in Southern Europe been influenced by Southern European cultures?

Living in God's World

1. Using Isaiah 55 or another section of Scripture, write an article that evaluates the state of religion in Southern Europe.
2. Write an essay to propose solutions to the environmental issues in Southern Europe.

CASE STUDY | Pollution in the Mediterranean Sea

Oil spills, plastic bottles and bags, industrial waste, and countless tons of other trash and pollutants have been dumped or otherwise transported to the Mediterranean Sea for decades. Contributing nations range from Spain in the west to nations in the Middle East and North African nations to the south. In addition to the damage to water quality, the effect on marine life, from tiny fish to large whales, has been devastating.

The Mediterranean also serves as a highway for extensive commercial shipping and cruise lines that transport tourists throughout this region. These huge ships churn up the waters and can adversely affect marine life. In addition to pollution caused by burned fuel to power these ships, oil spills and improper discharge of waste by unscrupulous companies intensify the contamination of the Mediterranean.

Agencies that monitor the ongoing pollution of the Mediterranean measure annual pollution by raw sewage, mineral oil, mercury, lead, and phosphates in thousands to millions of tons.

Nations that contribute to this enormous problem are formulating agreements on how to deal with the continued pollution in order to at least diminish the volume. A method for reversing the effects of generations of pollution is yet to be determined.

1. How has pollution in the Mediterranean Sea affected marine life?
2. How is annual pollution of the Mediterranean Sea measured?
3. Which pollutant do you think causes the most damage? Why?
4. What are nations doing to solve the pollution of this body of water?
5. If you were given the resources, what would you do to reverse the pollution of the Mediterranean Sea?

unit 5

AFRICA

GEODATA | Activity

Cultural Geography *Student Activities*

You will have the opportunity to complete a geodata activity for Africa in the Activities.

Background image:
Elephants roam across the savanna with Mount Kilimanjaro in the distance.

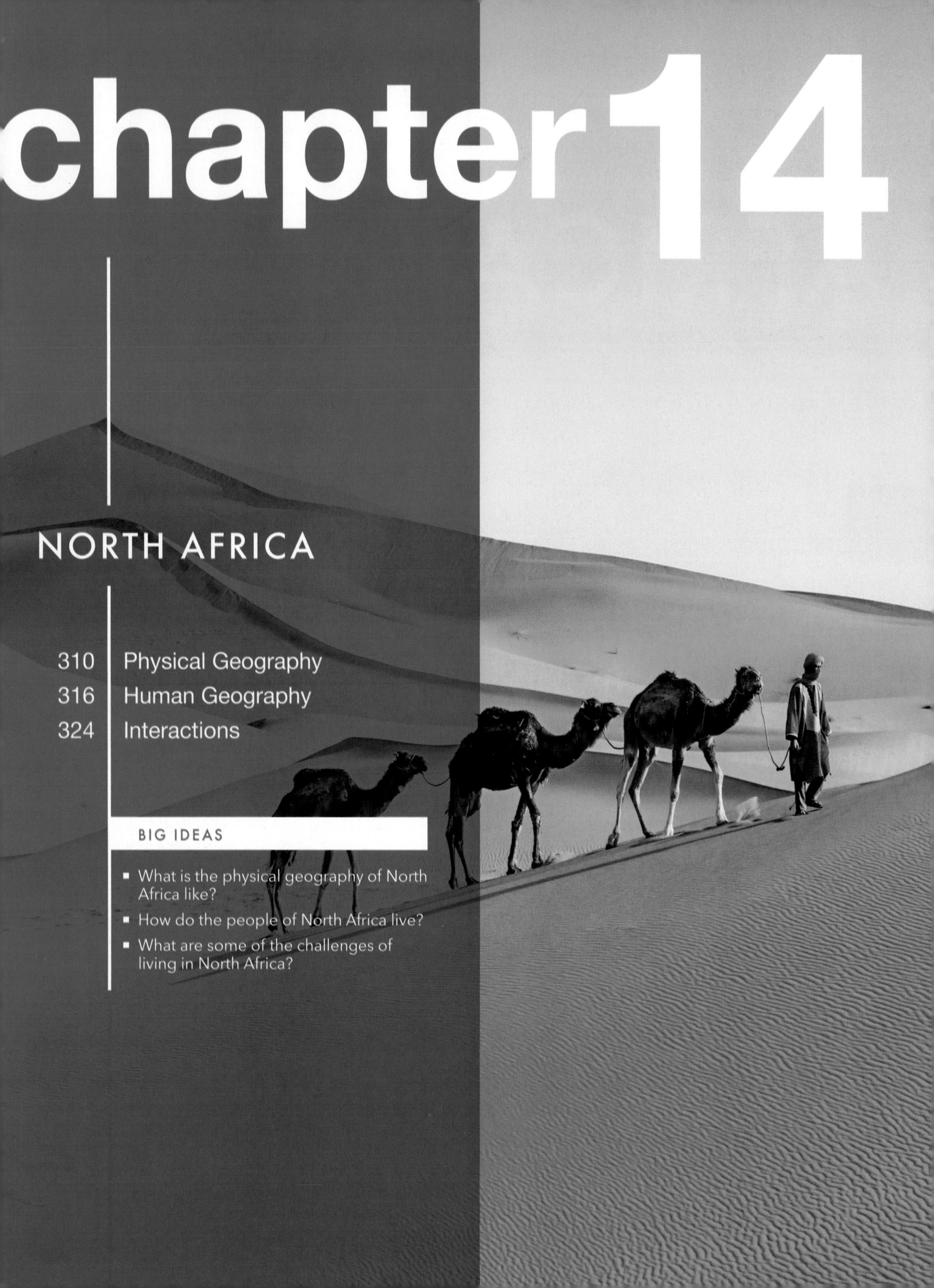

chapter 14

NORTH AFRICA

310 Physical Geography
316 Human Geography
324 Interactions

BIG IDEAS

- What is the physical geography of North Africa like?
- How do the people of North Africa live?
- What are some of the challenges of living in North Africa?

◂ A Hausa village in Tahoua, Niger

▾ A Berber-Roman arch in Djemila, Algeria, which dates to the third century AD

◂ The Valley of the Kings, Luxor City, Egypt

▾ Hassan II Mosque, Casablanca, Morocco

VALLEY OF THE KINGS

The desolate valley west of the Nile in southern Egypt contains more than sixty tombs of the pharaohs and their families. Most of the tombs were robbed long before archaeologists explored them, but in 1922 an English archaeologist discovered fabulous riches in the tomb of nineteen-year-old Tutankhamen, or King Tut. The most recent discovery, that of the mummy of Queen Hatshepsut, was in 2007. Archaeologists believe there are many undiscovered tombs yet to be found. The tombs were furnished with everything the pharaoh would need to enter the afterlife. They included treasures such as golden masks and jewelry but also common items such as furniture, clothes, food, and even pets. Other reminders of the ancient kings' glory are the ruins of their temples. The Temple of Karnak is the most well-known of these sites. Sphinxes once lined the avenue leading to the front gateway, flanked by towers 143 feet high.

◂ Tuareg tribesman with camels, western Sahara, Morocco

GUIDING QUESTIONS

- What are the regions of North Africa?
- What caused the landforms of North Africa?
- What bodies of water are important to North Africa?
- What is the climate of North Africa, and how does it relate to its location on the globe?
- What are the natural resources of North Africa?

ATLAS MOUNTAINS

The Atlas Mountains are a fifteen-hundred-mile chain which lies along the northwest coast of Africa. These mountains cover most of Morocco, northern Algeria, and northern Tunisia.

SINAI PENINSULA

Although most of Egypt lies in Africa, the Sinai Peninsula is part of Asia. It is divided from African Egypt by the Isthmus of Suez, a bridge of land between the Gulf of Suez and the Mediterranean Sea.

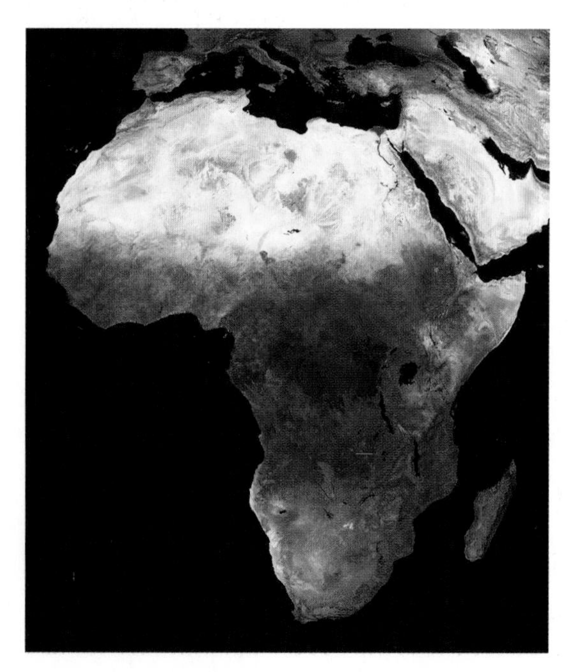

Though Africa is the second-largest continent, its size is not as important as its location. Eighty percent of Africa's land is between the Tropic of Cancer and the Tropic of Capricorn. This position makes the climate mainly warm, and it makes the climate in most areas consistent—there are no great temperature fluctuations. This position also determines the patterns of rainfall for the continent. The amount of rainfall decreases as you move north or south away from the equator, and near each end of the continent there are great deserts, the Sahara in the north and the Kalahari in the south. The Sahara is perhaps the single most important geographic factor in the history of Africa, dividing the continent into two regions with very different peoples and histories. Saharan Africa shows the strong imprint of Islam, while sub-Saharan Africa's history involves many tribal groups.

PHYSICAL GEOGRAPHY

What is the physical geography of North Africa like?

Regions of North Africa

North Africa has more in common with the Middle East than with the rest of Africa. They share the same landforms, people, and religion.

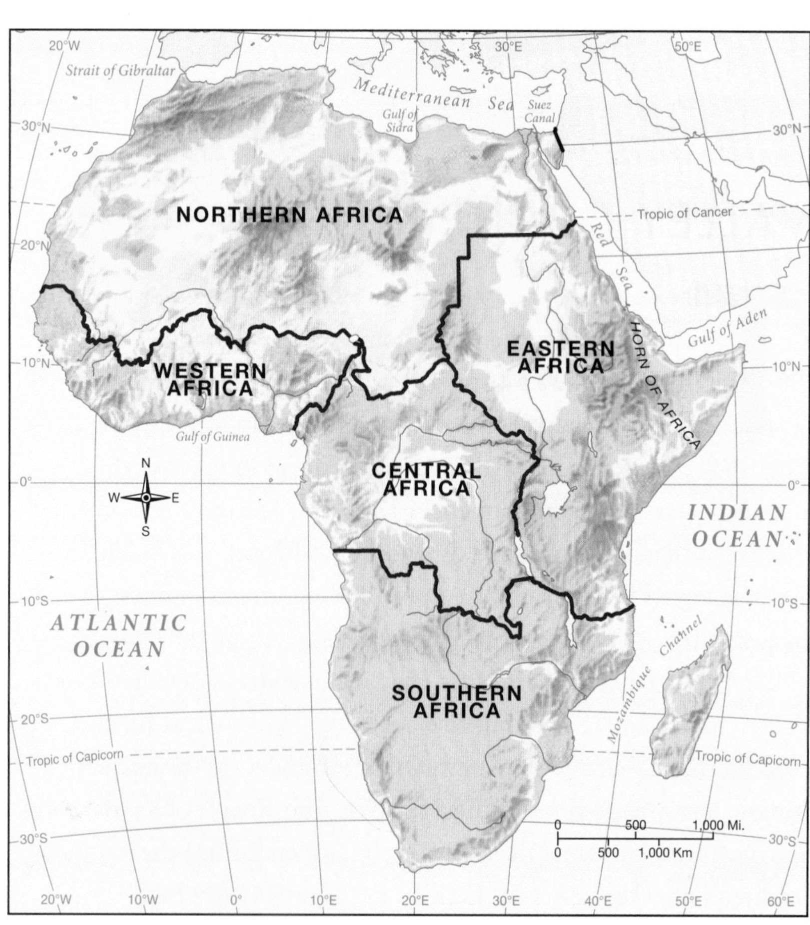

SAHARA

The **Sahara** is the world's largest desert. It is about the same size as the United States and is the only desert in the world that spans an entire continent from shore to shore. The Arabs looked at this vast, barren expanse and called it simply the "desert," or Sahara. Every country presented in this chapter is covered in large part by the Sahara.

Endless sand **dunes** like those found in the Grand Erg in central Algeria are what come to mind when one thinks of the Sahara. The dunes cover thousands of square miles, with only a few large oases to break the monotony. But the Sahara is not totally flat; it is interspersed with hamadas, which are elevated flat and rocky areas mainly devoid of sand. There are three main regions of these: the Tibesti Mountains in southern Libya and northern Chad, the Ahaggar Mountains in southern Algeria, and the Aïr Mountains in central Niger.

NORTHERN SAHEL

Between the Sahara and the jungles of Central Africa lies a transitional region called the **Sahel**. This band of grass-covered plains is about three hundred miles wide. The southern regions of four countries—Mauritania, Mali, Niger, and Chad—are part of the Sahel in North Africa.

NILE RIVER VALLEY

The Sahara hems in the Nile Valley on both sides. The Western Desert is a low plateau with hills, salt flats, and depressions. It covers two-thirds of Egypt. The Eastern Desert is rugged and covered by barren mountains reaching almost seven thousand feet. Although sometimes called the Arabian Desert, it is not the larger Arabian Desert that covers the Arabian Peninsula. The Nile River Valley averages ten miles wide in the south. The valley begins in Upper Egypt just north of the Aswan dam. Vegetation and farmland border the river. The valley is around 150 miles wide at the Nile Delta in Lower Egypt. This whole region resembles a lotus flower, the national flower of Egypt.

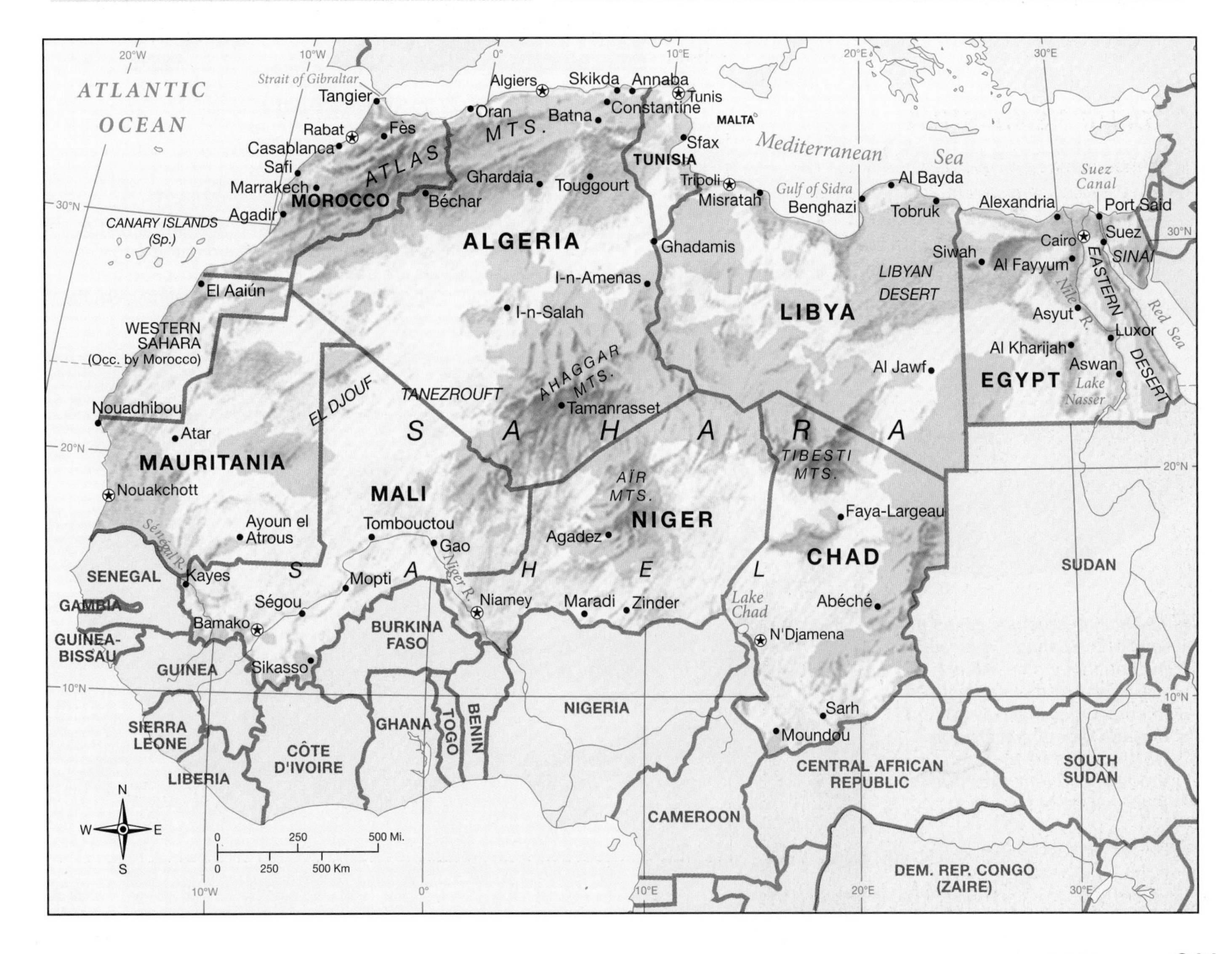

▲ *The Atlas Mountains rise to a maximum elevation of 13,661 feet at Jebel Toubkal in Morocco.*

Physical Landforms

While North Africa has three main physical and cultural regions, it also has three types of landforms. Rocky mountains are in the northwest, the Sahara in the center, and flat grasslands in the south.

▲ *Much more common than the dunes (ergs) are regs, which are flat desert areas covered with pebbles. The Tanezrouft Reg, on Algeria's southern border, is a monotonous plain that stretches hundreds of miles.*

▼ *The Qattara Depression in northwest Egypt drops to 436 feet below sea level. Covering an area almost as large as New Jersey, it was created through salt weathering and wind erosion. Salt weathering occurs when saline gets into cracks in the rocks, breaking them down.*

▲ *The Richat Structure, called the "eye of the Sahara," is located in central Mauritania. It is a geological dome made of sedimentary rock that was formed through differential erosion, which occurs when rocks erode at different rates due to their degree of hardness.*

Bodies of Water

The large bodies of water that surround North Africa are the Atlantic Ocean to the west, the Mediterranean Sea to the north, and the Red Sea to the east. Most of North Africa's people live along the coast of the Mediterranean Sea.

The Nile River is the lifeblood of Egypt. It is the longest river in the world, at 4,160 miles. It is one of the few large world rivers that flow north. The Nile Delta, where the river empties into the Mediterranean, is called Lower Egypt because it has the lowest elevation of the river. *Delta* is the term for the area at the mouth of a river where sediment accumulates called **alluvial deposits**. Nearly all of Egypt's population lives along the river where palm trees shade the houses and villages in the valley.

The Niger River is the third-longest in Africa and the most important river in the Sahel. It begins in the Guinea Highlands. The river lies mostly in Mali before finally emptying into the Atlantic in Nigeria. Most ancient and modern cities of Mali lie on this river. Bamako, the largest city in the Sahel and capital of Mali, is on the river, as is Niger's capital, Niamey. The Senegal River is the ninth-longest river in Africa; it flows through parts of Mauritania and Mali.

The Chari River and its tributaries, navigable only during the rainy season, provide a fertile region for agriculture in southern Chad. The Chari is fed by rivers that start in the jungles of the Central African Republic. The Chari flows into Lake Chad on the western border of Chad. The capital, N'Djamena, lies near the lake at the confluence of the Chari River and the Logone River.

Lake Chad is the most important body of water in the Sahel. Lake Chad once had a surface area of approximately 9,600 square miles, or roughly the size of Lake Erie. Since 1963, however, Lake Chad has shrunk to one-twentieth of its former size.

Oases are vital for life in the desert. They are areas of fertile land watered by a natural spring or other water sources like aquifers. They were places of rest for traders crossing the Sahara. They are home to farmers who grow dates, rice, corn, cotton, and other crops.

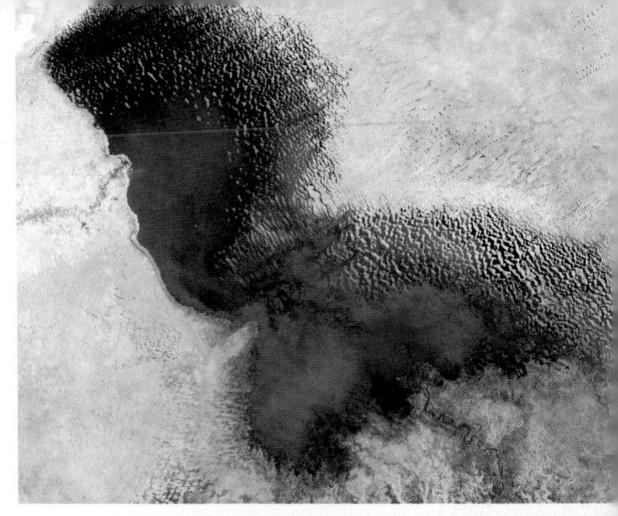

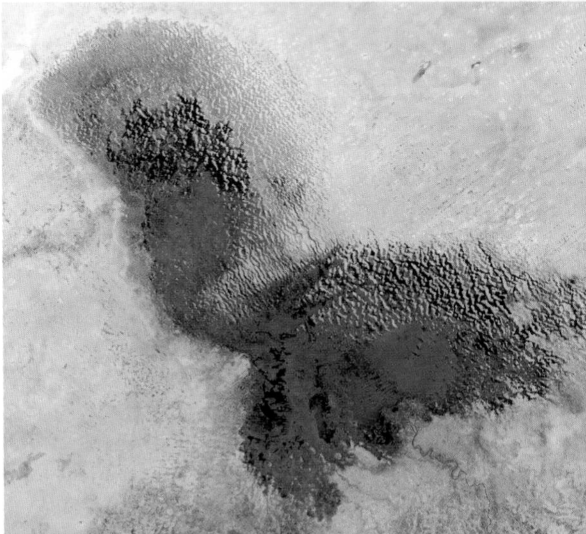

▲ *Satellite images taken in 1973 (top) and 2017 (bottom) show how much Lake Chad has shrunk. The combination of visible and infrared light helps to differentiate vegetation (red) and water (blue and slate gray).*

▲ *An oasis in the Sahara*

◂ *The Nile Delta from space*

Climates of North Africa

The people who live along the coasts of Morocco, Algeria, and Tunisia enjoy a pleasant mediterranean climate and scenery comparable to that of Southern Europe. Summers are dry but mild. Rains come in the winter, with snow falling in the high mountains. The mountains of Algeria and Morocco get enough snow to make operating ski resorts practical. The average temperature in the north varies from 52°F in winter to 79°F in summer. The mountain barrier blocks winds blowing off the sea, causing orographic rainfall. The water flows to the sea, bringing moisture to the valleys and coastal plains. Precipitation is near twenty inches annually, and this rainfall provides the only dependable water supply to support crops, livestock, and cities.

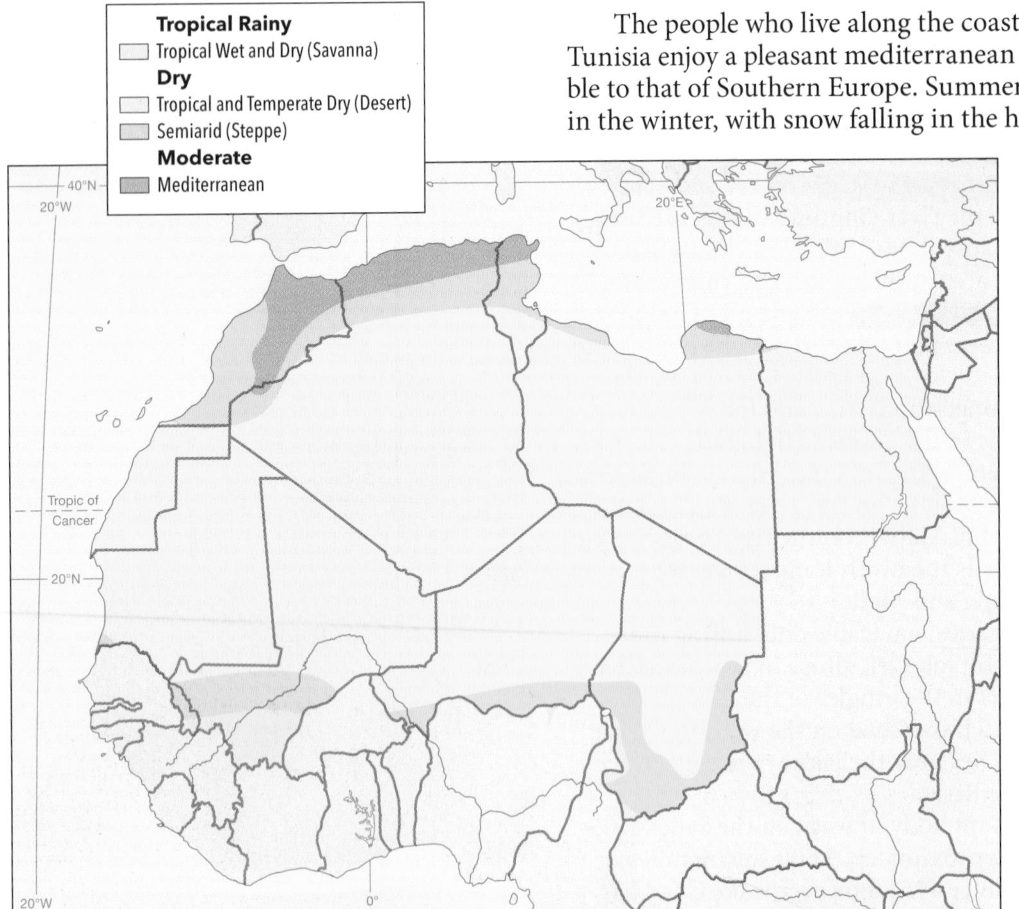

The Sahara climate is hot and dry, with summer temperatures averaging 90°F in the north and reaching 110°F in the south, though temperatures can frequently exceed 120°F. The annual rainfall ranges between one and five inches, and some parts are dry all year long. The hottest temperature ever recorded on earth happened in this region. Aziziya, Libya, recorded a temperature of 136°F on September 13, 1922.

The northern part of the Sahel near the Sahara has a semiarid climate and is drier than the southern Sahel, often receiving as little as four inches of rain annually. The short grasses in this area support scattered populations of Berber and Arabic nomads, who herd cattle and sheep. In the southern Sahel, there is a savanna climate. Here the grasses become more plentiful. This region sometimes receives up to twenty-four inches of rain per year.

Women selling freshly caught fish in Nouakchott, Mauritania

Resources of North Africa

North Africa does not have much arable land since desert is the dominant landform. Most of the agriculture is grown in and around the Atlas Mountains, the Nile, and the Sahel. Olives, dates, and grapes are the important crops of the Atlas Mountain countries. Cotton is a major crop in Mali, Egypt, and Chad. Egyptian cotton is known as the finest in the world.

Morocco, Egypt, and Mauritania are major fish-producing countries. The Atlantic waters off

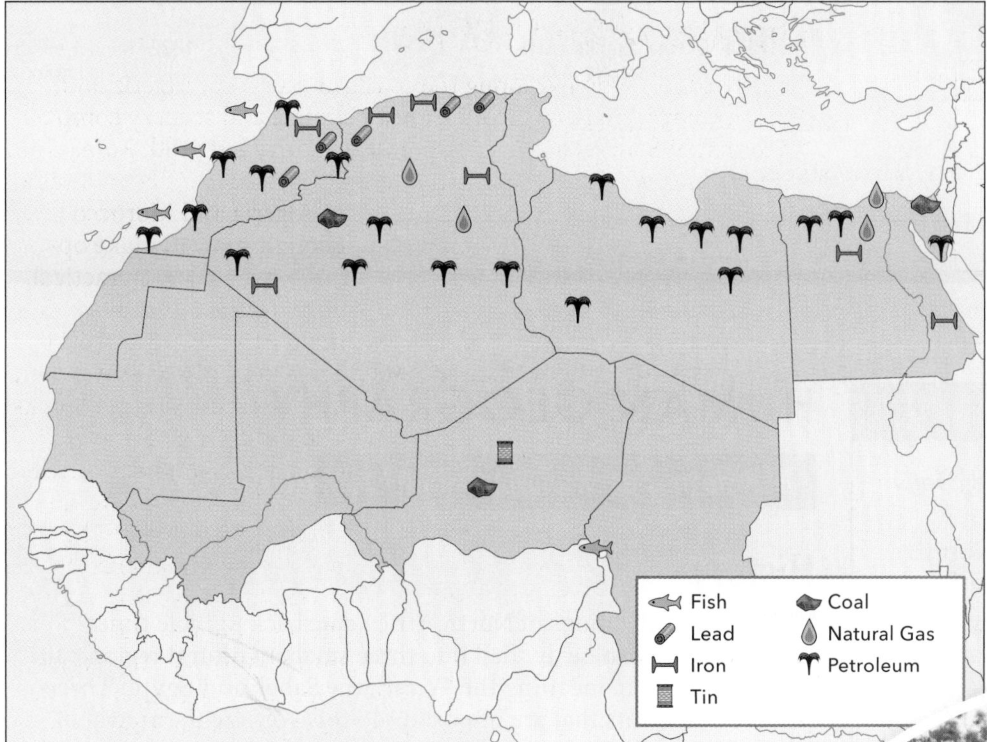

North Africa are home to over five hundred different species of fish. Egypt has less wild fishing but is a world leader in **aquaculture**, the farming of fish. Tilapia, mullet, and carp are the main types raised.

This region is important to world agriculture because it has an essential ingredient required for bountiful harvests. Northern Africa accounts for one-fifth of the world's phosphate deposits. Phosphate is a key ingredient in fertilizers.

Except for Libya, Tunisia, and Morocco, these countries have large amounts of uranium. Uranium is used as nuclear fuel. Niger has by far the largest uranium deposits of these countries. The deposits are located in the Aïr Mountains.

All of these countries except Mali produce some amount of petroleum and natural gas; Algeria and Libya are leading world producers. Petroleum was discovered in the Libyan Desert in 1959, just south of the Gulf of Sidra. Egypt's largest petroleum deposit lies near the Red Sea coast. Mauritania recently discovered offshore oil reserves, which are a welcome boost to the country's economy.

▲ *Cotton is widely cultivated in the Nile Delta and harvested in October each year.*

SECTION REVIEW

1. Which is farther north, Upper Egypt or Lower Egypt? Why were the regions given those names?
2. Distinguish an erg from a reg.
3. What African capitals lie on the Mediterranean coast? Why do you think they are located there?
4. Why is the Sahara an inhospitable place to live?
5. Why is North Africa important to world agriculture?

ca. 3100 BC Egypt unified under its first dynasty

1446 BC Hebrew exodus from Egypt

711 Muslim Arabs enter Africa

1324 Mansa Musa goes to Mecca

1574 Ottoman Empire asserts control over North Africa

1800

1822 Hieroglyphs deciphered using the Rosetta Stone

GUIDING QUESTIONS

- How has North Africa changed over time?
- How do the governments of North Africa interact with their citizens?
- What is the economic health of North Africa?
- What are the demographics of North Africa?
- What are the cultural characteristics and diversity of North Africa?
- What forms of religions are practiced in North Africa?

HUMAN GEOGRAPHY

How do the people of North Africa live?

History

The civilizations of North Africa date back to Bible times. This region can be divided into three smaller cultural regions: the Maghreb, meaning the "West"; the Sahel; and Egypt. Three key events that are important to this area are the arrival of Islam, colonization, and independence.

The Maghreb

The Berbers, or the Amazigh as they call themselves, comprise the many ethnic groups who are the pre-Arab inhabitants of the Maghreb. They first settled the Maghreb over three thousand years ago. Some farmed the coastal plains and valleys, while others kept livestock on the mountainsides or at the edge of the desert. They traded with the Phoenicians, Greeks, and Romans, and major ports arose along the coast. These port cities—Tangier, Algiers, Tunis, and Tripoli—were the foundation of what later became known as the Barbary Coast states of Morocco, Algeria, Tunisia, and Tripoli (modern Libya). In the seventh century, Arabs fleeing persecution migrated to the Maghreb, bringing the Islamic religion with them. Throughout the nineteenth and early twentieth centuries, France conquered, occupied, and colonized most of the Maghreb with one exception, Libya, which was taken over by Italy in 1911.

Two Amazigh men in the Atlas Mountains, Morocco

The Sahel

At one time, three great African empires—Ghana, Mali, and Songhai—occupied parts of the Sahel region. Most early caravan routes in the western Sahara stopped at a desolate basin in the northern tip of Mali, where salts were plentiful. The salt mines of Taghaza provided traders with a valuable commodity, prized among the people of the southern rainforests, who gladly traded gold for salt.

The Ghana Empire, which may have risen to power as early as the fourth century, was centered in Kumbi Saleh, a city at the southeast corner of Mauritania. The empire controlled all the western trade routes across the Sahel into the thirteenth century, keeping all the gold nuggets and allowing the gold dust to continue north. The ancient capital now lies in ruins.

The Mali Empire arose when it conquered Ghana around 1200. By taking control of the gold trade, the empire increased its riches to

1922	Egypt gains independence from Britain
1941–43	WWII fought across North Africa
1956	France and Britain withdraw from Suez; Tunisia gains independence from France
1962	Algeria gains independence from France
1967	Six-Day War between Israel and Egypt
1981	Anwar el-Sadat, Egyptian president, is assassinated for making peace with Israel
2011	Arab Spring

mythic proportions. Mansa Musa gained a reputation as the richest man in the world. When he made a year-long pilgrimage to Mecca in 1324 with a caravan of sixty thousand people, he was preceded by hundreds of slaves, each bearing a staff of gold, and hundreds of camels, each bearing bags of gold. His lavish gifts flooded Mecca's economy and caused gold to drop in value for a decade.

What became the largest African empire, Songhai, was born along the Niger River in the eighth century. This civilization grew slowly until its first great ruler, Sunni Ali, took over the declining Mali empire in 1464. Later, Morocco blamed Songhai for its economic decline and invaded in 1591. Morocco won easily because it was the first country to use firearms in a battle on African soil. Although this defeat ended the last empire of the Sahel, a reduced Songhai kingdom remained until France invaded in the nineteenth century.

▲ *The Sankore mosque in Timbuktu, Mali, is a reminder of the Mali Empire.*

Egypt

One of the world's oldest and most fascinating countries still thrives today along the Nile River. Located near the birthplace of civilization in the Middle East, Egypt seeks to maintain its rich ancient culture and heritage.

Most people associate Egypt with the ancient pyramids and temples that stand along the Nile Valley. As early as 3100 BC, Egypt was united as a state under one ruler. This began the long succession of dynasties and pharaohs who built the famous monuments. The ancient Egyptians invented one of the earliest writing systems, called **hieroglyphics**, which included over one thousand symbols to relate meaning. The dynastic period lasted until nearly five hundred years before Christ when Egypt endured a series of invasions by Persians, Greeks, Romans, and Arabs, who each brought a new culture.

▼ *The Great Pyramids of Egypt*

The Ottoman Turks controlled Egypt beginning in 1517 until an Albanian officer named Mohammed Ali won control in 1805. Ali's rule ushered in the modernization of Egypt, which included the building of modern Cairo and the completion of the Suez Canal in 1869. Unfortunately, the process drained much of Egypt's resources, and the British occupied the country until independence was granted in 1922.

▲ *The modern city of Cairo, Egypt*

Governments

Instability describes all the governments of the countries in this region. The lack of economic and political development in some African countries can be somewhat explained by the problems that have plagued Africa in the past few centuries. Some problems are due to natural causes and cannot be helped; others are caused by human decisions. North Africa has suffered from outside invasions, colonization, and civil wars throughout its past.

When colonies gained independence from European states, the Africans often had to establish their own national governments. They lacked self-governing experience since the Europeans had a paternalistic view of the Africans. Many of the new countries learned the hard lesson that socialism does not work. Also, tribal loyalties made it difficult to form a true federal government. As with any culture, access to power often exposed personal ambitions that ran counter to what was best for a nation. Thus the North African governments have been prone to corruption.

Western Sahara

The map on page 311 shows a large territory southwest of Morocco called Western Sahara. When Spain gave up this territory in 1975, Mauritania and Morocco moved in. Algeria opposed this illegal land grab and supported the Polisario, a native independence movement. In the bitter fighting, Mauritania withdrew its claim, but Morocco then claimed the entire region. While Morocco's troops captured the coastal cities, they could not defeat the nomads in the interior. Disputes continued until the United Nations imposed a ceasefire in 1991. Sovereignty over the area has not yet been resolved, although Morocco effectively retains control of 70 percent of this region.

◂ *United Nations helicopters arrive in the disputed territory of Western Sahara.*

GLOBAL IMPACT | Arab Spring

On December 17, 2010, Mohammed Bouazizi, a Tunisian fruit and vegetable street vendor, set himself on fire to protest the confiscation of his business by a city official. This single incident instigated a series of protests and revolutions across North Africa and the Middle East. The people were frustrated and felt powerless to effect change in their governments since after their independence from European nations they had been ruled by powerful dictators. Protests quickly gained steam, and in less than a month the Tunisian president had to flee the country. By the end of January, protests had spread to Algeria, Egypt, and Yemen. By February a civil war had broken out in Libya, and the long-time dictator of Egypt, Hosni Mubarak, had resigned. In March protests began in Syria, which led to a horrific civil war that left over 400,000 dead and millions as refugees. In October 2011 Libya's dictator, Muammar Qaddafi, was killed, leading to chaos. Both the Syrian and Libyan civil wars continue as of 2019.

▲ *The modern city of Cairo, Egypt Egyptians use their mobile phones to record celebrations in Cairo's Tahrir Square after the dictator, Hosni Mubarak, stepped down because of the Arab Spring protests.*

Social media played an important role in spreading the revolutionary spirit. Average people became news reporters, telling their stories on social networks. With smartphones, millions of people were now cameramen. The best videos were broadcast in a collaboration between traditional and new media. The governments tried to stop this reporting by shutting down the internet, which was largely ineffective since hackers found creative ways to bypass the blockages.

Ultimately, the Arab Spring left most of the countries in worse conditions than before. While the original reason for the Arab Spring seemed to be the people's desire for freedom, Islamists were able to use the upheaval in the governments toward their ends. Islamists tried to gain power by being elected or by inciting civil wars. Egypt elected an Islamist president, Mohamed-Morsi. He quickly went about radically changing the country. His changes to the constitution brought people back into the streets. Eventually the military took control of the government so that the nation went full circle in a matter of two years.

Morocco and Tunisia seem to have come out of the Arab Spring with some positive results. The Moroccan king started reforms that brought some transparency to government. In October 2014 Tunisia had a parliamentary election that put the secular Nidaa Tounes party in charge. This party appears to believe in some degree of religious, economic, and political freedom.

1. What was one reason the dictators were not able to put down these revolutions as they had done in the past?
2. Why would free elections lead to Islamic governments?
3. What conclusions can you draw from the Arab Spring?

Economies

Many of Africa's economic struggles are caused by the continent's geography. Much of the soil in Africa is infertile, especially in the Sahara and Sahel regions. As a result, proper nutrition is not always possible, adversely affecting the physical well-being of all people. This, in turn, affects the available workforce. In addition to malnutrition, Africa has high concentrations of diseases such as malaria, typhoid, tuberculosis, and AIDS.

The Maghreb

Morocco and Tunisia have the best economies of the entire North African region. The governments have made an effort to privatize businesses that were once owned by the government. These two countries have the largest service-sector economies in the region. They have high youth unemployment and are trying to create more jobs to ease the discontentment of the youth.

Algeria and Libya have the struggling economies in the Maghreb. Algerian leaders have squandered the nation's oil wealth and maintained a centralized economy. When Muammar Qaddafi ruled Libya, he offered free education, medical treatment, and electricity. The situation was much like that of Venezuela. The country thrived when the oil price was high, but it was artificial prosperity. In the end, Qaddafi's policies did not keep him from losing power, and he was eventually murdered. Libya remains economically and politically unstable.

▾ *Tourists at the Temple of Nefertari in Abu Simbel, Egypt*

Egypt

Egypt's economy is projected to boom in the coming years if the country can maintain political stability. The former general who was president as of 2019, Abdel El-Sisi, enacted policies to pay down national debts and balance the budget. His policies have created short-term pain but are praised by economists as policies that should set the country up for success. Egypt is heavily dependent on money from tourism. Islamic terrorists have tried to hinder tourism through bombings and organized attacks.

The Sahel

Nearly 90 percent of the people in the Sahel are engaged in subsistence farming, the raising of livestock, or fishing to make a living. Mauritania and Mali have relatively better economies in the Sahel although all four countries are extremely poor. Niger was once ranked the poorest country in the world.

Chad and Niger have some of the lowest per capita GDP and life expectancies in the Sahel. Because the people are subsistence farmers, they are threatened by the frequent droughts common to the Sahel. Niger's government provides minimal service to its people; all aid is received from foreign countries. Foreign aid provides for education and healthcare, especially HIV/AIDS relief.

▾ *A farmer in Niger*

Demographics

The fertility rate of the Maghreb compares to that of South America. Tunisia has the lowest fertility rate in Africa. In contrast, the Sahel nations have some of the highest fertility rates in the world, with Niger having the highest. In 1983 it was 7.83, and although it has been steadily declining since then, it is still among the highest in the world. The Maghreb has an average urbanization rate in the upper seventies. Niger and Chad are some of the least urbanized countries in the world.

As the Arabs spread across North Africa, they intermarried with the Berbers. The Arab-

Berber ethnic group now accounts for over 80 percent of the population in the Maghreb. Arabic is the official language. A small minority still speaks the Berber languages and continues traditional Berber farming practices, folk dances, and marriage customs. Many of the Berber tribes are **Bedouins**, which is the generic term for the thousands of nomadic tribes who live in the deserts of the Middle East and North Africa. The Tuaregs are the most significant Bedouin-Berber tribe in this region.

The Sahel is a transitional zone in more ways than just climate and agriculture. The four countries of the Sahel display a complex mix of peoples and cultures. Mauritania, for example, gets its name from its most significant people group, the Moors. *Moor* is another broad term applied to the many tribes who intermarried with the Arabs and the Spanish. The other three Sahel countries are composed of a variety of native indigenous groups.

The mix of languages in the Sahel is also complex. Arabic is the official language in the westernmost country, Mauritania. It is also an official language in the easternmost country, Chad, but 133 native languages are also spoken there. The Arabs had less impact on the two central countries, Mali and Niger, where tribal languages are common. Because these two countries were once part of French West Africa, French is the official language in both of them, and it is also an official language in Chad.

Culture and Diversity

The cultures of North Africa are high context. Meaning is expressed not so much in the actual words that are said but rather in how they are said. Societal roles are well defined, so one must understand his place in society and not cause conflict by acting outside of that role. The culture is **patriarchal** and hierarchal; fathers and elders have the final say.

The culture of North Africa is much like what is described in the New Testament. The defining characteristic is hospitality. Valuing hospitality originates from the fact that life in the desert is harsh, and people must help each other in order to survive. Guests are treated with the finest foods and greatest respect. A host considers every possible need of a guest in order to show respect and avoid insulting the guest.

As one travels further into the Sahel, the culture becomes less rigid. Women have more equality, although polygamy is more common. In Chad and Niger especially, up to one-third of marriages are polygamous, in this case men having more than one wife.

▲ *Tuareg tribesman in their trademark blue robes*

Hospitality is a defining characteristic of North Africa ▸

Moroccan fish tajine

Daraba, a vegetable stew, is popular in Chad.

The foods of the Maghreb and the Sahel can be differentiated by their staple. In the Maghreb the staple is *couscous,* a tiny pasta made of wheat or barley. *Tajine* is a popular dish that is named after the earthenware dish it is cooked in. It is a stew of sliced beef, chicken, or fish cooked with vegetables, fruits, and many spices.

The staple of the Sahel is millet, a whole grain seed that is easier to grow in the harsh conditions. It is high in protein and other vitamins. The women of the Sahel grind the millet into flour, which is a labor-intensive process. A popular dish in Chad is *daraba*, an okra, eggplant, and peanut stew. The Sahel peoples with access to a lake, river, or ocean eat a lot of fish.

Religion

Sunni Islam is the religion of North Africa. Religion as presented in a textbook and religion as practiced by people are often two different things. This is especially true of Islam in Africa. Officially, Islam centers on submission to the one god who controls all things. The Qur'an and the Hadith are the basis for Muslim teaching. Rites of prayer, cleansing, fasting, almsgiving, and pilgrimage are at the heart of the religion. Folk Islam maintains all of the teachings of official Islam, but it has other concerns, such as how to deal with sickness or famine or other negative events. Folk Islam is more concerned with spirits and ancestors. Often, folk Islam draws on the traditional religious practices of a region.

The Jinn play a large role in folk Islam. Jinn are believed to be spirits that stand between men and angels. Though these spirits can be good or bad, most are viewed as bad. For instance, in Egypt many Muslims believe there is a Jinn who will cause miscarriages. To be freed from a Jinn who has possessed a person or who is interfering with a person, a powerful person who can provide charms or curses is needed.

Major Religions of North Africa

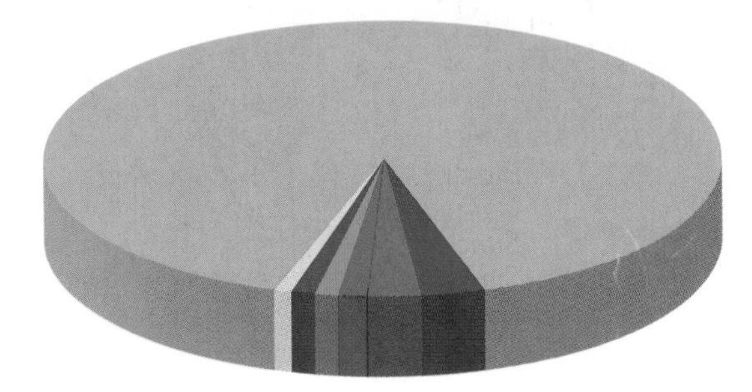

Islamic	**90.0%**
Orthodox	**3.1%**
Protestant Evangelical	**2.5%**
Ethnic	**1.6%**
Roman Catholic	**1.1%**
Protestant	**0.9%**
Unaffiliated	**0.8%**

African Muslims often practice divination to help with decision-making. For instance, they might open a Qur'an at random to see whether the words on the page provide direction. Or they might go to a fortune-teller to learn something of their future. Many Muslims practice both official Islam and folk Islam without seeing any inconsistency. However, some Muslims see folk Islam as a corruption. They think shrines to saints promote idolatry. They reject the idea that saints can intercede for people.

Morocco and Mauritania have the highest percentage of Muslims, almost 100 percent. They have fewer than ten thousand Christians. While missionaries are not allowed, some Christians work as tentmakers in Morocco and discreetly witness to the Moroccan people they interact with. Tentmakers are Christians who go to another country to minister but support themselves by holding a separate occupation in that country.

Christian satellite TV has become very popular in North Africa. Through this means and the personal witness of believers, many Muslims are converting to Christianity. Algerian believers are growing in numbers and winning many of their fellow countrymen to Christ. Algerians are producing literature in their languages and have developed vibrant outreach ministries. In 2008 there were as few as 10,000 believers; by 2019 the number was estimated to be 500,000.

While the other countries that border the Mediterranean also have percentages of Islam in the upper nineties, Egypt is only 87 percent Muslim and does have a large Christian minority, called Copts. Though their number has declined because of intense persecution, there may still be four to five million Copts in Egypt. They have strong historical ties to the desert. Ancient historical sites, including monasteries, are scattered throughout the desert, especially at oases. The religion of the Copts is one of ritual and tradition, similar to Roman Catholicism and Eastern Orthodoxy.

Christianity spread throughout Egypt soon after the time of Christ, and it survived after the Arab conquest. The Coptic Church claims to have been founded by Mark, the Gospel writer. During the fifth century, the church broke with orthodox Christian doctrine by claiming that the divine and human natures of Christ mixed in a single nature. The Coptic Church flourished until the Muslim invasion in the seventh century. Because of Muslim pressures, many Copts converted to Islam.

The Sahel nations have the lowest percentages of Islam, but it still represents the majority belief system of the region. Since Chad's borders reach the farthest south, it has the largest religious diversity of all of these countries. Missionaries are welcome, and their efforts have contributed to the growth of the Christian population. Outreach to Muslims is allowed and has resulted in a growing number of Muslims trusting Christ.

▲ *The Prince Tadros Coptic Church in Minya, Egypt, was burned in 2013. Christians live in fear because of attacks against their churches, businesses, and homes.*

▲ *Ethiopian Orthodox and Egyptian Coptic Christians take part in Palm Sunday celebrations at the Saint Simon Church, "the cave church," Cairo, Egypt.*

SECTION REVIEW

1. Why was Arab arrival such an important event in North Africa?
2. Why is Western Sahara not an independent nation?
3. What conclusions can be made about Sahel nations after evaluating their economic health along with their fertility and urbanization rates?
4. Considering that hospitality is a value for this region, how should one behave as a guest in a North African home?
5. Compare the religious practices of Latin America and North Africa.
6. What country in the Sahel has the largest Christian population? Why is this the case?

GUIDING QUESTIONS

- How do the economies and demographics of North Africa affect how the citizens interact with the environment?
- What are the environmental issues of North Africa?
- What are the causes and effects of environmental issues in North Africa?
- What are possible solutions to environmental issues in North Africa?

INTERACTIONS OF PEOPLE AND PLACES

What are some of the challenges of living in North Africa?

It may seem that the Sahara serves no purpose and that it would be a great idea to somehow turn it into a garden, but God set the earth's ecosystems in perfect balance. The Saharan phosphate deposits are not only an essential ingredient for world agriculture but also the essential ingredient for keeping the Amazon green. The desert dust, rich in phosphorus, is picked up by winds and moved from the Sahara across the Atlantic to naturally fertilize the Amazon jungle. Scientists believe as much as 27 million tons of dust falls in the Amazon each year, replacing the phosphorus that is lost in the process of decay and leaching.

Aswan High Dam, Egypt

The greatest environmental concern of the North African countries is how to obtain and manage what little fresh water they have. Until the early twentieth century, the Nile flooded every year, bringing with it precious silt. The farmers channeled the floodwaters into their fields to sustain their crops of grain and cotton. The population was restricted to about ten miles on either side of the Nile, where the floodwaters could be channeled. Beginning in 1902, new dams ended the flood patterns. The largest, Aswan High Dam, was finished in 1970. The dam and Lake Nasser behind the dam have stopped the flooding and allow year-round irrigation. Now two or three crops can be raised in one year. However, the dam also traps the rich sediments in Lake Nasser, preventing the replenishment of soil downstream. Egyptian farmers must now rely on fertilizers.

In 1953 while oil companies were looking for oil in the Libyan Sahara, the companies found oil along with a large amount of water in an aquifer. Qaddafi undertook a massive project in 1984 called the Great Man-Made River Project to bring the water to the northern farmlands, and he was initially successful. Presently it is the world's largest irrigation project, costing $35 billion. It was to be completed in five phases; phase three was completed in 2009. The project became a casualty of the civil war. It was a target of bombs and a resource to be captured by warring factions. Its future is as unstable as the country. Whether it was a long-term solution to Libya's water needs is also in question. Some scientists claim that once emptied the aquifer would never refill, while others say it is showing signs of recharging, although slowly.

Morocco and Egypt, having become more wealthy and stable recently, have undertaken renewable energy projects. Morocco completed the world's largest solar plant in 2016. It generates 580 megawatts, enough to power a large city. Egypt built the largest wind farm in Africa at the time in 2015; it generates 200 megawatts.

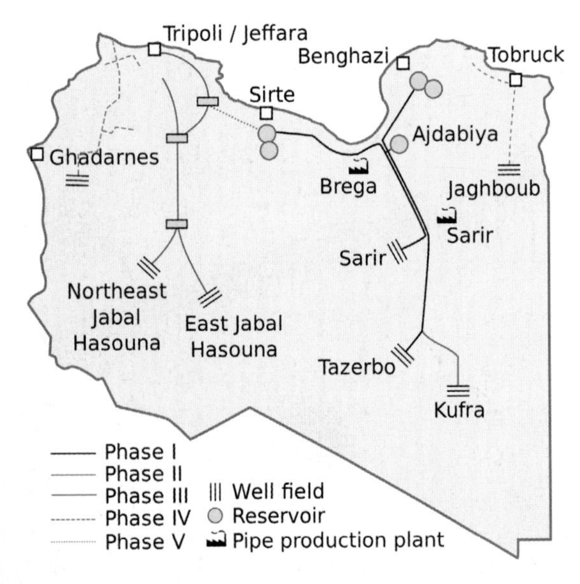

The Great Man-Made River Project of Libya

Interaction with the Environment

Water

Even though they have little fresh water, North African countries continue practices that lead to water pollution. In Egypt small worms called *schistosomes* live in the murky Nile and spread a disease known as *bilharzia*, which affects the liver and blood vessels. Scientists are concerned that Lake Chad will eventually disappear and with it a vital source of water and wildlife.

Air

While Africa has a major problem with air pollution, North Africa has less than the rest of the continent. The significant area of concern is seven cities in Tunisia and Morocco that rank high for air pollution.

Land

At one time, scattered acacia, mahogany, and baobab trees made the Sahel a true savanna. But recent droughts and famines have caused a fear that the Sahara is swallowing the savanna as it spreads southward. This process is called **desertification**, or *desiccation*. While it is difficult to measure the amount of land that is lost to the desert each year, desertification has caused food shortages that have killed thousands and forced many others to flee to the cities. In Egypt valuable farmland is being lost to urbanization. The Sahel region has to deal with plagues of locusts in the autumn months. The wildlife populations of the Sahel, including elephants, hippopotamuses, giraffes, gazelles, addaxes, and lions, are in sharp decline.

▾ *An addax in the Sahara*

▾ *Desertification in Nouakchott, Mauritania*

Reasons for Environmental Issues in North Africa

There are three main causes of water pollution in North Africa that may seem familiar. These countries continue to dump raw sewage into the rivers and seas. Excess fertilizer travels from the fields into the rivers. And chemicals used in the oil extraction process are dumped either directly into the water or on the ground, where they seep down and eventually reach the water.

There are two reasons for Lake Chad disappearing. First, because the surrounding region is susceptible to food shortages, water from the lake has been used to irrigate massive areas of farmland in Chad and neighboring countries. Also, the average rainfall has decreased since the 1960s. The lake bed is flat and shallow and is therefore naturally vulnerable to the slightest change.

Two conditions may contribute to desertification. One is human abuse of the land. Since the 1960s, the number of people in the Sahel has more than doubled. Newly drilled wells attracted herders who settled permanently for the first time. With this increased population came an increased demand for pasture, firewood, and cropland. Poor farming techniques and overgrazing compounded the loss of soil through erosion. The loss of trees and soil opened the way for the desert to invade. Another often-ignored factor in desertification is the earth's natural cycles. During the time of its population increase, the Sahel also experienced extreme, prolonged droughts. Droughts are a fact of life, depleting soil and vegetation wherever they strike.

▾ *A swarm of locusts*

Locusts are an ancient problem that has gotten worse. The planting of more crops provides the insects with a greater food supply. The locusts migrate from Libya and Algeria to the Sahel. In the past, those countries have been able to kill the locusts before they reach the Sahel, but because of instability, those countries have not been eradicating the pests as well as they did in the past.

Wild animals in the Sahel are under threat from several sources, and the animals have few protectors. Their habitat is under pressure from the desert, farms, and oil companies. Poachers kill the animals since their materials are valuable on the black market. Boko Haram, an Islamic terrorist group, has been a threat to the wildlife and the people of the region since 2011.

Proposed Solutions

A stable government, a better economy, and education on more efficient environmentally friendly practices would go far in solving many of these issues. Transaqua is the name for a proposal to refill Lake Chad. It is a project proposed by two companies, Bonifica from Italy and PowerChina, the company that built the Three Gorges Dam. The project would cost 50 billion dollars, and the United Nations has endorsed this plan. It would redirect part of the Congo River to the Chari River, thus adding water to the lake. A Canadian solar company presented a proposal in 2018 to use solar energy to pump water into the lake and supply energy for the people.

Some measures are now being taken to reduce desertification in the Sahel, such as new farming techniques and planting trees in rows to slow down wind erosion.

Niger has enacted a permanent ban on hunting, and the country uses its limited resources to enforce the ban. They have begun using drones to maximize their efforts and help with enforcement of the hunting bans.

SECTION REVIEW

1. What term describes the expansion of the desert toward the savanna?
2. Why would a better economy benefit both the people and the environment?
3. How are the political, economic, and environmental issues of North Africa related?
4. While considering the limitations of outside countries and agencies to help in Africa, what initiatives might be successful?
5. What is significant about where the solutions for Lake Chad are coming from?

A young man planting a tree for a campaign against the advancing of desert in sub-Saharan Africa

(bottom) Giraffes feeding from an acacia tree at the Kouré Giraffe Reserve, Niger

14 CHAPTER REVIEW

SUMMARY

1. North Africa has five regions, the most important one being the Sahara, which also defines the geography of the continent. The Atlas Mountains and northward have a mediterranean climate while the Saharan climate is very hot and dry. Phosphates, uranium, and petroleum are three important resources found in this region.
2. Pivotal events include Islam's arrival, colonization, and independence. The cultural geographic regions are the Maghreb, the Sahel, and Egypt. The governments of North Africa are unstable and prone to corruption. The Arab Spring was transformative for the entire region in 2011. Morocco, Tunisia, and Egypt are enjoying growth and economic health, while the Sahel countries remain very poor. This region, on the whole, is not urbanized and becomes more diverse as one travels south. North Africa has a high-context culture that values hospitality. Sunni Islam is by far the principal religion.
3. Desertification, lack of water, and disappearing wildlife are the main environmental issues of this region. Outside countries are trying to save Lake Chad. Lack of stability and poor economies are key reasons for the poor environment. Niger and Chad are trying to use their limited resources to save their wildlife.

Terms to Know

- ❑ Sahara
- ❑ dune
- ❑ Sahel
- ❑ alluvial deposits
- ❑ oasis
- ❑ aquaculture
- ❑ hieroglyphics
- ❑ Bedouin
- ❑ patriarchal
- ❑ desertification

Making Connections

1. What kind of earth-shaping process is responsible for the Emi Koussi? the Qattara Depression? the Richat Structure?
2. What climate is common on the northern coast of Africa in addition to desert? What geographic feature makes this climate possible?
3. What are some major sources of water in North Africa?
4. What were the three empires of the Sahel? What valuable resources did they trade?
5. Who are the Berber people?

Developing Geography Skills

1. Using the satellite image on page 310, the map on page 311, and the text, explain why the Sahel's population is concentrated in the south of each country.
2. Using the map on page 311, determine which nations will be directly affected by the shrinking of Lake Chad.

Thinking Critically

1. What factors contribute to the process of desertification? What measures can be taken to slow or reverse this destructive process?
2. Why did the people rise up against their governments during the Arab Spring? How should Christians think about revolution from a biblical worldview? Is there an alternative to revolution?

Living in God's World

1. Why are missionary opportunities limited in North Africa? What may be an effective method of reaching the North African people with the gospel?
2. How should a Christian living in a prosperous country approach the issue of poverty in places such as Niger, one of the poorest countries in the world?

CASE STUDY | The Suez Canal

The Suez Canal was the longest canal in the world when it was opened in 1869. It stretches almost 120 miles from the Red Sea at Suez to the Mediterranean Sea, where a new commercial center, Port Said, was built. As the shortest route between Europe and the Indian and Pacific Oceans, the canal is one of the busiest waterways in the world.

The canal is 66 feet deep. In 2014 it was widened from 590 feet wide to 1023 feet to allow ships to pass through going both directions at its most narrow points. It does not require the use of locks since the land between the Mediterranean Sea and the Red Sea is at the same elevation. Thousands of workers took ten years to complete the original construction, many of them dying in the arduous work of building the canal. The canal put Egypt back at the forefront of world affairs since it saved countries time and money in shipping. Neither was it as hazardous as traveling around the Cape of Good Hope in the Southern Ocean.

Interestingly, the French engineer Ferdinand de Lesseps was not the first to dig a canal here. Pharaoh Necho lost many slaves in his attempt to build the canal in the seventh century BC. King Darius of Persia conquered Egypt and completed the job around 522 BC. The Romans made improvements to the canal, but it eventually filled with silt.

Since a country can use its navy to project power far away from its borders, blocking a canal like the Suez can be a means to check that power. Warships and cargo ships alike depend on canals, so the country controlling the canal can determine which countries have access. In 1956 the British gave up control of the canal to the Egyptian government, who promptly attempted to nationalize it. This caused a crisis that led to a UN peacekeeping force being placed there. In 1967 Egypt ejected the UN force and closed the canal in its war with Israel. It sank fifteen cargo ships to block the canal and ensure that no one used it. It was not opened again until 1975. Today an average of fifty ships a day pass through the canal.

The USS Dwight D. Eisenhower *transits the Suez Canal en route to the Mediterranean Sea.*

1. Why is the Suez Canal so important?
2. What is the key difference between the Suez and the Panama Canals?
3. How has the Suez Canal influenced Egypt's economy?
4. How has the canal made Egypt influential in world affairs?

chapter 15

EQUATORIAL AFRICA

332 Physical Geography
340 Human Geography
348 Interactions

BIG IDEAS

- What is the physical geography of Equitorial Africa like?
- How do the people of Equatorial Africa live?
- What are some of the challenges of living in Equatorial Africa?

Rainforest in the Congo

Antelope on the African savanna

PATROLLING THE CONGO BASIN

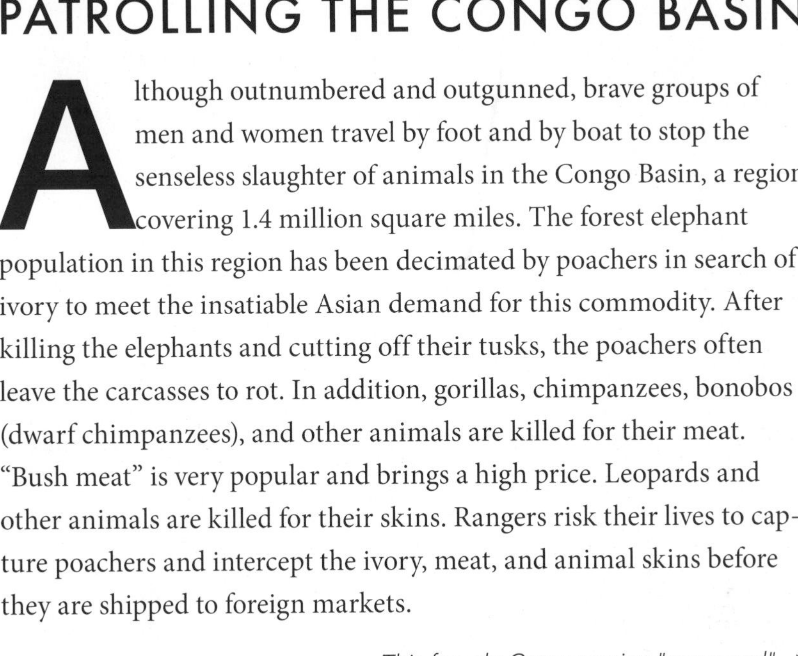

Although outnumbered and outgunned, brave groups of men and women travel by foot and by boat to stop the senseless slaughter of animals in the Congo Basin, a region covering 1.4 million square miles. The forest elephant population in this region has been decimated by poachers in search of ivory to meet the insatiable Asian demand for this commodity. After killing the elephants and cutting off their tusks, the poachers often leave the carcasses to rot. In addition, gorillas, chimpanzees, bonobos (dwarf chimpanzees), and other animals are killed for their meat. "Bush meat" is very popular and brings a high price. Leopards and other animals are killed for their skins. Rangers risk their lives to capture poachers and intercept the ivory, meat, and animal skins before they are shipped to foreign markets.

This female Cameroonian "ecoguard" is part of a binational group from Cameroon and Gabon that looks for evidence of wildlife poaching.

Zebra on the savanna

GUIDING QUESTIONS

- What are the regions of Equatorial Africa?
- What caused the landforms of Equatorial Africa?
- What bodies of water are important to Equatorial Africa?
- What are the climates of Equatorial Africa?
- What natural resources are found in Equatorial Africa?

Jungles and savannas dominate the landscape and lifestyles of the twenty nations in western and central Africa. The equator runs through the center of this region.

Unlike mediterranean climates and river valleys in the Sahel, tropical rainforests and dry savannas cannot generally support intensive agriculture. Traditionally, the people in this region have survived by being hunters and gatherers. When necessary, they practiced slash-and-burn agriculture to produce enough food for their families and tribe. The transition from small villages to cities has been difficult and remains a challenge in some countries.

PHYSICAL GEOGRAPHY

Regions of Equatorial Africa

What is the physical geography of Equatorial Africa like?

WEST AFRICA

The Cape Verde islands and an island associated with Equatorial Guinea were formed from volcanic activity and are the only landforms of that type in West Africa. Eleven of the other countries in this region have a variety of landforms ranging from coastal lowlands to plains and plateaus. Some even have highlands and mountains. Burkina Faso stands apart in this region of Africa as the single landlocked country of West Africa. Much of the country is located on a savanna and desert plateau in the northern part of the country. A **savanna** is a grassy plain in tropical and subtropical regions.

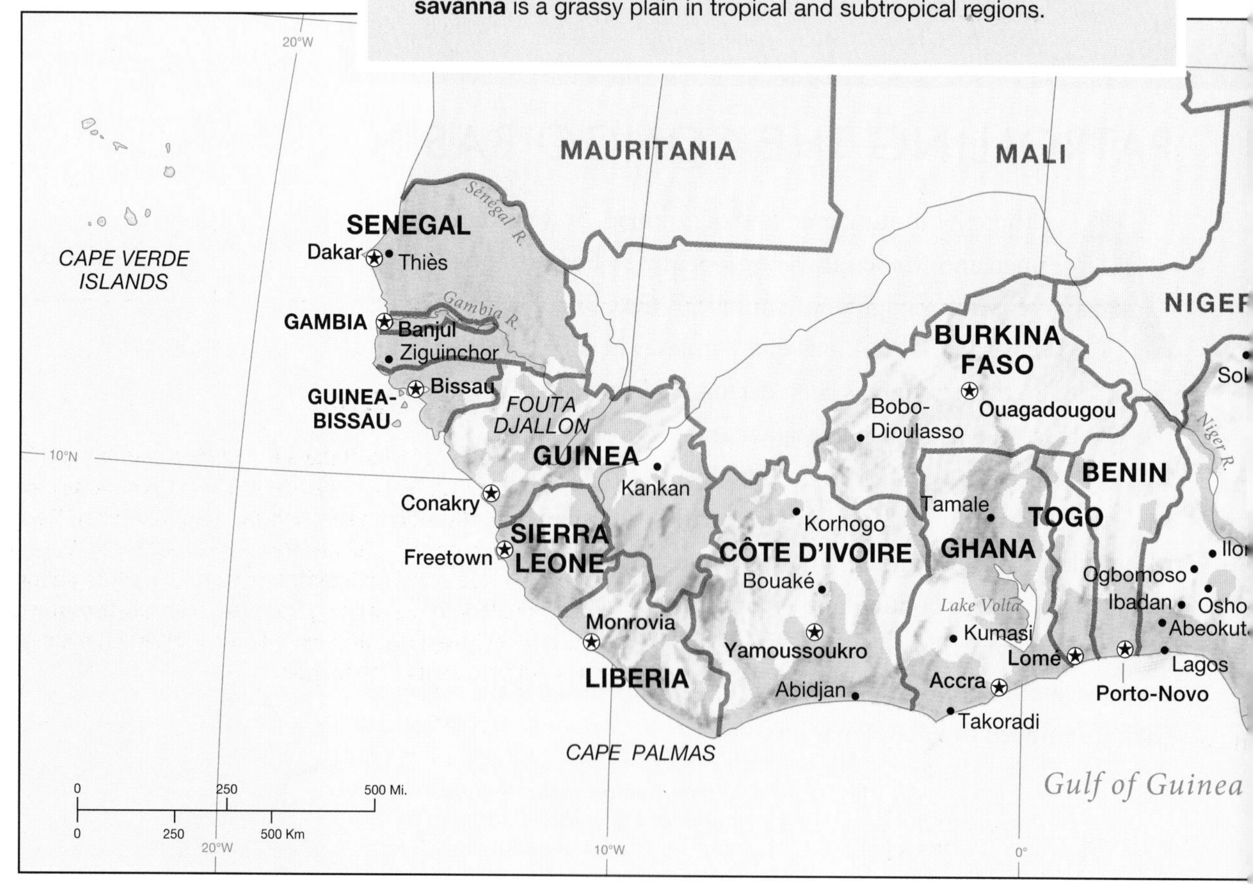

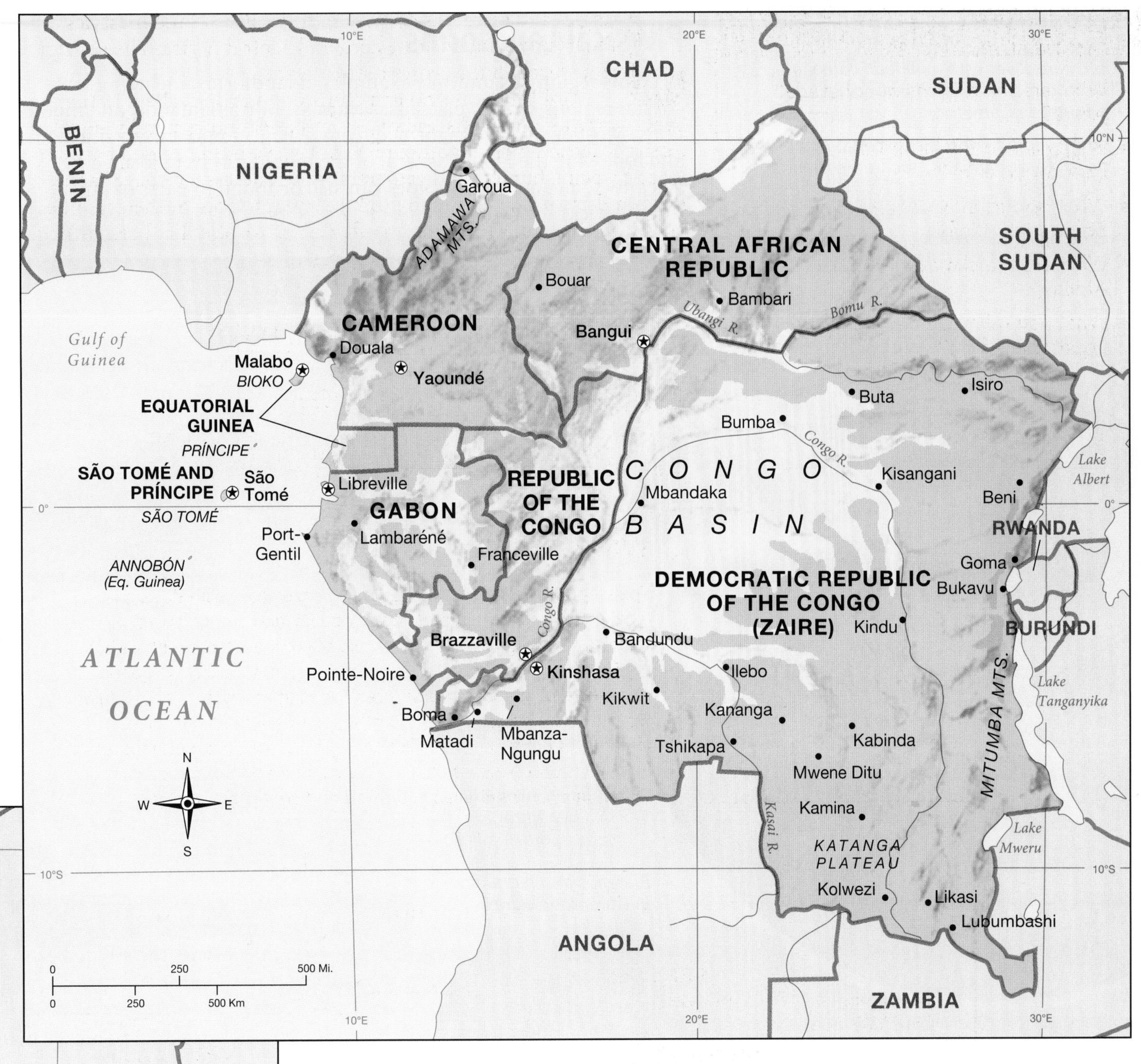

CENTRAL AFRICA

The island nation of São Tomé and Príncipe was formed by volcanic activity. Five of the other Central African nations have some access to the Atlantic Ocean, and the Central African Republic is the single landlocked nation in this region of Africa. While the Central African Republic is primarily a plateau, the other nations enjoy a variety of landforms ranging from low coastal areas to plateaus, savannas, hilly regions, and mountains. Cameroon even has an active volcano as its highest point.

Physical Landforms

This region has multiple examples of landforms, including low coastal regions, plains, plateaus, savannas, hills, highlands, and mountains. Most of Africa was formed from plate tectonic activity during and following the Flood. Several of the mountains were formed by volcanoes, and active volcanoes can still be found in parts of Equatorial Africa.

- (left) Faro River with a plateau in the background near Faro National Park, in Northern Cameroon
- (right) Pico do Fogo is a volcano on the island of Fogo in the Cape Verde islands.

African village huts in a desert region of Burkina Faso

Plateaus and highlands in Cameroon, Africa

Bodies of Water

In addition to the Atlantic Ocean, West and Central African nations have a number of important rivers that make life possible in this region. The rivers provide water for irrigation, transportation, fishing, and energy production in the form of hydropower. Some of the rivers also serve as national boundaries. For example, the Congo River serves as a national boundary and is navigable for one thousand miles, from Kinshasa to Kisangani. The sedimentary basin of the Congo River, the **Congo Basin**, is home to one of the world's largest rainforests. Many species of plants and animals are found only in this basin. The Niger River provides a major passage for commercial shipping in West Africa from the Atlantic to the interior of Africa. Another important river is the Ubangi River, which is a tributary of the Congo River and serves as a national boundary for the Central African Republic. Other significant rivers include the Ogooué River in Gabon, the Benue River in Nigeria, and the Senegal and Gambia Rivers in Guinea and Senegal.

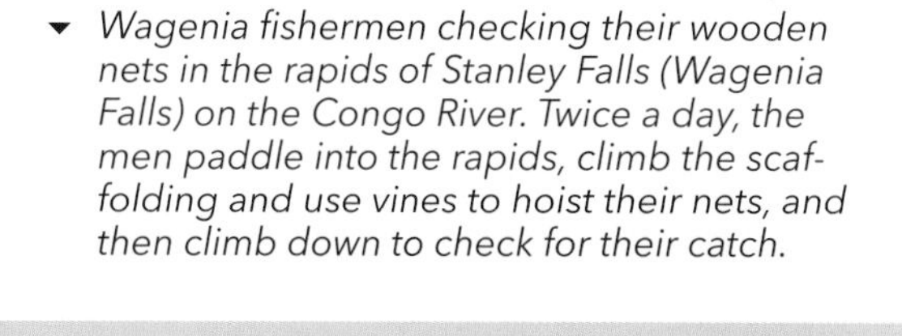

▾ *Wagenia fishermen checking their wooden nets in the rapids of Stanley Falls (Wagenia Falls) on the Congo River. Twice a day, the men paddle into the rapids, climb the scaffolding and use vines to hoist their nets, and then climb down to check for their catch.*

- *Asejire Dam near Ibadan in Nigeria*
- *A woman and a teenage boy fishing on Lake Nokoue near Ganvie in Benin*

Though this region has no large lakes, the Democratic Republic of the Congo has several small lakes. Senegal also has two notable lakes, and one of these can be considered unique. Lake Retba is a manmade saltwater lake, and the water is pink. The salty water attracts algae, and the interaction of the algae with the salt produces a red pigment that gives the water a pink hue. Besides its unique color, this lake provides a seemingly endless supply of salt that is extracted and exported.

- *People at Lac Rose (Pink Lake) collecting salt to be sold across the region, especially for preserving fish. Known for its high salt content, the lake has a pink or sometimes orange color that is caused by algae.*

Climates of Equatoral Africa

West Africa

Located north of the equator, Western Africa experiences shifting winds. These winds result in alternating tropical rainy and dry climates. The highlands receive more rainfall than the lowlands, and the northern regions in proximity to the Sahara receive the least amount of rain and record the highest temperatures.

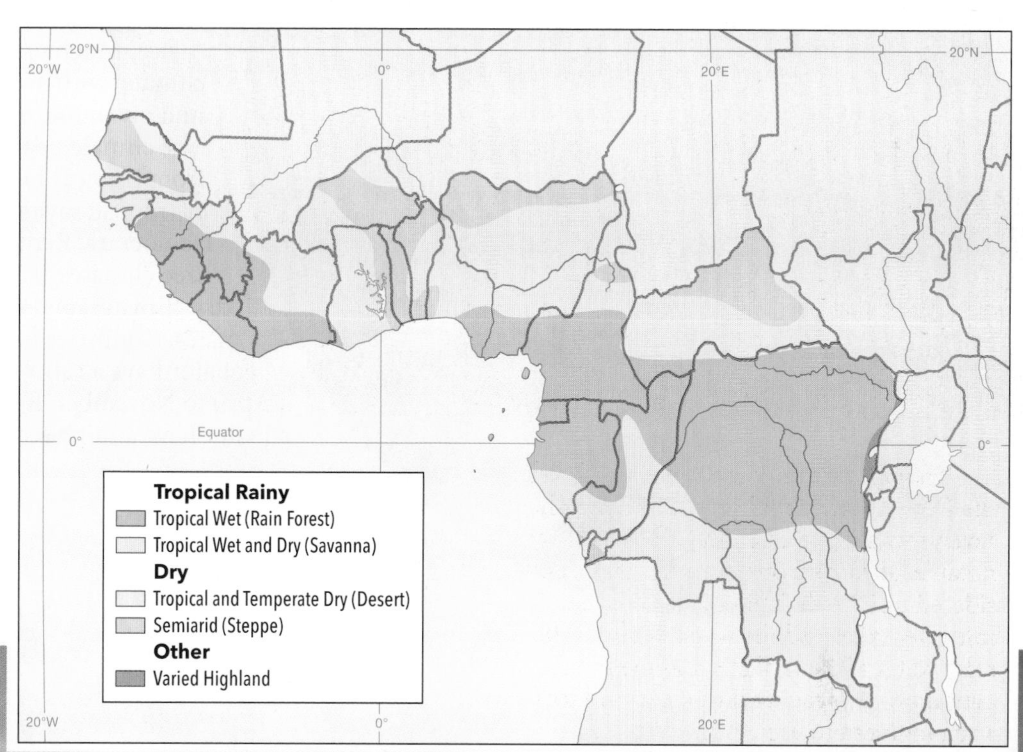

▾ *Baobab trees, like this one in Burkina Faso, thrive in a tropical dry climate.*

▾ *Kpatawee Waterfall and the rich vegetation in Liberia, West Africa, typify a tropical rainy climate.*

Central Africa

The equator crosses the heart of Central Africa. Much of the region has a tropical wet climate, with average temperatures of 80°F and one hundred inches of rainfall each year. The climate near the equator varies slightly, from tropical rainforest to tropical monsoon or tropical savanna. Large countries such as the Democratic Republic of the Congo experience all three climates. The highlands experience cooler, dry climates, and mountains have cold, alpine climates. Countries in this region that are north of the equator have a rainy season that generally lasts from April to November. Regions a few degrees south of the equator have a rainy season from October to May.

Mt. Rwenzori (16,762 feet), the third-highest mountain in Africa, has an alpine climate.

A highlands region in the Congo

Rainforest of the Congo Basin

Resources of Equatorial Africa

Many of the countries in Equatorial Africa have an abundance of common and precious resources. Common resources include fish, salt, timber, phosphates, iron ore, natural rubber, and petroleum. Precious resources include gold, uranium, and diamonds.

◂ *Radioactive uranium mineral from the Democratic Republic of the Congo*

▾ *Raw bauxite stone, from which aluminum is extracted*

WEST AFRICA

Cape Verde Islands: fish, salt

Senegal: fish, phosphates

Gambia: fish, titanium, tin, zircon, silica sand, clay, petroleum

Guinea-Bissau: fish, timber, phosphates, clay, granite, limestone

Guinea: bauxite, iron ore, gold, uranium, diamonds

Sierra Leone: diamonds

Liberia: natural rubber, palm oil, timber, diamonds, iron ore, gold

Côte d'Ivoire: petroleum, natural gas, diamonds, manganese, iron ore, bauxite, and copper

Burkina Faso: manganese, limestone, marble, phosphates, pumice, and salt

Ghana: bauxite, manganese, silver, gold, diamonds, timber, fish

Togo: fish, phosphates, cement, textiles

Benin: petroleum, limestone, timber

Nigeria: timber, petroleum, rubber

CENTRAL AFRICA

Cameroon: petroleum

São Tomé and Príncipe: fish, timber, petroleum

Equatorial Guinea: petroleum, fish, gold, bauxite, diamonds, tantalum, timber

Gabon: timber, manganese, gold, uranium, petroleum

Republic of the Congo: potash, lead, zinc, uranium, copper, phosphates, petroleum

Democratic Republic of the Congo: petroleum, tin, copper, cobalt, diamonds, uranium, gold, silver, zinc

Central African Republic: diamonds, uranium, gold, petroleum

SECTION REVIEW

1. Between which two major lines of latitude does most of Equatorial Africa lie?
2. How does Equatorial Africa's location on the globe affect its climate?
3. How were the islands of São Tomé and Príncipe formed?
4. Why is the Congo River so important to Equatorial Africa?
5. What energy-producing resource is abundant in Equatorial Africa?
6. What resources are abundant in Equatorial Africa?

White-gray, uncut diamonds

700 800 900 1000 1100 1200 1300

700–1200 Ghana Empire

1200–1500 Mali Empire

3000 BC Migration to Africa

GUIDING QUESTIONS

- How has Equatorial Africa changed over time?
- How do the Equatorial African governments interact with their citizens?
- What is the economic health of Equatorial Africa?
- What are the demographics of Equatorial Africa?
- What are the cultural characteristics and diversity in Equatorial Africa?
- What forms of religion are practiced in Equatorial Africa?

HUMAN GEOGRAPHY

How do the people of Equatorial Africa live?

The village, a self-contained group of families living in close proximity in a rural area, is an important concept in understanding life in Africa. In the traditional African village, each person plays a vital role in the survival of the whole community. Having more than one wife is viewed by many as a sign of wealth, so polygamy is common. Young children pull weeds or sort vegetables; older children herd livestock or do household chores. Loyalty to the village extends to larger social units. Several villages that are descended from a common ancestor form a clan. Two or more clans, in turn, form a tribe. A headman wields the highest authority in the village. A strong tribal chief unites several villages, using headmen as his administrators.

Whenever people are isolated in small groups, their speech patterns diverge quickly. Dialects arise and then turn into new languages. Africa has about 15 percent of the people of the world and about 20 percent of the languages. Strong identification with a tribe that speaks the same language or dialect is called **tribalism**. In spite of European influence, tribalism continues to be a central feature of sub-Saharan Africa. Individuals often feel more allegiance to their tribe than to their nation-state.

Moving from rural areas to the cities in Equatorial Africa has increased following independence. People move to find better employment opportunities and for many other reasons. As of 2018, Kinshasa, the capital of the Democratic Republic of the Congo, was the largest

- *(left) Local people trading foods and goods at a small village market in Benin*
- *(right) Kinshasa is the capital and largest city in the Democratic Republic of the Congo.*

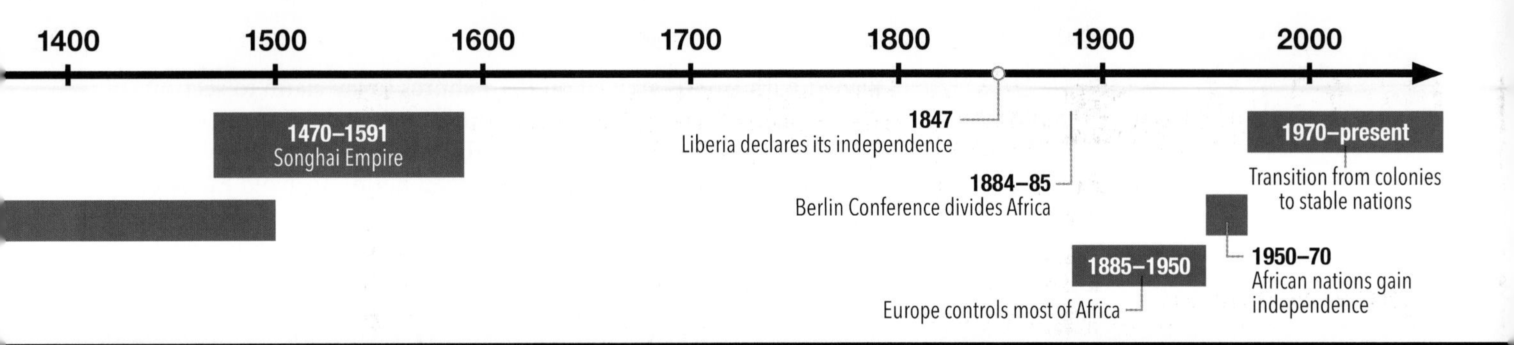

city in Equatorial Africa, with a population of 11.3 million people. With the growth of cities come modern conveniences that are found in many Western cities, including high rises, shopping malls, and multinational corporations. In some of these countries, urbanization is nearing 50 percent of the population.

History

People may have migrated to Africa as long ago as 3000 BC. Evidence of early civilizations has largely disappeared due to the climate and centuries of weathering. What may be the oldest city in Western Africa, Djenné-Djeno, was located along a tributary of the Niger River.

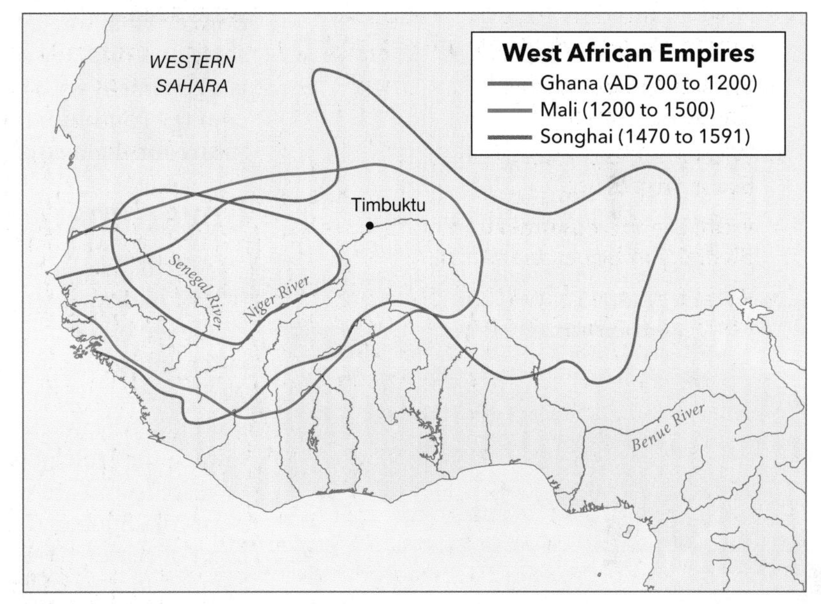

Tribes handed down their history primarily through stories, and each generation shared its oral history with the next. In addition to tribal information, creation and flood accounts were part of African history. Written history about Africa began, in large part, with the arrival of European explorers and traders. For example, voyages along the western coast of Africa increased European awareness of Africa's size and resources even as Africans became aware of other civilizations beyond the Atlantic Sea.

As Europe descended into the Middle Ages, three kingdoms emerged in West Africa—Ghana, Mali, and Songhai. Each successive kingdom became larger than the previous. These kingdoms built prosperous civilizations financed by gold mines and caravan trade in gold, salt, and other precious commodities carried by camels across the Sahara. The Niger River also provided a steady flow of merchants and goods through this region. Each of these kingdoms accumulated great wealth by charging a tariff on the goods passing through their lands. The kingdom of Mali added agricultural goods and copper to the thriving trade of gold and copper. During this kingdom's dominance, Timbuktu became the capital, and Mansa Musa became its most famous ruler. The Mali Empire fell to invaders in the fifteenth century and was succeeded by the Songhai Empire, which conquered even more territory under the leadership of Sunni Ali. Ali's accidental death by drowning weakened the Songhai Empire. By this time, European explorers were visiting West African ports and establishing trade agreements with African tribes.

For a time, Europeans satisfied themselves with exploration and trade. However, in 1884 European nations met in Berlin and secretly divided Africa among themselves. No Africans were present at these meetings, and they were unaware of such plans until European ships loaded with troops arrived on their shores to lay claim to sections of Africa. The region was forcibly divided among the Portuguese, French, British, and Germans. Some of the descendants of these invaders now call Africa home. The only West African nation to avoid European imperialism was Liberia. This nation was formed from slaves repatriated by groups in the United States. Liberia escaped foreign occupation because of its ties with America.

African nations chafed under foreign rule and pressed for independence, especially following World War II. Most of the countries in this region gained their independence between 1950 and 1969. Cape Verde was the last country in West Africa to gain its independence in 1975.

Following independence most of these African nations struggled to form national governments out of many tribes and language groups that had previously been held together by European forces. Some countries experimented with socialism and communism. Others tried to continue the European models that had been imposed on them. The recent history of many of these countries has been marked by revolution or tribal warfare. Others have slowly transitioned from dictatorships and military control to democracies and civilian control. Africa is a continent with incredible human and natural resources, and each country continues to work toward a stable government and a better future for the next generation.

▾ A Nigerian man and woman jointly cast their ballots at a polling station in Daura, Katsina State, during presidential elections on March 28, 2015.

Governments

Terms like *democratic*, *democracy*, and *republic* are found in the title of many governments in West and Central Africa. Despite the challenge of forming governments following independence in the latter half of the twentieth century, the goal of the citizens of these African nations remains to elect their leaders and to restrict leaders' powers with laws. Some of these nations have made steady progress toward the realization of these goals, while others have suffered from civil strife and are still denied representation and a stable government.

Most Equatorial African nations have an elected leader and some form of representation. In some countries the elections are carefully controlled to ensure the reelection of the ruler and his party. In these countries opposition candidates risk arrest and imprisonment or worse. In other countries free elections are ensured, and the people are able to choose their leaders.

Several African nations have a form of government that is similar to that of the United States, with an elected leader who controls the executive branch and separate houses of government that control the legislative branch. Other African nations have a semi-presidential republic. This system of government has a popularly elected president plus a prime minister and cabinet. The president is largely ceremonial; legislation is enacted by the cabinet and carried out by the prime minister. Still other countries have a unitary form of government, with a single assembly (unicameral) rather than two assemblies (bicameral).

Government Interaction with Its Citizens

The treatment of citizens in Equatorial Africa differs radically depending on the nation. Nations in West Africa that are stable, including Cape Verde, Senegal, Ghana, and Nigeria, tend to protect human rights and treat their people with dignity, although human trafficking remains a serious problem. Citizens of nations that are plagued with power struggles and military dictatorships often suffer abuse from political leaders and their followers.

Likewise in Central Africa, nations that are stable, such as Cameroon and the tiny nation of São Tomé and Príncipe, tend to protect the rights of their citizens. To that end, Cameroon is working hard to defeat the Islamic terrorist group Boko Haram, which has carried out violent attacks and mass kidnappings of girls. Tragically, the other Central African countries continue to battle corruption and violence that often result in the abuse of their citizens. Equatorial Guinea has one of the worst human rights records, resulting from authoritarian rulers and large-scale human trafficking.

Education and Health Care

The goal of each of these countries is universal and free education. However, the reality in many Equatorial African countries falls far short of this lofty goal. Poverty, violence, and insufficient resources to accommodate the high birthrate are just some of the obstacles that many African nations must overcome in order to provide an adequate education for their children. In addition to suffering from national poverty, often due to corruption, many children must choose between getting an education and working to support their family. In some of these African countries, there are simply not enough teachers or enough buildings to meet the educational needs of the children. Even stable and prosperous African nations struggle to set aside enough funds for their growing educational needs.

The level of health care and government funding varies dramatically in Equatorial Africa. Health care tends to be better in cities than in the expansive rural areas, and its quality varies by location and by the level of stability of the local government. Most health care has been provided by government-funded clinics, medical missionary teams, and nonprofit organizations that send trained medical personnel into areas to treat or prevent diseases such as AIDS, sleeping sickness, yellow fever, and malaria.

Economies

The agricultural sector drives most of the Equatorial African economies, and most Africans work in this sector. **Cash crops**, crops that are raised specifically for sale, constitute much of this sector. Many of these countries are striving to diversify and modernize their economies. Countries in West Africa process a large variety of goods that are exported. Products include timber, salt, phosphates, iron ore, gold, diamonds, titanium, ship construction, and textiles. Gambia has also developed a tourist industry. Central African economies thrive on the processing of fish, timber, petroleum, textiles, palm oil, bauxite, manganese, uranium, and cobalt.

▲ *(top) These refugees in Nigeria were driven from their homes by attacks from the Islamic group Boko Haram.*

▲ *(middle) A public school for girls in Lagos, Nigeria*

▲ *(bottom) Girls walking home from a Muslim school in Nigeria*

The economies of the Equatorial African countries vary significantly in size and diversity. The GDPs of the West African nations in 2017 varied from Gambia's $1.01 billion to Nigeria's $376 billion.

The GDPs of Central African nations in 2017 varied from $375 million in tiny São Tomé and Príncipe to $38.6 billion in the Democratic Republic of the Congo. Petroleum revenues helped boost the GDP of several Central African countries.

The economies of Equatorial Africa are mixed, with some industries (including petroleum) often being controlled by the government. The freedom or regulation of the economy is frequently tied to the type of government in power. Dictatorships and authoritarian rulers tend to control the most lucrative exports and channel much of the nation's wealth to their own accounts. Political and economic corruption is a huge problem in Africa, and the end result is extreme wealth for a few and poverty for many in these countries.

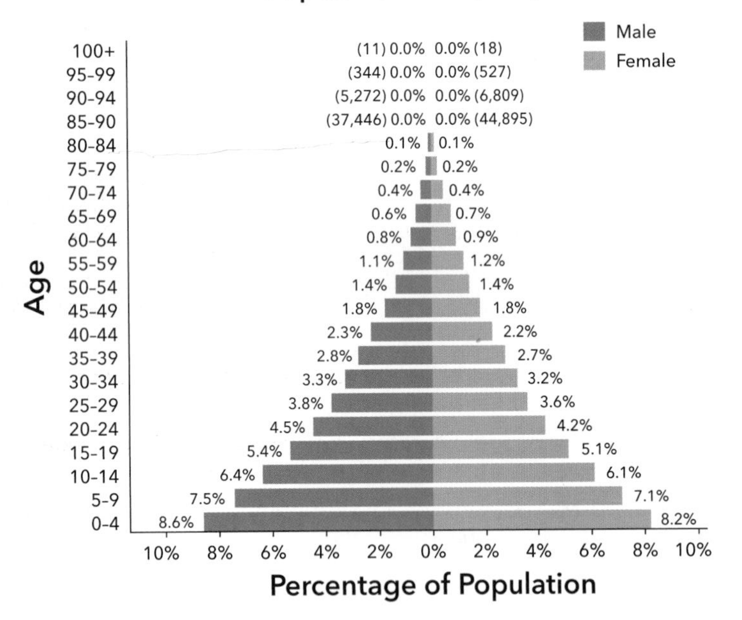

Demographics

In 2017 the combined estimated population of Equatorial Africa was 445 million. The country in West Africa with the largest population was Nigeria, at 191 million people. The country in this region with the smallest population was Cape Verde, with 0.6 million people. The Democratic Republic of the Congo had the largest population in Central Africa, with 83.3 million people, and São Tomé and Príncipe had the smallest, with 0.2 million people.

Equatorial countries tend to have high birthrates, and their populations are increasing rapidly. The example of Nigeria's population pyramid shows that over half of the population is less than twenty-four years old, and a small number of people are above sixty. This population imbalance is due to many factors, including diseases, war, and famine. It also helps to explain why some children are forced to become apprentices to learn a trade and help support their families rather than receive an education.

Equatorial African populations are based on hundreds of tribes, and the populations are almost exclusively native African, with some tiny exceptions of those descended from European settlers. Cape Verde, however, was not populated prior to its discovery by the Portuguese. As a result, 73 percent of Cape Verde's population is mixed Portuguese and African, with only 25 percent having purely African heritage.

Culture and Diversity

The variety of cultures in these regions ranges from less than twenty to a few hundred, depending on the country. Nigeria has over 250 tribal groups that speak over five hundred languages. Many people in these regions identify as Bantu, but there are many subgroups within that designation, and each might speak a different dialect. This variety in languages has resulted in a vast number of diverse cultures. Style of dress differs, as do customs, traditions, and even the materials used to build a home. Areas where forests are abundant provide resources that might be scarce on savannas and plateaus. People have adapted to their environment, and their cultures have been shaped, in part, by their natural surroundings and resources.

▲ (above) Young man in Senegal playing a Kora, a stringed instrument made from a calabash gourd

◂ (top left) A man playing a balophon, a traditional African musical instrument

◂ (left) Diola boys playing drums in Kaschouane Village, Senegal

As in other cultures, the people of Equatorial Africa enjoy music and express themselves in various forms of dance. While some musical instruments might be familiar, others are unique to Africa.

Meals in West and Central Africa are typically a combination of locally grown cereal grains, available fruits and vegetables, various types of meat, and milk products. One meal commonly served in West Africa is a stew called *mafé* that is made with chicken, fish, or lamb and ground peanuts. A popular meal in the Central African Republic is "fish and greens with fufu." Many African countries have their own

▾ *Mafé, or peanut stew, an example of Senegalese African cuisine*

▾ *Fufu, in the large dish, is a common food in West and Central Africa. It is made from the cassava root.*

Puff puff, a popular sweet snack, on a Nigerian party buffet

Egusi soup, an example of Nigerian cuisine

version of jollof rice. For example, Nigerians enjoy jollof rice and a thick soup known as *egusi*. They also enjoy "puff puff," a dough-based snack.

It should come as no surprise that one of the most popular sports in Equatorial Africa is soccer. Basketball is also popular. Other popular sports include *kokawa* (wrestling), *abula* (a form of volleyball), and *dambe* (boxing).

Two wrestlers engage in the traditional Nigerian kokawa contest.

Religion

Six of the countries in West Africa are dominantly Muslim, with the other seven being a combination of Christian majority with a significant Muslim minority. None of the Central African countries have a Muslim majority. Most of these countries have some traditional African or animist presence, with Togo having the highest percentage at nearly 36 percent.

Religions of Nigeria

Religion	Percentage
Islamic	**43.5%**
Protestant Evangelical	**23.5%**
Roman Catholic	**15.8%**
Protestant	**11.7%**
Ethnic	**5.2%**
Unaffiliated	**0.3%**

BELIEFS

▲ *This witch tree near Kumasi, Ghana, is covered with pieces of personal property, often clothing or sandals, from witches that have been cleansed. The items must be left there forever, according to animist practice.*

African Traditional Religions

African traditional religions are difficult to label and to describe. They are sometimes called primitive religions, but devotees of these religions find that label offensive. Christians reject it because it presumes that religions evolved from primitive beginnings, whereas the Bible teaches that humanity began with knowledge of the true God and fell away. Furthermore, African traditional religions are often complex, having developed over long periods of time.

Animism is another term used to describe African traditional religions. **Animism** is the belief that all things have a spirit and that these spirits exercise great control over the world. A person must perform certain religious rituals or the spirits will become angry and he will experience bad luck. Worshiping the objects whose spirits are dominant in his locality will supposedly please the spirits and bring the person good luck.

There are many religions included under the broad category of African traditional religions. Each one is associated with a specific people group. Though these groups do not send out missionaries or proselytize, their beliefs and practices may spread as people intermarry with other groups or move to new areas.

Traditional religions do not have scriptures. They function by oral tradition and rituals that are carefully passed down from generation to generation. The rituals touch every aspect of life. This is a challenge for Christian missions. African converts to Christianity often attempt to merely add Christianity to their animistic beliefs. They may profess faith in Christ but then turn to a traditional healer to perform the traditional rituals if they become ill. Even true converts struggle to break with the religious traditions of their people. For instance, they may struggle with superstitions about the evil influence of owls even though they know the superstition to be false.

African traditional religions often include a belief in a high god who is a personal spirit, the creator, omniscient, omnipresent, and eternal. But this god typically is not approachable. In some cases, only the community can pray to this god in dire circumstances. The individual may never appeal to him. Or it may be possible to appeal to this god through intermediary gods. Even when it is possible to pray to the high god directly, the spirits of ancestors and the spirits of objects and places are of greater concern. These religions do not focus on a right relationship with the high god. They focus, rather, on appeasing the spirits so that daily life progresses well rather than poorly.

SECTION REVIEW

1. How has Equatorial Africa changed over time?
2. How well do the Equatorial African governments provide for the education, health, and safety of their citizens?
3. How would you describe the economies of Equatorial Africa?
4. Describe the demographics of Equatorial Africa.
5. What are some cultural characteristics and examples of diversity in Equatorial Africa?

INTERACTIONS OF PEOPLE AND PLACES

What are some of the challenges of living in Equatorial Africa?

GUIDING QUESTIONS

- How do the Equatorial African economies and people interact with the environment?
- What are environmental issues in Equatorial Africa?
- What are causes and effects of environmental issues in Equatorial Africa?
- What are possible solutions to environmental issues in Equatorial Africa?

Interaction among People

This region has a variety of cultures and governments. Stable governments and unified countries provide the best opportunity for people to interact positively with each other. Fractured governments and unstable societies, however, often have the opposite effect. The people of the Democratic Republic of the Congo have suffered from terrorist groups that forcibly recruit thousands of child soldiers. Rival groups in some of these countries have kidnapped and brutalized boys and turned them into brutal killers to defeat opposing forces. This horrific practice has resulted in the immense loss of life and lasting harm to these children. Human trafficking is another negative interaction within African society. While the kidnapping and enslaving of people has ancient roots and is not confined to Africa, these practices are still a horrible abuse of fellow humans in exchange for profit. Women and children are especially vulnerable to human trafficking.

GLOBAL IMPACT | AIDS

AIDS is a global epidemic that by 2017 had resulted in the deaths of about 77.3 million people. **AIDS** is a disease that weakens the body's immune system and increases the body's vulnerability to infection and terminal illness.

Sub-Saharan Africa has one of the highest rates of AIDS in the world. Approximately 69 percent of the people infected with HIV/AIDS live there, even though their countries make up about 15 percent of the world's population. The first step for African countries has been to recognize the problem. Because of the stigma attached to the disease, many people were not being tested, and some governments have, until recently, refused to acknowledge the enormity of the problem. For example, the president of South Africa initially denied that HIV causes AIDS. Education is an important part of the battle. Some countries, such as Uganda, have implemented programs that encourage sexual abstinence outside of marriage. Unfaithfulness of even one partner can affect an entire family. Many women get HIV through an unfaithful partner. Others contract it through sexual assault. Because of the physical method of transmission, women are more likely to get HIV than are their partners. A majority of sub-Saharan Africa's AIDS patients are women.

The AIDS epidemic has taken a huge toll on the labor force in sub-Saharan Africa, devastating the economies of those countries. The average life expectancy in the region initially dropped to only forty-seven years, although that number is rising.

Currently, about 11 million children in Africa have been orphaned by AIDS. And many children are infected themselves.

▲ *A sign promoting HIV testing for pregnant women in Sierra Leone*

Children can contract the disease simply by being born to an infected mother. Aggressive medical treatment has greatly reduced the number of children born with AIDS.

Certainly, Christians should be sympathetic toward those who have HIV/AIDS. Just as Christ healed the lepers of His day, Christians should be willing to minister to those from all levels of society. Could God be calling you to minister to AIDS victims in Africa?

1. Define AIDS.
2. Why are AIDS victims reluctant to report their condition?
3. How do many African women contract this disease?
4. How should Christians respond to this disease?

Interaction with the Environment

Following colonial rule, African countries faced many obstacles, including the struggle to unify nations that contain multiple tribes and languages. For many individual Africans, however, a greater struggle is simply surviving and laboring to produce enough food and raise enough livestock to feed their families. This lifestyle is known as **subsistence farming**. Some Africans are fortunate enough to live where resources are plentiful and rainfall is adequate to meet human needs and support crops. Others have labored under less favorable climate and soil conditions; their lives remain very difficult. For many in Africa, wood has been their main resource. Forests have been cleared to provide an income from logging, to increase the amount of land available for growing food, or simply to provide fuel for cooking. Land has often been cleared by "slash and burn," a process where trees and bushes are cut down and then burned. Given their limited resources, people viewed this practice as the only option. In addition to growing crops, many Africans practice **pastoralism**, or the raising of large herds of animals, especially sheep, goats, or cattle.

▲ *A woman, with her son, works in a small fenced garden in rural Senegal. This is an example of subsistence gardening.*

In African cities, industries have developed and transportation has expanded to move raw materials to factories and finished goods to ports. Automobiles have multiplied to transport workers and goods, and Africa is becoming a mobile society. As in other cultures, traffic congestion has become a way of life for a growing number of Africans. When cities and industries develop, waste is produced in large volumes, and the tendency is to drain household, human, and industrial waste to the nearest flowing body of water for disposal. All of these things negatively affect the environment unless properly handled.

In some areas of Equatorial Africa, **poaching**, the illegal killing of animals, is a serious problem. Animals are killed for ivory, skins, or meat. Some Africans depend on the meat to feed their families or seek to make money from these highly sought items. Many African governments attempt to limit poaching, with varying degrees of success. Given the large amounts of money at stake in poaching, many officials are tempted to take a bribe and look the other way. As a result, endangered species edge closer to extinction.

▲ *This 2014 photo of seized ivory at a port in Togo gives evidence of the country's intensified efforts to crack down on ivory trafficking.*

Reasons for Environmental Issues

Given the brief history of independence for most of Equatorial Africa and the struggle to develop true representative democracies, there has been a mixed response to the environmental issues that confront them. Lack of funds or corruption that siphons off designated funds intended to address environmental issues has resulted in a steady increase of pollution and inadequate efforts to solve environmental issues.

Water

Clean water is essential to life, but it is also difficult to find or sustain in many African nations. Water is often a scarce resource, and the rivers contain manmade pollutants and natural infestations that make the water dangerous to drink. Villages often have to resort to drilling to find safe water from underground reservoirs. As in other countries, agricultural runoff and human and industrial wastes often find their way into open water supplies, and few nations in this region have adequate resources to filter the water and remove contaminants.

Air

Much of the air pollution in African cities results from factory and automobile exhaust. However, many Africans also suffer from air pollution in their own homes. Up to 90 percent of African homes burn solid fuels and have poor ventilation, resulting in a toxic environment. Solid fuels include wood, crop waste, dung, or coal, and these substances contaminate the air in homes with a concentration that may exceed levels found in industrial cities. Air pollution in homes is a leading cause of death for African children.

City traffic in Kinshasa, DRC ▸

▾ Mounds of burning trash in Port Harcourt, Nigeria, contribute to a growing air pollution problem.

Land

Deforestation has produced large regions in Equatorial Africa that no longer have the vital cover of trees. This has led to loss of habitat for animals, destruction of plant life that contains much potential food and medicinal value, and the inevitable erosion and loss of topsoil. **Overfarming**, the practice of clearing land or grazing animals to excess, has done serious short-term damage to the land. Slash-and-burn practices have also taken an extensive long-term toll in exchange for short-term advantages.

Proposed Solutions

Several things need to occur in Equatorial Africa in order to address environmental problems. Each country needs a stable government with a growing economy. These countries need to firmly oppose corruption and ensure that wealth will be wisely stewarded. Greater emphasis needs to be placed on educating the children and empowering them to succeed and strengthen their country. An economically prosperous and politically stable nation can begin to address its many environmental problems.

Another essential step is addressing the rate of deforestation and making a concerted effort to plant new trees. They also need to develop other fuel sources for African homes so that solid fuels will not be required for cooking. Countries must develop the resources they have and build a transportation system to get cleaner fuel sources, such as natural gas, to the homes.

Other types of fuels, including hydropower from dams, need to be developed to tap the enormous energy potential from Equatorial Africa's many rivers. Another energy source that is readily available in some regions of Africa is wind. Cape Verde is developing wind farms to take advantage of the ocean breezes that sweep across the islands. West and Central African nations have enormous potential and vast human and natural resources. Wise stewardship of these resources will be key to properly dealing with the environmental challenges.

▲ *A young man fills water jugs from a water pump near his home in Liberia. This well provides clean drinking water to the entire neighborhood.*

SECTION REVIEW

1. What are three environmental issues in Equatorial Africa?
2. What role have many governments played in dealing with environmental issues in Equatorial Africa?
3. How has Equatorial Africa adjusted from agricultural to diversified economies?
4. Explain how the Equatorial African economies and people have interacted with the environment.
5. What solutions to current environmental issues in Equatorial Africa would you propose?

15

CHAPTER REVIEW

SUMMARY

1. The physical geography of Equatorial Africa was shaped by tectonic activity and volcanic eruptions. Equatorial Africa's abundant natural resources hold great economic potential.
2. The people of Equatorial Africa are ethnically varied by tribe and language and yet similar in the enjoyment of common activities, including ethnic foods, regional music, and sports. These societies are transitioning from a third-world status to developed societies but are threatened by instability and corruption.
3. A major challenge in Equatorial Africa is the need to make wise use of human and natural resources in ways that build strong economies without further endangering the environment. A goal for Equatorial Africa would be to develop cleaner resources for energy production and find ways to ensure the protection of their fragile environment.

Terms to Know

- ❑ savanna
- ❑ Congo Basin
- ❑ village
- ❑ tribalism
- ❑ cash crops
- ❑ animism
- ❑ AIDS
- ❑ subsistence farming
- ❑ pastoralism
- ❑ poaching
- ❑ overfarming

Making Connections

1. Describe the poaching problem in the Congo Basin and provide an example of one animal species that is endangered.
2. What earth-shaping process is at work on the islands of Equatorial Africa?
3. How do landforms affect climates in Equatorial Africa?
4. How has deforestation affected Equatorial Africa?
5. Why do you think Equatorial African economies are in transition?
6. Identify political issues in Equatorial Africa.
7. What factors have influenced religion in Equatorial Africa?

Developing Geography Skills

1. How do landforms influence the distribution of population in this region?
2. What role have rivers played in the concentration of population in Equatorial Africa?

Thinking Critically

1. Though many people oppose human trafficking, why is a biblical worldview best equipped to address this issue?
2. The main goal in African traditional religion is to appease the spirits and avoid bad luck. What are the problems with this kind of relationship? How does a Christian's relationship with the God of the Bible differ?

Living in God's World

1. Write a paragraph explaining how you would help provide clean water for African villages.
2. If you were able to travel to Equatorial Africa and demonstrate the love of Christ by working with AIDS patients, what types of things could you do?

CASE STUDY | Malaria

Perhaps you have heard a missionary from Africa report an encounter with malaria, a mosquito-borne disease that has sickened and even killed many people. The missionary might describe some of the symptoms: a severe headache, chills and sweating of the skin, a fever, and a dry cough. The victim of malaria also suffers from muscular fatigue and pain in every muscle. Malaria causes nausea and vomiting and can enlarge the spleen. Any movement is extremely difficult and painful, and the patient is extremely weak. There are two basic levels of malaria: uncomplicated and severe.

Treatment for uncomplicated malaria includes quinine and antimalarial drugs in pill form. People who have some level of immunity or have experienced malaria before might have this less severe form of malaria.

Treatment for severe malaria is normally administered intravenously, which gets the medicine into the blood system more rapidly and avoids upsetting the stomach with the higher dosage needed. This form of malaria progresses rapidly and needs to be treated quickly.

Recovery from both levels of malaria can take from one to two weeks, depending on factors such as immunity and type of treatment. However, many people are unable to resume normal activities for up to one month due to lingering dizziness, fatigue, and joint pain.

Since nearly 216 million people contract malaria each year, it is a significant health issue, especially in Africa. About 655,000 of those who contract malaria will die from the disease. Even though these are alarming numbers, the actual death rate is 0.3 percent due in part to the combination of medicines that are now available to treat malaria.

▲ *Covering beds with mosquito netting helps to protect people from being bitten by malaria-carrying mosquitoes.*

1. On what continent would you be most likely to contract malaria?
2. How is malaria spread?
3. Which level of malaria requires more urgent and extensive care? Why?
4. Why does it take so long to recover from malaria?
5. What percentage of malaria patients survive?

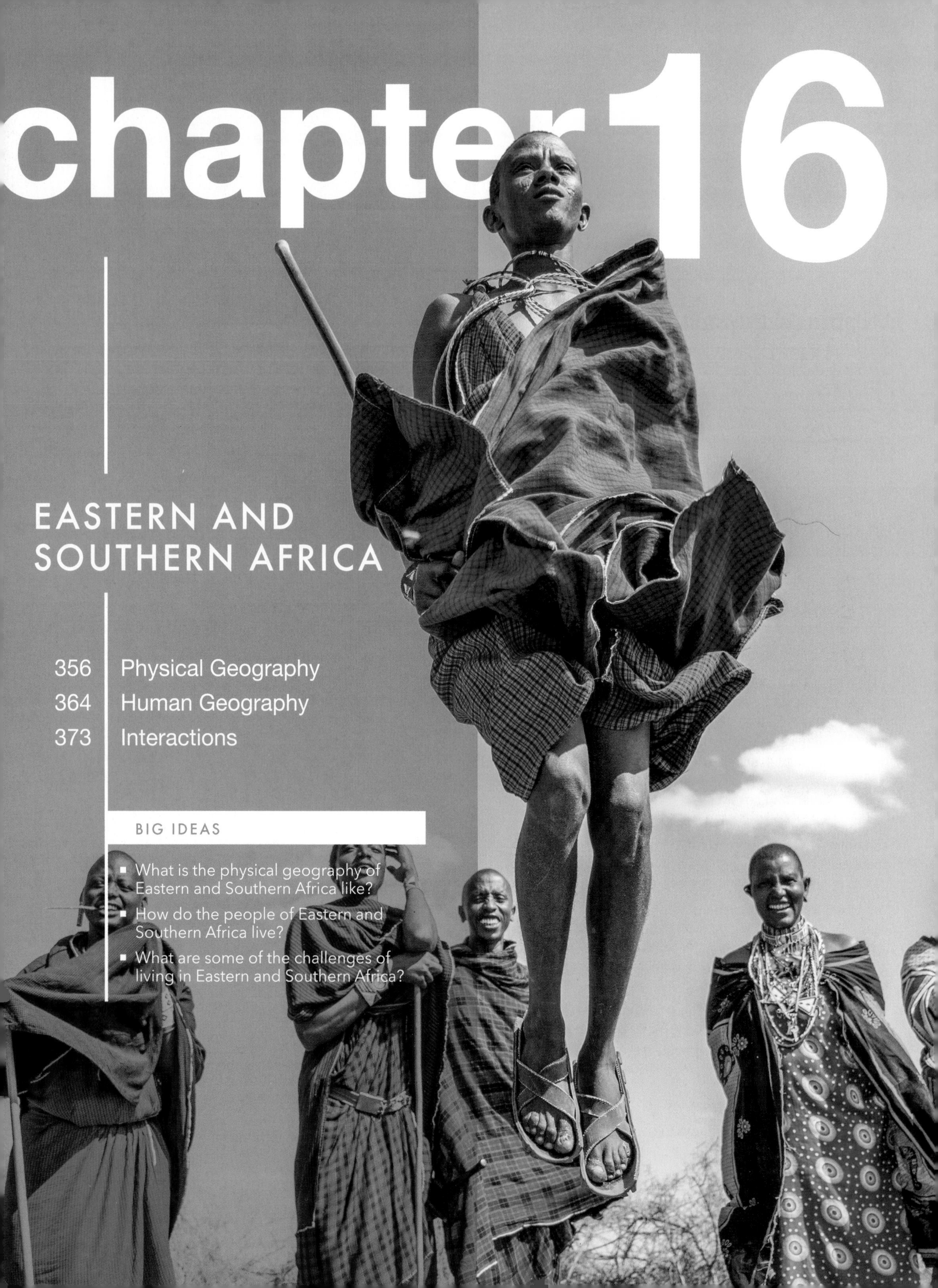

chapter 16

EASTERN AND SOUTHERN AFRICA

356 Physical Geography
364 Human Geography
373 Interactions

BIG IDEAS

- What is the physical geography of Eastern and Southern Africa like?
- How do the people of Eastern and Southern Africa live?
- What are some of the challenges of living in Eastern and Southern Africa?

Cape Town, South Africa ▸

◂ Masai tribe members perform a traditional dance in Kenya.

▾ The Ssese Islands in Lake Victoria, Uganda

▴ (middle) The Deadvlei, or "dead marsh," in the Namib Desert, Namibia

▴ (bottom) Botswanans work in a diamond finishing factory in Gaborone, Botswana.

THE LAND OF DIAMONDS

A diamond is a significant gift to give to someone you love. Though a diamond ring is usually considered an essential element in the marriage proposal, this was not always the case. Before the 1940s diamonds were not the important symbol they are today. In 1867 a fifteen-year-old boy, Erasmus Jacobs, found a diamond on his father's farm along the Orange River in South Africa. This discovery started people on a quest to find all the diamond wealth of Africa. Slowly the diamond mining industry became more efficient, creating a plentiful supply of the gem. In 1888 all diamond mining operations were consolidated under one European-owned company, the De Beers Group. De Beers hired an advertising company to create a market for their product. In 1948 they launched a successful advertising campaign with the slogan, "A diamond is forever."

Illegal diamond mining has been used to pay for civil wars. These diamonds are called *conflict diamonds*. Jewelers try to ensure that they do not sell conflict diamonds, but they are difficult to differentiate. Most African countries have not seen much return from their diamond wealth because corruption is rampant and European companies have historically taken the raw diamonds to Belgium where they are refined. But this is changing. Botswana charted a new path, limiting corruption and investing in a national diamond finishing industry so that most of the diamond wealth stays within the country.

GUIDING QUESTIONS

- What are the regions of Eastern and Southern Africa?
- What caused the landforms of Eastern and Southern Africa?
- What bodies of water are important to Eastern and Southern Africa?
- What are the climates of Eastern and Southern Africa, and how do they relate to the regions' location on the globe?
- What are the natural resources of Eastern and Southern Africa?

Eastern and Southern Africa is a massive area. People sometimes mistakenly think of Africa as one country, yet the continent contains fifty-four countries. If you could overlay the land areas of Europe, the United States, India, Japan, and China on that of Africa, those lands would all fit in Africa with room to spare. While the African people have suffered from famines, civil wars, and racial unrest, they are a hopeful people, and God is working. Africa has more Christians than any other continent. It is demonstrating positive growth in most economic and health indicators.

PHYSICAL GEOGRAPHY

What is the physical geography of Eastern and Southern Africa like?

Regions of Eastern Africa

Eastern Africa is home to Africa's highest mountain, its Great Lakes, and some of its most dramatic landscapes. The region includes eleven different countries.

THE GREAT RIFT VALLEY

The Great Rift Valley is the key physical feature of East Africa as well as the largest subregion. Beginning in the Middle East, this gash in the earth divides the Horn of Africa. The Horn was so named because the peninsula is shaped like an animal horn; it includes Eritrea, Ethiopia, Djibouti, and Somalia. The **Rift Valley**, caused by the junction of tectonic plates, continues southward through all of East Africa and ends at the border of South Africa.

The rift runs through the center of Ethiopia and creates an area of rugged highland plateaus called the *Ethiopian Highlands,* which rise to 14,928 feet at Ras Dashen in the far north. The Great Rift Valley dominates the interior of Kenya. It divides into the Eastern and Western Rifts at Lake Turkana in northern Kenya. The rifts rejoin at Lake Malawi in southern Tanzania. The Eastern Rift parallels the Indian Ocean in Kenya, while the West Rift Valley contains the Great Lakes of Africa as well as Uganda, Rwanda, and Burundi. The Western Rift runs along the western edge of East Africa, bordering the Democratic Republic of the Congo. The land between these rifts drops to form a large basin containing the Serengeti Plain and Lake Victoria.

SWAHILI COAST

This narrow lowland region runs along the coast of the Indian Ocean, beginning in southern Somalia. The region includes the coasts of Kenya, Tanzania, and Northern Mozambique. Zanzibar, Pemba, and Mafia are three large tropical islands off the coast that belong to Tanzania.

SAHARA

Desert covers northern Sudan and northern Eritrea. West of the Nile is the Libyan Desert, while the Nubian Desert lies to the east. The Darfur region of western Sudan contains the Marra Mountains. Near the east coast are the Red Sea Hills.

SAHEL

The Sahel continues from Chad across central and southern Sudan. It covers the extreme north of South Sudan and most of Eritrea. The Dahlak Archipelago in the Red Sea consists of more than one hundred islands that belong to Eritrea.

The Great Rift Valley in Kenya

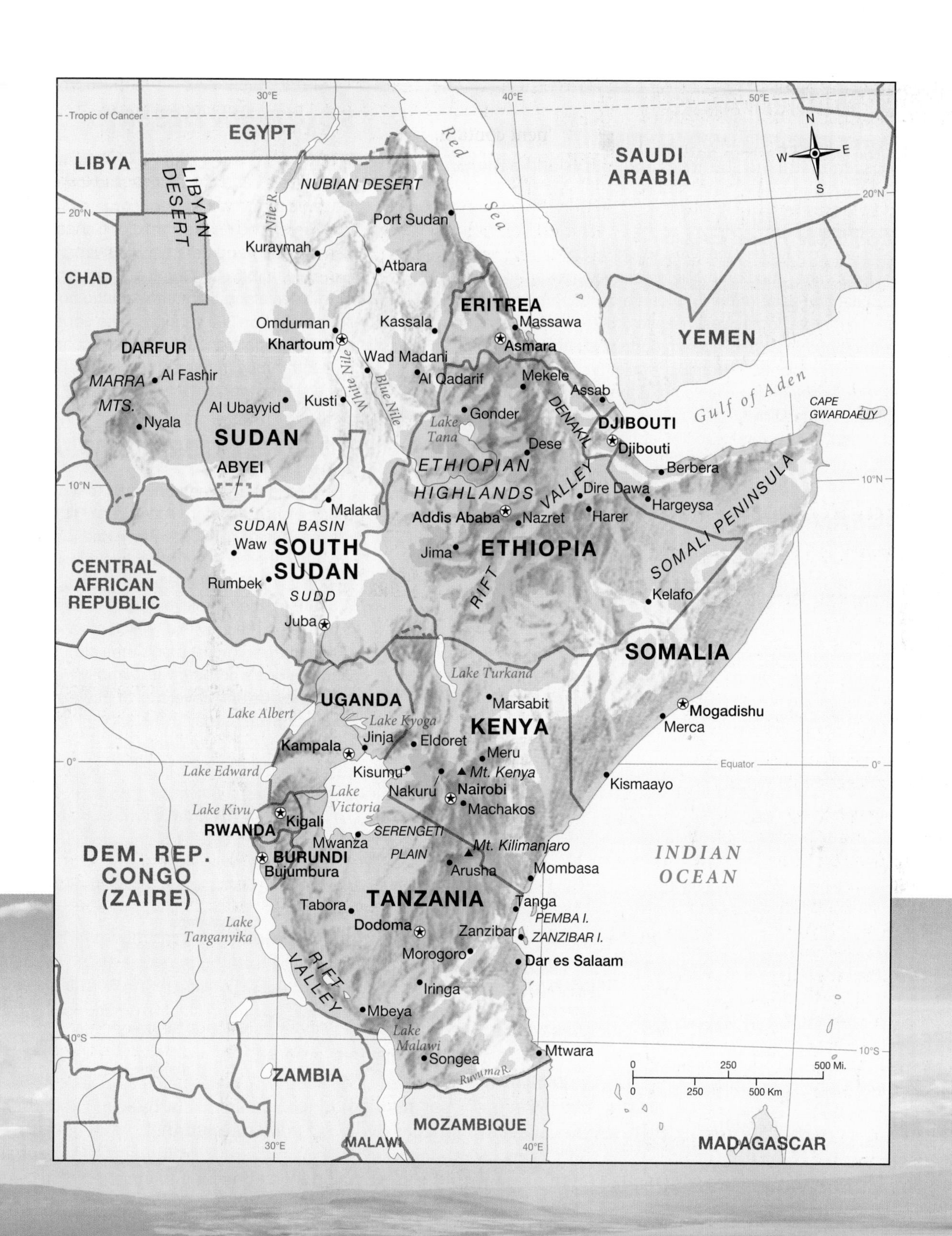
EGYPT
LIBYA
LIBYAN DESERT
NUBIAN DESERT
Red Sea
SAUDI ARABIA
CHAD
Port Sudan
Kuraymah
Atbara
Nile R.
ERITREA
Massawa
Asmara
Kassala
Omdurman
Khartoum
YEMEN
DARFUR
Wad Madani
Al Qadarif
MARRA MTS.
Al Fashir
Nyala
Al Ubayyid
Kusti
White Nile
Blue Nile
Mekele
Assab
Gonder
Lake Tana
DENAKIL
DJIBOUTI
Djibouti
Gulf of Aden
CAPE GWARDAFUY
SUDAN
ABYEI
Dese
ETHIOPIAN HIGHLANDS
Berbera
Dire Dawa
Hargeysa
Harer
Malakal
Addis Ababa
Nazret
SUDAN BASIN
SOUTH SUDAN
Waw
Jima
ETHIOPIA
SOMALI PENINSULA
RIFT VALLEY
CENTRAL AFRICAN REPUBLIC
Rumbek
SUDD
Kelafo
Juba
SOMALIA
Lake Turkana
UGANDA
Marsabit
Mogadishu
Merca
Lake Albert
Lake Kyoga
KENYA
Jinja
Eldoret
Kampala
Meru
Kisumu
Mt. Kenya
Nakuru
Nairobi
Lake Edward
Lake Victoria
Machakos
Kismaayo
Equator
Lake Kivu
Kigali
RWANDA
Mwanza
SERENGETI PLAIN
Mt. Kilimanjaro
DEM. REP. CONGO (ZAIRE)
BURUNDI
Bujumbura
Arusha
Mombasa
INDIAN OCEAN
TANZANIA
Tabora
Tanga
PEMBA I.
Dodoma
Zanzibar
ZANZIBAR I.
Lake Tanganyika
Morogoro
Dar es Salaam
RIFT VALLEY
Iringa
Mbeya
Lake Malawi
Mtwara
Songea
ZAMBIA
Ruvuma R.
MOZAMBIQUE
MALAWI
MADAGASCAR
Tropic of Cancer
30°E
40°E
50°E
20°N
10°N
0°
10°S
N
S
E
W
0
250
500 Mi.
500 Km

Regions of Southern Africa

Southern Africa is located south of the rainforests of the Congo Basin. It includes ten mainland countries and four island nations.

SOUTHWESTERN PLATEAUS

Angola, Namibia, Botswana, and Zambia lie on plateaus in southwest Africa. The west coast and parts of the interior are desert, and the rest is grassland. The Bié Plateau in the west rises to 8,800 feet. It is shaped somewhat like a boomerang, with its apex in northwest Angola. One part runs inland parallel to the Atlantic in Namibia, while the other part ends in western Zambia. The Angola Plateau is south of the Bié Plateau and is a series of high plateaus with altitudes averaging 6,000 feet. Savanna covers most of the land except for rainforests in the far north and deserts in the southwest.

INDIAN OCEAN ISLANDS

There are four independent island nations and one principality of France in the Indian Ocean. Africa's largest island is Madagascar. Northwest of Madagascar are the Comoros islands, the largest being Grande Comore. It is a high plateau with Mount Karthala, a volcano. The 115 tropical islands of the Seychelles are sprinkled in an archipelago northeast of Madagascar. Many of these islands are granite mountains, while others are low coral islets and atolls. Mauritius is a volcanic island east of Madagascar. Reunion Island, between Mauritius and Madagascar, is a principality of France.

SOUTHERN DESERTS

The Kalahari Desert is the sixth-largest desert (over 200,000 square miles) in the world. It lies on the Tropic of Capricorn, much as the Sahara lies on the Tropic of Cancer. The desert basin is centered in Botswana. The barren Namib Desert stretches eight hundred miles along the entire Atlantic coast of Namibia as well as a piece of the southern coast of Angola and the northern coast of South Africa. It has some of the tallest dunes in the world.

SOUTHEASTERN PLATEAUS

The veld is the savanna plateau that covers much of Southeastern Africa. The Highveld makes up most of South Africa and Zimbabwe. On either side of the Highveld lies the Middleveld. While the Highveld averages 4,500 feet, the Middleveld plateau averages 3,500 feet. The Lowveld, which reaches 600 feet at its lowest point, runs along South Africa's borders with Zimbabwe and Mozambique and covers all of Eswatini, formerly Swaziland.

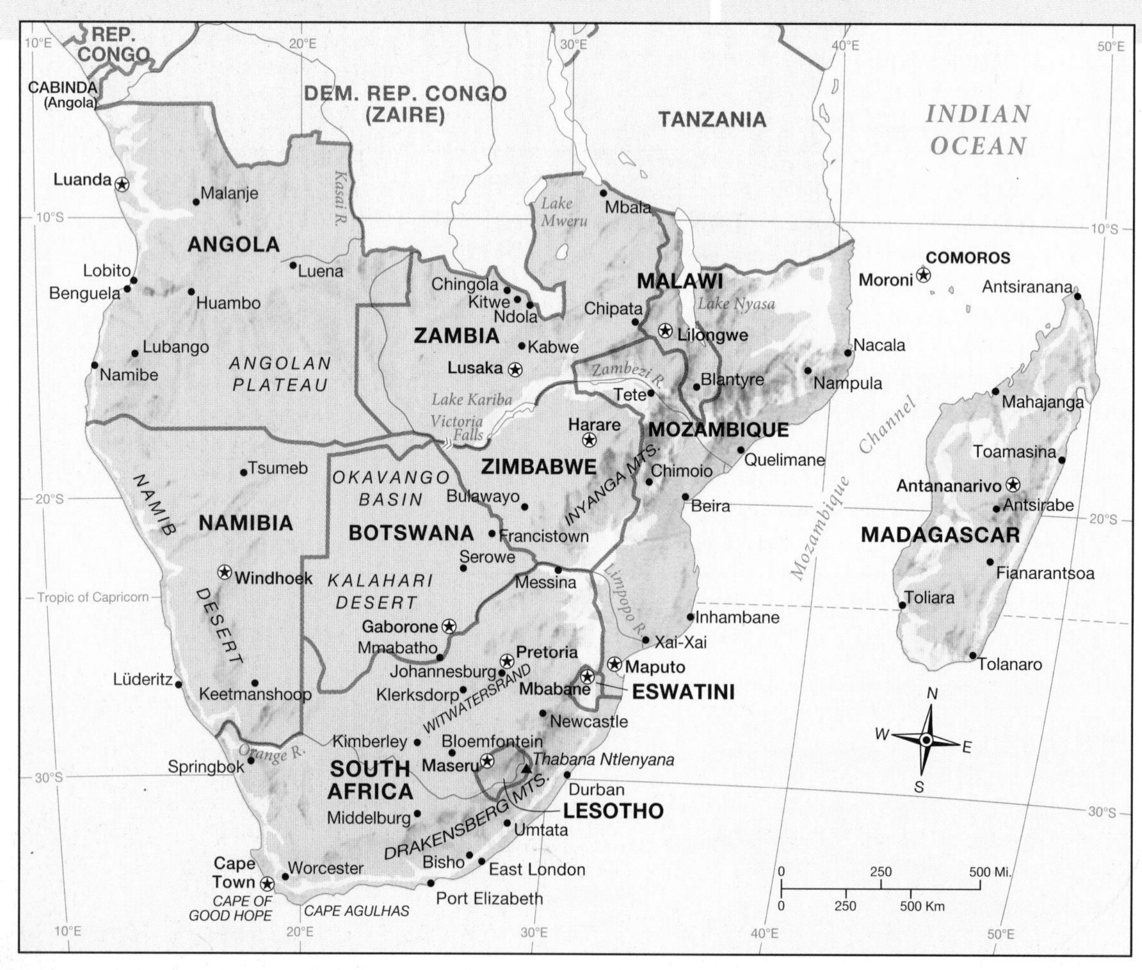

Physical Landforms

Plateaus, cliffs, and mountains dominate Eastern and Southern Africa.

The Afar Triangle is the northernmost portion of the Rift Valley. It is a geological depression located in Djibouti and formed by the triple junction of three tectonic plates.

The Danakil Desert in the Afar Triangle sinks 509 feet below sea level. It is the lowest spot in Africa and one of hottest places on earth. The colorful deposits are potash, green acid, iron oxide, and sulfur.

Mount Kilimanjaro rises to 19,341 feet near the Tanzania border with Kenya. This massive volcanic peak is the highest mountain in Africa. Snow falls on this mountain even though it is near the equator.

The dome-shaped Brandberg Massif stands alone in the northwestern Namib Desert. It is made of basalt magma from a previous volcano. Erosion has formed the rock's current shape.

Bodies of Water

Oceans and Seas

East Africa includes the Red Sea and the Indian Ocean. The Red Sea joins the Indian Ocean at the twenty-mile-wide Bab-el-Mandeb strait, controlled by Djibouti. The warm waters of the Indian Ocean meet the cooler waters of the Atlantic Ocean at 20°E near Cape Agulhas in South Africa.

Victoria Falls ▸

Rivers

Unlike most world rivers, African rivers do not permit navigation from the coast to the interior because of great falls and rapids. Consequently, European settlers remained along the coast in many areas. The rivers, however, do allow navigation within the interior and therefore play an important role.

The Nile River and its tributaries, which flow west of the Great Rift Valley, constitute the most significant river system in Africa. The Nile **cataracts** are areas of shallow water where boulders break the surface. These along with dams prevent ships from sailing up the river from Sudan, thus isolating the south from Egypt.

Two rivers join at Khartoum, Sudan, to form the Nile: the Blue Nile and the White Nile. The Blue Nile begins near Lake Tana in the mountains of Ethiopia. It circles through the northern highlands before its descent west to Sudan. Heavy summer rains cause the Blue Nile to flood and carry silt downstream to Khartoum. The silt makes the plain the most fertile area in the country.

The White Nile is the longer of the two rivers. It does not flood because its waters spread over a large marsh called the Sudd, where much water is lost through evaporation. The source of the White Nile lay hidden until 1862 when John Speke, a British officer, pushing ever deeper into the interior, traced the source to Lake Victoria. While that information is still true in a sense, the source has been traced to its remotest starting point near the Rwanda-Burundi border where the Ruvironza and Nyabarongo Rivers begin, eventually emptying into Lake Victoria.

▾ Cape Agulhas, South Africa

The Zambezi River is the fourth-longest in Africa but the main east-flowing river. It begins in the wetlands of Mwinilunga in northwestern Zambia near the Angola and Congo borders. On the Zimbabwe border is Victoria Falls, one of the most spectacular waterfalls in the world. The falls drop 355 feet over a crest that spans more than one mile. The roar is audible twenty-five miles away. Even the twelve-hundred-foot-high mist is visible at that distance. The falls are called Mosi-oa-Tunya, meaning "The Smoke that Thunders." After the falls the Zambezi continues and forms the northern border of Zimbabwe before it divides Mozambique and empties into the Indian Ocean.

The two main rivers in South Africa are the Limpopo and the Orange. The Limpopo is characterized as sluggish, carrying a lot of silt. It begins in northern South Africa, creating that country's border with Botswana and Zimbabwe before flowing into the Indian Ocean in Mozambique. The Orange River is the longest river in South Africa, flowing through the steppe to the west coast. It forms the northwestern border with neighboring Namibia. Ships on the Atlantic Ocean cannot navigate up the river because of the powerful Augrabies Falls, which drop a total of 625 feet near the coast.

Kibirizi, Tanzania, on Lake Tanganyika is near the town where Henry Stanley found David Livingstone.

Lakes

Some of the largest Great Lakes of Africa by size include Victoria, Tanganyika, Malawi, Turkana, Albert, and Kivu. They far exceed the North American Great Lakes in water volume but have less surface area. Lake Victoria is the largest in Africa and third-largest in the world; it borders Uganda, Kenya, and Tanzania. The capital of Uganda, Kampala, lies on the northern edge of the lake.

Lake Tanganyika lies on Burundi's western border, with Burundi's capital, Bujumbura, on the northern shore. The lake supplies the country with ten thousand tons of fish annually. In Ujiji, Tanzania, on the shore of the lake, the reporter Henry M. Stanley discovered David Livingstone, whose whereabouts had become a mystery. Their encounter on October 28, 1871, began with the now-famous words "Dr. Livingstone, I presume." Lake Malawi is the eastern border of Malawi. Over half of the world's flamingos live in Africa.

Flamingos congregate at Lake Nakuru in Kenya.

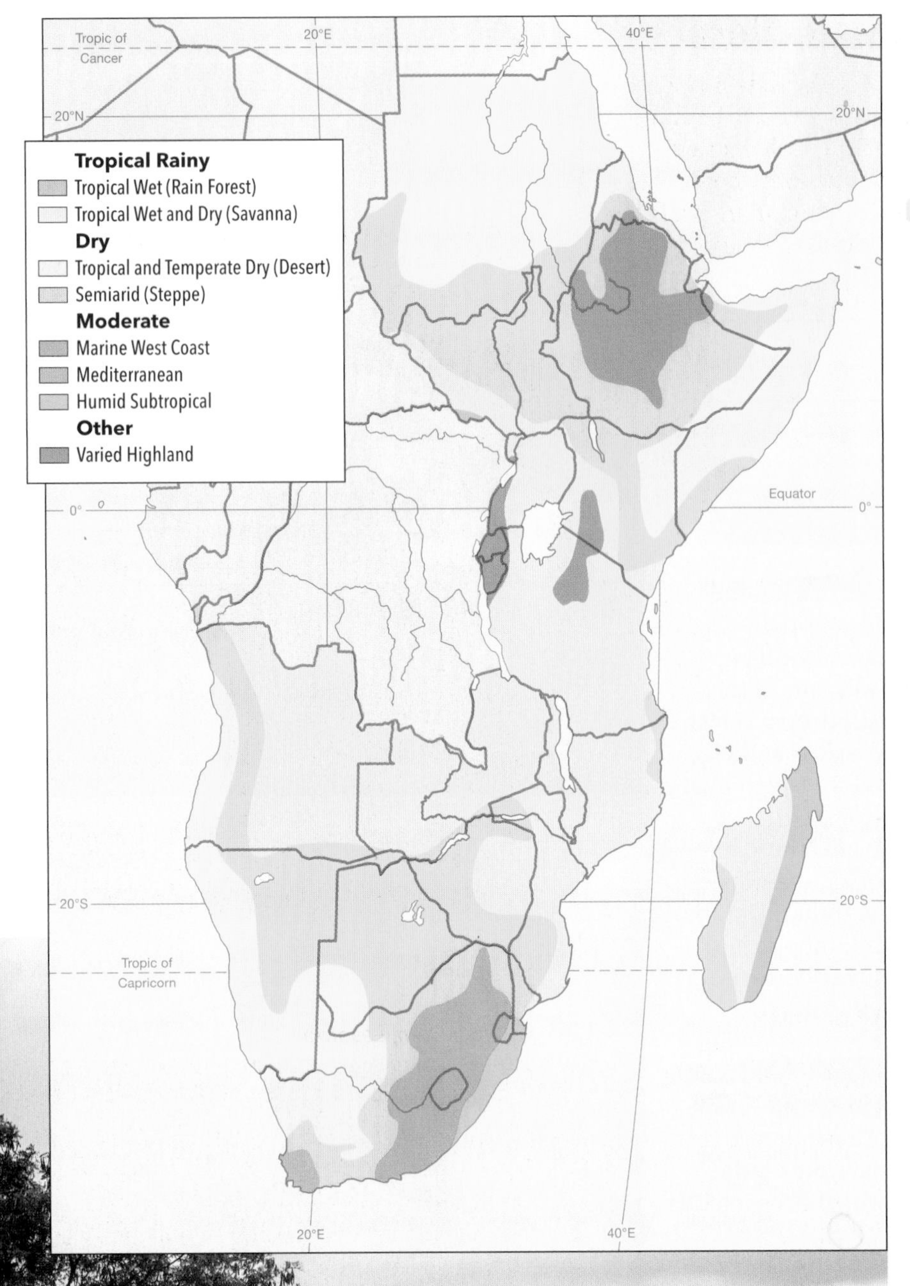

Climates of Eastern and Southern Africa

The climate of Eastern Africa is generally hot on the coast but cooler inland where most people choose to live since the higher altitude creates a more comfortable climate. The capitals of sub-Saharan Africa are some of the highest in the world. Addis Ababa, Ethiopia, the fourth-highest capital city, is well over a mile high, as are Asmara, Eritrea; Nairobi, Kenya; Windhoek, Namibia; and Maseru, Lesotho. The cities of Kigali, Rwanda; Gitega, Burundi; and Harare, Zimbabwe are all higher than the capital of Nepal but are not quite a mile high. The weather is temperate even though the cities are on or near the equator. Another positive aspect of the highland climate is that sicknesses related to mosquitoes and the tsetse fly are less common.

In northeastern and southern Africa, there are many desert regions that have a hot and dry climate. In general, sub-Saharan Africa has two seasons, rainy and dry. Rainfall is unreliable in many areas of the continent because of the wind currents found in the tropics, and these weather fluctuations have made the life of the African farmer very difficult. There is a long dry season followed by a season of torrential downpours. In Namibia, a cold ocean current keeps the air very dry and causes temperature inversions and thick fogs. The frequent fogs, resulting in many shipwrecks, have given the northern shore the nickname Skeleton Coast.

▼ *Tea fields in Kenya*

▲ *A shipwreck on the Skeleton Coast in Namibia*

Resources of Eastern and Southern Africa

Eastern Africa has a large percentage of arable land, while Southern Africa has more mineral wealth. Coffee was first discovered in Ethiopia. Kenya is a world leader in tea production; unlike other tea producing countries, Kenya has small farms that are known for researching how to maximize crop yields and growing more profitable teas. The best soils are around the lakes. Sorghum is a popular cereal crop somewhat like corn but able to handle drier climates. Sorghum can also be turned into a sweetener. In Southern Africa the land is better suited for pasture. The Indian Ocean island nations and the countries around the lakes depend on the hundreds of varieties of fish found in their waters. Though diamonds and gold are the most valuable resources found in the south, there is also a large copper belt in the center of southern Africa. Lesotho has made use of its water supply by exporting water to South Africa and using the water to produce electricity. Lesotho produces enough electricity to be self-sufficient and to export excess electricity to South Africa.

A sorghum farmer inspects her crop, which thrives in the dry conditions.

SECTION REVIEW

1. Compare the physical regions of Eastern Africa with those of Southern Africa.
2. How did the Great Rift Valley form? What landforms did it create?
3. Identify one river that runs north, one that runs east, and one that runs west.
4. How does the climate affect where people live in Eastern and Southern Africa?
5. How do the resources of Eastern Africa differ from those of Southern Africa?

Katse Dam, Lesotho

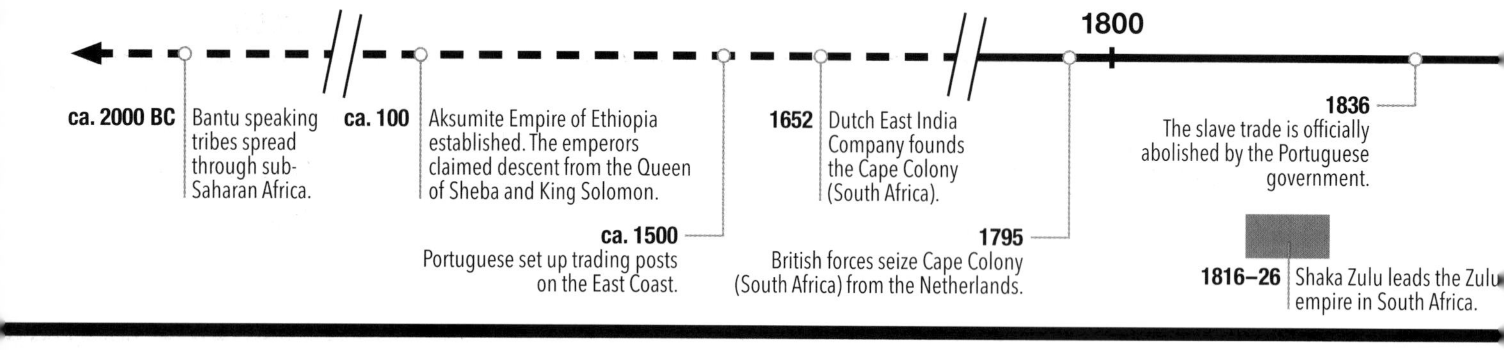

GUIDING QUESTIONS

- How have Eastern and Southern Africa changed over time?
- How do the governments of Eastern and Southern Africa interact with their citizens?
- What is the economic health of Eastern and Southern Africa?
- What are the demographics of Eastern and Southern Africa?
- What are the cultural characteristics and diversity of Eastern and Southern Africa?
- What forms of religions are practiced in Eastern and Southern Africa?

Colonization of Africa

Belgian
British
French
German
Italian
Portuguese
Spanish

Mediterranean Sea
Nile R.
Red Sea
Niger R.
Lake Chad
Congo R.
Lake Victoria
Lake Nyasa
Lake Tanganyika
Zambezi R.
Orange R.
ATLANTIC OCEAN
INDIAN OCEAN

HUMAN GEOGRAPHY

How do the people of Eastern and Southern Africa live?

History

Sudan's history is similar to that of North Africa. When Arab Muslims conquered Egypt in the Middle Ages, they pushed south into Sudan, bringing their religion and language. The Arab-Islam push was stopped in Ethiopia, which is a buffer zone between Arab North Africa and sub-Saharan Africa. Everything south of Ethiopia was colonized by Europeans. At the Battle of Adwa in 1896, the Ethiopians defeated the Italians, making Ethiopia one of the two African nations never to be colonized.

Colonization

The Scramble for Africa is the term for the time in the late nineteenth century when Europeans were grabbing up pieces of Africa. In Eastern and Southern Africa, Britain controlled the majority of the territory, while Portugal and Germany controlled colonies on both coasts. The modern-day business languages and religions of these countries are a reminder of their colonial influence. For example, the people of Mozambique and Angola speak Portuguese and are primarily Catholic, while in Botswana, Zambia, Uganda, and Kenya the people speak English and are primarily Protestant.

Independence

The vast majority of the countries in these regions gained independence in what was called **decolonization** during the late 1950s through the 1960s. A few countries had to wait until the mid-70s. South Africa was the first in sub-Saharan Africa to gain independence. The first Europeans to settle there were the Dutch, called Boers. The British followed and settled the land. They lived separate from the Boers, but when diamonds and gold were discovered, a conflict ensued called the Boer War (1899–1902), which the Boers lost. The Boers and the English made

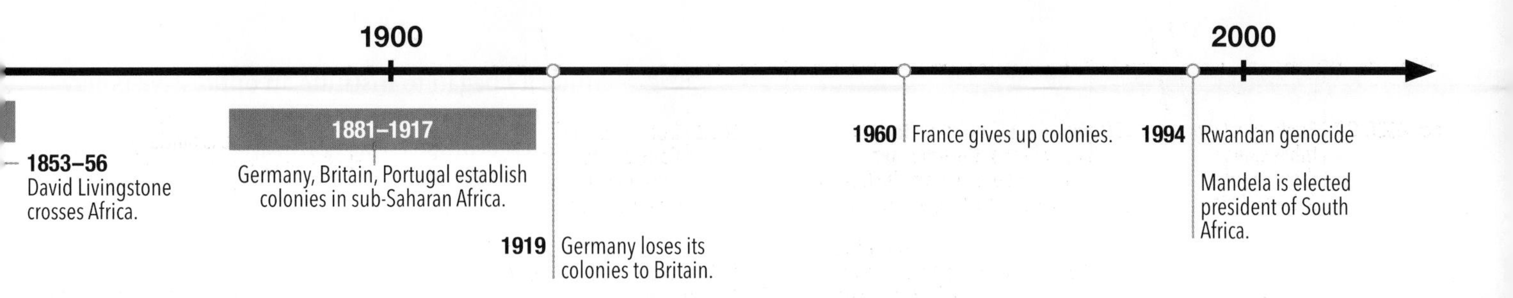

peace, and in 1910 the Union of South Africa was formed. In 1961 the name changed to the Republic of South Africa.

The major push for independence among the rest of the countries began after World War II. In general, the British colonies were given independence without war. In Kenya, however, the eight-year-long Mau Mau Rebellion was successfully suppressed by the British. Portugal was not so quick to give up its colonies; both Angola and Mozambique fought guerrilla wars for over a decade before gaining independence in the mid-70s.

Governments

Since gaining independence these countries have shared many of the same issues. Although progress has been uncertain at times, it seems that they are overcoming their common challenges. Most of the governments in these regions are representative democracies, with a president heading the executive branch. Eritrea is a dictatorship, while Eswatini and Lesotho have constitutional monarchies.

Civil War

Civil wars and insurgencies (revolts or uprisings) have been a defining characteristic for many years. Botswana, Zambia, and the Indian Ocean islands are the only countries to escape some sort of conflict during the past forty years. Generally, major conflicts are in decline in Africa, but as of 2019 war continued in Somalia, and Islamic insurgencies were ongoing in South Sudan and Tanzania.

The civil war between Christians and animists in the south of Sudan and Muslims in the north ended in 2011. The people of southern Sudan voted to form a separate nation, making South Sudan the newest country in the world. Since 1991 Somalia has been in chaos. The government disintegrated, and clan warfare engulfed the south. Two years later, famine laid waste to the land. Later that year, the UN sent troops into Somalia to restore peace and bring famine relief. The UN withdrew in 1995, and anarchy and famine returned to Somalia. In 2004 a transitional government was formed, bringing some hope for the war-ravaged country, but peace has been elusive.

Racism

Ethnic division has been a major hindrance to peace and stability in Southern Africa. The countries of South Africa, Namibia, and Rhodesia were ruled by white minorities after independence. In Rhodesia black rebels fought the white rulers until they won control in 1979, changing the name to Zimbabwe. Most white people fled the country.

South Africa clung to white rule until 1994. In a system called **apartheid,** the Afrikaner (descendants of the Boers and English)

▲ *During apartheid, buses in South Africa were segregated.*

minority began to institute an oppressive policy of ethnic separation. The Afrikaners contended that each ethnicity was culturally different from all others. Thus it was best to keep all ethnic groups separate so that each could develop. Nevertheless, apartheid severely regulated life for non-white majorities. Non-whites could not vote in national elections, could not own land, and, after 1959, had no representation in the South African Parliament. Because opposition groups were banned, the oppressed groups had no organized voice.

Under apartheid, every area of life was segregated: restaurants, stores, buses, trains, and so forth. The apartheid government also forced black people to live in reservations called "homelands." Homeland citizens had to carry identity documents at all times. Any protest was met with swift and brutal retribution. As a result of these policies, the international community condemned apartheid. South Africa was isolated through embargoes and sanctions.

In 1989 President De Klerk responded to the international criticism and pressure by easing the apartheid restrictions. In 1990 he released the jailed opposition leader, Nelson Mandela. De Klerk and Mandela began negotiations to make a smooth transition away from apartheid. Mandela was elected president of South Africa in 1994. The number of official languages rose from two to eleven, and a new constitution went into effect in 1997. The constitution included the idea that the government should provide for the people materially rather than ensuring the right of people to provide for themselves. There was hope for the future, but although apartheid ended over two decades ago, South Africa still exhibits an uneven distribution of wealth. Although more black families have entered the middle class, unemployment remains high among black people. Rather than embracing the idea of reconciliation and forgiveness, many black groups are seeking revenge, and some white groups are trying to continue to live separately in "whites only" private towns. Lawmakers promote a policy called *land expropriation without compensation* (taking white-owned farms). According to experts on Africa, South Africa is being isolated from the rest of the continent because of its continued internal strife.

Tribalism

Tensions between ethnic groups are not the only source of conflict. When Europeans drew the borders of the large countries, they did not account for the different tribal lands that were being joined under single governments. In many cases, the colonial powers used tribal conflicts to their advantage. These conflicts have played a large part in limiting the success of these countries and, in some cases, have led to the death of millions.

When Belgium ruled Rwanda and Burundi, the government registered everyone according to tribe, either Tutsi or Hutu. In reality, the two tribes were not that different. The Tutsis, though in the minority, were wealthier. However, before the Belgians left Rwanda, they put the Hutu majority in charge of the government, and the animosity increased for many years.

African Union chief Moussa Faki and Rwanda's president Paul Kagame light a remembrance flame for the twenty-fifth commemoration of the 1994 genocide.

In 1994 following the murder of the presidents of Rwanda and Burundi, the Hutus organized for retaliation via the radio. They distributed machetes to their people and killed eight hundred thousand Tutsis, political moderates, and even other Hutus. It was eventually declared a genocide. With international assistance, the Tutsis managed to restore order. Since then Rwanda has made significant progress, and the country is rebuilding its infrastructure. The country is now considered safe for international travelers, and tourism is increasing. But the peace has come through heavy-handed authoritarian rule.

Socialism

The majority of the newly formed African countries looked to the socialist model of government because it was not associated with their colonizers. This resulted in man-made famines, atrocities, and the degradation of the infrastructure. Many infamous dictators stole what little wealth the countries had. An official in the Robert Mugabe government of Zimbabwe honestly expressed the thoughts of these governments by saying, "In Zimbabwe, socialism means what is mine is mine but what is yours we share it!" Nevertheless, entrepreneurship is a key aspect of African culture, and anywhere small businesses are allowed, they multiply.

(below) A man in Johannesburg, South Africa, displays and sells shoes that he has made.

(bottom) Older students in Somalia attend primary school. Sixty-seven percent of Somalia's population is under the age of 25.

Economies

Many people view Africa as ancient or as a place with "happy animals and miserable people." Yet most of the countries were founded relatively recently. The majority of the people are under twenty years old. Africa has enormous growth potential.

Growth

In recent years, African economists have developed a concept called *Africapitalism*, in which Africa stops looking abroad for aid and forgoes socialist economic models. Instead, Africans invest in private energy, transportation, building, and agricultural projects to benefit the greatest number of people. While East African economies are growing rapidly, Southern African economies are slow, and Zimbabwe's economy is continuing to decline. Two reasons that Southern African economies are not growing is that the countries were already more developed and they have suffered to a greater extent from the AIDS epidemic.

Ethiopia, Rwanda, Djibouti, Uganda, and Kenya are some of the fastest-growing economies not only in Africa but in the world. Ethiopia's growth is largely based on infrastructure projects and manufacturing. International companies have been moving some of their factories to Ethiopia so that it is

▲ *Kigali, Rwanda, is known for its cleanliness.*

being called the new China. Rwanda and Djibouti are trying to follow the Singapore model of governance, which is a combination of authoritarian rules and pro-business economic policies. Rwanda now has strict laws on gender equality in the workplace as well as cleanliness. Because of these laws, Kigali, Rwanda, is one of the cleanest cities in Africa. Rwanda also has a growing number of women in managerial positions. Djibouti is trying to leverage its favorable geopolitical location to be a financial, transportation, and military center since it has no natural resources. Djibouti acquires income by allowing foreign militaries to operate bases on its soil; it now has the most foreign bases of any country in the world. The United States and China currently have the largest military footprints in Djibouti. Nairobi, Kenya, is the center of trade, finance, and communication for East Africa. Tourism is a key generator of wealth in sub-Saharan Africa. The national parks in these countries draw more and more tourists each year.

Debt

Debt is the biggest economic concern for Africa in the foreseeable future. China holds more of that debt than any other foreign country. Critics claim that China is behaving as harshly as the European colonizers did. Using debt to gain power and influence in Africa, China is also extracting resources unfairly and importing Chinese workers rather than hiring Africans. In Zambia, the first nation to build a relationship with China, the mining industry, most of the media, power plants, and the airport are all owned by Chinese firms because of Zambia's loan defaults. Africans prefer to do business with China because it does not attach government reform requirements to the loans as other countries do.

GLOBAL IMPACT | Technology Changing Life in Africa

New technologies are an important element behind the economic growth of Africa. The invention of the cell phone, for example, has allowed some nations to skip certain development steps that other countries had to navigate through. In East Africa, people use their mobile phones to pay for everyday goods rather than cash or credit cards. The infrastructure for using credit cards is not available. This is not only convenient but safer since the people do not have to carry cash. Mobile companies also provide microloans so the people can build small businesses. The majority of the people had no access to banking before these services were offered. One Kenyan mobile company alone averaged over $162 million a day in transactions in 2018. Africans are also able to access government services through their phones. Mobile banking stands dot the streets, providing many employment opportunities. Because most of the people have unreliable power at home, an innovator invented a small efficient wood-burning stove with a USB charger attached.

▲ *M-PESA is the leading mobile phone financial service company in Africa.*

1. In what other ways might the smartphone improve the lives of Africans?
2. Why would access to banking be important to bringing people out of poverty?
3. What potential drawbacks can you see with a heavy use of mobile financial services?

Demographics

Sub-Saharan Africa has an average fertility rate that is double what is needed for population replacement. People in countries with better economies tend to have fewer children, while those with poor economies have more children. One reason for this difference is that in countries that lack other sources of wealth, children are seen as an investment. Eastern Africa has urbanization percentiles in the 20s and 30s. Southern Africa has a higher urbanization rate averaging in the 50s, with Botswana being the highest at 71 percent. Rwanda and Burundi are the most densely populated mainland countries, while Namibia, Botswana, and Zambia are some of the least densely populated in the world.

The map on page 364 shows each country's unifying language. Though not the case with Tanzania, German is still used to some extent in Namibia even though Germany lost that colony to the British after World War I. Almost everyone in sub-Saharan Africa is bilingual. Many are multilingual.

The peoples of sub-Saharan Africa belong to many different tribes, most falling under the umbrella of Bantu, which includes hundreds of tribes. Linguistic studies trace the Bantus to the Benue River in Cameroon. Whether because of drought, war, or a need for more land, the Bantus are believed to have begun their Bantu migrations around 2000 BC, reaching South Africa by AD 1000. Swahili is the most common Bantu language.

Since Ethiopia was never colonized, its official unifying language is Amharic, the language of the last emperors. Amharic also includes a unique alphabet. In South Africa, the Boers simplified the grammar of their High Dutch language and incorporated words from other

▲ *Ethiopian Amharic script*

languages, such as Zulu, a Bantu language. The resulting language is quite different from Dutch and is called *Afrikaans*. The people of Madagascar are a mixture of Africans and Indonesians whose ancestors arrived about two thousand years ago. Malagasy is the term for the people as well as the language, which is similar to Malay and Indonesian.

Three notable tribes, the Masai, San, and Himba, continue to live as they have for centuries. The nomadic Masai people of Kenya are famous for their ritual dances and their skills as warriors. Bantus and Europeans drove the San, or Bushmen, out of South Africa and into Botswana. The San have survived as hunter-gatherers in the Kalahari Desert. The Himba are a semi-nomadic tribe in Namibia.

Malagasy women walk the Avenue of the Baobabs in Madagascar. The Baobab tree is a national symbol of Madagascar.

Africans, like these two waiters in Cape Town, South Africa, are known for being friendly.

Culture and Diversity

In general, sub-Saharan Africans are friendly and courteous. Relationships take precedence, as with other high-context cultures. For example, when a person waits in a long line and finally reaches the front, he can be assured that he will get the full attention and courtesy of the attendant in spite of the many people still waiting.

Another aspect of Africa's high-context culture is that the group is valued over the individual. Family is the most important group. In Southern Africa there is a Bantu saying, *Lefura la ngwana ke ho rungwa*, which means "children benefit from serving their elders." This concept is biblical, yet it can be abused when it is not grounded in the Word, as when parents force their daughters to be child brides.

Music and dance are central in African culture, not only as a means of entertainment but also for communication and for passing on history. There is a diversity of foods in sub-Saharan Africa. *Nyama choma,* which means "grilled meat" in Swahili, is one of the most popular dishes in all of Africa. The grilled goat or beef can be ordered in the finest restaurant or the smallest street-side stand. For side dishes, *ugali* and *plantain* are common. Ugali is a staple food served at most meals; it is ground maize, or corn, boiled to make a mash. Africans eat ugali by scooping up a handful and rolling it into a ball. The ball is then dipped in the accompanying dish, called *ndiwo,* which is a sauce made from vegetables or meat. Plantains are like bananas but need to be cooked to be eaten. *Injera* is the common food of Ethiopia. This flat sourdough bread is served on one large plate placed in the center of the table with different vegetable pastes on top. Each person at the table tears a piece of the bread while folding in some of the savory vegetable and bean paste.

▲ *Injera and vegetable pastes is a common meal in Ethiopia.*

▼ *A meal of nyama choma accompanied by kachumbari salad, sukuma wiki, chapati, and roasted potatoes*

▲ *The African Bible College trains future pastors and Christian workers.*

Religion

Christianity arrived early in Eastern Africa when the Ethiopian eunuch returned home with the Good News after meeting Philip the evangelist (Acts 8:26–40). David Livingstone, the renowned missionary-doctor, is known for being the first to take the gospel into the interior of sub-Saharan Africa. He explored the continent, taking Christianity and hoping to open the interior to legitimate trade, thus destroying the slave trade. Following decolonization, most of the cities and landmarks were renamed, but Livingstone, Zambia, remained and demonstrates the respect Africans still have for Livingstone.

While Islam is growing at a slightly faster rate than Christianity, it is still predicted that by 2050 there will be over a billion Christians in sub-Saharan Africa. The growth of Islam and the lack of biblically trained leaders are the main threats to Christianity in Africa.

In countries where Islam is over 80 percent, Christians are heavily persecuted. Tanzania, Ethiopia, and Kenya are in the Islam-Christian buffer zone; here the religions seem to be able to coexist. In the public schools of Tanzania, Muslim and Christian students pray side-by-side during morning exercises, one group praying to Allah and the other to God. The students attend religion classes according to their beliefs.

But Islam is not the only threat to Christianity in sub-Saharan Africa. Africans are receptive to evangelistic preaching. The Christians have a teachable spirit and believe that the Bible is God's Word. Yet since there are few biblically trained pastors, many fall prey to deception. Many Africans have accepted prosperity theology, which appeals to their animistic worldview. The people are taught that there are layers between them and God. A "breakthrough" is required to get past those layers so that God can bless them, giving them what they desire. The breakthrough is accomplished by the powerful prayers of the pastor. Media and literature imported from the United States support this teaching. Because of the lack of leadership, churches are unable to challenge violence in the culture, such as the Rwandan genocide. Countering this trend are courageous African pastors and Bible schools seeking to change the direction as more leaders are trained.

Religions of Eastern and Southern Africa

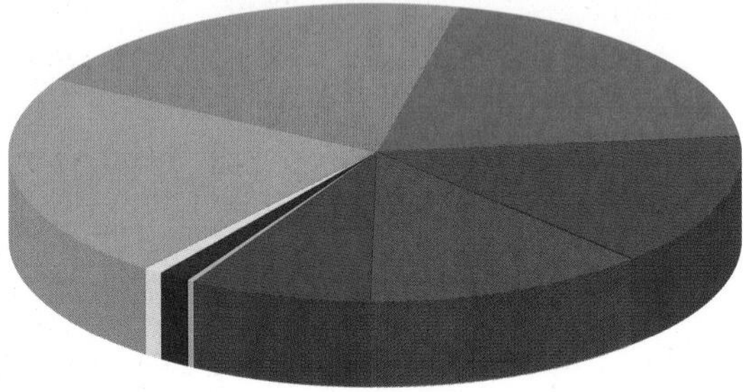

Religion	Percent
Islamic	**22.6%**
Roman Catholic	**20.4%**
Protestant Evangelical	**19.7%**
Protestant	**14.5%**
Ethnic	**12.3%**
Orthodox	**8.0%**
Hindu	**0.5%**
Other	**1.4%**
Unaffiliated	**0.6%**

Majority Catholic: Angola, Seychelles, and Burundi
Majority Protestant: Botswana, Namibia, and Eswatini
Majority Muslim: Comoros, Somalia, Sudan, and Djibouti

SECTION REVIEW

1. What East African country was never successfully colonized by a European power? How was it able to avoid it?
2. Describe the government of South Africa and its interaction with its people.
3. How has European imperialism left its mark on African nations?
4. Compare Africapitalism with socialism.
5. How are economic health and birthrates related? What reasons not mentioned in the chapter might also account for this?
6. How does the method of serving food in Ethiopia display the people's cultural values?
7. Why is prosperity theology appealing to those with an animistic worldview?

INTERACTIONS OF PEOPLE AND PLACES

What are some of the challenges of living in Eastern and Southern Africa?

GUIDING QUESTIONS

- How do the economies and demographics of Eastern and Southern Africa affect how the citizens interact with the environment?
- What are the environmental issues of Eastern and Southern Africa?
- What are the causes and effects of environmental issues in Eastern and Southern Africa?
- What are possible solutions to environmental issues in Eastern and Southern Africa?

Eastern and Southern Africa are some of the last places in the world where giant animals still roam wild and hunter-gatherer tribes still exist. Because of this, many sub-Saharan countries have reserved 20 to 30 percent of their land as parks and reserves. Uganda and Rwanda have parks high in their rugged mountains to protect the endangered mountain gorilla, whose numbers are slowly increasing after a steep decline. The Serengeti Plain in Tanzania and Kenya has more large land animals than any other place on earth. It is also the only place left in the world where vast herds of large mammals still migrate. Elephants, lions, rhinoceroses, cape buffaloes, leopards, giraffes, monkeys, and others roam the park, while vultures, storks, and egrets soar overhead. In the Masai Mara Game Reserve, Kenya's portion of the Serengeti is home to the Masai tribe. By attempting to preserve these wild places, the governments are keeping the tourist industry intact while also serving future generations.

▾ *A hippo mother with her baby in the Masai Mara National Park, Kenya*

▾ *Zebras and wildebeest on the banks of the Mara River during the annual migration from Tanzania to Kenya*

▲ A water hyacinth harvester on Lake Victoria

Interaction with the Environment

Water

Much of the surface water around population centers in sub-Saharan Africa is polluted. Hundreds of people die each day in Africa from water-related diseases. Only 16 percent of sub-Saharan Africans have access to tap water. Many animals and fish are dying because the surface water is overused and the wetlands have been drained for farmland. Around the Indian Ocean islands, coral reefs are dying. Water hyacinth plants have overtaken Lake Victoria, killing fish and native plants.

▼ Mountain gorillas are protected in Virunga National Park, Rwanda.

Air

Many of the large cities in these regions suffer from air pollution. Much of Southern Africa does not meet minimum standards set out by the World Health Organization. The homes in the villages have the additional problem of indoor air pollution from the burning of solid fuels for cooking.

Land

All of these countries have problems with deforestation, and the areas on the edge of deserts are suffering from further desertification. Soil erosion and loss of soil fertility are problems. Proper disposal of solid waste is not a priority. Some countries accept waste from around the world to recycle, but they do it without considering the health of the workers or the people. Many of the southern countries have toxic waste and heavy metal pollution from poor mining practices.

All the animals of sub-Saharan Africa are threatened to some extent. Rhinoceroses are the most endangered animal; there are only five white rhinos left in Africa. Zimbabwe once had a large number of black rhinoceroses, but not anymore. Zebras, African wild dogs, mountain gorillas, giraffes, chimpanzees, African penguins, elephants, lions, and cheetahs are some of the other most endangered animals.

Reasons for Environmental Issues

The air pollution is a result of coal power plants, vehicle emissions, indoor cooking and heating fires, and the use of individual diesel generators. South Africa gets over 90 percent of its energy from coal power plants. Many people use diesel generators because the public electric supply is unreliable. Deforestation has occurred for many of the same reasons as in South America: demand for hardwoods, farmland, and fuel for cooking and heating. In many parts of Africa, there is a destructive cycle occurring. Trees are cut, and the soil is worn out from farming or overgrazed by livestock. This makes the soil vulnerable to erosion by water and wind. Desertification follows as the exposed soil becomes unable to support vegetation. Deserts form or grow in size, and the amount of life-supporting land is reduced. People are forced to move to other areas, and the cycle is repeated. The water pollution is caused by the usual suspects: chemical runoff from farms, industrial and mining waste runoff, and unfiltered human waste. Hyacinth is an invasive species that came from South America. It doubles its mass every five days. Animals are declining because they are losing their habitat to development in unprotected areas. Poaching is a major problem as Asian countries especially use parts of these animals to produce health products.

Rwandan widows weave hyacinth into useful products.

Proposed Solutions

Transitioning to alternative forms of energy such as nuclear, solar, and hydroelectric would greatly reduce air pollution and blackouts. South Africa was one country that could afford nuclear power and had committed to building more nuclear plants, but those plans have stalled. In Zambia, the schools are training the children early in conservation. Students also learn how to grow fruits and vegetables.

Many African countries are trying to reverse desertification by planting trees and other vegetation. At Lake Victoria, millions of dollars have been wasted in corruption to solve the hyacinth problem. But individuals have been able to make and sell paper and baskets made from the plant. Fishermen devised a buoy system that they tow behind their boats, bringing the hyacinth to shore. Wildlife conservation vacations are becoming more common as a way to bring help and attention to the issue of endangered animals. The key to helping the wildlife is eliminating lawlessness.

SECTION REVIEW

1. Why are national parks important in the Lakes region?
2. What are some of the environmental challenges that Eastern and Southern Africa face?
3. Why does a lack of electric infrastructure cause more air pollution?
4. What other solutions can you think of to protect wildlife?
5. What do the effective solutions to the hyacinth problem reveal about solutions to environmental problems in general?

16 CHAPTER REVIEW

SUMMARY

1. Eastern Africa's most significant feature is the Great Rift Valley. Plateaus and deserts make up Southern Africa. The Afar Triangle, formed by a triple junction of tectonic plates, is the beginning of the Rift Valley. Rapids and falls prevent travel from the coast to the interior via the many rivers. There are several Great Lakes in Africa. Most cities are located in the highlands because of the climate. Eastern Africa has more agricultural resources, while Southern Africa has more mineral resources.
2. Every country south of Ethiopia was colonized during the Scramble for Africa. They gained their independence during the period of decolonization in the late twentieth century. Civil war characterized the time after decolonization. Apartheid was practiced by the white minority in South Africa. Most of the governments followed a socialist model because it was different from colonial governments. Africa is the continent with the most growth potential. Debt is the major hindrance to growth. The Bantu peoples are the majority in these regions. Africans value relationship and families. Sub-Saharan Africa has many Christians, but Islam and prosperity theology are the two obstacles to the gospel.
3. Southern and Eastern Africa have treasures in people, wildlife, and land that they are trying to protect. There is a cycle of desertification caused by humans. Most animals in Africa are endangered. Water pollution is rampant, and Lake Victoria is suffering from invasive species. Education, law enforcement, and a healthy economy would help to solve environmental problems.

Terms to Know

- ❑ Rift Valley
- ❑ cataracts
- ❑ decolonization
- ❑ apartheid

Making Connections

1. What geographical feature has divided Africa and, consequently, had the greatest effect on the continent?
2. Why did early settlers remain along the coasts of Africa rather than sail to the interior using the rivers?
3. Who are the Afrikaners, and where did they come from?
4. In what three ways is Ethiopia unique in these regions?
5. What is the Danakil Desert, and how was it formed?

Developing Geography Skills

1. Based on the maps on pages 357 and 358, what three major deserts are found in Southern and Eastern Africa?
2. Based on the map on page 357, what countries border Lake Victoria?

Thinking Critically

1. What role did Nelson Mandela and F. W. de Klerk play in ending apartheid in South Africa? Have all South Africans benefited equally from the end of this practice? Explain your answer.
2. If scientists were able to make the mosquito and tsetse fly extinct, how might that impact sub-Saharan Africa? You may refer to the map on page 80 of Chapter 4.

Living in God's World

1. How does preserving land, animals, and ways of life in parks and reserves fulfill the Creation Mandate?
2. Imagine you are a pastor in an African country overrun with the prosperity gospel. You have been given the opportunity to write a column in a national newspaper about the prosperity gospel. Compare it to the true biblical gospel explaining why the latter is better.

CASE STUDY | Botswana versus Zimbabwe

Botswana and Zimbabwe border each other, share many of the same natural resources, and should be very similar; yet in every indicator, one country is outperforming the other. Zimbabwe once had the nicknames "jewel" or "breadbasket" of Africa, but that is no longer true because of corrupt governance. The socialist dictator Robert Mugabe grossly mismanaged the economy and forced land redistribution. Consequently, Zimbabwe experienced up to 90 percent unemployment and inflation exceeding 150,000 percent. The country was ruled as a police state; those who spoke out were jailed. When Mugabe stepped down in 2017, there was hope that his handpicked successor would allow more freedom, but that has not been the case.

It is not by chance that Botswana is the most successful country in Africa during the past thirty years. When it became independent in 1966, it was considered a wasteland. Today the economy is healthy, utilities work, and modern glass buildings line the streets of Gaborone, the capital. This success is a result of wise leadership following independence. Seretse Khama, the first president of Botswana, married an English woman and set an example for social harmony. At that same time, the neighboring countries had white minorities imposing segregation or being forced out by black majorities. Khama also combined the best governing practices of the British with the traditional village tribal government that emphasized transparency and consensus. Khama set an example of service rather than seeking personal enrichment. Botswana had the advantage of witnessing the negative results of socialist economic policies in other countries, so they left the free markets intact.

▲ *Seretse Khama, his wife, Ruth Williams Khama, and their children*

1. How are the people of Zimbabwe suffering as a result of unwise leadership?
2. Why is it important for a new country, especially after it gains independence, to have a wise first leader?
3. Do you think that natural resources are all a country needs to be successful? Explain.

unit 6

GEODATA | Activity

Cultural Geography *Student Activities*

You will have the opportunity to complete a geodata activity for the Middle East and Central Asia in the Activities.

Background image:
The city of Yerevan with Mount Ararat and the lesser Ararat mountains in the background

THE MIDDLE EAST AND CENTRAL AND SOUTH ASIA

chapter 17

THE MIDDLE EAST

383 Physical Geography
388 Human Geography
399 Interactions

BIG IDEAS

- What is the physical geography of the Middle East like?
- How do the people of the Middle East live?
- What are some of the challenges of living in the Middle East?

Muslims praying at the Suleymaniye Mosque in Istanbul, Turkey

Orthodox Jewish man praying at the Wailing Wall in Jerusalem, Israel

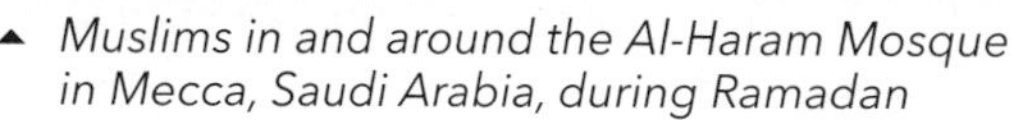

Muslims in and around the Al-Haram Mosque in Mecca, Saudi Arabia, during Ramadan

JOURNEY TO MECCA

Of all the religious activities a Muslim performs in an effort to please Allah, the journey to Mecca is one of the most important and exhausting. Many Muslims save money for years to be able to travel to Mecca in Saudi Arabia. While on this four-day pilgrimage (*hajj*), they will visit the Al-Haram Mosque that surrounds the Kaaba and will join up to two million Muslims who walk counter-clockwise seven times around this stone building in the middle of the massive courtyard. The pilgrims will run between two hills in Mecca to represent Hagar running in search for water. They then travel to Mount Arafat, where Muhammad was said to have preached his last sermon, and then to Mina, near Mecca, to cast seven stones at each of the three concrete pillars that represent Satan. Animals are sacrificed as a reenactment of Abraham's sacrifice of Ishmael. On the last day, the Muslim pilgrims return to Mecca to run between the two hills and walk around the Kaaba seven more times.

Good Friday procession on the Via Dolorosa in Jerusalem

GUIDING QUESTIONS

- What are the regions of the Middle East?
- What caused the landforms of the Middle East?
- What bodies of water are important to the Middle East?
- What are the climates of the Middle East?
- What natural resources are found in the Middle East?

While the jagged peninsulas of southern Europe have plentiful harbors and a mild mediterranean climate, the coasts along the nations of the Middle East have few good ports, scarce fresh water, and a limited number of natural resources. Yet the strategic location of this region has placed it at the center of the world stage.

The countries of the Middle East touch three continents. Turkey is anchored in Europe, nations west of the Persian Gulf border Africa, and the region as a whole is on the southwest border of Asia. Ancient cultures from all three continents have blended in the Eastern Mediterranean and the Persian Gulf for thousands of years.

Three major religions—Judaism, Christianity, and Islam—began in this region. Conquering armies have swept back and forth seeking

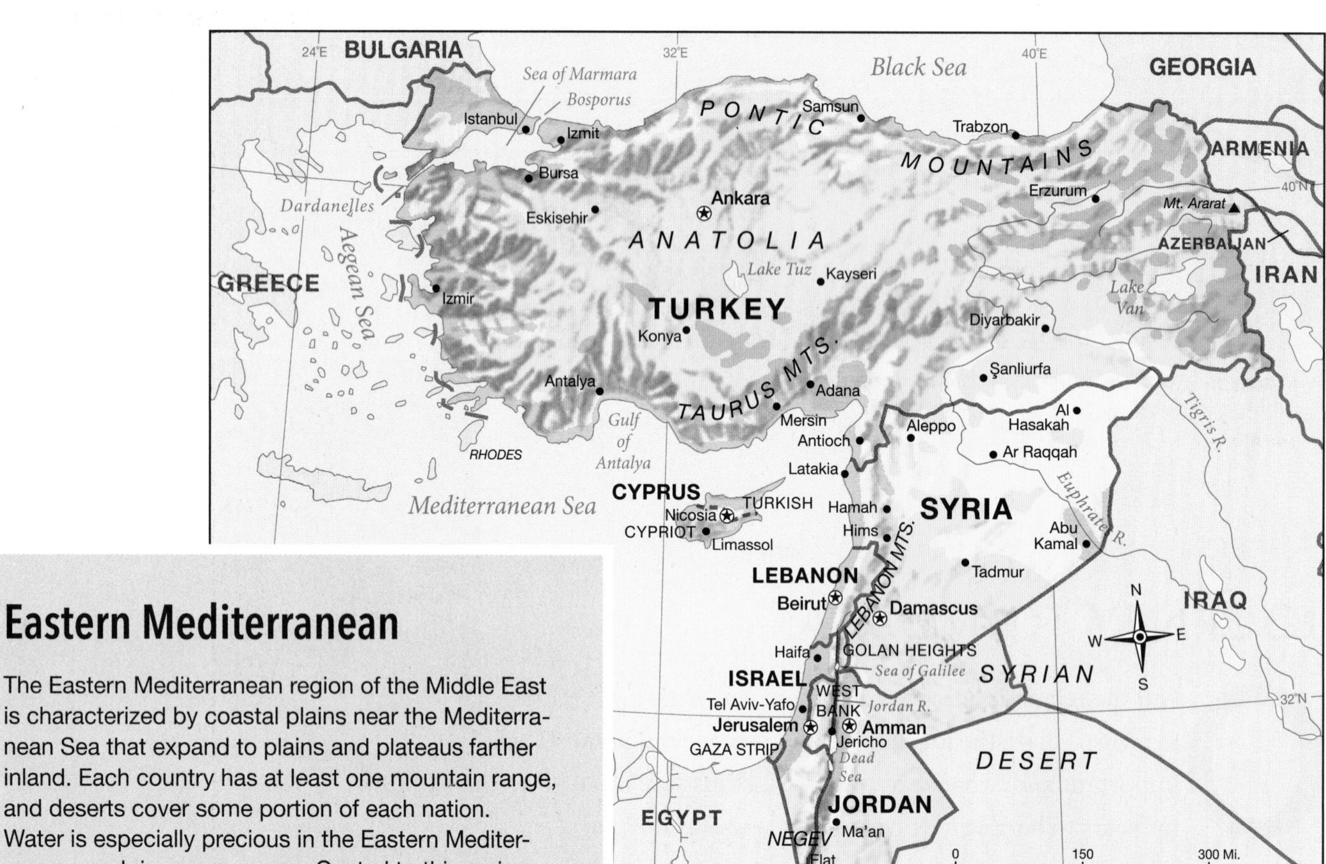

Eastern Mediterranean

The Eastern Mediterranean region of the Middle East is characterized by coastal plains near the Mediterranean Sea that expand to plains and plateaus farther inland. Each country has at least one mountain range, and deserts cover some portion of each nation. Water is especially precious in the Eastern Mediterranean, and rivers are scarce. Central to this region is the area between the Tigris and the Euphrates, historically known as Mesopotamia, the land between the rivers. While much of the physical geography of the Eastern Mediterranean has resulted from tectonic activity, volcanic activity also played a role in parts of this region, including Turkey, Lebanon, and Jordan.

Side View of Israel

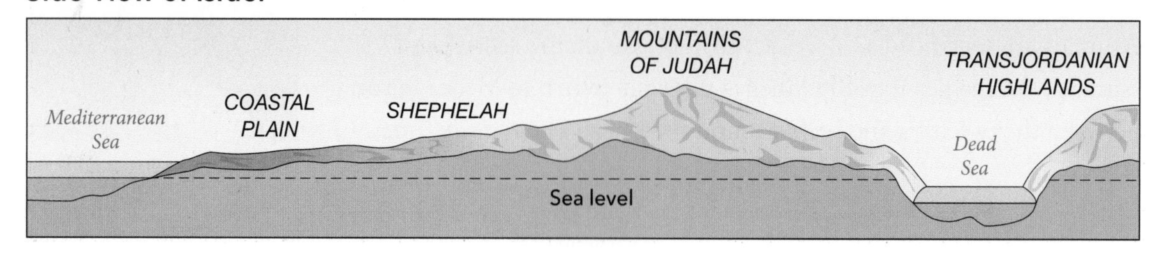

to control the ancient trade routes and bathing the land in blood. The nations of the Middle East are at once regions of great wealth and great poverty, characterized by beauty and terror, and a mixture of ancient ways and modern industry.

The Persian Gulf

The nations surrounding the Persian Gulf have coastal plains near the Red Sea and the Persian Gulf. Lowlands, plateaus, highlands, and mountains are also found throughout this region. The Persian Gulf nations have extensive regions covered with some of the world's driest deserts. In addition to extensive tectonic activity, there is evidence of volcanic formation in Yemen and other nations.

PHYSICAL GEOGRAPHY

Regions of the Middle East

What is the physical geography of the Middle East like?

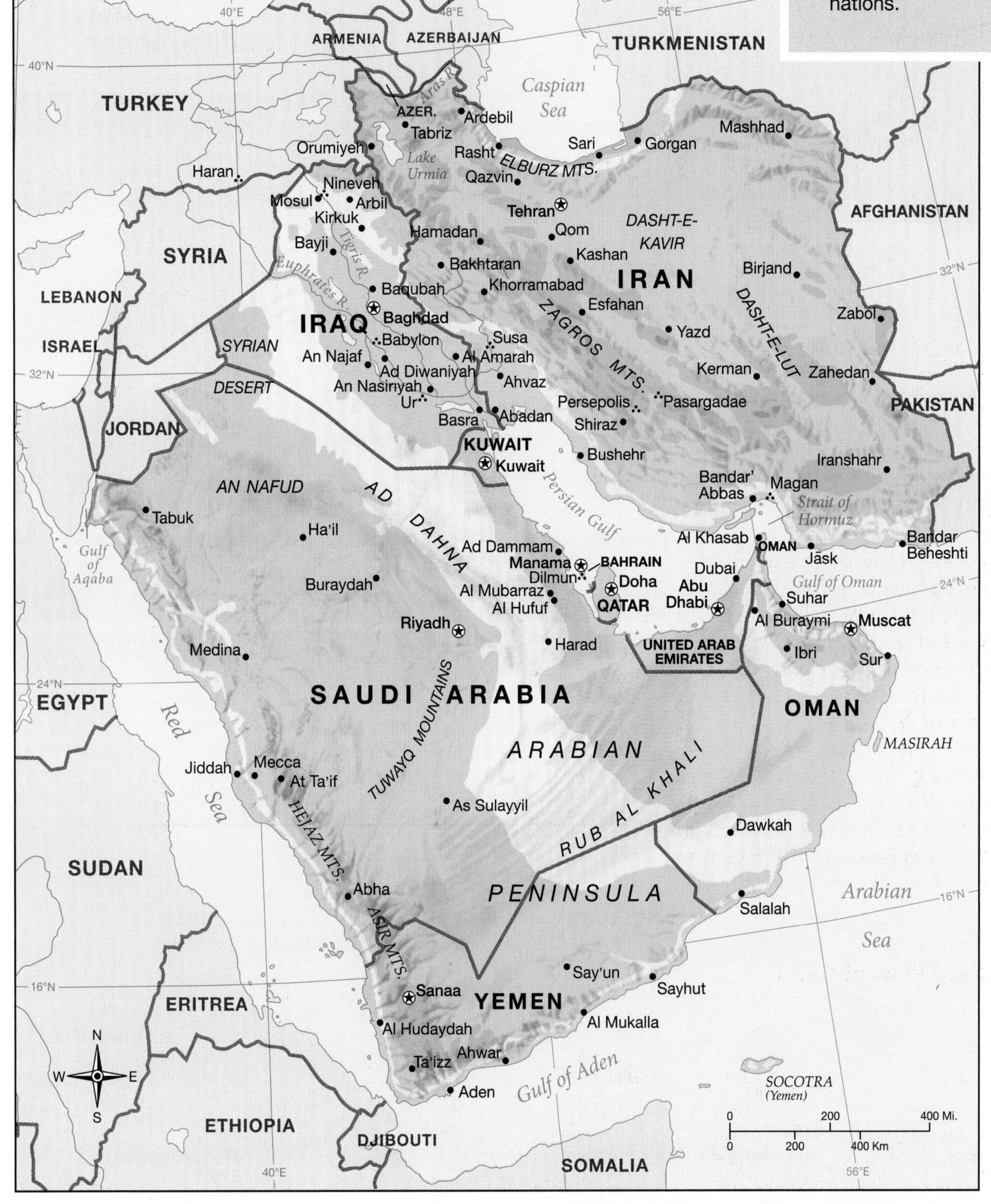

Physical Landforms

The Middle East sits astride several tectonic plates, including the African, Turkish, Arabian, and Eurasian Plates. This helps to explain the formation of mountains, valleys, and rifts in this region, as well as the ongoing tectonic activity that results in earthquakes.

Eastern Mediterranean

Turkey is home to the biblical Mount Ararat, which towers to 16,584 feet. This mountain range was formed by volcanic activity. ▸

Jordan Rift Valley

The Persian Gulf

▲ The Rub al Khali, also called "the Empty Quarter," covers most of the Arabian Peninsula. This and other deserts are often shaped into dunes.

▲ A ***wadi*** is a dry streambed that fills up with water after rainstorms.

Bodies of Water

Water in the Middle East has provided transportation in the past and still serves to provide irrigation and hydropower through the building of dams in key areas. There are few rivers in this region; chief among them are the Tigris and Euphrates, which originate in the mountains of Turkey and then cross several countries before emptying into the Persian Gulf. Seas in the Middle East include the Black Sea, the Aegean Sea, the Mediterranean Sea, the Red Sea, and the Caspian Sea. Important

Tigris and Euphrates basin ▶

▲ *Edge of the Dead Sea with the coast of Jordan in the background*

◀ *Doha, Qatar, along the Persian Gulf*

Tropical Rainy
Tropical Wet and Dry (Savanna)
Dry
Tropical and Temperate Dry (Desert)
Semiarid (Steppe)
Moderate
Mediterranean
Humid Subtropical

40°E 60°E 40°N 20°E Tropic of Cancer 20°N

gulfs include the Persian Gulf and the Gulf of Oman. Lakes include the "Sea" of Galilee, Tharthar and Milh (manmade lakes in Iraq), and Lake Urmia and Maharloo Lake in Iran. Maharloo Lake is pink from the algae interaction with the salt water. It is very shallow and evaporates in the summer.

An important river for Israel and Jordan is the Jordan River, which forms a boundary between the two nations and supplies much of the water for irrigation. The Dead Sea provides several minerals for Jordan and Israel that are extracted from the salty water.

Climates of the Middle East

The climate is generally hot and dry over most of this region. More rainfall occurs near the coastal regions and large bodies of water, but little moisture reaches into the continent. Summer temperatures vary from 85°F to 100°F, but temperatures reaching 124°F have been recorded in the Iraqi city of Basra.

Resources of the Middle East

Many of the nations in the Middle East have an abundance of petroleum and natural gas. Other resources found in this region include coal, iron ore, copper, phosphates, manganese, and zinc. Bahrain's natural resources have largely been depleted, and the country has had to restructure its economy around banking and other human resource industries. Yemen has an unusual resource in **khat**, a shrub whose leaves are harvested and chewed as a narcotic.

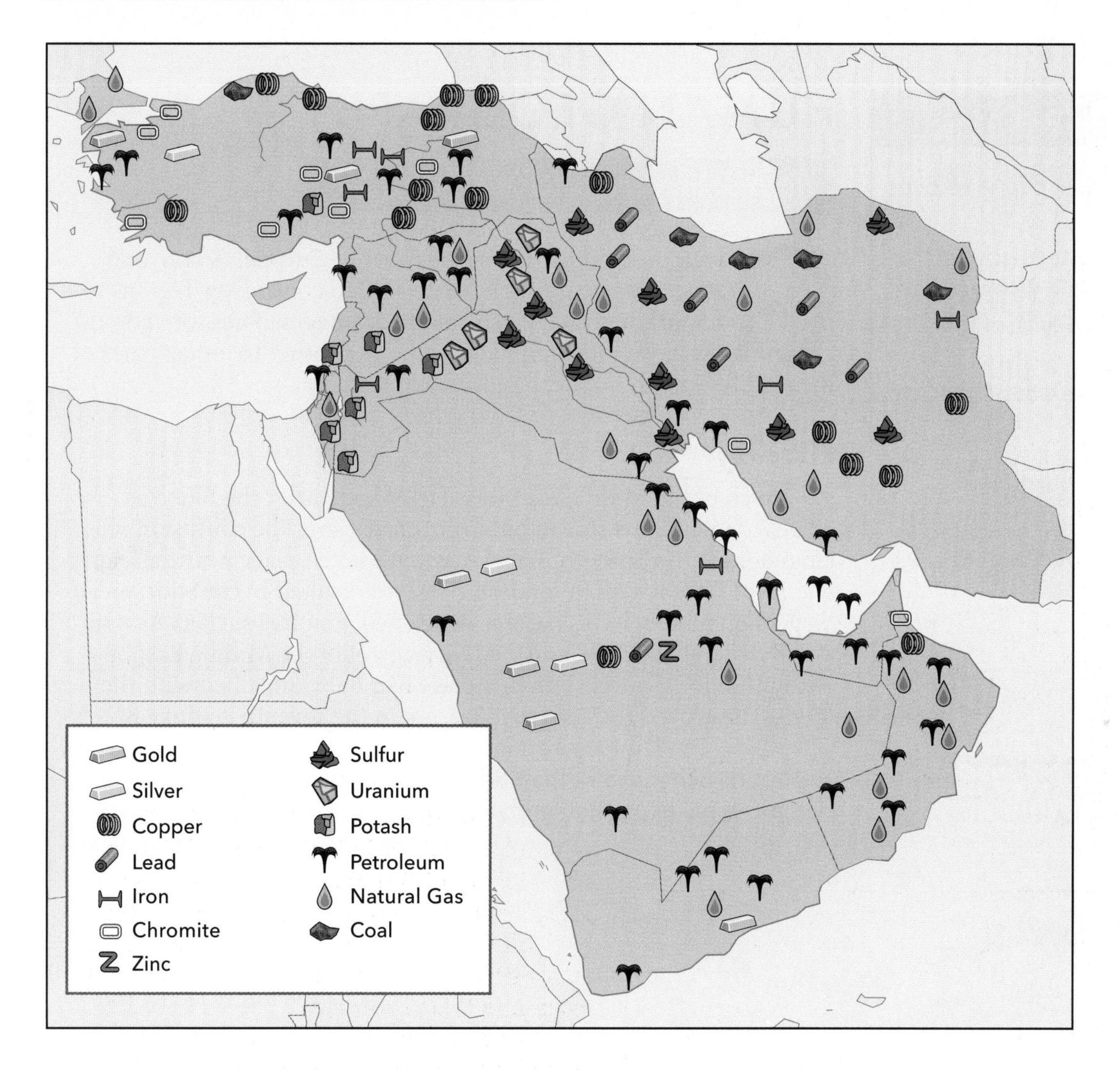

SECTION REVIEW

1. Between which two major lines of latitude does most of the Middle East lie?
2. How does the Middle East's location on the globe affect its climate?
3. Why are the Tigris and Euphrates Rivers so important to the Middle East?
4. How do the resources of the Middle East affect the world?
5. What resources are abundant in the Middle East?

1500	1000	500	0

- **ca. 3000 BC** Settled after the Flood
- **ca. 1200–612 BC** Assyrian Empire
- **612–539 BC** Babylonian Empire
- **529–323 BC** Persian Empire
- **336–ca. 100 BC** Greek Empire

GUIDING QUESTIONS

- How has the Middle East changed over time?
- How do the Middle Eastern governments interact with their citizens?
- What is the economic health of the Middle East?
- What are the demographics of the Middle East?
- What are the cultural characteristics and diversity in the Middle East?
- What forms of religion are practiced in the Middle East?

HUMAN GEOGRAPHY

How do the people of the Middle East live?

Given the Middle East's proximity to Europe, Africa, and Asia, many empires have desired to control key regions to maintain military and trade advantages. Thus foreign powers have often grappled with one another to annex parts of the Middle East to their expanding empires.

History

Much of the Middle East was settled soon after the Flood as Noah's descendants spread out over this region. The confusion of languages at the Tower of Babel may have taken place near the Tigris and Euphrates Rivers in modern Iraq and resulted in the widespread dispersion of people. As nations developed, empires such as Assyria and Babylon developed and vied for control of the Middle East between the twelfth and sixth centuries BC. Babylon, allied with the Medes, destroyed the Assyrian Empire in the seventh century BC. The Medo-Persian Empire conquered Babylon in the sixth century BC and controlled much of the Middle East for two centuries, until the rise and rapid expansion of the Greek Empire under Alexander the Great. After two hundred years of Greek dominance, the Roman Empire expanded into the Middle East and dominated this region until the expansion of Islam out of the Arabian peninsula during the seventh century AD. Islamic forces led by the Ottoman Turks steadily gained control over much of the Middle East until they destroyed Constantinople in 1453. Islam remained dominated by the Ottomans until their empire was dismantled after World War I. Syria and Palestine were placed under the control of European nations as protectorates after World War I but gained their independence following World War II.

▾ *A Syrian man rides a bicycle past a destroyed building in a village on the outskirts of Damascus.*

Jewish-Arab strife increased exponentially beginning in 1948, when the United Nations recognized Israel as an independent nation. Arab nations fought several wars to destroy Israel and drive

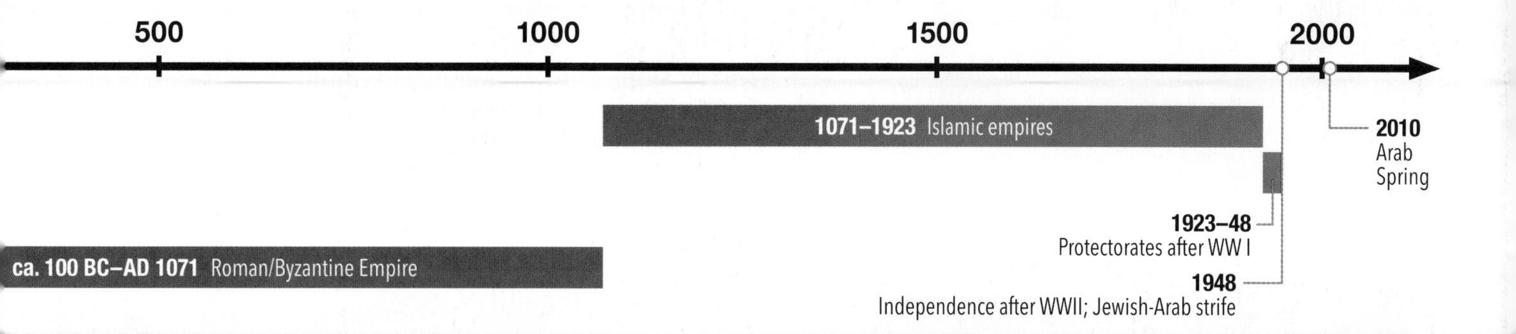

the Jewish people from their homeland, but Israel proved resourceful and successfully repulsed each attack. Although Israel is one of the smallest countries in the Middle East, its historical, religious, political, and economic importance is immense.

Beginning in 2010, a series of uprisings against authoritarian governments in the Middle East, known as the Arab Spring, resulted in the overthrow of some dictators and the demand for more representation in other countries. Yemen and Syria participated in these uprisings but have little to show for their efforts. Both countries continue to suffer from power struggles, and many of their citizens have been killed or driven into exile.

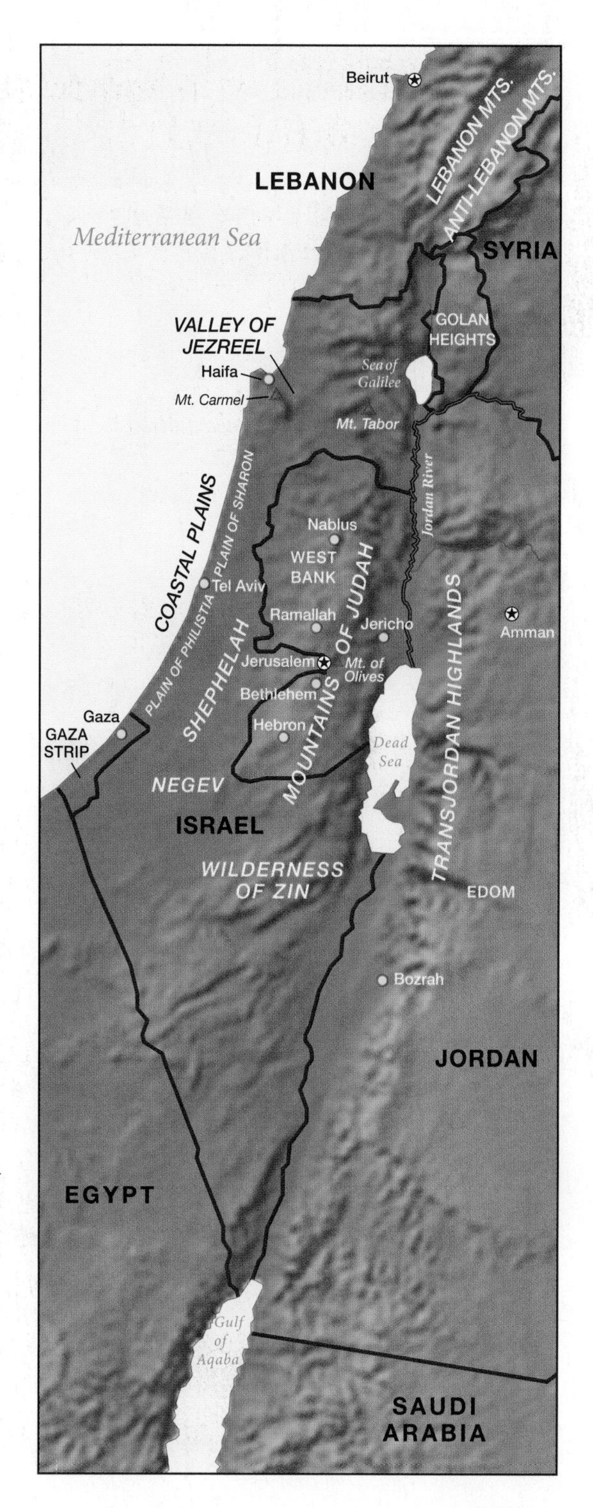

Government

Types of government vary across the Middle East. The Eastern Mediterranean countries of Turkey, Cyprus, Lebanon, and Israel have representative democracies or republics. Syria has a unitary republic in name only, as the ruling family tightly controls the government and rules with extreme brutality. Jordan has a constitutional monarchy, with the king holding extensive executive and legislative powers. Fortunately, Jordan's monarchs have ruled in a manner that demonstrates great concern for their people.

Most of the governments of the Persian Gulf countries are monarchies. Saudi Arabia, Oman, and Qatar have absolute monarchies. The United Arab Emirates are ruled by seven constituent monarchs. Yemen is distinguished in that it has been a semi-presidential, representative democratic republic. However, ongoing strife has resulted in an unstable government and an uncertain political future. Iraq and Iran are Islamic republics, meaning that they follow **sharia** law based on the Qur'an and the Hadith, which are sacred books to Islam. Muslim clergy play a strong role in Iran's government and make decisions on proposed legislation and government policies, making Iran, for practical purposes, a theocracy.

Government Interactions with Its Citizens

Governments across the Middle East vary in how consistently they protect the rights of their citizens. Some countries are classified as secular, meaning they are not following any particular religious guidelines in governing. Nations that are dominated by Islam include sharia law in their treatment of citizens. Depending on how diligently these nations apply sharia law, their citizens, in particular their women, can be subject to strict and brutal enforcement of law. Everything from the type of clothing worn in public to a woman being unaccompanied by her husband in public is subject to strict regulation, with harsh punishments being meted out for violation of sharia law.

- (top) Male Saudi students taking their final high school exams
- (middle) Female Saudi elementary students
- (bottom) Dedicated in 2012, the Hadassah Medical Center in Ein Kerem, Jerusalem, Israel, was built to withstand conventional, biological, and chemical attacks.

In many of the Muslim-dominated countries, persecution of religious minorities also occurs, often with government sanction. Levels of persecution can vary from discrimination and harassment to violence and even murder. One of the worst examples was the attempted genocide of Armenians by the Turks prior to World War I.

Education and Health Care

Most Middle Eastern countries provide compulsory and free education for their children, with priority given to the education of males. These countries vary in the number of years offered, from 8 to 12 years. Oman's education is free but not compulsory, and unstable countries such as Yemen and Syria are not able to enforce compulsory attendance. In the Muslim dominated countries, an Islamic-based education is an essential element, with great emphasis on memorizing large portions of the Qur'an.

Health care across the Middle East varies from universal health care to subsidized health care with personal copay. In Syria, because of the civil war, health care has been incapacitated, with the destruction of medical facilities and the killing of hundreds of health-care workers. In Yemen and Iraq health care has been significantly diminished by war and political instability. Iran's health care consists of three pillars: public, private, and NGOs (non-government organizations). Wealthy nations such as Saudi Arabia, Oman, Kuwait, and Qatar provide free health care for their citizens. These oil-rich nations have spent lavishly on hospitals and medical facilities to meet the needs of their people. As a result, a phenomenon known as **medical tourism** brings thousands of people from neighboring countries each year to purchase a level of health care not available in their own countries. Though Israel lacks the petroleum resources of the Arab countries, it has developed excellent health-care facilities and also attracts medical tourists who can pay for advanced medical procedures.

Economies

Petroleum-related industries drive many of the Middle Eastern economies. At the same time, these countries are working to diversify their economies to become less dependent on a single product. Turkey, Cyprus, Lebanon, Israel, Jordan, and Bahrain have free-market economies. The other countries in this region have mixed economies, due in large part to their concentration on petroleum production. Most of the countries in the Middle East would be classified as developing economies. Two notable exceptions are Israel and Bahrain. Israel is classified as a high-tech, advanced market economy. Bahrain has developed a banking- and financial-based economy to replace the lost income from its depleted oil reserves.

The economies in the Middle East vary significantly in size. The GDPs of Eastern Mediterranean nations in 2017 varied from Cyprus's $31.8 billion to Turkey's $2.2 trillion. The GDPs of the Persian Gulf nations in 2017 varied from Yemen's $736 billion to Saudi Arabia's $1.8 trillion. Petroleum revenues are pivotal in most Middle Eastern economies.

Given that Israel does not have a significant income from oil, its people have been forced to find creative ways of developing

◂ *Aerial view of Kibbutz Geva in the Harod Valley in Israel*

▾ *Aerial view of Nahalal, the first Moshav in Israel, in the Jezreel Valley, Israel. A* ***moshav*** *is a community settlement of farmers established by the Labor Zionists party in Israel. Moshav is the Hebrew word for "settlement" or "village."*

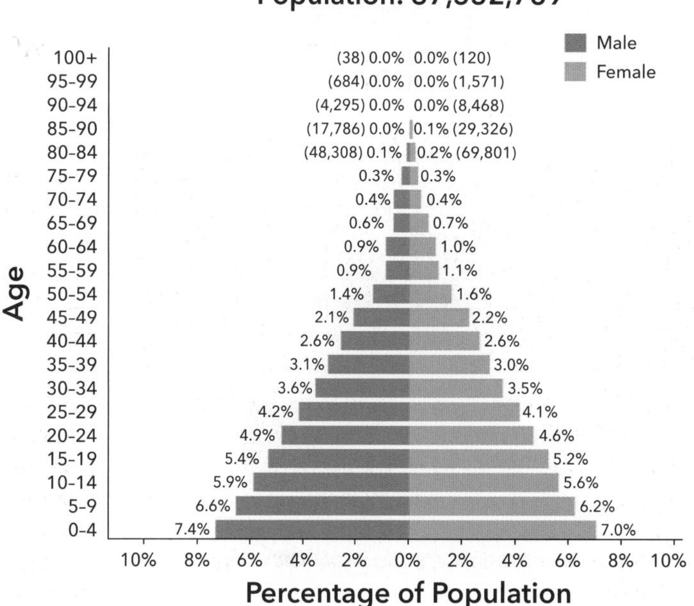

their tiny country since its inception in 1948. One element of Israel's success has been the development of the **kibbutz**, a collective community where labor, housing, and resources are shared. For many years these communities concentrated on converting desert into productive farmland and making other agricultural improvements. There are still over 270 kibbutzim in Israel today, and they have diversified from agriculture to hotels and specialized industries. Many kibbutzim have also been privatized and are no longer communally owned.

Demographics

In 2017 the combined estimated population of the Middle East was 329 million. The country in the Eastern Mediterranean with the largest population was Turkey, at 80.6 million people. The country in this region with the smallest population was Cyprus, with 1.2 million people. Iran had the largest population in the Persian Gulf, with 81 million people, and Bahrain had the smallest, with 1.49 million people.

Several Middle Eastern countries have high birthrates. The Eastern Mediterranean country with the highest birthrate is Jordan at 25.5/1000, and Yemen has the highest birthrate in the Persian Gulf region at 31.6/1000.

Various countries in this region also have young populations, including Turkey, Israel, and Iran. However, Iraq's population pyramid shows that nearly 60 percent of its population is under the age of twenty-five, making it the Middle Eastern country with the largest percentage of young people.

Iraq (2017)
Population: 37,552,789

Age	Male	Female
100+	(38) 0.0%	0.0% (120)
95-99	(684) 0.0%	0.0% (1,571)
90-94	(4,295) 0.0%	0.0% (8,468)
85-90	(17,786) 0.0%	0.1% (29,326)
80-84	(48,308) 0.1%	0.2% (69,801)
75-79	0.3%	0.3%
70-74	0.4%	0.4%
65-69	0.6%	0.7%
60-64	0.9%	1.0%
55-59	0.9%	1.1%
50-54	1.4%	1.6%
45-49	2.1%	2.2%
40-44	2.6%	2.6%
35-39	3.1%	3.0%
30-34	3.6%	3.5%
25-29	4.2%	4.1%
20-24	4.9%	4.6%
15-19	5.4%	5.2%
10-14	5.9%	5.6%
5-9	6.6%	6.2%
0-4	7.4%	7.0%

Percentage of Population: 10% 8% 6% 4% 2% 0% 2% 4% 6% 8% 10%

The Middle East has broad ethnic diversity. A large percentage of people in the Middle East are of Arabic origin or are the descendants of various Turkish tribes. In addition, many trace their heritage back to Assyrian, Greek, Phoenician, or Chaldean civilizations. As an example of the region's diversity, the majority of people living in Turkey are of Turkish nationality, but this country also has fifteen minority groups. Israel has the largest Jewish population in the Middle East but also has a significant number of Arabs and other nationalities among its citizens.

One group that has spread over several countries in the Middle East is the Kurdish people. Originally from Iran, the **Kurds** have dispersed to parts of Turkey, Iraq, and Syria. They have suffered much at the hands of others due to their minority status, the violence of some Kurds, and their perceived threat by many political leaders. While most Kurds are Muslim, some follow Shia Islam and others follow Sunni Islam. Still other Kurds are Christians. Estimates on their population size varies from 30 to 45 million.

▾ *Palestinian girls, wearing traditional clothing, dance during a celebration of Palestinian culture in Khan Yunis in the southern Gaza Strip.*

THE PALESTINIANS

The term *Palestine* is probably derived from the Greek term *Palaistínē* or the Arabic *Filastin*. In the Bible the term *Philistine* is used and is similar to the Arabic term. Outside of the Bible, *Palestine* has historically been used to refer to the region between Egypt and Phoenicia. Gradually, the people who lived in this region became known as Palestinians. The name was associated with where people lived rather than their nationality or religion, since Jews, Christians, and Muslim Arabs lived in this region for centuries.

By the start of the twentieth century, the term began to be used to refer to the Arab population living in this region, and the transition was completed by the re-formation of the nation of Israel in 1948. After this time, Jewish people referred to themselves as Israelis, and the term *Palestinian* was used almost exclusively by the Arab population of this area.

The Palestinians rejected the creation of the nation of Israel and, along with neighboring Arab nations, engaged in four wars to drive out the Jews. In the first war, Israel conquered West Jerusalem and annexed it. Thousands of Arab Palestinians were forced into exile. These refugees became a source of bitterness between the two sides, a constant "thorn in the flesh" for Israel.

Most Palestinians now reside in either the Gaza Strip (on the west coast of Israel) or the West Bank (on the west side of the Jordan River). Israelis also live in communities on the West Bank, and violent protests have erupted over controversial housing construction and terrorist attacks on Jewish settlers. While a large majority of Palestinians are Muslim, there is a tiny minority of Palestinian Christians who endure abuse and persecution.

1. What is the probable origin of the term *Palestine*?
2. Following 1948 whom did the term *Palestinian* refer to?
3. Why has strife between the Jewish and Palestinian people persisted?
4. What do you think it would be like to be a Palestinian Christian?

Turkish students perform a folk dance during the celebration to mark the 100th anniversary of Ataturk Youth and Sports Day in Izmir, Turkey, on May 19, 2019.

Culture and Diversity

The Middle East is a blend of many cultures that extend back over three thousand years. Varieties of languages, traditional forms of music and dance, and favorite foods have been handed down from one generation to the next. One cultural feature that has endured is the role of the extended family.

Food, Dance, and Sports

Meals in the Middle East are typically a combination of locally grown grains, fruits and vegetables, and various types of meat, including chicken and lamb. Dates are grown in abundance in the Middle East and are often found in favorite dishes. In Turkey slices of meat are grilled and served along with grilled vegetables in a dish called *kebap*. This is similar to a familiar method of preparing food known as *shish kabab*.

A dish commonly served in Arab homes is *maqlubbeh*, which is Arabic for "upside down." This meal is made with steamed rice and chicken or lamb and then inverted when served.

What meal is complete without dessert? Various forms of baklava are served in the Middle East. Another dessert, called *geshd* in Saudi Arabia or *rangeena* in Iraq, includes dates, flour, oil, and walnuts.

Traditional oriental Adana kebap and shashlik skewer

Dates are a main ingredient in geshd and rangeena.

Freshly prepared and flipped maqlubbeh

▲ *Syrian-Kurdish refugees play volleyball at the Quru Gusik (Kawergosk) refugee camp.*

As in many other parts of the world, the people of the Middle East love to participate in or watch their favorite sports. Once again, soccer tops the list of popular sports. In addition, many countries in this region enjoy basketball, volleyball, wrestling, rugby, various water sports, and even skiing (in Lebanon and Iran).

Family

The extended family has been a central focus in the Middle East for millennia. Prior to the existence of a central government, the typical Middle Eastern family resolved most issues and punished most transgressors. Today the average extended family involves at least three generations and can include other relatives such as aunts and uncles.

In modern Middle Eastern families, those who are financially able live in separate housing from their parents and grandparents. However, several characteristics of the extended family continue. The male leader of the family retains great authority and makes important decisions for the family. The welfare of the group continues to take priority over the desires of an individual in the family. In addition, social activities are largely contained within the extended family group. It would be unusual to see a family entertain others in a restaurant or gather at a public event. Another aspect of the traditional extended family that continues is the care given for family members in need. This would include the elderly, sick, divorced, widowed, or handicapped. Emotional and financial support is often provided for these family members.

CHILD MARRIAGE

Marriage between a young girl and an adult man is not exclusive to Islam and existed in Arabia long before Muhammad. However, Muhammad's marriage to Aisha, a child between six and nine years old, established a precedent that all Muslims could follow. Most Muslims today do not engage in child marriage, and many might even oppose it, but this horrific practice is considered a legitimate part of Islam and continues to be advocated and practiced far beyond the Middle East. Beyond denying a girl a normal childhood, the practice forces young girls into an adult relationship as little more than slaves. These traumatized women will bear physical and emotional scars for life, and many will try to escape or choose to end their lives rather than endure such abuse.

1. How did child marriage become acceptable in Islam?
2. Contrast child marriage and adult marriage.
3. What, if anything, can be done to help those trapped in child marriages?

Religion

As the birthplace of Judaism, Christianity, and Islam, the Middle East is dominated by religion. With the expansion of Islam beyond Arabia, the Middle East came under Muslim domination. Non-Muslims were given a choice of submitting to Islam and paying a tax, converting to Islam, or dying as unbelievers.

Islam permeates life in most Middle Eastern countries today, even those that, like Turkey, have secular governments. Every city has at least one **mosque**, an Islamic worship building. Criers or loudspeakers call the people

◀ *The Theology Mosque in Istanbul, an example of a modern mosque*

Islam

Islam, one of the world's largest religions, emerged on the Arabian Peninsula in the seventh century. At the center of Islam is the confession "There is no god but Allah, and Muhammad is the prophet of Allah."

Muhammad was born in Mecca on the Arabian Peninsula. As a young man, he supervised the caravans of a wealthy widow in their trade with Syria. At age 25 Muhammad married the widow, and her wealth gave him more time for contemplation. He claimed that the angel Gabriel visited him during times of meditation in a cave. Muslims claim that the Qur'an is the collection of the messages given to Muhammad by Allah. They declare that Muhammad is the last in a line of prophets that includes Adam, Abraham, Moses, and Jesus. Because Muhammad is the final prophet, Muslims insist that the Qur'an corrects corruptions in the revelations passed down from other prophets. Muhammad passed these revelations to his followers orally. This oral tradition was written down during his life and over the twenty years after his death. In its written form the Qur'an has 114 suras, or chapters. Beginning with Sura 2, the suras are arranged from longest to shortest, not in chronological order. And yet the chronology of the suras is important because the Qur'an contains contradictions. Muslims attempt to resolve these contradictions by saying that later revelation supersedes earlier revelation. The Hadith, collected sayings of Muhammad and stories about him, also play a foundational role in Muslim thought. The different sects of Islam have their own collections of Hadith. The collections of Hadith were written down by the late ninth century.

Parts of the Bible are also significant for Muslims, especially the Torah (Pentateuch), the Psalms, and the Gospels. Nevertheless, Muslims claim that the Bible has been corrupted and needs correction by the Qur'an. Muslim scholars disagree about whether this means that the actual text of the Bible has been corrupted or that Jewish and Christian interpretations of the Bible are corrupt.

The oneness of Allah is one of the most important teachings of Islam. Although Muhammad grew up in a polytheistic society, Islam rejects polytheism. Islam also rejects the biblical teaching that the One God exists in three Persons: Father, Son, and Spirit. Muslims say that Allah has no companions and no Son. Though Muslims believe that Jesus was a prophet, they deny His deity. They accept the virgin birth and miracles of Jesus. However, in Muslim teaching Jesus is unable to intercede for people. Only Muhammad can successfully intercede between Muslims and Allah. Muslims also deny that Jesus died for the sins of mankind. In Muslim teaching everyone is responsible for his own sins. Humans are considered to be, at the root, good. However, people are weak and they sin. Salvation is offered by Allah to those who follow the path of Islam, although no Muslim can be sure of salvation apart from a martyr's death.

The religious practices of Muslims are often described as the Five Pillars. The first pillar is the daily recitation of the Shahadah: "There is no god but Allah, and Muhammad is the prophet of Allah." The second pillar is prayer. Muslims pray three to five times a day, facing toward Mecca. These prayers are set recitations that give glory and thanks to Allah in Arabic. The third pillar of Islam is fasting. Muslims fast during the month of Ramadan. During this month Muslims do

▲ *The national flag of Saudi Arabia, with the shahada (the Muslim confession of faith)*

Minaret of a mosque in Oman ▶

▼ *(bottom) Muslim family in Syria eating an evening meal during the holy month of Ramadan*

not eat or drink between sunrise and sunset. The fourth pillar is alms giving. The zakat, or alms, can range from 2.5% to 20% of what one owns. Giving the alms is supposed to indicate that Allah owns all things as well as to benefit the poor. The fifth pillar is the pilgrimage, or hajj. Every Muslim is to make a pilgrimage to Mecca at least once if at all possible. Central to the pilgrimage is the circling of the Ka'bah. The Ka'bah is a black stone building believed to be located near the well that sprang up when Hagar and Ishmael faced death in the wilderness. Muslims teach that Abraham built this structure as a place of worship.

The most controversial Muslim practice is called *jihad*. Jihad is the Arabic word for struggle. Some Muslims insist it can refer to the struggle that each Muslim wages against his sin. But it is almost always used to refer to the Muslim "holy war" to spread Islam throughout the world. Some modern Muslims argue that this spread of Islam should take place only through peaceful means. They teach that Muslims should seek to persuade others to become Muslims. But other Muslim groups practice a violent jihad against those they view as enemies of Islam, including other sects of Islam. The Qur'an and Hadith give mixed messages on this matter. The Qur'an teaches "there is to be no compulsion in religion" (2:256). But the Qur'an also teaches that Muslims should fight and subdue Jews and Christians who do not submit to Muslim rule (9:29).

When considering this threat, Christians should balance a number of considerations. They must consider legitimate dangers that violent segments of Islam present while rejecting fear that prevents Christians from reaching out and evangelizing Muslims. Many of the Muslims that American Christians meet in their communities harbor no ill will toward them and would be willing to establish a friendship with a Christian. Christians should not neglect these opportunities.

▲ *(top) Zakat (alms giving) is one of the five pillars of Islam.*

▲ *(bottom) Special provision is made for disabled Muslims who desire to pray at the Ka'bah in Mecca, Islam's holiest site.*

to prayer up to five times daily from the minarets (towers) beside the mosques. Businesses stop for prayer at dawn, noon, midafternoon, sunset, and night. On Friday, the Muslim holy day, people meet at noon in the local mosque to recite their prayers together.

All countries in the Middle East have a Muslim presence, and Islam is the clear majority in every country except Cyprus, Lebanon, and Israel. Members of the Greek Orthodox Church constitute the majority in Cyprus, Muslims have only a slim majority in Lebanon, and Judaism enjoys a 77 percent majority in Israel. Every Middle Eastern country also has a minority of Roman Catholics, evangelicals, and nonreligious, although these groups endure persecution in some Middle Eastern countries.

Major Religions of Jordan

Islamic	**96.3%**
Orthodox	**1.5%**
Roman Catholic	**0.5%**
Protestant Evangelical	**0.4%**
Unaffiliated	**1.3%**

BELIEFS

Judaism

The religion of Judaism emerged in the wake of the destruction of the Jewish temple in AD 70. Though the roots of Judaism reach back to Moses and Abraham, AD 70 proved to be a decisive turning point. With the temple destroyed, sacrifices ceased and the influential priestly class fell from power. The crushing response of Roman military power also led the rabbis to discourage messianic movements, which stirred up the people against Rome and led to the kind of retribution experienced in Jerusalem in AD 70. In addition, the emerging Judaism faced competition from followers of Jesus, who claimed that Jesus was the Messiah—the one who fulfilled the Old Testament Scriptures and inaugurated the era of the New Covenant.

In this time of upheaval, the Pharisees, a Jewish sect that focused on keeping the Law of Moses, gained ascendency. The rabbis who emerged from this tradition developed rules for interpreting the Jewish Scriptures. These rabbis collected interpretations of laws about agriculture, holy days, rituals, and civic life in a collection known as the *Mishna*. The Mishna was completed in AD 200. Additional traditions about the application of the law can be found in the *Gemara*. Together the Mishna and the Gemara form the *Talmud*. Some Jews believe that the Talmud is inspired just like Scripture. Others deny its inspiration, but they do accept it as an authority for Judaism.

Central to Judaism are monotheism, the Torah, and the election of the nation Israel. **Monotheism** means that adherents to Judaism believe there is only one god. They believe that God created all that there is and that His laws govern the way that all people should live. Evil exists in God's world, but God will one day raise all people from the dead. He will judge the world with justice and mercy. The wicked will be judged for their wickedness. The just will be rewarded. One authority on Judaism notes, "If the balance is equal, then God inclines the scale to forgiveness." Because of the future judgment, humans must choose to do right and repent when they do wrong. Many in Judaism believe that people who work hard enough to overcome sin will be able to do it if they ask God for help. Judaism teaches that God chose Israel to be his special people because of the merits of the patriarchs.

They are unique because God gave them the Torah (Law) and because they worship the one true God instead of idols. Obedience to the Torah is thus a very important part of adhering to Judaism. It identifies a person as being a part of Judaism, which in turn marks him or her as being specially related to God.

▲ A Jewish man reading the Torah in a synagogue

▲ An Ultra-Orthodox Jewish man is helped by one of his children as he lights candles on the eighth and last night of the Jewish holiday Hanukah.

Judaism celebrates many holy days. Each week Jews observe a Sabbath. *Rosh Hashanah* begins the Jewish year (in September or October) with a time of reflection and repentance. *Yom Kippur*, the Day of Atonement, ceased being a day of special sacrifice with the destruction of the Temple. Today it is a day of fasting, repentance of sins, and synagogue attendance. *Sukkoth*, or the Feast of Booths, occurs five days after Yom Kippur. It is a remembrance of the wilderness wanderings after deliverance from Egypt. Closely following Sukkoth is the celebration of *Simchat Torah*. This marks the completion of the yearly reading of the Torah in the synagogue. The Torah scrolls are brought out and carried in a procession. *Hanukah*, or the Feast of Lights, takes place in December. It celebrates the rededication of the temple after it was recovered by the Maccabees in 142 BC. In February or March the feast of *Purim* is held. This feast celebrates the deliverance of the Jews from Haman as recounted in the book of Esther. One of the most important feasts for Jews is *Passover*. The Passover is the remembrance of God's deliverance of Israel from Egypt. Fifty days after Passover is *Shavuot*, the feast that celebrates the giving of the Law to Moses on Sinai.

◀ Hurva Synagogue in Jerusalem, Israel

Judaism, like Islam and Christianity, teaches that there is only one God. However, there are significant differences between Christians and Muslims regarding the identity of God and their relationship with Him. For the Muslims, Allah is only their lord and master. For Jews and Christians, God is also their Father.

From the period when the Jewish people were separated from the temple during captivity in Babylon and since the destruction of the temple in the first century AD, the Jewish people have met in a building to study the Law and worship God. This building became known as a **synagogue**, from a Greek word that means "to meet together."

SECTION REVIEW

1. How has the Middle East changed over time?
2. How well do the Middle Eastern governments provide for the education, health, and safety of their citizens? Choose two and contrast them.
3. What exports contribute to the economic success of the Middle East?
4. Describe the demographics of the Middle East.
5. What are some cultural characteristics and examples of diversity in the Middle East?

INTERACTIONS OF PEOPLE AND PLACES

What are some of the challenges of living in the Middle East?

Much of the Middle East endures harsh climatic conditions and limited arable land. In addition, water is a precious resource in many Middle Eastern countries. The people who live in this region must be creative and resourceful to meet their daily needs.

GUIDING QUESTIONS

- How do the Middle Eastern economies and people interact with the environment?
- What are environmental issues in the Middle East?
- What are causes and effects of environmental issues in the Middle East?
- What are possible solutions to environmental issues in the Middle East?

Interaction among People

In many Muslim societies women are expected to wear a covering, such as a hijab, niqab, or burqa, depending on how stringently sharia law is interpreted. Even in countries where these practices are not strictly observed, few jobs are open to women because they are not permitted to socialize with men other than their relatives. Education for females is limited. In many of these countries, women are not allowed to vote or run for office. Muslim women are taught to hold the family honor in the highest regard, and women are pressured to follow these cultural restrictions to ensure that they avoid any improper actions that might dishonor the family. Maintaining honor is very important in Muslim society. Bringing dishonor for any reason can result in the death of the offender at the hands of the head of the home. These deaths are known as honor killings.

According to Sura 4:3 a Muslim man may have up to four wives, depending on his financial resources. Sura 65 provides the circumstances under which a Muslim man may divorce his wife. In contrast, a Muslim woman may not have multiple husbands, and there is no procedure for a Muslim woman to divorce her husband.

A Bedouin woman wearing a hijab

A Turkish woman wearing a niqab

A Muslim woman wearing a burqa

Interaction with the Environment

Over the centuries poor farming methods and deforestation have contributed to the expansion of desert conditions across much of the Middle East, and people have been forced to move to more habitable regions. This has resulted in crowded cities and overuse of limited land and water resources. Solid fuel is used for cooking in many countries and presents challenges to preserving remaining wooded areas.

▲ *A desalination plant in Ashkelon, Israel*

The discovery of oil has brought enormous wealth to many countries of the Middle East. One benefit of this wealth is the ability to purchase technology to provide drinking water through **desalination** (the removal of salt from seawater). This process produces millions of gallons of water each day to supply the needs of people throughout the Middle East. Another benefit of oil wealth is climate-controlled housing and buildings to offset the oppressive heat that affects much of this region. Automobile use has expanded significantly across the Middle East as well.

Reasons for Environmental Issues

Several factors contribute to the environmental problems facing the Middle East. These factors include negative side effects from both industry and desalination.

Water

While desalination has provided millions of gallons of drinking water, this process has also increased salinity of sea water once the waste is returned to the ocean. As in other nations where industry is expanding, countries in the Middle East tend to pour their chemical waste into rivers and oceans. In addition, household and human waste often flows into bodies of water because most Middle Eastern countries lack the technology or the resources to properly capture and dispose of the various forms of waste.

Air

Air quality in the urban areas of Middle Eastern countries is often poor due to high levels of chemicals, dust, or other particles. Most desalination plants consume vast amounts of petroleum to purify the water, and that, in combination with an exponential increase in automobile use, has compounded air pollution.

Land

Typical land issues include coastal degradation near large bodies of water, erosion due to loss of vegetation and the encroachment of a desert climate, and deforestation. Countries that still have significant

▼ *Some Middle Eastern countries dump their garbage in the desert.*

wooded areas, such as Turkey, tend to remove trees for processing or to provide additional land for agriculture. Inevitably this leads to loss of topsoil and degradation of arable land. Another form of land pollution found throughout the Middle East is the improper disposal or processing of trash. Dumping of trash in the desert is a growing problem.

Proposed Solutions

For many countries in the Middle East, solutions will come when governments change their priorities and use their vast wealth to effectively solve environmental issues. Given the great wealth produced by petroleum along with the significant pollution that results, this will be a great challenge and will require wise leaders. In countries characterized by political instability, the end of violence and abuse must be the first step, followed by political and economic improvements that lead to a growing economy. These efforts will also require great expenditure of wealth and human resources to reverse the damage done to this region's environment.

Some countries, including Turkey, are planning to increase energy production through wind, solar, and hydroelectric power, in addition to pursuing other clean technology. Another encouraging example is found in the United Arab Emirates. Officials and average citizens have joined forces in this country to plant trees and other outdoor plants to reclaim portions of the desert. Water from desalination plants (as well as groundwater projects, including the one in al-Khazna) is used to sustain the plants. As a result, Abu Dhabi now has several thousand acres of grass. The nearby al-Ayn oasis has forty parks with pools or fountains. The increased vegetation appears to have slightly moderated the intense heat and has attracted additional birdlife.

SECTION REVIEW

1. What role does religion play in the treatment of women in the Middle East?
2. What are three environmental issues in the Middle East?
3. What role have many governments played in dealing with environmental issues in the Middle East?
4. Explain how the Middle Eastern economies and people have interacted with the environment.
5. What solutions to current environmental issues in the Middle East would you propose?

Urban park in Abu Dhabi, the United Arab Emirates

17 CHAPTER REVIEW

SUMMARY

1. The physical geography of the Middle East was shaped by tectonic activity and volcanic eruptions. Development of the Middle East's limited natural resources has fundamentally changed this region's economic potential.
2. The people of the Middle East are ethnically varied by tribe and language and yet similar in the enjoyment of common activities, including ethnic foods, regional music, and sports. These societies are transitioning to developed societies but are also threatened by radicalism and terrorism.
3. A major challenge in the Middle East is the need to make wise use of human and natural resources in ways that maintain strong economies without further endangering the environment. Goals for the Middle Eastern countries would be to diversify industry, steward their limited resources, and find ways to protect their fragile environment.

Terms to Know

- ❑ Mesopotamia
- ❑ wadi
- ❑ khat
- ❑ sharia
- ❑ medical tourism
- ❑ Kurds
- ❑ moshav
- ❑ kibbutz
- ❑ mosque
- ❑ monotheism
- ❑ synagogue
- ❑ desalination

Making Connections

1. Describe the *hajj* to Mecca that each Muslim is expected to take at least once in his life.
2. What earth-shaping process is at work in much of the Middle East?
3. How do landforms affect climates in the Middle East?
4. How has deforestation affected the Middle East over the last three thousand years?
5. Why do you think Middle Eastern economies are in transition?
6. Identify political issues in the Middle East.
7. What role has religion played in the Middle East?

Developing Geography Skills

1. How do landforms influence the distribution of population in this region?
2. What role have rivers played in the concentration of population in the Middle East?

Thinking Critically

1. Though many people oppose child marriage, why is a biblical worldview best equipped to address this issue?
2. The main goal in Islam is to please Allah and escape eternal punishment. What kind of relationship does a Muslim have with Allah? How does a Christian's relationship with the God of the Bible differ?

Living in God's World

1. Write a paragraph explaining how worldview influences a nation's approach to reclaiming desert land in the Middle East.
2. Given the opportunity, how could you demonstrate the love of Christ to Syrian refugees?

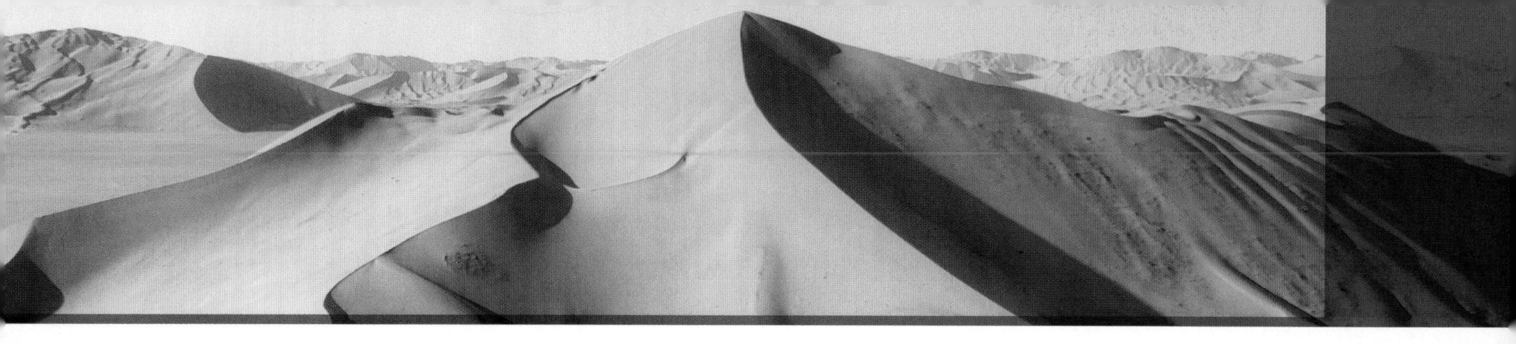

CASE STUDY | Sunni versus Shia

When Muhammad died in 632, Abu Bakr, an early follower of Muhammad, used military force to prevent the splintering of Islam into separate parties. After two more leaders succeeded Bakr, Islam split into two groups. Those who became known as the Shiites (followers [of Muhammad]) declared that the ruler of Islam must be a direct descendant of Muhammad. They also wanted this leader to serve as both political and religious ruler, as Muhammad had done. The other group, which became known as the Sunnis (adherents [of custom]), insisted that any worthy Muslim could serve as Muhammad's successor, or caliph, and that there should be separate political and religious leaders, as Abu Bakr and others had been.

These factions went to war, and the Sunnis retained a solid majority of 80-90 percent within Islam. In most countries, Sunni Muslims are in the majority and Shia Muslims are in the minority. Notable exceptions are Iran, Azerbaijan, and Iraq, where Shia Muslims are in the majority.

Much of the violence that has occurred between these groups can be explained by the fact that each group considers the other group to be heretical. While Shia Muslims have often been portrayed as violent and Sunni Muslims are frequently described as peaceful, both groups have participated in violence against their opponents.

Over the centuries, the differences between Sunnis and Shias have become more complicated, and there are even multiple divisions within each group. However, the great divide between Sunni Islam and Shia Islam remains undiminished.

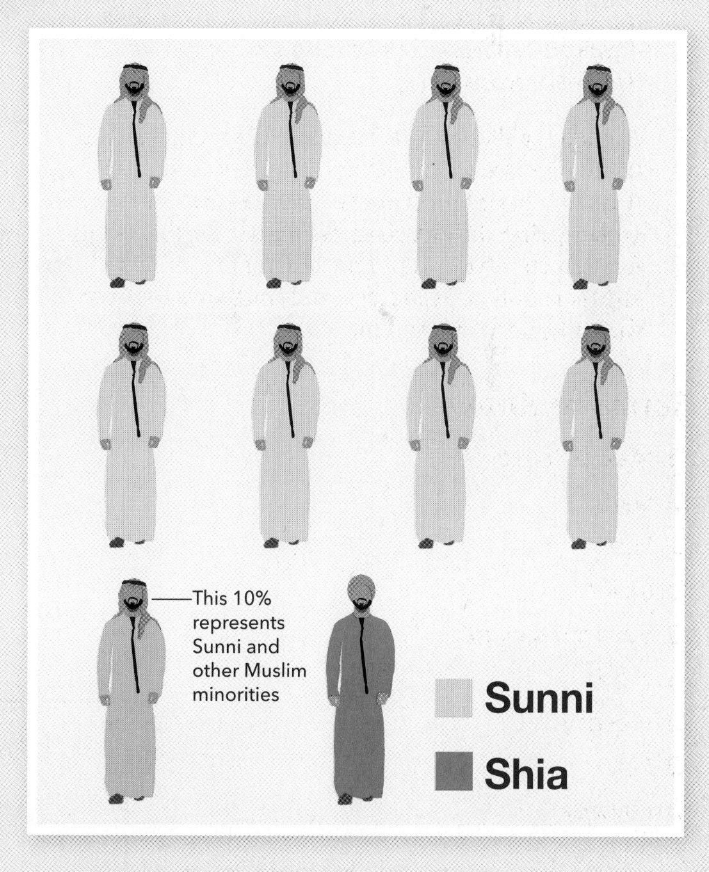

1. Who succeeded Muhammad upon his death?
2. Which group's name implies they are followers of Muhammad?
3. Which group believes that any worthy Muslim can be appointed to lead Islam?
4. Which group represents about 10 percent of Muslims?
5. Why do Shiites and Sunnis carry out violent attacks against one another?

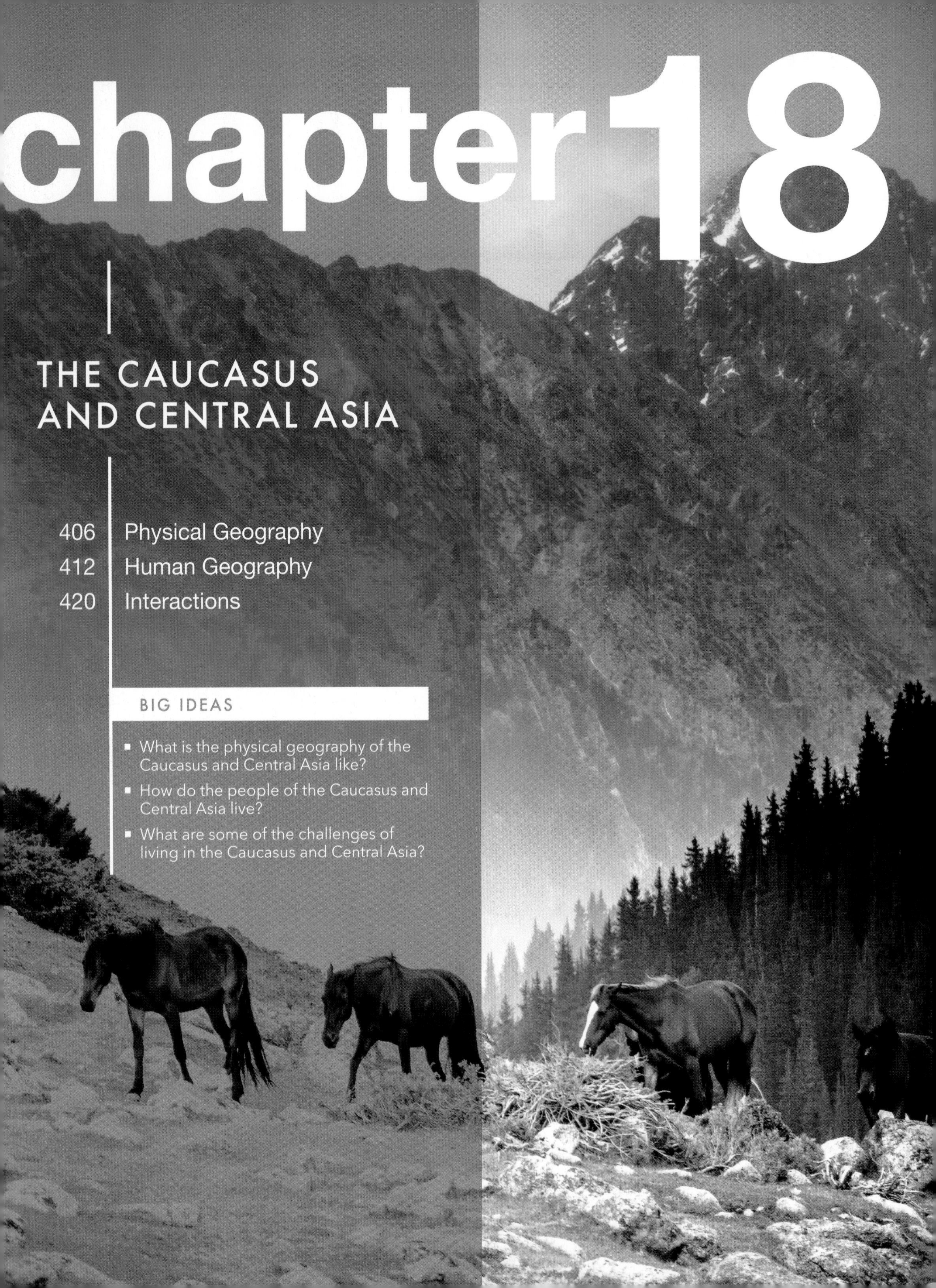

chapter 18

THE CAUCASUS AND CENTRAL ASIA

406 Physical Geography
412 Human Geography
420 Interactions

BIG IDEAS

- What is the physical geography of the Caucasus and Central Asia like?
- How do the people of the Caucasus and Central Asia live?
- What are some of the challenges of living in the Caucasus and Central Asia?

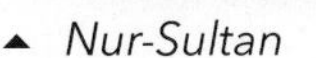

▲ Nur-Sultan

▲ The Ananuri church and fortress in Georgia

The Fan Mountains ▶ and Alaudin Lakes in Tajikistan

◀ Wild horses in Karakol, Issyk-Kul, Kyrgyzstan

FLY KITES, NOT DRONES

Kite flying is the ancient hobby and national pastime of Afghanistan. Children and adults enjoy flying colorful kites in the autumn when the mountain winds are strong. In kite fighting contests participants try to break their opponent's kite string with glass-coated string for better cutting. Other contests reward the kite flyer who can get his kite the highest without losing it. When the Taliban took over the country in the 1990s, they banned kite flying along with other sports. They called them a waste of time and money. The traditional day to fly kites was Friday, which conflicted with the Muslim holy day. One of the first signs that freedom had returned was the sight of kites once again gracing the skies. The sport provides economic relief for war widows who find employment in making and selling kites. A popular motto is "fly kites, not drones," in reference to the military drones.

▲ An Afghan boy prepares to fly a kite during a kite battle on a hillside in Kabul.

GUIDING QUESTIONS

- What are the regions of the Caucasus and Central Asia?
- What caused the landforms of the Caucasus and Central Asia?
- What bodies of water are important to the Caucasus and Central Asia?
- What is the climate of the Caucasus and Central Asia, and how does it relate to its location on the globe?
- What are the natural resources of the Caucasus and Central Asia?

The Caucasus region lies between the Black and Caspian Seas, while Central Asia includes the area between the Caspian Sea and western China. These two regions have a great variety of landforms, including deserts, steppes, valleys, mountains, and plains. All of these countries except for Afghanistan belonged to the Soviet Union. These are some of the most isolated and little known places in the world.

PHYSICAL GEOGRAPHY

What is the physical geography of the Caucasus and Central Asia like?

Regions of the Caucasus and Central Asia

These regions sit at the crossroads of Europe, Asia, and the Middle East. There are three Caucasian countries and five Central Asian countries. Also included in this chapter is Afghanistan, a country hard to place in a particular region. It is a buffer country, sometimes categorized as part of South Asia, Central Asia, or even the Middle East.

CAUCASUS MOUNTAINS

The region consists of two mountain ranges, the Greater Caucasus and the Lesser Caucasus. They run from the northwest to the southeast and are separated from each other by the Kura River Valley. The Caucasus includes the countries of Georgia, Armenia, and Azerbaijan.

CASPIAN DEPRESSION

This depression covers a large area of Kazakhstan to the northeast of the Caspian Sea. This region is a barren wasteland. At its lowest spot, the Caspian Depression is 433 feet below sea level.

CENTRAL ASIAN DESERTS

The Ustyurt Plateau is a clay desert covering parts of Turkmenistan, Uzbekistan, and Kazakhstan. The Kara-Kum Desert is south of the Ustyurt Plateau and covers 80 percent of Turkmenistan. Kyzyl-Kum is a vast desert that covers 80 percent of Uzbekistan. Though most of the Kyzyl-Kum is a wilderness, there are a few oases.

CENTRAL ASIAN MOUNTAIN REGIONS

There are three high mountain ranges in southwest Central Asia: the Pamir, Hindu Kush, and Tien Shan ranges. The Pamir Mountains cover the eastern half of Tajikistan. This range is sometimes called the Pamir Knot because it is where the three ranges mentioned above come together along with the Himalayas and the Kunlun Mountains. The Hindu Kush, Persian for "Hindu Death," is a mountain barrier extending southwest from the Pamirs along the border with Pakistan and into central Afghanistan. Kyrgyzstan is dominated by the Tien Shan, or the "Celestial Mountains." This northern range runs one thousand miles from Tashkent, Uzbekistan, to Urumqi, China, dividing Kyrgyzstan from China.

THE KAZAKH STEPPE AND KAZAKH UPLANDS

This is the largest area of Kazakhstan, the largest country of Central Asia and the ninth-largest in the world. It is also the largest dry steppe region in the world. **Steppes** are unforested grasslands. The Kazakh Uplands cover the eastern lake regions around Lake Balkhash and Lake Zaysan.

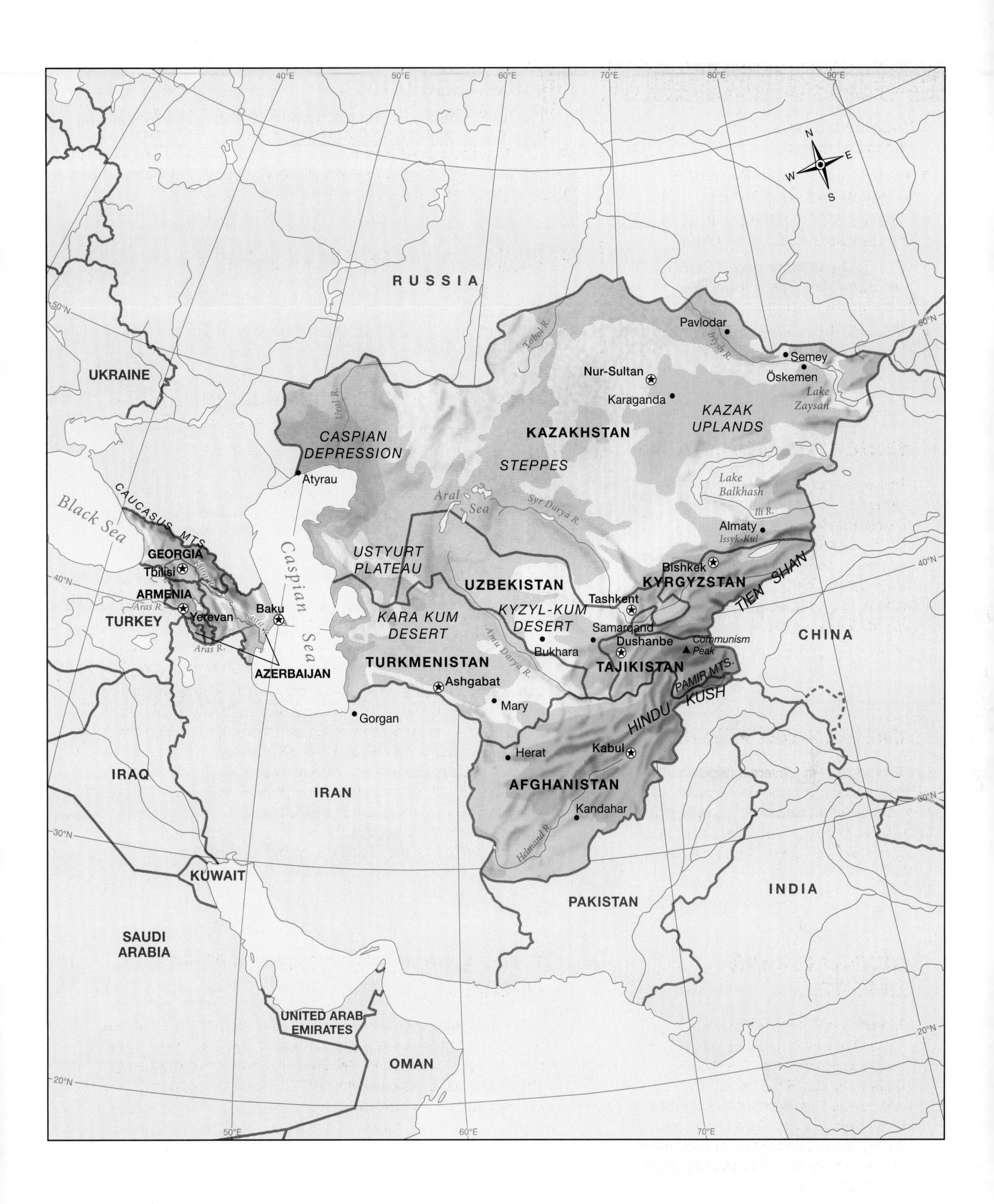
RUSSIA
UKRAINE
KAZAKHSTAN
CASPIAN DEPRESSION
STEPPES
KAZAK UPLANDS
Pavlodar
Semey
Öskemen
Nur-Sultan
Karaganda
Lake Zaysan
Lake Balkhash
Ili R.
Almaty
Issyk-Kul
Tobol R.
Irtysh R.
Ural R.
Atyrau
Aral Sea
Syr Darya R.
Black Sea
CAUCASUS MTS.
GEORGIA
Tbilisi
Kura R.
ARMENIA
Aras R.
Yerevan
Baku
TURKEY
AZERBAIJAN
Caspian Sea
USTYURT PLATEAU
UZBEKISTAN
KYZYL-KUM DESERT
KARA KUM DESERT
Amu Darya R.
Bukhara
Samarqand
Tashkent
Bishkek
KYRGYZSTAN
TIEN SHAN
Dushanbe
Communism Peak
TAJIKISTAN
PAMIR MTS.
HINDU KUSH
TURKMENISTAN
Ashgabat
Mary
Gorgan
Herat
Kabul
AFGHANISTAN
Kandahar
Helmand R.
CHINA
IRAQ
IRAN
KUWAIT
PAKISTAN
INDIA
SAUDI ARABIA
UNITED ARAB EMIRATES
OMAN
N
E
W
S
40°E
50°E
60°E
70°E
80°E
90°E
50°N
40°N
30°N
20°N

Physical Landforms

The high mountains and vast steppes of these regions make for dramatic vistas and unusual landforms.

▾ *The Veryovkina Cave (7,257 ft.) in Georgia is the deepest in the world. It is made of limestone.*

▴ *Jenish Chokusu, on the Kyrgyzstan-China border, is the highest peak in the Tien Shan range, at 24,406 feet.*

▾ *Torysh, Kazakhstan, is known as the "Valley of Balls." The balls, called concretions, are made of sedimentary rock. They are formed when sediment is deposited and cemented around some kind of nucleus, such as a fossil.*

The beautiful Charyn Canyon in Kazakhstan is made of sedimentary red sandstone. It was formed through water and wind erosion.

Bodies of Water

The Caucasus and Central Asia contain three inland seas: the Black, Caspian, and Aral. Only the Black Sea has access to the ocean; this differentiates it from the other two, which are technically lakes. Georgia's ports on the Black Sea permit greater opportunities to trade with Russia and Ukraine, as well as other nations. The Caspian Sea is the largest lake in the world. It provides key resources, such as fish and salt. Azerbaijan's capital, Baku, is the leading port. Several rivers flow into the Caspian Sea, which is ninety-two feet below sea level, but no waters flow out. The resulting "deadness" makes the Caspian Sea salty, although it is not as salty as ocean water. The Aral Sea is disappearing, in much the same way as Lake Chad.

The most important river in the Caucasus is the Kura, which empties into the Caspian Sea. Tbilisi, the capital of Georgia for more than fifteen hundred years, is on the Kura River. The three main rivers of Central Asia are the Amu Darya, Syr Darya, and Helmand. The Amu Darya is the longest river (1,500 miles) completely within Central Asia. It begins in the Pamirs of Tajikistan, forming part of its border with Afghanistan. It flows through Turkmenistan and Uzbekistan before fading out near the Aral Sea. The Syr Darya is north of the Amu Darya. It starts in the Tien Shan range in Kyrgyzstan and flows 1,374 miles through Uzbekistan and Kazakhstan into what is left of the Aral Sea. The Helmand River is totally within the borders of Afghanistan. It begins in the Hindu Kush and ends in a marsh and lake region on the Iran border.

▾ The Kura River flows through Tbilisi, Georgia.

The Helmand River in Afghanistan ▸

Karakul Lake in the Pamirs of Tajikistan

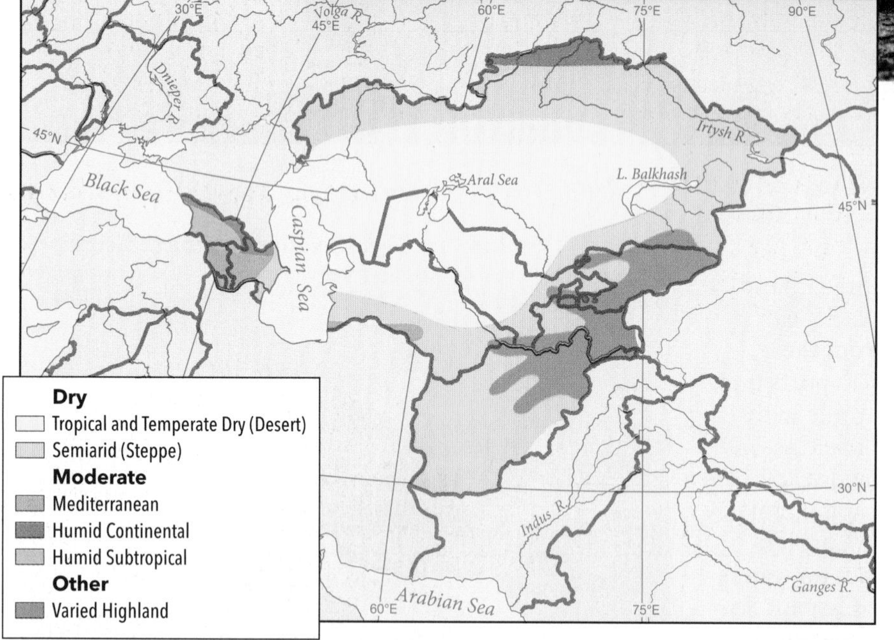

Karakul Lake in the Pamirs of Tajikistan is one of the highest navigable lakes in the world, at 12,990 feet. In 1987 after studying imagery of the lake taken from space, scientists concluded that a meteorite impact created the lake basin.

Climates of the Caucasus and Central Asia

While the Caucasus has a generally pleasant, humid climate because of its proximity to the Black Sea, Central Asia has a generally dry climate. As in other mountain regions, the elevation greatly affects the climate.

Resources of the Caucasus and Central Asia

These countries vary in their percentage of arable land. The mountain regions have very little farmland, but the plains and plateaus contain productive land for farming and grazing. The good soil and moderate climate of the Caucasus allow for the production of tea, grapes, citrus fruits, and cotton. All the Central Asian countries are major cotton producers, with Uzbekistan being the leader. It is believed that apples were first domesticated in Kazakhstan. In fact, the name of the former capital, Almaty,

A worker harvests grapes at a vineyard in Georgia.

means "father of apples." Kyrgyzstan has the largest natural walnut forest in the world. The mountains and plains support livestock. Between the valleys, herders graze sheep and goats for milk, mutton, and wool. In the high mountains, the people raise yaks for their milk, meat, and fur.

Armenia is a major molybdenum producer. This metal can withstand extreme temperatures without losing strength, so it is useful in airplane parts and military armor. Since Kazakhstan is one of the largest countries in the world and blessed with a vast amount of mineral wealth, it is a world leader in mineral production. Uzbekistan also has many of the same minerals, which include gold, silver, copper, lead, coal, iron ore, bauxite, chromite, and zinc. Kazakhstan ranks at the top for uranium reserves. Kazakhstan, Kyrgyzstan, and Tajikistan have reserves of rare earth minerals (a group of seventeen elements) required in the production of most electronics. Like Kazakhstan, Afghanistan has an abundance of assorted minerals, from gold to iron ore; it is said that the value exceeds $3 trillion. Lapis lazuli is a semiprecious stone unique to Afghanistan.

The Caspian Sea region is home to vast reserves of oil and gas, enriching the countries that border the sea. Kazakhstan, Azerbaijan, and Turkmenistan have the largest reserves of oil and natural gas. Azerbaijan is known for being the oldest oil-producing region. Oil wells here date back to 1594. Kyrgyzstan, Tajikistan, and to a lesser extent Georgia have abundant hydropower capacities. Some of the world's highest dams are here.

▲ *Yaks in the Pamir-Alay Mountains in Kyrgyzstan*

◂ *Molybdenum*

▲ *Lapiz lazuli*

SECTION REVIEW

1. Compare the dominant landform of Kazakhstan with that of Kyrgyzstan.
2. How do the mountains in this chapter compare to the Alps?
3. How are seas and lakes differentiated? Why would a lake be called a sea?
4. How are the climates of these regions affected by their location on the globe?
5. Why might these regions be important for technological industries?

ca. 900 The Samanids set up their capital in Bukhara.

1800

1838 Britain invades Afghanistan.

ca. 130 BC–1453 AD The Silk Road is a major trade route.

1848 First modern oil well drilled near Baku, Azerbaijan

GUIDING QUESTIONS

- How have the Caucasus and Central Asia changed over time?
- How do the governments of the Caucasus and Central Asia interact with their citizens?
- What is the economic health of the Caucasus and Central Asia?
- What are the demographics of the Caucasus and Central Asia?
- What are the cultural characteristics and diversity in the Caucasus and Central Asia?
- What forms of religion are practiced in the Caucasus and Central Asia?

HUMAN GEOGRAPHY

How do the people of the Caucasus and Central Asia live?

History

These regions share a characteristic: conquest or attempted conquest by foreign powers, including the Mongols, Turks, Persians, Russians, and Soviets. Many countries fell to Muslim conquerors at some point in their history. They also became the battleground between Western imperialists and other Asian states. A few proved impossible to conquer.

Ever present in the daily life of the Caucasians and Central Asians is their ancient history. These countries were dramatically affected by the **Silk Road**, a major trade route that linked two great ancient empires: Rome and China. Europeans gladly traded gold, silver, wool, jewels, and anything else of value to the Chinese in return for silk. Eventually, European traders discovered a water route to China that avoided Central Asia and the Caucasus. Little is left on the dusty Silk Road network except struggling cities and memories of past greatness.

▲ *Armenians lay flowers at the genocide memorial in Yerevan on April 24, 2009, in honor of the 94th anniversary of massacres by the Turks.*

Caucasus

Georgia and Armenia are unique among the countries in this chapter as Christian majority nations. Georgia enjoyed a period of independence and prosperity from about AD 1000 to 1212. But for most of their history, Georgia and Armenia endured frequent invasion and conflict as Byzantine forces opposed Turkish forces and Russian forces fought the Persians. Leading up to World War I, Turkish leaders decided to eliminate the possibility that Armenians would side with Turkey's enemies, the Russians. By 1917 Turkish forces and their allies had murdered up to 1.5 million Armenian men, women, and children in the Armenian genocide. Part of Armenia's tension with Turkey today stems from Turkey's continued denial of these atrocities. Azerbaijan has been influenced most by Iran (formerly Persia). Persians controlled the region from 700 BC to AD 600 (except for the brief interruption of the Greek Empire) and from the sixteenth century to 1813 (except for a brief period under the Ottoman Turks).

1900 — 2000

1922–36 Countries become Soviet Republics.

1979 The Soviet Army invades Afghanistan.

1991 Countries gain independence when the USSR collapses.

2001 Coalition forces support the Northern Alliance to oust the Taliban in Afghanistan.

Central Asia

The "stan" ending means "land of," so *Kazakhstan* means "land of the Kazakhs." This region, isolated by deserts and high mountains, was settled by Asian nomads and by Muslim conquerors from the Middle East. Various tribes of fierce nomads left an imprint of war and conquest on Central Asia. The Huns from this region threatened ancient Rome in the fourth and fifth centuries AD. The Mongols briefly dominated the region when they terrorized all of Eurasia during the thirteenth and fourteenth centuries. But it was the Turkic peoples, who migrated across most of Central Asia between the fifth and tenth centuries, that had the longest-lasting impact. Many of the modern-day countries in Central Asia have mainly Turkic populations.

▲ *A necropolis in Samarkand, Uzbekistan*

Kabul, Afghanistan, became important because of the thirty-three-mile Khyber Pass, one hundred miles southeast of the city, which allows easy passage through the Hindu Kush. At its narrowest point, the pass is around fifty feet wide. Great conquerors and their armies came through the pass, including Genghis Khan and possibly Alexander the Great. A southern extension of the Silk Road brought goods from India to Samarkand through this pass. Samarkand is in Uzbekistan near its eastern border with Tajikistan. Ancient Arab manuscripts called it "the Gem of the East." It is famous for its excellent examples of various types of architecture. Alexander the Great destroyed the city in 329 BC, but it was rebuilt and became a leading city on the Silk Road.

The Russian Empire conquered Central Asia in the nineteenth century but allowed the region some autonomy. After Russia became the USSR, Central Asia was divided into separate republics that are the same as the current countries. Like Ukraine, Kazakhstan suffered from forced starvations between 1931 and 1933, a terrible genocide that took between 1.3 and 1.75 million lives. It was part of Stalin's effort to collectivize the Kazakh people and end their traditional nomadic lifestyle. When the Soviet Union dissolved and the Central Asian countries became independent, Uzbekistan hoped that the Turkic peoples of Central Asia would unite into a single nation called Turkistan. Uzbekistan, with its large population, weak economy, and lack of trade opportunities, had much to gain from a union. However, no other nation shared Uzbekistan's enthusiasm.

▲ *Turkmenistan's president Gurbanguly Berdymukhamedov takes part in celebrations for the Day of the Horse in Ashgabat on April 28, 2018.*

Governments

These regions share common governing and economic characteristics but with some exceptions. The countries are cursed with authoritarian governments of different degrees. These all rank at the bottom for freedom of the press. Turkmenistan has the most outlandish government, similar to that of North Korea. The dictator leads a personality cult. The first president after the end of the USSR wrote a "holy" book, the Ruhnama, which is studied diligently in school and must be recited to obtain driver's licenses and other privileges. Television is limited to three state-run channels. Uzbekistan also has a very repressive government. For years children and most adults, including teachers and doctors, were forced to harvest cotton for little wages, the profits enriching the dictator. The former president of Uzbekistan even imprisoned his daughter, who was also corrupt but was poised to take power after her father. While not all governments of the Caucasus and Central Asia are as extreme as these two, they are all highly restrictive and resemble their former Communist selves more than the Eastern European countries. Georgia and Kyrgyzstan stand out for making genuine efforts at democratization. Georgia is trying to build closer ties with Europe, while Kyrgyzstan sees its traditional nomadic form of government as a kind of democracy. The actions of all of these governments have been largely overlooked by the rest of the world because of their isolation and their willingness to fight Islamic extremism within their borders. They have all assisted in the war on terror.

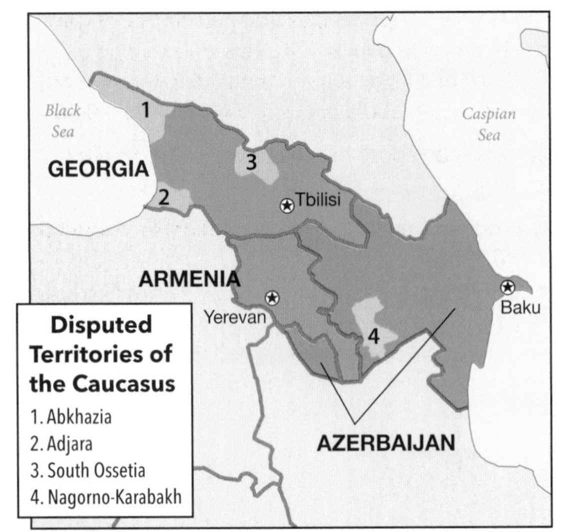

Enclaves, Exclaves, and Autonomous Regions

These two regions, in particular, are home to several **enclaves**, **exclaves**, and **autonomous regions**. An enclave is a country or portion of a country surrounded by another country. An exclave is a land separated from the main body of the country it belongs to. For example, Alaska is an exclave of the United States and Lesotho is an enclave in South Africa. Nagorno-Karabakh can be considered a large exclave of Armenia. While the land belongs to Azerbaijan, the people are Armenian, which is a source of conflict. In Georgia, dissatisfied Muslim minorities are concentrated in Abkhazia and South Ossetia, which are autonomous regions, or areas of a country that have been allowed self-rule, usually gained through rebellion. Autonomous regions sometimes have stronger loyalties to another country, but that country has no official rule over the lands. When Georgia tried to exert control over South Ossetia in 2008, Russian forces invaded Georgia, humiliated the government, and briefly occupied the country. In Tajikistan, the Gorno-Badakhshan Autonomous Oblast in the Pamirs makes up almost half of the country in the east. It is home to the Pamiri people, who fought a failed war for independence with the Tajiks in 1992. The agriculture-rich Fergana Valley, mainly within the borders of Kyrgyzstan, is home to many Uzbek exclaves.

A convoy of Russian troops makes its way through the mountains toward the armed conflict between Georgian troops and separatist South Ossetian troops, August 9, 2008.

GLOBAL IMPACT | Afghanistan, Graveyard of Empires

Afghanistan is often associated with holding off conquest since world powers throughout history have spent human and material capital to invade and control the country. Ancient invaders of Afghanistan include Alexander the Great, the Persians, the Arabs, the Mongols, and others. Afghanistan was not always successful in defeating invaders, but it did outlast them. In the nineteenth century, Afghanistan became a **buffer state**, which is a neutral state between two rivals who agreed to keep their armies out. In this case, the two were the Russian and British empires. Worries about Russia led the British into a futile war from 1878 to 1880. Later, Britain ended its efforts to control this region, and the world recognized Afghanistan as a sovereign nation. It was independent but remained politically weak. Despite usually controlling much of the territory and cities, these foreign powers learned that as long as the enemy can fight another day there is no victory.

▲ *Ahmad Shah Massoud (center) was a military and political leader in the war with the Soviets and later in the war with the Taliban. Bin Laden's men assassinated him on September 9, 2001.*

From 1978 to 1989, the Soviet Union waged a costly and ultimately unsuccessful campaign to set up and maintain a Communist dictatorship in Afghanistan. The United States supported the opposition to the Soviets, a coalition of Muslim tribes known collectively as the **Mujahideen** ("strugglers"). After the Soviet Union gave up and withdrew its troops, Afghanistan broke into warring factions, and anarchy reigned. Islamic extremists known as the **Taliban** ("seekers," or "students") eventually prevailed and restored order by enforcing rigid adherence to sharia law. They allowed Islamic terrorists to set up training camps in the country, and students from these camps carried out attacks against the West, including the attacks on the World Trade Center and the Pentagon on September 11, 2001. Consequently, the United States invaded Afghanistan, overthrew the Taliban, and chased down terrorists who had taken refuge in the mountains along the Afghan-Pakistani border. Despite fighting the longest war in American history, with over two thousand American casualties and trillions of dollars devoted to rebuilding the country, the United States was unable to achieve stability in Afghanistan.

1. Why do you think many countries have wanted to control Afghanistan?
2. In what ways does this constant fighting affect the people of the country?
3. What global impact has Afghanistan had?

Economies

The legacy of the Soviet Union is evident everywhere. In some ways during the latter years of the USSR, the people of these regions were more prosperous than they are now since the USSR subsidized industry and since many of these places were popular tourist destinations for Russians. When the USSR collapsed, these regions experienced a trauma as all the capital was quickly taken away. All of the people struggle with poverty to different degrees. The key economic driver is the extraction of natural resources, especially petroleum in the Caspian Sea countries. Handmade carpets are an important export. There are three main styles from this area: Caucasian; Buchara, indigenous to Turkmenistan, Uzbekistan, and Afghanistan; and Afghani. The women who make the carpets are paid by the number of knots they do per hour. Making the carpets takes great skill and is labor intensive. A large carpet could sell for up to $50,000. Kazakhstan is home to Russia's main spaceport, the Baikonur Cosmodrome, which provides income for the country since Russia leases the land.

▲ *Artisans weave hand-knotted silk carpets on looms in Samarkand, Uzbekistan.*

▲ *White marble buildings in Ashgabat, Turkmenistan*

Corruption

Georgia, Armenia, and Kyrgyzstan have made progress in fighting corruption and enforcing the rule of law, but other countries have not. Corruption can happen in small ways behind the scenes, as when a person bribes an official in order to get permission to open a business. But corruption can also happen openly and on a large scale, as when the dictator of Turkmenistan built Ashgabat as a monument to himself, with buildings of expensive white marble. In Kazakhstan the president moved the capital from Almaty to Astana, and he undertook one of the world's most ambitious building projects, using oil income to erect government buildings, a presidential residence, parks, and monuments. Critics compared the president to a child playing with toys; the country has yet to see a return on the investment of building a new capital. In March 2019 Astana was renamed Nur-Sultan after the president who built it.

Trade

▼ *An Afghan farmer harvests opium sap from a poppy in the Nangarhar province.*

The oil-producing countries are looking for new ways to get their product to the buyers, which is difficult since they are landlocked. Azerbaijan is hoping to complete a Southern Gas Corridor, a network of pipelines, between it and Europe. Kazakhstan is a corridor between the oil-rich Caspian Sea and China. China is seeking ways to gain the fuel it needs for its expanding industrial economy and to end its dependence on long ocean routes, so Kazakhstan is of great strategic importance. Kazakhstan has granted China sole rights to exploration and exploitation of oil along its border with the Caspian. The region could become a major battleground in the twenty-first century, as nations—including China—compete for the Caspian's oil wealth. In 2017 Uzbekistan devalued its currency to make it a more attractive trading partner. All these nations are heavily dependent on the money sent back from family members working abroad, called **remittances.**

Afghanistan's Economy

Afghanistan is the poorest of all these countries resulting from a weak government and lack of infrastructure. After 2001 there was an influx of foreign aid, and the economy grew artificially to support the 100,000 foreign troops stationed there. Much of that has ended. The major export of Afghanistan is opium, which is used to make heroin. In fact, Afghan farmers grew poppies in such large quantities they produced 90 percent of the world's opium and generated almost $7 billion in revenue, representing more than a third of the Afghan GDP in 2017. Despite concerted efforts to eradicate the crop, cultivation doubled from 2004 to 2017 and was present in all of the country's thirty-four provinces. As of 2019 the Afghan and American governments have yet to find an effective policy to combat this harmful practice. One method that has enjoyed limited success is showing the farmers the benefits of growing saffron, the most expensive spice in the world (averaging over $120 per ounce). Unlike opium, saffron has no narcotic value.

Demographics

The fertility/birthrates of these countries follow the pattern presented in previous chapters. Georgia and Armenia, being Christian and more "European," have negative population replacement rates. The Muslim and formerly Soviet states have higher rates, but because of the Russian influence, they rank in the middle compared to the rest of the world. Afghanistan has high fertility/birthrates.

The vast majority of the people of Afghanistan, Kyrgyzstan, and Tajikistan live in rural settings, and that is projected to be the case for the foreseeable future. The other countries in these regions have a slim majority living in urban areas. Azerbaijan is the most densely populated country, but none are very densely populated compared to the rest of the world. Uzbekistan is the most populous country in this region.

Afghanistan is the most ethnically diverse country of this chapter. Every other country has a majority ethnic group relating to its name along with a large minority of ethnic Russians and Koreans that Stalin forced to migrate there. Georgia is made up of a majority of Georgians, Kazakhstan is majority Kazakh, and so forth. But the mountains of Afghanistan harbor more than twenty ethnic groups, including Turkic, Mongol, Arab, Aryan, and Persian peoples. The two largest groups, the Pashtuns and Tajiks, constitute about three-quarters of the Afghan population. Southern Afghanistan and western Pakistan are the land of the Pashtuns, but an independent Pashtunistan has never been a reality. This is the home territory of the Taliban.

Each country has its official language, and Russian is spoken everywhere. The Central Asian languages are Turkic except for Pashto and Tajik, which are similar to Persian. The Georgian and Armenian languages and scripts are different from all other world languages. Georgian is the largest of the Kartvelian languages, which are not related to any other language tree. Armenian is its own branch of Indo-European.

Culture and Diversity

Pashtunwali is the strict ethical code of the Pashtuns; it predates Islam. The code includes eleven elements: hospitality, sanctuary, revenge, bravery, loyalty, righteousness, faith, respect, protection of women, honor, and country. The code means everything to Pashtuns, and they will go to great lengths to follow it. The idea of hospitality and sanctuary means more than just being friendly to guests. It means protecting them with your own life, if necessary. But acts of vengeance can go on for generations, and the protection of women can be taken to the extreme of locking them away.

Kyrgyz culture revolves around Manas, their national hero, whose story is told in the Epic of Manas, the longest epic poem in the world, which takes three days to recite. The poem is over a thousand years old and was passed down through "Manas-tellers" who memorized it. The poem was not written down until the 1920s.

▲ *(top) A young Azerbaijani girl from a village in the northern Caucasus*

▲ *(bottom) A young Kyrgyz in traditional clothes*

Uzbek plov is oiled rice with yellow carrots, quail, horse meat sausages, and shaved beef.

Kazakh horsemen playing Buzkashi

Khachapuri is a traditional Georgian food that consists of dough boats filled with sulguni cheese and egg.

A popular sport native to Central Asia is Buzkashi. It is a fierce game similar to polo in which two teams on horseback compete to get a goat carcass across their goal. Riders carry a whip to keep the opposing players and horses away. In former times riders would wear Soviet tank helmets for protection. The rules of the game have been codified in modern times, and there is a referee.

In the Caucasus, Armenians love chess and are known for being masters of the game. The small country has a disproportionate number of champions. New Year's is a favorite holiday in Armenia; celebrations go on for a week. People visit their families and neighbors and share traditional dishes. They also exchange gifts, usually fruits.

Major Religions of Caucasus and Central Asia

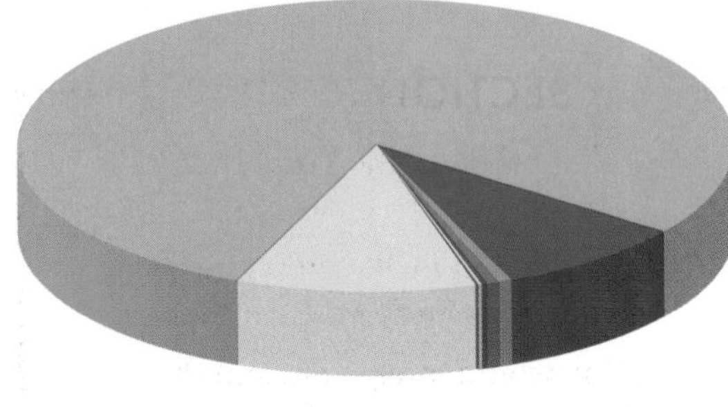

Religion	Percentage
Islamic	**79.0%**
Orthodox	**8.8%**
Roman Catholic	**0.5%**
Protestant Evangelical	**0.5%**
Protestant	**0.2%**
Buddhist	**0.1%**
Ethnic	**0.1%**
Unaffiliated	**10.8%**

Majority Orthodox: Armenia and Georgia
Majority Muslim: Azerbaijan, Afghanistan, Kazakhstan, Kyrgyzstan, Tajikistan, Turkmenistan, Uzbekistan

Religion

In the fourth century, Armenia became the first country in the world to officially adopt Christianity. The legacy of the Armenian Apostolic Church has endured for over seventeen hundred years. While many Armenians identify with the church for traditional reasons, a growing number of Armenians are embracing the truth of the gospel. There are more evangelical Christians here than in any other country in the Middle East or Central Asia. Christian Armenians are taking up the call to bring the gospel to their traditional enemies, the Turkish people. The Georgian Orthodox Church is a type of Eastern Orthodoxy. For many Georgians, membership in the Orthodox Church is a way to identify with their ancestors. As such, it is a form of patriotism rather than spiritual faith.

Sunni Islam is the religion of Central Asia, while Azerbaijan is majority Shia. For centuries this region was an important locale for Islamic study. For example, Samarkand, Uzbekistan, was the capital of a Muslim dynasty, the Samanids, and was second only to Mecca as an Islamic holy place. It still boasts Ulugh Beg Madrasa (an Islamic seminary), the oldest in Central Asia, dating from 1418. But during the twentieth century, all of that religious importance was suspended as the atheistic Soviet government restricted religion. Islam lost a lot of its influence, was forced out of the public square, and was mainly practiced at home. This history has given Islam in Central Asia a different complexion from that of the Middle East. The governments tend to be more secular, and the Arab Spring did not come here. This may change as the madrasas have reopened. The non-Muslim minorities have also diluted some of the influence of Islam. Islam in Afghanistan resembles that of the Middle East and Pakistan. A king ruled from 1933 to 1973, during which time the country was modernizing and becoming more secular. Not until the Soviets invaded was sharia law strictly enforced. Following the Soviet withdrawal, Islam became the only unifying force, and the most fervent students of that religion, the Taliban, took power.

▲ *A church service in the Astvatsatsin church of the Sevanavank monastery in Armenia*

One thing that has not changed in Central Asia is the persecution of Christians. Since Kyrgyzstan is more democratic, Christianity is allowed but is still looked down upon. The few Christians in Turkmenistan, Uzbekistan, and Afghanistan suffer tremendously for their faith. There are fewer than three thousand Afghani Christians. Central Asians equate ethnicity with religion, a common misconception worldwide. Ironically, because of this idea the Muslims thought their former Soviet persecutors were Christians. New archaeological discoveries are being used to prove that Christianity predated Islam in Central Asia, so the ethnic groups will understand their ancestors were not always Muslim.

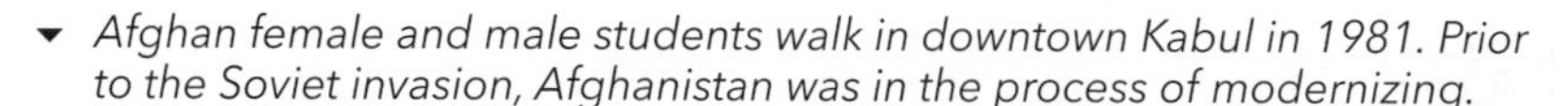

▼ *Afghan female and male students walk in downtown Kabul in 1981. Prior to the Soviet invasion, Afghanistan was in the process of modernizing.*

SECTION REVIEW

1. What product ruled trade across Central Asia?
2. What might be the difficulties of living in an enclave or exclave?
3. Why would foreign aid and the economic stimulus of the foreign soldiers not have helped the economy of Afghanistan for the long term?
4. Compare and contrast the religions and languages of Armenia and Ethiopia.
5. Which nation speaks a language closer to Iranian than to Turkish?
6. Evaluate Pashtunwali's positives and negatives.
7. How was the practice of Islam changed during the Soviet years?

GUIDING QUESTIONS

- How do the economies and demographics of the Caucasus and Central Asia affect how the citizens interact with the environment?
- What are the environmental issues of the Caucasus and Central Asia?
- What are the causes and effects of environmental issues in the Caucasus and Central Asia?
- What are possible solutions to environmental issues in the Caucasus and Central Asia?

INTERACTIONS OF PEOPLE AND PLACES

What are some of the challenges of living in the Caucasus and Central Asia?

Many of the people in these regions live as they have for centuries, close to nature and familiar with the natural rhythms that God instituted. The people of the Talysh Mountains in Azerbaijan are famously known for living very long lives. They credit the mountain air, temperate climate, and diet. Their diet consists of many fruits and vegetables, yogurt, and fermented goat milk. Generally they abstain from drinking alcohol or smoking. All these countries have paid a huge price for the forced industrialization during the Soviet years. The problems are similar to those of Eastern Europe. Central Asia has some of the most unusual and surreal environmental problems in the world, including a burning gas crater in Darvaza, Turkmenistan, called the "door to hell." There are also lakes created by exploding nuclear bombs.

▲ *Caucasians are known for living long. Antisa Khvichava, a Georgian woman, was purported to be the oldest person in the world at age 130 on July 8, 2010.*

Interaction with the Environment

Water

Water is more precious in Central Asia since it is not evenly distributed among the different regions. The mountains have plentiful amounts of water, while the drier steppe and desert countries have an abundant supply of fossil fuels but no water. The two areas meet at the Aral Sea, which is 10 percent of its former size and is considered by many to be one of the greatest environmental disasters in history. The loss of income and productivity has devastated the region around the Aral Sea. Since water is depleted, the salt in the seabed gets picked up by the wind and contaminates wherever it gets blown, causing desertification and respiratory problems for the people. Though the Caspian Sea is not being depleted as much as the Aral, it

▼ *(left to right) Satellite views of the Aral Sea in 2000, 2008, and 2018*

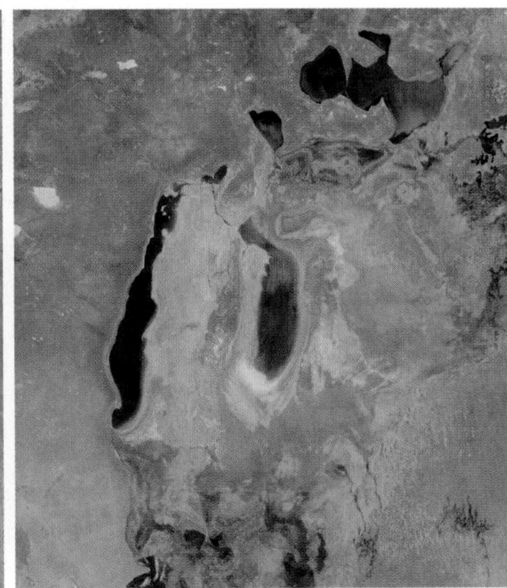

also has serious problems. It is polluted by industrial and municipal wastewater. Another source of pollution is the chemical waste and oil spills from offshore and onshore oil extraction. In the mountains the people use the river water that their herds have contaminated with their waste.

Air

Baku, Azerbaijan, and Almaty, Kazakhstan, have the unfortunate distinction of being some of the most polluted cities in the world. The people in the rural areas heat their homes with coal-burning stoves since electricity is unreliable. These home stoves do not cause huge amounts of smog, but the indoor pollution is hazardous for children, especially.

▲ *Baku, Azerbaijan, is one of the most polluted cities in the world.*

Land

The Polygon, near Semey, Kazakhstan, was the Soviet Union's primary nuclear weapons testing location from 1949 to 1989. The place was chosen because Moscow claimed it was uninhabited. Unfortunately, they were off by one and a half million people. There were 456 nuclear explosions here. In the early days the people would be instructed to go outside when the bombs went off. They did not realize that they were test subjects for the effects of radiation on humans. In a program called "Nuclear Explosions for the National Economy," bombs were exploded for mining projects and to create reservoirs. The bombs were most effective in extinguishing oil well fires. Children in the region are born with birth defects, and the people living here still do not understand the seriousness of the issue, partly because there is no exclusion zone like there is in Chernobyl. People eat fish from the lake created by the explosion, waters that are heavily irradiated. Afghanistan is littered with land mines, estimated to be as many as 640,000. As in other areas of the world, wild animals are endangered in these regions, particularly the snow leopards, whose numbers are estimated to be less than 500.

▲ A gas crater in Darvaza, Turkmenistan, called the "door to hell"

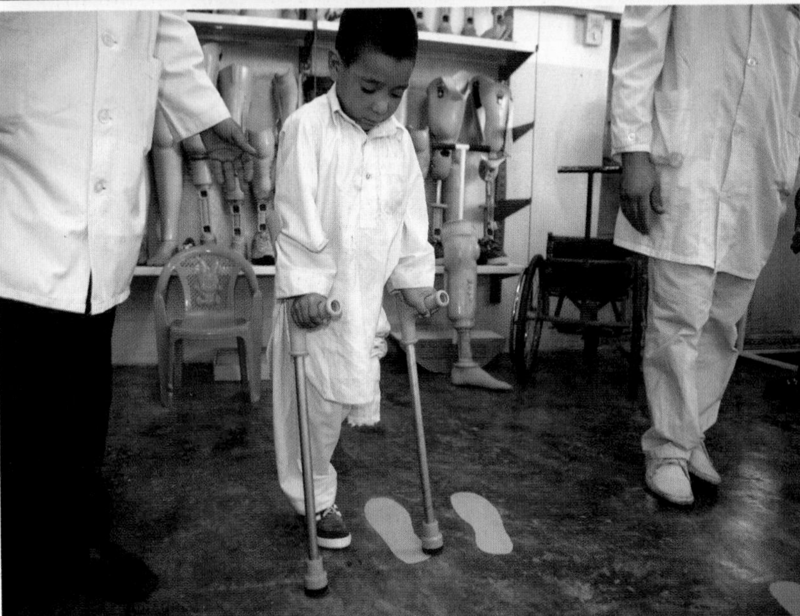

▲ A young land mine victim receives physiotherapy at the International Red Cross Orthopedic Rehabilitation Center in Kabul, Afghanistan.

Reasons for Environmental Issues

The Aral Sea dried up because the Soviets diverted the Syr Darya River in the 1960s, a river that had flowed into the Aral Sea. They did so to use the water to irrigate the cotton fields. Like the Caspian Sea to the west, the Aral Sea was a salt lake with no outlet to the ocean. Although it was once the world's fourth-largest lake, diverting the water flowing into the lake reduced it to a tiny fraction of its former size. The declining waters of the Aral Sea left salt deposits as they evaporated, and crop production has dramatically fallen as the soil quality in the area has deteriorated.

Baku and Almaty are so polluted because they are centers of oil and natural gas production, but companies show little concern for the environment, even allowing for oil spills. The burning gas crater in Darvaza, Turkmenistan, is the result of scientists lighting the crater in 1971 to dissipate methane. They thought it would burn for only a couple of days.

International organizations have been able to find and remove 80 percent of the land mines left by the Soviets in their pre-2001 war. The mines left by the Taliban fighters after 2001 are more difficult to find and are also more dangerous. From 1979 to 2018, over 31,000 people were killed or injured by land mines.

Snow leopard in the mountains of Kyrgyzstan

Proposed Solutions

The Kazakh government and the World Bank teamed up to build a dam and dike system on the Syr Darya River in 2005 called the Kokaral Dam. The $86 million project aimed to restore the North Aral Sea, which has just begun to show positive effects from the dam. There has been an 18 percent increase in fish, and there is decreased salinity. Kazakhstan is looking to begin phase II in 2020, hoping to reunite one of the port cities with the sea. Some people who are aware of the issue with the Aral Sea are boycotting cotton grown in Uzbekistan. Russia, Kazakhstan, and the United States began cleanup of Polygon test site in secret in 1995. It took seventeen years to complete and cost $150 million dollars. To help protect and restore the number of snow leopards, Kyrgyz park rangers use motion detection cameras in the mountains.

SECTION REVIEW

1. What do environmental issues in these regions reveal about how the governmental leadership can affect the environment?
2. Why might the Kazakh locals not take the problem of irradiated land and water seriously?
3. Why do you suppose the countries continued to drain the Aral Sea after it began to shrink?
4. Why would the United States be interested in investing millions in the cleanup of the Polygon, and why would they do it secretly?
5. What environmental solutions would you propose, after considering the problems as a whole?

The Kokaral Dam in Kazakhstan was built to save the North Aral Sea.

18 CHAPTER REVIEW

SUMMARY

1. The three Caucasus countries sit in the mountains between the Black and Caspian Seas. Central Asia is made up of mountain, steppe, and desert regions. There are three inland seas in these regions. The general climate is continental. These regions are mineral rich, and the area around the Caspian Sea has fossil fuel deposits.

2. These countries occupied a major trade route between China and Rome called the Silk Road. They were a part of the Soviet Union during the twentieth century, while Afghanistan was occupied by the Soviet Union in the 1980s. The governments are authoritarian. These countries depend on exporting their natural mineral wealth. Every country except Afghanistan has a majority ethnic group. Armenia and Georgia are Christian, while all the other countries are Muslim.

3. These countries are home to some of greatest environmental disasters in the world, the two worst being the depletion of the Aral Sea and the radioactive contamination around Semey, Kazakhstan. Oil extraction without concern for the environment is a problem. There are efforts to replenish the North Aral Sea as well as an international effort to clean up the nuclear waste.

Terms to Know

- ❑ steppes
- ❑ Silk Road
- ❑ enclaves
- ❑ exclaves
- ❑ autonomous regions
- ❑ buffer state
- ❑ Taliban
- ❑ remittances

Making Connections

1. What role did the Silk Road play in Central Asia in the past? What caused this route to become insignificant?
2. Which group left the longest-lasting impact on Central Asia: Huns, Turkic peoples or Mongols?
3. Compare and contrast the demographic issues of Afghanistan with those of the Balkans.
4. What is the difference between an autonomous region and an exclave?
5. Why do Afghani farmers grow opium?
6. What are ways that the Soviet Union affected this area economically and environmentally?

Developing Geography Skills

1. Looking at the map on page 407, identify what is unique about Uzbekistan's geographical situation.
2. Why could the Caspian region become a battleground in Central Asia? What countries are likely to become involved should a conflict occur?

Thinking Critically

1. With your current understanding of the complexities of Afghanistan, what solutions would you propose to bring peace and stability to the country?
2. What are two conditions common among Christians in Central Asia?

Living in God's World

1. What were the specific cases of corruption mentioned in this chapter, and how should we respond to these incidents of corruption from a biblical worldview?
2. What are some specific ways that Scripture enables Christians to endure persecution without rejecting their faith in Christ?

CASE STUDY | Education in Afghanistan and Central Asia

▲ *Girls attend a class on the Qur'an at the Speena Adi school in Afghanistan.*

"What do you want to do when you grow up?" This is a common question for children around the world, but not in some rural parts of Central Asia and all of Afghanistan, especially for girls since the answer is obvious. Girls have fewer educational opportunities for multiple reasons. The strictest religious leaders teach that girls only need to learn some verses from the Qur'an. Since schools cost money and these areas are very poor, parents often cannot afford to educate their daughters, who are going to just get married anyway. The quality of education is poor, especially in Afghanistan. In the public schools the teachers barely know how to read and write themselves. Traveling great distances in Afghanistan is dangerous for females, so unless the school is nearby, parents do not allow their daughters to walk to school. Literacy rates here are extremely low, with only 52 percent males and 24 percent of females being able to read in 2015. Compare these numbers to those of Kazakhstan, where 99.8 percent of both males and females are literate. In Afghanistan only 15 percent of girls study past fifth grade. In spite of having extremely low quality facilities and teachers, students still desire to go to school and overcome every hindrance to do so.

1. Why do both girls and boys have limited opportunities in Afghanistan particularly?
2. Considering what you read in Chapter 10 about many "-stan" countries not allowing head coverings in school, why do you think countries would not want the girls to wear the hijab in school?
3. What might be the effect of increased literacy percentages in Afghanistan?

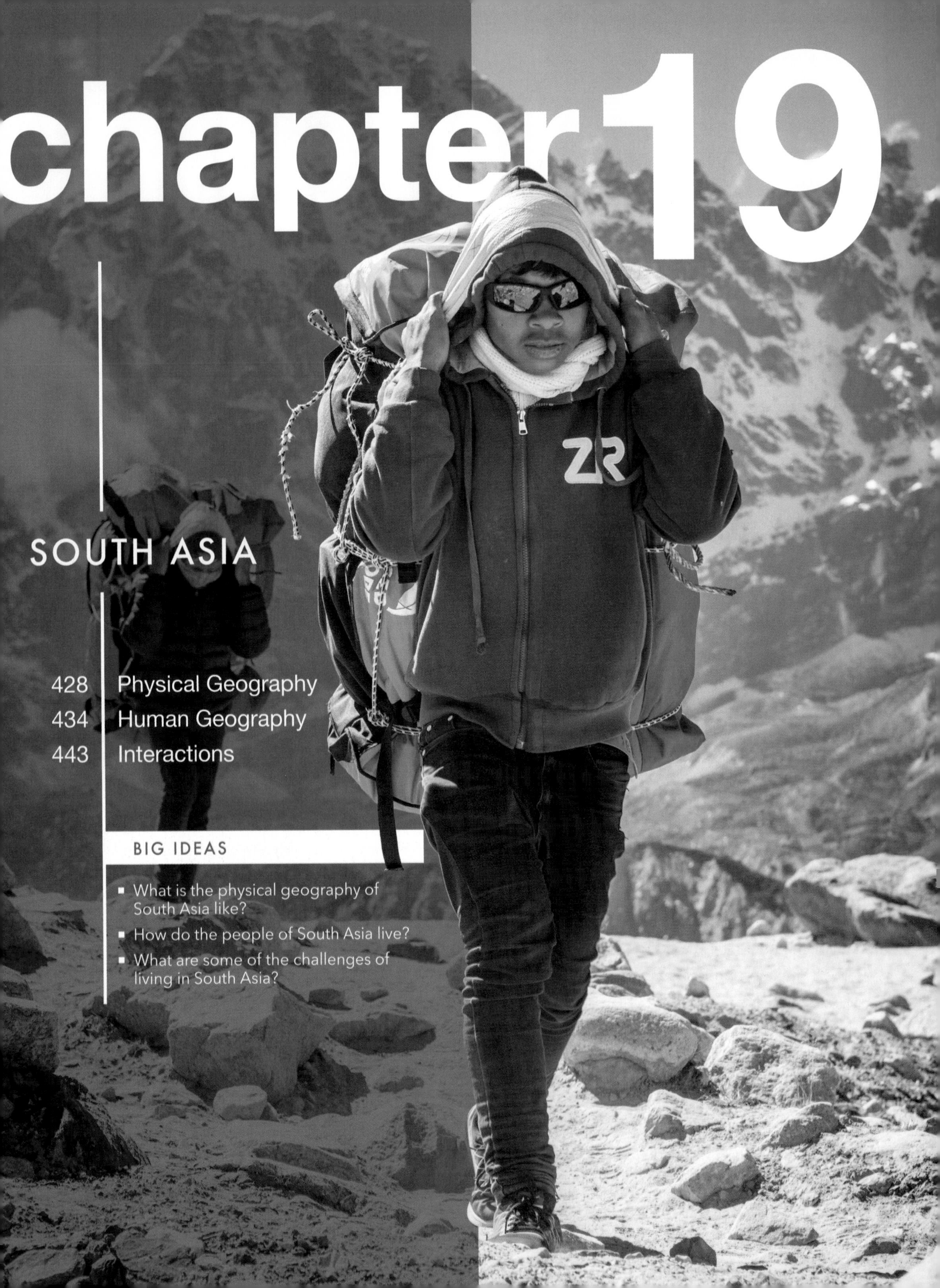

chapter 19

SOUTH ASIA

428 Physical Geography
434 Human Geography
443 Interactions

BIG IDEAS

- What is the physical geography of South Asia like?
- How do the people of South Asia live?
- What are some of the challenges of living in South Asia?

▲ *The Taj Mahal*

▼ *The Pink Palace in Bangladesh*

◀ *Sherpa porters on the Ngozumpa Glacier in Nepal*

CROWN OF THE PALACES

Travel in your mind with me to one of the most beautiful structures ever built by man, the Taj Mahal. *Taj Mahal* is Hindi for "Crown of the Palaces." We would travel to India to see this amazing tribute built by Mughal ruler Shah Jahan as a resting place for his favorite wife, Mumtaz Mahal. She died during the delivery of their fourteenth child.

Constructed of white marble, this huge structure reaches a height of 155 feet at the top of the dome and has a garden and reflecting pool on the grounds around the building. About 22,000 workers labored to construct this magnificent structure, and 1,000 elephants were used to transport the building materials to the 42-acre site along the Yamuna River. Four functioning minarets frame the tomb and rise to a height of 130 feet. They were built far enough from the tomb to avoid damaging the main structure in the event of their collapse.

Decorations inside the tomb include intricate calligraphy of Persian poetry, carvings of flowers in the marble walls, and large quantities of inlaid precious and semiprecious stones. Floors are tiled in a variety of geometric patterns.

In 1983 the Taj Mahal was declared a UNESCO World Heritage Site and is considered one of the finest examples of Mughal architecture in the world. Between seven and eight million people visit this site every year.

▲ *Vendors selling fresh vegetables at Lea Market in Karachi, Pakistan*

South Asia is an exotic region of contrasts between wealth and poverty, high culture and paganism, insurmountable peaks and broad river plains. Mountains and deserts have long isolated this region from the West, creating distinct differences in culture and history. South Asia is separated from the rest of Asia by the formidable Himalayas on the north and by the Indian Ocean on the south.

GUIDING QUESTIONS

- What are the regions of South Asia?
- What caused the landforms of South Asia?
- What bodies of water are important to South Asia?
- What are the climates of South Asia?
- What natural resources are found in South Asia?

PHYSICAL GEOGRAPHY

Regions of South Asia

What is the physical geography of South Asia like?

South Asia is classified as a subcontinent. A **subcontinent is** a large landform that is bigger than a peninsula and smaller than a continent. India covers most of the subcontinent of South Asia and has geographical forms that vary from towering mountains to a vast plateau, river valleys, coastal plains, and the Great Indian Desert. While India by far has the largest area, several other South Asia countries, including tiny Nepal, have a variety of landforms varying from lowlands to hills and mountains. Nepal and Bhutan are distinguished by being landlocked nations with no access to the Arabian Sea or the Indian Ocean.

Nepal's Mount Everest, at 29,029 feet, is the tallest mountain above sea level in the world. Given the ongoing pressure between the Indian and Eurasian plates, this mountain continues to rise. Everest's height was listed as 29,028 feet in the previous edition of this text.

Water has been a scarce resource in many of the countries discussed in previous chapters. However, other than in desert regions, water is abundant in South Asia due to snow and glacial melting and seasonal rains that inundate much of the region. Many important rivers flow across this region and provide vital moisture for agriculture to support the 1.76 billion people who live there.

▾ *The Deccan Plateau in India*

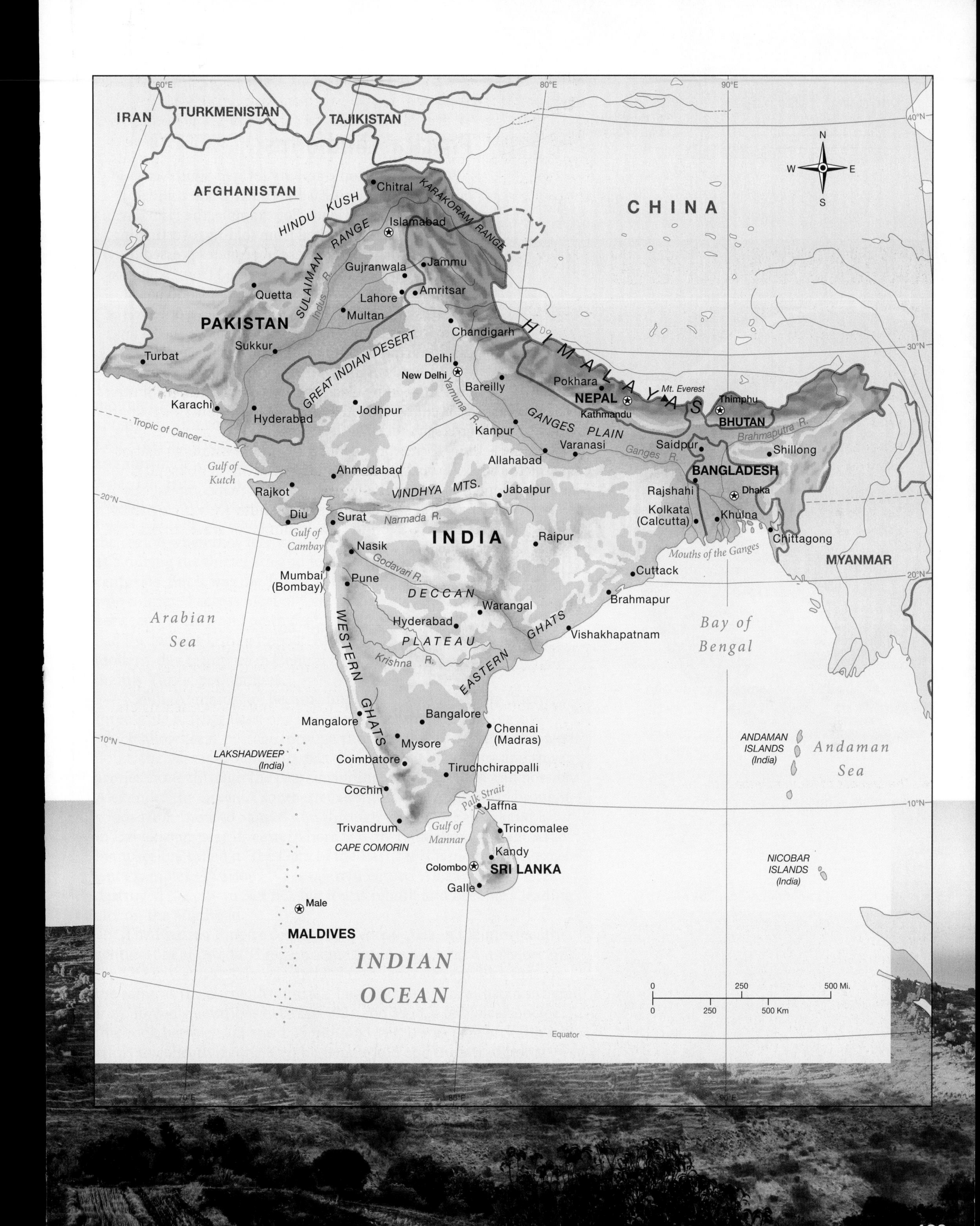

IRAN
TURKMENISTAN
TAJIKISTAN
AFGHANISTAN
CHINA
PAKISTAN
INDIA
NEPAL
BHUTAN
BANGLADESH
MYANMAR
SRI LANKA
MALDIVES
HINDU KUSH
KARAKORAM RANGE
SULAIMAN RANGE
HIMALAYAS
GREAT INDIAN DESERT
GANGES PLAIN
VINDHYA MTS.
DECCAN PLATEAU
WESTERN GHATS
EASTERN GHATS
Chitral
Islamabad
Jammu
Gujranwala
Lahore
Amritsar
Quetta
Multan
Chandigarh
Sukkur
Turbat
Delhi
New Delhi
Bareilly
Pokhara
Kathmandu
Mt. Everest
Thimphu
Karachi
Hyderabad
Jodhpur
Kanpur
Varanasi
Allahabad
Saidpur
Shillong
Ahmedabad
Rajkot
Jabalpur
Rajshahi
Dhaka
Kolkata (Calcutta)
Khulna
Chittagong
Diu
Surat
Raipur
Nasik
Mumbai (Bombay)
Pune
Cuttack
Brahmapur
Warangal
Hyderabad
Vishakhapatnam
Bangalore
Mangalore
Chennai (Madras)
Mysore
Coimbatore
Tiruchchirappalli
Cochin
Jaffna
Trivandrum
Trincomalee
Kandy
Colombo
Galle
Male
CAPE COMORIN
LAKSHADWEEP (India)
ANDAMAN ISLANDS (India)
NICOBAR ISLANDS (India)
Indus R.
Yamuna R.
Ganges R.
Brahmaputra R.
Narmada R.
Godavari R.
Krishna R.
Tropic of Cancer
Gulf of Kutch
Gulf of Cambay
Mouths of the Ganges
Palk Strait
Gulf of Mannar
Arabian Sea
Bay of Bengal
Andaman Sea
INDIAN OCEAN
Equator
60°E
80°E
90°E
40°N
30°N
20°N
10°N
0°
N
S
E
W
0
250
500 Mi.
500 Km

◂ *Panoramic view of Ella Rock in Ella, Sri Lanka*

Physical Landforms

Massive tectonic activity formed South Asia's northern boundaries as the Indian Plate collided with the Eurasian Plate. For example, the Himalayan Mountain range resulted from folding, overturning, and over-thrusting as these huge plates pressed together. The **Deccan Plateau** resulted from extensive volcanic activity that spread a layer of flood basalt across much of the land. The plains developed as the many rivers in South Asia deposited layer upon layer of silt during flooding.

Mountains and valleys in this region have also been shaped by glacier activity. For example, Bhutan's physical geography is characterized by high, steep mountains that are divided by swift rivers and deep valleys.

Volcanic activity formed the submarine mountain range that became the Maldives. From these mountains nearly two thousand coral islands developed, as well as the twenty-six atolls that comprise the Maldives. With an average height of just under five feet above sea level, these islands have little protection against storms or wave surges.

▴ *The summit of Mount Everest, the highest mountain in the world*

▾ *Aerial view of Villivaru in South Male Atoll, Maldives*

▾ *Aerial view of the Maldives capital, Malé*

Indian Hindus bathing and worshiping on the banks of the Ganges in Haridwar, India

The Ganges River flowing through a Himalayan mountain range

Bodies of Water

In addition to access to the Arabian Sea and the Indian Ocean, South Asia has a vast series of rivers for transportation, irrigation, and hydropower. Many large cities in this region, including the national capitals, are located near a river. Some of the rivers are well known, such as the Ganges River, which flows through India and Bangladesh to the Bay of Bengal, and the Indus River, which traverses Pakistan and empties into the Arabian Sea.

Another significant river is the Brahmaputra, which originates in Tibet and flows into eastern India and Bangladesh before reaching the Bay of Bengal, a distance of at least 1,800 miles. The Yamuna River is the longest tributary river, originating in the Yamunotri Glacier and eventually merging with the Ganges River. The Godavari and Krishna Rivers begin in western India and cross the lower region of India to reach the Bay of Bengal along the eastern coast, covering nearly 900 miles.

Om Tsho Lake in Bhutan

Several rivers combine with the Indus as it extends the length of Pakistan. This river stretches nearly 1,800 miles before it empties into a delta near the Tropic of Cancer.

Nepal and Bhutan have several rivers that originate in the mountains and flow down to the Ganges Plain. In addition, Bhutan has over 2,600 glacial lakes that drain into rivers. Bhutan also has an unusual threat in the form of GLOFs (global lake outburst floods), which are due to the periodic collapse of walls of ice or sediment that hold these lakes in place high up in the mountains. When the restraints collapse, villages below are in danger of deadly flooding and have only minutes to evacuate. Many of the rivers in these countries are also sources of hydropower as they rush down the mountains.

Satellite image of the Ganges River delta

Bangladesh both profits and suffers from its rivers. Though they provide abundant water and rich soil, the rivers also experience frequent flooding that can wash away crops, homes, and anything else that is located on this floodplain.

Sri Lanka is an island nation with over one hundred rivers and over forty estuaries. This island also has nearly four dozen lagoons.

Monsoons in India

- **Northeast** (winter)
- **Southwest** (summer)
- **Intertropical Convergence Zone** (in June/July)

AFGHANISTAN, PAKISTAN, CHINA, NEPAL, BHUTAN, BANGLADESH, MYANMAR, INDIA, Arabian Sea, Mouths of the Ganges, Bay of Bengal, ANDAMAN ISLANDS, Andaman Sea, Palk Strait, Gulf of Mannar, SRI LANKA, INDIAN OCEAN, NICOBAR ISLANDS, Laccadive Sea, MALDIVES, INDONESIA, 15°, 75°, 90°, N, S, E, W, 0, 200, 400 Mi., 200, 400 Km

Climates of South Asia

The Himalayas dominate the weather system of the region. Because the cold air north of the mountains cannot rise over them to spill into South Asia, the cold temperatures do not reach into the subcontinent. As the summer heat rises in the south, a low-pressure system results, drawing warm, moist air from the Indian Ocean in the form of winds called monsoons. A **monsoon** is a wind that changes direction with the seasons. South Asia has the strongest monsoon winds in the world. The Himalayas cause the airborne moisture to fall as rain. Eighty percent of India's total rainfall comes during the four-month monsoon season. A reverse monsoon pushes cool, dry winds across the mountains into South Asia, causing a dry season. Some islands escape the dry season because the ocean provides moisture regardless of wind direction.

The monsoon rains begin in June or July and supply the rain necessary for the agriculture on which all South Asian countries depend. If the monsoons come late or with too little rain, the plants wither and die. If the rains are early or cause floods, the rice rots. Either way, the subcontinent often experiences famine since it is largely a subsistence economy.

The Jumna River near Agra (with the Taj Mahal in the background) during a dry monsoon

Traffic in India during a wet monsoon

Resources of South Asia

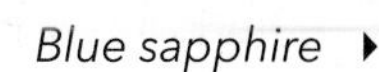

Blue sapphire ▸

India, Pakistan, and Bangladesh have reserves of petroleum and natural gas. India and Pakistan also have supplies of uranium and coal. Other resources include copper, iron ore, timber, and limestone. These nations have fish and other marine resources. Sri Lanka also has gemstones, such as sapphire and beryl.

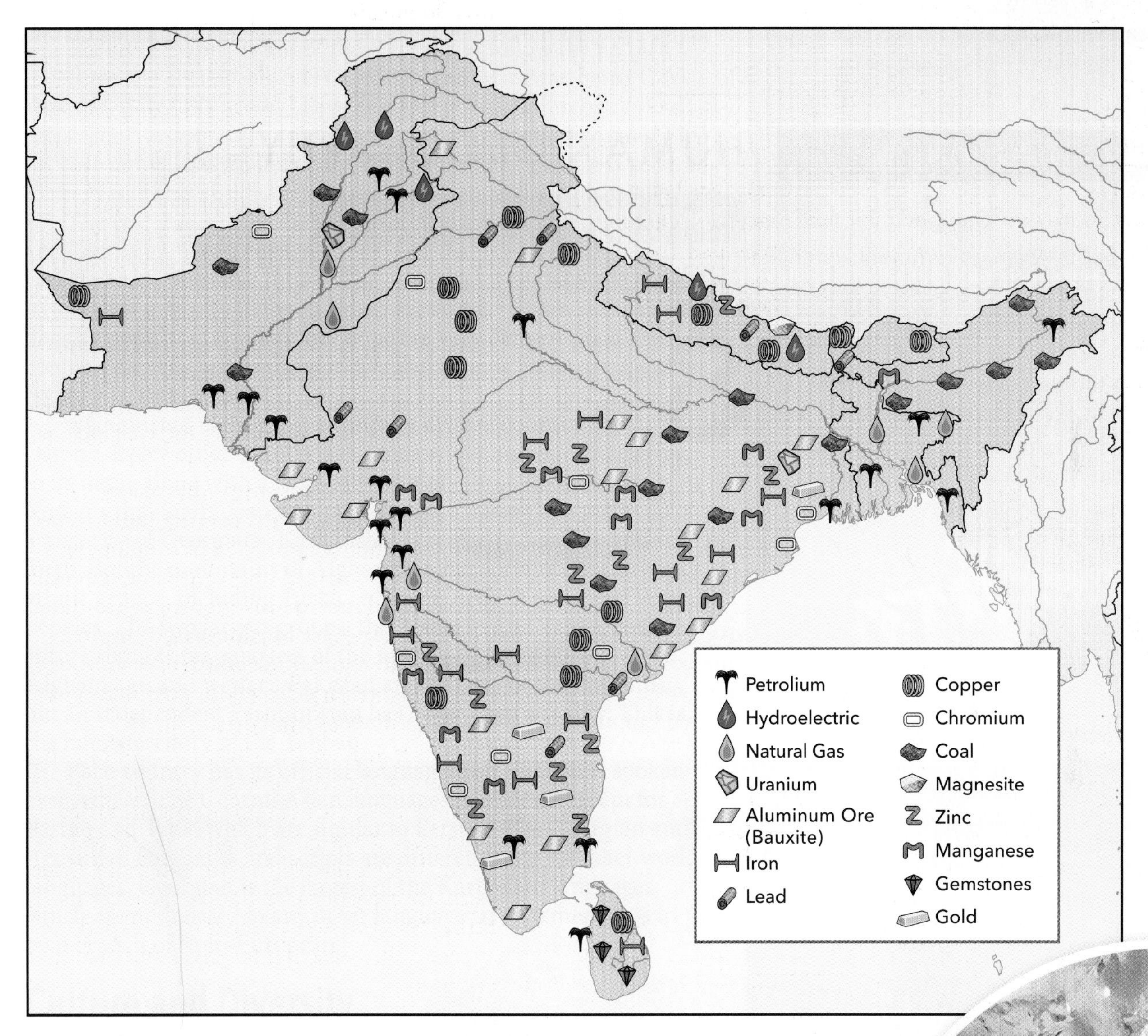

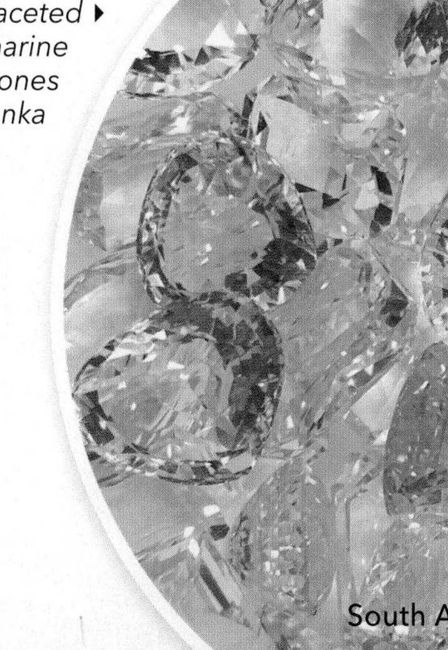
Faceted aquamarine beryl gemstones from Sri Lanka ▸

SECTION REVIEW

1. Between which two major lines of latitude does most of South Asia lie?
2. Why are the Ganges and Indus Rivers so important to South Asia?
3. How does South Asia's location on the globe affect its climate?
4. What resource that can be used for energy or weapons is abundant in some South Asian nations?
5. What other resources are abundant in South Asia?

1200 1300 1400 1500

ca. 3000 BC Settled after the Flood

ca. 2300 BC Asian civilizations flourish

ca. 1500 BC Aryan invasion

322–185 BC Mauryan Empire

AD 320 Gupta Empire established

1206–1526 Delhi Sultanate

GUIDING QUESTIONS

- How has South Asia changed over time?
- How do South Asian governments interact with their citizens?
- What is the economic health of South Asia?
- What are the demographics of South Asia?
- What are the cultural characteristics and diversity in South Asia?
- What forms of religion are practiced in South Asia?

HUMAN GEOGRAPHY

How do the people of South Asia live?

History

South Asia was settled as early as 3000 BC, and evidence for cities and kingdoms can be traced back to about 2300 BC. When the Maldives was originally settled remains a mystery, but there is evidence of Buddhists inhabiting these islands by the fifth century BC.

About 1500 BC a group known as Aryans invaded India and seized control. In 322 BC the Indians established the first Indian empire, the **Mauryan Empire**, which endured until 185 BC. Following a period of turmoil, the Gupta Empire emerged by AD 320 and led India into a period of prosperity that lasted until a Muslim invasion and the rise of the Delhi Sultanate in 1206. Another Muslim-based empire emerged as the **Mughal Empire** and maintained power over most of India from 1526 to 1858, when the British defeated the remnants of the Mughal Empire during the Age of Imperialism.

Lahore Gate at the Red Fort in Old Delhi, India

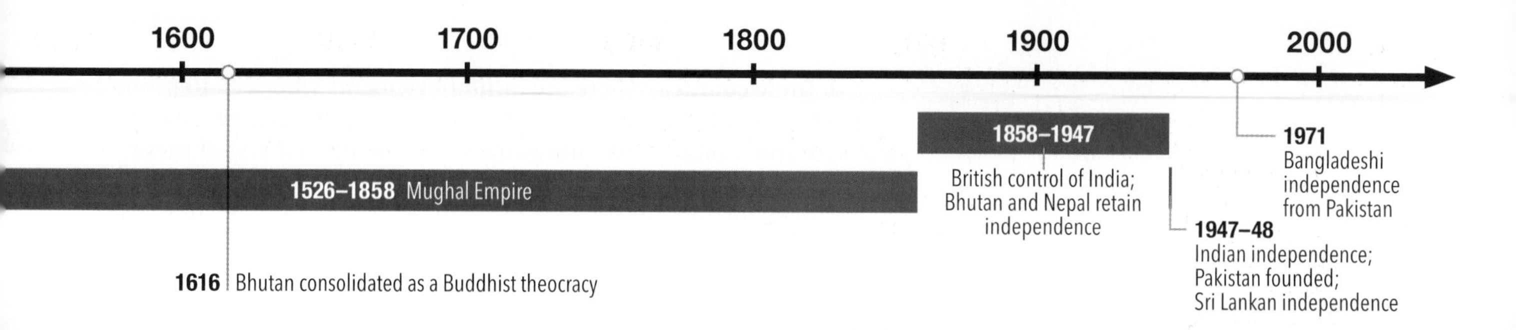

Britain maintained control of India, Sri Lanka, and the Maldives until after World War II. Indian resistance to British control had grown under the leadership of Mahatma Gandhi and others, who advocated passive resistance against British rule. **Passive resistance** is a means of achieving goals using protests, civil disobedience, and economic or political noncooperation. By 1947 India's demand for independence triumphed, and the British granted this nation independent status. From two regions in India the British created Pakistan to provide a homeland for Indian Muslims. Following three wars between the two regions of Pakistan, the eastern region gained its independence and became the nation of Bangladesh in 1971.

Nepal and Bhutan formed various kingdoms and dynasties through the centuries. During the *Age of Imperialism*, when many nations lost their freedom to Europeans, Nepal and Bhutan retained their independence and escaped colonial status. Nepal underwent a revolution in 1951 and a civil war beginning in 1997 that lasted for nine years. In 2006 the monarchy was abolished, and the assembly declared Nepal a democratic republic in 2008.

Bhutan's government was a Buddhist theocracy from 1616 to 1907, when a hereditary monarchy was formed. Successive rulers sought to modernize Bhutan, and international relationships developed beginning in the 1950s. Recently, Bhutan has opened its land to the world and is transitioning into a modern country.

▲ *Mohandas "Mahatma" Gandhi, leader of the Indian independence movement in British-ruled India, circa 1947*

Government

Thanks in large part to Britain's influence on this region, all of the South Asian governments are representative, and the people have the right to elect their leaders. All of the countries except Nepal have *parliamentary democracies* as their form of government. Nepal differs slightly by calling their government a *federal parliamentary republic*.

Government Interactions with Its Citizens

Forms of government that are similar in name do not always result in comparable levels of stability or equal protection of citizens. South Asian countries have enjoyed independence or a modern form of government for less than a century, and some for less than twenty years. Several of these governments struggle to represent their people in a way that commands respect for elected officials and demonstrates equality for all citizens regardless of ethnicity, religious preference, or social status.

In these countries there are militant elements who seek to promote their views while opposing, sometimes violently, the choices of others. For example, communism has gained a following in many of these countries, and its proponents have carried out various schemes to gain control of governments or destabilize the governments in power. Political corruption also plagues some of these countries, and public resources are misused for personal gain.

Education and Health Care

Educational opportunities vary among the South Asian nations. Some of the variables include urban versus rural and male versus female.

Given India's vast population and extreme range of economic levels, it has perhaps made the most significant improvements in its educational system. While most of India's children attend public school, a growing number of children are attending private schools. The current ratio of public to private education is seven to five, or seven public schools for every five private schools. Private education is increasing due to the superior quality of education offered in these schools and the growing wealth of Indian families who can now afford to pay for private education. This challenge to public education has forced educators to improve the historically weak performance of many public schools in India.

▲ *Indian students participating in an online classroom at a government school in Ahmedabad, India*

Education in Pakistan, Nepal, Bhutan, and Bangladesh varies based on the school's location in an urban or rural setting. Education for girls in rural areas tends to be of lower quality, and the drop-out rate tends to be higher for female students.

Health care in South Asia varies from universal in Sri Lanka and Bhutan to minimal in Bangladesh and the Maldives. The national government in India has assigned the responsibility for health care to the state governments. India's health care is free and subsidized for the poor, but its public health care is of very poor quality in comparison to private care. Pakistan and Nepal's health care varies dramatically in urban and rural regions, and there is a shortage of health workers in Pakistan. Most patients in Bangladesh pay for their own medical treatment.

Economies

South Asian economies are a mixture of agriculture, industry, textiles, and tourism. India, Nepal, and the Maldives have mixed economies. Pakistan, Bhutan, Bangladesh and Sri Lanka have free-market economies. All of these countries would be classified as developing economies, although India and Pakistan are also considered semi-industrialized.

The economies of South Asia differ significantly in size. The GDPs in 2017 varied from the Maldives's $6.9 billion to India's $9.5 trillion. The size of the workforce in each country varied from the Maldives' 222,000 workers to India's 522 million. With a combined workforce of 679 million people, South Asia is poised to play a significant role in the manufacture of the world's goods.

While agriculture remains a major element of many South Asian economies, the percentage of people employed in agriculture in 2017 varied from 42 percent in Pakistan and Bangladesh to 69 percent in Nepal. In many countries the percentage of workers in the services sector is growing, and the Maldives has the highest at nearly 70 percent. Increasing tourism industries in Bhutan, Sri Lanka, and the Maldives will play a significant role in the growth of service industry jobs.

Long bands of Indian textiles that are about 1500 feet long ▸

▾ *Weaver in a Pakistani cottage industry*

▴ *Tamil women picking tea leaves in Sri Lanka*

◂ *People climbing on the rock formation known as the Lions Gate of the Sigiriya Rock Fortress in Sri Lanka*

A crowded street in Delhi, India

Demographics

In 2017 the combined estimated population of South Asia was 1.76 billion. The country in this region with the largest population was India, with 1.34 billion. The country with the smallest population was the tiny island nation of the Maldives, with 436,330.

South Asian countries have sustainable birth rates that vary from a low of 15.5/1000 in Sri Lanka to a high of 22.3/1000 in Pakistan. The percentage of the population under the age of twenty-five varies from 18 percent in Sri Lanka to 27 percent in Pakistan. Nepal is a close second, with 26 percent of its population below the age of twenty-five. India's huge population means that over 321 million people are under this age even though its percentage is a mere 24 percent.

Most countries in this region are ethnically diverse. In sheer numbers most South Asians are of Indo-Aryan descent, although the many other ethnic groups include Punjab, Pashtun, Bengali, and Sinhalese. Some of these groups can trace their heritage back over thirty-five hundred years. For example, nearly 75 percent of Indians are descendants of those who merged from the intermarrying of the first Indians and the Aryan invaders around 1500 BC. While 98 percent of the people of Bangladesh are ethnic Bengali, there is also a tiny minority of other groups who have settled in this country.

Mutton (lamb) biryani in authentic copper serving ware with salad (raita), gravy, and eggs

Culture and Diversity

South Asia is a blend of many cultures that have continued for three millenia. Many languages and cultural distinctives are found in this region. South Asian people celebrate their culture and diversity in many ways, including music, dance, and ethnic foods. For most cultures in South Asia, the extended family is also central to South Asian society.

Food, Dance, and Sports

Common meals in South Asia include staple items such as rice, vegetables, and chicken. Many of the favorite meals in Pakistan start with chicken. For a different menu one could travel to Bangladesh, where the meat choices include chicken, beef, fish, goat, duck, and pigeon. While it might sound strange to many in the West, people in South Asia refer to sweets or desserts as *sweetmeats*.

Handheld portion of papri chat

Mixed dish of Pakistani sweets

▲ (top left) Indian women performing a traditional dance

▲ (top right) A Black Hat dancer at a monastery in Bhutan

◀ The Puneri Paltan (white) and Jaipur Pink Panthers (pink) in competition during a Pro Kabaddi League match in Jaipur, India (2019)

Popular sports include badminton, soccer, volleyball, basketball, and various water sports (in the Maldives). Unlike many other countries, soccer is not the favorite sport in any of the South Asian countries. The British influence surfaces in the sport of cricket, which is popular in some countries in this region. Rugby is also popular in Sri Lanka. Bhutan is unusual in that its favorite sport is archery.

Perhaps the most popular game in South Asia is Kabaddi, a contact team sport played on a court with two teams of seven players. The goal is for a member of one team, a raider, to cross the line approaching the opposing team and try to tag as many members of that team as possible without being tackled. In some forms of this sport, the raider must accomplish this and return to his side of the court in a single breath. This game can be played inside or outside, and the court can be rectangular or circular. This is the national sport in Bangladesh and is also popular in India and Pakistan.

Multi-generational family in Pakistan

Family

The extended or joint family has been the building block of South Asian nations for many centuries. These family units tend to be multi-generational and ruled by a patriarch. As these nations become more urbanized, extended families tend to be diminished and live in their own homes rather than in a family compound.

Religion

Hindu tradition assigns people to different classes, each with its own privileges and responsibilities but also limitations. Each class, called a **caste**, strictly determines its members' social status. According to the Hindu caste system, a Hindu must fulfill his or her role. Brahmins (priests and teachers) and Ksatriyas (rulers and warriors) occupy the highest castes. Merchants, skilled craftsmen (artisans), and farmers—the Vaisyas—belong to the midlevel caste. Sudras (unskilled laborers) are the lowest caste. Some despised occupations, such as tanners and garbage collectors, are considered so low that they are beneath caste. They are called "**untouchables**" and make up approximately one-sixth of the Indian population.

Today, the basic castes are divided into hundreds of subcastes, called *jatis*. A Hindu is born into the jati of his parents, and he will be pressured to marry someone from that jati. He will also be expected to hold an appropriate occupation, with scant hope of changing his caste. The system allows for little, if any, upward mobility in society.

Religions of India

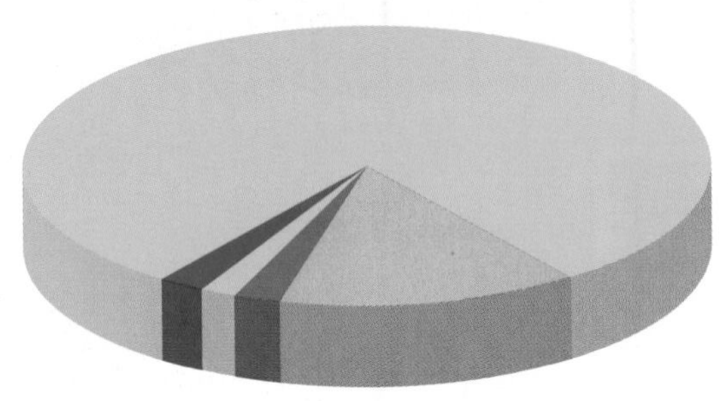

Hindu	**79.8%**
Islamic	**14.2%**
Protestant	**2.3%**
Sikh	**1.7%**
Other, including Jainist	**2.0%**

A Hindu mystic is an example of high-caste society in India.

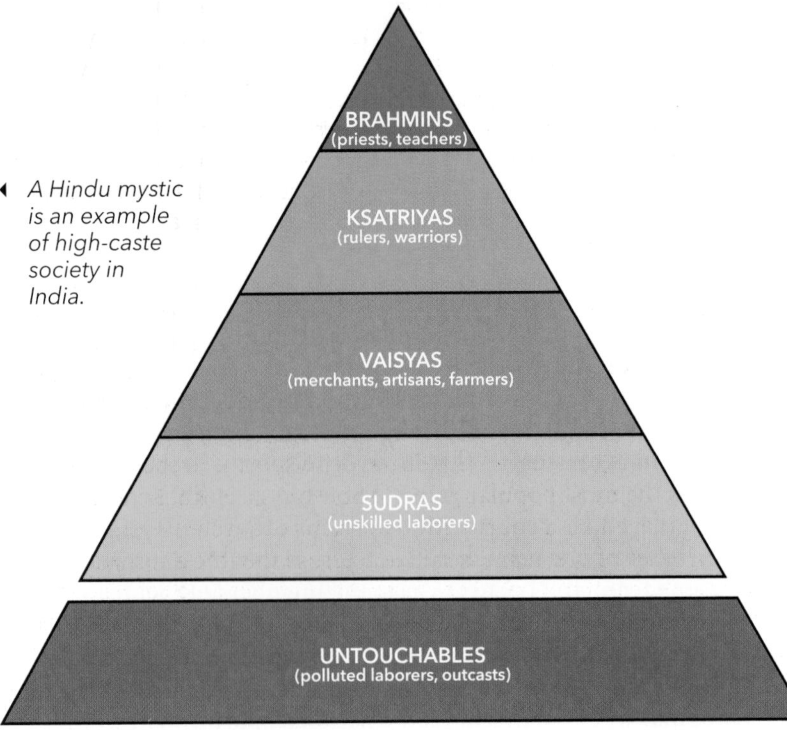

BELIEFS

Hinduism

Hindu temple ▸

Hinduism is often used to describe the religion of India. Though not every religion in India is considered Hindu (Buddhism for example), the Hindu religions do not all share the same beliefs or practices. Sometimes the beliefs of various Hindu groups contradict each other. These contradictions do not bother Hindus. They think what seems contradictory may actually harmonize in another dimension of reality.

The Hindu belief in god provides an example of these contradictions. Some Hindus believe in a personal god. Other Hindus believe that god is not a person but a divine being that pervades everything. They are pantheists. Brahman is the name given to the divine being. Whatever view is taken of Brahman, Brahman is both the cause and the material of creation. There is no creation out of nothing as in the Bible's record of creation.

Most Hindus do agree on two key beliefs: samsara and moksha. Samsara is the law of reincarnation—a cycle of birth, death, and rebirth—governed by karma. Doing good works gives a person good karma. Bad actions give a person bad karma. A Hindu accepts the caste into which he is born as the reward or punishment for his works in his past lives, and he tries to do good works so that his future lives will be better. Hindus believe that good karma might allow them to be reborn as a Brahmin or a rich man. Bad karma would cause them to be reborn into a lower caste, as an untouchable, or even as an animal. Moksha means "release" and refers to freedom from the law of samsara. Hindus wish to be freed from the cycle of reincarnation. Freedom from reincarnation means the person is absorbed back into full oneness with Brahman.

Hindu beliefs vary greatly because Hinduism has three sets of holy books and no single founder or teacher. The first book, *Rig-Veda*, was written approximately 1200 BC and is the basis of the caste system. The Upanishads, written a few centuries later, teach about the Hindu gods—Brahma, Vishnu, and Shiva—as well as reincarnation and karma. The Bhagavad-Gita, which appeared even later, focuses on Krishna (a human manifestation of Vishnu). Some Hindus believe in one god; others believe in many gods. Many gurus (spiritual leaders) attract followers to their own teachings. Their followers try to escape reincarnation by repeating prayers, seeking spiritual wisdom from the gurus, helping others, or enduring strict discipline and self-denial.

Hindus claim to be very tolerant of other religions. A Christian who shares the gospel with a Hindu may find him ready to accept that Jesus is a god and that Christianity contains much truth. But in fact Christianity and Hinduism are incompatible at their foundations. The Christian concept of God differs greatly from the Hindu conceptions of Brahman. The Christian God is personal and exists apart from His creation. Brahman is not personal for many Hindus and is both the material of creation as well as its cause. For the Christian, the fundamental problem is not being trapped in the material world. The fundamental problem is sin and broken fellowship with God. For the Christian the human person is sinful. For the Hindu he is part of the divine being. This leads to a different conception of salvation. The Hindu seeks to escape life in this world so he can be absorbed back into Brahman. The Bible teaches that God will redeem His fallen Creation. The Christian hopes for a resurrected body, a new earth, and a restored relationship with God for all eternity. The means of salvation is also different. For much of Hinduism, salvation is achieved by performing the right deeds to gain good karma or by achieving the right state of meditation to know Brahman. Though some strands of Hinduism stress grace from a god as a means to escape samsara, the need for redemption from sin is not present.

Statue of the goddess Savitri in India ▸

BELIEFS

Sikhism

Sikhism (from the Punjabi term meaning "disciple" or "learner") was founded around 1500 by a Hindu man named Nanak (1469-1539) in the Punjab region of India. Sikhs retained ideas of reincarnation and karma but rejected the caste system. Nanak and ten other successive leaders were known as gurus (teacher, guide, expert). The tenth successor of Nanak declared himself the final guru and placed his authority in the Sikh scriptures, Granth Sahib, composed of hymns. These scriptures also contain the traditions and teachings of several Hindu Bhakti saints. Sikhs meditate on the words of the Sikh scriptures through music or by silently repeating their god's name. They believe that this enables the disciple to sense their god's presence and maintain control over the "Five Thieves"—lust, rage, greed, attachment, and conceit. Positive Sikh attributes include being truthful, faithful, self-controlled, and pure. This religion formed in a region of India controlled by the Mughal Empire and experienced treatment varying from patronization (during Akbar's reign) to violent persecution (during Aurangzeb's reign). Mughal rulers executed two of the ten gurus who succeeded Nanak, and many Sikhs became skilled warriors to preserve their way of life. One of the desired qualities of a Sikh was to become a "sant-Sipahi"—a saint-soldier. Members of the khalsa (army of the pure) distinguished their appearance by refraining from cutting their beards or their hair, wearing a steel bracelet on the right wrist, and carrying a sword.

Sikh soldier guarding the Golden Temple in Punjab, India

While Indian leaders have enacted legislation to make it possible for people in lower castes to improve their lives, little actual progress has been made. Discrimination, and even violence, against Indians near the bottom of the social system persists.

SECTION REVIEW

1. How has South Asia changed over time?
2. How well do the South Asian governments provide for the education, health, and safety of their citizens? Choose two and contrast them.
3. How would you describe the economies of South Asia?
4. Describe the demographics of South Asia.
5. What are some cultural characteristics and examples of diversity in South Asia?

An Indian woman working as a road sweeper is an example of low-caste society in India.

INTERACTIONS OF PEOPLE AND PLACES

What are some of the challenges of living in South Asia?

GUIDING QUESTIONS

- How do the South Asian economies and people interact with the environment?
- What are environmental issues in South Asia?
- What are causes and effects of environmental issues in South Asia?
- What are possible solutions to environmental issues in South Asia?

Much of South Asia is subject to the climate swings caused by the monsoon winds or the effect of living near mountain ranges. Natural conditions determine the success or failure of raising adequate food supplies.

Interaction among People

Treatment of women, or more accurately the mistreatment of women, is a serious issue in several South Asian countries. Sex-selective abortions have led to the deaths of countless female babies in India, Pakistan, Bangladesh, and Sri Lanka. In some of these countries, female babies are killed shortly after birth. Child brides are also common in some nations, including India, especially in rural areas.

Women who live in some parts of South Asia are in greater danger of kidnapping, abduction, torture, and human trafficking. Some violence against women, known as dowry violence, is the result of families not paying a bride's promised dowry to the groom's family. Sadly, crimes against women in this region are on the rise and often are met with apathy from media, political, and social officials.

Interaction with the Environment

For centuries the people of South Asia have lived by subsistence farming and the practice of trades passed down by their predecessors. They have used wood to heat their homes and cook their food. Hindus have bathed, washed their clothes, and cremated the dead along the sacred Ganges and Indus Rivers. Cattle, monkeys, and other animals, including rats, roam freely in cities and villages and are regarded by many as manifestations of Hindu gods. With around 20 percent of the world's population living in this region, the urban areas are densely populated, and access to clean water and sanitation is woefully inadequate.

▲ *Hindu pilgrims bathing and praying in the Ganges River*

Waste has become a monumental problem in several South Asian countries. Many of the poor in these nations, most notably in India, scavenge for recyclable material such as plastics and aluminum. Children and adults make a modest living of around $2 per day by selling their collection to companies that will turn this waste back into useful material.

Reasons for Environmental Issues

Several factors combine to negatively affect the environment in South Asia. Byproducts of industry, expanded use of automobiles, and ever-growing amounts of waste have created serious environmental issues that must be addressed. In addition, consumption of resources, such as trees and other vegetation, has resulted in damage to the environment.

Indoor air pollution in India

Water

While there is an abundance of water in much of South Asia, industrial, agricultural, human and animal pollutants have turned most rivers into toxic waterways. Lacking the resources to process water and remove harmful contaminants, industries and individuals pour various pollutants and raw sewage into the rivers once they pass through populated regions. Drinking contaminated water and using it to irrigate crops has led to a variety of health issues and a reduced lifespan, especially for infants and young children.

Air

The usual suspects, including industrial and automobile exhaust, have created significant air pollution in most countries in South Asia. An attempt to deal with mountains of trash has led many people to burn it, both to dispose of it and to provide a source of fuel in homes. In addition to burning trash, most homes burn solid fuels such as wood to cook food, and dangerous indoor pollution makes the air in many homes toxic, leading to serious respiratory problems. Furthermore, every country in this region has at least one cement plant, and some have several plants. These plants are not equipped to prevent large amounts of dust from entering the air and intensifying the smog problem.

Dusty cement factory in Karachi, Pakistan

Land

Trash in several of the countries in this region literally forms small mountains in urban areas. India

is estimated to produce over 120,000 tons of waste every day, and that number appears to be growing. At times these vast piles of trash catch fire and add to the air pollution problem.

Another land issue is the all too familiar problem of deforestation. India, as the region's largest nation, has the greatest number of acres stripped of trees each year, at 33.9 million. However, Pakistan's percentage of land deforested is greater given its much smaller size. At just over 100,000 acres per year, Pakistan's forested land is diminishing at an alarming rate. Because of the large number of trees cut down and the accompanying vegetation that is destroyed, massive erosion results. This is an especially significant problem in light of the monsoon rains and the seasonal flooding.

Proposed Solutions

While the countries in South Asia can trace their history back for a few thousand years, their transition from traditional to modern societies is ongoing and has many obstacles. This is especially true when these countries attempt to solve environmental problems. Proper sanitation, effective disposal and recycling of trash, removal of contaminants from water, and reforestation will require enormous resources and incredible political discipline. There are many demands on a nation's financial resources, and solving environmental problems must receive priority if the environments in these countries are to improve. Obvious solutions include disciplined recycling, development of cleaner energy, especially for homes and factories, and replacement of the forests that hold the land in place during the intense and prolonged rains that come to South Asia every year.

▲ *Burning trash mountain in India*

One solution to illegal dumping in some Indian cities is the encouragement of citizens to use their smart phones and a helpline to report infractions. The people take photos of the offender in action and send the evidence to local authorities. Then field officers drive to the offending merchant, for example, and give him a ticket, which he promptly pays. First-time offenders pay a modest fine, and repeat offenders pay higher fines. This system discourages illegal activity and makes a tiny dent in the growing problem.

▼ *Public trash bins for garbage and recyclable waste in New Delhi, India*

SECTION REVIEW

1. What role does religion play in the treatment of women in South Asia?
2. What are three environmental issues in South Asia?
3. How have governments in South Asia dealt with environmental issues?
4. Explain how the South Asian economies and people have interacted with the environment.
5. What solutions to current environmental issues in South Asia would you propose?

19

CHAPTER REVIEW

SUMMARY

1. The physical geography of South Asia was shaped by tectonic activity, volcanic eruptions, and glaciers. Continued development of South Asia's natural resources will profoundly enhance this region's economic potential.
2. The people of South Asia are ethnically varied by tribe and language and yet similar in the enjoyment of common activities, including ethnic foods, regional music, and sports. These societies are transitioning to developed societies but are also threatened by corruption and ethnic strife.
3. A major challenge in South Asia is the need to make wise use of human and natural resources in ways that maintain strong economies without further endangering the environment. Goals for South Asia would include diversifying industry, developing cleaner resources for energy production, and finding ways to protect their environment.

Terms to Know

- ❑ subcontinent
- ❑ Deccan Plateau
- ❑ monsoon
- ❑ Mauryan Empire
- ❑ Mughal Empire
- ❑ passive resistance
- ❑ caste
- ❑ untouchables
- ❑ reincarnation

Making Connections

1. What earth-shaping process formed Mount Everest?
2. How was the Deccan Plateau formed?
3. How do landforms affect climates in South Asia?
4. Why do you think South Asian economies are in transition?
5. Identify political issues in South Asia.
6. What role has religion played in India?
7. What are some causes of deforestation in South Asia?

Developing Geography Skills

1. How do landforms influence the distribution of population in this region?
2. What role have rivers played in the positive and negative developments of Bangladesh?

Thinking Critically

1. Though many people oppose abuse of women, why is a biblical worldview best equipped to address this issue?
2. The ultimate goal in Hinduism is to escape the cycle of reincarnation and be absorbed into full oneness with Brahman. How does a Christian's relationship with the God of the Bible differ?

Living in God's World

1. Write a paragraph explaining how worldview influences a nation's approach to the killing of female babies.
2. Given the opportunity, how could you demonstrate the love of Christ to the untouchables in India?

CASE STUDY | A Nutty Solution to Deforestation in Bhutan

Replanting trees is an obvious way to reverse the deforestation of a country. However, an enterprising company has developed another way to replace the ground cover in Bhutan, restore eroded landscapes, and help the people make a living at the same time. A company called Mountain Hazelnuts is working with farmers in rural areas in Bhutan to plant millions of hazelnut trees on their land and harvest the nuts for sale. This company has planted over 10 million trees and is working to establish at least 15,000 orchards across Bhutan. In addition to farmers, recipients of the trees include religious groups such as monasteries.

Why hazelnuts? Hazelnuts provide the growers with a high-value crop, and they are already indigenous to the country. Bhutan's climate is perfect for growing these plants because of the monsoon rains that provide enough moisture in the summer and cold winters that cause the trees to become dormant. The nuts harden during this period of dormancy.

Once the nuts are harvested, the company buys them from the people and guarantees them a rate that protects the growers from price instability. Farmers are embracing this relationship because they make more money growing hazelnuts than they would if they grew other crops. This system also helps to sustain the rural economy with orchards that can produce hazelnuts for at least fifty years.

1. What type of trees are being planted in Bhutan to reverse deforestation?
2. Why are these trees profitable for the farmers?
3. What makes Bhutan a suitable place to grow these trees?
4. Who buys the product harvested from these trees?
5. How does this process contribute to the rural economy of Bhutan?

▾ *Hazelnut tree nursery near Jakar, Bhutan*

GEODATA | Activity

Cultural Geography *Student Activities*

You will have the opportunity to complete a geodata activity for East Asia in the Activities.

Background image:
Thai wooden longtail boat at Koh Poda island in Krabi province, Thailand

EAST AND SOUTHEAST ASIA

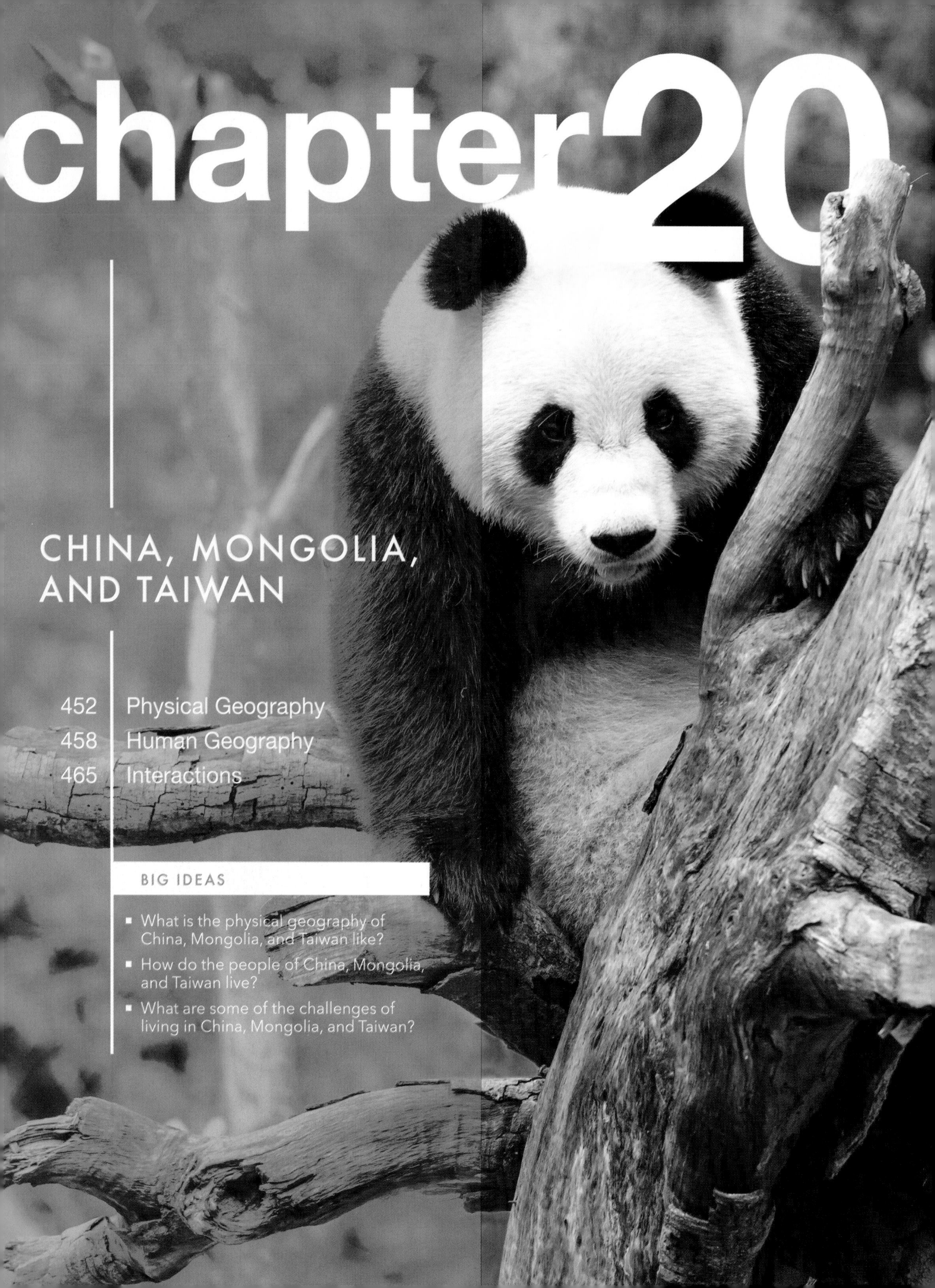

chapter 20

CHINA, MONGOLIA, AND TAIWAN

452 Physical Geography
458 Human Geography
465 Interactions

BIG IDEAS

- What is the physical geography of China, Mongolia, and Taiwan like?
- How do the people of China, Mongolia, and Taiwan live?
- What are some of the challenges of living in China, Mongolia, and Taiwan?

▲ *Great Wall of China*

◀ *Arkhangai province, Mongolia*

CHINA'S ENDURING WALL

If you had the opportunity to travel to China, one of the places you would want to visit is the Great Wall of China. Sections of this wall were built about 3,500 years ago, and some parts of the wall have proven to be quite durable. Scientists have discovered that Chinese workers combined the secret ingredient of sticky rice soup with the mortar to form an especially strong bonding agent. The enhanced mortar has enabled parts of the wall to resist the destructive effects of weather, human assault, and even earthquakes. Scientists refer to this as an organic-inorganic composite material, with the lime serving as the inorganic element and the rice soup as the organic part. The sticky mixture has proven to be so effective that workers still use it to restore ancient masonry. In addition to the Great Wall, Chinese masons constructed tombs and pagodas with this unique mortar, and some of these structures have remained intact to the present.

▲ *Taipei, Taiwan*

◀ *Giant panda in China*

East Asia is a region of great wealth and extreme poverty, with ancient cultures and religious practices. It is marked with extended mountain peaks and broad plateaus and plains. Mountains, deserts, and seas have long isolated this region from the West, creating distinct differences in culture and history. This region is bounded by Russia on the north and the Indian subcontinent and Southwest Asia on the west, and it has coasts on the Yellow Sea and the Japanese Islands on the east and the South China Sea on the south.

GUIDING QUESTIONS

- What are the regions of China, Mongolia, and Taiwan?
- What caused the landforms of China, Mongolia, and Taiwan?
- What bodies of water are important to China, Mongolia, and Taiwan?
- What are the climates of China, Mongolia, and Taiwan?
- What natural resources are found in China, Mongolia, and Taiwan?

PHYSICAL GEOGRAPHY

Regions of China, Mongolia, and Taiwan

What is the physical geography of China, Mongolia, and Taiwan?

China covers most of this region and has geographic forms that vary from the Himalaya Mountains to the high Plateau of Tibet in the west and the Gobi Desert in the north. Mongolia is primarily mountains and plateau, with the Gobi Desert stretching across the southern portion of the country. Taiwan is covered with mountains and rolling hills.

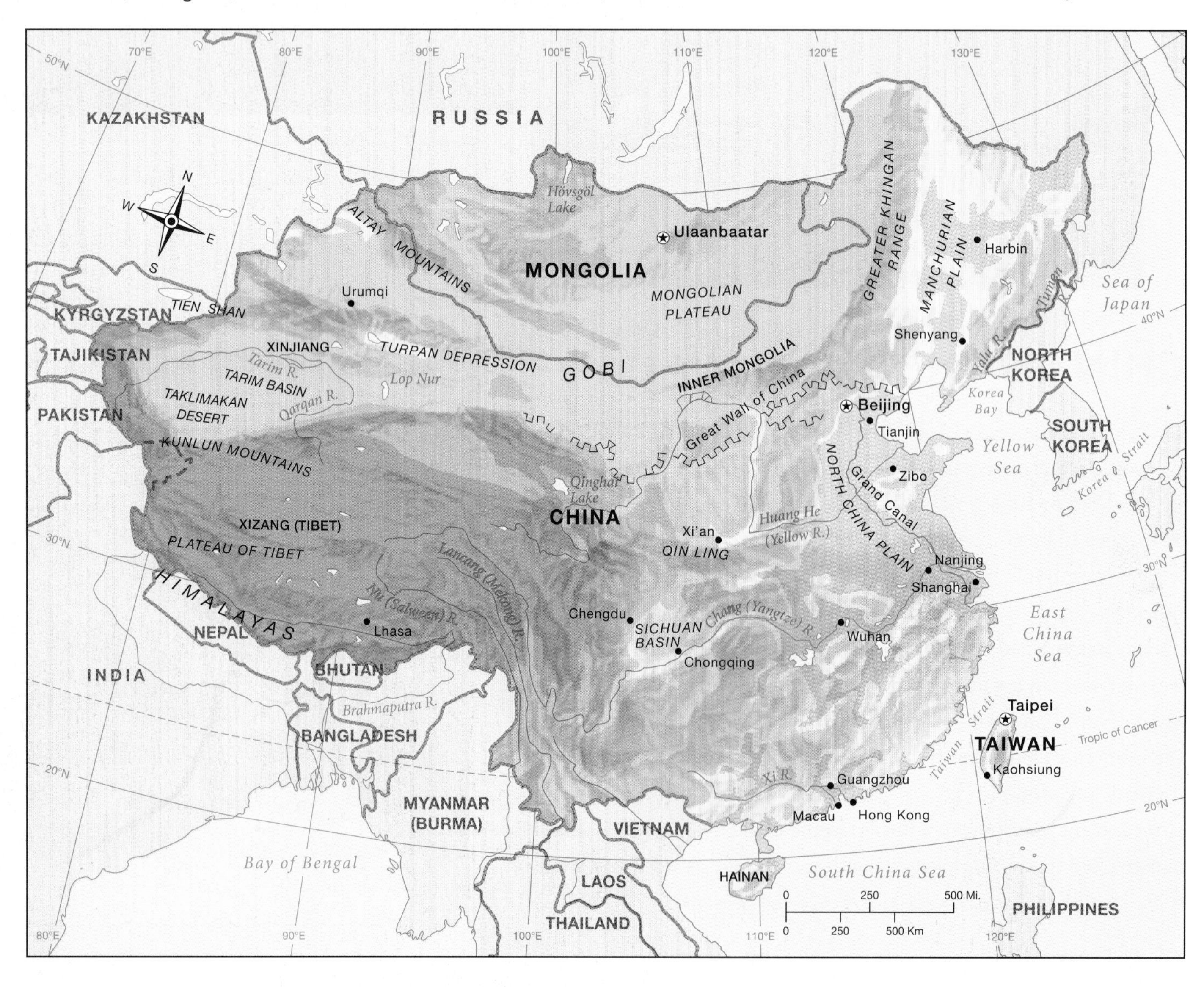

Physical Landforms

Massive tectonic activity during the Flood resulted in the landforms of this region. One of the dominant features of China, the **Tibetan Plateau**, is the highest plateau in the world. With an average elevation of 16,000 feet, this region is appropriately called the "roof of the world." Also known as the "Asian water tower," the Tibetan Plateau has 37,000 glaciers that supply water to several countries and nearly two billion people.

▲ *Fisherman with cormorants on the Li River in China*

◀ *Tibetan Plateau*

▼ *Glacier on the Tibetan Plateau*

◂ *Hot spring in Taipei, Taiwan*

Mongolia's terrain was also formed by tectonic activity, glaciers, and volcanoes. The Mongolian Plateau extends over one million square miles. Taiwan may have been formed by the convergence of the Philippine Sea Plate and the Eurasian Plate and remains geologically active, with 15,000 to 18,000 earthquakes each year. Other geological activity includes hot springs.

▴ *Lake on the Mongolian Plateau*

◂ *Volcanic landscape in China*

Sun Moon Lake in Taiwan

Bodies of Water

In addition to access to the South China Sea, the East China Sea, and the Yellow Sea, China has thousands of rivers that provide important transportation routes. Three key bodies of water in China are the Yangtze River, the Huang He (Yellow) River, and the Grand Canal that connects the two. In addition, China has dozens of lakes, with the Qinghai Lake being distinguished as the largest lake in China (salt lake).

Mongolia has several rivers and lakes. Most of Mongolia's lakes are seasonal and salty. Hövsgöl is the largest freshwater lake in Mongolia. Taiwan is surrounded by water and is separated from mainland China by the Taiwan Strait. This strait varies from 81 to 112 miles wide. Taiwan has twenty rivers, and its largest lake is the Sun Moon Lake.

Work on the Grand Canal began in the fifth century BC. The different portions were connected during the seventh century AD. Between 1271 and 1633 various Chinese dynasties rebuilt and widened the canal. It is the oldest and longest canal in the world and extends 1,100 miles.

The Yellow Sea

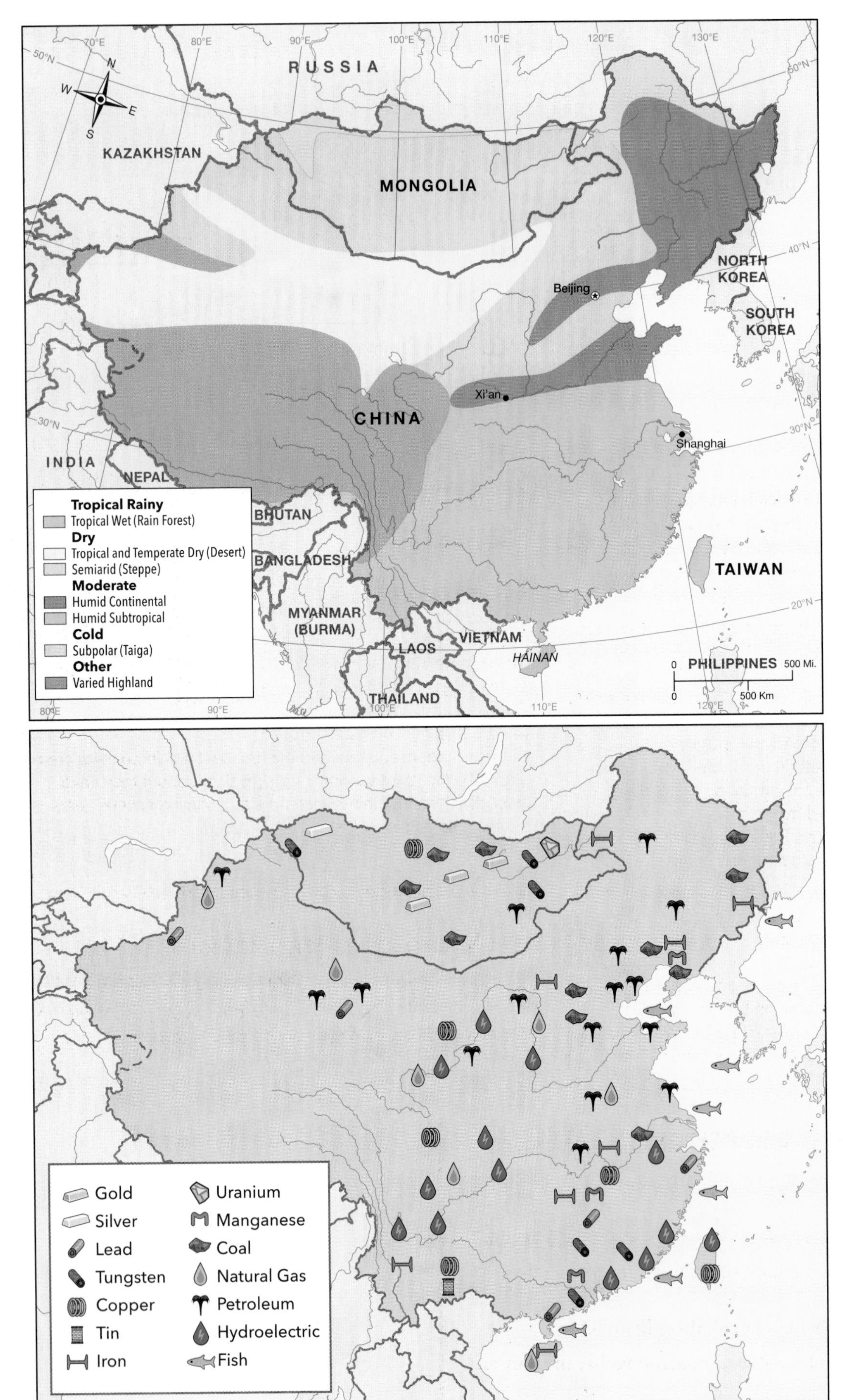

Climates

China covers a vast region and has a variety of landforms that result in multiple climate zones. While the southernmost territory of China is a tropical monsoon climate, the largest zone is the highland climate zone over the Tibetan Plateau. Other climates include semiarid, arid, humid monsoon, and cool temperate in the far north. China and Taiwan are subject to monsoon winds that either bring in immense amounts of moisture or provide seasonal periods of dry weather. This region is also subject to typhoons, the eastern version of hurricanes, and several of these storms sweep in each year from the Pacific Ocean in the east.

Mongolia's climate can be described as variations of cold, including cold desert, cold semiarid, and cool continental. Taiwan's climate varies from tropical to temperate. Near the coast, Taiwan enjoys a marine tropical climate. At higher altitudes the climate is temperate.

Resources

These countries have common resources such as coal, petroleum, natural gas, iron ore, and zinc. They also have precious resources, including rare earths, silver, and gold. China and Taiwan have abundant supplies of fish and other marine resources.

GLOBAL IMPACT | Three Gorges Dam

Three Gorges Dam (with a ship lift on the right end)

Tourists on board a cruise ship viewing the ship lift at the Three Gorges Dam

Both the Huang He and the Chang begin high on the Plateau of Tibet in Qinghai, the largest and least populated of China's provinces. As the Chang River drops down into the North China Plain, it passes through a series of three gorges, known as the Ichang Gorges. Scenic limestone cliffs rise two thousand feet above the rushing water.

In the 1990s, Communist China began a controversial project to dam the river and flood the gorges. The **Three Gorges Dam** became fully operational with a lock for ships in 2012; a ship lift (for ships weighing less than 3,000 tons) was completed in 2015. At capacity it generates electricity equivalent to the output of eighteen nuclear power plants. At 1.3 miles long and 607 feet high, it is one of the most powerful dams in the world, almost three times as powerful as America's most powerful dam, Grand Coulee. The electricity produced by the dam replaces 31 million tons of coal consumption per year and eliminates approximately 100 million tons of greenhouse emissions.

The project has been controversial in that it involved the involuntary displacement of at least 1.3 million people, whose homes were submerged by the reservoir. Several historical sites were also lost. Some environmentalists have condemned the destruction of the beautiful scenery, the increasing threat of landslides in the region, and effective extinction of the Yangtze river dolphin. Others have expressed concern about sewage from former factory sites that is polluting the reservoir. Upstream, the people of Chongqing are concerned about buildup of sediment in the city's harbor. The cost of constructing the dam exceeded its initial $17 billion estimate, with a final cost of $37 billion. Chinese authorities predicted that the cost would be recovered within the first ten years of energy production, but they have since reported that this milestone was achieved several years ahead of schedule on December 20, 2013.

1. Where does the water that flows to the Three Gorges Dam originate?
2. Why would a ship lift and locks be needed?
3. How is the Three Gorges Dam reducing pollution in China?
4. Given the 2007 estimate that the dam would pay for itself in ten years, how many years did it take to reach this goal?

SECTION REVIEW

1. Between which two major lines of latitude does most of China and Mongolia lie?
2. Why are the Yellow and Yangtze Rivers so important to China?
3. How do China and Mongolia's locations on the globe affect their climates?
4. What precious metal is found in all three nations?
5. What resources are abundant in China, Mongolia, and Taiwan?

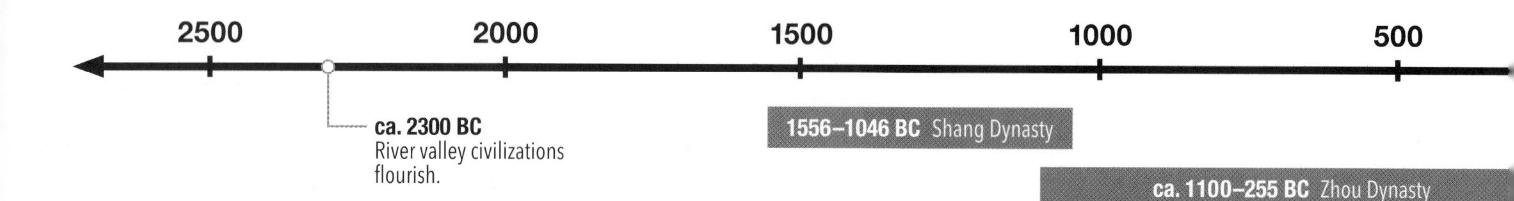

GUIDING QUESTIONS

- How have China, Mongolia, and Taiwan changed over time?
- How do China, Mongolia, and Taiwan's governments interact with their citizens?
- What is the economic health of China, Mongolia, and Taiwan?
- What are the demographics of China, Mongolia, and Taiwan?
- What are the cultural characteristics and diversity in China, Mongolia, and Taiwan?
- What forms of religion are practiced in China, Mongolia, and Taiwan?

▲ *A retouched picture of Mao Zedong at the standing committee of the State Council in Beijing in 1957*

HUMAN GEOGRAPHY

How do the people of China, Mongolia, and Taiwan live?

History

China's early history was one of river-valley civilizations and isolation from outside groups for centuries. Because the Chinese began recording their history very early, much information is available, including information about eight Chinese dynasties (and one Mongol dynasty in China).

- Shang (1556–1046 BC)
- Zhou (ca. 1100–255 BC)
- Qin (221–206 BC)
- Han (206 BC–AD 280)
- Tang (618–907)
- Song (960–1279)
- Yuan [Mongol] (1279–1368)
- Ming (1368–1644)
- Manchu (1644–1911)

Various groups struggled for control of China after the end of the Manchu Dynasty, and two parties emerged: the conservative Nationalist Party under Chiang Kai-shek and the Communist Party led by Mao Zedong. The two forces called a truce in their fighting when Japan invaded China just prior to World War II. Following Japan's defeat in 1945, the fight for control of China resumed, and by 1949 the Communists had seized the major cities of China. The Nationalist Party was forced to relocate on the island of Formosa (Taiwan). Mao's twenty-seven-year reign was marked with agricultural, economic, and political disasters. While statistics vary, up to sixty-four million Chinese died unnatural deaths under Mao, most from starvation.

Mongolia was settled by nomadic peoples who survived by moving their lifestock from place to place for food and water. The nomads united into an empire under the leadership of Genghis Khan in 1206. From 1279 to 1368 the Mongols even controlled much of China during the Yuan Dynasty. Following the fall of the Yuan Dynasty, Mongol tribes returned to their land and remained divided by internal strife. By the end of the seventeenth century, Mongolia came under the control of the Manchu Dynasty. With the fall of the Manchu Dynasty in 1911, Mongolia renewed its struggle for independence. By the 1920s Mongolia came under Soviet influence and had a Communist government for nearly seventy years. During the revolution of 1990, the Mongol people rejected communism and established a multi-party system.

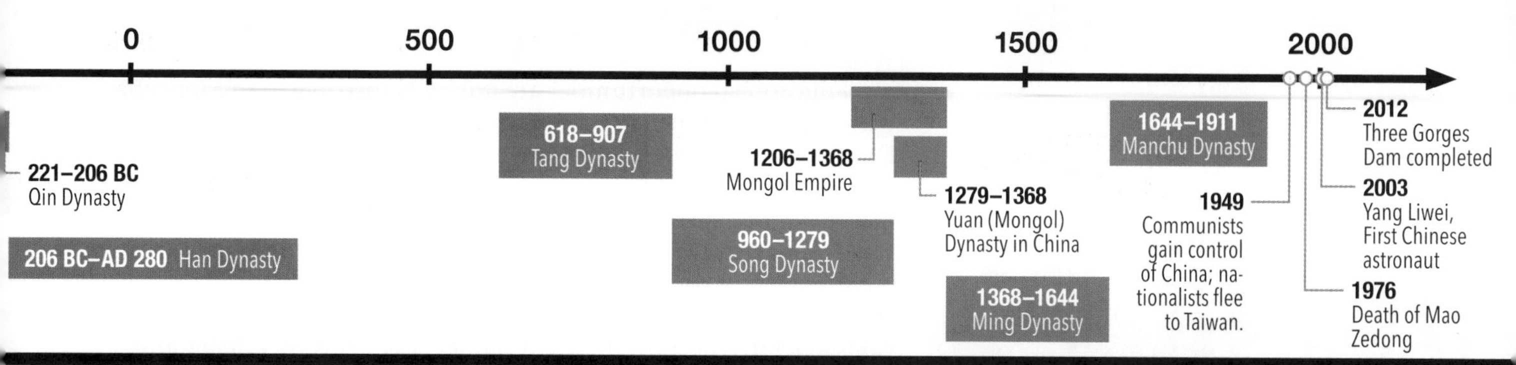

Taiwan may have been settled as early as 3000 BC. It was colonized by the Dutch during the 17th century. The nationalist government of China took control of the island in 1945 and moved to the island in 1949 when the Communists gained control of the mainland. Beginning in the 1960s Taiwan became one of the four "**Asian Tigers**," a reference to their phenomenal industrial and economic growth. (Hong Kong, Singapore, and South Korea are the other three Asian Tigers.)

▲ *Hong Kong*

Government

The forms of government in these three nations vary. The Chinese Communist government recently celebrated its seventieth anniversary and has a history of rule through violence and brutality. Having overthrown its Communist government nearly three decades ago, Mongolia now has a semi-presidential representative democratic republic. Its leaders are elected by the people, and Mongolian political leaders continue to struggle with corruption that has long been a part of Mongolia's history in the twentieth century. Taiwan's short political history began with a military dictatorship and transitioned into its current form as a representative democratic republic with broad freedoms for its citizens.

Government Interactions with Its Citizens

China's government closely monitors the activities and movement of its citizens and tries to restrict their access to information that contradicts the propaganda of Chinese officials. A growing number of Chinese people desire freedom of speech, but anything that is critical of the Communist regime faces brutal suppression. Chinese attempts to stamp out or neutralize religious expression have resulted in the imprisonment of millions and the deaths of many from varying religious backgrounds. The recent imprisonment and "re-education" of Uyghur Muslims in China reveal how Communists persecute various religious groups, including Christians, and have done so since communism's rise to power.

▼ *Students in class in central Shanghai, China*

Education and Health Care

Education in China is provided by the state, and nine years of education is compulsory. Though Chinese students may spend fewer years in school than those in other countries, the school day lasts about 9.5 hours. Students also attend Saturday classes to boost their science and math performance. In addition, many parents pay for tutoring to help their children survive in the rigorous educational program.

Educational opportunities are unevenly distributed in Mongolia, with overcrowded urban schools and sparsely attended rural schools. Dropout rates are higher in Mongolia's rural schools, due in part to the need for boys to tend to their families' herds and the presumption that males need little education to tend to farm needs. Taiwan has a state-supported twelve-year compulsory education program. Taiwanese students are under great pressure to succeed academically, given the limited number of high-paying technical jobs that are available. Consequently, the Taiwanese educational system is very demanding.

China's health care is a mixture of public and private, with the public sector tending to offer less care with longer waits and the private sector offering better and more extensive care for those who can afford it. Mongolia established a Soviet-style model of health care, and expectations were high. But the resulting levels of care proved to be disappointing, and there was a lack of medical facilities and qualified personnel. Taiwan instituted national health care and single-payer compulsory social insurance. Despite these actions the Taiwanese continue to struggle to have their health needs met due to a low doctor to patient ratio and a shortage of nurses. The result is long waits for appointments and limited options for procedures.

▲ *Chinese employees working on motors for mobile phones at a factory in Huaibei, China*

Economies

The reforms enacted in Communist China following the death of Mao Zedong have resulted in China's economy growing to become one of the top economies in the world. While political and personal freedoms are severely restricted, economic opportunities have led to incredible wealth in China. As of 2017 China's GDP was $23.21 trillion. China has 806.7 million workers and a growing economy. Forty-three percent of the workforce labors in the services sector, and 29 percent works in various industries, including a strong technology sector. The remaining 28 percent of the workforce is employed in agriculture.

Mongolia has recently transitioned to a market economy after its experiment with socialism. In 2017 its GDP was $39.7 billion. With 1.24 million workers, its economy continues to grow as the nation modernizes its industry. Just over half of the workers labor in the services sector, and 31 percent work in agriculture, including a thriving industry in cashmere wool. Mining is also a major industry in Mongolia.

Taiwan's capitalist market economy boasted a GDP of $1.19 trillion in 2017. This island nation has a workforce of 11.8 million workers, with nearly 60 percent engaged in the services sector. Taiwan is also a major producer of electronics, communication and information technology, petroleum refining, chemicals, textiles, and pharmaceuticals.

▲ *Mongolian goats, whose wool is used to make cashmere*

◀ *Cashmere socks*

Kaohsiung, Taiwan ▶

Demographics

China's estimated population in 2019 was 1.4 billion, with nearly 44,000 babies born each day. China's birthrate is 12.4/1000. Mongolia's estimated population in 2019 was 3.2 million, with a birthrate of 19.6/1000. Taiwan's estimated population in 2019 was 23.7 million, with the lowest birthrate in this region—8.3/1000.

China, Mongolia, and Taiwan are less ethnically diverse than many other countries. Ninety-one percent of Chinese identify as Han, with 8 percent belonging to various minorities. While Mongolia technically has twenty-seven ethnic groups, most of these are descended from the Mongols or Turks. Taiwan's citizens are nearly 97 percent Han, with about 2 percent descended from indigenous Taiwanese people.

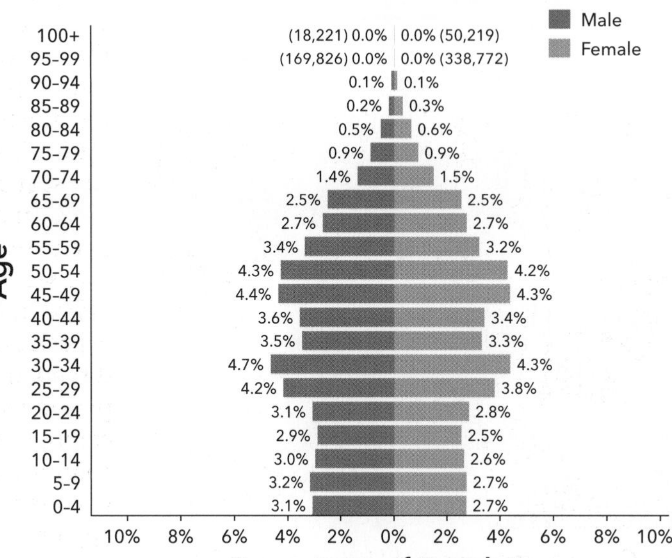

Culture and Diversity

While China has over two hundred dialects, the Chinese government has made Mandarin the official spoken dialect. The Chinese and Mongolian cultures have been handed down from generation to generation for nearly five thousand years. Even when China came under foreign control, the invaders tended to adopt Chinese culture rather than the reverse.

Food, Dance, and Sports

Typical of other regions in the world, these countries eat foods that are readily available, and rice is often a standard ingredient in their meals. Most foods are cooked in a wok with a mixture of vegetables and meats, especially pork.

▲ *(top) Tsuivan, a Mongolian dish of noodles with beef and vegetables*

▲ *(bottom) Buuz, steamed Mongolian dumplings*

▼ *Traditional dragon dance to celebrate the arrival of the new year in Foshan City, China*

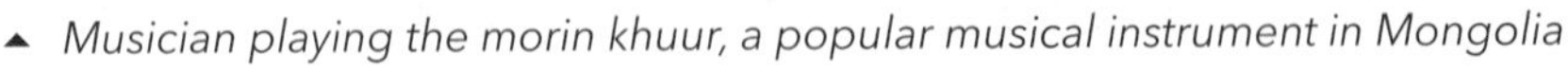

▲ Musician playing the morin khuur, a popular musical instrument in Mongolia

▲ *Young musician in traditional dress playing the pipa, a traditional plucked string instrument in China*

Musical instruments include the *morin khuur,* or Mongolian fiddle, and various Chinese musical instruments.

Favorite Chinese sports include table tennis, badminton, basketball, and soccer. Mongolians love to watch and engage in wrestling, archery, and horse racing. Taiwan's favorite sports include baseball, basketball, golf, tennis, and cycling.

▲ *This huqin erhu is another traditional Chinese stringed instrument.*

Family

Historically the extended family has been a building block of Chinese society. Even with the rise of communism, Mao Zedong initially encouraged couples to have at least two children in order to increase the national population. However, as Communists embraced various warnings that the world could not sustain a growing population, authorities instituted and vigorously enforced a one-child policy. This, along with the starvation of millions of Chinese as a result of government policies, severely damaged families and weakened Chinese society.

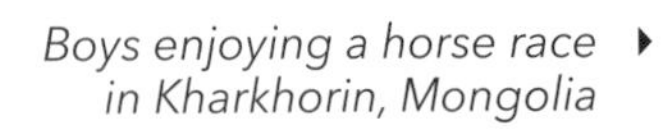

Boys enjoying a horse race in Kharkhorin, Mongolia ▸

GLOBAL IMPACT | One-Child Policy

An ongoing tragedy is China's attempt to stabilize its population growth. In the 1970s the Communist government instituted a policy that limited Chinese families to one child. The **one-child policy** resulted in the abortion of up to thirteen million Chinese babies each year for the next forty years. Some Chinese women traveled abroad to have their second child, a practice that is known as **birth tourism**.

One unintended consequence of this policy has been the imbalance of male and female babies born. Since many Chinese families prefer a male child so that the parents will be provided for in their final years, gender-selective abortion resulted in the death of many Chinese baby girls. There are now millions more Chinese men looking for wives than there are Chinese women to meet this need. It is projected that by 2025 China will have 96.5 million men in their twenties but only 80.3 million young women. Some Chinese men will go abroad to seek a wife. Others may seek wives by kidnapping or engaging in human trafficking.

Another long-term consequence of this imbalance is that by 2050 there will not be enough workers to support an aging Chinese society. Despite recent changes that allow families to have two children, forced abortions continue in many regions of China.

▲ *A young Chinese couple with their daughter*

1. Why was the one-child policy implemented?
2. What is the practice of traveling to another country to have a child called?
3. Which gender of baby have most Chinese parents preferred? Why?

Religion

The people of this region have historically been deeply religious, and their religious beliefs have shaped their societies for centuries. China has a large number of nonreligious or unaffiliated people, due in large part to the antagonism of communism toward Christianity and religion in general. Many Christians have been forced to go underground and worship in secret to avoid imprisonment.

Mongolia's period of experimenting with communism may explain the 25 percent who identify as nonreligious. About one-third of Mongolians continue to practice ethnic religions, and another third practice Buddhism. Christians may number around 3 percent.

Taiwanese embrace Buddhism at 35 percent, and about 33 percent identify as Taoists, although this is regarded as more of a philosophy than a religion. About 10 percent of the people continue to practice ethnic religions, and around 18 percent identify as nonreligious. Christians may constitute about 4 percent of the population.

Religions of China and Mongolia

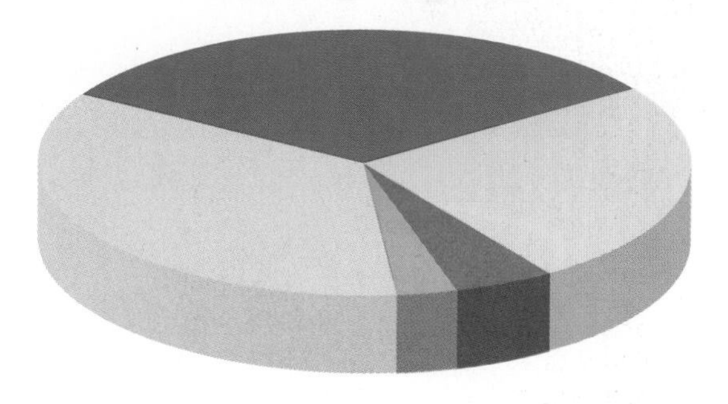

Ethnic	**32.0%**
Buddhist	**25.0%**
Protestant Evangelical	**5.0%**
Islamic	**3.0%**
Unaffiliated	**35.0%**

Philosophy

Confucianism

K'ung Futzu (551–479 BC) is the most honored teacher in Chinese history. The Chinese call him "the Master"; we know him as Confucius. His teachings became known as **Confucianism**. Confucius grew up in poverty during a time of social and political unrest in China. Prior to obtaining a political office, he devoted his time to teaching. Confucius believed that a moral government would produce a moral society. He sought to train men who, by entering government service and maintaining proper conduct, would bring about a moral

▲ *Statue of Confucius in a Confucian temple in China*

society. His disciples recorded and expanded upon his teaching, developing a system of ethics that became a major influence on Chinese culture.

Fundamental to Confucius's teaching was his belief in five basic human relationships: father and son, elder and younger brothers, husband and wife, friend and friend, and ruler and subjects. Confucius believed that maintaining proper relationships in these five areas would bring harmony and order to society. In addition, he placed great confidence in China's past, trusting it as the basis and guide for human behavior. Since right behavior was found in right relationships, Confucius concluded that the fundamental principle was "What you do not want done to yourself, do not do to others."

Confucius recognized the impossibility of living up to this standard. He observed that it would be difficult to live up to this standard for an entire day. Thus he rightly recognized that no one is truly good. Yet because he did not believe in God, who will bring all things into judgment, Confucius counseled his disciples to simply do the best they could.

Taoism

Second in importance to the teaching of Confucius was that of **Taoism**. According to Chinese legend, Laozi (also spelled Lao-tzu) taught that *tao* ("the way") was the pervading force in nature. He encouraged men to find peace and happiness by living in harmony with nature. According to Taoist teaching, men can achieve this harmony by ceasing to strive for power, wealth, and learning; instead they should adopt a lifestyle in which they learn to live with the flow of the natural order. By living in harmony with the order that is part of nature, men can accomplish great things. Taoists illustrated this teaching with the example of water: "There is nothing in the world more soft and weak than water, yet for attacking things that are hard and strong there is nothing that surpasses it. . . . The soft overcomes the hard; the weak overcomes the strong."

Confucianism became the guiding philosophy of China's educational, social, and political systems; Taoism became the basis of mystical, magical, and superstitious elements in Chinese society. In many ways, these two philosophies conflict with one another. Confucianism promotes living an active life and fulfilling one's social obligations. Taoism favors a more passive lifestyle and attempts to free man from the busyness of responsibility. Confucians strive for improved government, laws, and education, while Taoists minimize external authority and involvement in society.

▲ *Statue of Lao-Tzu, also called Laozi, at the Laojun Mountain in central China's Henan Province*

SECTION REVIEW

1. How have China, Mongolia, and Taiwan changed over time?
2. How well do the Chinese, Mongolian, and Taiwanese governments provide for the education, health, and safety of their citizens?
3. How would you describe the economies of China, Mongolia, and Taiwan?
4. Describe the demographics of China, Mongolia, and Taiwan.
5. What are some cultural characteristics and examples of diversity in China, Mongolia, and Taiwan?

INTERACTIONS OF PEOPLE AND PLACES

What are some of the challenges of living in China, Mongolia, and Taiwan?

GUIDING QUESTIONS

- How do the Chinese, Mongolian, and Taiwanese economies and people interact with the environment?
- What are environmental issues in China, Mongolia, and Taiwan?
- What are causes and effects of environmental issues in China, Mongolia, and Taiwan?
- What are possible solutions to environmental issues in China, Mongolia, and Taiwan?

For nearly five thousand years, the people of this region have grappled with difficult natural conditions and have developed empires that expanded well beyond their national boundaries. They found ways to grow enough food for their expanding populations and to feed their armies as they marched to conquer other lands. They have struggled with expanding deserts that threatened their ability to grow food and maintain herds and foreign invaders who threatened their personal freedom and way of life. The people of this region have demonstrated resilience and creativity to overcome obstacles and make full use of the resources available to them.

Interaction among People

Some Chinese businesses, with the tacit consent of the government, use children and political prisoners to manufacture goods. While statistics are unavailable, reports of children below the age of sixteen working up to eight hours a day continue to surface. In addition, political prisoners, including Christians, are forced to work for little or no pay under harsh conditions as part of their punishment.

Even more disturbing are the reports of detainees being executed and having their organs harvested. Voluntary organ donation runs counter to Confucian teaching because of the belief that the entire body is needed for the afterlife. However, organ harvesting is extremely profitable, and a growing number of people needing major organ transplants are traveling to China to acquire them. Investigators estimate that China makes $1 billion each year in this illegal activity. This has created a despicable trade known as **transplant tourism**. Members of the religious group Falun Gong and Chinese Muslims are among the many victims whose organs are harvested for sale. Statistics vary, but thousands of involuntary transplant surgeries are performed each year in China. The Coalition to End Transplant Abuse in China (ETAC) recently held a tribunal to document the forced organ harvesting and issued a report on June 17, 2019, at a conference in London.

▲ *An elderly ethnic Uyghur man walks in front of the Id Kah Mosque in Kashgar, China.*

Interaction with the Environment

Over the centuries some farming methods contributed to the growing desert that crosses China and Mongolia. Without active measures to plant vegetation that would stabilize the soil, desertification has become a greater problem in this region. Since many have continued to use wood for construction and fuel, loss of ground cover and

biodiversity has increased over the centuries. With the development of industry, the removal and processing of resources, and other human activity, the environment has often suffered. Industry demands resources and massive amounts of energy. In addition, industrial by-products and waste materials have often been disposed of improperly.

Reasons for Environmental Issues

As in other parts of the world, products of industry, the expanded use of automobiles, and ever-growing amounts of waste have created serious environmental issues that must be addressed. In addition, consumption of resources, such as trees and other vegetation, has resulted in damage to the environment.

As millions of Chinese continue flocking to the cities where there are jobs, more energy is consumed to supply the needed power. This leads to more pollution in the cities. Despite China's strict environmental controls, there is little enforcement at the local level.

Water

These countries have access to water, but, as in many other countries, industrial, agricultural, and human pollutants have turned many rivers into toxic waterways. This region lacks the resources or the will to process water and remove harmful contaminants. As a result, various pollutants and raw sewage pour into the rivers once they pass through populated regions. The damage that results from drinking contaminated water has led to health problems and a reduced lifespan for infants and young children.

Air

Industrial and automobile exhausts have created significant air pollution in these countries. A natural source of air pollution in this region is the Gobi Desert. Dust from this immense desert is swept up by the monsoon winds, seriously contaminating the air over vast regions before dropping into the sea. China and Mongolia also burn coal to produce about 80 percent of their electricity, and China tends to burn lower grades of coal that produce more sulfur dioxide and other pollutants.

In addition to domestically produced air pollution, Taiwan must also contend with pollution that blows across the strait from China. Proximity to mainland China makes Taiwan an unwilling victim of China's pollutants, and the people of Taiwan suffer when prevailing winds send them a heavy dose of China's contaminated air. Taiwan suffers a double dose of misery from air pollution due to its topography. Air pollution tends to become trapped in the cities and linger because of the nation's mountains, thus increasing the intensity of the pollution.

Foul-smelling foam resulting from chemical pollution covers a river in Jiangxi, China.

Land

China has an immense problem with soil contamination, due in part to its rapid industrialization. Chemicals have been routinely dumped following their use in industry or agriculture, with little regard for long-term consequences.

Another land issue is the all-too-familiar problem of deforestation. Many of the poor in these countries still rely on wood for fuel, and there is also an industrial demand for wood. Another source of deforestation is forest fires. Lacking the resources to effectively combat these fires, the people must rely on natural boundaries or weather to contain them. When vegetation is destroyed, massive erosion results, especially during the monsoon rains.

Proposed Solutions

We have already discussed one of China's solutions in the form of the Three Gorges Dam. Additional tapping of hydroelectric power will reduce China's need to build more coal-fired plants. In addition, China is working to build nuclear power plants, natural gas-powered plants, and other fuel plants to reduce air pollution. While China and Taiwan have the wealth and governmental resolve to resolve their environmental issues, Mongolia is struggling to match resources with the enormity of the challenge.

Although China has the national resolve to address environmental issues, local corruption remains rampant, and regulations continue to be downplayed or ignored. While some become rich, many in China suffer from the consequences of poor stewardship of resources. The challenge for China is to demand and ensure the care of its citizens while providing work for its teeming population. The Chinese government has also worked to end the use of plastic bags in supermarkets and to encourage its people to use reusable cloth bags instead. This change alone would reduce some of the country's hundreds of tons of waste produced each year.

Taiwan also struggles to balance the need for industry with the care of its citizens. One way the Taiwanese are trying to reduce pollution is the replacing of all gas- and diesel-powered vehicles with electric automobiles in the next twenty years.

A "Greenrunner" electric automobile at an exhibition in Taiwan. The Greenrunner weighs 1,190 pounds (with battery) and, after a recharge, can travel up to 132 miles.

SECTION REVIEW

1. Why do millions of Chinese continue to flock to the cities?
2. What are three environmental issues in China, Mongolia, and Taiwan?
3. How have the Chinese, Mongolian, and Taiwanese governments dealt with environmental issues?
4. Explain how the Chinese, Mongolian, and Taiwanese economies and people have interacted with the environment.
5. What solutions to current environmental issues in China, Mongolia, and Taiwan would you propose?

Sandstorm in Beijing, China, that originated in the Gobi Desert over six hundred miles away

20 CHAPTER REVIEW

SUMMARY

1. The physical geography of China, Mongolia, and Taiwan was shaped by tectonic activity, volcanic eruptions, and glaciers. Continued development of this region's natural resources is profoundly enhancing the economic prosperity of these nations and leading China and Taiwan to significantly influence the world's economy.
2. The people of this region have little ethnic diversity although they speak hundreds of languages. They enjoy similar activities, including ethnic foods, regional music, and sports. These societies continue to transition into developed societies. Common threats include desire for an expanded role in the world and political corruption.
3. A major challenge in China, Mongolia, and Taiwan is the need to make wise use of human and natural resources in ways that maintain strong economies without further endangering the environment. Close proximity of the nations results in shared pollution, potential strife for resources, and common desire for self-preservation. Goals for this region would include developing cleaner resources for energy production, caring for their citizens, and finding ways to protect the environment.

Terms to Know

- ❑ Tibetan Plateau
- ❑ Three Gorges Dam
- ❑ Asian Tigers
- ❑ one-child policy
- ❑ birth tourism
- ❑ Confucianism
- ❑ Taoism
- ❑ transplant tourism

Making Connections

1. What secret ingredient made buildings in China more durable?
2. Why is the Tibetan Plateau referred to as the "Asian water tower"?
3. How do landforms affect climates in China?
4. Why do you think Taiwan's economy has been successful?
5. Identify three political issues in China.
6. What role has Confucianism played in China?
7. What are some causes of deforestation in Mongolia?

Developing Geography Skills

1. Why is the population of China concentrated in the east?
2. What roles have glaciers played in this region?

Thinking Critically

1. Why do you think the people of Mongolia initially adopted Soviet-style communism? Why did they later reject communism in favor of representative government and a market economy?
2. Contrast Confucianism and Taoism.

Living in God's World

1. Write a paragraph explaining why the one-child policy is contrary to nature and Scripture.
2. Given the opportunity, how could you demonstrate the love of Christ to the cancer victims in China's cancer villages? (See Case Study on page 469.)

CASE STUDY | Cancer Villages in China

Twenty-seven percent of global cancer cases occur in China, with the top four cancers being lung, stomach, liver, and esophageal. Nearly 7,500 people a day die from conditions related to air pollution, and cancer has been the leading cause of death in China since 2010.

Many of these cancer villages are near chemical plants or coal-fired power plants. These plants produce massive amounts of air, soil, and water pollution. Often the contaminants contain heavy metals that are lethal to human and animal life.

The official local response ranges from some level of concern to outright denial. Local officials tend to discourage citizens from collecting samples and documenting the pollutants. Journalists and other outsiders who visit these villages in an attempt to document the pollution may be threatened, have their equipment confiscated, and be told to leave.

Two of the most polluted cities in the world are located in China. Some industrial communities in China now have cancer rates that are much higher than the national average, giving rise to the term *cancer villages*. The unofficial definition of a cancer village is a place where nearly every other household has had a family member die from cancer.

1. What is a cancer village?
2. In what country are cancer villages located?
3. What types of plants are most cancer villages located near?
4. How do chemical and power plants contribute to cancer villages?
5. How do officials typically respond to this environmental disaster?

chapter 21

JAPAN AND KOREA

472 Physical Geography
478 Human Geography
488 Interactions

BIG IDEAS

- What is the physical geography of Japan and Korea like?
- How do the people of Japan and Korea live?
- What are some of the challenges of living in Japan and Korea?

◂ *(top left) The Eikando shrine and bridge, Kyoto, Japan*

▴ *(above) The Mansudae Grand Monument in Pyongyang, North Korea, includes bronze statues of President Kim Il Sung and Leader Kim Jong Il.*

◂ *The Shibuya shopping district, Tokyo, Japan*

LIFE IN TOKYO

Tokyo is one of the most unusual and fascinating cities in the world. The Shutoken, or "Capital Region," includes Tokyo, Yokohama, and other cities that have blended seamlessly to form what is considered today to be the most populated metropolitan area in the world, with 36 million people. There is no excuse for being bored in Tokyo. There are numerous restaurants, stores, and museums to visit. There are hidden parks to explore and many cultural mysteries to solve. The trains will take you everywhere you need to go if you can interpret the colorful map with its labyrinth of crisscrossing lines and maneuver through the crowds, escalators, and tunnels. Since many things in the city are automated, it feels futuristic. Unlike many cities, Tokyo is ethnically homogeneous, very safe, and clean. As in other large cities, both natives and foreigners can feel insignificant or lonely.

◂ *A Japanese woman dressed in a traditional kimono in Sumida Park, Tokyo, Japan*

▴ *A Buddhist temple in Kwangju, South Korea*

GUIDING QUESTIONS

- What are the regions of Japan and Korea?
- What caused the landforms of Japan and Korea?
- What bodies of water are important to Japan and Korea?
- What is the climate of Japan and Korea, and how does it relate to their location on the globe?
- What are the natural resources of Japan and Korea?

Japan, North Korea, and South Korea occupy a relatively small portion of northeast Asia but have played a significant role in world history over the past one hundred years. The Japanese call their country *Nippon*, which means "source of the sun." According to their mythology, the rising sun first shone on the islands of Japan. Korea has been known as the "Hermit Kingdom," meaning it walled itself off from the rest of the world. While the North continues to hold to that nickname, the South has not. It is becoming an economic dynamo and is even challenging its much larger Asian neighbor, China.

PHYSICAL GEOGRAPHY

What is the physical geography of Japan and Korea like?

Regions of Japan and Korea

THE JAPANESE ISLANDS

Japan is a group of four main islands forming a crescent shape located due east from the coast of Russia and the Korean Peninsula. It also includes thousands of smaller islands that stretch southwest to northeast for twelve hundred miles.

The Main Islands

Hokkaido is the northernmost of the four main Japanese islands. Although it is the second-largest island and the largest **prefecture** (political division of Japan, similar to a province), it has a relatively small population. Japan's largest island, Honshu, is home to more than 80 percent of the Japanese people. Narrow coastal plains lie around the mountains of Honshu and support most of the population. The island contains thirty-four of the forty-seven prefectures and eight of the ten largest cities, including Tokyo on the fertile Kantō Plain. The smallest of Japan's four main islands, Shikoku, lies south of Honshu. With only 3 percent of the Japanese people, this mountainous and heavily forested island has only four prefectures. Southeast of the Korean Peninsula is Kyushu, the southernmost and second-most-populous of Japan's main islands. The earliest settlers built Japan's first cities here.

The Ryukyu and Ogasawara Islands

The Ryukyus are a curving chain of one hundred islands from Kyushu southwestward to Taiwan. Included among the Ryukyus is Okinawa, Japan's fifth-most-populous island and the only prefecture not on one of the four main islands. The thirty Ogasawara Islands are southeast of the main Japanese Islands. Notable islands in this group are Chichi Jima and Iwo Jima.

THE KOREAN PENINSULA

Korea is a peninsula that extends south from northeastern China. Mountains and hills cover most of the peninsula, which has been split since 1945 into two countries: North Korea and South Korea. A coastal plain extends down the west coast of Korea. All of the peninsula's major cities lie on that plain, including the respective capitals. Low rugged mountains cover the eastern half of the peninsula. Korea's highest mountain, Mount Paektu (9,003 feet), is at the north end of the Hamgyong Mountains. South of the Hamgyongs are the Nangnim Mountains. Running down the east-central portion of the peninsula are the Taebaek Mountains.

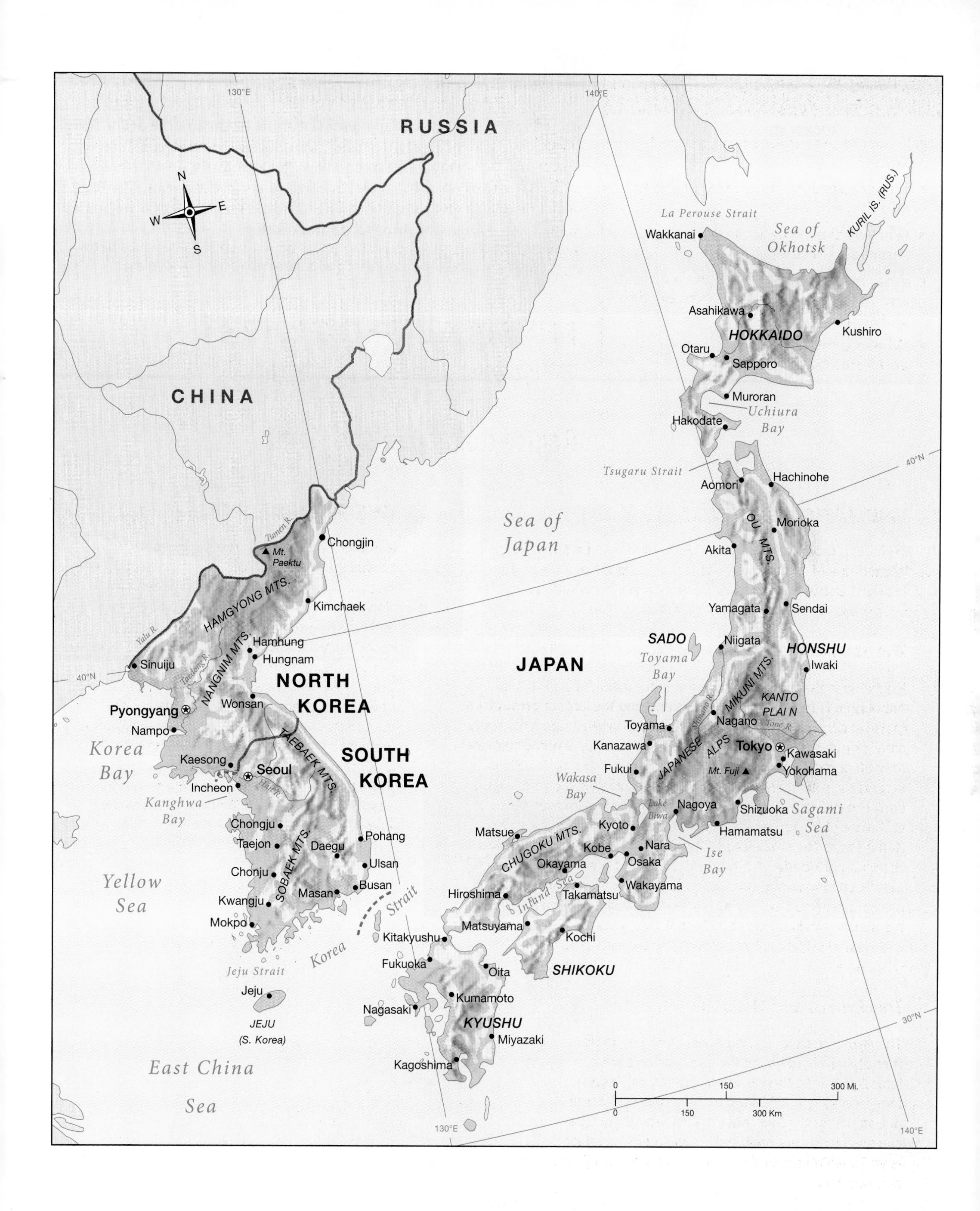
RUSSIA
CHINA
NORTH KOREA
SOUTH KOREA
JAPAN
N
E
S
W
130°E
140°E
40°N
30°N
La Perouse Strait
Sea of Okhotsk
KURIL IS. (RUS.)
Wakkanai
Asahikawa
HOKKAIDO
Kushiro
Otaru
Sapporo
Muroran
Uchiura Bay
Hakodate
Tsugaru Strait
Aomori
Hachinohe
Morioka
OU MTS.
Akita
Sea of Japan
Yamagata
Sendai
SADO
Niigata
HONSHU
Iwaki
Toyama Bay
MIKUNI MTS.
KANTO PLAIN
Shinano R.
Tone R.
Nagano
Toyama
Kanazawa
JAPANESE ALPS
Tokyo
Kawasaki
Yokohama
Mt. Fuji
Fukui
Wakasa Bay
Lake Biwa
Nagoya
Shizuoka
Sagami Sea
Hamamatsu
Ise Bay
Kyoto
Nara
Osaka
Kobe
Wakayama
Matsue
CHUGOKU MTS.
Okayama
Inland Sea
Takamatsu
Hiroshima
Matsuyama
Kochi
SHIKOKU
Kitakyushu
Fukuoka
Oita
Kumamoto
Nagasaki
KYUSHU
Miyazaki
Kagoshima
Tumen R.
Mt. Paektu
Chongjin
HAMGYONG MTS.
Kimchaek
Yalu R.
NANGNIM MTS.
Hamhung
Hungnam
Sinuiju
Taedong R.
Wonsan
Pyongyang
Nampo
Korea Bay
TAEBAEK MTS.
Kaesong
Seoul
Han R.
Incheon
Kanghwa Bay
Chongju
Taejon
SOBAEK MTS.
Daegu
Pohang
Ulsan
Chonju
Busan
Masan
Kwangju
Mokpo
Yellow Sea
Korea Strait
Jeju Strait
Jeju
JEJU (S. Korea)
East China Sea
0
150
300 Mi.
0
150
300 Km

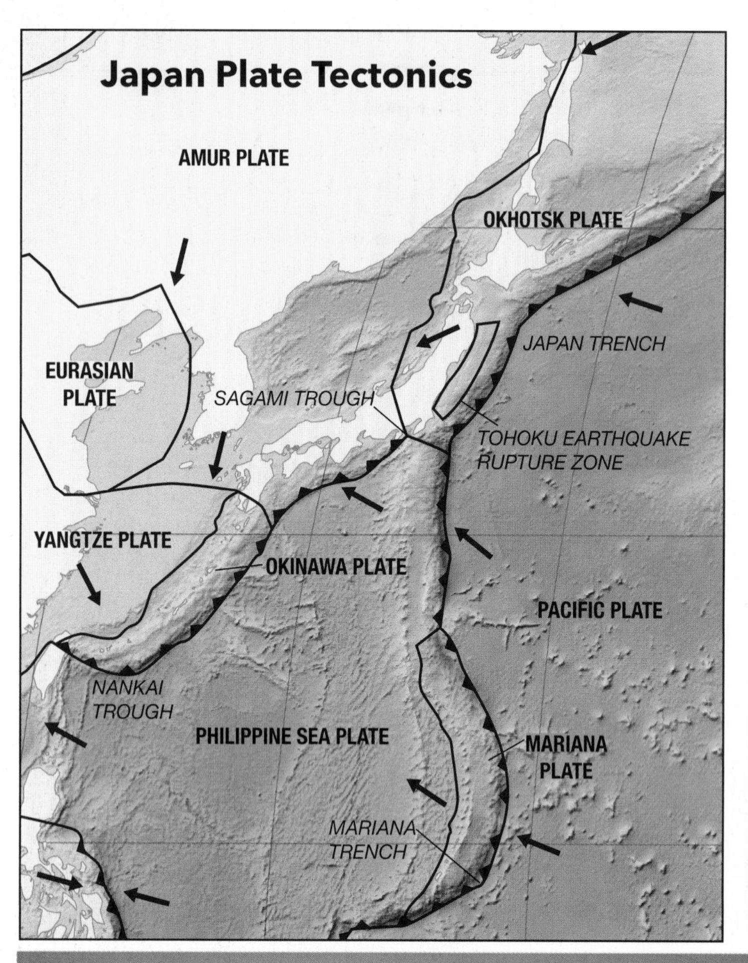

Physical Landforms

The Japanese Islands lie in the middle of the Ring of Fire. As a result, they suffer from the constant threat of earthquakes and **tsunamis**, destructive waves resulting from an earthquake in the ocean. The islands are dotted with one hundred and ten active volcanoes just waiting to be awakened.

Aogashima is a Japanese volcanic island in the Philippine Sea.

Mount Fuji, at 12,389 feet, is a stratovolcano like Mount Saint Helens.

Numerous thermal hot springs are a result of the volcanic activity of the islands. A notable spring is Jigokudani, known as "hell valley," in southern Hokkaido. Japanese macaques enjoy the springs during the wintertime.

▲ *Mount Halla-san is an extinct volcano located on Jeju Island and is the highest mountain in South Korea at 6,398 feet.*

▲ *The Hwanseongul Cave in the Taebaek Mountains in South Korea is one of largest caves in Asia; it is over four miles long and made of limestone.*

Bodies of Water

The Japanese Islands face the open Pacific Ocean to the east. To the west the islands create the Sea of Japan, or East Sea, which separates them from the Korean Peninsula. Because the East Sea is almost entirely enclosed by the islands and the mainland, it has almost no tide. Areas of the sea have a higher concentration of dissolved oxygen resulting from the convection current, which occurs when the cold oxygen-rich water sinks under the warm water during the wintertime. This makes the sea a desirable home for fish. The Yellow Sea separates China from Korea. During the spring when the Gobi Desert sandstorms blow from China, they turn the surface of the water yellow. Tides on the Korean west coast are notable for having a wide variation, similar to those of Canada's Bay of Fundy. Though Japan is surrounded by water, it lacks a large internal river system for cargo transport. For southern Honshu and the two smallest main islands, however, the Seto Inland Sea serves the role of a large river.

▼ *The Seto Ohashi Bridge crosses the Seto Inland Sea and connects various islands.*

The Lotte World Tower stands in the distance along the Han River in central Seoul, South Korea.

Heaven Lake in North Korea is the mythical birthplace of the Korean people.

North Korea has the largest and longest rivers in this region, but in general, both Japan and Korea lack significant rivers when compared to other regions of the world. The Yalu and Tumen Rivers divide the Korean Peninsula from China and Russia. These are the largest rivers in Korea. The Han River, along its delta, forms part of the border between North and South Korea in the west; it also divides Seoul in half. The largest river in South Korea is the Nakdong, which begins in the Taebaek Mountains and flows into the sea at Busan.

A beautiful, culturally significant lake for all of Korea is Heaven Lake, which occupies the caldera of Mount Paektu on the border of North Korea and China. It is the mythical birthplace of the Korean people.

Climates of Japan and Korea

Most of Japan has four seasons, with a cool temperate climate in the far north and a tropical climate in the far south. While the ocean and seas moderate the weather for both Japan and Korea, Hokkaido has long and severe winters and cool summers because of the influence of the cold Oyashio (or Kuril) Current, which flows from north to south.

In Korea, Jeju Island in the far south has a humid subtropical climate, and Busan on the southern mainland gets very little snow in the winter. But as one moves north toward the main body of the Asian continent, the temperature decreases significantly. Pyongyang is five degrees cooler on average than Seoul even though the cities are only 120 miles apart.

Resources of Japan and Korea

Of the three countries highlighted in this chapter, North Korea has the most natural resources and arable agricultural land. Yet it cannot produce enough food to feed its people. Japan can only grow crops on its coastal plains, which make up less than 12 percent of the land. Consequently, farmers rely on technology to maximize crop yields as the Dutch do. South Korea has a greater percentage of arable land than Japan. Most of the farmland is dedicated to growing rice. The favorable climate and irrigation permit two rice harvests a year. The most important crops for North Korea are rice and corn. Almost 20 percent of the land is arable, but mismanagement and a cooler climate mean that crop yields lag significantly behind those of the other two countries.

Because Japan has only a negligible amount of mineral resources, it is one of the largest importers of fossil fuels. One of the reasons Japan invaded Southeast Asia in World War II was to harvest the mineral resources there. South Korea also lacks large amounts of mineral resources, although it does have some reserves of coal. North Korea has large amounts of coal and tungsten. Tungsten is a hard element used to make tools such as saw blades and drill bits. It is also used in bullets and rocket parts. Tungsten jewelry is becoming more popular. It is believed that there may be a wealth of rare-earth minerals under the ground in North Korea. The value may exceed six trillion dollars.

▲ *(top) A Japanese farmer uses his tablet computer to maximize his strawberry harvest.*

▲ *A South Korean farmer drives a rice transplanter to plant the rice seedlings in the paddy.*

◀ *North Korean peasants cultivate rice fields at dawn.*

A white tungsten steel ring ▶

▼ *Tungsten*

SECTION REVIEW

1. What is a common landform of Japan and Korea?
2. Why are earthquakes and volcanoes so common in Japan?
3. Why is the Sea of Japan rich in fish and other marine life?
4. How does the sea affect the climate of Japan and Korea?
5. Compare the natural resources of Japan and South Korea with those of North Korea.

1100 | 1200 | 1300 | 1400 | 1500

1192–1590 Medieval Japan

GUIDING QUESTIONS

- How have Japan and Korea changed over time?
- How do the governments of Japan and Korea interact with their citizens?
- What is the economic health of Japan and Korea?
- What are the demographics of Japan and Korea?
- What are the cultural characteristics and diversity in Japan and Korea?
- What forms of religions are practiced in Japan and Korea?

HUMAN GEOGRAPHY

How do the people of Japan and Korea live?

History

Both Japan and Korea have similar histories. During ancient times both were made up of small regions ruled by competing clans. The clan was the basic unit of social, religious, and political organization. Both countries were unified by powerful leaders. They both learned from China's advanced culture, writing, literature, and philosophy.

Japan

The Yamato clan on the island of Honshu became the most powerful and forged a unified Japanese state in the sixth century AD. In the twelfth century, Japanese warriors called **samurai** protected the estates of feudal lords (daimyo), whose rivalries escalated into civil war. When the Yoritomo clan established itself as the country's strongest clan in 1192, the emperor granted Yoritomo the title of **shogun**, meaning "great general" of the people. Shoguns ruled Japan in the emperor's name until 1867. Japan wanted to remain isolated from the world, but American admiral Matthew Perry arrived in Tokyo Bay and, with the threat of force, made Japan open itself to trade. Japan decided on the "if you cannot beat them join them" philosophy. In 1868 the emperor was restored. Emperor Meiji reigned until his death in 1912. He embarked on a modernization program so that Japan would be an empire rather than a colony. Japan wanted the Western nations to see it as their equal, but despite its achievements, Japan was not accepted. Emboldened by an apparent victory over Russia in the Russo-Japanese war and a successful occupation of Korea, Japan invaded Manchuria (northeast China) on September 18, 1931, an act of aggression that was arguably the beginning of World War II in the Pacific.

The samurai were the military nobility of pre-industrial Japan.

Korea

The Korean peninsula is a bridge between the larger, more powerful countries on every side. It has been conquered at various times by China, the Mongols, Japan, and the Manchus. These invaders wanted not only to expand their borders but also to protect

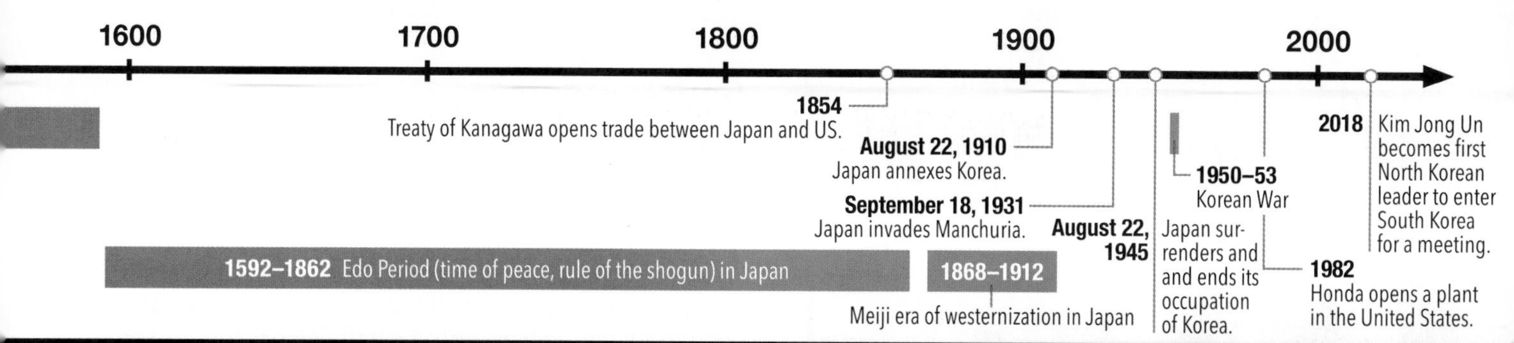

their respective countries from attack. However, the Koreans drove out each wave of invaders. In AD 668 the peninsula was unified under the Silla dynasty, but after 220 years it disintegrated. In 935 it was united again under the Koryŏ dynasty, which is where the name *Korea* comes from. The Koryŏ dynasty modeled itself after China, developing a bureaucracy. It was during this time that the country formed a unique culture and identity. The Joseon dynasty ruled from 1392 to 1896. The Korean navy repelled a Japanese invasion in 1592. In 1910 Japan finally gained control of Korea and governed it as a colony. The Japanese initiated an extensive modernization program in Korea, building railroads and developing industries. The Korean people, however, resented Japan's repressive government.

Admiral Yi used a fleet of his famed turtle ships to keep the Japanese from taking over Korea in the sixteenth century.

After World War II, the country was divided at the thirty-eighth parallel. The United States supervised the southern half, and the Soviet Union oversaw the northern half. Free elections were supposed to be held to set Korea back on its feet as an independent nation; however, the Soviet Union refused to give up its territory. Instead, the Soviets established a Communist satellite nation. Hoping to unify the peninsula under communism, the superior North Korean army invaded South Korea in 1950. United Nations troops, a majority of whom were Americans, were rushed to the peninsula. Initially, it seemed like they were too late as the forces were pushed into the southeast corner at the city of Busan. But the North's invasion had run out of steam, and when General MacArthur performed a counter-invasion at Inchon, just west of Seoul, it seemed the war was almost over. Just as the American forces reached the border with China, that country decided to come to the North Koreans' aid. They launched a massive invasion that forced the American troops back down the peninsula. The city of Seoul was devastated as it changed hands four times throughout the war. After three years of warfare, there was a truce. The boundary between North and South Korea, the thirty-eighth parallel, is a **demilitarized zone** (**DMZ**), a strip of land in which no troops or weapons are allowed. A peace treaty was never signed, although one was proposed in 2018. Technically the two nations are still at war. The United States has its largest single overseas base in South Korea. Over twenty thousand personnel are stationed on bases and camps throughout the country.

South Korean and American soldiers face North Korean soldiers at the DMZ.

▲ Emperor Naruhito is enthroned in a ceremony at the Imperial Palace on October 22, 2019, in Tokyo, Japan.

Governments

Japan and South Korea both have representative governments. Japan is a constitutional monarchy with a parliament, like Britain. Japan's constitution was largely the work of the American occupation force after World War II. Key specifications included protecting civil liberties, stripping the emperor of all but ceremonial power, and allowing Japan to have only a small defense force. (The latter may change, as many would like to see Japan take on a larger role in the world.) South Korea is a democratic republic with a three-branch system of government, more like the United States. In the years after the Korean War, South Korea saw a lot of upheaval in the government. The country went through six different republics; many included dictatorships and military rule. The current republic began in 1987. Much of the turmoil in the government has resulted from continual North Korean subversion. North Korea's official name is the Democratic People's Republic of Korea; however, it is neither democratic nor a republic. Nor is it for the people. The entire focus of the government is on the glorification of Kim Jong Un, his father Kim Jong Il, and his grandfather Kim Il Sung, the "Great Leader." Kim rules with unlimited power based on the idea that North Korea is the greatest, most prosperous nation on earth.

▼ New cars in Yokohama, Japan, wait to be loaded on a ship.

Economies

Japan

Japan is one of the leading economies in the world. Following World War II Japan reinvented itself as it had done during the Meiji period. The economic recovery was called the Japanese economic miracle. They built a thriving industrialized nation, importing raw materials and converting them into high-tech, high-quality goods that were in great demand. There was close cooperation between government and business. The well-educated populace provided a diligent and intelligent workforce, willing to sacrifice personal happiness for the success of the nation. Japanese brands, especially its automobiles, became the standard and gained a well-deserved reputation for safety and quality of craftsmanship. Toyota is one of the largest automakers in the world. It was the first automaker to sell more than 10 million vehicles in a year. Many other Japanese automakers, such as Nissan,

Honda, and Suzuki, are huge worldwide. By the 1980s it looked like Japan would again take over the world, this time economically. But growth declined significantly in the 1990s, a time period the Japanese refer to as "the lost decade." The government got more involved in the economy by printing money. Japan is the most indebted country in the world when debt to gross GDP is compared. It has one of the highest costs of living, which contributes to the demographic crisis of low birthrates, thereby increasing economic woes by not providing enough potential employees.

South Korea

Following the Korean War, South Korea was one of the poorest countries in the world. As late as 1965 North and South Korea were almost equal economically. Much like Japan, South Korea underwent a period of rapid economic transformation that was called the "miracle on the Han River." The economic growth revolved around *chaebols*, huge companies that have close relations with the government. The most well-known chaebols worldwide are Samsung, Hyundai, and LG. These companies were founded by families who continue to have the final say in business decisions. They are huge conglomerates. Samsung specializes in electronics but is also involved in insurance, construction, and shipbuilding. An employee of a particular chaebol will often live in an apartment built and owned by that chaebol. Hyundai is not only one of the world's leading car manufacturers; it also makes ships and trains and even operates department stores.

▲ *Companies like Samsung have many high-rise apartments for their employees and others.*

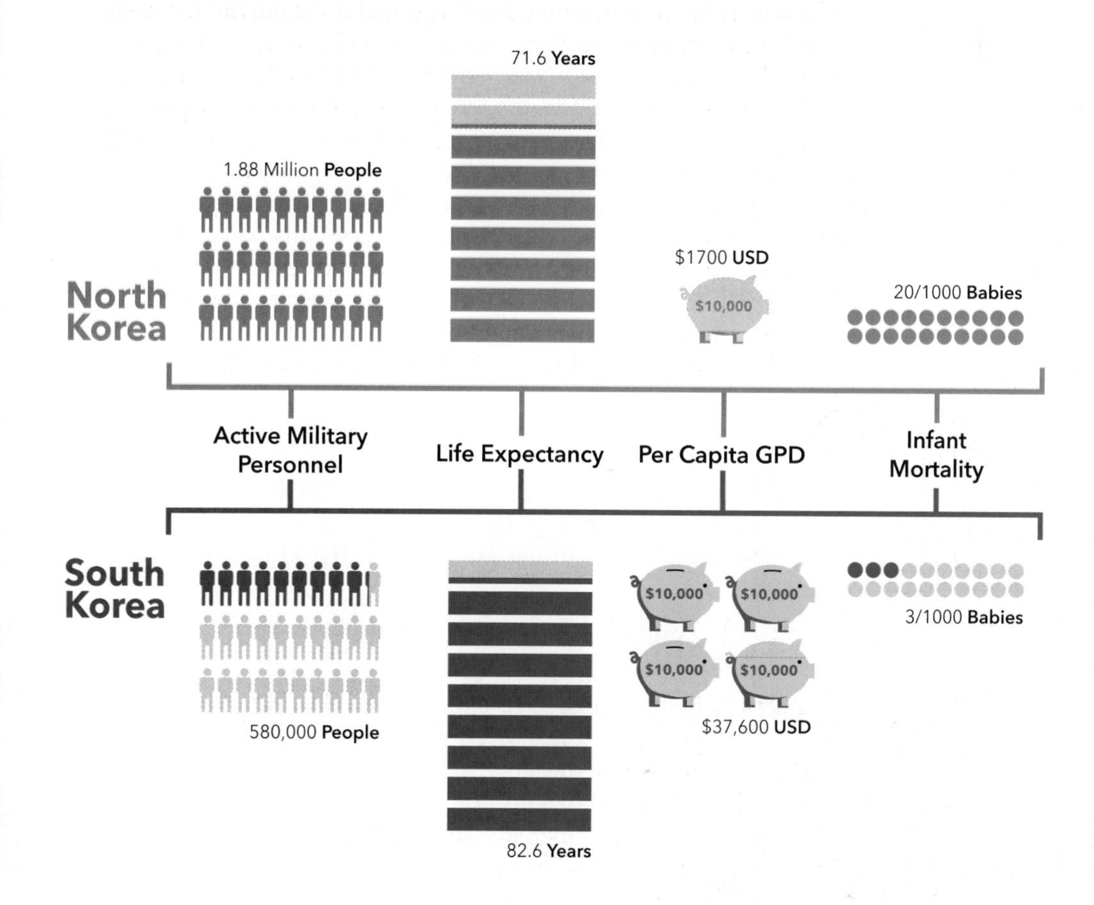

GLOBAL IMPACT | Nuclear Proliferation

"BALLISTIC MISSILE THREAT INBOUND TO HAWAII. SEEK IMMEDIATE SHELTER. THIS IS NOT A DRILL." On January 13, 2018, everyone with a cell phone in Hawaii received this text message. Thankfully it was a false alarm and did not create mass panic, being Saturday morning. But it put in sharp focus the threat of a nuclear armed North Korea. For several months there had been a war of words and actions between North Korea and the United States. North Korea had been testing nuclear bombs and launching missiles, some passing over Japan. In response, the president increased sanctions on North Korea and stepped up military exercises in South Korea.

By 1964 only five nations possessed nuclear weapons. World leaders saw the need to stop the spread before an irresponsible country obtained them. In 1968 the Non-Proliferation of Nuclear Weapons Treaty (NPT) was completed and signed by almost all the countries of the world, including North Korea. The treaty had three goals: stopping more countries from gaining weapons, moving toward the disarming of those who had them, and emphasizing the peaceful use of nuclear power. By 1991 all nuclear weapons had been taken out of South Korea, and it signed the Joint Declaration on the Denuclearization of the Korean Peninsula with North Korea. But all along the North was progressing in its effort to produce a nuclear bomb.

Kim Jong Il's fear of losing power greatly increased with the end of the Cold War. In 2006 the North completed its first nuclear weapons test. His son, Kim Jong Un, saw keeping his nuclear weapons as the only means of staying in power as he witnessed what happened to dictators who did not possess weapons of mass destruction. For instance, Saddam Hussein did not have a nuclear bomb, and his country was invaded. Muammar Qaddafi renounced his weapons of mass destruction program, and he was eventually killed. The United States has tried both rewards and threats to stop North Korea's weapons program; to date, both methods have been unsuccessful.

1. Why would the world want to limit the spread of nuclear weapons?
2. How did the nonproliferation treaty prove to be ineffective?
3. What solutions would you suggest to get North Korea to give up its nuclear weapons?

North Korean leader Kim Jong Un inspects the test-fire of the intercontinental ballistic missile Hwasong-14 on July 4, 2017. It is capable of reaching most cities in the United States.

North Korea

The North Korean government owns all industries and farms. Everything is centrally directed. Kim Jong Un demonstrates little concern for his people; however, he has allowed a black market to exist for more than ten years because it brings some capital into the country. This black market trades mainly with China. On average one person per household works in the black market. The North Korean government is also known to operate illicit industries such as counterfeiting currency, manufacturing illegal drugs, and trafficking humans and weapons.

Demographics

Japan and South Korea have some of the lowest fertility/birth rates. In 2009 Japan had a negative population growth rate for the first time; it has averaged negative 0.01 percent growth since then. The country has lost more than a million and a half people. While other nations replace their missing babies through immigration, Japan has largely rejected this option, although that may be changing. South Korea, which is not projected to see population decline until 2021, has also resisted allowing large-scale permanent immigration. North Korea has a higher fertility rate, but it has a significantly smaller population. Due in part to the effects of communism, a devastating famine from 1994 through 1998 killed as many as 3.5 million.

Japan is over 90 percent urbanized; the rate has gone almost straight up since the 1950s. South Korea's urbanization rate is in the 80s and has been going up rapidly since the 1970s. North Korea's rate is in the 60s and is not projected to dramatically increase. South Korea is one of the most densely populated nations in the world, with over 1,300 people per square mile.

The Korean language is slightly different between the North and South. The South has adopted newer words from English and other languages with little change to the pronunciation, while the North prefers to borrow new words from the Russian language or to create Korean alternatives.

Unlike other countries Japan and the Koreas have almost no other ethnicities living in them. Japan does have a native minority in Hokkaido: the Ainu, Japan's original inhabitants. They number over 17,000. Although the Japanese have traditionally considered the Ainu an inferior people, the Japanese government has begun to compensate the Ainu monetarily for the years of mistreatment and discrimination. It has officially recognized the Ainu as an indigenous group.

Culture and Diversity

These cultures are at the same time fascinating, frustrating, and mysterious to the outsider. Japan and the Koreas are similar since Korea was colonized by Japan and both were influenced by China. One benefit of the homogeneous society is the feeling that everyone is family. Almost 50 percent of Koreans have the last name Kim, Lee, or Park. The family aspect of the culture makes for a relatively safe society. It is not uncommon to see elementary children walking alone in downtown Tokyo or Seoul. But as in any family, there are many rules. Foreigners will be excused for not following many of the rules, but one rule that can never be broken is no shoes in the house, apartment, hotel room, or even certain restaurants.

Of course, there are many differences between Japanese and Korean culture. Japanese tend to live in houses, while Koreans seem to prefer the high-rise apartment life. Japanese are known for what seems to the outsider as being excessively polite in public and in the workplace, while at home children are casual with their parents. Koreans hold strictly to the trait of showing honor to one's elders, including parents. South Korea has a greater number of people with English language skills than Japan, perhaps a result of having closer ties to the United States over the past seventy years.

- Children in Japan and South Korea generally make their way to and from school by themselves, even walking downtown.
- (bottom) Japan is known for its Kawaii "cute" culture. Even ordinary things like trains, parking lots, and construction sites can be decorated in this fashion.

▲ *Sushi and sashimi are types of Japanese cuisine that have become popular worldwide.*

Japanese Culture and Foods

Cultural anthropologists have placed Japan on the extreme end of the high-context cultural scale. So, as expected, we see a society in which social harmony is of the highest value; the group is more important than the individual. Communication depends heavily on nonverbal cues. But we would also expect to find a seemingly chaotic disordered environment and a place that accepts "good enough" in exchange for keeping harmony. Yet the cities and rural areas of Japan resemble those of their counterparts on the extreme low-context scale, Germany and Switzerland. One would not expect a company like Toyota to come from a high-context culture. What can explain this contradiction? The Meiji period was a time when the Japanese changed their culture. They wanted to learn from others who were doing things better but also retain their own identity. They particularly admired German culture.

▲ *Another type of Japanese cuisine is tempura, which is deep fried fish, vegetables, or chicken.*

Korean Culture and Foods

Koreans are proud of their unique culture and inventions. The Korean alphabet, Hangul, is one of the most efficient alphabets in the world. Because it is phonetic, the letters have consistent sounds. It was invented in the fifteenth century by King Sejong. Before that Koreans used Chinese characters to represent their words, which resulted in high illiteracy rates because of the complexity of Chinese characters. Ondol is the unique Korean home heating system, invented in ancient times. It uses hot water pipes under the floor to radiate heat. Because of this, activities such as eating and sleeping can

The diagram shows how the Ondol system worked in ancient times. Today rather than heating rocks with a wood fire, they heat water using electricity or gas, but it is the same principle. ▶

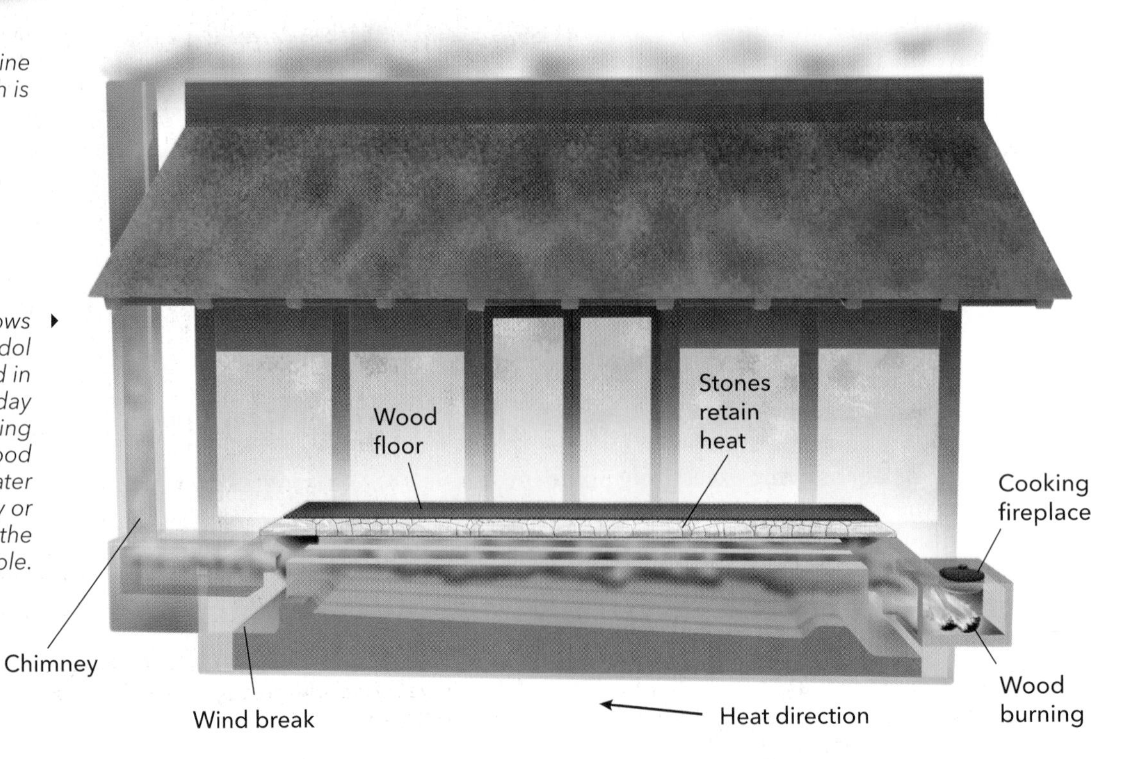

Koreans eat in the traditional manner, sitting on the floor with a low table.

take place on the floor. Although most people have incorporated beds and dining tables, some still live traditionally, using bedding on the floor and eating at the very low dining table with seating on the floor. They return to this tradition especially when guests visit. Yeogwans, hotels without beds, are still common around South Korea.

A special meal includes many small side dishes of vegetables, seaweed, and other mysteries. The main dish is barbecued meat cooked in the center of the table. Individuals can pick from the side dishes or the meat. One will eat the meat by wrapping it in a cabbage or chwi-namul leaf.

Korean food is very spicy. Kimchi, fermented cabbage mixed with spices, is usually eaten with every meal.

Religion

The majority religion of this region is Buddhism. Throughout Japanese history Shintoism and Buddhism slowly merged until 1868 when the two were separated. Most people continue to follow both without sensing a contradiction. For instance, weddings are often Shinto ceremonies, while funerals are almost always Buddhist. Since Buddhism lends itself to being practiced loosely, very few who call themselves Buddhists are fervent followers.

While large numbers of Chinese and Koreans are Christians, that is not the case in Japan. In the seventeenth century there were as many as 300,000 Christians in Japan, mainly on Kyushu, but because the rulers feared foreign involvement, the Christians were brutally persecuted and virtually wiped out. There were reports that the emperor offered to convert and declare Christianity the official religion following World War II. This might have made a great difference since the Japanese tend to act as one, but those reports were probably the result of General MacArthur and others misinterpreting Japanese politeness and high-context communication. In any case, despite allowing missionaries to work in the nation for over seventy-five years, Japan has a very small percentage of Christians.

Christianity in Korea is a special story. The gospel did not arrive by foreign missionaries but via Korean laypeople who heard it while they were in China in the early nineteenth century. They brought it back to their home and were heavily persecuted because Christianity was considered a threat to Confucianism. As more people converted, however, missionaries were invited. The first two came from the United States, one Presbyterian and one Methodist. Their ministries resulted in those denominations being the largest in Korea to this day. In 1907 Korea was facing a powerful Japan poised to annex it. In light of this reality, a revival broke out in Pyongyang after the leader of a church there, Kil Sun-Ju, confessed his sin, relating himself to Achan (Josh. 7:18). This revival marked the beginning of massive church growth. Ironically, it began in what is today North

Religions of East Asia

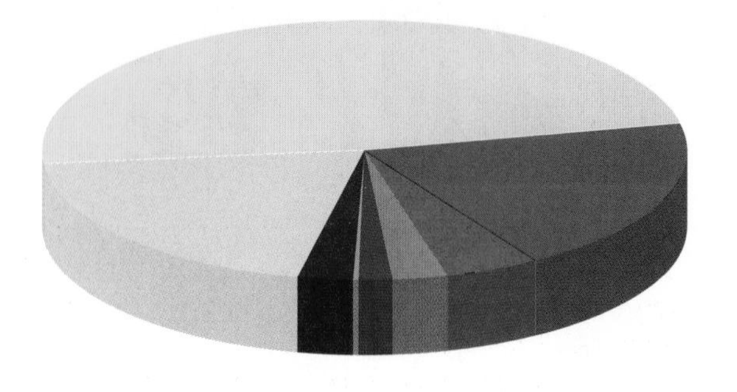

Buddhist	**48.5%**
Ethnic	**19.4%**
Protestant Evangelical	**4.7%**
Roman Catholic	**2.9%**
Protestant	**1.5%**
Islamic	**0.3%**
Other	**2.8%**
Unaffiliated	**19.9%**

Majority unaffiliated: North Korea
Majority Buddhist: Japan

Billy Graham held his largest crusade in Seoul. Over 1.1 million attended on June 3, 1973.

BELIEFS

▲ *A Shinto gate, Hiroshima, Japan*

Shintoism

The Shinto religion is the national Japanese religion but is followed equally with Buddhism. Shinto mythology describes the formation of Japan itself. The gods, or kami, emerged out of primordial chaos. In the seventh generation, the brother and sister Izanagi and Izanami emerged. They created the islands of Japan, but they also quarreled. The curses they pronounced on each other brought about the existence of death. From Izanagi emerged three of the most powerful kami: the sun goddess, the moon god, and the storm god. The sun goddess is the source of life and harmony. The storm god is the source of evil, but his evil comes about through ignorance rather than ill intent. The sun goddess's grandson descended to Japan, and his great-grandson became Japan's first emperor. Thus Shinto has a very close connection to the state in Japan.

In the late nineteenth and early twentieth centuries, the Japanese government claimed that Shinto was not a religion. Religions were human creations, but Shinto was said to come directly from the gods. Shinto received a setback with Japan's defeat in World War II. The Americans required the Japanese emperor to confess that he was not divine. Nonetheless, it is the central religion of many Japanese.

Shinto identifies disharmony with nature as the basic problem of the world. Shinto ritual plays an important role in bringing about harmony with nature. The world is pervaded with kami, which are gods or spirits. Humans themselves may become kami. They are good but are a great distance from becoming kami. The Shinto religion is not philosophical, and it rarely involves ethics. It is a religion of tradition and ritual.

Korea. Christianity became an indigenous religion and stood on three important pillars: 성경 연구 Seong-gyeong yeongu (Bible study meetings), 새벽 기도회 saebyoeg gidohoe (dawn prayer meetings), and 통성 기도 tongseong gido (collective audible prayer).

Today red crosses on the tops of churches blaze across the South Korean skyline. The percentage of evangelical Christians in South Korea rivals that of the United States. During the past forty years, South Korea has sent out a larger percentage of missionaries than any other country. But as in the United States, youth are abandoning the church in large numbers because of urbanization, materialism, secularism, and church scandals.

North Korea is officially atheist. Juche, created to be the official state ideology, is supposed to be an indigenous Marxism distinct from Leninism (USSR) and Maoism (China). North Korea needed to find its own place since it was caught in the middle of the Sino-Soviet split of 1960. In theory, Juche involves three principles: political independence, economic self-sustenance, and self-reliance in defense. In practice, Juche is the worship of the Kim family. In 2019 Kim Jong Un made this more obvious by replacing Juche language in the constitution with references to himself. The years of Kim family rule have resulted in the deaths of hundreds of thousands of Christians. Parents cannot tell their children about Christ until they are sure the children will not report them since the children may inadvertently reveal the secret or turn in their parents to avoid prison for themselves. Yet the church survives underground and may number up to 300,000.

SECTION REVIEW

1. How did the Korean peninsula get split into two countries?
2. Why might North Korea have had an easier time subverting the South's government instead of vice versa?
3. What factors enabled Japan to recover so quickly from World War II and become the economic power it is today?
4. Evaluate the causes of the demographic crisis of population decline in Japan and South Korea.
5. Evaluate why Japanese and South Korean societies are relatively safe.
6. Compare two of the religions described in this chapter.

GUIDING QUESTIONS

- How do the economies and demographics of Japan and Korea affect how the citizens interact with the environment?
- What are the environmental issues of Japan and Korea?
- What are the causes and effects of environmental issues in Japan and Korea?
- What are possible solutions to environmental issues in Japan and Korea?

INTERACTIONS OF PEOPLE AND PLACES

What are some of the challenges of living in Japan and Korea?

Because of their Buddhist beliefs, the Japanese and Koreans are known for living in harmony with nature. An example of this is the Japanese garden, which has become a world-famous type of public garden. The gardens often include arched footbridges, small pagodas, flowers, conifers, and ponds. They are always clean, uncluttered, and carefully laid out. Korea is called the "land of the morning calm." Hiking in the mountains is a popular pastime in South Korea. While the people of this region want to live this ideal of harmony, it is not always the reality. Urbanization, industrialization, and a densely packed population make for social and environmental challenges. South Korea tries to preserve its ancient way of life in

South Koreans love to go hiking and enjoy nature, but it is impossible to avoid crowds since the nation is densely populated.

A Japanese garden in Kyoto, Japan

various folk villages, yet the irony is that the place that seems to have the most calm is the Daeseongdong peace village, which is located in the DMZ less than a mile from North Korea and is under the threat of an artillery barrage. South Koreans celebrate Arbor Day (tree planting day) more seriously than other nations. Until 2005 it was a national holiday. They make tree planting a high priority because during their years under Japanese control almost all the trees were cut down.

▲ *This sign at Seoul's Seongsan Bridge promotes a phone counseling service for those who are considering suicide by jumping into the Hangang River. It is appropriately labeled "life line."*

Interaction among People

A major social/political issue in South Korea and Japan is the high suicide rate. The age groups most at risk are teenagers and the elderly. Suicide is the main cause of death for 15- to 24-year-olds. High school students in Japan and South Korea are expected to excel in academics. They spend much of their waking hours studying. Success in life depends on getting accepted into a handful of universities, which only a small percentage can do. Many teens and young adults cannot handle that pressure. A growing number of elderly in Japan and South Korea are finding themselves alone and impoverished. In the past, their children would have taken care of them, but as families have fewer children and those they do have live less traditionally, the support system for the elderly disappears. The South Korean pension system did not begin until 1986, so many who built the nation and are now reaching advanced age do not have enough credit in the system to survive on.

The South Korean government and churches are trying to decrease the number of deaths by suicide. Churches reach out to the elderly, visiting them at home and delivering meals. The government has placed encouraging signs, phones, and cameras on the bridges in hopes of keeping people from jumping. In 2011 a common pesticide that was used as a means to commit suicide was banned. The action decreased the suicide rate by 15 percent, but the number is still high.

Interaction with the Environment

Japan is regarded as one of the cleanest countries in Asia, but it exists as a paradox. The people go to extensive recycling efforts yet produce huge amounts of unnecessary garbage. For example, fruits and vegetables are individually wrapped. They want to save endangered animals yet hunt and eat whales. Still, Japan and South Korea are some of the cleanest industrialized nations in the world. In contrast, the outside world knows little about the environment in North Korea, and what is known is devastating.

▲ *Individually wrapped bell peppers for sale in Tokyo, Japan*

Water

There is some amount of groundwater pollution in Japan and South Korea. Japan is trying to contain the contamination of the seawater from the Fukushima nuclear plants. The East Sea has less fish and sea life. Fish catches have been smaller every year.

Air

Of these three countries, Japan has the best air quality. The Korean peninsula has air pollution comparable to that of Eastern Europe, and the North is ten times worse than the South. Acid rain is blamed for killing trees in northern Honshu. Dioxins released into the air by trash incinerators are an issue in Japan.

▲ *A picture taken March 24, 2011, shows the damage to two of the reactors at the Fukushima Daiichi nuclear plant.*

▼ *Yellow dust storms blowing in from China's Gobi Desert are a common springtime occurrence in Korea.*

Land

The soil in North Korea is significantly degraded. Forest cover dropped 17 percent from the 1970s to 1990s. Satellite images reveal how barren the North is. Even at the DMZ the South side is forested while the North side is barren. The few scientists who were able to visit the national parks in the North noted the eerie absence of any birds or wildlife. The mountain where North Korea has done its nuclear tests collapsed in 2018, probably releasing radiation into the air. Most of the trees in and around the testing area are dead.

Before 2011 Japan depended heavily on nuclear power. Thirty percent of its power came from nuclear plants. On March 11, 2011, the country suffered an earthquake measuring 9.1, the fourth most powerful ever recorded. The resulting tsunami was unprecedented, killing 22,000. The Fukushima nuclear plant was located precariously on the east coast, right in the path of the tsunami wave. An ironic issue with nuclear plants in operation today is that they require an outside power source. When the power at the Fukushima plant went out, the backup generators came on but were soon swamped. The workers were able to rig car batteries together to restore backup power, but it was too late. Three reactors melted down compared to just one at Chernobyl. These were the only level seven nuclear disasters in history, yet Chernobyl was far more destructive because it did not have a containment structure as Fukushima did.

Reasons for Environmental Issues

The lack of sea life in the East Sea is blamed on overfishing by the surrounding countries and the dumping of chemicals. The primary cause of air pollution in South Korea and Japan is dust that is picked up in the Gobi Desert in China and Mongolia and carried by wind in the springtime. Secondary causes of air pollution are diesel vehicle emissions, dioxin from burning garbage, and emissions from coal power plants. North Korea has pledged to build more coal power plants. North Korea suffers soil degradation and deforestation because the people need to use every piece of wood for fuel. They do not use twentieth-century farming techniques for reducing erosion.

Proposed Solutions

The Japanese probably have some of the most ingenious solutions to environmental issues. They are using freshwater mussels to clean up dirty rivers; the mussels feed on the chemicals. Clams were harvested in Tokyo Bay in 2008 for the first time in forty years after the Japanese made serious efforts to clean the water. They have cleaned the Kyu-Otagawa River in Hiroshima with pillars made of coal ash from power plants; the pillars decompose the sludge.

South Korea declared fine dust a social disaster and enacted different measures to control it. They use airplanes to seed clouds and clear the air. South Korean public and private organizations went to China and Mongolia to plant trees in the desert. Many inventors have tried to resolve the issue of diesel emissions. In 2002 some Japanese inventors claimed to have a device that removed 90 percent of the pollutants from diesel exhaust. Inventions like this have helped to make new diesel vehicles dramatically cleaner. Japan has reduced the amount of trash it needs to burn through aggressive recycling. Japan is using trash to create new land. The trash is carefully processed and spread into the sea as it is layered with soil. South Korea pledged to get 35 percent of its power from renewable energy by 2040. The country has closed twenty aging coal plants.

After the Fukushima disaster Japan shut down its many nuclear plants but soon realized that the country could not get along without the power. The government allowed many reactors to be restarted, while putting in place safety measures so the plants could withstand the worst possible natural disaster. Newer types of nuclear plants are much safer than the Fukushima and Chernobyl type, both of which were built in the 1970s. Thorium and molten salt reactors are safer, do not require water for cooling, and produce much less waste.

The Maishima Incineration Plant in Osaka, Japan, is decorated to make it an attraction rather than an eyesore.

SECTION REVIEW

1. How might Japan and South Korea be victims of their success?
2. Why do senior citizens and teens commit suicide at such high numbers?
3. How does the yellow dust problem and lack of fish in the East Sea show that solutions need to be found regionally?
4. What may be some cultural reasons North Korea continues to degrade the environment?
5. What creative solutions to environmental problems have Japan and South Korea implemented?

21

CHAPTER REVIEW

SUMMARY

1. Japan is a crescent comprising four main islands, and Korea is a peninsula. Located on the ring of fire, Japan experiences many earthquakes. The seas and the Pacific Ocean are the most important bodies of water. Rivers are not as significant here as in other places in the world. The climate is temperate but subtropical in the extreme south. This region has limited arable land and natural resources.
2. Japan and Korea both were influenced by China and wanted to be isolated from the rest of the world. North and South Korea fought a bitter war which technically is ongoing. Japan and South Korea have representative governments and experienced rapid economic transformation. North Korea is Communist and is one of the poorest countries in the world. The countries are experiencing or anticipating negative population growth. These are high-context cultures, yet Japan has borrowed from European culture. Buddhism is the primary religion. South Korea has seen major church growth.
3. North Korea has the most serious environmental issues with deforestation and soil degradation. Japan has devised many solutions for environmental issues. Korea suffers from yellow dust blowing from China. Japan experienced a nuclear disaster after a tsunami in 2011.

Terms to Know

- ❑ prefecture
- ❑ tsunami
- ❑ samurai
- ❑ shogun
- ❑ DMZ

Making Connections

1. What are the four main Japanese islands?
2. Why are earthquakes and volcanoes largely not present in Korea?
3. What was the culmination of Meiji Japan's effort to modernize and become an empire?
4. What are the commonalities of the Japanese and Korean economic miracles?
5. Why are Korea and Japan homogeneous?
6. Compare the Chernobyl and Fukushima disasters.
7. What are the environmental issues in North Korea?

Developing Geography Skills

1. How do the mountains influence the economy and where people live in this region?
2. How have the history and culture been influenced by the region's seas?

Thinking Critically

1. What could result from the two Koreas reuniting?
2. Evaluate Shintoism's understanding of the problem with the world.

Living in God's World

1. Briefly compare North and South Korea in terms of environment. What are some solutions to North Korea's problems?
2. Evaluate the impact of childlessness in Japan and South Korea according to a Biblical worldview.

CASE STUDY | A Prison State

North Korea is a prison state, but within that prison there are degrees of prisons. Life in Pyongyang has been somewhat open to the outside world, and even photos of North Korean rural life have been leaked. But to date very little is known about what goes on in the many concentration camps. We know they exist through the testimony of escapees and through satellite images taken of the large complexes. Camps like Yodok are comparable to Auschwitz. An estimated 130,000 people live in these camps. Their life there is unimaginable. Regular beatings and torture are normal. Whole families are placed in these camps. Children can grow up never knowing what life outside of prison walls is like. They suffer for the political crimes of their parents, grandparents, or great-grandparents because of the rule that three generations are punished for one person's "crime." They are forced to work twelve hours a day at hard labor. The guards in the camp treat the people worse than animals. Everyone is forced to watch the executions. An escapee put it this way, "Death was part of our life." There are an estimated 70,000 Christians in these camps.

A United Nations report stated, "Systematic, widespread and gross human rights violations have been and are being committed by the Democratic People's Republic of Korea, its institutions and officials. In many instances, the violations of human rights found by the commission constitute crimes against humanity. . . . The gravity, scale and nature of these violations reveal a State that does not have any parallel in the contemporary world."

1. Why would North Korea punish three generations for one person's "crime"?
2. Why would the remainder of the world be largely quiet about these atrocities?
3. What can Christians do to support their brother and sisters in these camps?

A rare ground-level image of a North Korean prison camp

chapter 22

SOUTHEAST ASIA

497 Physical Geography
502 Human Geography
512 Interactions

BIG IDEAS

- What is the physical geography of Southeast Asia like?
- How do the people of Southeast Asia live?
- What are some of the challenges of living in Southeast Asia?

▲ *The Bagan Valley in Myanmar is filled with Buddhist temples.*

◂ *(top left) Beach in the Philippines*

◂ *(left) The "singing trees" at the Gardens by the Bay in Singapore*

▲ *The Cloud Forest at the Gardens by the Bay*

SINGING SUPERTREE GARDENS

The Gardens by the Bay in Singapore are a modern engineering and biological wonder reminiscent of Nebuchadnezzar's famous hanging gardens in ancient Babylon. These gardens were built on 250 acres of reclaimed land. The most amazing elements of the gardens are the cloud forest, the flower dome, and the supertrees. The cloud forest is a cool moist greenhouse with a 150-foot manmade mountain full of thousands of different species of plants. It has the highest manmade waterfall in the world. Visitors can reach the top of the mountain via suspended walkways. The flower dome is the world's largest glass greenhouse. It has a cool dry environment. Together the two greenhouses are home to over 250,000 different plant species from around the world. The engines for this ecosystem are the eighteen supertrees in the center of the garden that range in height from 80 to 160 feet. These tall structures covered with plants offer shade and collect rainwater and solar energy. Skywalks connect the trees, allowing visitors to take in the full expanse of the gardens and the city of Singapore. In the evening music is played in the "trees" as they light up.

◂ *The Golden Bridge in Danang, Vietnam, opened June 2018.*

GUIDING QUESTIONS

- What are the regions of Southeast Asia?
- What caused the landforms of Southeast Asia?
- What bodies of water are important to Southeast Asia?
- What is the climate of Southeast Asia, and how does it relate to its location on the globe?
- What are the natural resources of Southeast Asia?

Southeast Asia is a resource-rich and culturally rich region. It was the focus of intense competition and power struggles among European colonial powers. The large population centers cluster around rivers and along the narrow coastal plains where available harbor facilities make trade more feasible. Steep highland areas are heavily terraced to enable the production of abundant crops. The dense forests, steamy jungles, and rugged mountains tend to inhibit land travel between the various countries. Today, Southeast Asia is developing into an economic powerhouse, but the stresses of poverty, political corruption, and Chinese influence weigh heavily on the region.

MAINLAND SOUTHEAST ASIA

The mainland region extends out of the main body of the Asian continent into the sea like a claw. The claw is formed by two peninsulas, the Malay Peninsula in the west and the Indochina Peninsula in the east.

The Malay Peninsula

The Malay Peninsula contains the countries of Myanmar, Thailand, and half of Malaysia. Both Myanmar and Thailand have a mountainous area in the north, a central fertile river valley, and a large plateau to the east. The Hengduan Mountains straddle the China/Myanmar border. South of the Hengduans is the Shan Plateau, which is the largest physical feature of Myanmar. Thailand's large plateau in the east, the Khorat Plateau, opens into Laos.

The Indochina Peninsula

Indochina is so-called because of its neighbors, India to the west and China to the north. Laos, Cambodia, and Vietnam make up this region. Mountains cover most of Laos and Northern Vietnam. The Luong Prabang Mountains are in the north, while the Annam Highlands run parallel to the South China Sea. Cambodia, in the south, is mostly flat. The large Mekong Delta in southern Vietnam is that country's flattest area.

PHYSICAL GEOGRAPHY

What is the physical geography of Southeast Asia like?

Regions of Southeast Asia

Southeast Asia is divided into two large regions, mainland Southeast Asia and island Southeast Asia, each of which is further divided into two subregions, making for a total of four regions.

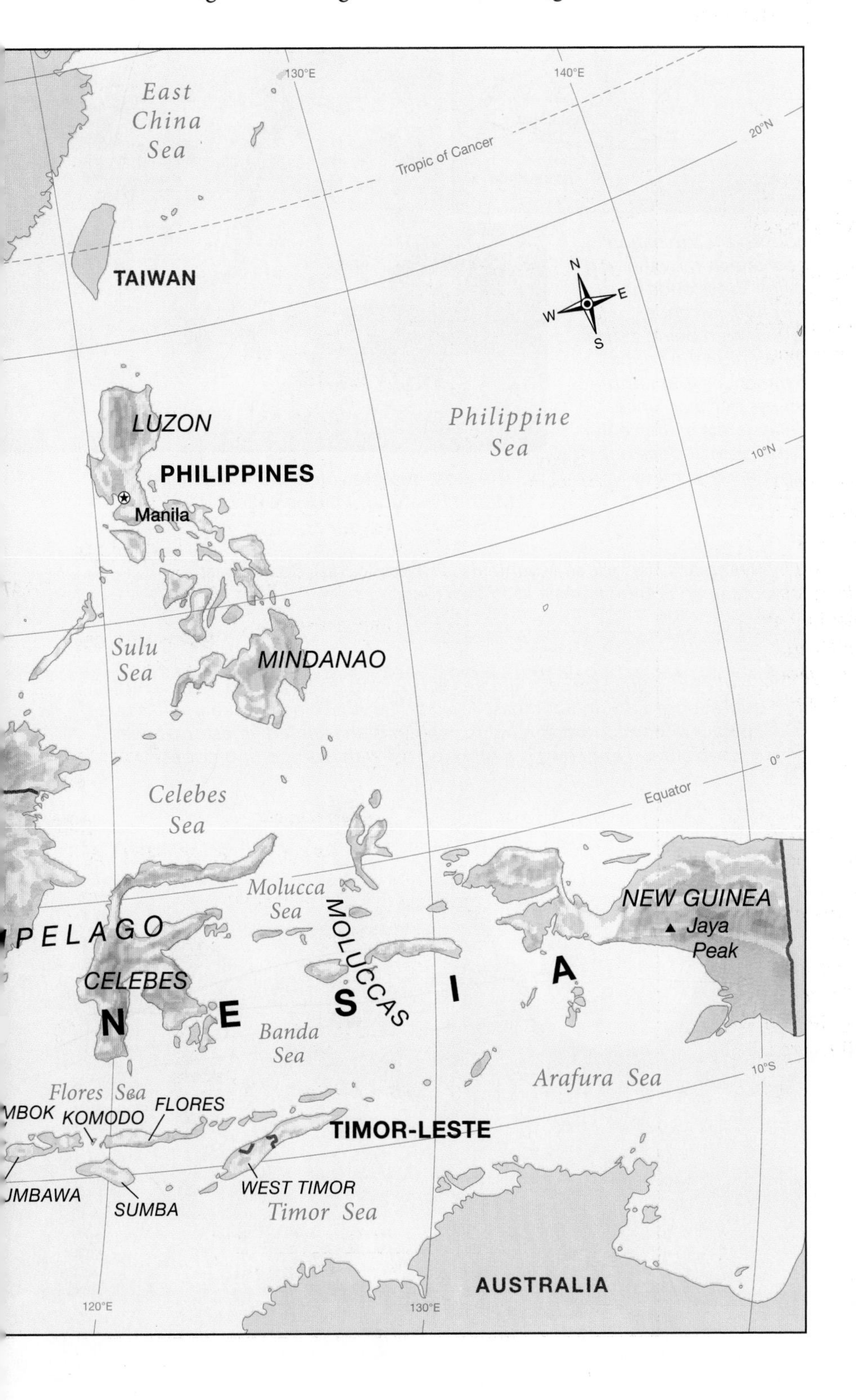

ISLAND SOUTHEAST ASIA

Island Southeast Asia is made up of the Malay and Philippine archipelagos, which contain some of the largest islands in the world.

The Malay Archipelago

The Malay Archipelago has five main islands: Sumatra, Borneo, Java, Sulawesi, and New Guinea. Most of the islands are mountainous and have many volcanoes. This archipelago contains five and a half countries. Indonesia is the largest country, with 17,508 separate islands. Only 6,000 are permanently inhabited. They stretch across more than three thousand miles, from Sumatra and the Indian Ocean in the west to New Guinea and the Pacific Ocean in the east. Singapore is a city-state that includes one large island and sixty-two smaller islands. Brunei shares part of northern Borneo with Malaysia. Timor-Leste is the eastern half of Timor Island.

The Philippine Archipelago

The Philippines is an archipelago made up of 7,641 islands, of which about 900 are inhabited. The two largest islands, Luzon and Mindanao, bookend the country. The islands stretch over a thousand miles from north to south. The country has over 21,000 miles of coastline, with pristine, secluded beaches.

Physical Landforms

Southeast Asia lies at the collision point of four main plates: the Indian, Eurasian, Philippine, and Australian. There are many other minor plates. All of this makes for some intense earthquake and volcanic activity. This region is on the western side of the Ring of Fire.

▲ *Indonesia is the nation most affected by the ring of fire. The islands have over 400 volcanoes, 150 of them being active. On average the country experiences four earthquakes per day. Since Malaysia sits in the center of the plate, it does not experience as many earthquakes.*

▲ *The most notable volcano of the Philippines is Mount Pinatubo, which erupted in 1991.*

◂ *In Myanmar's Hengduan Mountains is Hkakabo Razi, the highest mountain in Southeast Asia at 19,295 feet.*

▾ *The weathered limestone mountains at Hạ Long Bay, Vietnam, are examples of karst topography. In Southeast Asia and South China this feature has two forms called fengcong and fenglin. Fenglin is an isolated limestone tower with steep sides. Fengcong is a rounded hill with overlapping ridges.*

Bodies of Water

▲ The Saigon River flows through Ho Chi Minh City and enters the sea as part of the Mekong Delta.

Every part of Southeast Asia is influenced by its bodies of water. A glance at the map reveals that it is filled with seas, straits, gulfs, and rivers. This region serves as the boundary between the Indian and Pacific Oceans. There are also important resource-rich geopolitical flashpoints such as the South China Sea and the Malacca Strait. The seas and oceans serve as the most stable boundaries for these nations.

Several major rivers drain the mainland. The Mekong River begins in Tibet and flows through every mainland country except Malaysia. It is 2,700 miles long, the region's longest river. The Mekong's delta is the key feature in southern Vietnam, providing the people around Ho Chi Minh City, formerly Saigon, with fertile agricultural land. The Salween River is the second-longest (1,749 miles); it also begins in Tibet and flows through Myanmar, emptying into the Andaman Sea. It drains a more narrow basin than the other rivers. A more important river to Myanmar is the Irrawaddy River. The Irrawaddy Valley is the key feature of the country and is where the majority of people live.

Two smaller rivers whose deltas provide fertile land for the people are the Chao Phraya in Thailand and the Red River in Vietnam. The Chao Phraya flows from the northern highlands and empties into the Gulf of Thailand near the capital, Bangkok. Rice farming is prevalent in the valley. The Red River provides the space for the major population center in northern Vietnam. It flows through the capital, Hanoi, and empties at a delta into the Gulf of Tonkin.

▼ Boats travel down the Irrawaddy River, Myanmar.

▾ *Equatorial glaciers of Gunung Jaya Wijaya in Papua, Indonesia*

▴ *Many cities like Bangkok, Thailand, suffer seasonal flooding because of monsoon rains.*

▾ *A Komodo dragon in the Komodo National Park, Indonesia*

Climates of Southeast Asia

Because this region is in the tropics, at or around the equator, the weather is hot and muggy year-round, with small seasonal variations. Humidity is usually at 80 to 90 percent. The elevation can dramatically affect the weather, making the mountain areas near the Chinese border on the mainland relatively cool. In island Southeast Asia, some mountains are snowcapped with glaciers in Papua, Indonesia, formerly Irian Jaya. Apart from those highland areas, all of the islands have a tropical wet climate with two seasons: dry and rainy. The rainy season is caused by seasonal wind changes. This climate is perfect for sustaining rainforests and the animals that live in them. The monsoon season lasts from May to September for most of the region. It can bring a great amount of flooding to the river valleys where people live.

Resources of Southeast Asia

The Japanese called Southeast Asia, and particularly the islands of Indonesia, the southern resource area because of its many natural resources. This region has a great amount of fertile, arable land. Thailand, Vietnam, and Cambodia have the most arable land, while Laos, being mountainous, has far less. Singapore and Brunei, being very small, have the least. The rivers and deltas provide perfect conditions for growing the main crop, rice. Rice as a staple food is one of the reasons for the large population. It provides 11 million calories per acre, while wheat provides only 4 million. Rice can be harvested multiple times a year in Southeast Asia, whereas in temperate climate regions, wheat can be harvested only once a year. Ash from volcanic eruptions has made the soil in Indonesia very fertile. Almost all of the palm oil in the world comes from this region; the oil is used in a variety of food products. Other important crops are cassava (tapioca), peanuts, cacao, coconuts, and coffee.

Plant and animal life is very diverse here. Almost forty thousand different flowering plants are grown in Indonesia alone. Elephants, monkeys, orangutans, tigers, and Komodo dragons can still be found in the wild throughout this region. Fish and other marine life are a valuable resource for sustaining not only the local population but people around the world. Hardwood forests are a key renewable resource along with rubber, which remains a valuable crop despite the invention of synthetic rubber.

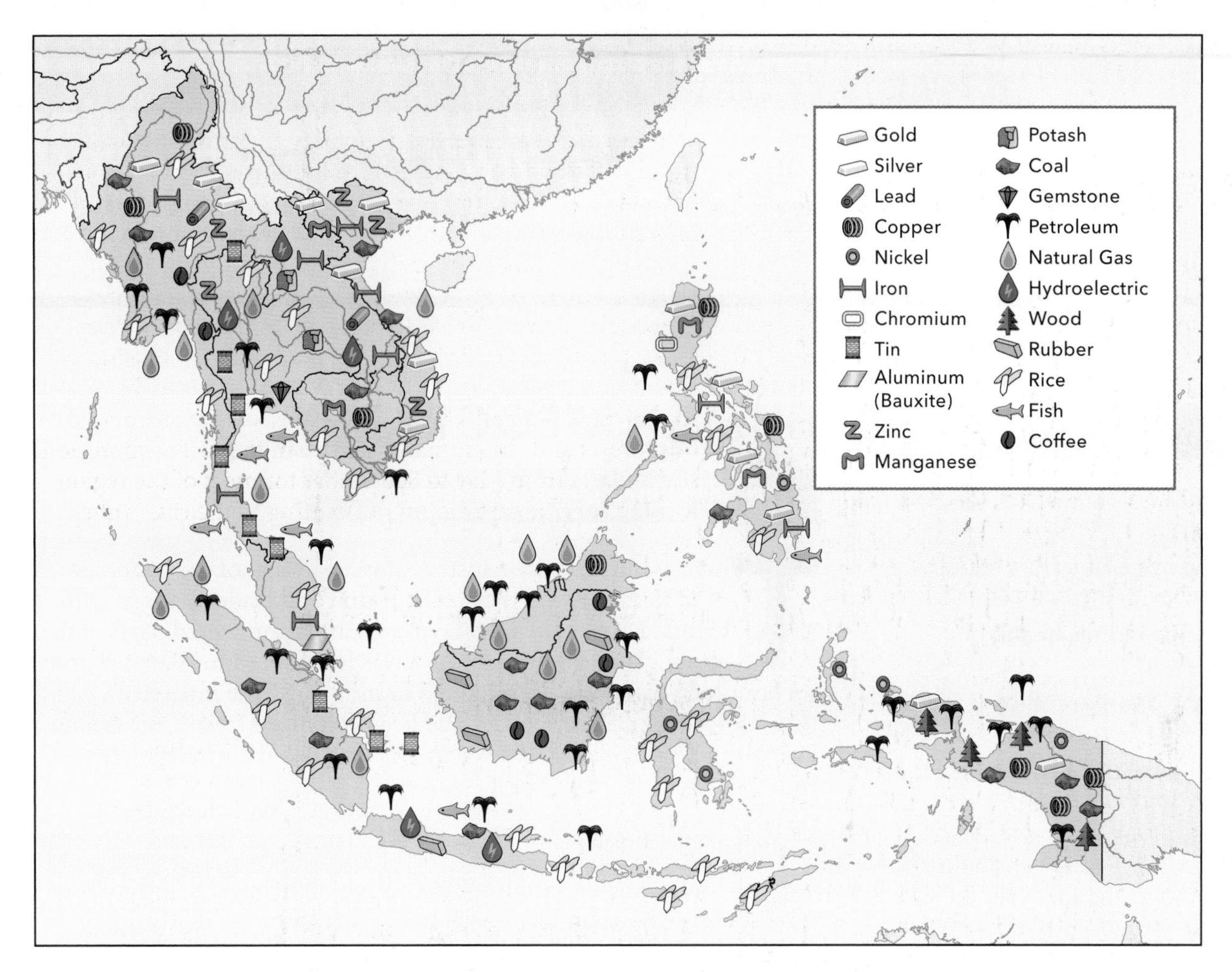

While this region does not have as much mineral wealth as other regions, there are amounts of gold, copper, nickel, tin, and gemstones. Indonesia has the world's largest sulfur mine. The miners harvest the sulfur by hand from an active volcano. Many Southeast Asian countries have supplies of oil and gas, with the most being in Indonesia and the South China Sea. The rivers that descend from the mountains in the northern regions of the mainland provide hydropower. Laos plans to be the battery of the region.

A sulfur miner inside the crater of Ijen volcano, East Java, Indonesia ▸

SECTION REVIEW

1. Determine which country is landlocked by looking at the map on pages 496–97.
2. Why does island Southeast Asia have so many volcanoes and earthquakes?
3. Which river not only forms much of the border between Laos and Thailand but also flows through Cambodia and Vietnam?
4. Why would most of the people of Myanmar and Thailand live in and around the central river valleys?
5. How might the floods during the rainy season every year affect the people and the economy?
6. What are two resources found in Southeast Asia that have not been mentioned as being found in other regions?

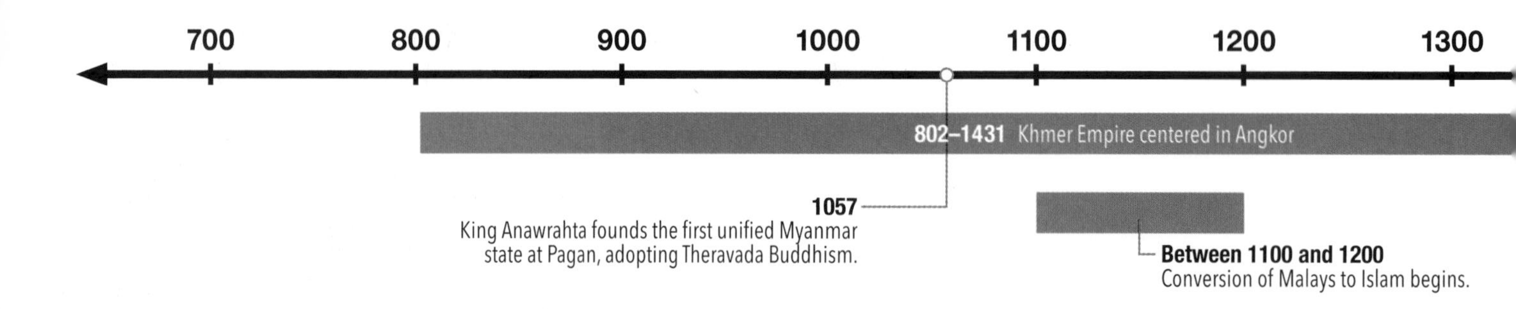

GUIDING QUESTIONS

- How has Southeast Asia changed over time?
- How do the governments of Southeast Asia interact with their citizens?
- What is the economic health of Southeast Asia?
- What are the demographics of Southeast Asia?
- What are the cultural characteristics and diversity in Southeast Asia?
- What forms of religions are practiced in Southeast Asia?

HUMAN GEOGRAPHY

How do the people of Southeast Asia live?

These countries have a history similar to that of the countries of Africa. Early on they had cultural and trade relations with China. During the Han Dynasty China conquered parts of the region. Island Southeast Asia was introduced to Islam around six hundred years after the religion's founding. By the nineteenth century, almost all of the countries had been colonized by the Europeans. Following World War II some countries received their independence, while others had to fight for it.

Mainland History

Thailand is the only country in this region to avoid being colonized. It served as a buffer zone between British forces in Myanmar and French forces in Indochina. The Japanese controlled the entire region during World War II. One positive result of colonialism was the unifying influence exerted among various tribal groups throughout Southeast Asia, which made independence possible and practical.

Vietnam was a central conflict zone of the Cold War from the mid-1950s through the early 1970s. In 1954 the Communist Viet Minh rebels led by Ho Chi Minh defeated the French at the Battle of Dien Bien Phu. At the same time, a conference in Geneva decided that Vietnam would be split at the 17th parallel, with the north under the authority of the Viet Minh and the South governed by Emperor Bao Dại. In what seemed

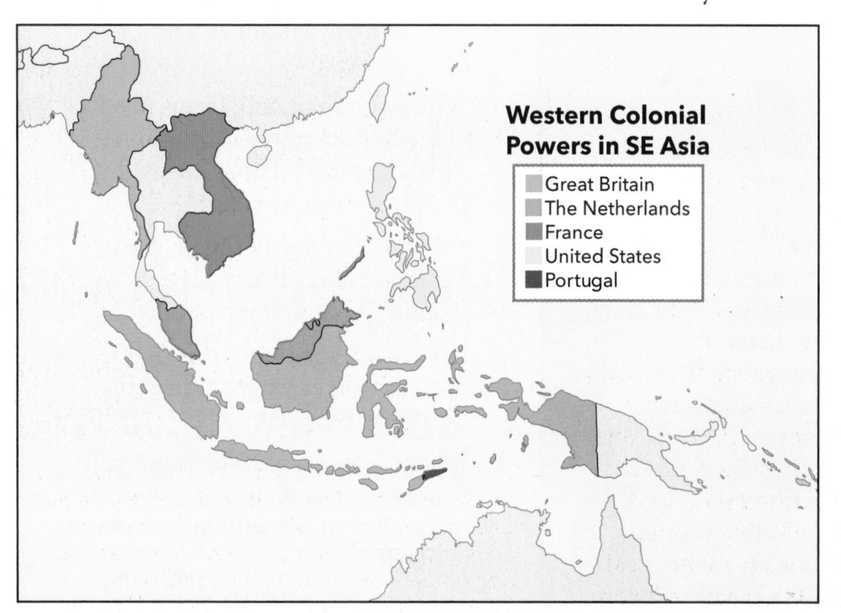

The Opera House in Hanoi, Vietnam, is a reminder of the French colonization.

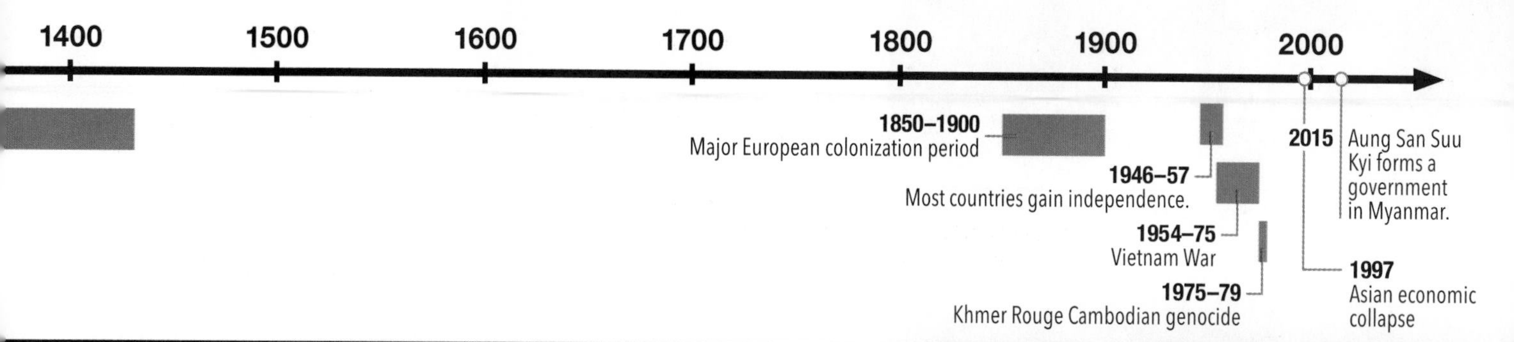

like a sequel to the Korean War, the United States supported the government of South Vietnam against invasion from the North and helped them fight the Communist insurgents in the South, the Viet Cong. The driving force for American intervention was the **Domino Theory**, the belief that if South Vietnam fell to communism the rest of Southeast Asia would fall, followed by the rest of Asia, and eventually the world. The United States sent progressively more troops to help the South, but in 1973 it signed the Paris Peace Accords with the North, virtually ending American involvement in Southeast Asia. In 1975, the South fell to the North, and over a million South Vietnamese were killed.

With the defeat of South Vietnam, the Communist Pathet Lao took over Laos and the Communist Khmer Rouge took over Cambodia in 1975. During the rule of the Khmer Rouge from 1975 to 1979, the capital, Phnom Penh, was emptied, and the country was forced into a primitive lifestyle. Authorities killed one-fifth of the population, including the educated, Christians, Buddhist monks, and anyone who appeared to threaten the regime. The people were indoctrinated into communism to the point that children thought they were doing right by killing their parents. The countryside was filled with skeletons and became known as the "killing fields." Vietnam invaded Cambodia in 1978 after the Khmer Rouge crossed the border and killed Vietnamese villagers. Vietnam drove the Khmer Rouge into the jungles near Thailand and occupied Cambodia for the next ten years. The Khmer Rouge finally surrendered in 1999, and the United Nations put the leaders on trial for crimes against humanity.

▲ *Unearthed skulls reveal the extent of the atrocities committed by the Khmer Rouge.*

Island History

The Philippines was the first Southeast Asian country to be colonized and the only one to be colonized by Spain. It has been influenced by Western nations more than any other Southeast Asian country. It was a Spanish colony for 334 years, followed by 47 years as a colony of the United States, one of the few with that distinction. The Japanese occupation during World War II delayed the Philippines' scheduled independence, but the country gained full independence in 1946.

The hub of Indonesian civilization has been the island of Java. It has been at various times under the control of Arab traders, the Dutch, the Japanese, and various regional warlords, dictators, and military juntas. With the end of Portuguese rule of East Timor in 1974, Indonesia took over the island, but the East Timorese fought a war for independence that resulted in the deaths of over one hundred thousand Timorese. In 1999 the East Timorese people overwhelmingly voted for independence. In response, Indonesian forces in league with local militia destroyed about 75 percent of the region's infrastructure before the UN intervened to stop the fighting. The new country Timor-Leste gained international recognition in 2002.

▲ *The Bell House in Baguio City, Philippines, is a reminder of the American colonization. Baguio City was built by the Americans in the mountains and established as the summer capital. Bell House was the summer home of the US administrator, and during World War II it became the headquarters of the commanding Japanese general, Yamashita.*

- (top) Thai Red Shirts supporters wave clappers and national flags during a rally at a stadium in Bangkok on November 19, 2013. They represent the working class and are left leaning.
- (bottom) These demonstrators are part of an opposition movement known as "yellow shirts," which is made up of royalists, the upper and middle class, and members of the military.

Governments

Ten of the eleven nations are members of the **Association of Southeast Asian Nations** (**ASEAN**), which was founded in 1967 to promote political and economic cooperation and regional stability. The organization's Secretariat is located in Jakarta, Indonesia. Timor-Leste is in the process of membership as of 2020.

All of the countries except Vietnam, Laos, and Brunei officially have some form of representative government. Brunei is a constitutional sultanate, which is like a dictatorship. It officially adopted sharia law in 2013. Thailand and Malaysia are constitutional monarchies. Instability characterizes most of these governments.

The effective head of Thailand's government is the prime minister, and although he is supposed to be elected, in many cases since 1932 he has gained power through coup d'état. In recent years two groups have engaged in counter-protests to vie for power: the Red Shirts and Yellow Shirts. The Red Shirts are made up of the rural poor and students, while the Yellow Shirts consist of the middle and upper classes.

Myanmar had free elections in 2015 for the first time in twenty five years. The country had a totalitarian government led by generals who suppressed the minority tribes by force. In 2006 the generals moved the capital from Yangon to Naypyidaw in the center of the country. The city is notable for its empty twenty-lane street. Aung San Suu Kyi, the leader of the opposition democracy movement, lived under house arrest for many years. Because of her tireless efforts, she was elected State Counselor in 2015. Myanmar had new hope with Suu Kyi's rise to power, but persecution of the Rohingyas, a Muslim minority, continued.

Of the Indochina countries, Cambodia, a constitutional monarchy, is the freest. Vietnam and Laos still have Communist governments that retain tight control and limit civil freedoms, but the governments do allow for economic freedom to a large extent. Because of this policy, Vietnam has experienced massive economic growth, as has Laos to a lesser extent.

Singapore is a parliamentary republic that pays governing ministers multi-million dollar salaries to keep them from being tempted by corruption. The people have accepted the restriction of certain freedoms, such as gum chewing or singing an obscene song in public, in order to enjoy a seemingly ordered and stable city-state that has continued to experience economic growth. Malaysia has a unique system in which nine sultans rotate as head every five years.

- Aung San Suu Kyi and the Myanmar military chief Senior General Min Aung Hlaing arrive for the handover ceremony at the presidential palace in Naypyidaw on March 30, 2016.

The Rohingya people arrive by boat in Bangladesh from Myanmar, escaping genocide.

Indonesia is a republic with a directly elected president and a bicameral legislature. After independence, it had a constitution that gave the president most of the power. From 1949 to 1998, Indonesia had only two presidents, Sukarno and Suharto, both military dictators. Following the economic crisis of 1997 and 1998, riots caused Suharto's government to fall. The president is now limited to two terms.

The Philippines is a republic with an elected president, somewhat like the United States. The government has been unstable since independence and has suffered several coups. In 2016 there was a notable change in leadership as the people elected the first president from Mindanao, Rodrigo Duterte. He was elected on a platform of anti-crime and anti-corruption. In 2019 he made peace with the Muslim insurgents in the south and granted them autonomy in a western section of Mindanao.

Filipino nurses attend the mass oath-taking ceremony in Manila. Filipino nurses work in hospitals all over the world.

Economies

Today all of the ASEAN countries are seeing continued growth, but in 1997 most of them suffered an economic collapse. It began in Thailand, as the currency lost much of its value, and then spread to Indonesia, South Korea, Malaysia, the Philippines, Laos, and other Asian countries that were affected to a lesser extent. The crisis resulted in massive inflation. For example, in Thailand something that cost $1 in October 1997 cost $2 by January. The **IMF (International Monetary Fund)** stepped in to manage the economies. Although the nations appreciated the financial assistance, they resented the loss of their sovereignty since the money came with certain demands for reform.

The tourism industry has grown for the whole region. Bangkok was the world's most visited city for most of the 2010s. Indochina is seeing a higher number of visitors as well. The tourists come to see the ancient temples and ruins and to enjoy the relatively unspoiled natural wonders. ASEAN nations are trying to transition from economies centered on agriculture and the export of raw materials to high-tech, consumer-driven economies. Most of these nations are involved in the manufacture and exportation of clothes and shoes.

Because of the historically high poverty levels, all of these nations have large economic **diasporas**, groups of people who work abroad and send money back home through

Tourists visit the Angkor Wat temple, Cambodia.

▲ *Singapore is one of the most advanced cities in the world. It is considered the hub of Southeast Asia.*

remittances, which helps the economy. But the diasporas also hurt the economy, as there is a **brain drain** when the smartest people of the nation emigrate to more developed countries. In 2013 over ten million Filipinos were living and working abroad, constituting 11 percent of the population. Other problems that inhibit growth include an underdeveloped infrastructure, corruption, and ineffective tax systems.

Singapore and Brunei are by far the richest of these countries. Singapore is the financial and high-tech hub of Southeast Asia. It has been a major trade and shipping location since the time of Christ and remains the focal point of trade in the region today. It is rated as one of the most competitive countries for business in the world and is noted for being corruption-free. Brunei is wealthy because it has successfully harvested its large oil and gas reserves. Bruneian citizens pay no personal income taxes.

The Myanmar economy suffered for many years because of sanctions imposed on it as a result of the government's persecution of ethnic minorities. The United States eased sanctions in 2011 but renewed them after forces started persecuting the Rohingya people. Timor-Leste has the greatest economic challenges since it is a very small nation and has to rebuild its infrastructure.

Demographics

The Philippines has the highest fertility/birthrate in Southeast Asia, but the rate is only above average when compared to the rest of the world. The Indochina countries are having children above the replacement rate, but the Malay Peninsula countries average below the replacement rate. The mainland is one of the least urbanized regions in the world. Thailand is barely over 50 percent urbanized, while the rest of the countries average in the 20s and 30s. In island Southeast Asia, Singapore is 100 percent urbanized, while the rest of the island countries have a slim majority of people that live in urbanized areas. Indonesia is the fourth most populated country in the world, and it is projected to rank there beyond 2030. Singapore is one of the most densely populated nations in the world, with over three thousand people per square mile. Laos is one of the least densely populated, with over eleven people per square mile.

Southeast Asia is as heterogeneous (consisting of many kinds) as East Asia is homogeneous (consisting of one kind). ASEAN has over 1,319 officially recognized distinct people groups, which may be more than any other region in the world. In general, we can say that each ASEAN nation has a couple of main ethnic groups, but in the mountains or isolated island regions, there are many additional ethnic minority groups. A minority group might have as little as one hundred people while still possessing a distinct culture and language. As in Africa, the national borders do not respect the ancient ethnic territories. Cambodia and Thailand are the most homogeneous, with one ethnicity making up more than 90 percent of the population. The Philippines and Indonesia are the most heterogeneous. In the Philippines, Tagalogs are the largest people group, making up 28 percent of the population. In Indonesia, Javanese constitute 40 percent of the population.

With so many ethnicities and languages, it can be hard to build a unified nation. All of the countries have one or two official languages that are used in school and for business. The Philippines and Malaysia have English as one of their official languages. Other official languages of the ASEAN nations are Burmese, Vietnamese, Thai, Chinese, Lao, and Malay. Because of this diversity of languages, most people are bilingual or trilingual.

Culture and Diversity

These cultures are complex and probably the most difficult for outsiders to understand. Since they are high-context, there are so many opportunities to be misunderstood and to misunderstand. When this happens on an international level, the result is war. There are four broad attributes of ASEAN culture: showing respect, avoiding shame, treasuring one's family, and having an easy-going attitude toward life. In general, these traditional values are held to more firmly in rural areas, while those living in urban areas tend to live a less culturally distinct life.

Respect is shown in many ways, but one obvious example is in the greeting. With the exception of Filipinos, Southeast Asians greet with their palms together in a prayer-like fashion. In Thailand, it is called the *Wai*; in Cambodia, it is called the *Sampeah*. There are three different forms of the Wai depending on status. Although they are Muslim, Indonesians also use the gesture, which they call the *Sembah*. Filipinos show respect by using the words *kuya* (big brother) or *ate* (big sister) when addressing family elders or even older strangers. Another subtle way of showing respect is to hand someone something using both hands.

Shame avoidance seems more important here than in other regions of Asia. In Myanmar, the fear of being shamed is called *Āna*, which means "cheek hurts." It is the concept of saving face, trying your utmost to avoid hurting the feelings of others, not getting embarrassed or embarrassing someone else. It is said that "face is more important than truth or justice." The way this plays out in society is that any criticism must be done privately and usually through a third party. Someone may say "yes" when they really want to say "no." Outbursts of anger are unthinkable.

Families are usually very close. Members of one's extended family may live under the same roof or nearby. Loyalty to the family is higher than any other loyalty.

An easy-going, light-hearted attitude pervades most of these cultures. The Philippines is known as "the smile of Asia," and Thailand is known as the "Land of Smiles." Thais have a concept called *sanuk*; the direct translation is "fun," but is much more than that. It affects all work and social life. Other cultures might split work and play. Thais, on the other hand, are lighthearted and view all aspects of life that way. Frequent parties and a love for karaoke demonstrate the laid-back lifestyle in ASEAN countries.

▲ *A Thai man offering the Wai gesture*

▼ *The Filipino practice of* Mano Po*, or "bless," shows respect to family elders. When arriving home a child will perform this gesture.*

◀ *A distinct trait of the Burmese is the application of Thanaka cream on their faces. It is made from the bark of a tree by the same name and is used to prevent sunburn.*

Foods

Southeast Asians take pride in their various dishes. A common greeting in many of these countries is, "Have you eaten?" Even when it is feasible to use things like microwaves and make quick meals, it is not something they take advantage of. Food must be prepared in the traditional way, which is labor intensive. The task of cooking may be an all-day chore, usually for the women of the family.

▲ *Burmese food is influenced by their Indian neighbors. A meal will usually include meat curries and soup. Other foods include preserved fish and vegetables dipped in fermented sauce.*

Insects are an important delicacy in Cambodia, more than in other Asian nations. Cambodia's rice was voted the best in the world, and its foods are noted for being fresh and organic. ▶

▼ *Thai cuisine has been exported around the world. There are four tastes that every Thai dish must have: sweet, sour, spicy, salty.*

▲ *Phở is the popular soup of Vietnam.*

▼ *Filipino cuisine manifests the mixture of cultures that have influenced the country. Soups and fish are a common part of meals. For celebrations, the main course is Lechon, a whole roasted pig.*

Religion

The people of ASEAN countries tend to be very religious, even in officially atheist Vietnam. Buddhism is the religion of the mainland; Islam is the religion of Indonesia, and Catholicism is the religion of the Philippines and Timor-Leste.

Mainland Southeast Asia

Buddhist countries are not tolerant of other religions, whether that be Christianity or Islam. A popular saying is "to be Thai is to be Buddhist." This makes it extremely difficult to reach these people for Christ since to become a Christian means facing the possibility of being disowned by one's family. Missionaries to this area must sacrifice and dedicate their lives with the prospect of few results. While Thai people are not as openly hostile toward Christians as other nations, it still can take years and years of building a relationship with a Thai person before he or she comes to Christ. The mainland Buddhism is mixed with spiritism. Villages have spirit houses and sacred trees. Ancestor worship is a part of life. Men are expected to spend time in one of the many monasteries each year. Thais are taught that if "a boy becomes a novice monk, his mother will not enter hell; if he becomes a full monk, his father will also not enter hell."

Religions of Southeast Asia

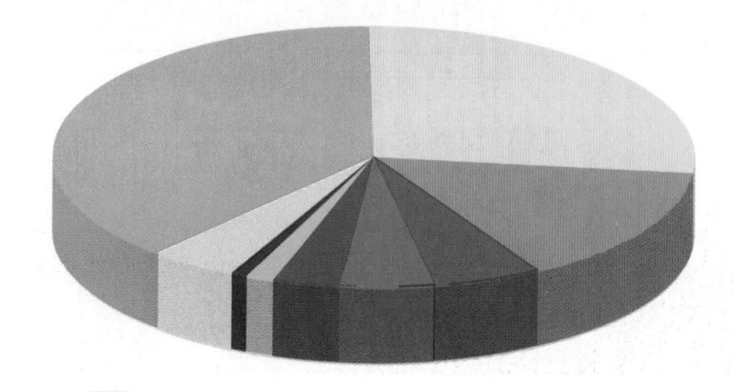

Religion	Percentage
Islamic	**38.2%**
Buddhist	**27.0%**
Roman Catholic	**14.6%**
Ethnic	**5.5%**
Protestant Evangelical	**4.7%**
Protestant	**3.6%**
Hindu	**1.2%**
Other	**0.9%**
Unaffiliated	**4.3%**

Majority Catholic: Philippines and Timor-Leste
Majority Buddhist: Myanmar, Thailand, Laos, and Vietnam
Majority Islamic: Malaysia, Brunei, and Indonesia

Thais celebrate the Songkran Festival where people pour water over a monk's hands, asking for a blessing. Eventually the festival turns into a countrywide water fight that lasts for weeks because it is the hottest time of the year.

While the mainland ethnic majority populations have been resistant to the gospel, the minority mountain and hill tribes such as the Karen, Chin, Kachin, Naga, and Akha, who were animist, have largely accepted Christ. This is mainly the result of the work of a handful of missionaries, including Adoniram Judson, who came during the 1800s. Many of these tribes are now 80 to 90 percent Christian. Myanmar is home to the second-largest population of Baptists in the world, after the United States. It seems possible that these peoples were more receptive to the gospel because they understood their spiritual poverty more than the Buddhists.

The Karen people in Myanmar pray during a Baptist church service. A quarter of the Karen people are Christians.

BELIEFS

◂ *Golden Buddha statue, Phuket, Thailand*

Buddhism

Buddhism is a religion that promotes the teachings of Siddhartha Gautama, who lived about five hundred years before Christ. Buddha means "enlightened one." Gautama gained this title by claiming to be enlightened and claiming he could help others become enlightened.

Buddha lived in India and was influenced by Hindu ideas such as karma and samsara (the cycle of reincarnation). But Buddhism is not considered a Hindu religion because Buddhists reject the Hindu scriptures. Buddhists use collections of Buddha's sayings as their scriptures. Buddhists also reject the idea of a soul or even of self. Buddhists believe that what are thought of as persons are the aggregates of matter, sensation, cognition, mental formations, and consciousness. When the body dies, these aggregates affect the cycle of samsara. Buddha's denial of the soul is important to his teaching about salvation. Buddha's diagnosis of the world's problem and the way of salvation is called the Four Noble Truths.

First, Buddha taught that suffering, impermanence, dissatisfaction, and emptiness (dukkha) afflict everything. Second, the reason dukkha afflicts everything is desire. The existence of desire leads to suffering. Third, the way to escape suffering is to cease from desiring. This is one reason Buddha denied the existence of souls. Denying the existence of the soul is necessary to cease from desiring. Fourth, desire and suffering cease when one follows the Noble Eightfold Path: (1) right view, (2) right intention, (3) right speech, (4) right action, (5) right livelihood (one that does not harm others), (6) right effort, (7) right mindfulness, (8) right concentration (meditation). The goal is to escape from samsara into nirvana. Nirvana is not mere nothingness; it is ultimate reality. But because of this, Buddhists teach that nothing can be said about it.

Christians would say that Buddha recognized an important truth when he said that suffering, impermanence, dissatisfaction, and emptiness afflict everyone. Solomon made precisely this point in the book of Ecclesiastes. But Buddha made a grave error when he traced the root of suffering to desire. A person is certainly disappointed when he loses something he greatly desires. But the Bible points out that the root cause of suffering, impermanence, dissatisfaction, and emptiness is sin. Desire remains good. Love for God and love for others are the two great commandments, according to Jesus. Obedience to these commands includes desire for God to be glorified and desire for the good of others.

▲ *Buddhist novices walk to collect alms and offerings in Mandalay, Myanmar.*

In contrast to the Buddhists of Burma and Thailand, Cambodians have been open to the gospel since the end of the twentieth century. When a woman accused of crimes against humanity during the Khmer Rouge years came to Christ, it made headlines worldwide. She proclaimed her innocence, and eventually the charges were dropped. In 2018 she was baptized by a survivor of the death camps.

In Vietnam Communism is the official ideology; Buddhism is tolerated, but Christianity is not. Heavy persecution continues. Christianity is viewed as an element of Western colonialism. Ironically, Communism is actually the Western ideology and Christianity has its origins in the east.

Indonesia and Malay

The factor that tends to unite so many different peoples of such different languages and cultures over such vast distances is religion. In Indonesia it is Islam. Indonesia is the largest Muslim country in the world. Although Indonesians are Sunni by name, they follow a form of Islam called *kebatinan,* which brings in aspects of Hinduism and Buddhism. This accounts for the moderating of the religion when compared to how it is practiced in the Middle East. Like other ASEAN countries, Indonesia has a minority population that is predominantly evangelical because of the work of missionaries. The Indonesian side of New Guinea (West Papua) is Christian.

Elinor Young, a missionary to the Kimyal people in Papua, Indonesia, worked to translate the Bible into their language. She suffered from polio as a child but did not let that deter her from missionary service. Since she could not climb the rugged trails, the tribesmen helped her.

Philippines and Timor-Leste

These two are the only Catholic-majority nations in Asia, a result of Spanish and Portuguese colonization. Filipinos are fervent followers of the Catholic church and have included a kind of spiritism with it. However, the Philippines also has the most evangelical Christians of any ASEAN country. Filipinos are very open to hearing the gospel, and Bible classes can be taught in public schools. Churches there have enthusiasm but are challenged by a lack of trained leadership and the influence of the prosperity gospel.

SECTION REVIEW

1. Did Vietnam prove or disprove the Domino Theory? How?
2. What are two common characteristics of ASEAN governments?
3. How does having a large diaspora help and hurt the economy?
4. What may be one strength and one weakness of being a very heterogeneous nation?
5. What do Southeast Asians try to avoid above all else? Why?
6. Why is it difficult for the mainland majorities to turn to Christ?

GUIDING QUESTIONS

- How do the economies and demographics of Southeast Asia affect how the citizens interact with the environment?
- What are the environmental issues of Southeast Asia?
- What are the causes and effects of environmental issues in Southeast Asia?
- What are possible solutions to environmental issues in Southeast Asia?

INTERACTIONS OF PEOPLE AND PLACES

What are some of the challenges of living in Southeast Asia?

Southeast Asia has beautiful landscapes and people, yet it faces numerous political/social/environmental challenges. In order for each nation to succeed at meeting these twenty-first-century challenges, the leaders must turn from corruption and cooperate to find long-term solutions for their nation and the region.

Interaction among People

Human trafficking and the domination of China are two significant issues in this region. ASEAN is one epicenter of the worldwide human trafficking problem. There are more people in slavery today than at any other time. Over four million people in the ASEAN region live in some form of slavery, whether for labor or sex. A Cambodian saying that "boys are like gold, girls are like cloth" implies that boys never lose their value but girls can be used and thrown away.

Control of the waters in the middle of the South China Sea is hotly disputed between Vietnam, Malaysia, the Philippines, Taiwan, Brunei, and China. These waters are important for two reasons: one-third of all global shipping travels through here, and the waters are believed to conceal a treasure trove of oil and gas. Coral reefs called the Spratly Islands are the only type of land here. While the other nations argue over ownership, China with its resources has taken the initiative to build up the islands through dredging and crushing the coral. The Chinese have built landing strips and placed military equipment on the manmade islands, creating not only an environmental disaster but also a situation that could lead to war. The United Nations' World Court has ruled that the rightful owner for most of the area is the Philippines since they are closest, but the ruling has had no effect.

▲ *Satellite images show the extent to which the Chinese have built up the Subi Reef in the Spratly Islands.*

On the Myanmar/China border, there is a lawless autonomous area called Mong-La where many illegal activities occur. The Chinese use the city, and the Myanmar government looks the other way. Products from many endangered species are sold here, such as elephant tusks, leopard skins, and tiger claws. People and drugs are sold, and casinos are used to launder money. The **Belt and Road Initiative** (**BRI**), the Chinese plan to build a series of roads, seaports, airports, and power plants around the world, is especially significant in Southeast Asia. As China has done in Africa, it uses this initiative to put the countries in debt and then takes over control of the projects they have built, thus gaining more influence in the region.

Environmental Issues in Southeast Asia

Water

Except for Singapore, all of these countries have the same water pollution problems to different degrees. Most people living in rural areas do not have access to potable water or wastewater services. The Citarum River in Indonesia is one of the world's most polluted rivers. Many parts are so filled with trash that you cannot see the water. Fish stocks are declining for the whole region. Coral reefs are dying.

Since rivers travel through many countries, one country can dramatically impact another's ecosystem by changing a river. For the rivers on the mainland, this has been happening as China, without consulting the other nations, has built seven dams and plans to build twenty-one more, mostly on the Mekong. In the early 1990s, scientists predicted that the dams would cause droughts in Southeast Asia to gain in intensity. That is one prediction that came true. In 2016 Vietnam suffered one of its worst droughts.

▲ *The Citarum River in North Jakarta, Indonesia, is one of the most polluted rivers in the world.*

▼ *The slash-and-burn method is used to clear forests in South Kalimantan, Indonesia.*

Air

Air pollution is greatest in the cities. Jakarta leads the way with the highest pollution levels. It is said that on average children here lose two and a half years of their lives because of the air pollution.

Land

Deforestation is the major land environmental problem everywhere in this region. The forests have some of the most valued hardwoods in the world, such as teak and mahogany. The lands where the forests lie are also valuable for producing palm oil. With deforestation comes soil erosion and a loss of biodiversity. In Laos and Cambodia, there are many land mines and other unexploded ordnance. Cambodia has the highest per capita number of amputees because of all the land mines. Wildlife populations are threatened by illegal hunting. The "Golden Triangle," where the borders of Myanmar, Laos, and Thailand meet, is a place where poppies are grown for opium.

▲ *Jeepneys and buses fill the streets of Manila. Jeepneys are the most common form of public transportation in the Philippines; passengers sit on bench seats, facing each other. Jeepneys originated during World War II, when jeeps were converted for carrying passengers.*

Reasons for Environmental Issues

The water pollution is from farming and factory wastes and inadequate water treatment facilities. Some places have raw sewage flowing into the rivers and seas. Fish are decreasing because of overfishing, dynamite fishing, and a loss of their natural feeding grounds in the coastal mangrove swamps because of pollution and logging. Sediment flowing into seas also kills the fish.

There are many forms of motorized transportation in ASEAN countries which cause traffic congestion and are the main source of air pollution. The other major cause of air pollution is the intentional burning of the forests in Indonesia.

Much of the deforestation is illegal. It is done either to clear land for agriculture, to log the hardwood forests, or both. Burning of the forests is the worst possible thing to do. When they are gone there is nothing to hold the soil, so it flows into the rivers. When the forests are gone, the animals lose their home. The mass of garbage collecting all over the countryside is the result of rapid urbanization.

Proposed Solutions

The Mekong River Commission was formed by the involved nations to collectively deal with the problems related to control of the river. China, however, has refused to participate. In places like northern Thailand, farmers have learned how to use the land more efficiently, using better irrigation practices and managing erosion by replanting trees. Sometimes the

▼ *Southeast Asian leaders from Cambodia, Laos, Thailand, and Vietnam link arms during the opening ceremony of the Mekong River Commission Summit in Hua Hin, Thailand, on April 5, 2010.*

▲ *The Banaue Rice Terraces, northeast of Baguio, Philippines, are called an "eighth wonder of the world." These terraces were carved by hand into the mountains by the indigenous people possibly two thousand years ago. They are an example of sustainable interaction with the land.*

poor environmental policies are a result of the local people's lack of education and their desire for income. Other times it is the result of a corrupt central government that does not care about either the people or long-term effects. A grand strategy called the **Poverty Environment Initiative (PEI)** is being undertaken by eight of the eleven countries. They hope not only to find solutions to the environmental issues but also to solve the underlying cause by finding other means of income for the people. Nonprofit organizations are working hard to remove land mines and unexploded ordnance from Cambodia and Laos.

SECTION REVIEW

1. What are three of the major economic and environmental threats to ASEAN countries?
2. Evaluate how coming to Christ could change the culture, resulting in economic and environmental progress.
3. How is the loss of fish and marine life the end of a chain of environmental problems?
4. Why is something like the Poverty Environment Initiative important?

22

CHAPTER REVIEW

SUMMARY

1. Southeast Asia contains eleven countries and is divided between mainland and island sections. This region is at the collision point of four plates. The majority of this region sits very close to large bodies of water and rivers, providing fertile land. The climate is humid-tropical. The main resource is the arable farmland.

2. All the countries were colonized except for Thailand. The Vietnam War caused great upheaval for the mainland. Except for Timor-Leste, all the nations are members of ASEAN. Instability characterizes the governments. There was an economic crisis in 1997, but today the economies are growing. Southeast Asia is extremely heterogeneous. An easy-going attitude, concern for face, close families, and respect for elders characterize the cultures. The three main religions are Buddhism, Islam, and Catholicism.

3. Human trafficking and conflicts in the South China Sea are major political issues. Water pollution in the rivers from untreated waste is a problem. Air pollution from vehicles and fires is a problem. Deforestation, soil degradation, and land mines in Indochina are other issues. The countries are trying to find broad regional solutions that consider the poor.

Terms to Know

- ❑ Domino Theory
- ❑ ASEAN
- ❑ IMF
- ❑ diaspora
- ❑ brain drain
- ❑ Belt and Road Initiative
- ❑ Poverty Environment Initiative

Making Connections

1. What crop is critical to all Southeast Asian countries?
2. Which three Southeast Asian countries were ruled by the French?
3. What are some examples of cultural diffusion in Southeast Asia?
4. How do the countries of Southeast Asia hope to change their economies?
5. What are four characteristics of Southeast Asian culture?
6. How does China influence this region?

Developing Geography Skills

1. Based on the map on pages 496–97, why would it be difficult to have a cohesive government and economy in Indonesia and the Philippines?
2. Compare and contrast ethnic and religious characteristics in Southeast Asia and Eastern Europe.

Thinking Critically

1. Evaluate the idea that if "a boy becomes a novice monk, his mother will not enter hell; if he becomes a full monk, his father will also not enter hell," on the basis of biblical teaching.
2. How might the embrace of a biblical worldview reduce brain drain in the countries with large diasporas?

Living in God's World

1. What do the atrocities committed by the Khmer Rouge reveal about human nature?
2. Write out a plan for the evangelization of the mainland Buddhist majority. Take into account their many folk beliefs and their loss of community when they turn to Christ.

CASE STUDY | 2004 Indian Ocean Tsunami

Banda Aceh, Indonesia, on January 5, 2005, after being hit by the December 26 tsunami

On December 26, 2004, an earthquake measuring 9.1 on the Richter scale struck off the west coast of Sumatra. This was the third most powerful earthquake in recorded history. It caused a rupture in the earth's crust under the Indian Ocean that was more than six hundred miles long.

There was a several-hour interlude between the earthquake and the tsunami wave hitting the shores, yet most people were taken by surprise because no early warning system was in place. The tsunami resulted in an estimated 227,898 deaths. Damages exceeded $10 billion. Millions lost their homes and were left without food or water. Indonesia suffered by far the most casualities, the majority of which were in the town of Banda Aceh on Sumatra. To this day, large fishing boats sit well inland on top of houses as a reminder of the tsunami and its power. Many tourists were spending their Christmas vacation at the beaches of Thailand. Phuket, a popular resort area, was hit especially hard by the tsunami.

Some of the tourists and locals were afflicted with normalcy bias, the belief that the disaster is not really happening even as imminent death is seconds away. Some tourists stood on the beach mesmerized by the waves while others were screaming for them to run.

Not everyone was taken by surprise. Few animals died because they fled for higher ground well before the wave struck. The Moken people of Myanmar and Thailand live by the sea and depend on it for their livelihood. They knew earlier than anyone else that something was wrong, and so they were able to escape to safety. Tilly Smith, a British girl on vacation, was able to warn as many as one hundred people since she realized a tsunami was coming. She had just learned about them in geography class, and when she saw the water dramatically recede, bubble, and sizzle, she realized what was coming.

1. What could officials do to be better prepared for a tsunami?
2. Why did the Moken people and Tilly Smith survive the tsunami?
3. Why might a person fall victim to normalcy bias?

unit 8

GEODATA | Activity

Cultural Geography *Student Activities*

You will have the opportunity to complete a geodata activity for Oceania in the Activities.

Background image:
Tasman Lookout, New Zealand

OCEANIA AND ANTARCTICA

AUSTRALIA AND NEW ZEALAND

523 | Physical Geography
528 | Human Geography
537 | Interactions

BIG IDEAS

- What is the physical geography of Australia and New Zealand like?
- How do the people of Australia and New Zealand live?
- What are some of the challenges of living in Australia and New Zealand?

▲ *Sydney Opera House*

THE HOUSE WITH SAILS

Many consider the Sydney Opera House the most beautiful building in the world. Built on a point that juts into Sydney Harbor, the opera house looks like a huge ship flying into the harbor with open sails. The "sails" are high partial domes.

A Danish architect provided the winning design in a worldwide competition. The original design called for wide sails, but they proved impossible to make. The engineering problems were finally overcome after thousands of hours of computer simulations. Unfortunately, the $7 million budget blossomed to $102 million. Queen Elizabeth presided at the formal opening on October 20, 1973.

One million ceramic tiles, specially made in Sweden to remain bright white and free of fungus, cover the concrete sails. The interior design mixes 67,000 square feet of Gothic tinted glass with space-age steel ribs and concrete fans. There are five performing halls, a theater, and two restaurants. The theater's wool curtains are some of the largest in the world. In addition, the world's largest mechanical tracker organ sits in one of the concert halls.

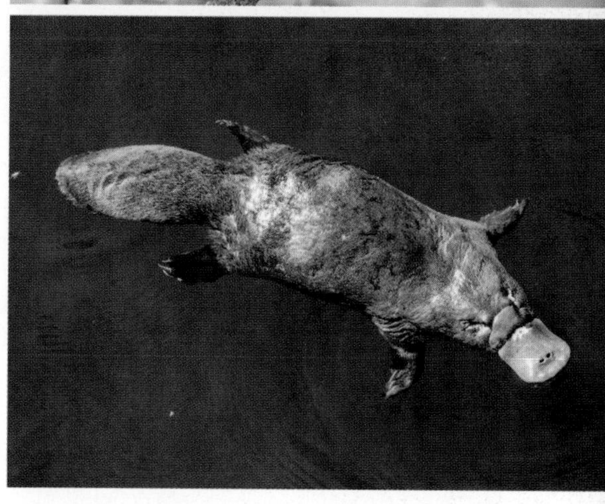

▲ *(top) A wild kangaroo with a joey in its pouch*

▲ *(middle) Baby koala "up a gum tree" (eucalyptus) in New South Wales, Australia*

▲ *(bottom) Platypus swimming in the river*

◀ *Young indigenous dancer in Australia*

GUIDING QUESTIONS

- What are the regions of Australia and New Zealand?
- What caused the landforms of Australia and New Zealand?
- What bodies of water are important to Australia and New Zealand?
- What are the climates of Australia and New Zealand?
- What natural resources are found in Australia and New Zealand?

Hidden by the broad Pacific, the islands of Australia and New Zealand were among the last lands settled by the Europeans. Australia is often referred to as "the land down under" because it lies on the opposite side of the earth from Europe and North America and in the Southern Hemisphere, where the seasons are opposite of those in the Northern Hemisphere.

New Zealand is a beautiful island country isolated from the rest of the world. Its nearest neighbor, Australia, is twelve hundred miles to the west, across the stormy Tasman Sea. New Zealand has many

AUSTRALIA

Australia is a land with a variety of geographic forms. It can be divided into western plateau, central lowlands, coastal plains, and eastern highlands (where the Great Dividing Range is located). Mount Kosciuszko is the highest point in Australia at 7,310 feet. The sparsely populated areas beyond the coastal cities of Australia are collectively known as the **outback**. The outback crosses a variety of climate zones, but common denominators include a small human population and limited land use, such as grazing.

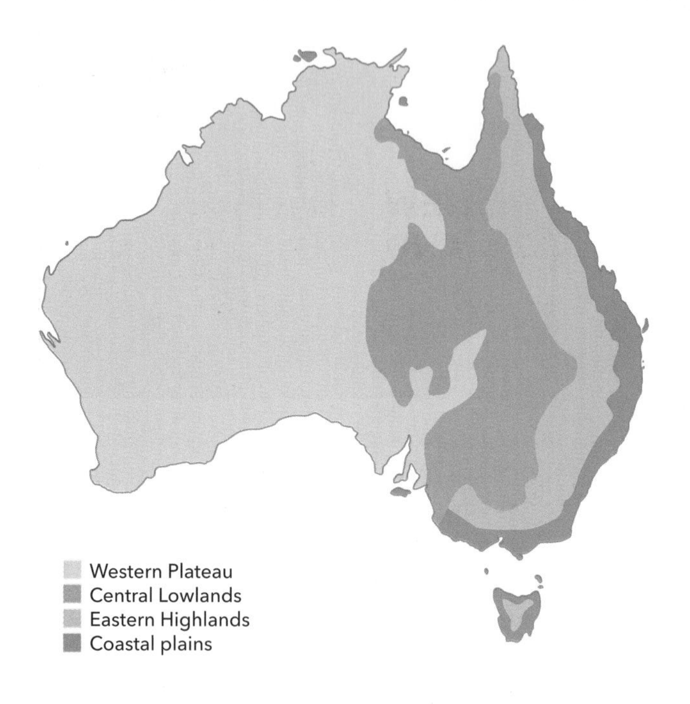

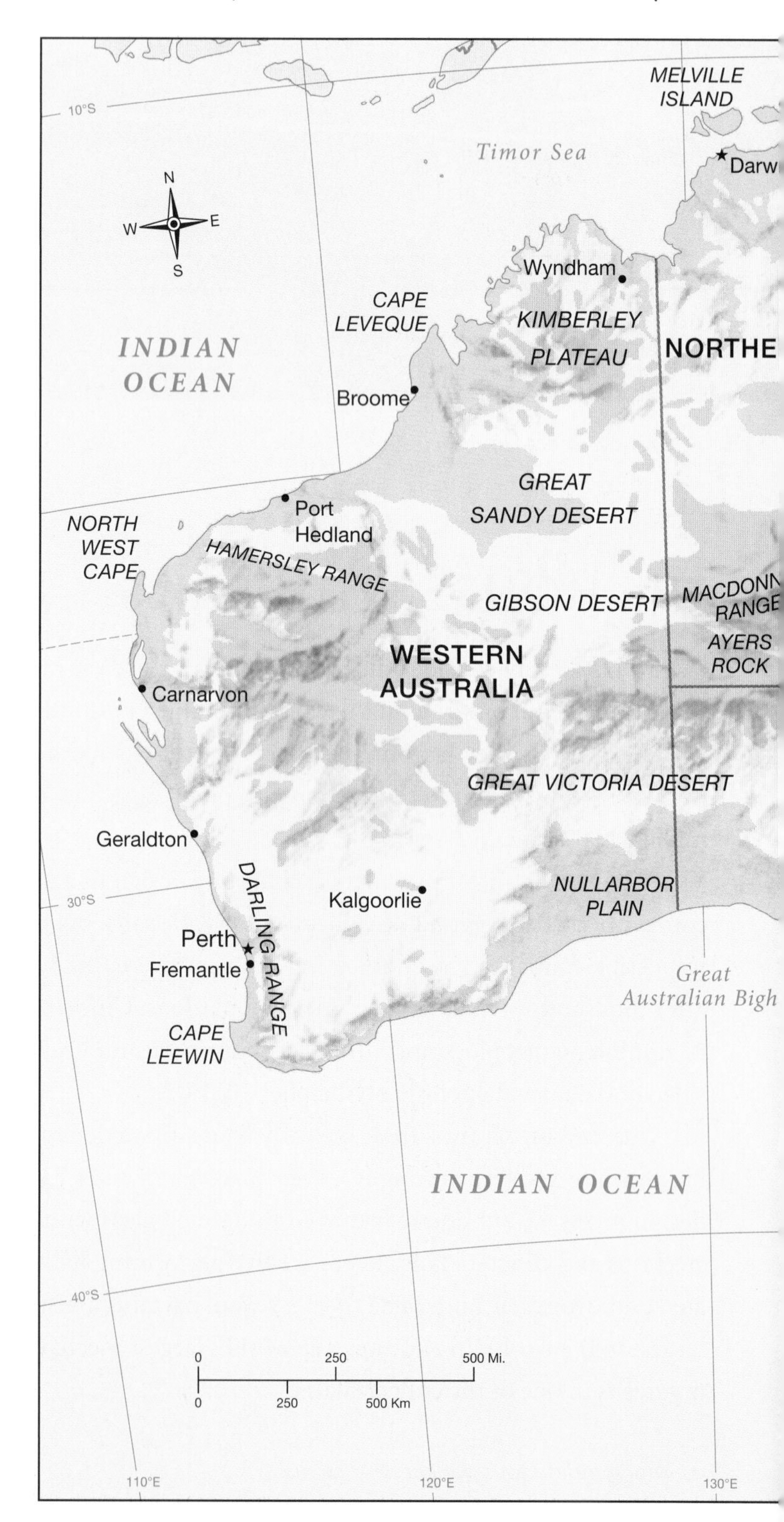

similarities to Australia, including a British heritage and a similar history.

PHYSICAL GEOGRAPHY

Regions of Australia and New Zealand

What is the physical geography of Australia and New Zealand?

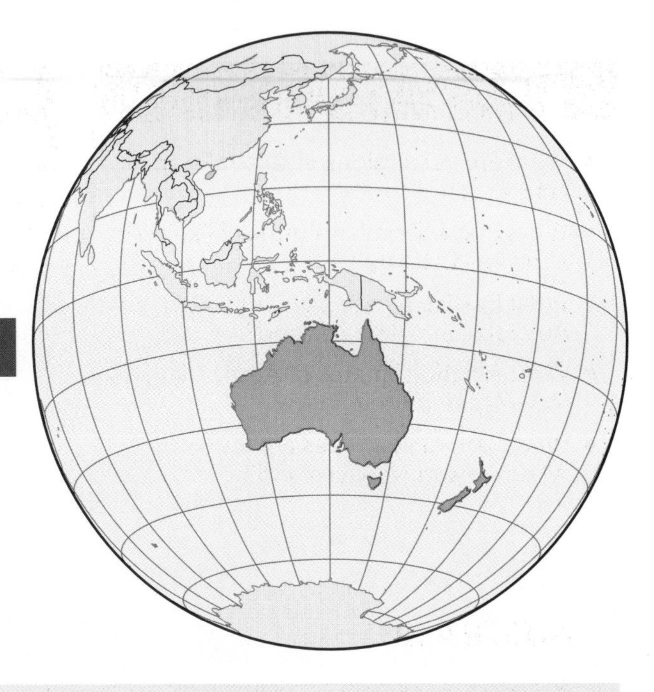

NEW ZEALAND

New Zealand is part of the Ring of Fire that wraps around part of the Pacific Ocean. It is a land of fjords, volcanoes, and nineteen mountains that exceed 10,000 feet. Mount Cook is the highest mountain in New Zealand at 12,316 feet. New Zealand is also a land of contrasts, with glaciers and hotsprings.

▲ *New Zealand is shown here approximately 136% larger than it would be in comparison to Australia.*

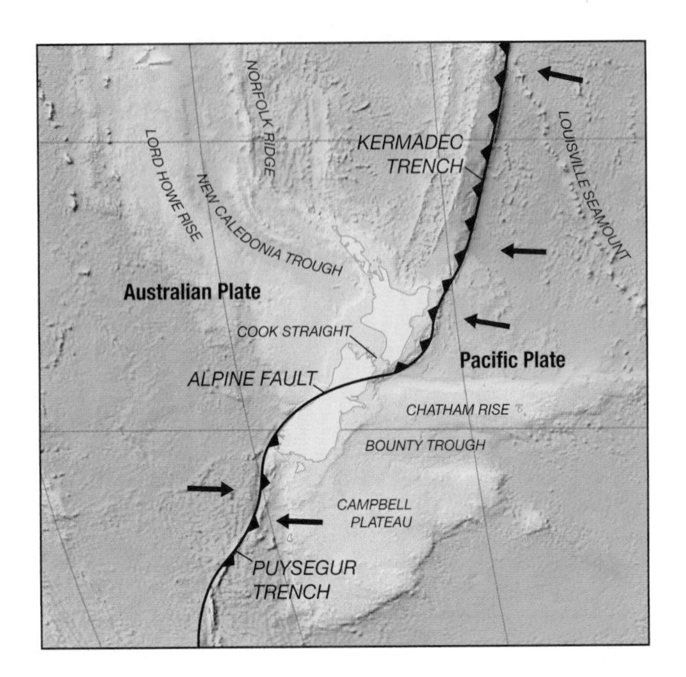

Physical Landforms

The lands of Australia and New Zealand were formed during the Flood, as massive sections of the earth's crust ruptured. Marine fossils reveal that sea life was suddenly buried with sediment and became part of the landmass of these two islands. While Australia is near the center of a major tectonic plate, New Zealand lies at the edge of the Australian and Pacific tectonic plates. The Pacific Plate is gradually moving toward and being subducted below the Australian Plate. This has resulted in ongoing geothermal and tectonic activity in New Zealand. In addition, glaciers in New Zealand's high mountains have shaped the landform, producing many fjords.

Both nations are regularly shaken with some level of tectonic activity. While one might expect Australia to avoid earthquakes, given its location in the middle of a large tectonic plate, the island continent registers about one earthquake per day with a magnitude of 2.0 or greater. Scientists cannot explain what causes this frequent tectonic movement.

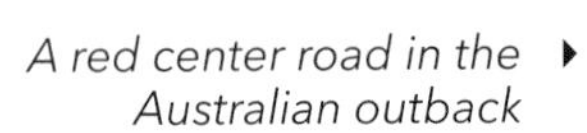

A red center road in the Australian outback ▸

▾ *Uluru (Ayers Rock)*

▲ Franz Josef Glacier, New Zealand

Geothermal activity in Rotorua on New Zealand's North Island ▶

▼ Aerial view of Lake Eyre in South Australia when it is full of water

Bodies of Water

Australia

Australia is surrounded by large bodies of water, including the Indian Ocean, the Timor Sea, the Arafura Sea, the Coral Sea, the Tasman Sea, and the Great Australian Bight. Fresh water is a precious commodity on this island despite the presence of some lakes and rivers.

Lake Eyre is Australia's largest lake and is located in the northeast corner of South Australia. It is the lowest point on the continent, at fifty-two feet below sea level. Most rivers of the Central Lowlands, including the Great Artesian Basin, drain into this lake. These rivers—and the lake itself—are dry most of the time. A few times each century, heavy rains fill the rivers and lake. Within a period of two years, however, the lake returns to a barren salt bed. Given the scarcity of surface water in many areas of Australia, every effort is made to capture water runoff, recycle water, and access artesian wells to meet the nation's water needs.

Despite large areas of arid land, Australia does have surface water in some regions. The Murray River is the longest river in Australia, at nearly 1,500 miles in length, with 1,234 miles being navigable. Other significant rivers include the Murrumidgee River, Darling River, Lachlan River, Warrego River, Cooper Creek, and Paroo River. About 7.5 percent of Australia's electricity is produced by hydroelectric power.

A classic paddlewheeler makes its way down the Nepean River, passing houses in Penrith along the way. ▶

GREAT BARRIER REEF

Just off the northeast shore of Queensland is the largest coral formation in the world. The **Great Barrier Reef** stretches up to sixteen hundred miles—as far north as Papua New Guinea. The "barrier" makes travel hazardous for ships sailing to the coast. Captain Cook, the European explorer, ran aground on the reef and was nearly shipwrecked. Because of the navigational hazards, numerous lighthouses have been constructed.

This underwater garden is actually 2,900 separate reefs. It includes more than 900 islands, including 300 coral cays (small, low-lying coral islands), 213 unvegetated cays, 43 vegetated cays, and 44 low wooded cays. Similar to tropical rainforests, the reef is home to a large variety of life forms, including more than 1,500 kinds of fish, 400 types of coral, 4,000 kinds of mollusks, and at least two endangered species, the sea cow and the large green sea turtle.

Such variety provides unique research opportunities for many types of scientists. In the 1960s, scientists began warning that the reef was disappearing. It was under attack by a poisonous starfish that devoured the polyps by the millions. Also, insecticides from farms onshore were washing into the ocean and destroying the coral. Some fertilizer companies were even mining the reef for limestone. To protect the reef, the Australian government in 1975 set aside most of it as a national park. Up to two million people visit Queensland every year to see the reef, generating over $3 billion annually.

1. Why is it dangerous to sail near the Great Barrier Reef?
2. How has Australia responded to the danger posed to ships by the Great Barrier Reef?
3. To what has the Great Barrier Reef been compared?
4. What types of marine life exist along this series of reefs?
5. What threatens the survival of the Great Barrier Reef?

▲ *Aerial photo of the Great Barrier Reef*

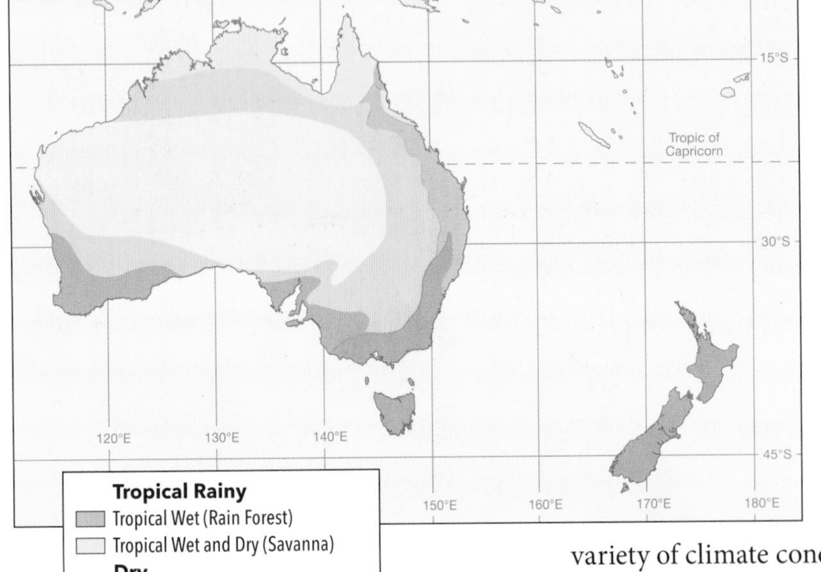

New Zealand

New Zealand is bordered by the Tasman Sea on the west and the Pacific Ocean on the East. This country has several lakes that are fed, in part, from melting glaciers. Lake Taupo is the largest, and others include Lake Wakatipu, Lake Te Anau, and Lake Ellesmere. New Zealand also has approximately 110,000 miles of rivers. One thousand miles of these rivers are navigable, and 50 percent of electricity in New Zealand is produced by hydroelectric power.

Climates

Australia's vast terrain, covering nearly three million square miles, experiences a variety of climate conditions that vary from temperate dry (desert) to marine west coast. Climate and terrain have made much of the continent too harsh to support large populations. This fact, in addition to the location of initial settlements, has resulted in most Australians living in more temperate regions of the island along or near the coast.

New Zealand enjoys a marine-west-coast climate. Prevailing winds blow off the Tasman Sea, bringing warm, moist air that showers the islands 150 days of the year. Because clouds are so common, the native islanders called their home Aotearoa, or "land of the long white cloud."

ANALYZING A CLIMATE MAP

Based on the climate map on the previous page, answer the following questions.

1. Which coast has a dry climate?
2. Which coast has a tropical climate?
3. What climate appears directly west of the Great Dividing Range?
4. What is the most widespread climate in Australia?

▾ *Australian opal*

Resources

Australia and New Zealand share several common resources, including coal, petroleum, natural gas, fish, and iron ore. They also have precious resources, including gold. Australia additionally has silver, opal, and diamonds.

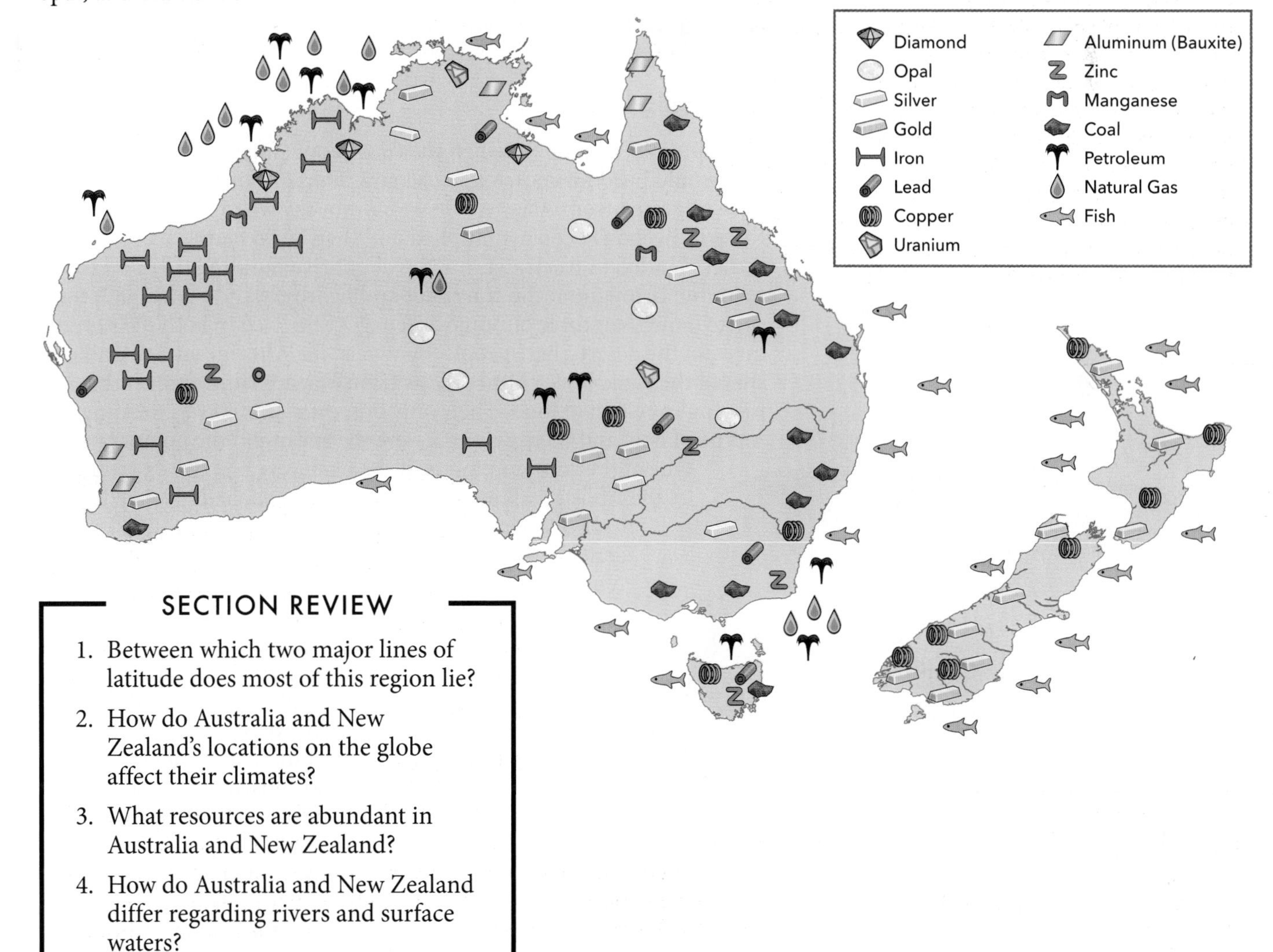

SECTION REVIEW

1. Between which two major lines of latitude does most of this region lie?
2. How do Australia and New Zealand's locations on the globe affect their climates?
3. What resources are abundant in Australia and New Zealand?
4. How do Australia and New Zealand differ regarding rivers and surface waters?
5. How do you think rivers are used in New Zealand?

1700 | 1800

1642 Dutch navigator Abel Tasman explores the region.

? Arrival of first people to Australia

600–1300 Migration of the Maori from Polynesian islands (New Zealand)

1769–70 English explorer Captain James Cook

1787–88 The First Fleet sailed from Britain to Australia, and European settlement began.

GUIDING QUESTIONS

- How have Australia and New Zealand changed over time?
- How do Australia and New Zealand's governments interact with their citizens?
- What is the economic health of Australia and New Zealand?
- What are the demographics of Australia and New Zealand?
- What are the cultural characteristics and diversity in Australia and New Zealand?
- What forms of religion are practiced in Australia and New Zealand?

HUMAN GEOGRAPHY

How do the people of Australia and New Zealand live?

History

Both of these island nations were first inhabited by people who migrated from other islands or continents. They established settlements centuries before Europeans explored this region of the earth.

Australia

Opinions vary about when the first people migrated to the island that would become known as Australia. These Aboriginal peoples may have migrated from Asia. While we cannot say when they arrived, these indigenous people multiplied and thrived. When the first British settlers landed in Australia in 1788, about five hundred tribes were scattered throughout the continent and nearby islands. Although they spoke more than three hundred languages and lived in both the rainforests and the desert, these people, known as the **Aboriginal Australians,** shared the same basic culture. Each tribe was nomadic, frequently moving in search of food. Their only domestic animal was the dingo, a type of dog, and their weapons were the spear and the boomerang. One of the common foods in the bush was a fat, white grub that the Aboriginals ate raw or after being cooked in heated ashes.

Following the arrival of the First Fleet in 1788, several convoys of British ships continued to bring British convicts and settlers to Australia. Gradually more settlements were established, and in 1803 a British ship first circumnavigated the island. Men in South Australia over the age of twenty-one gained the right to vote in 1855, and this right was expanded as various territories across Australia were populated and organized. Gold was first discovered at Gympie in Queensland in 1867, and subsequent discoveries resulted in a rapid increase of people coming to Australia. The Aboriginal Australians suffered greatly from this influx of Europeans and the European insensitivity toward, and even murder of, these indigenous people. In 1869 the Australian government began a tragic and ill-conceived plan to deal with the Aboriginal people by removing children from indigenous families and raising them in government or

▲ *The Australian **boomerang** is a curved wooden device that can be thrown and will return to the thrower.*

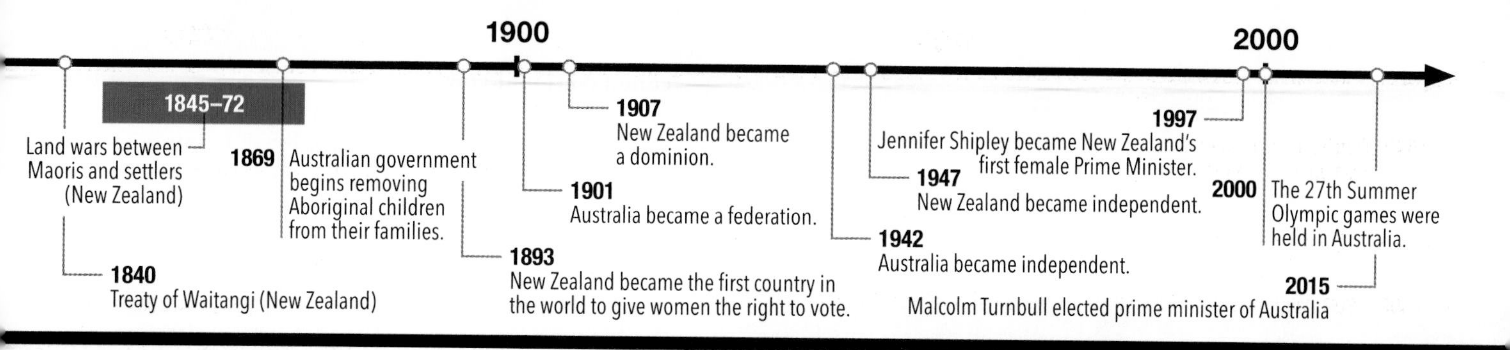

religious institutions. This travesty continued for a century, and the victims have become known as the **Stolen Generation**.

In 1901 Australians gained their independence from Great Britain and achieved dominion status. While Australia was no longer subject to Great Britain, the nation provided strong military assistance to Great Britain during World Wars I and II. Following the attack on the United States on September 11, 2001, Australia sent troops to aid in the fight against terrorism in Afghanistan and later to Iraq in 2005. Australia remains a strong ally of Western Europe and the United States.

▲ *Stolen Generation children at the Kahlin Compound in Darwin, Northern Territory, Australia in 1921*

New Zealand

Many believe that Polynesians settled the island that became known as New Zealand about seven hundred years ago and developed the Maori culture. At first, they lived by hunting and fishing. After the "moa hunters" hunted the moas to extinction, they cleared forests and planted crops. They also became skilled woodcarvers using stone tools.

Frequent wars and superstitious rituals were central to Maori life. It was not uncommon for them to eat their defeated foes. The Maori proved to be a difficult challenge for the Dutch explorer Abel Tasman, who discovered the islands in 1642 while searching for a fabled continent south of Australia. When Tasman attempted to land, the Maori killed several of his men. In 1769 the British explorer Captain James Cook landed and established relations with the Maori. He succeeded in mapping the coasts of the two main islands.

The first European settlers on the islands were escaped convicts from Australia and deserters from British ships. Whalers and seal hunters also built small stations along the coast to resupply their ships. Christian missionaries soon followed. English traders gave rum and guns to the Maori in return for flax, a strong fiber used for ropes. The introduction of guns led to bloody fighting among Maori tribes and between the Maori and the Europeans. The settlers unknowingly also introduced diseases to which the Maori had no immunity, greatly reducing the Maori population.

In response to the growing violence, British settlers asked Great Britain to annex New Zealand and bring the law and order it needed so badly. On February 6, 1840, a group of Maori chiefs signed the Treaty of Waitangi in which they recognized the British monarch as their sovereign. In return, the Maori received full property rights over their land. They also agreed to sell land only to the British crown. New Zealanders celebrate the signing of the treaty each year in a holiday

▲ *Illustration of the flightless moa bird*

▲ (top) Canberra, the capital of Australia

▲ (bottom) Wellington, the capital of New Zealand

called National Day.

Tensions remained high on the North Island, where most of the Maori people lived. Complicating the situation, shiploads of settlers continued to arrive, and many purchased land illegally. In 1845 opposition to land sales resulted in a Maori uprising. This marked the start of the Land Wars. Much like the outnumbered American Indians, the Maori put up a stiff, though futile, resistance. When war ended in 1872, Maori power was broken, and the government seized the land. After the Maori wars, the British colony grew rapidly. In 1872 the development of refrigerator ships enabled New Zealand to begin shipping meat to Europe. New Zealand has become one of the world's leading exporters of mutton (lamb). At New Zealand's request, Great Britain granted the colony dominion status in 1907.

Following New Zealand's independence, it remained a loyal member of the British Empire and supplied troops during World Wars I and II. During the 1980s new political leaders worked to reduce the role of government in the economy, while increasing its role in social issues, including an attempt to reduce the pay gap between men and women in the workplace. A labor-led coalition formed in 2017 to address domestic issues, including a growing housing shortage.

Government

Australia has a federal parliamentary constitutional monarchy. The continent is divided into six states, with a national capital at Canberra. Legislative authority is invested in the parliament, which is composed of two chambers, the House of Representatives and the Senate. Every three years half of the senators stand for reelection.

New Zealand has a parliamentary constitutional monarchy. The country is divided into sixteen regions. The government of New Zealand is similar to those of other independent nations within the British Commonwealth. The British crown is represented by a governor-general. The legislative authority is the parliament, which consists of one chamber called the House of Representatives. Every three years members are elected to represent ninety-one general districts and four Maori districts. Wellington is the national capital of New Zealand.

Government Interaction with Its Citizens

Many of the troubling interactions between the governments in these countries and the indigenous peoples occurred in the previous two centuries, and problems are being addressed. However, the taking of Aboriginal children from their parents, for example, left a deep scar on the Australian society, and extensive damage takes time to heal. Official apologies and efforts to remove all forms of discrimination from society will not occur overnight. Past violence between the European immigrants and Maoris also requires a concerted and sustained effort to bring about genuine equality.

Education and Health Care

▲ A 2018 march in Sydney to draw attention to past abuses of Aboriginal children

Australia provides compulsory education, and students attend from ten to twelve years depending on the state and territory. New Zealand has a combination of state public, state integrated, and private education. (State integrated schools are formerly private schools that have been integrated into the state education system; many of these are Roman Catholic.) Attendance is compulsory from a student's sixth birthday to his sixteenth.

In the area of health care, both countries have a combination of taxpayer funded and private insurance to pay for health needs. New Zealand tried a public health system beginning in the 1930s but has recently moved to a mixed public/private system. Australia is predicted to have a serious shortage of doctors and nurses by 2025, and patient out-of-pocket expenses in Australia are among the highest in the world as the government is failing to increase taxpayer-funded percentages. Not-for-profit organizations help to fill the gap to meet health care needs in Australia, but rural and remote health care is still very poor. As in other countries where government is involved in health care, patients using the public facilities often face long wait times and have limited options, especially for certain medical procedures. In New Zealand, a patient may have to wait up to 300 days before receiving treatment, unless the illness is life-threatening.

▼ Large earth-moving machine in the outback of Australia

Economies

Australia has a high-income market economy that places an emphasis on exports. Industries include mining, manufacture of industrial and transportation equipment, food processing, chemical production, commercial fishing, and steel production. Australia has a thriving tourism industry, and 79.2 percent of its 12.9 million (2017) labor force works in the service sector. In 2017 Australia's GDP was $1.25 trillion.

New Zealand has a highly developed free-market economy. Industries include aluminum production, food processing, metal

▼ A group of tourists enjoy a camel ride on an Australian beach.

fabrication, wood and paper products, manufacture of industrial and transportation equipment, mining, chemical production, commercial fishing, and steel production. New Zealand has 73 percent of its 2.7 million (2017) labor force employed in the service sector. New Zealand also has a growing tourism industry. In 2017 New Zealand's GDP was $189 billion.

Demographics

Australia's estimated population in 2018 was 23.5 million, and its birthrate was 12/1000. New Zealand's estimated population in 2018 was 4.5 million, with a birthrate of 13.1/1000. Australia is highly urbanized at 86.1 percent, with 67 percent of the population living in or around capital cities including Sydney, Melbourne, Brisbane, Perth, and Adelaide. New Zealand is also highly urbanized at 86.6 percent. Approximately one-third of the population lives in Auckland, the largest city in New Zealand. Along with Auckland, Christchurch, Wellington, Hamilton, and Tamanga constitute the five largest cities. Just over 75 percent of New Zealanders live on the North Island.

About 56 percent of the Australian population is of European descent (English, Irish, and Scottish), while 33.5 percent are of Aboriginal descent. Chinese and other ethnic groups make up the rest of the population. Those of European descent make up 71 percent of New Zealand's population. Maoris represent about 14 percent, and those of Asian descent constitute about 11 percent of the population.

▲ *(top) Tourists enjoy kayaking at the Abel Tasman National Park, on South Island, New Zealand.*

▲ *A worker grades freshly dried sheets of veneer for pressing into plywood in New Zealand.*

Cultures and Diversity

Cultures vary in Australia and New Zealand, depending in large part on ethnic descent. Those of European descent tend to embrace a European culture, while the Aboriginal Australians and Maoris tend to continue the cultural practices handed down by their ancestors. The Aboriginals have a number of languages, while English is the most widely spoken language in both countries.

Australians have four broad goals for their country. The first is social equity, which encourages Australians to treat one another as equals. The second, cultural respect, requires appreciation for other cultures. The third is productive diversity, a uniquely Australian phrase that refers to recognizing the value of a diverse population. The fourth, live life large, can have several meanings. Given the challenging environment across much of Australia, it might refer to living life to the fullest despite harsh conditions and an arid environment.

Food, Dance, and Sports

Chicken continues to be the meat of choice in Australia, while New Zealanders raise vast herds of sheep and thus prefer lamb (mutton). Ready access to the ocean also provides this region with a great variety of seafood, including New Zealand green-lipped mussels. Locally grown vegetables provide nourishment and add color to the typical dishes served in these countries. Aboriginal Australians have traditionally eaten whatever was available, including kangaroos and lizards.

▲ *Mussels steaming in a pan*

◂ *Lamb dinner*

Among the original inhabitants of Australia and New Zealand traditional dance is very important. While Aboriginals have a variety of ceremonial dances for marriage ceremonies and story-telling, these dances are often collectively referred to as *corroboree*. Different types of body painting indicate the particular dance being performed.

▾ *Lockhart River community dance troupe at the Laura Aboriginal Dance Festival in Queensland, Australia*

New Zealand women's soccer team performing the Haka during the 2017 Women's World Cup Final

A popular dance among the Maori is the *haka* (sometimes referred to as a war dance). This dance has also become popular among many New Zealanders, regardless of ethnic background, and involves making a fierce or war-like face as part of the dance. Haka is also performed as a sign of respect (or perhaps frustration) following a loss or tragedy.

Music is an essential part of Aboriginal and Maori culture. One of the more unusual instruments in Australia is the **didgeridoo**, a long hollow wooden wind instrument that produces a deep sound. Another unusual device used for music and communication is the bullroarer, a wooden spindle attached to a cord that is spun rapidly to produce a deep moaning sound. The bullroarer has also served as a means of communication across distances.

The Maoris developed forms of flutes and trumpets as part of their music. The *koauau* and *nguru* are two types of Maori flutes.

Bullroarer

Aboriginal musician playing the didgeridoo on a street in Sydney, Australia

A nguru (wooden nose flute) in New Zealand

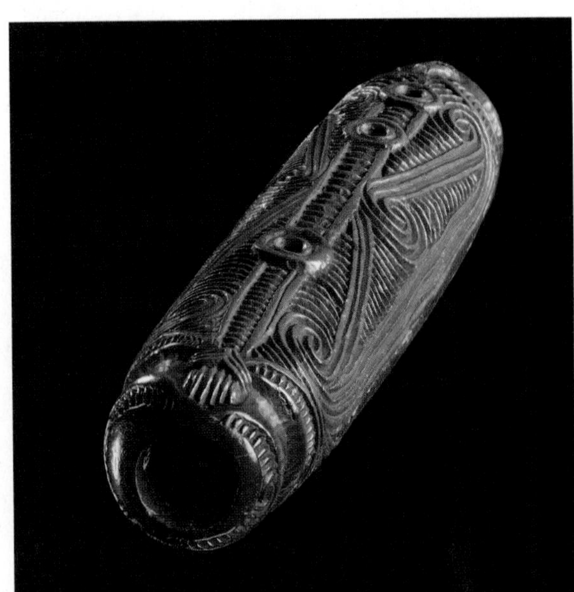

(far right) A koauau (wooden flute) in New Zealand

▲ *Australian Rules Football game in Perth, Australia*

▲ *Cricket match between the women's teams of England and New Zealand*

Australians have developed their own version of football called *Australian Rules Football*. Other popular sports include rugby, cricket, and soccer. New Zealanders love to play rugby, netball (a version of basketball), soccer, and cricket.

Family

While the role of the family remains important to society in Australia and New Zealand, the extended family has historically been central among the Aboriginal Australian and Maori tribes. Several generations formed the local clan, and family members governed the communal structure of these groups. The Maori word for extended family is *whanau*.

▼ *Extended Aboriginal family in Australia*

Religions

Depending on ethnic background, the people of Australia and New Zealand embrace various types of religious practice. Those of European descent vary from typical European religious affiliations to secular. The Aboriginal Australians and Maoris tend to retain the religious customs handed down by their ancestors in the form of ethnic religions.

Major Religions of Australia and New Zealand

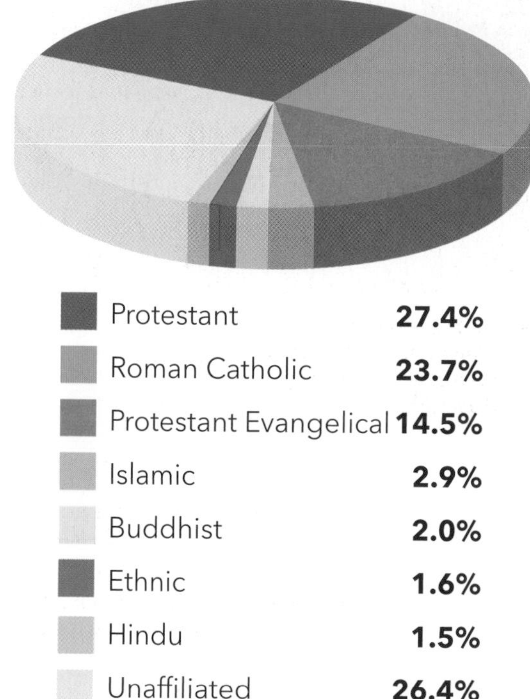

BELIEFS

Ecumenical Christianity

A distinctive feature of Australian religious life is the Uniting Church in Australia. The Uniting Church was formed in 1977 by the union of the Congregational, Presbyterian, and Methodist churches in Australia. It is an expression of the ecumenical movement, which was particularly strong in the 1960s and 1970s. The goal of the ecumenical movement is the external unity of the church. Proponents argue that the Bible necessitates this unity because Christ prayed for the unity of the church in John 17:21. In addition, in the New Testament the church was unified in particular locations (e.g., the church of Ephesus). Ecumenists also make practical arguments. They claim that church union eliminates duplicated efforts made by the denominations, and it avoids competition among Christian groups. An example is found in missions. Ecumenists believe it is a scandal for different denominations to compete on the mission field for conversions. However, this argument has been weakened by those in ecumenical circles who teach that all religions lead to salvation.

Critics of ecumenism point out that the ecumenists' foundational text, John 17:21, is taken out of context. John 17 speaks as much about the calling out of disciples from the world and their sanctification in the truth as it does about unity. Thus it defines the people who are to be unified, and these people are Christians. They are unified because they are in Christ and believe the truth of the gospel. The ecumenical embrace of theological liberalism offends many Christians because liberalism denies the inspiration and authority of Scripture and ignores Christ's emphasis on truth and separation from the world. Critics of ecumenism readily admit that the early church was not divided into denominations, but they recognize that denominations can play an important role in carrying out the Great Commission (Matt. 28:19–20). In addition, Christians have often worked across denominational lines without sacrificing their convictions, recognizing that their unity in Christ enables cooperation in many areas. Unity is maintained within local assemblies where members hold the same views on issues such as church government and the method and significance of baptism.

1. What denominations joined together to form the Uniting Church?
2. What is the goal of the ecumenical movement?
3. What should unify a group of people in a church or denomination?
4. What are some areas in which Christians of different denominations can cooperate without sacrificing their convictions?

▲ (top) The Queenscliff Point Lonsdale Uniting Church in Queenscliff, Australia

▲ Bangalow Uniting Church building in a village in northern New South Wales, Australia

SECTION REVIEW

1. How have Australia and New Zealand changed over time?
2. How well do the Australian and New Zealand governments provide for the education and health of their citizens?
3. How would you describe the economies of Australia and New Zealand?
4. Describe the demographics of Australia and New Zealand.
5. What are some cultural characteristics and examples of diversity in Australia and New Zealand?

INTERACTIONS OF PEOPLE AND PLACES

What are some of the challenges of living in Australia and New Zealand?

GUIDING QUESTIONS

- How do the Australian and New Zealand economies and people interact with the environment?
- What are environmental issues in Australia and New Zealand?
- What are the causes and effects of environmental issues in Australia and New Zealand?
- What are possible solutions to environmental issues in Australia and New Zealand?

Following the arrival of the first people and the later settlement by Europeans, these groups had to find ways to live together and develop a civilization on these islands in the South Pacific. Conditions in much of Australia are harsh, and safe water supplies are limited. Resources abound, but accessing them has proven to be very challenging. New Zealand presented its own set of challenges, with much of the main islands covered with mountains. Both of these countries have found ways to adapt to their environments and use their resources with great economic success.

Interaction with the Environment

Australia and New Zealand have been characterized by agricultural and population growth. The people have cleared land and increased agricultural production, with the result that they can provide for their own needs and export products to other countries as well. Australian ranches, called **stations**, can cover thousands of acres. These ranches raise large numbers of livestock that live primarily by grazing. In New Zealand about half of the land is used for agriculture. To feed these growing herds, ranchers import copra, which is dried coconut meat. New Zealand ranchers are known as **graziers**. In addition to vast numbers of sheep, they also raise cattle.

Population growth has resulted in additional land being needed for housing and the expansion of cities. The use of automobiles and the expansion of power stations to meet electricity needs impact the environment. Growing industrial output and manufacturing also consume resources and produce byproducts that negatively affect the environment.

Australian jumbuck (male sheep)

(bottom) Deforestation in Australia

Reasons for Environmental Issues

The bumpy terrestrial cane toad, or marine toad, is one of the invasive species creating problems in Australia.

Increasing use of land for agriculture, removal of vegetation and trees, and the introduction of invasive species all have environmental consequences. In Australia, the removal of trees increases erosion and results in increased salinity of the soil. Clearing of brush and other vegetation also contributes to the loss of biodiversity and reduces soil stability.

A number of invasive plants and animals have been brought to Australia, with unexpected negative results and the loss of some native species of plants and animals. Invasive species include toads, rabbits, willow trees, black striped mussels, and red fire ants. For example, Australians imported rabbits for hunting, but the rabbits multiplied rapidly due to a lack of natural predators. The rabbit population has become uncontrollable and destructive of much vegetation.

The mussels and other invasive forms of marine life often arrive in ballast water from ships arriving in Australian ports. These marine predators have multiplied and endangered Australia's marine ecosystem.

The Australian government has been slow to enact and enforce laws to protect the environment. Until recently the nation has sought to expand and increase industrial and agricultural production without fully weighing the environmental cost. Australian authorities are now working to solve many of the nation's environmental issues. New Zealand's leaders have also taken aggressive steps and are working to manage natural resources in a sustainable way.

Water

With the growth of agriculture, water supplies in Australia have been contaminated. Up to 19,000 tons of phosphorus and up to 140,000 tons of nitrogen seep into the water every year. These chemicals are applied to crops and wash into the rivers. As in other developed countries, industrial waste often ends up in water supplies. Dairy farming has become a growing industry in New Zealand, and the runoff results in further pollution.

Air

Air pollution in Australia is caused primarily by coal-fired power stations and exhausts from industry and automobiles. New Zealand has a relatively low level of air pollution, but a growing use of automobiles has become a major source of concern.

Land

Deforestation through logging, naturally occurring bush fires, and the clearing of land for grazing and construction continues to harm the land in both countries. Increased demand for farming and raising of livestock depletes the physical resources of Australia and New Zealand. Erosion is a constant problem that occurs with or without human activity. Ranchers with large herds tend to allow their livestock to overgraze, with negative environmental consequences.

Rabbits imported to Australia have multiplied and extensively damaged the vegetation in South Australia.

▲ *Geothermal power plant in New Zealand*

Proposed Solutions

The Australian government is aggressively working to eliminate coal-burning power plants and is seeking cleaner energy sources. Both nations are producing energy through hydroelectric power, but New Zealand has more potential to capitalize on this resource. Both countries are installing wind-powered generators and expanding the use of solar panels to produce electricity. New Zealand is aggressively working to replace most, if not all, vehicles with electric cars in the next decade. Both countries are encouraging improved recycling to reduce the volume that ends up in landfills. New Zealand also has increased its energy potential by continued development of geothermal energy. Engineers are developing high-efficiency electric motors to get the most energy out of the electricity consumed.

SECTION REVIEW

1. How has the introduction of rabbits to Australia had a negative environmental impact?
2. What are three environmental issues in Australia and New Zealand?
3. How have the Australian and New Zealand governments dealt with environmental issues?
4. Explain how the Australian and New Zealand economies and people have interacted with the environment.
5. What solutions to current environmental issues in Australia and New Zealand would you propose?

23 CHAPTER REVIEW

SUMMARY

1. The physical geography of Australia and New Zealand was shaped by tectonic activity, volcanic eruptions, and glaciers. Continued development of this region's natural resources is profoundly advancing economic prosperity. Harsh geographic conditions across much of Australia continue to hinder access to the continent's resources.
2. The people of this region are primarily of either European or indigenous descent. They have come to realize the need to treat one another as equals and to embrace ethnic diversity. They enjoy similar activities, including ethnic foods, regional music, and sports.
3. A major challenge in Australia and New Zealand is the need to make wise use of human and natural resources in ways that maintain strong economies without further endangering the environment. Goals for this region would include developing cleaner resources for energy production and developing technology to protect the environment.

Terms to Know

- ❑ outback
- ❑ Great Barrier Reef
- ❑ Aboriginal Australians
- ❑ boomerang
- ❑ Stolen Generation
- ❑ didgeridoo
- ❑ Uniting Church
- ❑ station
- ❑ grazier
- ❑ coral bleaching

Making Connections

1. What earth-shaping activity formed these two island nations?
2. Why does New Zealand have ongoing volcanic, earthquake, and geothermal activity?
3. How do landforms affect climates in Australia?
4. Why do you think the Maoris hunted and fished at first rather than grow crops?
5. Identify a political issue in Australia and New Zealand's past.
6. What role has dancing played in Aboriginal Australian culture?
7. What are some results of deforestation in Australia?

Developing Geography Skills

1. Why is the population of Australia concentrated along the coasts?
2. What role have glaciers played in the geography of New Zealand?

Thinking Critically

1. From a biblical worldview, what was wrong with the Australians taking Aboriginal children from their parents?
2. Australians seek to treat all people as equals. Can true equality be achieved without a commitment to the biblical view of human beings bearing the image of God? Why or why not?

Living in God's World

1. While it is good and biblical to promote unity among various Christian denominations, what are the dangers of ecumenism for spreading the gospel?
2. Given the opportunity, how could you demonstrate the love of Christ to the Aboriginal Australians or any other group in this region that has been mistreated?

CASE STUDY | Coral Bleaching

Coral is composed of tiny marine creatures that secrete calcium carbonate to form a hard skeleton. Coral reefs are formed by groups of coral polyps that live in colonies, and these reefs support marine life. Coral polyps have algae that live inside them and provide their color. The coral provides the algae with carbon dioxide and ammonium, and the algae's work of photosynthesis nourishes the coral.

Under certain stressful conditions the coral polyps expel the algae. This process is known as **coral bleaching** because the coral loses its color. The expelling of the algae removes about 90 percent of the coral's food source, and it begins to starve. One common cause of coral bleaching is a change in water temperature (increasing or decreasing). Other causes include increased sedimentation, bacterial infections, herbicides, and other pollutants such as oil spills.

Coral does not die during a brief absence of the algae, but the coral needs algae to re-enter the polyps and carry out photosynthesis to nourish the polyps and preserve the health of the reef. While human carelessness and naturally occurring erosion play a part in this process, natural weather cycles such as El Niño have extensively damaged coral reefs around the world. Scientists estimate that an El Niño event lasting from 2014 to 2017 damaged over 70 percent of the world's coral reefs.

Australia's Great Barrier Reef has suffered from nine stress-related events in the last forty years. In some locations along the Reef, the mortality rate for the coral approached 90 percent. However, new coral has replaced much of the destroyed coral polyps. While bleaching has destroyed some of the coral, much of this damage resulted from tropical cyclones and the predatory work of crown-of-thorns starfish that consume large quantities of the polyps.

Coral bleaching is truly a global problem, given the damage occurring to coral reefs in Florida, Hawaii, Japan, the Indian Ocean, and many other areas of the world. However, there are exceptions. Coral in the southern part of the Red Sea has proven to be immune to bleaching despite warm summer water temperatures in this region.

Scientists are monitoring sea temperature changes, and organizations such as the US National Oceanic and Atmospheric Administration (NOAA) collect data on sea surface temperatures. Other scientists are observing coral that appears to be resistant to bleaching and are working on ways to encourage the rebuilding of coral reefs. Efforts include growing corals in special tanks and then transplanting them to areas where reefs are in decline. One scientist, Madelaine Van Oppen, is working to produce a variety of algae that will be less sensitive to temperature change.

▲ *(top) Healthy coral*

▲ *Bleached coral on the Great Barrier Reef*

1. What are coral reefs formed from?
2. Why does coral bleaching occur?
3. What weather event recently damaged large areas of coral?
4. What are scientists doing to help strengthen coral reefs?
5. Why should Christians care about the health of coral reefs?

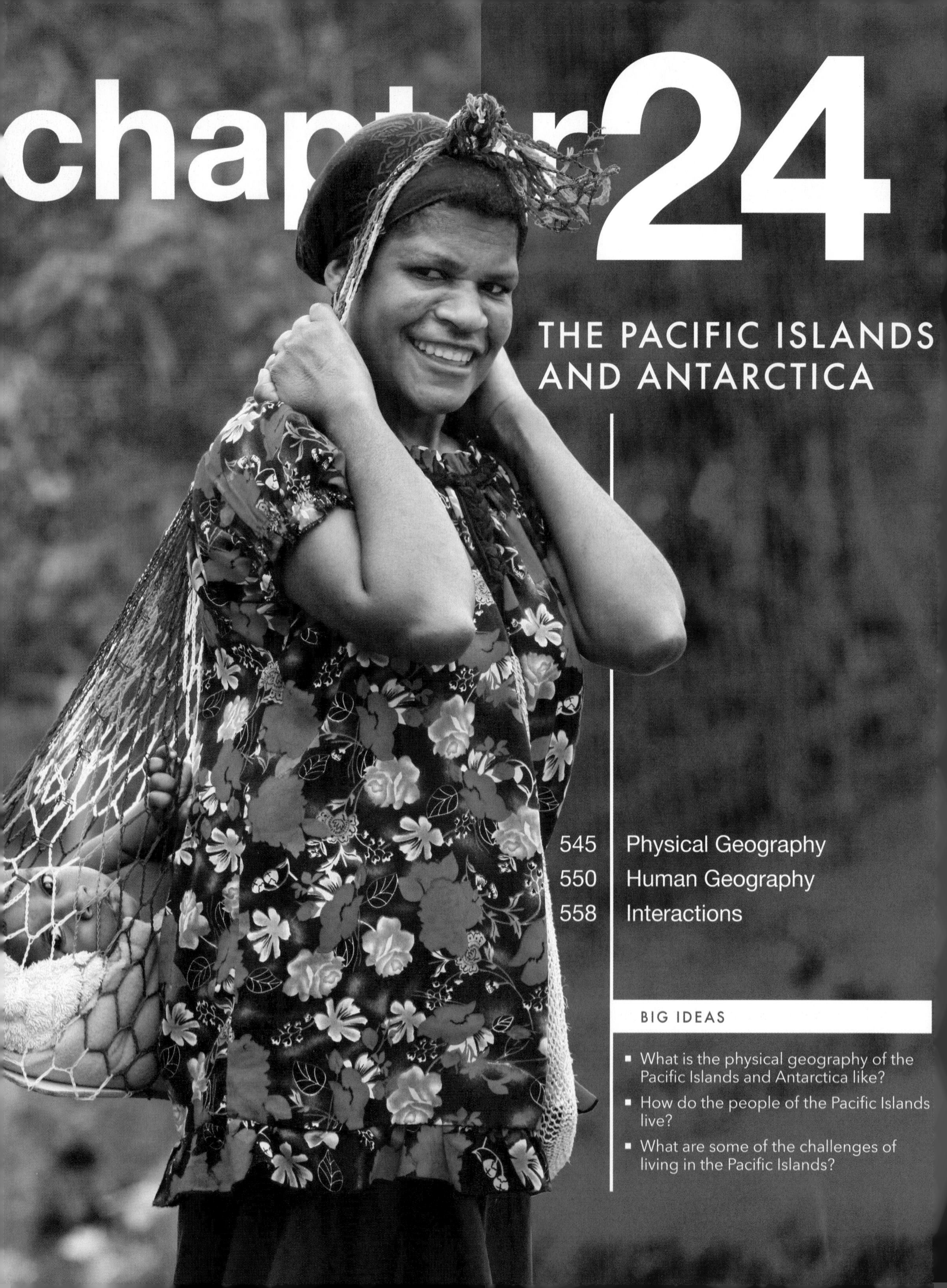

chapter 24

THE PACIFIC ISLANDS AND ANTARCTICA

545 Physical Geography
550 Human Geography
558 Interactions

BIG IDEAS

- What is the physical geography of the Pacific Islands and Antarctica like?
- How do the people of the Pacific Islands live?
- What are some of the challenges of living in the Pacific Islands?

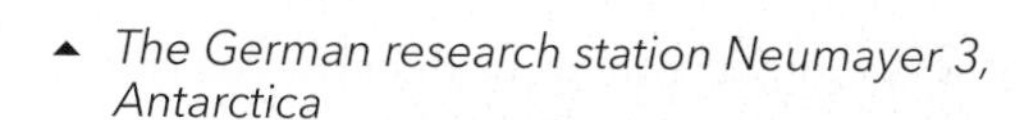

▲ The German research station Neumayer 3, Antarctica

◀ (top left) Mount Otemanu towers above a resort in Bora Bora, French Polynesia.

◀ Children on Wakaya Island, Fiji

OCEANIA PATHFINDERS

People settled the Pacific Islands long before European explorers arrived. When one island became overcrowded, a group set out for another island. Polynesians developed exceptional navigation skills to travel on the open seas across great distances and locate other islands. They made pathways in the vast ocean using the stars, planets, clouds, and ocean currents. For the Polynesians, the ocean was not empty and uncrossable but a place to journey in as one would on land. They sailed double-hulled canoes. They ate preserved taro root in the form of *poi* and caught fish for food. They used hollowed-out gourds to carry fresh water and collected rainwater throughout the trip. As the years went by, the settlers of various islands developed distinct cultures and languages. At the same time, they retained certain similarities that made it possible to group them into three broad people groups: Melanesians, who migrated from Southeast Asia, and the Polynesians and Micronesians, who migrated from Taiwan.

▲ The Hokulea, a replica of an ancient Polynesian boat, sails near Honolulu.

◀ A mother in Papua New Guinea carries her baby in a traditional woven bilum hanging from her head.

GUIDING QUESTIONS

- What are the regions of the Pacific Islands and Antarctica?
- What caused the landforms of the Pacific Islands and Antarctica?
- What bodies of water are important to the Pacific Islands and Antarctica?
- What are the climates of the Pacific Islands and Antarctica, and how do they relate to their locations on the globe?
- What are the natural resources of the Pacific Islands and Antarctica?

Although the Pacific Ocean is larger than all seven continents combined, the twenty-five thousand islands scattered across its vast expanse have a very small combined land area. The Pacific connects the people of Oceania rather than dividing them. The first Europeans to visit the islands described the region as a paradise on earth, with warm breezes, sandy beaches, friendly natives, and abundant tropical fruits. But the reports were misleading. Islanders faced the threat of typhoons, disease, and isolation.

During the twentieth century, modern technology opened Antarctica and other new frontiers for scientific study. Scientists discovered not only a wealth of new knowledge but also new areas of competition for scarce resources and military advantage.

MICRONESIA

This is the smallest region of the three and does not have any large islands. Guam, the largest island, measures almost 32 miles long and just over 9 miles wide, a little smaller than Chicago. Micronesia is made up of four and a half countries and two territories, including Nauru. There are four main island groups: the Caroline, Mariana, Marshall, and Gilbert Islands. The Caroline Islands include two countries: the Federated States of Micronesia and Palau, whose main island, Babelthuap, is the largest Caroline Island. The Mariana Islands extend 350 miles from north to south and are part of a partially submerged mountain range in the Pacific. They include the United States territories of Guam and the Commonwealth of the Northern Marianas (CNMI). The Gilbert Islands are the western half of Kiribati. Tabiteuea, a narrow coral atoll of fifteen square miles, is the largest of Kiribati's islands. The Marshall Islands is one country and includes 1,156 islands.

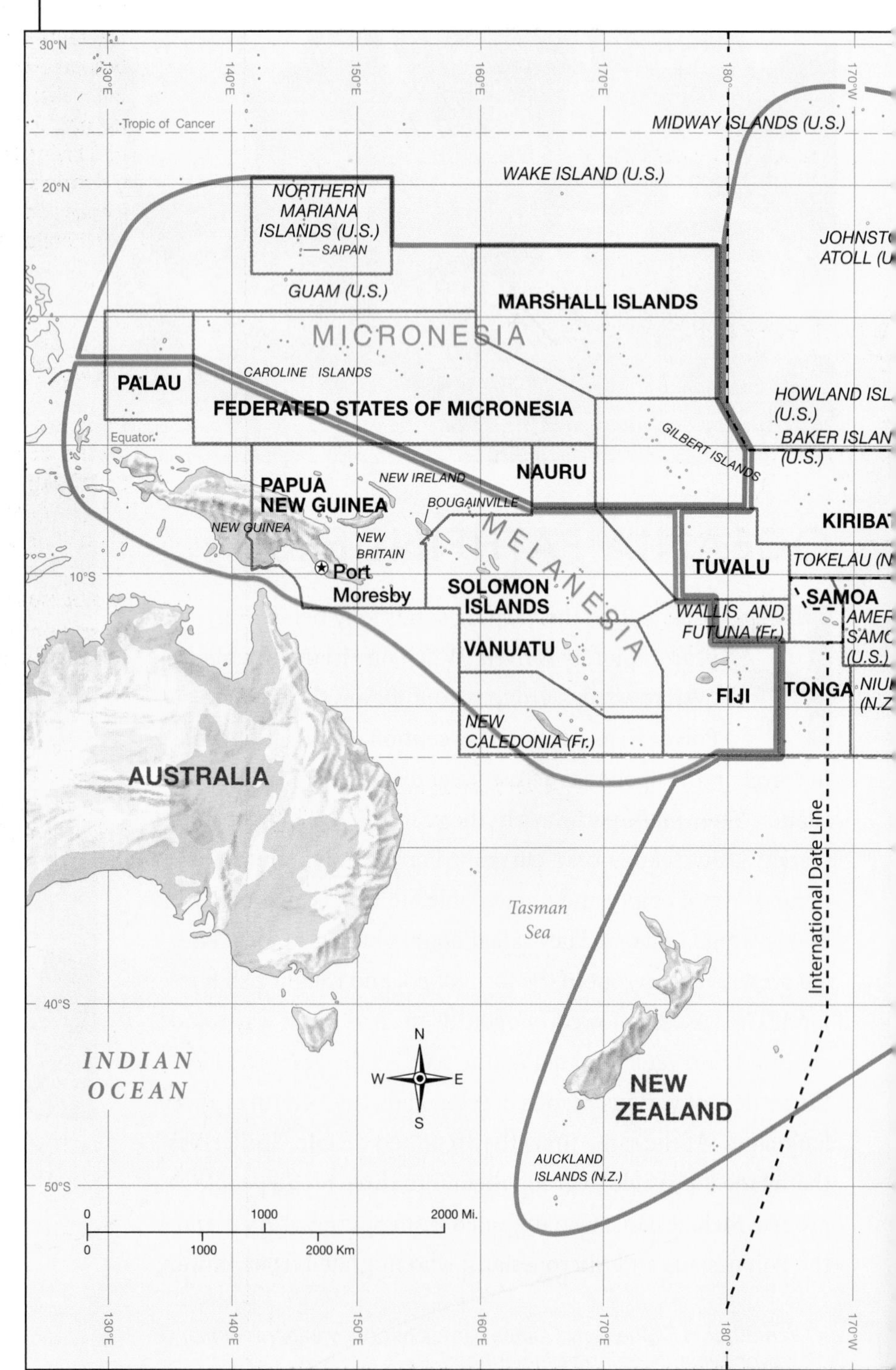

PHYSICAL GEOGRAPHY

What is the physical geography of the Pacific Islands and Antarctica like?

Regions of Oceania

This chapter covers three of the four regions of Oceania: Melanesia, Micronesia, and Polynesia. The majority of islands in these regions are very small.

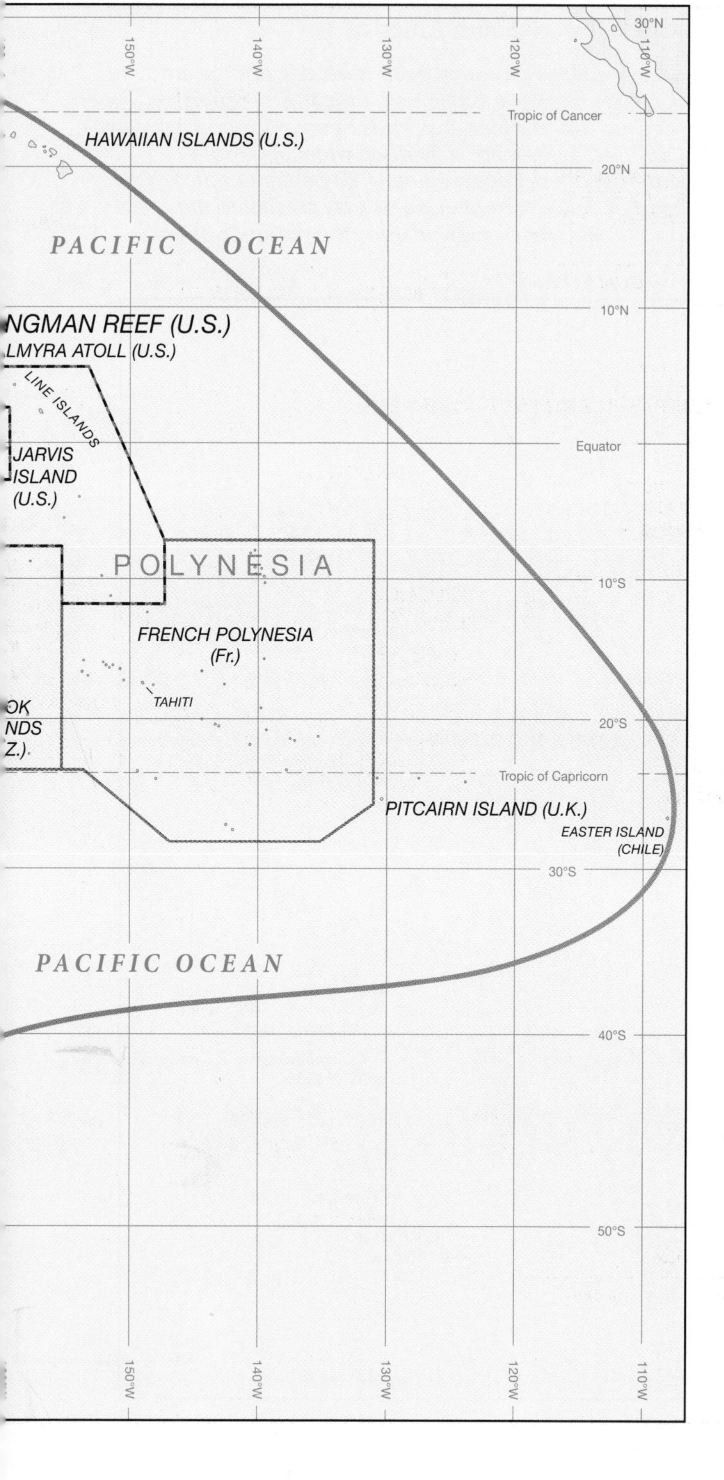

MELANESIA

Melanesia includes four countries and one French dependency. The largest Melanesian island, New Guinea, is also the third-largest island in the world. Western New Guinea belongs to Indonesia, while the eastern half is part of the country of Papua New Guinea (PNG), a country of 600 islands. The Solomon Islands number over 900. Guadalcanal is the largest. To the southeast is Vanuatu, an archipelago of 83 islands, Espiritu Santo being the largest. New Caledonia is a part of France. Fiji is in the center of Oceania, consisting of 330 islands, with Viti Levu and Vanua Levu being the largest.

POLYNESIA

Polynesia is the largest of these three regions. The most significant island groups of Polynesia are New Zealand and Hawaii. There are four and a half independent nations. The Phoenix and Line Islands are half of Kiribati. Tuvalu is a chain of nine low-lying coral atolls. Tonga is an archipelago of 169 islands, and Samoa is a group of six islands. There are many other individual islands and island groups controlled by a handful of nations. The most significant of these is French Polynesia, which includes six major island groups: the Society, Gambier, Tubuai, Tuamotu, Marquesas, and Austral Islands. Tahiti, in the Society Islands, is the largest. Easter Island, part of Chile, sits by itself as the eastern vertex of the Polynesian triangle.

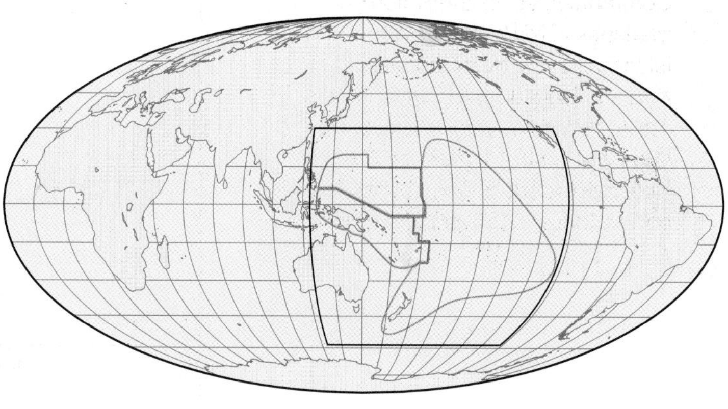

Regions of Antarctica

Antarctica has two regions, West Antarctica and East Antarctica. The regions are divided by the 1,900-mile-long Transantarctic Mountain Range. East Antarctica is a high plateau covered by a thick icecap that is more than a mile deep. West Antarctica is mountainous and is cut in on both sides by the Ross and Weddell Seas. Glaciers that flow into the Ross and Weddell Seas slide out onto the water to form solid ice shelves. The Ellsworth Mountains near the Weddell Sea—the highest mountains on the continent—peep up above the icecap. At the tip of West Antarctica is the Antarctic Peninsula, the most coveted piece of property on the continent. It is the only part of the continent that extends beyond the Antarctic Circle toward South America.

◀ *In the open seas, icebergs can be a major hazard. Icebergs are jagged chunks of ice that have broken off, or "calved," from a glacier as it reached the sea. Icebergs have been measured as large as two hundred miles long, sixty miles wide, and more than a thousand feet deep. Because nearly 90 percent of an iceberg lies hidden below the water, ships may crash into the underwater portion before the crew realizes the danger is there.*

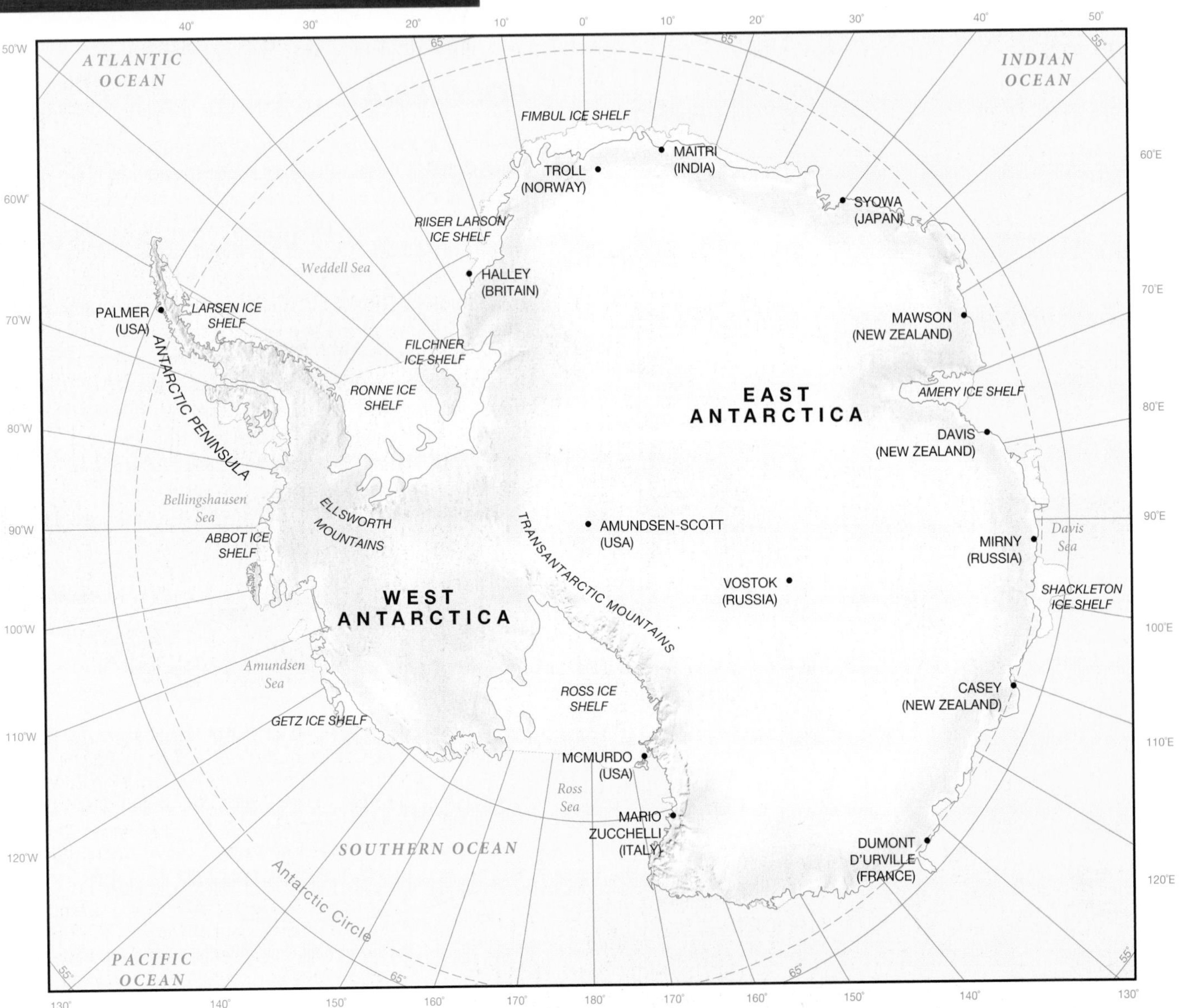

Physical Landforms

There are two types of islands in the Pacific, **high islands** and **low islands**. New Guinea, a high island, is huge and has a rugged mountain system that extends the length of the island and continues into the ocean. The low islands are sometimes just a few feet wide and a few feet above the water.

Low islands, or atolls, like this one near Chuuk, Micronesia, are rings of coral on the submerged cones of volcanoes. The coral sand lacks organic material, so it is a poor soil. Few plants grow well.

Moorea, French Polynesia, is a high island. The high islands have volcanoes on them; the larger islands like New Guinea and Hawaii have many volcanoes that can rise over ten thousand feet. The rich volcanic ash provides fertile soil.

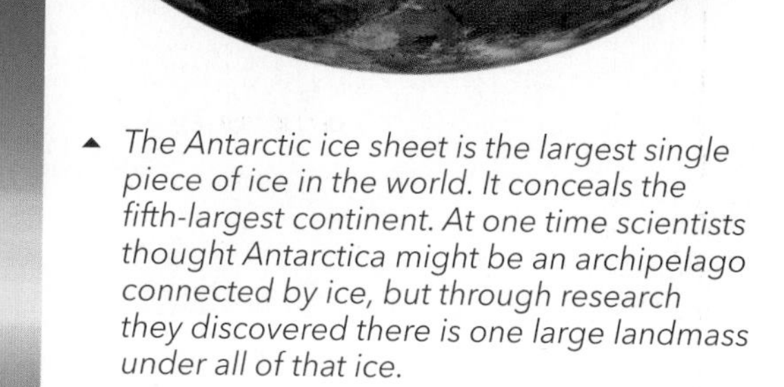

The Antarctic ice sheet is the largest single piece of ice in the world. It conceals the fifth-largest continent. At one time scientists thought Antarctica might be an archipelago connected by ice, but through research they discovered there is one large landmass under all of that ice.

Although New Guinea is a tropical island, a few mountains, such as the 14,793-foot Wilhelm Mountain, remain cold year-round. Steep valleys lie between the mountain ranges.

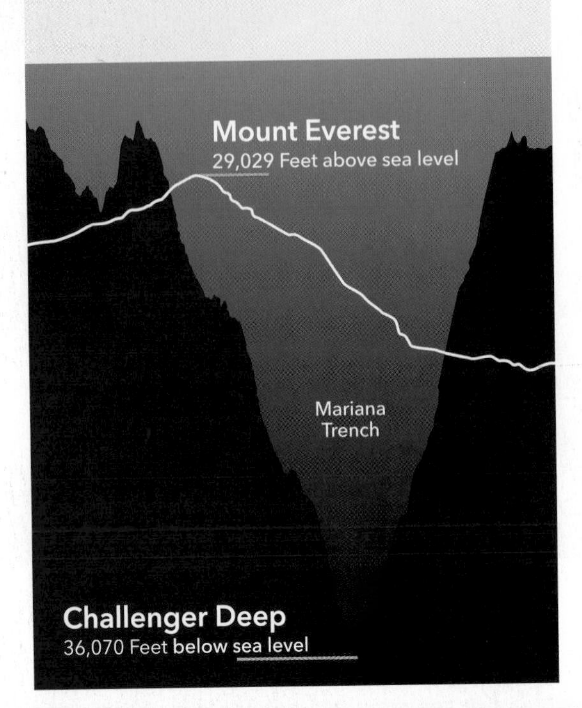

Bodies of Water

The Pacific Islands

This region's body of water is the Pacific Ocean, the largest in the world, covering one-third of the earth's surface. At sea level, the ocean looks like endless miles of blue water, but concealed below are mountains, plateaus, and plains. The average depth of the Pacific is fourteen thousand feet. The plains, known as **abyssal plains**, are the flattest areas on earth and make up about half of the ocean floor. A few plateaus and hills, usually extinct volcanoes, rise above the abyssal plains.

The Pacific sea floor has more deep canyons, called trenches, than all the other oceans combined. The word **deep** refers to a place in a trench that exceeds the depth of eighteen thousand feet. The deepest deep in the world is the Mariana Trench, and its deepest point is the Challenger Deep, the deepest point on earth, which is up to 36,070 feet below sea level. Mountain ranges form along the oceanic ridges. Isolated underwater volcanoes, called **seamounts,** dot the basins. Sometimes a new volcano breaks through the ocean surface, forming an island. The Pacific Island region includes thousands of **lagoons,** which are areas of the ocean surrounded by coral. The waters are calmer than on the open ocean, and the lagoons provide a home for marine life.

Papua New Guinea is the only island with significant rivers. The rivers are the Sepik and the Fly. The Sepik is the longest river in PNG. By water volume, the Fly River is the largest in Oceania. The Fly River forms part of the border between Indonesia and PNG. Unlike those in other regions, the rivers of PNG have no major cities.

▲ *Jeep Island is located in the Truk Lagoon. A lagoon is an area of the ocean surrounded by coral.*

▲ *Bicolor fairy basslets swim at the bottom of Truk Lagoon around the wreck of the Shinkoku Maru, a Japanese cargo ship sunk during World War II.*

Antarctica

Technically, Antarctica is surrounded by three oceans—the Atlantic, Pacific, and Indian Oceans. Yet, a band of polar water circling the continent is much colder and less salty than the subtropical waters next to it. A gigantic ice pack covers this band. Pieces of the pack that break off are called **ice floes**. The open water between floes is called a **lead**. In places, the ice extends as far as nine hundred miles from the coast. The waters are deep—from 13,123 to 16,404 feet—with the deepest point being 23,738 feet at the South Sandwich Trench.

Climates of the Pacific Islands and Antarctica

The climates of the Pacific Islands and Antarctica would seem very dissimilar, yet they have the similarity of consistency: one consistently hot, one consistently cold. The Marianas hold the world record for having the most consistent weather, between 82°F and 84°F year-round. As with other tropical climates, all of the islands have a rainy season and a dry season caused by the trade winds. The islands north of the Equator and west of the Antimeridian (180°) lie in an unofficial area called typhoon alley because they suffer frequent typhoons from June through October.

The Antarctic Plateau is famous for its cold cyclonic storms that whirl almost endlessly from east to west. Gales can reach two hundred miles per hour. The average temperature of the interior during the coldest months is -94°F (compared to -22°F on the coast). The extreme cold of the interior prohibits life. Nothing lives here—not even a bush or an insect. Nevertheless, the cold is a blessing. Because cold air cannot hold much moisture, the interior receives less than two inches of snow per year. The desert conditions prevent snow from building up and depleting the world's water level.

Resources of the Pacific Islands and Antarctica

Taro root ▸

▴ (top) During the typhoon season of 2015, storms came one after another. In this July 9 satellite image, severe tropical storm Linfa, typhoon Chan-hom, and typhoon Nangka are pictured moving across the ocean.

▴ A taro field in the Hanalei Valley, Kauai, Hawaii

The islands lack significant amounts of arable land. All of these islands have two products for export: coconuts and marine products such as fish, seashells, pearls, shrimp, and seaweed. Coconuts are exported in the form of copra, dried coconut meat. The coral reefs and wide ocean waters provide valuable fishing grounds. For their own sustenance, the islanders grow taro plants and sweet potatoes. These islands, especially Nauru, are home for migrating birds, and through the centuries the bird droppings accumulated so much that the valuable phosphate could be mined. High islands such as the Solomons and New Guinea have valuable hardwood forests.

The Melanesian islands have many mineral resources. New Guinea has quantities of gold, silver, and copper. New Caledonia is a world-leading supplier of nickel and cobalt. Ten percent of the world's nickel reserves are buried beneath the mountains of the main island. Strip mines now dot more than half of the island's landscape. Nickel is used in stainless steel. Cobalt is an important ingredient in the lithium batteries that are used in many electronics. Fiji, Samoa, and French Polynesia are noted for their advances in small hydropower.

In Antarctica, core samples and radio soundings have provided tantalizing clues about what is under the icecap. Extensive coal fields and mineral resources may lie under the ice, awaiting the development of economically feasible and environmentally safe methods of mining. Some nations have even set up pretend research stations to ensure a right to participate in any bargaining over mining and land claims.

▾ A nickel factory on New Caledonia

SECTION REVIEW

1. What two nations are the Caroline Islands divided into?
2. What is another name for a low island? Why is soil so poor on such islands?
3. What is a deep?
4. What are the positive and negative aspects of the tropical island weather?
5. What mineral compound made Nauru rich? How did it get there?

1500 | 1600 | 1700

1519–21 Magellan sails around the world.

1643 Dutch explorer Abel Tasman is the first European to visit Fiji.

1219–1266 Polynesians settle Hawaii.

GUIDING QUESTIONS

- How have the Pacific Islands and Antarctica changed over time?
- How do the governments of the Pacific Islands interact with their citizens?
- What is the economic health of the Pacific Islands?
- What are the demographics of the Pacific Islands?
- What are the cultural characteristics and diversity in the Pacific Islands?
- What forms of religion are practiced in the Pacific Islands?

HUMAN GEOGRAPHY

How do the people of Melanesia, Micronesia, and Polynesia live?

Ferdinand Magellan was the first European to chart the Pacific during his voyage around the world in 1519–21. After battling the stormy seas on the southern tip of South America, Magellan reached a calm ocean, which he called the Pacific ("peaceful"). However, for ninety-eight days his men sighted only two islands, both of which were uninhabitable. Provisions ran out, and the crew was forced to eat rats and leather. Finally, the starving men reached Guam, where they took on fresh supplies. During the next two centuries, few expeditions braved this forbidding "empty" quarter of the earth.

Between 1768 and 1779 Captain James Cook filled in many empty spaces on the world map. He charted the east coast of Australia and discovered New Caledonia and the Hawaiian Islands, which he named the Sandwich Islands. Since that long-ago encounter, the people of these islands have struggled to find their place in the larger world. The islanders were thrust into the difficult process of acculturation—the exposure of one group of people to the values and lifestyles of a foreign group of people and their adoption of those ways as their own. Following Captain Cook, European traders and whalers came in search of coconut oil, sandalwood, pearls, and provisions. Congregational missionaries came to evangelize the islanders. The missionaries brought the gospel, medicine, and education. Continental nations vied for control over the islands as they were discovered.

A painting of Captain Cook's ships, the Resolution *and the* Adventure, *in Matavai Bay, Tahiti, French Polynesia*

Hawaii and New Zealand were the first to complete this cycle of discovery and colonization. All the Oceania islands followed this cycle to some degree. From the 1800s to today, Hawaii and New Zealand have been the most prosperous of all the islands in this region. For over one hundred years, Hawaii tried to remain independent, but the islands were annexed by the United States in 1898.

Melanesia experienced the cycle in the mid-nineteenth century. The French explorer Dumont d'Urville named the region Melanesia, the "Black Islands," in 1831 because he was struck by the dark appearance of the land rising from the green sea. There were more than twelve hundred different tribes in Melanesia, each with its own language and

1800	1900	2000

1768–79 Captain Cook explores Oceania for Great Britain.

1820 First missionaries to the Pacific arrive in Hawaii.

1840–1900 Europeans vie for control of the islands.

December 7, 1941-September 1945 WWII is fought in this region.

1968–94 Majority of islands gain independence.

GLOBAL IMPACT | The Mystery of Easter Island

▲ *Moai statues on Easter Island*

Easter Island is an unusual volcanic island over two thousand miles off the coast of Chile, far from the other inhabited islands of the Pacific. The Dutch admiral Jacob Raggeveen discovered the island on Easter Sunday, 1722. He found on the coast rows of mysterious stone heads, called *moai*. The massive heads had very long ears and flat noses. On the larger heads were red stones that looked like hats or crowns.

Most of the moai are ten to twenty feet tall and weigh up to fifty tons. The largest finished head is thirty-two feet high and weighs one hundred tons, but one of the unfinished heads is more than sixty feet high and weighs more than three hundred tons. How did the natives carve the moai out of the volcanic rock at the crater Rano Raraku, transport them to the coast, raise the heads to an upright position, and place the red stones on top? Oral tradition said the statues walked to their location. In 2011 two scientists proved that using three groups of people, one on each side of the statue and one in the back to stabilize, they could walk the statues.

When Captain Cook visited the island in 1774 and talked to the natives, they told him that their Long Ear ancestors had made the statues twenty-two generations previously—about the thirteenth century. They called their island Rapa Nui and considered it the navel of the world. By that time many of the statues had been toppled. The natives said it happened during wars with Short Ear invaders from islands far to the west.

Where did the statue-builders come from? Where did the invaders who toppled the moai come from? If South American legends are true, perhaps the statue builders came from Lake Titicaca. A legend from the Gambier Islands, twelve hundred miles west of Easter Island, may explain the origin of the tribe that toppled the statues. The legend tells of a defeated chieftain who took his tribe in two large canoes to a solitary island in the east.

Easter Island has another mystery that has not yet been explained. It is the only Pacific island with an ancient writing system, but no one has been able to decipher the rongorongo tablets. Many of these tablets were hidden in caves, along with idols and skulls.

1. What is special about Easter Island's location?
2. What are some of the mysteries of the island?
3. Why would it seem logical for the people to think the island was the navel of the world?

▲ (top) US Marines land on Pavuvu in the Solomons in 1943. On many Pacific islands, the artifacts of the war are still visible.

▲ Roald Amundsen, first to reach the South Pole, fixes his position at the pole in 1911.

rituals. Headhunting and cannibalism were common practices even into the twentieth century in some remote parts. The British, Dutch, and Germans vied for control of the Melanesian islands.

During the 1930s and 40s, Japan controlled most of Oceania's islands, except for Hawaii, New Zealand, and French Polynesia (which was attacked by the German navy). Little islands such as Tulagi, Wake, Guadalcanal, Tarawa, Saipan, and many more became well known in the United States during World War II as US forces pursued an island-hopping campaign to reach Japan. After World War II, the United Nations divided the islands among the Allied countries. They were governed as **trust territories** to help the islands recover from their losses and develop stable governments.

Antarctic History

Captain Cook circumnavigated the Antarctic region in 1773 in search of a fabled southern continent, but his ship could not penetrate the ice pack. In 1820 an American sealing ship, a Russian sealing ship, and an English sealing ship each claimed to be the first to sight Antarctica. Finally, in 1895 a Norwegian businessman named Henryk Johan Bull became the first human to set foot on the continent. On December 14, 1911, Roald Amundsen planted the Norwegian flag at the South Pole. At the same time, a British explorer named Robert Scott was struggling to reach the site. He did reach it; however, his entire party perished on the return trip. Admiral Richard Byrd flew a plane over the South Pole on his 1928–29 survey expedition. In 1958 Vivian Fuchs successfully crossed the 1,550-mile width of the continent.

Foreign powers began establishing bases on Antarctica in the 1940s. Once they started, no seafaring nation wanted to be left out. Scientists from the United States and other countries prevailed on their governments to reserve the earth's last great wilderness for pure science, unspoiled by Cold War tensions. From 1957 to 1958, twelve nations coordinated their efforts in building sixty scientific bases and sharing all their findings. The following year, twelve nations signed the Antarctic Treaty, agreeing to ban military bases and weapons testing on the continent, to freeze all land claims, to exchange all information freely, and to open all camps for inspection at any time. Many other nations later signed the treaty. In 1991 the Antarctic Treaty Parties extended the treaty indefinitely and agreed to ban mining for fifty years.

Governments

Although most of these countries are independent, their governments are still related to the Allied nations of Britain, France, and the United States in differing degrees. The majority of the Melanesian islands are part of the British Commonwealth. Of the three groups these countries have the most independence. The islands related to France have the least independence. It is very difficult for small islands to survive as independent nations since they have populations equivalent to small or medium-sized cities. Running a national government is costly and requires many diplomats, legislators, lawyers, economists, judges, and generals. In many cases, family members take turns serving in the government. It is not uncommon for visitors to these smaller islands to meet the president or members of parliament.

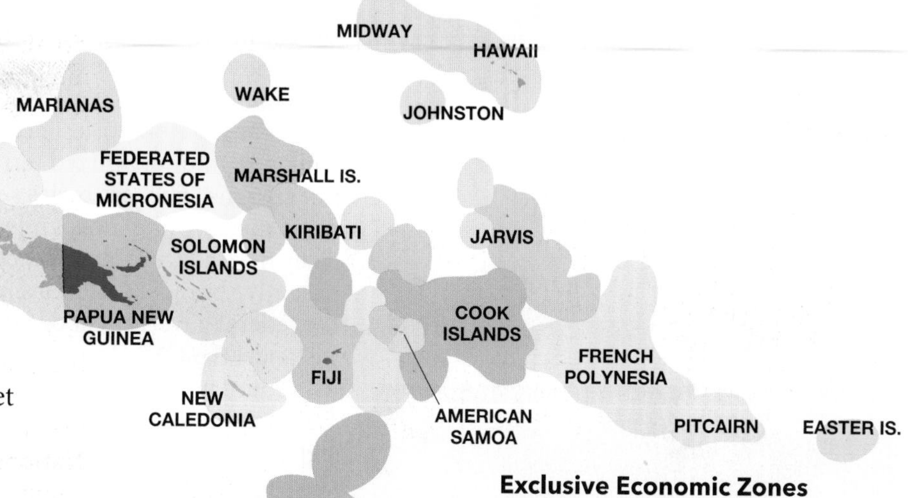

Exclusive Economic Zones of the Pacific Islands

France, Federated States of Micronesia, Great Britain, USA, Vanuatu, Kiribati, Samoa, Tuvalu, Papua New Guinea, New Zealand, Fiji, Tonga, Palau, Solomon Islands, Chile, Nauru, Marshall Islands

Britain

Papua New Guinea, the Solomon Islands, Tonga, and Tuvalu are constitutional monarchies. Tonga has a king, while the others have the queen of England as head of state. Although Tonga was under a protected status with Britain during the twentieth century, it is the one country that never totally lost its independence. Fiji, Nauru, Samoa, and Vanuatu are parliamentary republics. Kiribati is the lone presidential republic of these. Since all of these are part of the British Commonwealth, they have governments similar to Britain's, with a parliament.

The people of Papua New Guinea, the Solomon Islands, and Fiji suffer ethnic tension and struggle for unity within their countries. A large percentage of Papua New Guineans have no contact with the government and live as they have for centuries. The PNG government put down a revolt on the island of Bougainville in 1997 but has since allowed the island some autonomy. The Solomon Islanders have not yet developed a strong sense of national identity. Ethnic tensions that developed between the peoples of Guadalcanal and immigrants from Malaita became violent in 1998, and a civil war occurred between 1998 and 2003. The fighting ended when Australian forces intervened and disarmed the militias. When Fiji gained independence, the government tried to balance the rights of the large Indian minority and those of the Fijian natives. The main conflict was religious, as the Indians are Hindu and Fijians are Christian. In 1987 the first Indian managed to gain a majority in parliament and became prime minister. That victory frightened the Fijians and led to a coup. Fiji has since endured two more coups. Voreqe Bainimarama, a Fijian naval officer who led the most recent coup of 2006, won a parliamentary election in 2014 with 59 percent of the vote, which gave his government some legitimacy.

Fiji's new caretaker, Prime Minister Jona Senilagakali, signs the oath of office on December 6, 2006, after a coup. Coup leader Voreqe Bainimarama looks on.

(bottom) The capitol building of Palau

France

New Caledonia and French Polynesia are French possessions. It seems the people prefer to stay a part of France. In 2018 New Caledonia voted to remain part of France, and in 1958 French Polynesia voted the same way.

United States

Palau, the Federated States of Micronesia, and the Marshall Islands are self-governed in "free association" with the United States. Under this system, the countries control their internal and foreign affairs, but the United States has promised to defend them. In return the countries have agreed to keep out foreign military forces. These countries are republics with a president, much like the United States.

Guam and the Commonwealth of Northern Marianas (CNMI) are organized territories; people born there are US citizens. American Samoa is an unorganized territory; people born there are US nationals, not citizens. The territories seem to lie in a gray area legally. In some cases they are like independent countries, but in others they are not. They have a legislature, judiciary, and executive. A governor leads the executive branch. They have more independence than states unless the federal government decides otherwise on a particular issue. For instance, the CNMI ran its own immigration department until 2009. The country offered temporary work visas that were not given in the US. Many Asians took advantage of these visas hoping it was a first step in immigration to the mainland of the United States. In 2009 the Department of Homeland Security took over immigration to the CNMI and has been trying to phase out the work visas, which has caused turmoil for those who settled on the islands. The US government required American Samoa to follow the federal minimum wage, not their own. As a result, the island lost one of its two tuna canneries that had employed many of the islanders.

▲ *Fiji Water is a brand of bottled water derived, bottled, and shipped from Fiji.*

Economies

For all the islands, most products are expensive since goods must be imported from great distances and in small quantities. Because of the high costs, many people grow fruits and vegetables and fish to supply their families with food and a small income. Large numbers of islanders are employed by their governments. Two-thirds of the citizens of the Federated States of Micronesia work for the government. Tourism and remittances are a large part of the economies of Polynesia and Micronesia, while in Melanesia mining and logging are most important. All of the islands get income from selling fishing rights to their waters, and they depend heavily on foreign aid. Micronesians depend largely on aid from the United States, while Melanesians depend on aid from Australia and New Zealand. Tuvalu, Kiribati, the Marshall Islands, and others have wisely set up sovereign funds (state-owned investment funds), in which they invest money overseas to stabilize their economies.

Many islands have niche industries that provide a great deal of income. Fiji has a bottled water industry. Vanuatu has an offshore banking industry. Papua New Guinea has coffee and natural gas industries. Nauru was one of the richest nations in the world because of its phosphate deposits. The government was able to provide its citizens with many free services, and they did not pay taxes. The phosphates, however, are mostly gone now, and the wealth obtained from their sale was mismanaged so that Nauru is now one of the poorest nations. Nauru has a detention facility for illegal immigrants to Australia which provides some income, but it is also a source of societal strife as the islanders do not want the immigrants there and vice versa. Guam's main source of income is its large American air force and navy bases. The Commonwealth of the Northern Marianas had a garment industry for many years because it could label the clothing "Made in the USA." That industry ceased for many reasons and has since been replaced by an economy focused on one casino that opened in 2015. Polynesia, and especially American Samoa, has a representation of professional football, players that is out of proportion to the population. Some of these players make 5 to 10 million dollars a year. When they send some of this money back home, it has a big impact on the economy.

The University of Arizona's Faitele Faafoi leads his teammates in a performance of the Samoan war dance called the Haka. Samoans are heavily recruited into the NFL.

Those islands in typhoon alley typically suffer at least one devastating typhoon every decade. The Northern Marianas was unfortunate enough to be directly hit in 2014 by super typhoon Soudelor and again in 2018 by super typhoon Yutu. Fiji, Vanuatu, and Tonga suffered their most destructive storm in 117 years in 2016 when Cyclone Winston hit. Governments have to spend capital on rebuilding and bringing back tourists.

Demographics

This region has broad ranging urbanization rates. In Guam and Nauru the rates are 95 and 100 percent respectively. In Papua New Guinea and Pitcairn Island they are 13 and 0 percent respectively. All the Pacific Islands have birthrates well above replacement level, and while the Melanesian countries are experiencing population growth, most of the Polynesian and Micronesian islands have minimal or negative population growth.

More people live in PNG than in all the other Pacific islands combined. Many hundreds of tribes coexist, each speaking its own language. PNG represents about 12 percent of the world's languages. Tok Pisin, also called Pidgin English, is the unifying language. With some effort an English speaker can understand it. The smallest nation in this chapter and one of the smallest in the world, Nauru has an area of only eight square miles and a population of around ten thousand. It is one of the most densely packed countries in the world.

Most of the islands have a majority ethnicity related to the islands. For example, the Marshall Islands are 92 percent Marshallese, and Nauru is 89 percent Nauruan. The islands that are not independent have a significantly smaller indigenous population. For example, the Mariana Islands are less than 30 percent Chamorro, the native ethnicity. Only 21 percent of the population of Hawaii has some amount of native Hawaiian blood.

Chuukesse women and a baby stand in front of a produce stand on Weno Island, Federated States of Micronesia.

(bottom) Melanesian children on Guadalcanal in the Solomon Islands

Boys in Tonga, wearing traditional skirts, enjoy snacks after school.

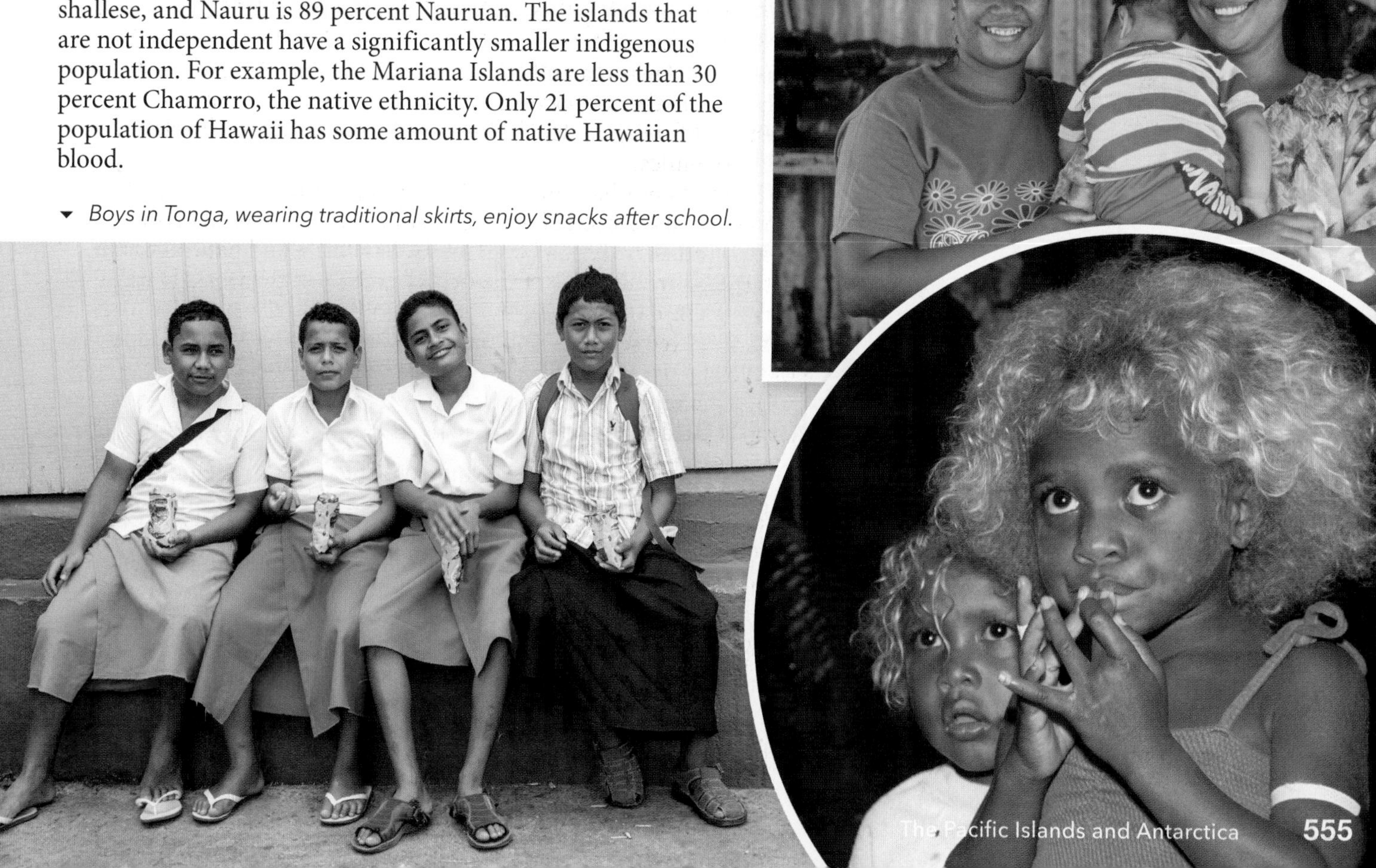

Culture and Diversity

Island life is known for having a slower and more relaxed pace than life on the continents. For most of the islands, this is still true. The people are known for being very friendly. On the island of Rota, people wave at every passing car, and the drivers wave back. On the more developed islands, this culture has rapidly changed because of immigration from the mainland and the Internet, which allows people there to be as busy as they are everywhere else. Traffic congestion is becoming more common.

A family enjoys a day at the beach on Fuakea island, Tuvalu.

Breadfruit

Families spend a lot of time at the beach and enjoy "talking story." Outdoor barbecues are common. Water sports such as surfing, swimming, canoeing, and fishing are other popular pastimes. The Polynesians invented surfing, and it was first observed during Captain Cook's expedition to Tahiti. There are still some who know the art of traveling the ocean by canoe via natural landmarks. People from all over the world fly to the Pacific Islands to enjoy snorkeling and scuba diving. Palau's reefs, for example, are one of the "seven underwater wonders of the world." Like Australia's Great Barrier Reef, Palau's waters are filled with coral, exotic fish, undersea caves, lava tubes, and shipwrecks. Although diving excursions are usually too expensive for the average islander, those who guide the tourists are scuba experts.

Coconuts, fish, breadfruit, sweet potatoes, and taro are the staples. The people use coconut meat, milk, and oil in different recipes. The mixed plate lunch is a feature of Polynesia. It includes grilled or barbecued meat, rice, macaroni salad, and green vegetables.

A common meal in Polynesia is a barbecue mixed plate; this one includes chicken katsu, korean kalbi beef short ribs, rice, and macaroni salad.

Religion

All of the islands followed some type of animist religion in which the people worshiped a host of gods and spirits. Violence and class and gender inequality were the key aspects of these religions. In 1819 the Hawaiian king Kamehameha I died. Queen Ka'ahumanu convinced the leaders that it was the late king's wish that she share power as co-regent with Kamehameha II. Upon obtaining this role, she convinced the king to break the religious rules, in effect ending Hawaii's traditional religion. Providentially, the first missionaries from New England arrived in 1820 with no knowledge of what had just happened. The queen enthusiastically welcomed the missionaries, and

▲ Sunday morning church service at a boy's school on Tongatapu Island, Tonga

▲ The Haili Church in Hilo, Hawaii, was the largest Protestant church in the world for a time in the 1840s, with over ten thousand members.

most of the Hawaiians believed the gospel. By 1840 Kamehameha III declared Hawaii a Christian kingdom. The official motto is, "The life of the land is perpetuated in righteousness."

American and British missionaries, many of whom were children of those who came to Hawaii, went on to the other islands in the region. The missionary effort culminated in the twentieth century with a push to reach the people of New Guinea. Bible translators are still at work there today. Beginning in the mid-nineteenth century, Mormon missionaries arrived in the Pacific Islands. By the twentieth century they had many converts, and a large Mormon following exists on the islands to this day.

While secular influences have diluted the Christian witness, many islands seek to hold on to their Christian heritage. In 2003 congregations in the Solomon Islands used their influence to seek an end to a six-year-long civil war. Christian leaders have counseled thousands who were affected by the violence. Church leaders also convinced the government to form the Truth and Reconciliation Commission to help resolve issues between the warring factions. Vanuatu's motto is "In God We Stand," and many of this tiny nation's leaders are Christians who played an important role in securing the nation's independence. Because Tonga considers itself a Christian nation, the constitution strictly prohibits all trade, games, and work on Sunday. Despite a need for money from tourism, the king and others discourage it for fear the nation will lose its identity: "If too much tourism happens, we will become like Hawaii, where there are no more Hawaiians," warned King Tupou IV, who was crowned in 1965.

SECTION REVIEW

1. In what way is Antarctica the world's most unusual territory?
2. What are ways Britain, France, and the United States still influence the islands?
3. What are the commonalities of all the economies?
4. What could explain the existence of high birthrates yet minimal or decreasing population growth in Polynesia and Micronesia?
5. Why might life seem slower and more relaxed on the islands?
6. Why were the Hawaiians more open to the gospel in 1820?

Major Religions of the Pacific Islands

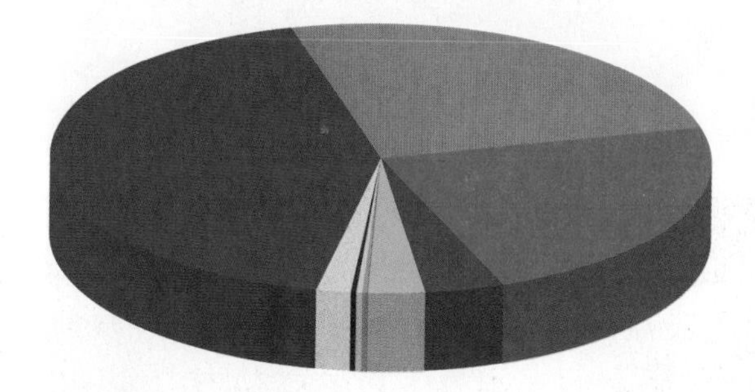

Religion	Percentage
Protestant	42.6%
Roman Catholic	25.3%
Protestant Evangelical	23.1%
Ethnic	3.9%
Hindu	2.6%
Islamic	0.5%
Buddhist	0.1%
Other	0.4%
Unaffiliated	1.5%

GUIDING QUESTIONS

- How do the economies and demographics of the Pacific Islands affect how the citizens interact with the environment?
- What are the environmental issues of the Pacific Islands and Antarctica?
- What are the causes and effects of environmental issues in the Pacific Islands?
- What are possible solutions to environmental issues in the Pacific Islands?

INTERACTIONS OF PEOPLE AND PLACES

What are some of the challenges of living in the Pacific Islands?

Despite the idyllic setting, it is dangerous to live here; safety margins are small. The people live in the reality that life is fragile. Basic medical care can be a long flight away. On the mainland people can drive inland to avoid a hurricane, but on these islands people can only close the shutters and wait out the storm. Islanders must learn to make do without needed supplies or medicines for long periods since ships can be delayed. Outdated foods that would be disposed of in other places are salvaged and sold. A storm can cut off Internet and telephone communication for a long time. If a business closes, it is difficult to find another job since employment opportunities are limited. It is much easier just to migrate to the mainland or a more prosperous island and find work. Islands like Nauru, Yap, and Pohnpei have been largely forgotten by the rest of the world, but others like Bora Bora in French Polynesia, Palau, and Kauai are too well known. These islands have millions of visitors every year and suffer all the negative issues associated with too many tourists, such as piles of garbage, traffic, and over-development.

The Northern Marianas suffered their second devastating typhoon in three years in 2018. Typhoon Yutu destroyed many buildings like these on the island of Tinian.

Environmental Issues of the Pacific Islands and Antarctica

As Kazakhstan was the Soviet location for testing nuclear bombs, so the Marshall Islands and French Polynesia were testing sites for American and French bombs, respectively. From 1946 to 1962 the United States exploded 105 nuclear bombs in the air and undersea. Most of the islands where the tests took place will be contaminated for years to come. The residents were evacuated and compensated, but those who lived in supposedly safe zones still suffer from higher percentages of cancer because of the tests.

For islands like Kiribati, all the headlines and attention focus on the island's imminent disappearance due to sea level rise and the effect of such an event on the citizens. While it is thought that these fragile islands would lose land, the opposite has actually been observed. Even *National Geographic* admitted, "Some islands grew by as much as 14 acres in a single decade, and Tuvalu's main atoll, Funafuti—33 islands distributed around the rim of a large lagoon—has gained 75 acres of land during the past 115 years." What does cause loss of land is over-development that destroys the natural barriers to storm surges.

The nuclear bomb was detonated at ninety feet underwater on July 25th, 1946, at the Bikini Atoll. The purpose of the test was to investigate the effect of nuclear weapons on naval ships. Water filling the cavity formed by the bubble caused a hollow column of water, called the chimney or plume, to rise six thousand feet in the air.

Antarctica

Scientists have studied all sorts of phenomena in Antarctica. But more than in any other place, the studies here have demonstrated the need to take scientific pronouncements with a grain of salt, as there is still so much to be learned. In 1985 the discovery of an ozone "hole" above the continent raised fears that the atmosphere might be warming. The ozone layer prevents harmful UV light from passing through the earth's atmosphere. Researchers found that higher UV levels harmed the Antarctic plankton and marine life. It was thought the use of CFC chemicals was the cause of the hole, so these chemicals were banned. In 2016 scientists found that the hole had dramatically closed up. Over the years they learned even more. The holes can be caused by seasonal changes, and gases from volcanoes in the 1990s may have been more to blame for the holes than CFC chemicals.

In recent years the greater concern is melting sea ice in Antarctica. About 90 percent of the world's ice is locked in the icecap of Antarctica. This represents about 70 percent of the world's fresh water. Many scientists predict that if the icecap were to melt, the sea level around the world would rise as much as two hundred feet, sinking many islands and every major coastal city. In 2014 scientists were surprised to find that the ice in the eastern Antarctic was increasing while the western ice was slightly decreasing. So, on the whole, there was an increase.

Water

Many of the Micronesian islands are so small they lack natural freshwater sources, and even the "fresh" water tastes salty. Some of the lagoons, like that at the south Tarawa atoll and the Majuro lagoon in the Marshall Islands, are polluted with human waste. For all of the islands, what little groundwater exists has levels of contaminants that are not acceptable. Many of the islands' reefs are damaged.

▾ *The islands of New Caledonia are scarred from nickel mining.*

Land

Papua New Guinea, the Solomon Islands, Tonga, and Fiji are suffering the chain reaction of rainforest loss, with the resulting erosion and soil degradation. Closed mining operations in Papua New Guinea, New Caledonia, and Naura have left the land a scarred and barren wasteland. All of the islands struggle to know what to do with their trash and how to prevent invasive species. Oceania is dealing with 571 different invasive species, ranging from little plants to rats and snakes. None of the islands had snakes prior to modern times. Somehow a brown tree snake arrived on Guam and killed most of the native bird population. There were no mosquitoes in Hawaii until 1826, when a ship carried them there accidentally in some barrels of water.

▲ *Trade winds blow onto the shores of Molokai, Hawaii, regularly bringing with them piles of plastic that have been floating around the Pacific Ocean for years.*

Reasons for Environmental Issues

Most of the islands lack advanced sewer and waste water treatment facilities. Lagoon latrines and open-pit dumping still occur in some places. This was not a problem when there were fewer people, but now it is a problem. The rainforest loss is a result of a growing commercial demand for tropical timber. The loggers need to change to sustainable logging practices. Mining projects in Melanesia also impact the forests and water. The growing trash problem is the result of a greater use of plastics worldwide, and the cost of shipping away trash is too great.

Proposed Solutions

The answer to the lack of fresh water is desalination. The process of changing saltwater to fresh previously required a lot of space and energy, but the technology has progressed rapidly. The American navy has already shown that desalination is viable. In a United States Navy bulletin Dr. J. Paul Armistead said, "We plan to build prototype desalination units that will use 65 percent less energy and be 40 percent smaller by weight and by volume relative to current navy reverse osmosis systems. They should require roughly 75 percent less maintenance." These machines have already helped civilians after typhoons when the navy has brought relief. With wise leadership, an island government could set the standard by implementing similar technology rather than depending on rainwater catchment systems.

▼ *Members of the Royal New Zealand Defense Force pump seawater into large holding tanks ready to be used by the desalination plant in Funafuti, Tuvalu.*

On Guam inspectors use trained snake-detecting dogs to find invasive snakes in cargo, conduct nighttime spotlight searches, and promote public education. Since 1993, they have removed more than 150,000 brown tree snakes from Guam's ports, including specimens found on outbound cargo planes and ships.

The leaders of Palau have shown foresight in protecting their island environment. They have reduced the number of charter flights allowed from China to limit tourists and control over-crowding. They also want to help the tourists learn more about the culture and the people of the island so they care about the island rather than just spending time at the beach. Palau is also farming fish to satisfy the demand of tourists without depleting the supply of wild fish. Many islands have made significant efforts to fight invasive species. New arrivals have their bags checked at the airport and must walk on a foot wash to clean their shoes. But it is a never-ending concern, and with some islands receiving millions of visitors every year, it is difficult to catch everything.

In 2019 Lucy Hughes, a British woman, won an award for inventing a biodegradable plastic called Marina Tex, made out of fish waste. Hopefully inventions like this can ease the growing trash pressure on the ocean and the islands.

A ship tows the first floating waste collection device toward the Golden Gate Bridge. Like tentacles, the cleaning system's 600-meter-long plastic pipes are designed to surround and extract plastic waste.

SECTION REVIEW

1. Why might it be surprising that living on a tropical island is dangerous?
2. Was the United States government right to detonate nuclear devices on some of the Marshall Islands? Why or why not?
3. What environmental problem is not a significant issue in the Pacific Islands and Antarctica? Why might that be?
4. How might a relaxed culture affect environmental issues?
5. How might you address the various environmental issues in the islands?

24 CHAPTER REVIEW

SUMMARY

1. Melanesia has the largest islands of the three Oceania subregions. Micronesia is made up of mostly small, low islands. Antarctica has two regions divided by the Transantarctic Mountains. High islands have volcanic mountains; low islands are coral rings. The Pacific has mountains, plateaus, and plains below the surface. Both the Pacific Islands and Antarctica have consistent climates. Copra and marine products are major exports of these regions. Melanesia has mineral resources.
2. Ferdinand Magellan and Captain Cook are the most significant European explorers of the Pacific. The islands followed a cycle of discovery, trade, evangelization, and colonization. The islands are related to the three Allied powers of Britain, France, and the United States. The majority are independent. Tourism and remittances are important sources of income for Micronesia and Polynesia. Mining and logging are important to Melanesia. People living here are known for being friendly and laid-back. The islands have Christian majorities.
3. The challenges to living on these islands are a lack of medical care, a lack of supplies, and a lack of employment. The Marshall Islands were the location for American nuclear bomb testing. Key environmental issues are the lack of fresh water, treatment of human waste, and a growing amount of garbage. Desalination is a solution to the need for fresh water. Wise leadership is needed to conserve the islands' tranquility and resources. New inventions are a solution to the problem of plastic trash.

Terms to Know

- ❑ high island
- ❑ low island
- ❑ abyssal plain
- ❑ deep
- ❑ seamount
- ❑ lagoon
- ❑ ice floe
- ❑ lead
- ❑ trust territory

Making Connections

1. On which type of island would you best be able to survive if you were marooned in the Pacific: high island or low island? Why?
2. Which is a major export for many Pacific islands? What is this product made from?
3. How are low islands formed?
4. How did Captain Cook's explorations affect the islands?
5. Why might it be expensive to have a national government?
6. What do most scientists fear will happen to some of the islands? What has been the reality so far?

Developing Geography Skills

1. Based on the map on pages 544–45, how are American Samoa and Samoa affected by the International Dateline?
2. Based on the map on page 544, why might Fiji be known as "the crossroads of the South Pacific"?

Thinking Critically

1. Should every parcel of land in the world be occupied by people, despite the difficulties of living there? Why or why not?
2. How did becoming part of the United States affect the native Hawaiians? How did the King of Tonga seek to take a different course?

Living in God's World

1. Missionaries have been criticized as oppressors because they sought to convert islanders from their traditional cultures to Christianity. How should Christians respond to this criticism?
2. How does family life among the islands differ from other regions? What cultural factors contribute to the differences?

CASE STUDY | Sustainable Fishing

Huge, beautiful, and profitable fish like marlin and swordfish are fished in the Pacific for sport and food. Four kinds of tuna are commercially harvested in the South Pacific: yellowfin, skipjack, bigeye, and albacore. Fish are these nations' most profitable renewable resource. Skipjack and albacore meat are sold in the canned form, which has declined in popularity, while yellowfin and bigeye meat are sold fresh and are in great demand since sushi is so popular worldwide.

▲ *A school of yellowfin tuna*

Fishing technology has maximized yields for fishermen around the world. They use three methods of fishing: purse seine, pole and line, and longline. Purse seine involves circling the school with a dragnet up to a mile long. Very few fish in the school can escape. Pole and line is the way most sport fishermen and women fish. The longline method involves letting out a line with hundreds of bated hooks. The first method has many downsides, but the main one is bycatch, when dolphins, whales, and other marine life get caught unintentionally.

Fish factories—huge ships that patrol areas with large amounts of fish—can catch, fillet, and freeze several tons of fish a day. But the problem is that there are too many fishing boats and not enough fish. Fish are being caught and killed faster than the fish can reproduce and grow. Pollution has also taken a toll on fish populations. Waters that once throbbed with life are falling silent. Marine biologists estimate that the number of fish in the world's oceans may have reduced by as much as 80–90 percent in the past forty years.

But there is hope for the future. Government officials and marine biologists are teaming up to create rules and zones for sustainable fishing. They are capping the amount of fish that people can take from the ocean. Fishermen are returning to more primitive fishing practices, such as harpooning and pole and line fishing, to avoid wiping out whole schools of fish. The result is a rebounding fish population in regulated areas where sustainable fishing is enforced, such as Alaska. Palau is leading the way with initiatives to protect their wild fish population, even setting up a learning exchange between the fishermen of Palau and fishermen of Papua New Guinea. Good and wise use of God-given resources involves thinking about how actions affect the future. Conserving world fisheries through sustainable fishing is an example of exercising good and wise dominion with a mind for the future.

1. How is tuna meat sold?
2. Why would the fishing industry be interested in more sustainable methods?
3. How would you handle the issue of overfishing?

GLOSSARY

A

Aboriginal Australians The first people to migrate to Australia

abyssal plain A broad, level area on the ocean floor

acid rain Sulfur dioxide and nitrogen oxide combined with water vapor that falls to the earth as rain

AIDS A disease that weakens the body's immune system and increases the body's vulnerability to infection and terminal illness

alluvial deposits Sediment that is deposited by a river

animism Religious belief that ascribes spiritual powers to animals, plants, and other aspects of nature

apartheid An oppressive political system of segregation in South Africa

aquaculture Cultivation or farming of fish in a controlled artificial environment

aquifer Underground layer of water-bearing rock or sediment from which groundwater can be extracted

archipelago A large group of islands

ASEAN Association of Southeast Asian Nations; founded in 1967 to promote economic and political cooperation

Asian Tigers A name given to Hong Kong, Taiwan, Singapore, and South Korea because of their phenomenal industrial and economic growth

atmosphere The layer of gases that surrounds the earth

autocracy A government whose ruler has unlimited authority

autonomous regions Areas of a country that have greater loyalties to another country or a desire for independence and have been given limited autonomy

avalanche A large amount of snow that detaches and moves down a mountain

axis Line about which the earth rotates

B

Balkanization The tendency of ethnically and religiously diverse territories to break up into small, hostile nations

Bedouin The generic term for the thousands of nomadic tribes who live in the deserts of the Middle East and North Africa

Belt and Road Initiative The Chinese plan to build a series of roads, seaports, airports, and power plants around the world

biome Any large region where distinct populations of plants and animals are found living together

biosphere Consists of all the different areas on the earth where life can exist

birthrate The number of children born each year per one thousand people

birth tourism The practice of traveling to another country to give birth

black market An illegal underground or shadow economy

boomerang A curved wooden device that can be thrown and will return to the thrower; used as a weapon

brain drain When the smartest people of a nation emigrate to more developed countries

buffer state A neutral state between two rivals that is intended to prevent conflict

C

capitalism A free market economy in which anyone may go into business in an attempt to make a profit; most businesses are privately owned instead of government owned.

Carnival Literally means "farewell to meat"; a festival that occurs before Lent

cash crops Crops that are raised specifically for sale

caste A system in India that determines a person's social status

cataclysm A violent upheaval or change in the earth's crust

cataracts Areas of shallow water in rivers where boulders break the surface

chernozem Rich, black topsoil located on the Great European Plain in Russia

Chinook winds A wind phenomenon in North America that causes dramatic warming during the winter

city-state A city and its surrounding territory; functions as an independent state

clan Several villages that are descended from a common ancestor

clear-cutting The total removal of trees in a given area

climate The average weather over an extended length of time

climate change Gradual changes in the world's climate

climate zone Zone that determines the climate of landmasses in that region

collectivization An action whereby the state takes ownership of the farms and puts people there to work the land

command economy A system in which government determines what industries are developed, where they are built, and what they produce

communism The most radical form of socialism in which the government owns everything and allows no private property or free-market business transactions

compass rose A symbol that displays the orientation of a map

Confucianism The teachings of the Chinese philosopher K'ung Futzu

Congo Basin The sedimentary basin of the Congo River

continental divide Line of mountains that determines where the waters flowing from each side will drain on a continent

continental drift The idea that the continents were once one landmass but at some point drifted apart (see also **plate tectonics theory**)

continentality Climate conditions that form over the interior of a large landmass and are characterized by temperature extremes, such as hot summers and cold winters

continents The seven primary landmasses of the earth's surface

contour lines Lines of separate colors on a relief map to indicate all points on a map that have the same altitude

convection A process of heat transfer that occurs in the mantle when particles carry thermal energy as they move from one place to another

coral bleaching Loss of color that results when algae is expelled from coral due to stress or change in temperature

cordillera A chain of mountains

core The central portion of the earth that lies below the mantle

core values Ideals that forge a common culture and bind a people together

Coriolis effect The influence of the earth's rotation on wind direction

coup d'etat A sudden overthrow of a government by a military leader or government official

Creation Mandate The unique calling of God to humankind to exercise dominion over the earth; based on Genesis 1:28

crust The solid outer part of the earth

cultural boundary A border drawn to segregate the people of different ethnicities

cultural diffusion The spread of cultural traits from one culture to another

culture The system of customs and traditions and habits that a group of people uses to make something of their world

culture hearths The locations where different cultures appeared around the world

culture region A distinct area in which a specific culture thrives

cylindrical projection Map projection based on tracing shadows cast when a paper is wrapped in the shape of a cylinder around a wire globe

czar Title similar to *emperor* or *king*

D

death rate The number of people who die each year per one thousand people

Deccan Plateau A plateau in India that formed when extensive volcanic activity spread a layer of flood basalt across much of the land

decolonization The process of gaining independence from a colonial ruler

deep A place in a trench that exceeds the depth of eighteen thousand feet

deforestation The process of removing trees for logging, farming, or grazing

democracy A form of government whereby the people rule themselves

demographic transition model A model used to describe what has happened with populations and to suggest what will happen

demography The study of population characteristics

desalination Process of removing salt from seawater to provide drinking water

desertification The changing of arable land into desert

developing country A country whose industries do not take full advantage of its natural or human resources

devolution A passing down or "de-evolution" of power after the fall of the Soviet Union

dew point The point at which water vapor begins condensation

dialects Local languages

diaspora Group of people who have left their home country to live and work abroad

dictatorship Rule by a person or group with the authority of military strength

didgeridoo A long, hollow wooden wind instrument that produces a deep sound

dikes Strong walls of stone and earth built to restrict or restrain the flow of water

diplomacy The art of negotiating agreements between nations

dissident A person who opposes official government policy in an authoritarian state

DMZ Demilitarized zone; a neutral zone separating hostile countries; used especially in reference to North and South Korea

Domino Theory The belief that if South Vietnam fell to communism, Southeast Asia would fall, followed by the rest of Asia and eventually the world

drainage basin The area drained by a river system

drought Extended period with little or no rainfall

dune Vast hill of sand with few plants to hold it down

E

earthquake A shaking, trembling, or concussion of the earth due to subterranean causes

economics The study of the process by which people make a living, buy and sell, grow crops, manufacture goods, and provide services

ecotourism Tourism that emphasizes exotic, natural environments with the goal of supporting conservation efforts

enclave A country or portion of a country surrounded by another country

equator Imaginary line that divides the earth into the Northern and Southern Hemispheres

equinox Point in time twice each year when the length of day and night are approximately equal all over the planet

erosion The natural breakdown and removal of materials on the earth's surface

escarpment A steep face or edge of a ridge

estuary The widening mouth of a river as it approaches the ocean, where it tends to form a delta

ethnic cleansing The mass killing or expulsion of an ethnic or religious group

ethnic group A people or nation that shares a common birth

European Union An organization of countries that seeks to form a single European community that can compete on the world stage economically and politically

euthanasia Physican-assisted suicide

eutrophication The increase of nutrients in a lake or stream that causes an increase in algae and bacteria, reduces oxygen levels, and increases the cloudiness of the water

evangelical Orthodox Protestants

exclaves Land separated from the main body of the country it belongs to

F

faults A crack in the earth's surface where two pieces of land have moved in different directions

First Nations The native peoples of Canada

fjord Long, narrow, deep inlet between steep cliffs that glacial motion carved into the land during the glacier's movement to sea level

foehn The term for a dry winter wind in Europe

foreign policy The set of principles that guides a government's international relations

front The line between two air masses where rain or snow falls

futsal An indoor version of soccer played in Portugal and Greece

G

G20 Countries with the largest economies

GDP Gross Domestic Product; the monetary value of all the goods and services produced in one year within a country's borders

geography The detailed study of the earth and how people relate to the earth and one another

geometric border A boundary usually drawn as a straight line to connect specific points or to follow a line of latitude or longitude

geothermal energy The energy in steam heated by magma intrusions that can be harnessed to generate electrical power and heat

geyser Hot spring formed from water heated by magma that rises to the earth's surface and shoots into the air

GIS Geographic information system technology used to make modern maps

glaciation The process whereby glaciers recede and sweep away material, creating U-shaped valleys

glasnost Russian term for "openness"; refers to the opening of the Soviet Union to the West

GPS Global positioning system of satellites

graziers New Zealand ranchers

Great Barrier Reef The largest coral formation in the world; located off the coast of Australia

green space An area of grass, trees, or other vegetation set aside in an urban area

groundwater depletion Drawing too much water from aquifers

H

headwaters Source of a river

hieroglyphics Egyptian writing system which included over one thousand symbols to relate meaning

high island Larger islands rising above sea level with volcanic mountains and hills

highly developed country A country with a wide range of industries that take full advantage of its people's skills

Holocaust Hitler's attempt to systematically murder every Jewish person within his sphere of influence

hot spring Spring formed from water heated by magma that rises to the earth's surface

hydroelectric energy Energy generated by the use of running water

hydrologic cycle The process of evaporation, condensation, and precipitation

hydrosphere All of the water that exists on or around the earth

I

ice floe A large, flat sheet of floating ice that has formed from seawater

IMF International Monetary Fund; an international organization whose goal is to foster monetary cooperation and secure financial stability worldwide

industry Human exertion of any kind employed for the creation of value

interrupted projection Map projection that is interrupted with gaps or cuts

Intertropical Convergence Zone The area encircling the earth at the equator in which the northeast and southeast trade winds converge

invasive species Plants and animals not native to a country that are brought into the country, with unintended consequences

isthmus Narrow land bridge that connects two larger landmasses

J

junta A council of military and civilian leaders who seize power, often resulting in civil wars

K

karst topography Topography produced by the erosion and collapse of solution caves in thick strata of chemical sedimentary rocks

khat Shrub grown in Yemen whose leaves are harvested and chewed as a narcotic

kibbutz Collective community in Israel where labor, housing, and resources are shared

Kurds Ethnic group originally from Iran that has spread to parts of Turkey, Iraq, and Syria

L

lagoon Area of the ocean surrounded by coral

land bridge Strip of land that connects two large landmasses

landform A feature of the land, such as a hill, peninsula, or mesa

language family A group of languages that share many common characteristics

latitude The distance north or south of the equator measured in degrees

latitude zones One of three zones in relation to the equator (tropics, temperate, or polar)

leaching The dissolving of soil minerals by water and their removal downward through the soil

lead The open water between floes

legend Part of a map that displays the meaning of the symbols on the map

lithosphere The area of solid matter on the surface of the earth

Llanos Broad grassy plains that cover the northeastern corner of Colombia and central Venezuela

loess A very fine silt that has been deposited by the wind

longitude The distance east or west of the prime meridian measured in degrees

low island Also called atolls; rings of coral left around a submerged volcano cone

M

magma Molten rock that flows because it is subjected to intense pressure and temperature

mantle The portion of the earth's interior lying between the crust and the core

Manufacturing Belt Region in the American Northwest and Great Lakes regions where manufacturing was concentrated until the 1960s

maquiladoras Plants built by American and Japanese companies in Mexico where goods are manufactured and then sent for final assembly to the companies that own the plants

massif Mountain formed by fault-line movement

Mauryan Empire First Indian empire; established in 322 BC

medical tourism The practice of traveling to another country to purchase health care not available in one's own country

mental map A person's perception of the world or a part of it based on available knowledge

Mesopotamia Area between the Tigris and Euphrates Rivers

mestizo Person of Amerindian-Spanish descent

migration Movement of people to a new area

mixed economy Attempt to combine elements of capitalism and socialism

monotheism The belief that there is only one God

monsoon A wind that changes direction with the seasons

moshav Community settlement of farmers in Israel established by the Labor Zionist party

mosque Islamic worship building

mountain A large mass of earth and rock that rises above the common level of the earth or adjacent land; higher than a hill

MTD Moralistic Therapeutic Deism; a modern religious philosophy in America

Mughal Empire Muslim-based empire in India that ruled from 1526 to 1858

multiactive A culture that has characteristics of both high and low contexts

multiculturalism The view that all cultures are equally valid and no culture is better than another

N

NAFTA North American Free Trade Agreement; 1993 pact that facilitated free trade between Canada, Mexico, and the United States

nation A group of people with a common heritage, culture, and homeland

NATO North Atlantic Treaty Organization; an alliance of European and North American nations committed to defending each other if one member is attacked

natural borders Borders such as oceans, mountains, rivers, or deserts

neocatastrophists Those who admit that the current condition of the earth's surface cannot be explained by gradual uniform processes alone

newly industrialized countries Countries that have transitioned from primarily agricultural industries to goods-producing industries

North Atlantic Drift Warm current that continues from the Gulf Stream, crosses the Atlantic Ocean, and flows along the coast of northwestern Europe

nuclear waste Radioactive byproducts of the manufacture of nuclear energy and nuclear weapons

O

oases Areas of fertile land watered by a natural spring or other water sources, such as aquifers in the desert

old-growth forests Forests that are populated with mature trees which have not experienced significant disturbance

oligarchy A small group of people who hold ultimate authority

one-child policy Policy of limiting Chinese families to one child; began in the 1970s to control China's growing population

orographic Precipitation related to mountains

outback The scarcely populated areas beyond the coastal cities of Australia

overfarming The practice of clearing land or grazing animals to excess

overfishing To exhaust the usable fish supply in certain waters

P

Pampas A region of South America with vast grasslands and a semiarid climate

parliamentary system A representative government led by a parliament and a prime minister

passive resistance A means of achieving goals using protests, civil disobedience, and economic or political noncooperation

pastoralism Raising of large herds of animals, especially sheep, goats, or cattle

patriarchal Having an organization of society in which the male head of the family exercises authority over all its generations

peat Dense layer of partially decayed plant material; usually found in bogs

perestroika A Russian term for the "restructuring" that brought more free-market policies and some private ownership of property to the Soviet Union in the 1980s

permafrost The layer of soil beneath the surface that remains frozen throughout the year

plain A broad, level expanse with no visible elevation

plateau A large, relatively flat area that is elevated above the surrounding landscape; a tableland

plate tectonics theory The view that large sections of the earth's crust move, producing earthquakes and volcanoes

poaching The illegal killing of animals

polar region Latitude zone that receives only a small amount of sunlight in winter

polder A parcel of land reclaimed from the sea

population density The population of a country divided by its area to reveal the average number of people per square mile or kilometer in the country

population distribution Term for where people choose to live

Poverty Environment Initiative An initiative in Southeast Asia to solve both environmental problems as well as the underlying causes

precipitation Concentrated water droplets falling to the earth

prefecture A political division of Japan

primate city The largest city in a country; also significantly larger than other cities in that country

prime meridian Line of longitude that passes through Greenwich, England, and is designated 0°

prime minister The executive of a parliamentary republic

privatization The change from government ownership to private ownership of industries

province A region of a country; a tract or district

Q

Québécois French speaking Canadians that live in Quebec

R

rainforests Dense jungles filled with biodiversity

rain shadow The land beyond the mountains that is usually very dry because little water vapor survives passage over the mountains

reforestation Replanting of trees

reincarnation A cycle of birth, death, and rebirth according to Hindu teaching

relief maps Maps that show specific changes in elevation

remittances Money sent to families from relatives or acquaintances working abroad

remote sensing Geographic information gathered by aircraft or satellites

Renaissance Rebirth of the arts that began in the fourteenth century

republic A government characterized by a representative system and operated according to a constitution

revolution The earth's trip around the sun once a year

rift valley A valley caused by the junction of tectonic plates

Ring of Fire A zone of earthquake and volcanic activity around the edge of the Pacific Ocean

river system A main river and all of its tributaries

rotation Movement of the earth on its axis 360° every twenty-four hours

S

Sahara The world's largest desert

Sahel A three hundred-mile-wide band of grass-covered plains in Africa between the Sahara and the tropical forests

samurai Japanese warriors who protected the estates of feudal lords

satellite states Nations, primarily in Eastern Europe, that were under the control of the Soviet Union

savanna A grassy plain in tropical and subtropical regions

scale Calibrated line that indicates distance on a map

seamounts Isolated underwater volcanoes that dot the ocean basins

secularism A belief system that rejects or excludes religion

sedimentation The washing of sediment from construction and farming sites by rain that transfers it to the ocean, where it settles in the reef system

sharia Law based on the Qur'an and the Hadith

shatter belt A region that is under continual political pressure and is often fragmented by warring internal factions and heavily influenced by surrounding rival countries

shogun A "great general"; ruled Japan in the emperor's name from 1192 to 1867

Silk Road A major trade route that linked the great ancient empires of Rome and China

smog Haze or cloud that results when smoke and other pollutants in the atmosphere combine

socialism An economic system in which the government owns the major industries and promises to make production decisions for the welfare of society; a command economy

solar system Composed of the sun, planets, small system bodies, and other objects held in orbit around the sun by the sun's gravity

solstice Event when the sun reaches its greatest angular distance from the equator twice each year

Soviet bloc A string of semi-independent countries behind the Iron Curtain that were ruled by puppet governments taking their orders from Moscow

station Australian ranch

steppes Unforested grasslands

Stolen Generation The indigenous children who were forcibly taken from their parents by Australian authorities and raised in government or religious institutions

subcontinent Large landform that is smaller than a continent

subduction The tectonic process by which the relatively thin and dense oceanic crust slowly slides down and under the more massive but less dense continental crust

subsistence farming Producing just enough food and raising just enough livestock to feed one's family

Sunbelt Region in the South and Southwest that manufacturing moved to during the 1960s

sustainable development Meeting the needs of the present generation without denying future generations the capacity to meet their needs

synagogue Jewish building for worship

syncretism The blending of aspects of various religions to form a new religion

T

Taliban Islamic extremists known as "seekers" or "students" of Islam; found in Afghanistan and Pakistan

Taoism The teachings of Chinese philosopher Laozi (also spelled Lao-tzu)

Temperate Zone Latitude zone with neither the constant warmth of the tropics nor the extreme cold of the poles

thematic map Map that records gathered information about climate, population, or resources of a nation or region

theocracy Government ruled by religious or divine authority

Three Gorges Dam One of the world's largest dams; constructed in China to produce hydroelectric power

Tibetan Plateau Extensive plateau located in western China

timberline The altitude of a mountain system at and above which trees do not grow

transplant tourism The practice of traveling to another country to obtain an organ transplant

Trans-Siberian Railway Russian railway that extends 5,778 miles from Moscow in the west to Vladivostok on the Pacific Ocean

tribalism Strong identification with a tribe that speaks the same language or dialect

tributary A river that flows into and feeds another river

tropics Latitude zone closest to the equator with consistently very warm temperatures

trust territory A territory under the trusteeship of the United Nations

tsunami Destructive waves resulting from an earthquake in the ocean

U

uniformitarianism The belief that only those forces that are presently acting on the earth have shaped the earth in the past

Uniting Church Formed in 1977 by the union of the Congregational, Presbyterian, and Methodist churches in Australia

untouchables People in India whose occupations, such as tanner or garbage collector, are considered so low that they are beneath caste

urbanization The movement of people from rural areas to cities and the growth of those cities

USMCA Trade agreement between the United States, Mexico, and Canada; signed December 2019

V

vertical climate zones Tropical regions in Latin America with specific patterns of growth based on elevation

village A self-contained group of families living in close proximity in a rural area

W

wadi A dry streambed that fills up with water after rainstorms and then dries up again

weather The condition of the atmosphere at a given time and place

weathering The degenerative process that contributes to the breaking up and alteration of rock materials

welfare state Country that assumes primary responsibility for the social welfare of its citizens "from the cradle to the grave"

world ocean The whole system of oceans that flow into each other

INDEX

A

Aboriginal Australians 528-30
aborigines 461
abortion 67, 250, 443, 463
absolute monarch 73
Abu Dhabi 401
abyssal plains 549
Academie française 226
acculturation 551
acid rain 113, 160
Acquired Immune Deficiency Syndrome (AIDS) 250
addax 325
Addis Ababa 362
Adelaide 532
Adriatic Sea 260
Aegean Sea 289
aesthetics 13, 15, 66, 70
Afghanistan 405–7; demographics 417; economy 416; environment 421–22; history 413; religion 419; resources 411; 415; water 409
Africa, *see* Central Africa; Northern Africa; Southern Africa; Western Africa
Africapitalism 367
Afrikaans 370
Afrikaner 365
agnosticism 228
agribusiness 235
agriculture 4, 36, 60; economy 79, 104, 128
Ahaggar Mountains 311
Aïr Mountains 311
Akha 509
Alabama 95
Alaska 22, 94-95, 120-21, 414, 563
Albania 260-61; demographics 273; economy 272; water 264
Alberta 120-25, 134
Alexander the Great 295, 388, 413, 415
Alexandria 12, 311
algae 114-15, 135-36, 336, 386, 541
Algeria 310-11; climate 314; economy 320; environment 326; history 316; religion 323; resources 315
Algiers 316
Al-Haram Mosque 381
Allah 73, 372, 381, 395-96, 398
alliance 75-76, 223, 280
alloy 38
alluvial deposits 313
alluvial plain 27, 168, 313
alluvium 27
Almaty 407, 410, 416; environment 421-22
almsgiving 322, 396
aloe 43
alpine climate 338
alpine lakes 219
alpine mountain system 215, 220, 226, 260
Alps 27, 215-17, 219–20, 267, 287–89
Altai Mountains 238
Altiplano Plain 27, 166
altitude 10, 55, 95, 149, 171, 362, 456
aluminum 38, 201, 203, 443, 532
Amazigh 316
Amazon Basin 165–66, 171
Amazonia 168, 257
Amazon rainforest 171, 182
Amazon River 32, 167, 170
amber 267
American revolution 106
American Samoa, economy 555, government 554
Amerindians 154
Amharic 369
Amman 382, 389
ammonium 541
amputees 513
Amsterdam 213, 215; climate 220; environment 230
Amundsen, Roald 120–21, 546–47, 552
Anak Krakatau 21
anarchy 73, 365, 415
ancestor worship 155
Andaman Sea 499
Andes Mountains 27, 33, 165–68, 171
Andorra 286–88; climate 291; culture 299–300; demographics 297; economy 297; environment 303; government 296; history 294–95; religion 301; water 290
Angel Falls 166, 171
Angkor Wat 505
Angola 358; water 361; history 364–65
animal husbandry 36, 40
animism 347
animist 133, 509, 556
animistic worldview 372
Ankara 382
Annam Highlands 496
annex 269, 272, 283, 388, 392, 486, 529, 550
anoxic 264
Antarctica 31, 546; climate 549; environment 558–59; history 552; resources 549; water 548
Antarctic Peninsula 546
Antarctic Plate 22
Antarctic Plateau 549
anthropogenic 135
anthropologist 68, 71, 187, 484
antibodies 180
Antigua and Barbuda 48
Antilles, Greater and Lesser 145, 153
antimalarial 353
Antimeridian 548
Antioch 12, 382
Antwerp 215
Aogashima 474
apartheid 365–66
Apennine Mountains 287
apologetic 132
Appalachian Mountains 95
aquaculture 37, 315
aquifer 99, 101, 324
Aquitaine 215
Arabian Desert 311
Arabian Peninsula 50, 311, 385, 388, 395
Arabian Plate 22, 359, 384
Arabian Sea 383, 428–29, 431
Arabic language 321
arable land 220
Arabs 311, 316–17, 320–21, 392, 415
Aral Sea 409
archery 439, 462
archipelago 28, 145, 358
Arctic Circle 120, 122, 193, 238
Arctic Ocean 120–21, 123, 134–35
Ardennes 214
Argentina 2, 166; climate 172; economy 176; environment 182; religion 180; resources 173; water 171
Arizona 89
Armenia 385, 406–407; culture 418; demographics 417; government 414; history 412; resources 410
artesian well 525
artisans 440
Ashgabat 407, 416
Asia, *see* Central Asia; East Asia; South Asia; Southeast Asia
Asia Minor 12
Asian Russia 239
Asian Tigers 459
Asmara 357, 362
aspen 245
asphalt 113
Association of Southeast Asian Nations (ASEAN) 504
Assyrian 388, 392
Aswan High Dam 324
Atacama Desert 166, 168–69, 172, 182
atheism 228
Athens 74, 287; history 295
Atlanta 163
Atlantic Ocean 32, 95, 100, 123–24
Atlas Mountains 310, 312, 314
atmosphere 20, 25, 43, 45, 51, 54, 58
atmospheric pressure 48
atoll 28, 430, 544, 558–59
atrocities 225, 367, 412, 493
Auckland 523, 527, 532
aurora 193
Auschwitz 493
Australia 497, 520–24; climate 526; culture 534; demographics 532; economy 531; environment 537–39; government 530–31; history 528; religion 535–36; resources 527; water 525–26
Australian plate 22, 498
Austral Islands 545
Austria 213–215
authoritarian 73–75, 246, 249, 343–44, 367–68, 389, 414
autocracy 73–74
automaker 480
automobile manfacturing 176, 201–2, 224, 480
autonomous regions 414
autonomy 248, 271, 413, 505, 553
Autumnal 46
avalanche 220
avian botulism 115
avocado 156
axis 46
Azerbaijan 385, 403, 406–7; demographics 417; economy 416; environment 420–21; government 414; history 412; religion 418; resources 411; water 409
azimuthal projection 8
Aziziya, Libya 314

B

Babel, Tower of 13, 67, 69, 388
Bab-el-Mandeb strait 360
Babelthuap 545
babies 225, 273, 443, 461, 463, 481–82
Babylon 73, 383, 388–98, 495
Bach, Johann 227
bacteria 114, 254
bacterial 160, 541
Baghdad, Iraq 12, 383
Baguio, Philippines 503, 515, 517
Bahamas 145, 147
Bahrain 383; demographics 391; economy 390; resources 387
Baja California 144
Baku 407; water 409, 414, 421–22
balance of trade 81
Balkanization 270
Balkan Mountains 260–61, 266
Balkan Peninsula 260, 287, 295
Balkan Region 270, 274, 276
ballet 251
ballistic missile 482
Baltic Canal 238
Baltic People 273
Baltics 274, 277–78
Baltic Sea 193, 218, 260, 264–65
Baltic States 271, 273
Bamako 311, 313
Banaue 515, 517
Banff National Park 119
Bangkok 81; climate 500; economy 505; water 499
Bangladesh 12, 87, 427, 429; climate 432; culture 439; demographics 438; education 436; environment 443; history 435; resources 433; water 431
bankrupt 136
Bantu 344, 369–70
baobab 325, 337, 370
baptism 110, 156, 181, 536
Baptist 110–11, 130, 156, 509–10
Barbados 145
Barbary Coast 316
Bárðarbunga 195
Barents Sea 238
barley 125, 149, 220, 266, 290, 322
barometer 48
barrier islands 24
baseball 462
Basque 68
bauxite 38
Bavarian Plateau 215
Bay of Bengal 431–32
Bay of Biscay 218, 286
Bay of Campeche 144
Bay of Fundy 123, 475
Bayou 29
Bedouin 321
Beethoven 227
Beijing 452, 458, 467
Beirut 382, 389
Belarus 260–63; culture 274; environment 278; government 272; history 269; resources 266–67; water 265
Belfast 192
Belgium 214–15, 355, 366; environment 232; government 223; religion 229; resources 220; water 218
Belgrade 261; water 264
Belize 145; demographics 154; economy 153
Belt and Road Initiative 512
Bengali 438
Benin 332; resources 339
Berber 314, 321
Bering Sea 239
Bering Strait 239
Berlin 215, 225, 341
Berlin Wall 222
beryl 433
Bethlehem 389
Bhagavad-Gita 441
Bhutan 428–29; culture 439; economy 437; environment 447; government 436; history 435; water 431
biblical worldview 106
bicameral 342, 504
bilharzia 325
bilingual 369, 506
binational 331
Bingham, Hiram III 165
biodegradable 560
biodiverse crops 277
biodiversity 144, 513, 538
biofuels 115
biome 57, 161, 257
biosphere 20, 40
birthrate 83–85, 105, 128, 131, 154, 225, 250, 344, 391, 417, 461, 532
birth tourism 463
Bishkek 407
bitumen 125, 134, 136–37
Black Forest 214–215, 218
Black Hills 103
black market 250, 482
Black Sea 218, 260, 264, 382, 385, 407, 409–10
block-fault 263
Blue Nile 360
Boer War 364
Boers 364–65, 369
Bogd Khan Uul National Park 75
Bogotá 171
Bohemian Forest 260
Boko Haram 326, 343
Bolivia 166–67; culture 178; demographics 177; environment 184; government 175; resources 173; water 170
boomerang 358, 528
Borglum, Gutzon 103
Borneo 497
borscht 252
Bosnia-Herzegovina 260; economy 272; environment 278; history 270; water 264
Bosporus 382
Boston 34
Botswana 355, 358, 377; demographics 369; government 365; history 364; water 361
Bouazizi, Mohammed, 319
Bougainville 553
Brahman 441
Brahmapur 429
Brahmaputra River 431, 452
Brahmin 440–41
Brahms 227
brain drain 505
Brandberg Massif 359
Bratislava 261, 264
Brazil 60, 166–68; climate 171; culture 178–79; demographics 177; economy 176; environment 182–85; resources 172–73
Brazil Current 52
Brazilian Highlands 166–68; climate 171
Brazzaville 333
breadbasket 121, 260, 377
breadfruit 556
Bremen 215, 225
Brisbane 532
Britain, *see* Great Britain
British 76, 318, 329, 342, 377, 434–35; automobile 201; colonies 14, 178, 365, 530; Commonwealth 530, 552–53; Empire 14, 415, 530; forces 502; heritage 522–23; Isles 51, 192, 196, 200; law 130; missionaries 557; North America Act 126; settlers 528–29
British Columbia 120, 124–25; culture 130; economy 128
Brittany 214–15
Brunei 496–97; economy 506; environment 512; government 504; resources 500
Brussels 215, 223, 225
Brutalist-style architecture 275
bubonic plague 148
Bucharest 261, 264
Budapest 261, 264, 274
Buddha 510
Buddhism 441, 463, 486–87, 509–11
Buenos Aires 172, 183
buffer state 415
buffer zone 294, 364, 372, 502
Bukhara 407, 412
Bulgaria 260–61; demographics 274; government 272; resources 266; water 264
bureaucracy 73–74, 222–23, 479
Burkina Faso 332, 334; climate 337; resources 339
Burma Plate 498
Burmese 115, 506–8
burqa 399
Burundi 356–57; climate 362; demographics 369; government 366–67; water 360–61
business 67, 77–78, 81–82, 104, 223, 319, 364, 367–68, 416, 480–81, 506
Butchart Gardens 130
Byrd, Richard 552
Byzantine Empire 252, 273

C

cabinet 132, 342
cacao 172, 183, 500
Cain 36–37
Cairns 19
Cairo 311, 318–19, 323, 364
calcite 39
Calgary 119–22, 131
California 80–81, 96–97; climate 100; demographics 105
California Current 52
calligraphy 427

Cambodia 496–97; culture 507–8; demographics 506; environment 512–15; government 504; history 503; resources 500
Cameroon 333–34; demographics 369; government 343; resources 339; water 335
Canada 119–22; climate 124; culture 129–32; demographics 128; economy 128; environment 134–37; government 126–27; religion 132–33; resources 125; water 123
Canadian Rockies 121
Canadian Shield 120–23, 125
Canary Islands 311
Canberra 530
canneries 554
cannibalism 551
cantons 223
Cape of Good Hope 358
Cape Town 355
Cape Verde 332
capitalism 77–78, 81–82, 104, 108
Caribbean Sea 144–45, 149, 167, 170
Carnival 179
Caroline Islands 544–45
Carpathian Mountains 260
Casablanca 309, 311
cash crop 343
cashmere 460
Casimir 259
Caspian Depression 406–7
Caspian Sea 33, 238, 383, 385, 406–7
cassava 345, 500
Castilian 294
caste 440
cataclysm 25, 40
Catalán 286
Catalonia 285
cataracts 360
Catholic, *see* Roman Catholic(ism)
Caucasus 404–24
Caucasus Mountains 238, 240, 460
Central Africa 330–51
Central African Republic 313, 333; culture 345, water 335
Central America 144–61
Central Asia 404–25
Central Lowlands 523, 525
Central Plains 95
Central Provinces 123
Central Siberian Plateau 239
Central Uplands 214–215, 219, 260
Chad 311; culture 321; demographics 321; economy 320; environment 325–26; religion 323; resources 314; water 313
chaebol 481
Challenger Deep 549
chancellor 222–23, 225
charcoal 39
Charlemagne 286, 294, 528
Charleston 34
Charlottetown 120–21
Chernobyl 261, 269, 278–81, 421, 490–91
chernozem 241
Chiang Kai-shek 458
Chicago 33, 175, 544
Chile 166–67, 545, 551; climate 171; economy 176; environment 182; government 174–75; resources 172–73
China 75, 135–36, 368, 451–54; climate 456; culture 461–62; demographics 461; economy 460; environment 465–67, 469, 478, 502, 512–14; government 459; history 458; religion 463; water 455
Chinook winds 124, 220
Chomolungma 26
Christian worldview 227
chromite 387, 411
chromium 38, 81, 173, 433, 501
Chuquicamata 173
Churchhill Falls 125
Churchill, Manitoba 123
circumnavigate 171, 528, 552
city-state 295
civilian 11, 225, 271, 342, 560
civilization 14, 19, 26, 32, 108, 228, 317, 503, 537
clams 31, 491
clan 340, 478
clear-cutting 114, 184
climate 54–55
climate change 59, 61, 81, 134, 257
climate zone 56
climatology 54, 56, 60–61
climograph 56, 61
coal 38–39
coal-burning 539
coal-fired 113, 206, 208, 254, 467, 469, 538
Coastal Mountains 95, 122
Coastal Plains 27, 95, 121, 314, 389, 428
coastline 10, 26, 120, 287, 389, 433, 497
cobalt 125, 339, 343, 550
cocaine 159, 175, 183
cocoa 172
coconut 537, 550–51, 556
Cold War 502
collectivization 269, 280
Cologne 215, 225
Colombia 13, 166–67; culture 179; demographics 177; economy 176; environment 182–84, 187; government 174–75; religion 180; resources 172–73
Colombo 429
colonial 106, 140, 150, 174, 349, 364, 366, 435, 496
colonialism 502, 510
colonization 316, 318, 364, 502–3, 511, 550
Colorado 96
Colorado Plateau 94
Colorado River 25, 89, 98
Columbia Plateau 94
Columbia River 35, 123
command economy 77
commercial farmers 36
commercial fishing 531–32
commission 3, 14, 223, 280, 493, 514, 536, 557
commodity 37, 111, 316, 331, 341, 525
Commonwealth 127, 247, 259, 272, 530, 545, 553–55
Commonwealth of Independent States (CIS) 247
communism 268–72, 274, 342, 436, 458, 462–63, 479, 483, 503, 510
communist 65, 78, 150, 175, 218, 222, 246, 250, 252, 254, 270–72, 276, 279, 414–15, 457–60, 463, 479, 502–504
Comoros Islands 358
compass 6–7, 9, 389
compass rose 9
concrete 39, 113, 381, 521
concretions 408
condensation 51
conductor 38
confluence 313
Confucianism 463–64
Confucius 463–64
conglomerates 481
Congo Basin 27, 335, 338, 358
Congo, Democratic Republic of, climate 338; economy 79, 344; environment 348; history 340; resources 339; water 336
Congo, Republic of the, 333
Congo River 27, 326, 335
Congregational 536, 551
conic projection 8
coniferous 159
coniferous forest 123
conifers 488
Connecticut 166
conquerors 260, 412–13
conquistadors 165, 178
conservation 80, 115, 134, 152, 185, 375
conservationists 37, 61, 160
Constantinople 12, 252–53, 295, 388
constitution 102
constitutional monarchy 73, 200, 296, 389, 480, 530
constitutional sultantate 504
constitutionality 248
consumer-driven 505
consumerism 111
container 81, 233
contaminants 113, 160, 350, 444–45, 466, 469, 559
continental air masses 53
continental divide 94; *see* Eastern Continental Divide; Western Continental Divide
continental drift 22, 168
continental shelf 22, 124
Continental Western Europe 212–33
continentality 244
continents 20
contour lines 10
convection 21
Cook, James 526, 529, 550–52
Cooper Creek 525
Copenhagen 193, 200
copper 38
Copper Canyon 146
copra 537, 549
Coptic church 323
Copts 323
coral 28, 145, 158, 358, 430, 525–26, 545, 548, 550
coral bleaching 541
coral reef 374, 512–13, 549, 556, 559
cordillera 120
Cordillera Central 166
Cordillera Occidental 166
Cordilleran Ice Sheet 122
core (of the earth) 20–21
core values 106
Corinth 12
Coriolis effect 49, 100
corroboree 533

corrosion 38
corruption 13, 79, 131, 151, 174, 255, 272, 297, 318, 322, 343–44, 349, 351, 355, 375, 416, 436, 459, 467, 496, 504–506, 512
Corsica 215, 287
Costa Rica 76, 145; water 147
Côte d'Ivoire 332, 339
Cotopaxi 168
cotton 60, 107, 153, 313–15, 324, 410, 414, 422–23
council 133, 247–48, 458
counseling 489
coup d'état 174–75, 504–5, 554
couscous 322
craftsmanship 480
Crater Lake 33
creation 3–4, 12–13, 19, 25, 35, 39, 43, 75, 77, 341, 441
Creation Mandate 3, 12–15, 35, 60, 65–66, 84
Creator 5, 19, 51, 77, 109, 347
cremation 157
Crete 287
cricket 439, 535
Crimean Peninsula 261, 269, 283
Croatia 260–261; water 264–65; government 271
crude birthrate 83
crude death rate 83
crust, earth's, 20–22, 25, 27
Cuba 145; demographics 154; government 150; religion 155
cultivate 315, 477
cultural boundary 76
cultural convergence 70
cultural diffusion 70, 82
cultivation 13, 37, 416
culture 12–15, 66–72
culture hearth 67
culture region 67
Curacao 145
cycling 230, 300, 462
cyclone 541, 555
cyclonic storms 549
cylindrical projection 7
Cyprus 302, 382; demographics 391; economy 390; government 389; religion 396
Cyrene 12
Cyrillic language 273
czar 246–47, 249, 252, 254
Czechia 260–61; culture 274; economy 272; environment 278; government 271; water 265

D

Daeseongdong 489
Damascus 12, 382, 388
Danakil Desert 359
Danube River 218, 261, 263–64, 280
Dardanelles 287, 382
Darfur 356–57
Darwin 228
Dasht-e-kavir 383
Dasht-e-lut 383
Dawkins, Richard 228
Deadvlei 355
death rate 83–85
Death Valley 97
Deccan Plateau 428, 430
deciduous forest 159, 245
Declaration of Independence 102, 107, 132, 482
decolonization 364, 372
deep 548
deforestation 159, 182–83, 185, 207, 277, 303, 351, 374–375, 399–400, 445, 447, 467, 490, 513–14, 538
deformational mountains 27
deism 109
Delhi 429, 434, 438, 445
delta 28, 60, 313, 431–32
demilitarized zone (DMZ) 479
democracy 74, 103, 108, 126, 150, 175, 296, 342, 414, 504
democratization 110, 271, 414
demographic transition model 85
demographics 65, 83, 86–87
demography 83
Denakil desert 357
Denmark 193, 195; climate 197; culture 204; economy 202; environment 209; government 200
Denuclearization 482
depositional 25, 28
depression 33
desalination 400–401, 560
desert 24, 30, 52, 54, 87
desert climate 400
desertification 325–26, 374–75, 420, 465
detail-oriented 72
Detroit 33, 121
developing countries 74, 79
devolution 247
dew point 51
Dhaka 429
dialects 27, 154, 340, 461
diaspora 12, 505, 511
dictatorship 73, 174–75, 272, 294, 296, 342, 344, 365, 415, 459, 480, 504
didgeridoo 534
Dien Bien Phu 502
diesel 233, 375, 490–91
diesel-burning 232
diesel-powered 208, 467
dikes 216, 231
Dinaric Alps 260–61
dioxins 135–36, 489–90
diplomacy 76
diplomat 132
discrimination 390, 442, 483, 530
disenfranchised 272
dissident 249
distortion 5–6, 8
district 174, 248, 471, 530
divination 322
divorce 83, 394
Djibouti 356–57, 359; economy 367–68; water 360;
Dnieper River 261, 263, 265
Dniester River 260–61, 265
doldrums 49, 171
dolphin 457
Dominica 145
Dominican Republic 145
Domino Theory 503, 511
Donbass 283
Donets Basin 261
Don River 238, 242
dowry 443
drainage basin 32–33
Drakensberg Mountains 358
drift 22, 40, 51–52, 168, 197
drought 36, 112
Duma 248
dune 28, 311–12

E

earthquake 21–22, 165, 195, 384, 451, 454, 474, 490, 498, 517, 524
earth-shaping 18, 21, 23, 25, 101, 125, 149, 173, 221, 267
East Antarctica 546
East Asia 448
East China Sea 452, 455, 473
Easter Island 545, 551
Eastern Africa 310, 356; climate 362; demographics 369; religion 372; resources 363
Eastern Continental Divide 32, 95, 99
Eastern Desert 311
Eastern Europe 258–83
Eastern Ghats 429
Eastern Mediterranean 382, 384; demographics 391; economy 390; government 389
Eastern Orthodoxy 252–53, 276, 323, 418
ecological 17, 280
economic systems 77–82
economics 14, 77
ecosystem 324, 495, 513, 538
ecotourism 152
Ecuador 165–67; climate 171; culture 178–79; demographics 177; environment 184; government 175; resources 172–73
ecumenism 536
Edinburgh Castle 3, 204
Egypt 19, 309–12, 329; economy 320; environment 324–25; government 319; history 316–17; religion 322–23; resources 314–15; water 313
elephants 307, 325, 331, 373–74, 427, 500, 512
Elbe River 218
elected government 74, 77
Ellsworth Mountains 546
El Niño 541
El Salvador 151
embargo 82
emeralds 173
Emerald Isle 192
Empty Quarter; *see* Rub al Khali 50, 385, 550
enclave 106, 414, 419
Energiewende 233
England 5, 104, 191–92, 535, 553, 556; environment 207, water 196
English Channel 192, 214, 218–19
entrepreneurs 77, 134, 136
entrepreneurship 367
equator 5, 7, 46–47, 49, 51–52, 54, 57, 79–80, 168, 171–73
Equatorial Guinea 332; government 343
equinox 46
ergs 312
Eritrea 356–57; climate 362; government 365

erosion 23–26, 30, 96–97
escarpment 169
Estonia 259–61; government 272, 283; resources 267; water 264
estuary 29, 171, 219, 432
Eswatini 358; government 365
Ethiopia 356–57; climate 362; culture 371; demographics 369; economy 367; history 364; religion 372; resources 363; water 360;
Ethiopian Highlands 356–357
ethnically 471
ethnic background 15, 534–35
ethnic cleansing 271
ethnic diversity 392
ethnic division 365
ethnic group 69, 76, 154, 251, 316, 321, 366, 417, 419, 438, 461, 532
ethnicity 106, 226, 270, 483
ethnic majority 509
ethnic minority 274, 506, 509
ethnic tension 553
ethnomusicology 180
ethnos 69
eucalyptus tree 57
Euphrates River 385, 388
Eurasia 22, 413
Eurasian continent 266
Eurasian plate 22, 146, 195, 384, 428, 430, 454, 474, 498
euro 49, 223, 364
Europe 191, 214; *see* Continental Western Europe; Eastern Europe; Northern Europe; Southern Europe
European Russia 238; climate 244
European Union (EU) 222–23
euthanasia 67, 201
eutrophication 114
evangelical 109–10
Evangelicalism 109
evangelism 180, 301
Everglades 115
evolution 228
exclave 414, 419
export 37, 120, 125, 202, 363, 415–16, 505, 537, 549
exportation 505
exported 173, 336, 343, 508, 550
exports 78, 81–82, 128, 172, 250, 344, 531
Eyjafjallajökull 195

F

family 14, 67
farming 36–39, 43
fascist 294–95
fault 22, 27, 72, 96
fault-block 27
faulting 22, 194, 240, 288
fault-line 288
favela 187
fengcong 498
fenglin 498
Fergana Valley 414
feudal 478
Fiji 544–45; economy 554; environment 559; government 553; resources 549
Finland 191–93; climate 197–98; culture 204; demographics 203; economy 202; environment 206; government 200; water 196
First Nations 131
fjord 24, 121, 169, 194, 196, 523–24
Flanders 215
flax 114, 125, 266–67, 529
Flood 21–23, 25–26, 30, 33, 39
Florida 51, 115, 541
flysch 262
foehn 220
foreign policy 75
forestry 35, 37, 125, 209, 254
Formosa 458
fossil 25, 122, 408, 524
fossil fuels 37, 39, 420, 477
fracking 112
France 81, 84, 174, 213–17, 316, 502, 553; culture 226; demographics 225; economy 224; environment 230, 232–33; government 223–24; history 222; religion 227–29; resources 220; water 218–19
Fraser River Valley 125
free-market 77, 175, 222, 247, 297, 436
French Revolution 227
front 53
fuel-efficient 115
Fukushima 489–91
furs 125
fútbol 179
futsal 300

G

G20 224
Gabon 331, 333; resources 339; water 335;
Gaborone 355, 358, 377
Galapagos Islands 173
Gambia 332; economy 343–44; resources 339
Gambia River 332, 335
Gandhi 435
Ganges River 429, 431–32, 443
Gaza 382, 389, 392
GDP 78
gender-selective 463
genealogical 110
Genesis 3, 14–15, 19, 25, 35, 40, 139
Geneva 215, 219, 301, 502
Genghis Khan 413, 458
genocide 365, 367, 372, 390, 412–13, 502–4
geographer 2, 4, 9
geographers 11, 26, 32
geographical 3, 267, 428
geographically 226, 249
geography 3–5
geometric border 76
Georgia 405–8; demographics 417; economy 416; government 414; history 412; religion 418; resources 411; water 409
geothermal energy 199, 208–9, 539
Germany 213–16, 246, 260, 268, 364, 369, 484; culture 226; demographics 225; economy 224; environment 230, 232–33; government 223–24; history 222; religion 227, 229; resources 220; water 218–19
geyser 195
Ghana 332; government 342; history 341; resources 339
Ghana Empire 316
GIS 9, 11
glaciation 24, 96, 240, 288
glaciers 9, 24–25, 30, 33, 56, 122, 169, 192, 194, 196, 219, 453–54, 500, 523–25, 546
glasnost 247
globalization 82
Gobi Desert 452, 466
Golan Heights 382, 389, 475, 490
gondola 187
Goode's projection 7
Gorbachev 247, 279
gores 6–7
Göteborg 193
government 14, 66, 69, 73–78
GPS 9, 11
Grand Coulee Dam 35, 457
Grant, Ulysses 93
graziers 537
Great Alföld 263–64, 266
Great Australian Bight 525
Great Barrier Reef 19, 526, 541, 556
Great Basin 94, 100
Great Belt 197
Great Britain 36, 73, 126, 166, 174, 192, 364, 415, 435, 480, 502, 529–30, 553; environment 206
Great Circle 5
Great Commission 536
Great Depression 104
Great European Plain 215, 240, 260, 266
Great Hungarian Plain 261
Great Indian Desert 428–429
Great Lakes, Africa, 356, 361
Great Lakes, North America, 33, 53, 95, 100, 121, 123, 125, 134–36, 243
Great Man-Made River Project 324
Great Plains 24, 27, 54, 94, 100, 120
Great Rift Valley 356, 360
Great Salt Lake 33, 98
Great Slave Lake 120–21, 123–24
Great Victoria Desert 522
Great Wall of China 451–52
Greece 74, 224, 287; climate 291; culture 300; economy 297; environment 303; government 296; history 295; religion 301; water 289–90
green space 207
Greenwich, England 5
Grenada 145
groundwater depletion 112
Guadalcanal 544
Guadeloupe 145
Guam 544; demographics 555; economy 554; environment 559; government 551; history 545;
Guatemala 145; demographics 154; environment 159
guerrilla 365
Guinea 332; water 335
Guinea-Bissau 332; resources 339
Guinea Highlands 313
Gulf of Aqaba 382–83, 389
Gulf of Guinea 332
Gulf of Mexico 27, 51, 53, 94–95, 99–100
Gulf of Saint Lawrence 125
Gulf of Sidra 310–11, 315
Gulf of Suez 310
Gulf of Tonkin 499
Guyana 166–67; culture 178; government 174
gypsy 274

H

habitat 114, 137, 170, 326, 351, 375
Hague, the, 215, 230
Haifa 382, 389
Hainan 452, 456
Haiti 145
hajj 381, 396
Hangul 484
Hanoi 499, 502
Hanukah 398
harbor 34, 287, 382, 457, 496
Havana 106, 145
Hawaii 10, 22–23, 36, 50, 94–95, 105, 482, 541, 545; demographics 555; environment 559; history 550, 552; religion 556–57
hazelnut 447
headwaters 32, 99
Helsinki 193, 206
hemisphere 5, 25, 46, 100, 172, 522
heterogeneous 506, 511
hierarchal 321
hieroglyphics 316–17
high-caste 440
high-context 71–72, 178, 226, 370, 484, 486, 507
high-density 89
high-efficiency 539
high island 547
highland 55, 63, 148, 166, 171, 197, 204, 220, 337, 356, 362, 410, 456, 496, 500
highly developed country 79
Highveld 358
hijab 399, 425
hill 28, 127, 509
Himalaya Mountains 26, 30, 406, 428, 430–32, 452
Hindu Kush Mountains 406–7, 413
Hinduism 76, 429, 440–43, 510, 553
hippopotamuses 325
Hiroshima 279, 473, 487; environment 491
Hispaniola 145
Hokkaido 472–74; climate 476; demographics 483
Holocaust 228, 237, 274
Holodomor 269
Honduras 145
Honshu 472–73; environment 489; history 478; water 475
Hormuz Strait 383–84
Horn of Africa 310, 356
hot springs 196
Houston 56
Hudson Bay 120–21, 123
human trafficking 82, 153, 342–43, 348–49, 443, 463, 482, 512
Humboldt Current 171
humidity 48, 51, 53, 58, 500
humid subtropical 55, 148, 172, 291, 476
Humphrey, John 132
Hungary 261, 263; demographics 273–74; government 271–72; history 268; resources 266; water 264
hunter-gatherer 373
Hussein, Saddam 482
hyacinth 374–75
hydrocarbon 39
hydroelectric energy 199, 208–9, 220–21, 242, 303, 375, 401, 467, 525, 539
hydrogen 38, 115, 233
hydrologic cycle 51
hydrologic fracturing 112
hydrology 26, 41
hydropower 196, 245, 290, 303, 335, 351, 385, 411, 431, 501, 550
hydrosphere 20, 40

I

Iberian Peninsula 286, 294
icebergs 6, 123–24, 547
icecap 195, 546, 549, 559
ice floe 548
Iceland 19, 193–95; climate 198; demographics 203; economy 203; government 200; religion 204; water 196
Idaho 93
idolatry 14, 68, 322
idols 397, 553
igneous 99, 120, 122
Iguacu 167
Illinois 110
IMF 505
immigration 83, 128, 130, 153, 163, 200, 272, 482–83, 554, 556
imperialism 150, 342, 412, 434–35
import 80–82, 537
Incas 165, 170, 174
India 13–14, 17, 67, 76, 427–31; climate 432; culture 439; demographics 438; economy 436; environment 443–45; government 436; history 434–35; religion 440–42; resources 433; water 431
Indian Ocean 31, 310, 329, 356–58, 360–61, 429, 497, 499, 517
Indian Plate 22, 26, 430, 498
individualism 106, 108
Indo-Aryan 438
Indochina 497, 502, 504–6
Indo-European 67–68, 273, 417
Indonesia 21, 496–98; climate 500; demographics 506; economy 505; environment 513–14, 517; government 504; history 503; religion 509, 511; resources 500–501
industrial revolution 85–86, 104
industry 35, 37–39
infant 185, 481
infertile 27, 319
inflation 128, 377, 505
infrastructure 79, 136, 230, 367, 369, 416, 503, 506
In-Situ 137
insurance 296–97, 460, 481, 531
insurgents 503, 505
intercontinental 482
intermarry 320–21, 347, 438
international relations 75–76
international trade 81
international waterway 218
interrupted projection 7
Intertropical Convergence Zone 171, 432
invasive species 114
Ionian Sea 287, 289
Iran 73, 383, 403, 412; culture 393; demographics 391–92; government 389–90; water 386;
Iraq 383; climate 386; culture 393; demographics 391–92; government 389; history 388; water 386
Ireland 192; demographics 203; economy 201; environment 206–8; government 200; religion 204; water 196
Irian Jaya 500
Iroquois 133
Irrawaddy River 499
Isaiah 304
Islam 132, 229, 252, 310, 316, 322–23, 372, 382, 388–89, 392, 394–98, 403, 417–19, 502–3, 509, 511, 535
Islamabad 429
Islamic 73, 204, 388–89
Islamic extremists 225, 414–15
Islamists 319
Isle of Wight 192
Israel 69, 76, 87, 110, 329, 381–82; demographics 391–92; economy 390; environment 400; government 389–90; history 388–89; religion 396–98; water 386
Istanbul 83, 253, 381–82, 394
isthmus 28, 144–45, 310
Italy 285, 287–88; climate 291; economy 297; environment 303; government 296; history 295; water 289–90

J

Jainist 440
Jakarta 504, 513
Jamaica 145, 147, 149
Japan 84, 470–74; climate 476; culture 483–84; demographics 482; economy 481; environment 488–91; government 480; history 478–79; religion 486–87; resources 477; water 475
Japan Current 124
Java 497, 501, 503
Jeepneys 514–15
Jefferson, Thomas 103, 107
Jeju 473, 475–76
Jerusalem 73, 381–82, 389–90, 397–98
Johannesburg 358, 367
John, Gospel of, 536
Jordan 73, 382, 385–86; government 389; economy 390; demographics 391
Jordan Rift Valley 384
Jordan River 386, 392
Juche 487
Judaism 14, 382, 394, 396–98
Jumna River 432
junta 174, 503
Jura Mountains 214–15
Jutland 193

K

Kaaba 65, 381, 396
Kabul 405; history 413
Kalahari Desert 168, 310, 358, 370
Kaliningrad 238
Kamchatka Peninsula 239
Kantō Plain 472–73
Karachi 427, 429, 444
Kara-Kum Desert 406
karma 80, 441–42, 510
Karst topography 262, 498
Kauai 558

Kazakhstan 406–408; demographics 417; economy 415–16; environment 421–23; history 413; resources 410–11; water 409
Kenya 57, 355–57; climate 362; demographics 370; economies 367–68; environment 373; history 364–65; landforms 359; religion 372; resources 363; water 361
Khama, Seretse 377
Khartoum 357, 360, 364
khat 387
Khmer Rouge 503, 510
Khyber Pass 413
kibbutz 391
Kiel 215, 218
Kiev 261, 265, 269
Kigali 357, 362, 368
Kīlauea 23
Kimchi 485
Kim, Jong Un 482, 487
Kinshasa 333; environment 350; history 340; water 335
Kiribati 544–45; economy 554; environment 558; government 553
Komodo 500
Korea, *see* North Korea and South Korea
Koryŏ 479
Kosovo 261; history 271
Kraków 259, 261
Kremlin 247
Kurds 69, 392
Kuwait 383; government 390
Kyi, Aung San Suu 504
Kyoto 471, 473, 488
Kyrgyzstan 406–408; demographics 417; economy 416; environment 423; government 414; religion 419; resources 411; water 409
Kyushu 472–73, 486

L

Labrador 120–21; current 123–24
lagoon 28, 290, 432, 549, 558–60
Lagos 332, 343
lake 29, 33, 113–14
Lake Athabasca 120–22
Lake Baikal 33, 237, 239, 243
Lake Chad 33, 311, 313, 325–26
lake-effect 124
Lake Karakul 410
Lake Maracaibo 166–67, 170
Lake Titicaca 33, 167, 170, 553
Lake Turkana 356–57, 361
Lake Victoria 33, 357, 360–61, 374–75
Lake Wakatipu 525
land bridge 144–45
land expropriation without compensation 366
landform 21–26, 28
landmass 22, 27, 54, 57, 100, 244, 524
landmines 278
language family 67
Laos 496–97; demographics 506; economy 505; environment 513–15; government 504; history 503; resources 500–501
Lao-tzu 464
lapse rate 55
Latin America 140–87
Latin culture 72, 226
latitude 5, 7–8, 76, 100, 148, 197
latitude zones 46–48, 52–53, 56
Latvia 260–61, 272; resources 266; water 264
Laurentide Ice Sheet 122
leaching 183, 324
lead 548
lead (mineral) 38, 125, 173, 254, 280, 292, 305, 411
Lebanon 382–83; culture 394; economy 390; government 389; religion 396
lechon 508
leeward 56, 124
legend 9
Lenin, Vladimir 246
Leninism 487
Lesotho 358; climate 362; government 365; resources 363
Lhasa 452
Liberia 332; climate 337; environment 351; history 342; resources 339
Libreville 333
Libya 311; climate 314; economy 320; environment 324, 326; history 316; resources 315
Liechtenstein 215
Lima 179
Lincoln, Abraham 103, 106
linguistic 369
linguists 67
Lisbon 286, 300
lithosphere 20, 23, 40
Lithuania 260–61; culture 274; water 264
Livingstone, David 361, 372
Llanos 167
lochs 196
lock 242, 457
Locke, John 107
loess 220
Loire River 215
Loire River Valley 219
longitude 5, 76
low-caste 442
low-context 71–72, 178, 226, 484
low island 547
Luxembourg 214–15; culture 227; economy 224; environment 233
Luzon 497

M

Mao Zedong 458–60, 462
Macau 452
Macedonia 295
Macedonians 273
Machu Picchu 165
Mackenzie River 120, 123
Madagascar 358; demographics 370
Madrasa 418–19
Madrid 286, 296
Maduro, Nicholas 175
Magellan 167, 171, 546–47, 551
Maghreb 316, 319–22
magma 21, 40, 199, 359
Magyar 273
Malacca Strait 499
Malagasy 370
malaria 80, 148, 161, 319, 343, 353
Malawi 335, 356–358, 361
Malay Archipelago 497
Malayo-Polynesian 68
Malays 502–3
Malaysia 497–98; demographics 506; economy 505; environment 512; government 504; water 499
Maldives 429–30; culture 439; demographics 438; economy 437; government 436; history 434
Mali 311; economy 320–21; history 316–17; resources 314–15; water 313
malnutrition 84, 185, 319
Malta 287; government 296; history 295; religion 301
Manchu Dynasty 458–459, 478
Manchuria 478
Mandarin 461
Manila 505; environment 514
Manitoba 120–21; water 123
Mansa Musa 317, 341
mantle 20–23, 40
Manufacturing Belt 105
Maoism 487
Maori 529–30; culture 532, 534–35
maquiladoras 152
Mariana Islands 544–45, 549; demographics 555
Mariana Trench 474, 548
marine fossils 524
marine life 114, 158, 305, 500, 538, 541, 548, 559
marine resources 433, 456, 549
marine-west-coast climate 55, 124, 148, 197, 220, 266–67, 526
Marquesas Islands 545
Marshall Islands 544; demographics 555; economy 554; environment 558–59; government 553
Marshall Plan 222
Maryland 105
Masai 57, 355, 370, 373
massif 288
Massif Central 214–16; water 219
Matterhorn 213, 215
Matthew, Gospel of, 117
Mauritania 311–12; demographics 321; economy 320; environment 325; government 318; history 316; religion 323; resources 314–15; water 313
Mauritius 358
Mauryan Empire 434
Mbabane 358
Mecca 65, 317, 381, 383, 395–96, 418
Medellín, Colombia 187
medical tourism 390
mediterranean climate 55, 63, 100, 148, 260, 266, 291, 314, 332, 382
Mediterranean Sea 34, 286–87, 382; environment 305
Medo-Persian Empire 388
megalopolis 70, 219
Mekong River 60, 452, 496–97, 499; environment 513
Mekong River Comission 514
Melanesia 543–44; demographics 555; economy 554; environment 560; government 552; history 550, 552; resources 549
Melbourne 532
mental map 6
mercator 7

Mercosur 176
mercy-killing 201
Mesopotamia 382
mestizo 154, 177
metamorphic 99, 120
meteorological map 9
meteorologists 48, 58
meteorology 58, 61
Methodist 109, 181, 486, 536
Mexico 143–45; climate 148–49; culture 155; demographics 154; economy 152–53; environment 158–61; government 151; history 150; religion 157; water 147
Michigan 105
microloans 369
Micronesia 544–45
Micronesia, Federated States of, 544, 551; government 553; economy 554
Mid-atlantic 195
Middleveld 358
Midwest US 95
migration 102, 104, 128, 154, 200, 373
militarize 136
militia 503, 554
Mindanao 497, 505
mink 125
missionaries 68, 82, 132, 156, 180, 276, 301, 323, 347, 486–87, 509, 511, 529, 550, 556–57
Mississippi River 32, 94, 99, 105
Mississippi Valley 95
Missouri 32, 99, 110
mixed economy 78, 128, 152, 201–203, 249
Mogadishu 82, 357
Mojave Desert 58, 93
moksha 441
Moldova 260–61, culture 274; demographics 273; environment 278; government 272; history 269; religion 276; resources 266; separatists 283; water 265
Monaco 87, 286
monarch 73, 127, 529
monarchy 294, 435
Mongol Empire 459
Mongolia 75, 451–54; culture 461–62; climate 456; demographics 461; economy 460; environment 465–67; government 459; history 458; religion 463; water 455
monotheism 397–98
Monrovia 332
monsoon 432; climate 456, 500; environment 443, 445, 447, 466–67
Montana 38, 93, 134
Montenegro 260–61; water 264
Montreal 121; culture 129, 131; demographics 128; government 126
Moor 321
Moravia 261
Mormon 109–10, 117, 557
Morocco 24, 309–12; climate 314; economy 319; environment 324–25; government 318–19; history 316; religion 322–23; resources 314–15
Moscow 237–38; climate 244–45; economy 249; government 247–48;
moshav 391
mosque 394
mountain 10, 26–28
Mount Chimborazo 168
Mount Fuji 473–74
Mount Kilimanjaro 357, 359
Mount Pinatubo 498
Mount Rushmore 103
Mount Saint Helens 19, 97, 474
Mozambique 356, 358; history 364–65; water 361
Mozambique Channel 310, 358
M-PESA 369
MTD 109
Mubarak, Hosni 319
Mugabe, Robert 367, 377
Mughal Empire 427, 434–35, 442
Muhammad 381, 394–95, 403
Muir, John 93, 96
Mujahideen 415
multiactive 72, 178, 226
multiculturalism 13, 130
multilingual 369
Murmansk 238, 255
Murray River 525
Muslims 109, 229, 300–301, 322–23, 364–65, 381, 394–96, 398, 403, 419, 435
Mussolini, Benito 295
Myanmar 497–98; culture 507; economy 506; environment 512–13, 517; government 504; history 502; religion 509–10; water 499

N

NAFTA 127, 152
Nagorno-Karabakh 414
Nairobi 357, 362, 368
Nakdong River 476
Namib Desert 355, 358–59
Namibia 355, 358; climate 362; demographics 369–70; government 365; water 361
Napoleonic wars 295
Nassau 145
nation 69
Nationalist Party 458–59
nationalize 175, 329
nation-state 69, 340
NATO 223, 271–72
natural borders 75, 238
Nauru 544; demographics 555; economy 554; environment 558; government 553; resources 549
navigable 32–33, 170–71, 196, 218, 243, 290, 313, 335, 410, 525
Naypyidaw 504
N'Djamena 311, 313
necropolis 413
Negev 382, 389
neocatastrophists 25, 40
Nepal 8, 26, 426, 428–29; demographics 43; economy 437; government 435–36; history 435; water 431
Netherlands, the 213–15; culture 227; environment 230–32, 235; resources 220; water 218–19
neutrality, policy of 223, 295
Newfoundland 120–21; resources 124–25
New Jerusalem 87
newly industrialized countries 79
New Mexico 105
New Testament 321, 536
New Zealand 521–24; climate 526; culture 533–34; demographics 532; economy 531–32; environment 537–39; government 530; history 529; religion 535; resources 527; water 526
Niagara Falls 90, 448
Nicaragua 76, 145; economy 153
Niger 311–12; culture 321; demographics 320–21; economy 320; environment 327; resources 315; water 313
Nigeria 333; culture 344; demographics 344; economy 343; government 342; religion 346; resources 339; water 335–36
Niger River 313, 317
Nile Delta 87, 311, 313, 315
Nile River 87, 313–15, 317, 360
Nile River Valley 311, 317
Nineveh 383
Nippon 472
nirvana 510
nitrates 39, 135, 173, 254
nitrogen 113, 538
NOAA 541
Noah 67
nomadic 36, 321, 370, 413–14, 458, 528
Non-Proliferation of Nuclear Weapons Treaty 482
nonreligious 155, 204, 227, 300–301, 396, 463
Nordic 191
nor'easters 100
Normandy 214
North Atlantic Drift 51–52, 197
North Korea 414, 471–73; economy 482; environment 489–90; government 480; history 479; religion 487; resources 477; water 476
North Macedonia 261; history 270; government 272
Norway 193; climate 197; economy 201; government 200; water 196
Northern Europe 190–211
Notre Dame Cathedral 227, 229
Nova Scotia 120–21; government 126; resources 124; water 123
Nubian Desert 356–57
Nubian plate 359
nuclear energy 255
nuclear reactor 39, 279
nuclear waste 255, 278
Nunavut 120–22
Nur-Sultan 405, 407, 416

O

oases 311, 313, 323, 406
oblast 242, 248, 283, 414
ocean-current 197
ocean floor 22
oceangoing 32
Oceania 519–63
oceanic ridges 548
oceans 20, 30–31
Oder River 261, 265
Ogasawara 472
Okinawa 472, 474
okra 322
okrugs 248
old-growth forests 114, 160

Old Testament 397
oligarchy 74, 77
Olympic National Park 93, 96
Olympics 131, 187, 252
Oman 383–84; government 389–90; religion 395; water 386
omnipresent 347
one-child policy 462–63
Ontario 120–122; government 126–27
opium 416–17, 513
Orange revolution 269
Orinoco River 167, 171
orographic 52–53, 314
orthodox Protestants 109
Oslo 193
osmosis 560
Ossetia 414
Ottawa 121, 126–27
Ottoman Turks 318, 388, 412
outback 522
overfarming 351
overfishing 124, 490, 514, 563
overpopulation 85, 113
oxygen-rich 124, 475
Ozark 94–95
ozone 559

P

Pacific Alliance 176
Pacific Coast 125, 149, 173
Pacific Islands 542–549
Pacific Mountain Ranges 94, 96, 100
Pacific Ocean 31, 95, 98, 123, 144–45, 147–48, 166, 170–71, 237, 475, 497, 499, 522–23, 526, 544, 548, 551–53, 556–58, 560
Pacific plate 22–23, 146, 474, 524
Pacific Rim 241
paganism 428
pagodas 451, 488
Pakistan 76, 429; culture 439; demographics 438; economy 437; environment 443–45; government 436; history 435; resources 433; water 431
Palau 545; culture 556; environment 558, 561, 563; government 553
Palestine 388, 392
Pamir Mountains 406, 409–10, 414
Pampas 167, 172–173
Panama 145; economy 153
Panama Canal 145, 148
panda 451
pantheism 133, 441
Papua Indonesia 500, 511
Papua New Guinea 526, 545; demographics 555; economy 554; environment 559; government 553; water 548
Paraguay 167; water 171; resources 173; economy 176; demographics 177
parasites 160
Paris 213, 215; water 219; climate 220; religion 227, 229; environment 232–33
Paris attacks 225
Paris Peace Accords 503
parliamentary constitutional monarchy 296, 530
parliamentary democracy 150, 435
parliamentary republic 200, 504, 553
parliamentary system 126–27
Pashto 417
Pashtun 417, 438
Pashtunistan 417
Pashtunwali 417
passive resistance 435
Passivhäus 230
pastoralism 349
Patagonia 166, 172
paternal 318
patriarch 440
patriarchal 321
peat 206, 254, 267
Peloponnesus 287
peninsula 28
Pennsylvania 112
Pentateuch 395
Pentecostalism 156, 180–81
perestroika 247
permafrost 124, 243
Perry, Matthew, 478
Persian Empire 295, 329, 388, 412
Persian Gulf 382–83, 385–86
Persian Gulf countries 389–91
Perth 23, 532
Peru 165–67; climate 171; culture 179; economy 176; environment 184; government 175; resources 172–73; water 170
Peru Current 52
pesticides 113, 233, 235, 254, 278, 489
Peter (Bible) 14
petroleum 39
pharaohs 309, 317, 329
Pharisees 397
pharmaceuticals 201–3, 460
Philadelphia 34
Philippine Archipelago 497–98
Philippines 495–98; culture 507; demographics 506; economy 505; environment 512, 515; government 505; history 503; religion 509, 511
Phoenician 298, 392
Phoenix 89, 545
phosphates 39, 305, 315, 324, 339, 343, 387, 550, 555
phosphorus 324, 538
Pinochet, Augusto, 174–75
Pinsk marshes 261, 263
Pitcairn Island 556
Pizarro 174
plains 26–27, 30
plankton 124, 559
plantain 371
plantation 107, 183
plateaus 26, 30
plate tectonics theory 21
Plitvice Lakes 265
poaching 331, 349, 375
Pohnpei 558
Poland 259–61; economy 272; environment 277–78, 280; government 271; history 268; resources 266–67; water 264–65
polar regions 47
polder 216, 231
Polisario Front 318
polygamy 67, 110, 321, 340
Polynesia 544–45; culture 556; economy 554–55; history 550–52
polytheism 395
Pompeii 288
Pope John Paul II 259, 268
Popocatepetl Volcano 146
population demographic model 85
population density 87, 128–29
population distribution 86
population growth 83, 463, 482
population pyramids 85, 344, 391
Portugal 166, 178, 286; climate 291; demographics 298; economy 297; environment 303, 364–65; government 296; history 294; religion 300; water 289–90
potassium 39
Poverty Environment Initiative 515
Prague 261, 268
prairie 125
precipitation 48, 50–54
prefecture 472
premier 127, 247
Presbyterian 111, 486, 536
presidential republics 150
Pretoria 358
primate city 154, 203
primary industry 35
prime meridian 5
prime minister 126–27
Prince Edward Island 121, 125
Pripyat, Ukraine 263, 279
privatization 249, 271–72
Promised Land 69, 87
prosperity theology 372
provinces 121, 126, 248, 472
Puerto Rico 145
pumice 339
Purim 398
purse seine 563
Putin, Vladimir, 247–48
Pyongyang 471, 473, 493; climate 476; religion 486
pyramids 317
Pyrenees 215, 217, 286, 288, 291

Q

Qaddafi 319–20, 324, 482
Qatar 78, 383; government 389–90; water 386
Qattara Depression 312
quail 418
Québec 119–121; resources 125; government 126–27
Québécois 130
Quechua 177–78
Queen Elizabeth 521
Queen Elizabeth Islands 120, 193
Queensland 526, 528
Quito 165, 171
Qur'an 322, 389–90, 395–96, 425

R

Rachmaninoff, Sergei, 251
racism 365
radiation 278–80, 421, 490
radicalization 229
radioactive 254–55, 339
radioactivity 39, 281
rainfall 54–56

rainforest 32, 52, 338; environment 559–560
rainforests 144, 161, 170, 526, 528; climate 500; environment 182–85, 332, 335, 358
rain shadow 53
Ramadan 381, 395–96
Ranchería River 183
ranches 537–38
ranching 36
rare-earth 477
reactor 279–81
reactors 39, 490–91
recycle 115, 374, 443, 445, 489, 491; water 112, 114, 525
referendum 127, 296
reforestation 160, 208–9, 445
reform 150, 187, 247, 368, 505
Reformation 214, 227, 301, 392
refugees 131, 203–4, 225, 271–72, 319, 343, 392, 394
Regina 120, 122
regs 312
reincarnation 441–42, 510
relief 104, 320, 365, 405, 560
relief maps 10
religion 12–15
religious groups 66, 68
remittances 416, 505, 554
remote sensing 9, 17
Renaissance 108, 285, 290, 295
renewable resource 37, 500, 563
representative 150, 223, 248, 389, 435, 459, 480, 504
representative democracy 74, 349, 365
republics 74, 77, 150, 200
reservation 133, 366
reservoir 33, 183, 350, 421, 457
resorts 70, 287, 297, 314
retribution 366, 397
revolution 46
Reykjavik 193, 203
Rhine River 215, 218–19
rhinoceroses 373–74
Rhodes 382
Rhodesia 365
Rhodope Mountains 260–61
Rhône River 219
Riachuelo River 183
Richat Structure 312
rift valley 356
Ring of Fire 146, 168, 474, 498, 523
Rio de Janeiro 86, 181, 187; culture 179
rivers 19, 26–27, 29–33
river system 32
Riyadh 383
Robinson's projection 8
Rockies 27, 94, 100, 121, 166
Roman; alphabet 273; civilization 34; Empire 200, 271, 285, 388; forces 294; Republic 285; ruins 285; soldiers 273
Roman Catholic 109, 144, 156–57, 179–80, 203, 227, 253, 270, 273, 276, 294, 300–301, 323, 396, 531
Romanesque 297
Romani 203, 274
Romania 260–61; demographics 273; environment 277–78; government 272; religion 276; resources 266; water 264
Romans (Bible) 19, 73, 84, 139, 228, 253
Rome 156, 253, 285, 287; history 295, 397
Roosevelt, Theodore, 93, 103
Ross Sea 523, 546
rotation 45–46, 49, 100
rugby 394, 439, 535
Ruhr Valley 218–19
rural areas 86–87
Russia 237–241; climate 243; culture 251; demographics 250; economy 249; environment 254–55; government 247–48; history 246; religion 252–53; resources 245; water 242
Russian Orthodox 252
Russian revolution 246, 249
Rwanda 356–57; climate 362; demographics 369; economy 368; environment 373–75; government 366–67; religion 372

S

Saab 202
Sabbath 398
sacrament 156
Sado 473
saffron 417
Sahara Desert 232, 309–16, 318–19, 323–25, 337, 341, 356, 358
Sahel 311, 313–14, 316–17, 319–23, 325–27, 332, 356
Saigon 499
Saint Basil's Cathedral 253
Saint Kitts and Nevis 145; demographics 154
Saint Lawrence Lowlands 121
Saint Lawrence River Valley 126
Saint Lucia 143, 145
Saint Petersburg 188, 238, 248, 255
Saint Vincent and the Grenadines 145; religion 157
salinity 170–71, 400, 423, 538
Salween River 452, 499
Samarkand 413, 415, 418
Samoa 545; government 553; resources 549
samsara 441, 510
Samsung 481
samurai 478
sanctification 536
sanctuary 417
sandalwood 551
San Diego 56
sanitation 85, 443, 445
San José 145
San Marino 287
Santeria 157
Sao Tomé and Principe 333; economy 344; government 343
sapphire 433
Sarajevo 261, 269–71
sardine 172
Sardinia 287
Saskatchewan 120–22, 127, 131, 136
satellite states 246
Saudi Arabia 73, 381, 383; culture 393; government 389; water 385
sauerkraut 252
savanna 19, 144, 169, 307, 325, 331–32, 334, 338, 358
scale 9
Scandinavia 192–93
Schengen Area 224
schistosomes 325
Schulze, Ernst-Detlef, 257
Scotland 192, 196, 204, 211
Scramble for Africa 364
seamount 548
Sea of Azov 238, 242, 261, 264
Sea of Galilee 382, 386, 389
seaweed 37, 485, 550
secularism 139, 204–5, 487
sedimentation 158, 265, 541
segregate 76, 187, 366
segregation 377
Seine River 215, 219
self-sustenance 487
Semey 407, 421
semiarid 54, 148, 172, 243–44, 291, 456
semi-presidential 342, 389, 459
Senate 126, 530
Senegal 332; government 342; resources 339; water 335–36
Senegal River 313
sensors 9
Seoul 70, 473, 483, 486; climate 479; water 476
Serbia 261; government 270–71; water 264
Serbs 270–71, 273
Serengeti Plain 356–57, 373
serfdom 247
service sector 319
Seychelles 358
Shahada 395
Shamanism 252
Shang Dynasty 458
Shanties 153
sharia law 389–99, 415, 419, 504
shashlik 393
shatter belt 260, 283
shellfish 122
Sherpa 427
Shetland Island 192
Shia 392, 403, 418
Shiites 403
Shikoku 472–73
Shintoism 486–87
shipbuilding 201, 286, 481
Shiva 441
shogun 478–79
shrimp 173, 550
shrine 103, 227, 471
Shutoken 471
Siberia 237–39, 244, 247, 252, 257
Sicily 12, 287
Siddhartha 510
Sierra Leone 332; resources 339
Sierra Madre Oriental 143–44, 146, 166
Sierra Nevada Range 27, 94, 98
Sierra Nevada (Spain) 286
Sikhism 442
Silesia 261, 265
silica 339
Silk Road 412–413
Sinai 310–11, 398
Singapore 368, 459, 495–97; demographics 513; economy 506; government 504; resources 500
sinkholes 262
Sino-Soviet 487
Sino-Tibetan 68

Six-Day War 317
Skeleton Coast 362
Skopje 261
slash-and-burn 332, 349, 351, 513
Slavic 246, 273
sleighs 204
Slovakia 260–62; government 271; water 264
Slovenia 260–62; government 271; water 264
smartphone 70, 319, 369
smog 113, 160, 207
snails 299
snorkeling 556
snowmobile 136
snowstorms 101
soccer 179, 204, 252, 300, 346, 394, 439, 462, 535
socialism 77–78, 318, 342, 367, 460
sociologists 205
Sofia 261
software 9, 17, 201
solar power 51, 115, 182, 324, 326, 375, 401, 539
solar system 31, 45
Solomon Islands 544–45; environment 559; government 553; religion 557;
solstice 46, 57
Somalia 82, 356–57; demographics 367; government 365
Somalian Plate 359
Somaliland 364
sonar 22
Songhai Empire 316–17, 341
Songkran Festival 509
Sonoran Desert 144
sorghum 363
sourdough 371
South Africa 355, 358; culture 370; demographics 369–70; environment 375; government 365–66; history 364–65; resources 363; water 360–61
South America 165–85
South American plate 22
South Asia 427–45
South China Sea 452, 455, 497, 499, 501, 512
South Dakota 103
Southeast Asia 495–517
southeastern 105, 358
Southern Africa 358–75
Southern Europe 284–303
Southern Hemiphere 5, 25, 46, 522
Southern Ocean 31
South Island 523
South Korea 70, 472–73; climate 476; culture 483–85; demographics 482; economy 481; environment 488–91; government 480; history 479; religion 486–87; resources 477; water 475;
South Pole 49
South Sudan 356–57; government 365
Southwest, US, 89, 100–101, 105
Southwest Asia 452
souvenirs 185
sovereign 529
sovereign funds 554
sovereign nation 127, 290, 415
sovereignty 271, 318, 505
Soviet bloc 268
Soviet Republics 246, 269
Soviet Union 222–23, 246–47, 268, 406, 415, 421, 479
spaceport 415
Spain 286; climate 291; culture 299; demographics 298; economy 297; environment 303; government 296; history 294; religion 300; water 289–90
Spanish Civil War 295
Spanish language 106, 154, 178, 294
sphere 5, 75, 205, 228
Sphinxes 309
spiritism 509, 511
spirit-prison 110
spleen 353
Spratly Islands 512
Sputnik 247
Sri Lanka 429-30; culture 439; demographics 438; economy 437; environment 443; government 436; history 435; resources 433; water 432
Stalin, Josef, 246, 269, 283, 413, 417
starfish 526, 541
starvation 85, 246, 269, 413, 458, 462
state-run 414
state-supported 460
station 537
steamboats 32
steel 38–39, 202, 531–32, 550
steppes 239; climate 266, 406–8
stewardship 15, 37, 59, 61, 112, 115, 158, 160, 254, 351, 467
Stockholm 193, 203
stocks 513
Stolen Generation 529
strata 25, 262
stratovolcano 474
Strauss 227
Stravinsky 251
strike-slip fault 22
Strokkur Geyser 195
subarctic 197–98, 243–44
subcastes 440
subcontinent 428, 432, 452
subculture 109
subduction 27
subpolar 54–55, 63, 123, 197, 245, 456
subranges 260
sub-saharan 310, 327, 340, 348, 362, 364–65, 368–374
subsidized 150, 390, 415, 436
subsistence farming 36, 320, 349, 443
subtropical 149, 291, 548
suburb 13, 87, 89, 105
Sudan 356–57; government 365; history 364; water 360
Sudd 360
Sudeten Mountains 260
Sudras 440
Suez Canal 311, 318, 329
sugar 153, 172, 184
sugar beets 220, 266
Suharto 504
suicide 250, 489
Sukarno 504
Sukkoth 398
Sulawesi 497
sulfur dioxide 113, 159, 195, 466
sultanate 434, 504
Sumatra 497, 517
Sunbelt 105
Sunni 317, 322, 341, 392, 403, 418, 511
supercontinent 22
superhighway 215
Sura 395, 399
Suriname 166–167; culture 178; government 174
sustainable development 161
Swahili 356, 369, 371
swamp 29, 58, 148
Sweden 193; climate 197–98; culture 204; demographics 203; economy 202; government 200; religion 204; water 196
Switzerland 214–16; culture 227; economy 226; environment 230, 484; government 223–24; religion 229; resources 220; water 218–19
swordfish 563
Sydney 521, 532
synagogue 229, 397–398
syncretism 157
Syria 225, 319, 382; history 388–89; government 389–90; demographics 392; religion 395
syrup 125, 299

T

tablelands 30
Taebaek Mountains 472, 475–76
Tagalogs 506
Taghaza 316
Tahiti 545, 556
taiga 63, 123, 197, 239, 244–45, 257, 456
tailings 136–37
Taipei 451, 452, 454
Taiwan 451–54; climate 456; demographics 461; economy 460; environment 466–67; government 459–60; history 458–59; religion 463; water 455
Tajikistan 406–7; demographics 417; government 414; history 413; resources 411; water 409–10
tajine 322
Taklimakan Desert 452
Taliban 405, 415, 417, 419, 422
Tallinn 259, 261, 264
Talmud 397
Talysh 420
Tampico 144, 163
Tang Dynasty 458–59
Tangier 311, 316
Tanzania 356–357; demographics 369; environment 373; government 365; religion 372; water 361
Taoism 464
Tarawa 559
tariff 82, 341
taro 543, 550, 556
Tashkent 406–407
Tasman, Abel, 529
Tasmania 523
Tasman Sea 522–23, 525–26
Tatar Mountains 250
Taymyr Peninsula 239
Tbilisi 407, 409, 414
Tchaikovsky 251
teak 513

technology 9, 11, 82, 84, 105, 160, 185, 209, 235, 249, 369, 400–401, 460, 477, 544, 560, 563
tectonic; activity 22, 33, 122, 243, 334, 382–84, 430, 453–54; forces 25, 27; plates 20, 22, 33, 144, 146, 524
Tegucigalpa 145
Tehran 73, 383
Tel Aviv 382, 389
telenovelas 177
telephone 108, 558
television 249, 414
tells 12, 110, 553
temperate 55–56, 63, 171–72, 362, 386, 410
temperate climate 291, 420, 456, 476, 500
temperate regions 100, 526
Temperate Zone 47, 53, 55, 57
tentmakers 323
tepui 169
terrace 213
territorial claims 136
terror-famine 269
terrorism 104, 111, 529
terrorist attacks 111, 213, 225, 392
terrorist groups 326, 343
tertiary industries 35, 78
Texas 105
textiles 339, 343, 436–37, 460
texting 70
Thailand 496–97; culture 507; demographics 506; economy 505; environment 513–14, 517; government 504; history 502–3; religion 509–10; resources 500; water 499
Thanaka 507
thematic map 11
theocracy 73, 88, 389, 435
thermal energy 21, 31, 46, 48–52, 55, 57
thermometer 48, 58
third-culture 71, 89
thorium 491
Three Gorges Dam 326, 457, 467
thunderstorm 43, 101
Tiahuanaco Empire 170
Tibesti Mountains 311
Tibet 431, 457, 499
Tibetan Plateau 30, 53, 452–53
Tien Shan 406–9
Tiergarten 213
Tierra caliente 149
Tierra fria 149
Tierra templada 149
tigers 500
Tigris River 382–83, 385, 388
timber 41, 201–2, 209, 242, 267, 302, 339, 343, 433, 560
timberline 123
timber-rich 220
Timbuktu 317, 341, 364
Timor Island 497
Timor-Leste 497; economy 506; government 504; history 503; religion 509, 511
Timor Sea 525
TIPNIS National Park 184
Tiranë 261
Titanic 281
titanium 199, 339, 343
Tocqueville, Alexis de, 108
Togo 332; religion 346; resources 339
Tokyo 471–73; culture 483
Tokyo Bay 478, 491
tolerance 132–34, 137–39
tolerant 204, 441, 509
tombs 259, 309, 427, 451
Tonga 545; economy 555; environment 559; government 553; religion 557;
topographic maps 17
topography 148, 197
topsoil 24, 160, 241, 255, 302, 351, 401
Torah 395, 397–98
tornadoes 58, 101
Toronto 120–21; climate 124; culture 130; demographics 128; environment 134
torture 443, 493
totalitarian government 74
tourism 128, 152–53, 175, 203, 224, 297, 320, 367–68, 436–37, 505, 531–32, 554, 557
toxic fungus 259
toxic gases 113
toxic waste 280, 374
toxic waterways 444, 466
toxins 249
Toyota 480, 484
traffic congestion 349–50, 432, 514, 556, 558
trains 38, 159, 366, 471, 481
Transaqua 326
transcontinental railroad 104
Transjordan 389
Transjordanian plateau 382
translation 507
translators 67, 557
Transnistria 283
transparency 319, 377
transplant tourism 465
transportation; land 159, 226, 230; public 226, 233; system 112, 158, 351; water 31, 33, 95, 170, 196, 242
Trans-Siberian Railway 237–39
Transylvania 259, 267
Transylvanian Alps 260–61
treaties 76, 248
trench 22, 474, 548
tribal 274, 341; council 133; government 377; groups 310, 344, 502; languages 321; loyalties 318; peoples 183; warfare 342
tribalism 340, 366
tribunal 465
tributaries 32, 99, 167, 360
Trieste 261
trilingual 506
Trinidad and Tobago 145
Trinity 181, 253
Tripoli 311, 316
Trivandrum 429
Tropic of Cancer 47, 197, 310, 358
Tropic of Capricorn 47, 310, 358
tropics 47, 144, 149, 171, 500
Trudeau, Justin, 127, 132, 134
Trudeau, Pierre, 128, 130
trust territory 552
Tsetse fly 362
tsunami 474, 490, 517
Tuareg 309, 321
tuberculosis 319
tubocurarine 161
tulips 220
Tumen River 473, 476
tuna 37, 554, 563
tundra 123–24, 197–98, 291
tungsten 38, 81, 477
Tunis 311, 316
Tunisia 310–11; climate 314; demographics 320; economy 319; environment 325; history 316; resources 315
Turkey 271, 382; culture 393; demographics 391–92; economy 390; environment 401; government 389, 412; religion 394; water 385
Turkic peoples 413, 417
Turkish; forces 412; government 229; people 418; plate 384; tribes 392
Turkistan 413
Turkmenistan 406–7; economy 415–16; environment 422; government 414; religion 419; resources 411; water 409;
Turks 203, 390, 412, 461
Tutankhamen 309
Tutsis 366–67
Tuvalu 545; economy 555; government 553
typhoid 319
typhoon 456, 546, 548, 555, 560
tyranny 78

U

Ubangi River 335
Uganda 356–57; economy 367; environment 373; history 364; water 361
Ukraine 81, 260–261; climate 266; environment 278–81; government 272; history 269; religion 276; resources 267; separatists 283; water 264–265
Ulaanbaatar 452
Ultra-Orthodox 398
unbiblical 131
UNESCO 427
unicameral 127, 342
uniformitarianism 25, 40
United Arab Emirates 73, 78, 383; environment 401; government 389
United Kingdom 75, 192; climate 197; demographics 203; economy 201; environment 206–8
United Nations (UN) 132, 271, 318, 388, 493, 503
United States 93–98; climate 100; culture 106–8; demographics 105; economy 104; environment 112–15; government 102–3; religion 109–11; resources 101; water 99
Uniting Church 536
untouchables 440
Uralic 68, 273
Ural Mountains 215, 239–41, 250, 273
uranium 39, 125, 136, 292–93, 315, 339, 411
urban areas 86
urbanization 86–87, 177, 226, 232, 273, 320, 325, 341, 369, 483, 487–88, 514, 556
urbanized 226, 272, 440, 532
Uruguay 167; culture 179; demographics 177; economy 176; resources 173; water 171
Uruguay River 167, 171

U-shaped valleys 24
USMCA 152
USSR, *see* Soviet Union
Utah 93–94, 110
Uyghur Muslims 459, 465
Uzbekistan 406–7; demographics 417; economy 415–16; environment 424; government 414; history 413; religion 418–19; resources 410–11; water 409;

V

vacation 375, 517
vaccinations 84
Vaisyas 440
Valley of balls 408
Valley of Jezreel 389
Valley of Mexico 143
Valley of the Kings 309
valleys 26–28, 33, 53, 94, 121
Vancouver 120–21; culture 130–31; demographics 128; environment 134
Vanuatu 544–54; economy 554–55; government 553; religion 557
Vatican City 156, 285–87, 300
Vatnajökull 194–95
veld 358
velocity 11
Venetian 290
Venezuela 75, 166–67; economy 176–77; environment 182; government 174–75; resources 173; water 170–71
Venice 287, 290
Verdun 223
Vermont 121
Vernal 46
vertical climate zones 149
Vesuvius 287–88
Victoria 120, 130
Victoria Falls 358, 361
Vienna 213, 215; culture 227; water 218
Vietnam 36, 60, 497–98; environment 512–14; government 504; history 502–3; religion 509–10; resources 500; water 499
Viking 191, 528
village 86, 340
Virginia 283
Virgin Islands 145
visa-free 224
Vistula River 265
vital statistics 83, 85
Vladivostok 237–39
volcano 21, 28, 33, 146, 195
Volga-Baltic Waterway 242
Volga-Don Canal 242
Volga River 238, 242, 244, 251
Volkswagen 224
volleyball 300, 346, 394, 439
Voodoo 157

W

Waddenzee 231
wadi 385
Wailing Wall 381
Wales 134, 192
Walesa, Lech, 268
Wallachia 261
walnut 393, 411
warlords 503
Warsaw 261, 265, 275
warships 329
Washington, George, 103,
wastelands 57
water-bearing rock 99
Waterton-Glacier National Park 134
Wawel Cathedral 259
Wayúu 183
weather 27, 43, 46, 48
weathering 23–26
Weddell Sea 546
wedding 156, 251, 486
welfare state 200
Wellington 530, 532
West Antarctica 546
West Bank 76, 382, 392
westerlies 47, 49
westerly winds 100, 220
Western Africa 310, 337, 341
Western Australia 23
Western Continental Divide 32, 94
Western Cordillera 120, 122, 125, 145, 166
Westernization 246–47
Western Plateau 522
Western Sahara 311, 316, 318
West Indies 145; climate 149; demographics 154; economy 153; religion 155
West Jerusalem 392
West Siberian Plain 239
westward 104, 108
wetland 29, 137, 167
wetlands 361, 374
whalers 529, 551
whales 305, 489, 563
whanau 535
wheat 54, 125, 220, 266, 290
White Nile 360
wife-carrying 204
wildebeest 373
wilderness 75, 87, 398, 406
Wilderness of Zin 389
Wilson, Woodrow, 148
wind belts 49
wind-deposited 28
Windhoek 358, 362
windmill 208–9
wind-powered 539
windstorms 24, 36
wind turbines 202, 220
Winnipeg 120–21
Winthrop, John, 107
Wirtschaftswunder 222
witch tree 347
wives 204, 399, 463
Wojtyła, Karol, 259
wood-burning 369
woodcarvers 274, 529
wool 36, 411–12, 460, 521
world ocean 31
World Trade Center 111, 415
worldview 25, 78, 210, 328, 352
Worthington Glacier 97
wrestling 346, 394, 462
Wycliffe Bible Translators 67
Wyoming 93

X

Xinjiang 452
Xizang 452

Y

yaks 411
Yamato clan 478
yams 60
Yamuna River 427, 429, 431
Yamunotri Glacier 431
Yangon 504
Yangtze Plate 474, 498
Yangtze River 455, 457
Yanukovych, Victor, 269
Yap 558
yellow fever 148, 343
Yellow Sea 452, 455, 475
Yellowstone National Park 75, 93
Yeltsin, Boris, 247
Yemen 73, 319, 383; demographics 391; education 390; government 389; resources 387;
Yerevan 407, 412, 414
Yodok 493
yogurt 220, 420
Yokohama 471, 473, 480
Yom Kippur 398
Yoritomo 478
Young, Brigham, 110
Yuan Dynasty 458–459
Yucatán Peninsula 144, 152
Yugoslavia 270
Yukon River 94, 98
Yukon Territory 120
Yushchenko, Viktor, 269

Z

Zagreb 261
Zaire 333
zakat 396
Zambezi River 361
Zambia 358; demographics 369; economy 368; environment 375; government 365; history 364; religion 372; water 361
Zanzibar 356
zebra mussels 115
zebras 373–74
Zelensky, Volodymyr, 272
Zimbabwe 358; climate 362; environment 374, 377; government 365, 367; water 361;
Zulu language 370

PHOTO CREDITS

Key: (t) top; (c) center; (b) bottom; (l) left; (r) right
(bg) background; (i) inset

Cover

front hadynyah/E+/Getty Images; **back** vwalakte/iStock/Getty Images Plus/Getty Images

Front Matter

ii–iii Trevor Reeves/Shutterstock.com; **v** Freder/iStock/Getty Images Plus/Getty Images; **vi** t Julien Hautcoeur/Shutterstock.com; **vi** i WPA Pool/Getty Images News/Getty Images; **vi** c loeskieboom/iStock Editorial/Getty Images Plus/Getty Images; **vi** b Freda Bouskoutas /iStock/Getty Images Plus/Getty Images; **vii** t Triff/Shutterstock.com; **vii** ct ARCTIC IMAGES / Alamy Stock Photo; **vii** cb Denis Brodeur /National Hockey League/Getty Images; **vii** b Adapted from Statistics Canada, Canadians and the outdoors, March 26, 2018. This does not constitute an endorsement by Statistics Canada of this product.; **viii** tl Olaf Kruger/Getty Images; **viii** tr mdulieu/iStock/Getty Images Plus /Getty Images; **viii** c Jon Vidar Sigurdsson/Nordic Photos/Getty Images Plus/Getty Images; **viii** i "Iceland Mid-Atlantic Ridge Fig16"/USGS /Wikimedia Commons/Public Domain/Map Resources; **viii** b Godong /Universal Images Group/Getty Images; **ix** l Universal Images Group North America LLC / Alamy Stock Photo; **ix** r SuperPuay/Shutterstock .com; **x–xi** bg Horizonman/Shutterstock.com

Unit Openers

xii–1 Georgijevic/E+/Getty Images; **90–91** Mike_Kolesnikov/iStock /Getty Images Plus/Getty Images; **140–41** Kryssia Campos/Moment /Getty Images; **188–89** yulenochekk/iStock/Getty Images Plus/Getty Images; **306–7** Elsen Karstad/500px/Getty Images; **378–79** Dmitriy Gutkovskiy/Shutterstock.com; **448–49** Preto_perola/iStock/Getty Images Plus/Getty Images; **518-19** NZSteve/iStock/Getty Images Plus /Getty Images

Chapter 1

2, 16–17t Caspar Benson/Getty Images; **3t**, ct NASA; **3cb** Andrew Merry/Moment/Getty Images; **3b** Ashley Cooper pics / Alamy Stock Photo; **4** Alex Potemkin/E+/Getty Images; **5** Art-Y/iStock/Getty Images Plus/Getty Images; **6–7** olli0815/iStock Editorial/Getty Images Plus /Getty Images; **8** Klaus Vedfelt/DigitalVision/Getty Images; **9** NOAA; **10t** Planet Observer/Universal Images Group/Getty Images Plus/Getty Images; **10b–11** Westend61 GmbH / Alamy Stock Photo; **12** Fabeha Monir/iStock Editorial/Getty Images Plus/Getty Images; **13t** loonger /E+/Getty Images; **13c** hadynyah/E+/Getty Images; **13b** Yasemin Yurtman Candemir/Shutterstock.com; **14** Werli Francois / Alamy Stock Photo; **15t** adisa/iStock/Getty Images Plus/Getty Images; **15b** mizoula /iStock Editorial/Getty Images Plus/Getty Images; **17b** Joe McDonald /Corbis Documentary/Getty Images Plus/Getty Images

Chapter 2

18, 40–41t Blue Planet Studio/Shutterstock.com; **19tl** Senderistas /Shutterstock.com; **19tr** Dene' Miles/Shutterstock.com; **19c** Max shen/Moment/Getty Images; **19b** Age Fotostock/Wolfgang Kaehler /Media Bakery; **21** tom pfeiffer / Alamy Stock Photo; **22** "Pangaea continents" by Kieff/Wikimedia Commons/CC By SA 3.0/labels added; **23** © Minyun Zhou | Dreamstime.com; **24t** Pavliha/iStock/Getty Images Plus /Getty Images; **24c** AlexZachen/iStock/Getty Images Plus/Getty Images; **24b–25** Dean Fikar/Moment/Getty Images; **26–27b** Kertu/Shutterstock .com; **27t** JordiStock/iStock/Getty Images Plus/Getty Images; **30t** junjun /Shutterstock.com; **30b–31** Posnov/Moment/Getty Images; **32** Adobe Stock/Cmon; **33t** jimkruger/E+/Getty Images; **33b** Julia Kuzenkova /Shutterstock.com; **34** Sven Hansche/Shutterstock.com; **35** Robbi Shobri Rakhman/Shutterstock.com; **36t** Sirisak_baokaew/Shutterstock .com; **36c** ALEXANDER JOE/AFP/Getty Images; **36b** Douglas Peebles Photography / Alamy Stock Photo; **37t** Matjaz Corel / Alamy Stock Photo; **37b** Kletr/Shutterstock.com; **38t** Adobe Stock/Jeffrey Daly; **38c** Aleksandr Pobedimskiy/Shutterstock.com; **38b** William Campbell /Corbis Historical/Getty Images; **39** Dazman/iStock/Getty Images Plus /Getty Images; **41b** US Army Photo / Alamy Stock Photo

Chapter 3

42, 62–63 john finney photography/Moment/Getty Images; **43tl** Anthony Murphy/Moment Open/Getty Images; **43tr** Rawpixel /iStock/Getty Images Plus/Getty Images; **43c** Andrey Larionov/500px /Getty Images; **43b** Timofey Zadvornov/iStock/Getty Images Plus /Getty Images; **44–45bg** Withan Tor/Shutterstock.com; **45** (Mercury), (Jupiter) right, (Saturn) Vadim Sadovski/Shutterstock.com; **45** (Venus), (Mars), (Jupiter) left, (Uranus) NASA images/Shutterstock.com; **45** (Earth) "The Earth seen from Apollo 17 with white background" by NASA/Wikimedia Commons/Public Domain; **45** (Neptune) © iStock .com/3quarks; **47** Steffen Schnur/Moment/Getty Images; **48–49bg** Mike Hill / Alamy Stock Photo; **48t** Adobe Stock/Tomas Ragina; **48c** Gannet77/E+/Getty Images; **48b** Adobe Stock/anoyo; **50l** Adobe Stock /naticus; **50r** Mlenny/E+/Getty Images; **51t** Daniel Wright/iStock/Getty Images Plus/Getty Images; **51b** gsagi/iStock/Getty Images Plus/Getty Images; **52t** Adobe Stock/BadBoyC; **52b–53** Tony Waltham/robert harding/Getty Images Plus/Getty Images; **56t** Triff/Shutterstock.com; **56b** ARCTIC IMAGES / Alamy Stock Photo; **57t** Steve Morgan / Alamy Stock Photo; **57c** Jim Reed/Corbis NX/Getty Images Plus/Getty Images; **57b** Stefonlinton/iStock/Getty Images Plus/Getty Images; **58t** VasekM /Shutterstock.com; **58b** sumikophoto/Shutterstock.com; **59** Grzegorz Radosław Maziarski/500px/Getty Images; **60t** barmalini/iStock/Getty Images Plus/Getty Images; **60c** Getty Images/iStockphoto/Thinkstock; **60b** hadynyah/iStock/Getty Images Plus/Getty Images; **61** Ramdan _Nain/iStock/Getty Images Plus/Getty Images

Chapter 4

64, 88–89t Helen Sessions / Alamy Stock Photo; **65tl** liveostock images/Shutterstock.com; **65tr** Adobe Stock/Jasmin Merdan; **65c** Enrique Díaz/7cero/Moment/Getty Images; **65b** david pearson / Alamy Stock Photo; **67** Amrish Saini/EyeEm/Getty Images; **68** Jim West / Alamy Stock Photo; **69** Elizabeth Fitt / Alamy Stock Photo; **70t** Image Source/Getty Images; **70c** Adobe Stock/kovop58; **70b** Time, Life, Enjoy.../Moment/Getty Images; **71** nadia mackenzie / Alamy Stock Photo; **73** Anadolu Agency/Getty Images; **74** vverve/Bigstock.com; **75t** Kraig Lieb/Lonely Planet Images/Getty Images Plus/Getty Images; **75b** PATRICK BAZ/AFP/Getty Images; **76** rglinsky/iStock/Getty Images Plus/Getty Images; **77** olli0815/iStock Editorial/Getty Images Plus/Getty Images; **78** Xinhua / Alamy Stock Photo; **79** Mike Robinson / Alamy Stock Photo; **80t** nechaev-kon/iStock/Getty Images Plus/Getty Images; **80b** Adobe Stock/peteri/Map Resources; **81t** Russell Kord / Alamy Stock Photo; **81b** Thatree Thitivongvaroon/Moment/Getty Images; **82** Africa Collection / Alamy Stock Photo; **83t** katatonia82/Shutterstock.com; **83b** Max Roser/Our World in Data/CC By 4.0/modified; **84t** BSIP /Universal Images Group/Getty Images; **84b** Our World in Data/CC By 4.0/modified; **85** Max Roser/Our World in Data/CC By 4.0/detail; **86** luoman/iStock/Getty Images Plus/Getty Images; **87** Harvepino/iStock /Getty Images Plus/Getty Images; **89b** Jason Finn/iStock/Getty Images Plus/Getty Images

Chapter 5

92 aijohn784/iStock/Getty Images Plus/Getty Images; **93t** bpperry /iStock/Getty Images Plus/Getty Images; **93cl** Universal Art Archive / Alamy Stock Photo; **93cr** TheBigMK/iStock/Getty Images Plus/Getty Images; **93b** James Randklev/DigitalVision/Getty Images; **96tl** Sunset Avenue Productions/DigitalVision/Getty Images; **96tr** Adobe Stock /Galyna Andrushko; **96c** CarbonBrain/iStock/Getty Images Plus /Getty Images; **96b** "Sevehah Cliff" by Jane S. Richardson/Wikimedia Commons/CC By 3.0; **97tli** Bruce M Herman/Science Source/Getty Images Plus/Getty Images; **97tri** David Lyons / Alamy Stock Photo; **97t** Adam Hardtke/500px/Getty Images; **97bli** inEthos Design/Shutterstock .com; **97bci** B Christopher / Alamy Stock Photo; **97bri** Adobe Stock /sherryvsmith; **97b, 116–17t** tonda/iStock/Getty Images Plus/Getty Images; **99r** Source: Secondary Hydrogeologic Regions of the Conterminous United States/Public Domain; **103** M. Kaercher/iStock /Getty Images Plus/Getty Images; **105** Joel Carillet/iStock Unreleased /Getty Images; **106** David Grossman / Alamy Stock Photo; **107** image BROKER / Alamy Stock Photo; **108t** wsfurlan/iStock/Getty Images Plus/ Getty Images; **108c** mbbirdy/iStock Unreleased/Getty Images; **108b** DebraMillet/iStock/Getty Images Plus/Getty Images; **109** AlbertPego/ iStock/Getty Images Plus/Getty Images; **110t** Juanmonino

/iStock/Getty Images Plus/Getty Images; **110**b Pictorial Press Ltd / Alamy Stock Photo; **111** "US Navy 010914-F-8006R-003 Aerial view of Pentagon destruction"/U.S. Navy/Wikimedia Commons/Public Domain; **112**t doranjclark/iStock/Getty Images Plus/Getty Images; **112**b BRANDONJ74/iStock/Getty Images Plus/Getty Images; **113**t helt2 /iStock/Getty Images Plus/Getty Images; **113**b Kenneth Keifer /Shutterstock.com; **114**tl Jason Finn/iStock/Getty Images Plus/Getty Images; **114**tr Diane Macdonald/Moment Open/Getty Images; **114**b J.K. York/Shutterstock.com; **115**tl iStock/Getty Images Plus/Getty Images; **115**tc Heiko Kiera/Shutterstock.com; **115**tr jamesbenet/iStock/Getty Images Plus/Getty Images; **115**c Wolfgang Hoffmann/Design Pics/Getty Images; **115**b 4kodiak/E+/Getty Images; **117**b pichitstocker/iStock /Getty Images Plus/Getty Images

Chapter 6

118 Rick Rudnicki / Alamy Stock Photo; **119**tl, **130**b Michael Wheatley / Alamy Stock Photo; **119**tr boonsom/iStock Editorial/Getty Images Plus/Getty Images; **119**c madsci/iStock Editorial/Getty Images Plus /Getty Images; **119**b A Kitisa/Shutterstock.com; **122**t, **131**b age fotostock / Alamy Stock Photo; **122**cl Mike Randolph/Radius Images/Getty Images; **122**cr "Athabasca Oil Sands map" by NormanEinstein /Wikimedia Commons/Public Domain/Map Resources; **122**b stockstudioX/E+/Getty Images; **123**t, ct Breck P. Kent; **123**cb Chris Hendrickson/Photographer's Choice RF/Getty Images; **123**b © Rkhalstad | Dreamstime.com; **124**t FilippoBacci/iStock/Getty Images Plus/Getty Images; **124**b Jun Zhang/iStock Unreleased/Getty Images; **125**t CAP53/iStock/Getty Images Plus/Getty Images; **125**ct alblec /iStock/Getty Images Plus/Getty Images; **125**cb lightasafeather/E+ /Getty Images; **125**b, **138–39**t Ron Nickel/Design Pics/Getty Images; **126–27**bg Julien Hautcoeur/Shutterstock.com; **127** WPA Pool/Getty Images News/Getty Images; **129**t Denis Brodeur/National Hockey League/Getty Images; **129**b Adapted from Statistics Canada, Canadians and the outdoors, March 26, 2018. This does not constitute an endorsement by Statistics Canada of this product.; **130**t Hemis / Alamy Stock Photo; **130**c LeonU/iStock Unreleased/Getty Images; **131**t "Cree students and teacher in class at All Saints Indian Residential School, (Anglican Mission School), Lac La Ronge, Saskatchewan, March 1945" by Bud Glunz/Library and Archives Canada/Flickr/CC By 2.0; **132** GEOFF ROBINS/AFP/Getty Images; **133**t kenneth-cheung/iStock/Getty Images Plus/Getty Images; **133**b © NativeStock / North Wind Picture Archives; **134**t milehightraveler/E+/Getty Images; **134**b dan_prat/iStock/Getty Images Plus/Getty Images; **135**t AP Photo/The Canadian Press, Jonathan Hayward; **135**bl, br "Oldest Arctic Sea Ice is Disappearing" by Joey Comiso/NASA/Wikimedia Commons/Public Domain; **136** louise murray / Alamy Stock Photo; **137** All Canada Photos / Alamy Stock Photo; **139**b Andrew Chin/Getty Images Entertainment/Getty Images

Chapter 7

142 Pauws99/iStock Editorial/Getty Images Plus/Getty Images; **143**tl Wildroze/E+/Getty Images; **143**tr Cameris/iStock/Getty Images Plus /Getty Images; **143**bl traveler1116/iStock/Getty Images Plus/Getty Images; **143**br KIKILOMBO/iStock/Getty Images Plus/Getty Images; **146**t jose carlos macouzet espinosa/iStock/Getty Images Plus/Getty Images; **146**b Arturo Peña Romano Med/iStock/Getty Images Plus /Getty Images; **147**l Matteo Colombo/Moment/Getty Images; **147**r, **162–63**t oriredmouse/E+/Getty Images; **148** Tiago_Fernandez/iStock Editorial/Getty Images Plus/Getty Images; **151**t EFE News Agency / Alamy Stock Photo; **151**b Xinhua / Alamy Stock Photo; **152**t bullsiphoto/iStock/Getty Images Plus/Getty Images; **152**b Guillaume De Kinderen/EyeEm/Getty Images; **153**t Charles Harker/Moment Open/Getty Images; **153**b artisteer/iStock/Getty Images Plus/Getty Images; **155**t, **156**b loeskieboom/iStock Editorial/Getty Images Plus /Getty Images; **155**b Freda Bouskoutas/iStock/Getty Images Plus/Getty Images; **156**t RudolfT/iStock/Getty Images Plus/Getty Images; **157** hydrangea100/iStock/Getty Images Plus/Getty Images; **158** Photo by Joel Sharpe/Moment Unreleased/Getty Images; **159**t stockcam/iStock /Getty Images Plus/Getty Images; **159**b National Geographic Image Collection / Alamy Stock Photo; **160** N8tureGrl/iStock/Getty Images Plus/Getty Images; **161**l Universal Images Group North America LLC / Alamy Stock Photo; **161**r SuperPuay/Shutterstock.com; **163**b Gerardo Tomas Alvarez Carmona/EyeEm/Getty Images

Chapter 8

164 Freder/iStock/Getty Images Plus/Getty Images; **165**t DoraDalton /iStock Unreleased/Getty Images; **165**c hadynyah/E+/Getty Images; **165**b DC_Colombia/iStock Editorial/Getty Images Plus/Getty Images; **168**t David Aguilar Photography/iStock/Getty Images Plus/Getty Images; **168**cl "Cratons West Gondwana" by Woudloper/Wikipedia /CC By-SA 3.0/modified/Map Resources; **168**cr PatricioHidalgoP /iStock/Getty Images Plus/Getty Images; **168**b, **177**tr imageBROKER / Alamy Stock Photo; **169**t Luc V. de Zeeuw/Moment/Getty Images; **169**c Steve Allen/DigitalVision/Getty Images; **169**b robertharding / Alamy Stock Photo; **170**t MediaProduction/iStock Unreleased/Getty Images; **170**c Novarc Images / Alamy Stock Photo; **170**b, **186–87**t Carlos Fabal /Moment/Getty Images; **171** Alice Nerr/Shutterstock.com; **172**t © Tomas Hajek | Dreamstime.com; **172**c Priscila Zambotto/Moment/Getty Images; **172**b chictype/iStock/Getty Images Plus/Getty Images; **173** J-Palys/iStock/Getty Images Plus/Getty Images; **175** Joe Raedle/Getty Images News/Getty Images; **176**t ULISES RUIZ/AFP/Getty Images; **176**b dpaH329icture alliance / Alamy Stock Photo; **177**tl Modoc Stories /Getty Images; **177**c hadynyah/iStock/Getty Images Plus/Getty Images; **177**b izusek/E+/Getty Images; **178** SCHNEYDER MENDOZA/AFP /Getty Images; **179**t Chrispictures/Shutterstock.com; **179**c jonnysek /iStock/Getty Images Plus/Getty Images; **179**b Jon Arnold Images Ltd / Alamy Stock Photo; **180**t RealyEasyStar / Fotografia Felici / Alamy Stock Photo; **180b–81** zxvisual/E+/Getty Images; **182**t abriendomundo /iStock/Getty Images Plus/Getty Images; **182**b Ildo Frazao/iStock/Getty Images Plus/Getty Images; **183** dpa picture alliance archive / Alamy Stock Photo; **184** Pawel Bienkowski / Alamy Stock Photo; **185**t MAURO PIMENTEL/AFP/Getty Images; **185**b Larry Larsen / Alamy Stock Photo; **187**b holgs/iStock Unreleased/Getty Images

Chapter 9

190 Rainbow79/iStock/Getty Images Plus/Getty Images; **191**tl Topi Ylä-Mononen/500px/Getty Images; **191**tr Bradley L. Cox/Moment /Getty Images; **191**bl Paul Thompson/Moment/Getty Images; **191**br Philippe Bourseiller/The Image Bank/Getty Images Plus/Getty Images; **194**t mantaphoto/iStock/Getty Images Plus/Getty Images; **194**c Claire Plumridge/Moment/Getty Images; **194**b leskas/iStock/Getty Images Plus/Getty Images; **195**tl Olaf Kruger/Getty Images; **195**tr mdulieu /iStock/Getty Images Plus/Getty Images; **195**c Jon Vidar Sigurdsson /Nordic Photos/Getty Images Plus/Getty Images; **195**b AdamMajor /iStock/Getty Images Plus/Getty Images; **195**i "Iceland Mid-Atlantic Ridge Fig16"/USGS/Wikimedia Commons/Public Domain/Map Resources; **196**tl John Clarke Photography/Shutterstock.com; **196**tr rpeters86/iStock/Getty Images Plus/Getty Images; **196**bl Westend61 /Getty Images; **196**br FrankRamspott/iStock/Getty Images Plus /Getty Images; **197** Alexey_Seafarer/iStock/Getty Images Plus/Getty Images; **197**i Planet Observer/Universal Images Group/Getty Images Plus/Getty Images; **198**t By Thomas E. Gunnarsson/Moment/Getty Images; **198**c Mint Images/Mint Images RF/Getty Images; **198**b Willy Pell/500px/500Px Plus/Getty Images; **199**t Aki Kipinä/iStock Editorial /Getty Images Plus/Getty Images; **199**b subtik/E+/Getty Images; **200** PhotographerCW/iStock/Getty Images Plus/Getty Images; **201**t Avpics / Alamy Stock Photo; **201**b PAUL ELLIS/AFP/Getty Images; **202**tl AFP /Getty Images; **202**tr aethernet/iStock/Getty Images Plus/Getty Images; **202**c klug-photo/iStock Editorial/Getty Images Plus/Getty Images; **202**b Jarmo Piironen/Shutterstock.com; **203** Planet Observer/UIG/Universal Images Group/Getty Images Plus/Getty Images; **204**tl Atlantide Phototravel/Corbis Documentary/Getty Images Plus/Getty Images; **204**bl George Sweeney / Alamy Stock Photo; **204**r GoranDomeij /iStock Editorial/Getty Images Plus/Getty Images; **205** Matthew Chattle / Alamy Stock Photo; **206**t PhilAugustavo/iStock/Getty Images Plus /Getty Images; **206**c Joe Fox/age fotostock/Getty Images Plus/Getty Images; **206**b Yevhenii Kravchuk/Shutterstock.com; **207**t Sorin Rechitan/EyeEm/Getty Images; **207**b Jeff Gilbert / Alamy Stock Photo; **208–9**b BerndBrueggemann/iStock/Getty Images Plus/Getty Images; **209**t, **210–11** brittak/iStock/Getty Images Plus/Getty Images

Chapter 10

212 Chinnaphong Mungsiri/Moment/Getty Images; **213**tl sborisov /iStock/Getty Images Plus/Getty Images; **213**tc stocklapse/iStock/Getty Images Plus/Getty Images; **213**tr Ken Welsh/age fotostock/Getty Images Plus/Getty Images; **213**b AlexKozlov/iStock Editorial/Getty Images Plus/Getty Images; **216–17**bg Ruud Morijn Photographer/Shutterstock .com; **216**l Andy Bryant/500Px Plus/Getty Images; **216**tr Alpha du centaure/Moment/Getty Images; **216**br nattrass/E+/Getty Images; **217** Petroos/iStock/Getty Images Plus/Getty Images; **218**t saiko3p/iStock Editorial/Getty Images Plus/Getty Images; **218**c Markus Hanke/Corbis /Getty Images Plus/Getty Images; **218**b–**19**b f11photo/iStock/Getty Images Plus/Getty Images; **219**t Francesco Bergamaschi/Moment/Getty Images; **220**t luiscarlosjimenez/iStock/Getty Images Plus/Getty Images; **220**b–**21, 234–35**t JacobH/E+/Getty Images; **222** Agencja Fotograficzna Caro / Alamy Stock Photo; **223**t AdrianHancu/iStock Editorial /Getty Images Plus/Getty Images; **223**b Pool FRANCOLON/SIMON /Gamma-Rapho/Getty Images; **224**t Lonely Planet Images/Getty Images Plus/Getty Images; **224**b Kiran Ridley/Getty Images News/Getty Images; **225**l BULENT KILIC/AFP/Getty Images; **225**r CHRISTOF STACHE/AFP/Getty Images; **226**t fotoember/iStock Editorial/Getty Images Plus/Getty Images; **226**b Nikada/iStock Unreleased/Getty Images; **227**l DIETER NAGL/AFP/Getty Images; **227**c DebbiSmirnoff /iStock/Getty Images Plus/Getty Images; **227**r Andy Christiani / Alamy Stock Photo; **228**t "Charles Darwin seated" by Maull & Fox/Wikimedia Commons/Public Domain; **228**b Don Arnold/Getty Images News/Getty Images; **229**tl kokoroimages.com/Moment/Getty Images; **229**tr Aziz Ary Neto/Cultura/Getty Images; **229**b Adobe Stock/REUTERS/Reuters Photographer; **230**t Marc_Osborne/iStock/Getty Images Plus/Getty Images; **230**c MIGUEL MEDINA/AFP/Getty Images; **230**b TonyV3112 /iStock Editorial/Getty Images Plus/Getty Images; **231** ©iStockphoto .com/DanielTaeger; **232**t julof90/iStock/Getty Images Plus/Getty Images; **232**b VladOrlov/iStock/Getty Images Plus/Getty Images; **233** Martyn Jandula/Shutterstock.com; **235**b RuudMorijn/iStock/Getty Images Plus/Getty Images

Chapter 11

236 mgrushin/iStock Editorial/Getty Images Plus/Getty Images; **237**tl DmitryNautilus/iStock/Getty Images Plus/Getty Images; **237**tr Anton Petrus/Moment/Getty Images; **237**c Novarc Images / Alamy Stock Photo; **237**b Vostok/Moment/Getty Images; **240–41**bg Aliyev Alexei Sergeevich/Cultura/Getty Images; **240**tl grizsys/iStock/Getty Images Plus/Getty Images; **240**tr, **256–57**t Dzhambulat Tkhazaplizhev/500px /Getty Images; **240**b oxygen/Moment/Getty Images; **241**t Maksim Kamyshanskii/iStock/Getty Images Plus/Getty Images; **241**b geyzer /iStock/Getty Images Plus/Getty Images; **242**t Images & Stories / Alamy Stock Photo; **242**b Alex Marakhovets/Shutterstock.com; **243**tl Planet Observer/Universal Images Group/Getty Images Plus/Getty Images; **243**tr Alexey Trofimov/500px Prime/Getty Images; **243**b AleksandrLutcenko/iStock/Getty Images Plus/Getty Images; **244**tl Vera Tikhonova/iStock Editorial/Getty Images Plus/Getty Images; **244**tr SeppFriedhuber/E+/Getty Images; **244**c SGV/iStock/Getty Images Plus /Getty Images; **244**b oixxo/iStock/Getty Images Plus/Getty Images; **245** Denis Privalikhin/iStock/Getty Images Plus/Getty Images; **247**t ANDRE DURAND/AFP/Getty Images; **247**bl, **250**c ITAR-TASS News Agency / Alamy Stock Photo; **247**br Kremlin Pool / Alamy Stock Photo; **249** scaliger/iStock/Getty Images Plus/Getty Images; **250**t, **251**cr ZUMA Press, Inc. / Alamy Stock Photo; **250**b Vladimir Godnik/Getty Images; **251**tl Buddy Mays / Alamy Stock Photo; **251**tr Sergei Butorin /Shutterstock.com; **251**cl Artyom Geodakyan/TASS/Getty Images; **251**b Lesyy/iStock/Getty Images Plus/Getty Images; **252**tl Fascinadora /iStock/Getty Images Plus/Getty Images; **252**tr matteodestefano/iStock /Getty Images Plus/Getty Images; **252**b picture alliance/Getty Images; **253**t Westend61/Getty Images; **253**b Alexey Borodin/Shutterstock .com; **254**t "Shatura steam power plant (2010)" by Burger/Wikimedia Commons/Public Domain; **254**b EvgenyMiroshnichenko/iStock/Getty Images Plus/Getty Images; **255**t alexalexl/iStock/Getty Images Plus /Getty Images; **255**c vicsa/iStock/Getty Images Plus/Getty Images; **255**b Alexander Khitrov/Shutterstock.com; **257**b "Amazon Tall Tower Observatory" by Jsaturno/Wikimedia Commons/CC By-SA 4.0

Chapter 12

258 Vladislav Zolotov/iStock Editorial/Getty Images Plus/Getty Images; **259**tl georgeoprea9/iStock/Getty Images Plus/Getty Images; **259**tr Ingus Kruklitis/iStock/Getty Images Plus/Getty Images; **259**c RStelmach/iStock/Getty Images Plus/Getty Images; **259**b Jaroslav Moravcik/Shutterstock.com; **262**tl jarino47/iStock/Getty Images Plus /Getty Images; **262**tr Avalon / Photoshot License / Alamy Stock Photo; **262**b–**63**b József Bartos/EyeEm/Getty Images; **263**t "Marsh. Polissia" by Ivan Shishkin/Wikimedia Commons/Public Domain; **264**t VvoeVale/iStock Editorial/Getty Images Plus/Getty Images; **264**c Pauline Lewis/Moment/Getty Images; **264**b porojnicu/iStock /Getty Images Plus/Getty Images; **265**t JaySi/iStock/Getty Images Plus /Getty Images; **265**b, **282–83**t Fesus Robert Levente/iStock/Getty Images Plus/Getty Images; **266**t igorwheeler/iStock/Getty Images Plus /Getty Images; **266**b–**67**b Model-la/iStock/Getty Images Plus/Getty Images; **267**t Evgeny_Kozhevnikov/iStock/Getty Images Plus/Getty Images; **267**c Erlend Haarberg/National Geographic Image Collection /Getty Images; **267**i AYImages/E+/Getty Images; **268**l CTK / Alamy Stock Photo; **268**r ullstein bild/Getty Images; **269**t UPI / Alamy Stock Photo; **269**b JOE KLAMAR/AFP/Getty Images; **270**c "Ethnic makeup of Bosnia and Herzegovina before and after the war" by Praxis Icosahedron/"Composition ethnique de Bosnie-Herzégovine" by Bourrichon/Wikimedia Commons/CC By-SA 3.0/modified; **270**b 992/Moment/Getty Images; **271**t MIKE PERSSON/AFP/Getty Images; **271**b Patrick Robert - Corbis/Sygma/Getty Images; **273**t Pawel Wewiorski/Moment/Getty Images; **273**ct Yanosh_Nemesh/iStock Editorial/Getty Images Plus/Getty Images; **273**cb Katiekk2/iStock Editorial/Getty Images Plus/Getty Images; **273**b PhotoStock-Israel / Alamy Stock Photo; **274**t Dennis Cox / Alamy Stock Photo; **274**b Luis Dafos / Alamy Stock Photo; **275**t Panama7/iStock/Getty Images Plus /Getty Images; **275**cl "Old Town Warsaw waf-2012-1501-31(1945)" /Wikimedia Commons/Public Domain; **275**cr nikitje/iStock Unreleased/Getty Images; **275**b Adobe Stock/sandsun; **276, 283**b NurPhoto/Getty Images; **277** © Kutizoltan | Dreamstime.com; **278**t European Environmental Agency (key moved and line added); **278**b Jasmin Brutus / Alamy Stock Photo; **279**t Wojtek Laski/Hulton Archive/Getty Images; **279**c Igor Kostin/Sygma/Getty Images; **279**b MediaProduction/E+/Getty Images; **280** AP Photo/Vadim Ghirda; **281** "1121-Txernobylgo zentral nuklearrerako sarkofago berria-en" by Berria/Wikimedia Commons/CC By-SA 4.0/modified

Chapter 13

284 massimo colombo/Moment/Getty Images; **285**t Photo by cuellar /Moment/Getty Images; **285**c Eloi_Omella/E+/Getty Images; **285**b lavendertime/iStock Editorial/Getty Images Plus/Getty Images; **288**t Kitti Boonnitrod/Moment/Getty Images; **288**c Volanthevist/Moment /Getty Images; **288**b Ary6/E+/Getty Images; **289**t Stocktrek Images /Getty Images; **289**b George Pachantouris/Moment/Getty Images; **290**t Moema Quintas - Fotografia/Moment/Getty Images; **290**c spooh /iStock Unreleased/Getty Images; **290**b Chloé Boulos/EyeEm/Getty Images; **291**t Luis Dafos/Moment/Getty Images; **291**ct StevanZZ /iStock/Getty Images Plus/Getty Images; **291**cb Mlenny/iStock/Getty Images Plus/Getty Images; **291**b Evgeni Dinev Photography/Moment /Getty Images; **292, 304–5**t RossHelen/iStock/Getty Images Plus/Getty Images; **293** GitoTrevisan/iStock Unreleased/Getty Images; **294** TRMK /Shutterstock.com; **295** FALKENSTEINFOTO / Alamy Stock Photo; **296**t EFE News Agency / Alamy Stock Photo; **296**b THIERRY BRETON /AFP/Getty Images; **297** peplow/iStock Editorial/Getty Images Plus /Getty Images; **298**t Jacek_Sopotnicki/iStock/Getty Images Plus/Getty Images; **298**b adamico70/iStock Editorial/Getty Images Plus/Getty Images; **299**tl T photography/Shutterstock.com; **299**tr ermess/iStock Editorial/Getty Images Plus/Getty Images; **299**c Studioimagen73 /iStock/Getty Images Plus/Getty Images; **299**bl tbralnina/iStock /Getty Images Plus/Getty Images; **299**br Photocuisine/Lawton/Media Bakery; **300**t Alexandre Sousa / Alamy Stock Photo; **300**b L'Osservatore Romano/Pool Photo via AP, File; **301** Hwa Cho Yi/Shutterstock.com; **302**t PhotoStock-Israel/Shutterstock.com; **302**b mrfotos/iStock/Getty Images Plus/Getty Images; **303** irakite/iStock/Getty Images Plus/Getty Images; **305**b chert61/iStock/Getty Images Plus/Getty Images

Chapter 14

308 hadynyah/E+/Getty Images; **309**tl HomoCosmicos/iStock Editorial /Getty Images Plus/Getty Images; **309**tr Siempreverde22/iStock/Getty Images Plus/Getty Images; **309**c, **328–29**t Tanatat pongphibool, thailand/Moment/Getty Images; **309**b ytwong/E+/Getty Images; **310** "Africa satellite orthographic"/NASA/Wikimedia Commons/Public Domain; **312**tl Paraponera/Shutterstock.com; **312**tr Zdenek Kajzr /iStock/Getty Images Plus/Getty Images; **312**bl "ISS-42 Richat Structure" /NASA/Wikimedia Commons/Public Domain; **312**br Universal Images Group North America LLC / DeAgostini / Alamy Stock Photo; **313**t, c NASA; **313**bl "Egypt (5635018418)"/NASA Goddard Space Flight Center/Wikimedia Commons/Public Domain; **313**br Frank Krahmer /DigitalVision/Getty Images; **314** frederic REGLAIN / Alamy Stock Photo; **315** Xinhua / Alamy Stock Photo; **316** monticelllo/iStock Editorial/Getty Images Plus/Getty Images; **317**t © iStock.com/oversnap;

317b sculpies/iStock/Getty Images Plus/Getty Images; **318**t Baloncici /iStock Editorial/Getty Images Plus/Getty Images; **318**b FAROUK BATICHE/AFP/Getty Images; **319** MOHAMMED ABED/AFP/Getty Images; **320**t R.M. Nunes/Shutterstock.com; **320**b Joerg Boethling / Alamy Stock Photo; **321**t Arco Images GmbH / Alamy Stock Photo; **321**b Eric Nathan / Alamy Stock Photo; **322**l iStock/Getty Images Plus /Getty Images; **322**r Fanfo/Shutterstock.com; **323**t AFP/Getty Images; **323**b KHALED DESOUKI/AFP/Getty Images; **324**t RGB Ventures / SuperStock / Alamy Stock Photo; **324**b "Great Man Made River schematic EN" by Danmichaelo/Wikimedia Commons/CC By-SA 3.0; **325**t Jose HERNANDEZ Camera 51/Shutterstock.com; **325**b Georg Gerster/SCIENCE SOURCE; **326** NHPA/SuperStock; **327**t commerce andculturestock/Moment Open/Getty Images; **327**b mtcurado/iStock /Getty Images Plus/Getty Images; **329**b "USS Dwight D. Eisenhower (CVN-69) transiting the Suez Canal in August 1990" by PH3 Frank A. Marquart, USN/NARA/Wikimedia Commons/Public Domain

Chapter 15

330 zsh Wang/500px/500Px Plus/Getty Images; **331**tl, **352–53**t Gleb _Ivanov/iStock/Getty Images Plus/Getty Images; **331**tr avstraliavasin /iStock/Getty Images Plus/Getty Images; **331**b Mike Goldwater / Alamy Stock Photo; **334**tl Michael D. Kock/Getty Images; **334**tr Anze Furlan/psgtproductions/iStock/Getty Images Plus/Getty Images; **334**c elenacastaldi77/iStock/Getty Images Plus/Getty Images; **334**b Fabian Plock/iStock/Getty Images Plus/Getty Images; **335** guenterguni /iStock Unreleased/Getty Images; **336**t bolarzeal/Shutterstock.com; **336**c Joesboy/iStock Unreleased/Getty Images; **336**b Frans Sellies /Moment/Getty Images; **337** Moiz_Cukurel/iStock/Getty Images Plus /Getty Images; **337**i himarkley/iStock/Getty Images Plus/Getty Images; **338**t, b guenterguni/iStock/Getty Images Plus/Getty Images; **338**c Pierre Galinier/500px/500Px Plus/Getty Images; **339**t MarcelC/iStock/Getty Images Plus/Getty Images; **339**c KrimKate/iStock/Getty Images Plus /Getty Images; **339**b Reimphoto/iStock/Getty Images Plus/Getty Images; **340**l peeterv/iStock Unreleased/Getty Images; **340**r mtcurado/iStock /Getty Images Plus/Getty Images; **342, 343**b PIUS UTOMI EKPEI/AFP /Getty Images; **343**t STEFAN HEUNIS/AFP/Getty Images; **343**c Frédéric Soltan/Corbis News/Getty Images; **345**tl commerceandculture stock/Moment/Getty Images; **345**tr Charles O. Cecil / Alamy Stock Photo; **345**c Anton_Ivanov/Shutterstock.com; **345**bl © Alexander Mychko | Dreamstime.com; **345**br GI15702993/iStock/Getty Images Plus/Getty Images; **346**tl Primestock Photography/Shutterstock.com; **346**tr bonchan/iStock/Getty Images Plus/Getty Images; **346**b AP Photo/Sunday Alamba; **347** ullstein bild/Getty Images; **348** Marco Di Lauro/Getty Images News/Getty Images; **349**t BOULENGER Xavier /Shutterstock.com; **349**b EMILE KOUTON/AFP/Getty Images; **350**t Ute Grabowsky/Photothek/Getty Images; **350**b Johnny Greig Int / Alamy Stock Photo; **351** MissHibiscus/iStock Unreleased/Getty Images; **353**b Salvador Aznar/Shutterstock.com

Chapter 16

354 Buena Vista Images/Photodisc/Getty Images; **355**t Ben1183 /iStock/Getty Images Plus/Getty Images; **355**cl © Brian Flaigmore | Dreamstime.com; **355**cr Gary_Schmid/iStock/Getty Images Plus/Getty Images; **355**b Per-Anders Pettersson/Getty Images News/Getty Images; **356–57, 359**cl miroslav_1/iStock/Getty Images Plus/Getty Images; **359**t "Topographic30deg N0E30"/Wikimedia Commons/GNU FDL, CC By-SA 3.0/labels added; **359**cr Stocktrek/Getty Images; **359**b, **361**b WLDavies/E+/Getty Images; **360** Mint Images - Art Wolfe/Mint Images RF/Getty Images; **361**t GeeeJay/iStock/Getty Images Plus/Getty Images; **361**c Eddie Gerald/Moment/Getty Images; **362** Jennifer Watson/iStock Editorial/Getty Images Plus/Getty Images; **362**i ARUBA48/iStock /Getty Images Plus/Getty Images; **363**t JEKESAI NJIKIZANA/AFP /Getty Images; **363**b deldew/iStock/Getty Images Plus/Getty Images; **366** Louise Gubb/Corbis Historical/Getty Images; **367**t YASUYOSHI CHIBA/AFP/Getty Images; **367**c Vladan Radulovic (RSA)/iStock Editorial/Getty Images Plus/Getty Images; **367**b NurPhoto/Getty Images; **368** Stephanie Braconnier/Shutterstock.com; **369**t Adobe Stock /Noor Khamis/REUTERS; **369**b mtcurado/iStock/Getty Images Plus /Getty Images; **370**t Monika Hrdinova / Dembinsky Photo Associates / Alamy Stock Photo; **370**b Image Professionals GmbH / Alamy Stock Photo; **371**t Photograph by Eric Isaac/Moment Open/Getty Images; **371**b Jen Watson/Shutterstock.com; **372** African Bible College; **373**t Henk Bogaard/iStock/Getty Images Plus/Getty Images; **373**b, **376–77**t Rixipix /iStock/Getty Images Plus/Getty Images; **374**t Tom Gilks / Alamy Stock Photo; **374**b Vicki Jauron, Babylon and Beyond Photography/Moment /Getty Images; **375** Tom Martin/AWL Images/Getty Images Plus/Getty Images; **377**b Keystone Press / Alamy Stock Photo

Chapter 17

380 Murat Taner/The Image Bank/Getty Images; **381**tl stefanofiorentino /iStock/Getty Images Plus/Getty Images; **381**tr Richmatts/E+/Getty Images; **381**b Hanan Isachar/Corbis Documentary/Getty Images; **384**t Lingbeek/E+/Getty Images; **384**b Suzuki Kaku / Alamy Stock Photo; **385**t, **402–3** Lukas Bischoff/EyeEm/Getty Images; **385**b tmprtmpr /iStock/Getty Images Plus/Getty Images; **386**t NickolayV/iStock/Getty Images Plus/Getty Images; **386**b Rob Atherton/EyeEm/Getty Images; **388** STRINGER/AFP/Getty Images; **390**t, **395**b AFP/Getty Images; **390**c Adobe Stock/Susan Baaghil/REUTERS; **390**b © Oren Gelbendorf | Dreamstime.com; **391**t Duby Tal / Albatross / Alamy Stock Photo; **391**b Jon Arnold Images Ltd / Alamy Stock Photo; **392** SAID KHATIB/AFP /Getty Images; **393**t, **396**b Anadolu Agency/Getty Images; **393**c busra İspir/iStock/Getty Images Plus/Getty Images; **393**bl Ferdinand Henke /EyeEm/Getty Images; **393**br LOVE_LIFE/E+/Getty Images; **394**t SAFIN HAMED/AFP/Getty Images; **394**b Ayhan Altun/Moment /Getty Images; **395**t Tramp57/Shutterstock.com; **395**c Kerrick/E+/Getty Images; **396**t, **397, 398**b Godong/Universal Images Group/Getty Images; **398**t MENAHEM KAHANA/AFP/Getty Images; **399**tl Joel Carillet /iStock Unreleased/Getty Images; **399**tr MindStorm-inc/iStock Editorial /Getty Images Plus/Getty Images; **399**b Frank Bienewald/LightRocket /Getty Images; **400**t Nir Alon / Alamy Stock Photo; **400**b ugurhan/iStock /Getty Images Plus/Getty Images; **401** Steve Heap/Alloy/Getty Images

Chapter 18

404 Photo by Ferdi Merkx, E-in-Motion/Moment/Getty Images; **405**tl janetheone/iStock/Getty Images Plus/Getty Images; **405**tr Arseniy Rogov/iStock/Getty Images Plus/Getty Images; **405**c victoriya89/iStock /Getty Images Plus/Getty Images; **405**b WAKIL KOHSAR/AFP/Getty Images; **408**tl "Veryovkina cave. Babatunda pit" by Petr Lyubimov /Wikimedia Commons/CC By-SA 4.0; **408**tr © Qumrran | Dreamstime .com; **408**b Moehring/Shutterstock.com; **409**t BNBB Studio/Moment /Getty Images; **409**c ShevchenkoAndrey/iStock/Getty Images Plus /Getty Images; **409**b BEHROUZ MEHRI/AFP/Getty Images; **410**t LUKASZ-NOWAK1/iStock/Getty Images Plus/Getty Images; **410**b VANO SHLAMOV/AFP/Getty Images; **411**t Evgenii Zotov/Moment /Getty Images; **411**bl Bjoern Wylezich/Shutterstock.com; **411**br Kerrick /iStock/Getty Images Plus/Getty Images; **412, 414**b, **419**b, **420**t AFP /Getty Images; **413, 424–25**t monticellllo/iStock/Getty Images Plus /Getty Images; **414**t IGOR SASIN/AFP/Getty Images; **415**t Patrick Robert - Corbis/Sygma/Getty Images; **415**b Bloomberg/Getty Images; **416**t Robert Wyatt / Alamy Stock Photo; **416**b NOORULLAH SHIRZADA/AFP/Getty Images; **417**t angela Meier/Shutterstock.com; **417**b Katiekk2/iStock Editorial/Getty Images Plus/Getty Images; **418**tl Sergio Amiti/Moment/Getty Images; **418**bl Anaiz777/iStock/Getty Images Plus/Getty Images; **418**r Ozbalci/iStock Editorial/Getty Images Plus/Getty Images; **419**t Eric Nathan / Alamy Stock Photo; **420**bl, bc, br NASA; **421** lawrence white / Alamy Stock Photo; **422**t Dale Johnson /500px/500Px Plus/Getty Images; **422**b Majid Saeedi/Getty Images News /Getty Images; **423**t Pavel Mikheyev/Shutterstock.com; **423**b The Asahi Shimbun/Getty Images; **425**b Christian Science Monitor/Getty Images

Chapter 19

426 fotoVoyager/iStock Unreleased/Getty Images; **427**l Tony Shi Photography/Moment/Getty Images; **427**tr Andrea Pistolesi/The Image Bank Unreleased/Getty Images; **427**br SM Rafiq Photography ./Moment/Getty Images; **428–29** manavision/Shutterstock.com; **430**t OscarEspinosa/iStock/Getty Images Plus/Getty Images; **430**cl Feng Wei Photography/Moment/Getty Images; **430**cr Maremagnum/Corbis Documentary/Getty Images; **430**b, **446–47**t Mohamed Abdulla Shafeeg /Moment Open/Getty Images; **431**t Tahir Ansari/iStock/Getty Images Plus/Getty Images; **431**c amlanmathur/iStock/Getty Images Plus/Getty Images; **431**b © Pascal Boegli/Moment/Getty Images; **432**t Universal Images Group North America LLC / Alamy Stock Photo; **432**c "India southwest summer monsoon onset map en" by Saravask/Wikimedia Commons/CC By-SA 3.0/modified/Map Resources; **432**bl Martin Puddy/Stone/Getty Images; **432**br Geoffrey Taunton / Alamy Stock Photo; **433**t Byjeng/Shutterstock.com; **433**b Darkydoors/Shutterstock .com; **434** Danny Lehman/The Image Bank/Getty Images; **435** Trinity Mirror / Mirrorpix / Alamy Stock Photo; **436** SAM PANTHAKY/AFP

/Getty Images; **437**t Tuul & Bruno Morandi/The Image Bank Unreleased/Getty Images; **437**cl Bashir Osman's Photography /Moment Unreleased/Getty Images; **437**cr Tuul & Bruno Morandi /The Image Bank/Getty Images; **437**b Claro Fausto Cortes/EyeEm /Getty Images; **438**t Atlantide Phototravel/The Image Bank Unreleased /Getty Images; **438**c solomonjee/iStock/Getty Images Plus/Getty Images; **438**bl Arindam Ghosh/iStock/Getty Images Plus/Getty Images; **438**br highviews/Shutterstock.com; **439**tl Peter Adams/The Image Bank Unreleased/Getty Images; **439**tr Christophe Boisvieux/The Image Bank Unreleased/Getty Images; **439**b NurPhoto/Getty Images; **440**t Agencja Fotograficzna Caro / Alamy Stock Photo; **440**b hadynyah/E+ /Getty Images; **441**t Selfiy/iStock/Getty Images Plus/Getty Images; **441**b Dinodia Photo/The Image Bank Unreleased/Getty Images; **442**t tscreationz/Shutterstock.com; **442**b Meinzahn/iStock Editorial/Getty Images Plus/Getty Images; **443** mrinalnag/iStock Editorial/Getty Images Plus/Getty Images; **444**t Mithun Kumar/500px/Getty Images; **444**b Pakistan Stock Footage/Shutterstock.com; **445**t iStock/Getty Images Plus/Getty Images; **445**b Tuayai/iStock Editorial/Getty Images Plus/Getty Images; **447** Charles O. Cecil / Alamy Stock Photo

Chapter 20

450 badboydt7/Shutterstock.com; **451**t, **468–69**t zhaojiankang/iStock /Getty Images Plus/Getty Images; **451**c Tuul & Bruno Morandi/The Image Bank/Getty Images; **451**b GoranQ/E+/Getty Images; **453**t Matteo Colombo/Moment/Getty Images; **453**c Fei Yang/Moment/Getty Images; **453**b Yiming Li/E+/Getty Images; **454**t Saif Faizullah/EyeEm/Getty Images; **454**c Zens photo/Moment Open/Getty Images; **454**b Yifan Li/EyeEm/Getty Images; **455**t RichieChan/iStock/Getty Images Plus /Getty Images; **455**c xia yuan/Moment/Getty Images; **455**b 500px Asia /Getty Images; **457**t 123RF; **457**b, **464**b Imaginechina Limited / Alamy Stock Photo; **458** AFP/Getty Images; **459**t loveguli/E+/Getty Images; **459**b Ryan Pyle/Corbis Historical/Getty Images; **460**t STR/AFP/Getty Images; **460**ct yenwen/iStock/Getty Images Plus/Getty Images; **460**cb Martin Vorel/Shutterstock.com; **460**b Shih Wei Wang/EyeEm/Getty Images; **461**t "Cujwan" by Marcin Konsek/Wikimedia Commons/CC By-SA 4.0/knocked out; **461**bl wind-moon/iStock Editorial/Getty Images Plus/Getty Images; **461**br Pavlacek_Jan/Shutterstock.com; **462**tl Bruce Yuanyue Bi/The Image Bank Unreleased/Getty Images; **462**tr James Caldwell / Alamy Stock Photo; **462**c Duc Mityagov photographer /Shutterstock.com; **462**b Pierre Jean Durieu/Shutterstock.com; **463** Billy Hustace/The Image Bank Unreleased/Getty Images; **464**t MirageC /Moment/Getty Images; **465** SOPA Images/LightRocket/Getty Images; **466**t humphery/Shutterstock.com; **466**b lionel derimais / Alamy Stock Photo; **467** PATRICK LIN/AFP/Getty Images

Chapter 21

470 RichVintage/E+/Getty Images; **471**tl, **492–93**t Pakkawit Anantaya /500px/500Px Plus/Getty Images; **471**tr mundosemfim/Shutterstock .com; **471**bl visualspace/iStock/Getty Images Plus/Getty Images; **471**br Jason Hosking/The Image Bank/Getty Images; **474**t Ippei Naoi /Moment/Getty Images; **474**c photography by Sanchai Loongroong /Moment/Getty Images; **474**b VittoriaChe/iStock/Getty Images Plus /Getty Images; **475**tl Askar Karimullin/iStock/Getty Images Plus/Getty Images; **475**tr Adobe Stock/Marcel; **475**b okimo/Shutterstock.com; **476**t fotoVoyager/E+/Getty Images; **476**b Yaorusheng/Moment/Getty Images; **477**t tdub303/E+/Getty Images; **477**cl znm/iStock Editorial /Getty Images Plus/Getty Images; **477**cr The Mariner 2392/Shutterstock .com; **477**bl rep0rter/iStock/Getty Images Plus/Getty Images; **477**br Van Rossen/Shutterstock.com; **478** CPA Media Pte Ltd / Alamy Stock Photo; **479**t Andreas Altenburger/500px/500Px Unreleased Plus/Getty Images; **479**b ED JONES/AFP/Getty Images; **480**t The Asahi Shimbun /Getty Images; **480**b CAPTAINHOOK/Shutterstock.com; **481** AFP Contributor/AFP/Getty Images; **482** AFP PHOTO/KCNA VIA KNS /Getty Images; **483**t Paul Quayle / Alamy Stock Photo; **483**b Shawn .ccf/Shutterstock.com; **484**t NatashaBreen/iStock/Getty Images Plus /Getty Images; **484**b, **485**b Ivan/Moment/Getty Images; **485**t Agencja Fotograficzna Caro / Alamy Stock Photo; **485**c Natta-Ang/Stock /Getty Images Plus/Getty Images; **486** AP Photo; **487** MasterLu /iStock Editorial/Getty Images Plus/Getty Images; **488**t Nghia Khanh /Shutterstock.com; **488**b SeanPavonePhoto/iStock Editorial/Getty Images Plus/Getty Images; **489**t Ki young/Shutterstock.com; **489**b Bloomberg Creative/Bloomberg Creative Photos/Getty Images; **490**t ZUMA Press, Inc. / Alamy Stock Photo; **490**b KIM JAE-HWAN/AFP /Getty Images; **491** jeremy sutton-hibbert / Alamy Stock Photo; **493**b Laura Kallfelz / Alamy Stock Photo

Chapter 22

494 83PM38/Shutterstock.com; **495**tl Carlo A/Moment/Getty Images; **495**tr, **516–17**t MartinM303/iStock/Getty Images Plus/Getty Images; **495**bl De Visu/Shutterstock.com; **495**br zonito/500px/500Px Unreleased/Getty Images; **498**tl National Geographic Image Collection / Alamy Stock Photo; **498**tr Stocktrek/Photodisc/Getty Images; **498**b Antonel/iStock/Getty Images Plus/Getty Images; **499**t ngoc tran /Shutterstock.com; **499**b Craig Lovell/The Image Bank Unreleased /Getty Images; **500**t Adobe Stock/Richard; **500**c lovingyou2911/iStock Editorial/Getty Images Plus/Getty Images; **500**b Ali Trisno Pranoto /Moment/Getty Images; **501** saiko3p/iStock Editorial/Getty Images Plus/Getty Images; **502**l "European colonisation of Southeast Asia" by Rumilo Santiago/Wikimedia Commons/CC By-SA 4.0/modified /Map Resources; **502**r Jon Arnold/Alloy/Getty Images; **503**t Roland Neveu/LightRocket/Getty Images; **503**b "Shooting Baguio: The Bell House" by Shubert Ciencia/Flickr/CC By 2.0; **504**t CHRISTOPHE ARCHAMBAULT/AFP/Getty Images; **504**ct Yvan Cohen/LightRocket /Getty Images; **504**cb YE AUNG THU/AFP/Getty Images; **504**b Allison Joyce/Getty Images News/Getty Images; **505**t ROMEO GACAD/AFP /Getty Images; **505**b LordRunar/iStock Unreleased/Getty Images; **506** Chanachai Panichpattanakij/Moment/Getty Images; **507**t David Fischer/Photodisc/Getty Images; **507**bl Mauro_Repossini/iStock Unreleased/Getty Images; **507**br Renato Borlaza/iStock Editorial /Getty Images Plus/Getty Images; **508**t Cat Box/Shutterstock.com; **508**cl Wichawon Lowroongroj/Shutterstock.com; **508**ctr hippostudio /iStock/Getty Images Plus/Getty Images; **508**cbr Максим Крысанов /iStock/Getty Images Plus/Getty Images; **508**b Christian Angelo Ipo /Shutterstock.com; **509**t KHellon/iStock Editorial/Getty Images Plus /Getty Images; **509**b Patrick AVENTURIER/Gamma-Rapho/Getty Images; **510**t Owner/iStock/Getty Images Plus/Getty Images; **510**b Patrik Dietrich/Shutterstock.com; **511** Copyright Elinor Young; **512** DigitalGlobe/ScapeWare3d/Getty Images; **513**t Barcroft/Barcroft Media /Getty Images; **513**b FADIL AZIZ/ALCIBBUM PHOTOGRAPHY/The Image Bank Unreleased/Getty Images; **514**t holgs/iStock Unreleased /Getty Images; **514**b STR/AFP/Getty Images; **515** Emilio Maranon III, Philippines/Moment Open/Getty Images; **517**b CHOO YOUN-KONG /AFP/Getty Images

Chapter 23

520 John Warburton-Lee Photography / Alamy Stock Photo; **521**tl simon bradfield/iStock Unreleased/Getty Images; **521**tr Jennifer A Smith /Moment/Getty Images; **521**c oversnap/iStock/Getty Images Plus/Getty Images; **521**b Lukas_Vejrik/Shutterstock.com; **524**t "Kermadec and Tonga Plates" by Sting and jpez315/Wikimedia Commons/CC0 1.0 /modified/Map Resources; **524**c Felix Cesare/Moment/Getty Images; **524**b Ignacio Palacios/The Image Bank Unreleased/Getty Images; **525**tl Delpixart/iStock/Getty Images Plus/Getty Images; **525**tr Apexphotos /Moment/Getty Images; **525**c JohnCarnemolla/iStock/Getty Images Plus/Getty Images; **525**b kokkai/iStock/Getty Images Plus/Getty Images; **526, 540–41**t Daniel Osterkamp/Moment/Getty Images; **527** Marc Dozier/The Image Bank Unreleased/Getty Images; **528** Michal Adamczyk/123RF; **529**t Matteo Omied / Alamy Stock Photo; **529**b Elaine Anderson/Getty Images; **530**t Steven Tritton/Shutterstock .com; **530**b JoshuaDaniel/Shutterstock.com; **531**t Richard Milnes / Alamy Stock Photo; **531**c Oliver Strewe/The Image Bank Unreleased /Getty Images; **531**b Tricia Muir/Moment Unreleased/Getty Images; **532**t Douglas Peebles/The Image Bank Unreleased/Getty Images; **532**b Lakeview Images/Shutterstock.com; **533**t Nolomo/Shutterstock .com; **533**c Aaron C Photography/Moment Open/Getty Images; **533**b Ozimages / Alamy Stock Photo; **534**t PA Images / Alamy Stock Photo; **534**cl Photo Italia LLC/iStock Editorial/Getty Images Plus/Getty Images; **534**cr fpwing/iStock/Getty Images Plus/Getty Images; **534**bl Heritage Image Partnership Ltd / Alamy Stock Photo; **534**br Museum of New Zealand Te Papa Tongarewa, Wellington, New Zealand/Bridgeman Images; **535**tl domonabike / Alamy Stock Photo; **535**tr TGSPHOTO / Alamy Stock Photo; **535**b The Sydney Morning Herald/Fairfax Media /Getty Images; **536**t Nils Versemann/Shutterstock.com; **536**b martin berry / Alamy Stock Photo; **537**t attaporn taweekeaw/Shutterstock.com; **537**b Ecopix/Shutterstock.com; **538**t Julie Thurston/Moment Open /Getty Images; **538**b John Carnemolla/Corbis Documentary/Getty

Images; **539** 4FR/E+/Getty Images; **541**c Marnie Griffiths/Moment /Getty Images; **541**b Brett Monroe Garner/Moment/Getty Images

Chapter 24

542 Friedrich Stark / Alamy Stock Photo; **543**tl, **562–63**t Lisa Mei Photography/Moment/Getty Images; **543**tr blickwinkel / Alamy Stock Photo; **543**c Holger Leue/The Image Bank Unreleased/Getty Images; **543**b, **557**l National Geographic Image Collection / Alamy Stock Photo; **546** Kathy Pflug; **547**t Travel Pix / Alamy Stock Photo; **547**cl Reinhard Dirscherl/Corbis/Getty Images; **547**cr NASA/Goddard Space Flight Center Scientific Visualization Studio The Blue Marble data is courtesy of Reto Stockli (NASA/GSFC).; **547**b Universal Images / SuperStock; **548**t nudiblue/Moment Open/Getty Images; **548**b Stuart Westmorland /Corbis Documentary/Getty Images; **549**t "Linfa, Chan-hom, and Nangka in the West Pacific - Jul 9 2015 0230z"/SSEC/CIMSS, University of Wisconsin–Madison/Wikimedia Commons/No Restrictions; **549**c PictureLake/iStock/Getty Images Plus/Getty Images; **549**i chengyuzheng/iStock/Getty Images Plus/Getty Images; **549**b Thomas Haupt/Shutterstock.com; **550** DE AGOSTINI PICTURE LIBRARY/De Agostini/Getty Images; **551** RachelKramer/iStock/Getty Images Plus /Getty Images; **552**t "Marine Raiders landing on Pavuvu"/US Marine Corps/Wikimedia Commons/Public Domain; **552**b North Wind Picture Archives / Alamy Stock Photo; **553**t "Territorial waters Oceania" by Kwamikagami/Wikimedia Commons/CC By-SA 3.0/modified; **553**c WILLIAM WEST/AFP/Getty Images; **553**b SeaTops / Alamy Stock Photo; **554** Sheila Fitzgerald/Shutterstock.com; **555**t AP Photo/John Miller; **555**c Greg Vaughn / Alamy Stock Photo; **555**bl © Hel080808 | Dreamstime.com; **555**br robertharding / Alamy Stock Photo; **556**tl sirichai_asawalapsakul/iStock/Getty Images Plus/Getty Images; **556**tr Miroku/Photodisc/Getty Images; **556**b rez-art/iStock/Getty Images Plus/Getty Images; **557**r Douglas Peebles / age fotostock / SuperStock; **558**t APFootage / Alamy Stock Photo; **558**b Science History Images / Alamy Stock Photo; **559** Arne Hodalic/Corbis Documentary/Getty Images; **560**t David Fleetham / Alamy Stock Photo; **560**b AP Photo /Alastair Grant; **561**t "20140402-APHIS-UNK-0006"/U.S. Department of Agriculture/Flickr/CC By 2.0; **561**b dpa picture alliance / Alamy Stock Photo; **563**b Mark Conlin / Alamy Stock Photo

All other maps were provided by GeoNova, Map Resources, or Precision Graphics.